What Others Have Written

"Captain Lunde is an outstanding Company Commander who has demonstrated superb leadership abilities. His unit is the farthest ranging, most aggressive, and most successful company in my Brigade. His men love him. He has been recommended for the DSC. Two Silver Stars, and one Bronze Star for valor in action. He is a model infantryman – courageous, disciplined, wiry, and tough. He possesses a keen understanding of soldiers' problems. If anyone can motivate young men, Captain Lunde can."—Lieutenant General Willard Pearson.

"LTC Lunde is one of the most extraordinary lieutenant colonels serving in the Army today... He should be promoted to colonel at once and given command of a mechanized infantry brigade in Europe. He is a future general officer."—Lieutenant General Robert L. Schweitzer

"Hank Lunde demonstrated great leadership and courage on many occasions. In my view he was the very best Company Commander I ever knew in Vietnam."—Colonel Dave Johnson

"I feel that the Infantry Commander [Hank Lunde] used the artillery very effectively and achieved the best results we have had to this date in the country."—Major Allen V. Stout, S-3 320th Artillery

"Hank Lunde was a very strong and outstanding leader. He was a brilliant tactician and displayed a low-key attitude and was very empathic towards the troops." —Colonel Karl Beach

IMMIGRANT WARRIOR

A Challenging Life in War and Peace

HENRIK O. LUNDE
COLONEL OF INFANTRY U.S. ARMY (RETIRED)

CASEMATE
Philadelphia & Oxford

Published in the United States of America and Great Britain in 2023 by
CASEMATE PUBLISHERS
1950 Lawrence Road, Havertown, PA 19083, USA
and
The Old Music Hall, 106–108 Cowley Road, Oxford OX4 1JE, UK

Hardback Edition: ISBN 978-1-63624-180-7
Digital Edition: ISBN 978-1-63624-181-4

A CIP record for this book is available from the British Library

Printed and bound in the United Kingdom by CPI Group (UK) Ltd, Croydon, CR0 4YY

Typeset in India by Lapiz Digital Services, Chennai.

For a complete list of Casemate titles, please contact:

CASEMATE PUBLISHERS (US)
Telephone (610) 853-9131
Fax (610) 853-9146
Email: casemate@casematepublishers.com
www.casematepublishers.com

CASEMATE PUBLISHERS (UK)
Telephone (0)1226 734350
Email: casemate-uk@casematepublishers.co.uk
www.casematepublishers.co.uk

Contents

Dedication

This book is first and foremost dedicated to my military family, those who served with me in A/2/502 in Vietnam. Furthermore, the dedication extends to my former wife, Florence, who struggled on the home front for over 47 years to raise a family, mostly in my absence. Finally, it is dedicated to my current wife, Truong, who was born and grew up in war-ravaged Vietnam.

Author's Notes

It is customary to begin a book with a list of those who helped make the work possible. I began discussing the subject matter with my former troops and superiors after I retired, in numerous telephone calls. After joining the family business and obtaining a commodity brokerage license in the mid-1980s, I was so busy that there was not much time for research and writing. The spare time was devoted to a promised two-volume genealogical venture with many spin-offs that I began in 1988. It ended up consuming most of my free time until 2002. We closed our family business at the end of 2003.

The end of the above period coincided with the appearance of cancer and other illnesses associated with Agent Orange. I had intended to resurrect the autobiography at that time. Still, since most of it dealt with my time in Vietnam, the doctors did not think it was beneficial to simultaneously deal with an emotional undertaking with my struggle to stay alive. Consequently, I began writing military history—producing four books and numerous lengthy articles—to keep my mind occupied.

After the publication of my fourth military history book in late 2014, I decided it would be too late if I did not restart my autobiography. The start was again delayed as I underwent open-heart surgery in 2015 and a hip replacement in 2020. In some ways, the delays were detrimental since many key individuals from my time in Vietnam had died. In other ways, it was also beneficial because I was able to avail myself of ever-increasing literature.

I cannot list the countless people who made this work possible. There are many, particularly if I include those I discussed the project with during the 1980s. I did not keep detailed notes as I did in Vietnam and it would be easy to unintentionally leave out names. Instead, I note just a few whose help was invaluable. I was unable to travel to military archives due to my medical condition. Lieutenant Colonel David "Skip" Perrine (U.S. Army, Retired)—the S-3 of 2/502 in 1967—was exceedingly helpful in providing many references. Perrine also reviewed chapters 7 to 19. Others have read parts of the manuscript covering events familiar to them, such as Colonel (Retired) Serge Demyanenko, who read chapters 2 and 3. Major (Retired) Adam Klys reviewed chapter 5. However, the only person who has read and commented on the whole manuscript is Timothy "Tim" Swain, Esquire, a prominent lawyer in Peoria, Illinois. Colonel (Retired) Henry Gole also provided help with the editing process.

Finally, I could not have completed this work without the tireless understanding, encouragement, and support of my wife Truong, who was born in Vietnam.

Despite the diligence of those who provided inputs, assistance, comments, and advice, I must stress that I take full responsibility for all conclusions and such errors as this book may inadvertently contain.

Introduction

There are several ideas behind this book and what I hope to accomplish. First, my siblings and I have lived on different continents since 1954. While they knew about my life in broad outlines, no one was familiar with the details of how my life unfolded. This lack of knowledge is particularly true for my siblings' many descendants. Therefore, one purpose of this book is to tell them about that part of my life with which they are not familiar—the good and the bad. I also considered it necessary to expand the manuscript somewhat to explain those aspects of American life they may not be familiar with, including governmental organization and a brief outline of the lives of high-ranking individuals I encountered during my service.

A second reason for writing this book is to tell the story of my three tours in Vietnam, which covered the better part of 38 months, and relate the significant activities of the units I served in or commanded. The emphasis is on my first tour, when I commanded an airborne infantry company-size unit for over 10 months. I considered those great troopers my military family and their achievements, sacrifices, and heroism needed recognition.

Third, most key officers and non-commissioned officers (NCOs) in the 2/502 during that battalion's first year in Vietnam have died. The three company commanders who brought their units to Vietnam were wounded or killed within six weeks, and I was among the three who replaced them. Now, there is only me left, as Thomas Taylor died in 2017 and Robert Murphy in 2020. So, I felt it essential that I, who was present for the longest time, should write about the outstandingly courageous soldiers with whom I served.

Finally, several of my superiors reminded me throughout my military career that I needed to blow my horn more often. Even one of our Founders, John Adams (1735–1826), wrote that "modesty is highly overrated as a virtue" and his motto was "Toot your own horn lest the same never be tooted."[1] I did not follow their advice since it seemed improper to brag and boast while troops were wounded or killed. I relied on my superiors to grant me the recognition I deserved. All this is now the distant past. Therefore, I will toot my horn and tell my story as I remember.

***

I looked at many memoirs and autobiographies by soldiers before deciding how to organize and write my account. The books by Charles B. McDonald (1922–1990),[2] David Hackworth (1930–2005),[3] and Anthony Herbert (1930–2014)[4] were helpful. My work is different in some respects because I have a foreign background that had to be covered. The organization of the book is chronological, not thematic.

This work is not a history but represents my recollections, supplemented or corrected by the memories of others who served with me and the available official reports. Even though it is not a history, I have, as far as possible, followed the manual of the style used for such books. References or explanatory notes are used whenever appropriate and are located with the other endnotes. Some of the endnotes are lengthy since they expand on the text or deal with tangential issues.

I have tried to make the combat part as correct as possible, a challenging task after more than half a century has passed. I mainly relied on my field notebooks[5] and letters to my wife, family, and friends. These are supplemented by thousands of pages of after-action (AA) reports, daily staff journals (SJs), studies, morning reports (MRs), rosters, casualty lists, verbal and written interviews, books in my possession, etc. I also used letters from the next of kin to the extent that privacy and common sense dictated. Maps are provided and inserted at relevant points.

To make the work more readable and exciting—giving a flavor of situations and personal conversations on the battlefield—I have used radio and other discussions as I remember them. While I have placed these in italics, I have not used quotation marks. The obvious reason for this is that I cannot swear to the exact wording.

I used real names when those were known to me. I felt it was an evasion not to do so. It is also the best way to recognize some of the heroism and achievements of my troops. When I could not recall the name after more than 50 years, I referred to the individual's position.

As this book will show, the notion that there was always unanimity between American commanders on the battlefield is erroneous. There are times when there are conflicts between how I recall events and how two of my subordinates recalled the same event. In those cases, I have given both sides of the story.

Finally, my notes frequently differ from the information found in the after-action reports (AA reports) and daily SJs at higher headquarters—battalion, brigade, and division. These were often prepared weeks after an event, while my notes were prepared within 24 hours in most cases, therefore virtually contemporaneous. I used my own shorthand form to make them useless to an enemy if captured or killed and so, after more than 50 years, they were challenging for me to read and decipher. The loose pages were destroyed after I transcribed the information needed.

While writing several military history books after I retired, I was often dismayed to find that the AA reports of the parties involved differed to such an extent that I had to double or triple check to make sure they were writing about the same action. My practical experience in Vietnam gave me a better understanding of how this situation can happen.

MRs I had access to can also be misleading. Soldiers wounded or killed are frequently not mentioned on the day of the action but several days later. Obtaining MRs was a lengthy process, in some cases taking more than a year between the time Lieutenant Colonel Perrine requested them and their arrival. Some reports are missing, while others are difficult to read as they were faded or smeared.

The letters to my wife Florence were also nearly contemporaneous. However, there are gaps between when these letters were written and mailed. I had to be careful not to say anything about future operations for security reasons. These letters provide a record of events and reveal my feelings about those events.

I wove into the narrative some of the problems that developed on the home front when there were no official organizations, as there are now, to support the families left behind. David Johnson's book, covering his three tours in Vietnam, provides much better treatment of the home front issue.[6]

My account of my service in the 101st Airborne Division is much more detailed than the period I spent in the 9th Infantry Division and at Pleiku. There are several reasons for this. First, my notes as commander of A/2/502 were three times more extensive than those for my time in the 9th Division and Pleiku were. Second, the notes I made in 1968–1969 were those most severely damaged in a flood we suffered in 1993. Two of the notebooks, kept on a lower shelf, floated away after the winter hurricane broke down the garage doors, destroyed one wall, and the home's downstairs filled with over 4 feet of seawater. Third, my service in the 9th Infantry Division was on a brigade and battalion staff and, at Pleiku, on a corps staff. My work precluded the close relationships with troops that existed when I was a company commander in 2/502. Fourth, I did not have Lieutenant Colonel Perrine to help me deal with the archives. I had to rely on what notes I had, my memory, copies of reports I wrote, and the 9th Division Operations Reports.

In my service in the Four Party Joint Military Team (FPJMT), I had the assistance of an excellent secretarial staff, who saved for me all unclassified materials suitable for writing an account of my time at the delegation. I am grateful for their effort. The problem for me was looking through the more than a thousand pages to determine what information they contained that would be helpful for the relatively short chapter on the FPJMT, in addition to my own notes and letters.

There will be errors in a book that relies on memories of events over 50 years ago. Some mistakes are unavoidable even when the sources are contemporaneous since they may be based on views of different parts of a battlefield. After-action reports and SJs, used whenever available, are other contemporary sources but are not always reliable since a single typing mistake—for example, in map coordinates—can give a false view of what transpired.

Moreover, despite my care in making notes, the reader must understand I was often unsure in Vietnam. We had some kind of action against the North Vietnamese Army (NVA) and Viet Cong (VC) virtually every day after we moved from Phan Rang to Tuy Hoa. For example, I was unsure on the night of 9/10 February 1966 when I took two soldiers with me into the creek to meet an approaching NVA group. I write that they may have been Misner and Ellis, but I was unsure. I am truthful, and the fact I could not remember who they were with certainty in the terror and confusion of a night engagement is, in my mind, excusable. Uncertainty in war is a given and in Vietnam it was especially so. I was nearly always unsure what confronted my men and me and often relied on instinct.

The reader should keep all these possible human errors in mind.

***

There is a certain amount of military terminology that I should address at the beginning. Many readers are undoubtedly unfamiliar with the unit designations used in this book. They are relatively simple. When speaking of specific companies of a battalion, they are written A/2/502 or C/1/327. The letter identifies the company. The first number is the numerical identifier of the battalion, while the second number specifies the regiment.

I often use the date/time system used by the military in documents such as AA reports and SJs. Many may be familiar with this system. The first two numbers give the month's date, while the following numbers provide the time in the 24-hour format. Finally, the month is written out in letters.

The maps I have used are topographical on a 1/50,000 scale. Map coordinates are usually given in six-digit numerals for maps this scale. The first three numbers show the west–east location, and the last three give the south–north location. Read the coordinates right and up. Preceding the six digits, you may find two letters. This is part of the Military Grid Reference System and is the 100-kilometer square identifier. We seldom used those two letters unless we were operating near the border of a square.

The precision level of a six-digit coordinate is 100 meters. This is sufficient for most operations and the pre-selected map reference points chosen before every operation for quick communications with subordinate units were in six digits. However, there were times when we had to use eight-digit coordinates with a precision level of 10 meters. This was most often the case when using close-in artillery support. If we had insufficient time, we would use a six-digit coordinate with a safety factor and then walk the strike ever closer to friendly positions. We could also use marking rounds if time allowed and the element of surprise was not imperative.

In pre-planning barrages around a night position, we asked for strikes in eight-digit coordinates, with each strike given an alphanumeric label for quick execution. It was usually the company commander's job to select the general location for these night strikes, but the attached Artillery Forward Observer (FO) would choose the exact location. He would coordinate this with the commander before sending the request to the supporting artillery. With my blessing, he would then notify the platoon leaders of any preplanned strikes near their lines. They, in turn, would alert their outposts.

Doing this work at night with a flashlight under a poncho was a time-consuming chore. A/2/502 had the most outstanding FO, which accounts for us being the only company in the brigade that did not have casualties from friendly artillery fire, except for two soldiers slightly wounded as we descended the steep hillside facing away from the artillery position to the Cambodian border on 14 May 1966.

As best I can recall, I have referenced many radio conversations with the help of my notes. Radio call signs changed periodically, but I chose those in use for the most prolonged period, *Hunter*. Thus, *Hunter 6* was my call sign as company commander. *Hunter 5* was the call sign for my Executive Officer (XO), and the platoon commanders were assigned *Hunter 1* through *4*.

***

This book was not intended to treat our involvement in Vietnam from a political perspective. The only times I deal with that subject are when political views and policies affected me or military operations. Of course, national and military strategies are linked, the latter being a component of the former. To write about military strategy without reference to national strategy is a futile exercise. In a democracy, we also must be attuned to the fact that domestic policies are often the determining factor in our national strategy. Historian Barbara W. Tuchman (1912–1989) deals with these subjects well in a book covering the historical spectrum, including Vietnam.[7]

My views about the war in Vietnam underwent an evolutionary change over the years I was there, which will become increasingly evident in later chapters. In a TV interview in July 1966, I stated we were winning the war. That statement was my honest belief since at the end of the first tour, I had concluded we were finally learning how to conduct the war at the tactical level. However, I also began to believe that the enemy's driving force was more nationalism than communism.

***

Like my father, who came to the United States in 1915, I felt the best way to repay my new country's opportunities was to serve the nation in some capacity. My father volunteered for service in France during World War I. I selected a military career, although it was not my first choice. I do not know if I have lived up to these family service ideals, but I kind of doubt it.

CHAPTER I

A Turbulent but Carefree Beginning

According to my mother, I was born early on Monday morning, 16 March 1936, in the middle of a severe late winter storm. Perhaps the day after the Ides of March and the weather were harbingers of how my life would unfold. My parents could not get to a hospital and a doctor could not get to our home. My birth, assisted by a neighborhood woman, took place on the small island of Risøy in the community of Fitjar in western Norway. I was the youngest of four children born to Oliva (1899–1989) and Anders Rolfsnes (1894–1968).

According to my parents, I was severely sick during the first year or two of my life and was not expected to make it. For that reason, they held a christening at home. The church ceremony was conducted almost two years later, at which time I was well enough to try to take the Bible away from the minister during the proceedings. Perhaps this was an early indication of my interest in history.

My childhood was happy, even though, in some respects, it was a lonely time and a difficult period for my parents. There was a decade or more separating me from my brothers and sister. My oldest brother Ole was born in 1923, my sister Anna in 1924, and my youngest brother Arthur in 1926.

When I began school, my siblings had grown up. There was only one other family on the island, and again there were no children my age—they were either older or younger than I was. There were only two girls in the whole school district that started the year I did. I learned to play, study, and dream by myself. I am sure this situation contributed to my description as an individualist and loner. It may also have been why two Norwegian journalists described me as "cold and unemotional" in 1966.

Our family was neither rich nor poor but shared with others the hard life associated with living on the then isolated islands on the west coast of south-central Norway. The 20th century had, in many respects, not reached this area during my childhood.

We had no electricity, no hot or cold running water, and no indoor plumbing. We had a battery-operated telephone and, after the war, a battery-operated radio. The heat was provided by large multi-story stoves in which we burned wood or peat.

We cut the peat out of the bogs in the spring and placed them in pyramid-shaped stacks where they were left to dry during the summer. We would carry them to a boat landing and transport them to our boathouse, where they were stored in the fall.

We would bring the peat from the boathouse to the basement in the winter as it was needed. Cooking was likewise performed on a wood stove. Water was collected from a well about 50 meters from the house. The well would freeze in the winter, so melted snow was often used as a primary water source. The well would also run dry in summers with little rain, and water had to be collected and moved by boat from a lake on a nearby island.

Reading and studying were performed in the light of paraffin lamps. The house was not insulated. I remember a thick layer of ice forming on the inside of the windows during winter. Mail was delivered by motorboat, and the mail carrier was my godfather, Knut Rolfsnes (1887–1991). My mother would often give him a list of groceries she needed, and he would pick them up in Brandasund, where he fetched the mail.

We had to use a boat to reach anyone except for the other family on the island. Even the school was on a different island. The distance was about 2 kilometers, but it could be challenging and dangerous to get there and back in winter. I remember my mother carrying hot water in a bucket from the house to where the rowboat was tied up in the winter to thaw the ropes securing the boat. She also took along rocks for ballast in winter. It was a hard life for my parents.

My father's family came from Bømlo and Skånevik, while my mother's family came from Tysnes, Fusa, and Kvinnherad. In these areas, an oral tradition traced the family on my father's and mother's side back for several centuries and included ancestors from well-known families in Norwegian history. The lineages also had many lesser-known family names, people who struggled from generation to generation to scrape out a meager living in farming and fishing.

We were proud of the heritage on both sides of the family but knew little about our ancestors. I completed a two-volume family history at my older brother Ole's urgings—written in Norwegian and English—but the mammoth project was not completed until 2002, 11 years after my brother died.

Many relatives on both sides of the family had immigrated to the U.S. in the 19th and 20th centuries. My paternal grandmother's older sister and younger brother immigrated to Iowa in the early 1880s. Two of my father's half-brothers and a half-sister emigrated in the late 19th century, and his brother Erik Rolfsness (1891–1981) in 1911. Erik returned to Norway to get married in 1915. When the young married couple set out again for the U.S., my father came along.

They settled near Ambrose, North Dakota, on the farm owned by their half-sister and her husband. They lived in a sod hut in the beginning. When World War I came along, Erik was drafted. Since he and his wife Lilly (1891–1968) already had one child and were expecting a second, my father arranged to switch places with his brother and went to France to participate in the last phases of that war. My paternal grandfather, Ola Nilsson Rolfsnes (1829–1917), died while his son was in France, as my father did while I served in Vietnam. After World War I, my father returned to Ambrose but soon headed to Norway to bring his mother to America.

There were also immigrants on my mother's side of the family. Her father's oldest brother settled in Florida, and two of my maternal grandmother's siblings came to Iowa in the early 1880s.

My mother was in Brandasund, helping her cousin, when my father returned from the U.S. after World War I. They met and were married in 1922 and lived in Rolfsnes for about two years. They sold their place in Rolfsnes in 1924 and my father returned to the U.S. for a couple of years in early 1924 to work and save up some money. The work was primarily in the building industry in Washington (state) and Alaska (not yet a state).

My mother, brother Ole (1923–1991), and my paternal grandmother, Gunnhild Rolfsnes (born Haugstøl) (1859–1947), lived in Tysnes with my mother's family while my father was in the U.S. My sister Anna was born in Tysnes. My father returned in 1925, and he and my mother bought that part of the island of Risøy called Lunde. They moved there with their children and my grandmother. My father planned to bring the family to the U.S. at this time had it not been for his mother's reluctance to leave Norway.

My paternal grandmother's family had moved from Skånevik to Bømlo in 1877. They were destitute. My grandmother had an older sister and a younger brother who had immigrated to the U.S. (Iowa) in the early 1880s. The Norwegian authorities were eager to remove people who presented a potential economic burden, and tickets to immigrate in 1890 were secured with the help of their children in the U.S. and the Norwegian government in Norway. However, when the time came to leave, my grandmother, her two sisters, and their mother changed their minds. Thus, the family remained in Norway.

In the 1920s, it was again the reluctance of my grandmother that kept the family in Norway. With her husband dead and her only other son in the U.S., no one could care for her if my parents left. They decided to remain with her in Norway. In my view, it was the right and honorable thing to do. Such decisions often determine the fate of entire families.

As with so many others from this area of Norway, my father was a part-time fisherman. However, for the most part, he was a boat builder, first as a worker for others and then for himself after the beginning of World War II. During the 1930s, he worked for Johannes Kvernenes (1902–1967), who was married to my mother's cousin. The Kvernenes boatyard was located about 5 kilometers from our home and my father would spend the nights in Kvernenes on a small motorboat he owned to save the cost of fuel involved in returning home each evening. The boat had a small cabin with a wood stove.

Living on a small boat was rough during the winter months. My father often woke to discover that moisture from his breath had formed icicles above his face. He would return home on Saturday afternoon and travel back to Kvernenes on Monday morning. My mother would cook enough food to last him for two or three days and then make a trip to Kvernenes in a rowboat in the middle of the week to take him meals to last him until he returned.

Our place in Lunde was large enough to support two or three cows, a dozen sheep, chickens, and one or two hogs. We grew our potatoes and vegetables. When my father worked, my mother, with the help of her mother-in-law and children, attended to the many chores associated with operating the small farm. The animals were kept inside during the winter, but in the summer they were turned loose on the island.

The cows had to be located each day and milked. However, most times, they wandered home by themselves when it came time for milking. Our neighbor and us would get together to round up the sheep each fall. The new lambs had to be marked and the sheep sheared.

In the fall, we would collect heather, of which there was a plentiful supply, to supplement the food for the animals during the long winter. My mother and grandmother would use wool to spin yarn for making clothing. Much of our everyday clothing was homemade in this manner. Footwear for daily use consisted of wooden shoes or clogs. My father or godfather made them. They were not comfortable and I would discard them most of the time during the summer.

In the 1920s and 1930s, my mother and one or more of the other wives on the islands would load a large rowboat with potatoes and carrots and take them to Bergen to sell. This trip was almost 80 kilometers. It was a strenuous trip—two days each way—involving several long stretches of open sea at the mouth of the fjords.

My first memory was from 1939, when my 16-year-old brother, Ole, left to go to sea. He was a naval cadet on the sailing ship *Statsråd Lehmkuhl.* He had an old dog that he and Arthur (1926–2007) used to hunt mink on the islands. As a kid, I was carrying on with the old dog when he snapped at me. I remember my brother punished the dog but, before he left, Ole hugged the dog for a long time. I would not see my brother again for 12 years, and 50 years would pass before seeing him display that kind of emotion again.

I do not remember much from the war in Norway. Still, we had frequent contacts with the German occupiers since we were situated in the gateway from Norway to Shetland, with considerable traffic in both directions. We often received surprise visits.

I remember specific incidents like the dive bombing of Slotterøy Light House in April 1940 and dogfights between German and English fighter planes. Later in the war, I witnessed large bomber formations passing over us on their way to bomb the U-boat pens in Bergen, as well as the surrounding forts from which they received heavy anti-aircraft fire. I also recall some of the visits to our island by the Germans.

One incident took place in 1944. There was a pre-arranged telephone signal given when Germans were expected. On this occasion, the Germans had first visited our neighbors on the island but had left there in two groups, preventing the neighbor from giving a pre-arranged signal and sufficient time to alert us.

When the warning came, my mother asked me to run down to the boatyard to alert my father and brother. I ran out the back door and towards the boatyard. The Germans approached the front of the house, saw me running out the back, and yelled for me to stop. I continued my mission, and it was not until my mother cried out for me to come back that I stopped. She had seen a couple of German soldiers aiming their rifles in my direction. My attempt to reach my father made the Germans, and particularly their Norwegian collaborators, suspicious.

They conducted a thorough search of the house and the five outbuildings. They paid attention to a large picture of my father's company in World War I when he served in the U.S. Army in France. The Germans or their Norwegian collaborators left a map on the dining room table while searching upstairs, where my grandmother lived, and told me to stay in the room. As I waited for their return, I noted three red circles on the map and one was our island.

This visit was after the Allied landings in Normandy, and a German officer asked my father whether he would support his former comrades if it came to that. My father must have been very annoyed by this visit because he answered "Yes", but quickly qualified it by saying that, in any case, he was too old for it to make any difference. This same officer noted we had tobacco plants growing in the yard and asked how they tasted. My father told him the truth—they had a foul taste. He complained there were no niceties since the Germans had arrived, and necessities were severely limited.

The search of the home and the outbuildings revealed nothing and, as they were leaving, the German officer came back to the basement door where my father was standing and handed him a pouch of tobacco. As soon as our uninvited visitors left, I told my father about the map I had seen. He thanked me but admonished me strongly to forget it and never tell anyone.

My maternal grandmother Anna Åse died in 1941, and we had difficulties getting to the funeral. This event was six months after the raid on Vågsøy, north of Bergen, by English and Norwegian commandos. This raid caused Hitler to order large reinforcements to Norway when he sorely needed those troops on the Eastern Front.

Severe travel restrictions were in force. To get to Tysnes, we had to pass the newly constructed German fortresses of Osternes and Flygansvær, commanding the entrance to Selbjørnsfjord and the interior waterway between Tysnes and Stord, called Langenuen. We decided to try the trip on a 42-foot fishing boat owned by my uncle Rasmus Waage (1894–1977). The trip took place at night. We crossed the fjord to Austevoll and followed the shoreline closely until we were out of sight of the two fortresses, then re-crossed the fjord and passed around the north end of the island Rekestern. The exhaust pipe on the boat was covered so that no sparks would give us away. We were not spotted, and all went well.

I remember my first day in school in 1942. My mother dropped me off, and I recall how frightened I was at being left alone among strangers. My teacher during the following seven years was Olav Sørvik. I remember him with great respect and fondness. He was an imposing, strict, but fair taskmaster and had a considerable influence on my life. He would teach at our school for two weeks and then instruct in a neighboring community for two weeks, during which time we were free. He was one of the first individuals I visited when I traveled to Norway from Germany in 1959. That was also the last time I saw him.

I had a keen interest in history and I read everything I could lay my hands on the subject. I read the *Kings Sagas* by Snorre Sturlason several times, as well as a copy in Danish of Edward Gibbon's *The Decline and Fall of the Roman Empire*—not exactly light reading.

The most significant limitation of my readings was the availability of books. There were no libraries or bookstores where we lived and one had to travel to Bergen to have access to either. The travel was at least a six-hour one-way trip by steamer and one I made only a couple of times before I was 12. However, I would borrow books from friends or my teacher. By the time I was 14, I had become quite familiar with the significant figures in history, from Alexander the Great to Winston Churchill (1874–1965).

The military side of history held a fascination in those formative years. Many of the games I used to play as a kid had military or adventurous overtones, and I guess they already pointed in the direction of my later life. However, I did well in all school subjects and Mr. Sørvik talked to my parents on several occasions and urged them to allow me to continue my education.

I was also interested in the religious classes—given once a week—in the public school, but that changed when I began the one-day-a-week studies for my Confirmation between May and October 1950. We were required to learn whole sections of the Bible verbatim and expected to regurgitate them when called on by the minister. It was like a pressure cooker for many of us who did not want to stand up and make fools of ourselves. I could not see the purpose of not summarizing and interpreting what we read instead of reciting it, as written in the Bible. I was also bothered by the fact that one girl from my class, who was a Jehovah's Witness, failed to get an exemption from attending the studies but was singled out to sit by herself on a side bench in the church.

In our view, the organized church had not taken a firm and uniform stand against the occupiers during the war. In short, the experience and feelings about the Church's activities during the war left us with a negative opinion about organized religion. That feeling stayed with me for most of my life. My Confirmation took place in October 1950.

As I became older, I began transporting myself to school by boat, except when the weather was severe. Nils Risøy, our neighbor's oldest son, who was three years younger than I, had by that time also begun school, to be followed a year later by a sister and then by his youngest brother in 1947.

I had a dog by this time named Kvikken ("the quick one"). He was attached to me, and when I left home for school in the morning he would follow along the shoreline as far as he could and, on several occasions, would then dive into the cold water and swim after the boat. We would usually turn around and pick him up or, if we did not see him follow, he would show up drenched on the school playground. It was quite a swim since the two islands were at least 500 meters apart at the narrowest point. I worried that one day he would drown and started locking him in the house before I left.

After school, if the weather permitted, I would often go fishing. If I were late coming home, I could count on my grandmother standing on a knoll near the house looking for me. I often remember her like that, dressed in an ankle-length black dress and with a black shawl on her head.

Later, I had lobster and crab pots, and I would check them after school. I would sell the lobsters at the end of the season. One autumn, the catch came to NOK 57 ($8.50). To me, this was a considerable sum of money. My sister Anna had helped me that year and I was supposed to split the money with her. I finally got around to sharing the wealth with her when I gave her a check for the principal and interest 30 years later.

Sometimes I would take the boat after school and search for driftwood along the many islands' shores. There were often exciting things to find, particularly during and immediately after the war. One time we found many items we believed to be blocks of butter, apparently from a torpedoed ship. We tried it for butter and frying, but it had a strong and unpleasant taste and was used primarily as a lubricant in my father's boatyard.

My cousins in Brandasund secured and dismantled many drifting sea mines during the war. It is a wonder they were able to do so without blowing themselves up. Mines torn loose from their fields were frequent, and the usual way to dispose of them was to blow them up with rifle fire. After the explosion, there were hundreds of dead fish floating in the water.

As mentioned before, many of my childhood activities and games had military overtones. I spent much time with bows and arrows, and became quite proficient in their use. However, I did not stop there, modernizing my arsenal by making rifles. These activities took place without my parents' knowledge and even without the knowledge of my siblings.

I would secure pieces of pipe of enough length from the boatyard, attach them to wooden stocks I made and drill a small touchhole in the tube. The result was a crude muzzleloader. My friend Nils participated in this endeavor—the most challenging part was securing powder. I found some in our basement, but relied primarily on my knowledge of chemistry from school and my readings. It was not too difficult to come up with a propellant in this manner.

My weapons manufacturing plant was in a small cave on the island. We shaved matches to come up with a simple system for the touchhole that worked. We made several weapons in this manner and Nils and I fired them on many occasions. To our delight, they worked. It scares me now to think of how easily we could have been badly hurt or even killed given how we experimented to come up with the appropriate amount of powder.

Of course, we had little knowledge of metallurgy to gauge the strength of either the pipes we were using or the stocks we had constructed. However, we were lucky and did not get hurt, although our faces were often black from the powder discharge. I imagine the remnants of our weapons production facility can still be found in that cave.

An illness a few days before the war ended in 1945 almost cost me my life. I had been with my mother and a neighbor named Ragna Tverderøy to cut peat on the western part of the island. After returning home and experiencing stomach cramping and vomiting, a doctor was called.

Sigurd Nilsson Hus, the doctor in the neighboring county, concluded I had appendicitis. Doctor Hus had been active in the resistance movement and spent time in a German prison. He wanted to get me to a hospital as soon as possible, but that proved to be a problem.

Transportation along the coast in those last days of the war had practically ceased. Salomon, our neighbor on the island, took us there in his fishing boat. I felt better when we got close to Bergen due to the fact—as I learned later—that the appendix had burst. My father was inclined to return home, but Salomon insisted we continue to the hospital.

Doctor Friedman Dahl operated on me immediately, despite the hospital staff having their hands full with war casualties, both Germans and Norwegians. He looked at the basement hallway full of patients waiting for treatment and said, "Let us take this boy first since he may have a future." By the time I came out of the hospital, the war was over.

After the war, my father and brother Arthur were busy repairing and rebuilding the fishing fleet that had either been damaged or neglected during the war and they had several employees working in the yard. However, this busy period ended within a few years.

My paternal grandmother died in 1947. Both my sister and Arthur were married in 1948. Fourteen other students and I started attending Framhaldskule (Continuation School) in Voss in October 1950 to prepare for higher education. I had a first-class headmaster named Sigurd Slyngstad and through his efforts, I obtained the top grades.

There were many debates within the family in this period. The subject dealt with whether to emigrate to the U.S. or stay in Norway. For a while, it looked like we might end up in Tysnes. My maternal grandmother Anna Gjellefall (1875–1941), married to Henrik Åse (1876–1963), inherited her father's farm in the 1930s. Anna and Henrik had not operated it themselves but leased it to others. It was eventually sold to Lars and Kristine Brekke in 1948.

My maternal grandmother was the oldest daughter in a family without surviving sons, so she inherited the farm. My mother was the oldest daughter in my grandparents' family and had not signed away her allodial rights. Therefore, my mother was entitled by law to buy the farm if she elected to do so within a specified period, which I believe was three years.

I remember the whole family traveling to look at the farm with this possibility in mind. Kristine was a childhood friend of my mother's and, in the end, my mother said she would not dispossess her friend in this manner. I believe this fit in well with my father's thinking since he felt the children would have a better future, with more opportunities, in the U.S.

The whole family made the final decision around the dining room table shortly after looking at the farm in Tysnes. My parents said that either we all stay in Norway, or we all immigrate. It was a unanimous decision to go. Since I was still in school in 1948 and considered a child, I did not vote on the matter. It is ironic that I, who did not get to vote, was the only one to end up staying in the U.S. permanently. However, there is no doubt I would have voted to go if I had an opportunity. It sounded like a great adventure.

I have always admired and respected my parents for the courage it took to make this life-changing decision. My father was 57 years old, and my mother was 51 when they left Norway. I do not think they had any high expectations of prospering in the new country. Nevertheless, they were willing to do this so their children and grandchildren could benefit. This decision was born out of love and consideration for the next generation. I will always admire them for the courage they displayed and the personal sacrifices they were willing to make on our behalf.

After deciding to emigrate, we started the paperwork to secure visas, which did not prove difficult since my father had been an American citizen and was a World War I veteran. My brother Ole had sailed on Norwegian and American ships during the war and had gone ashore and settled in Brooklyn in 1945. He had been born while my father was still a U.S. citizen, so Ole was American by birth.

Relatives of my sister-in-law Emma (1927–2008) provided the required employment guarantees for Arthur's family, and my brother-in-law Birger Bryn (1925–2003) received similar employment guarantees from Uncle Erik. Our home was listed for sale, and a buyer was found when emigration papers were in order in July 1951. We had also arranged to dispose of the personal property we did not intend to bring with us, and last visits were made to our closest relatives.

I remember the last day and night in our home distinctly. I had been excited about the adventure that lay ahead. But, on the last day, with the house empty, the gravity of the undertaking began to surface. My biggest problem was my 10-year-old dog that had lost an eye. He knew something was very wrong and would not let my mother or me out of his sight. However, my father did not want to kill the dog and arranged for our neighbors to care for him.

The last night at home was a beautiful summer night in late July with hardly any darkness. I felt despondent and told my parents I did not want to leave. My father explained to me that it was too late for us to change our minds.

I ran out of the house and climbed to the top of the highest hill on the island. I cried long and hard that night as I sat there with my dog. We remained there for the longest time. The air was warm and quiet, the sea was still and black, and everything I had taken for granted looked so beautiful. I was not to feel this sad and depressed again until 15 years later. Then, I was on the other side of the world and I had to say goodbye to troops who had shared so many dangers with me.

I sat on the hill until early morning when Arthur came to bring me home. As we left that morning, my dog followed us along the shoreline as far as he could. After we arrived in the U.S., my friend Nils wrote to tell me that his father had to kill the dog since it would not touch its food after our departure.

We went first to Bergen and after that by train to Oslo. We made a 15-minute stop at the Voss Railroad Station, giving us a chance to say goodbye to my sister, brother-in-law, and their two-year-old daughter Solveig. They were to follow us to the U.S. in a few months. Then, we changed trains in Oslo and continued to Gothenburg, Sweden, where we boarded our ship, the MS *Gripsholm* of the Swedish American Line.

While there, we had an incident that almost aborted our trip. After boarding the ship, my father went ashore to make a telephone call to the U.S. embassy. He returned only to discover he had forgotten our passports, visas, and wallet in the telephone booth. The ship was about to depart, and my father rushed ashore and found the papers where he had left them. He returned just as the crew was in the process of removing the boarding platform.

The lack of funds during our travel and initial period in the U.S. was a persistent problem. Norway had stringent currency restrictions in place at the time we emigrated. Each head of household was only allowed to bring $50.00 in U.S. currency, and there was no allowance for taking any Norwegian money. Taking Norwegian currency along in those days would not have helped. We would not have been able to exchange it after arrival in the U.S. What we could take along did not go far to meet the expenses associated with the move and resettlement in a new country.

CHAPTER 2

First Years in a New Country

We entered New York Harbor on a sunny 6 August 1951. We were all on the deck, looking at the sights. My father mentioned we would not have money or time to visit the attractions, such as the Statue of Liberty. Without thinking, I said, *We could see them when we go home to Norway.* My father gave me a quick and stern look, as he used to do when I had done something wrong. Then, with emphasis, he said, *I want all of you to remember that this is our home from now on.*

The medical and immigration processing took place on the ship and we docked in lower Manhattan instead of the usual place, Ellis Island. We stopped a couple of days in New York and then moved to Chicago, where my brother Arthur, his wife Emma, and their daughter Gunnlaug remained. Emma's aunt and uncle, who lived in Chicago, had obtained work for my brother under the guarantees provided when they received their visas. Although my brother Ole provided some sorely needed funds, my parents left most of these with Arthur. After three days in Chicago, my father, mother, and I proceeded to the West Coast by train. We could not afford sleeping accommodations, so it was a long trip, especially for my mother. However, we did pay for pillows and blankets for the six-day ride. My father, who knew much about the country's history, would tell my mother and me what he knew about the various places where we stopped or through which we passed. It was an adventure for me.

We arrived in Oakland, California, with less than $28 left. Then we made a mistake that brought our funds down to about $8. We assumed the train to Eureka, California, went from San Francisco and took the ferry across the bay but found it left from Oakland, where we had just been.

Since we had missed that day's train, we had to take a motel and wait for the next day. On the third-class coach of an old rickety train from Oakland to Eureka, we were seated among a group of Native Americans dressed in their traditional garb. I felt I was among those stoic heroes in James Fennimore Cooper or Zane Gray books.

To me, the trip from New York to Eureka was an unforgettable eight days, and I was fascinated by what we heard and saw. By the time we reached our destination, practically all our funds had been used. It was not much to start life in a new country, but we were with relatives and optimistic about the future.

Uncle Erik had purchased a used camping trailer that he parked on his property, and this became our home for the next five months. It was tiny but provided us with the necessities. My father obtained work as a carpenter and I was enrolled in Eureka High School within weeks of our arrival.

My biggest problem was that I could not speak, read, or write English. I had attempted to learn some, with my father's help, during the last few weeks in Norway and our trip, but my command of the language was limited to the most common and necessary phrases. In any of the larger cities in California, my inability to speak English would have been much less of a problem, but Eureka was a relatively small fishing and logging community near the Oregon border and did not have many immigrants. Therefore, the school system and teachers were not prepared or trained to handle this kind of problem.

My brother and sister and their families joined us in Eureka in early October and found housing in converted barracks near where we lived. Work was hard to find and keep due to a downturn in the economy. In the end, my father, brother, and brother-in-law leased an old boat and turned to fishing, primarily for crabs.

We would supplement whatever income we had from fishing by digging clams on the mudflats, which were exposed at low tide. We would get 50 cents for each large bucket of clams, but it was challenging to catch them. Sometimes I would sink into the mud up to my knees and needed help to get loose. I still remember the stench associated with these mudflats. I would help with this after school and during weekends. It was very unpleasant work and provided little money.

In school, I struggled with language problems. The teachers were helpful, but their responsibilities extended to the whole class and with a school population of over 800, there was only so much time they could spend helping one individual student.

Many Norwegians who had immigrated in the past had headed for already established Norwegian or Scandinavian communities. They, therefore, experienced fewer problems than those who migrated later to other areas of the country. Even as late as 1969, when I took my mother to visit her cousin in Mason City, Iowa, weekly newspapers in Norwegian were available, as was the case in New York and Seattle.

Kids tend to single out for harassment anyone who is, for some reason, different. This situation is not unusual, and it was prevalent at Eureka High School. I stood up to the harassment and prejudice as best I could, and it often resulted in fights, and I lost virtually all, due in part to being heavily outnumbered. The whole situation left scars and had a lasting effect on me. I came to appreciate more than most the destructive forces of prejudice, whether based on race, nationality, gender, or being in any way different from the majority.

The weather was unusually stormy on the northern coast of California in the autumn of 1951. My father, brother, and brother-in-law went out at times when the rest of the fishing fleet stayed in the harbor out of what they felt was a necessity. The locals referred to them as "the crazy Norwegians." Despite their efforts, the fishing season was a practical failure that year.

The family decided to move to San Francisco, where there were more opportunities for employment. My unhappiness in school had also reached a point in late November which caused my parents to consider sending me back to Norway to continue school and applied to Voss Landsgymnas.

We left Eureka in December 1951 and moved to San Francisco. We had no place to stay when we arrived there, but a Norwegian church minister helped us find temporary housing in what turned out to be a slum hotel in the lower Mission District of the city. The hotel's name was Ford—it was torn down long ago to make room for a four-story parking garage. The rent was cheap enough—I believe it was $1.50 per day for each of three rooms—but the conditions were terrible. Downstairs was a shoddy lobby that at night also served as a sleeping area (for 25 cents) for drunks, vagrants, and homeless people. One had to step over bodies to enter or exit.

The area was one of the worst in the city and one where you did not want to walk alone at night. There was one murder at the hotel while we lived there. It was no place to live, particularly for my brother and sister with their children. However, the lack of money forced us to stay at the Ford Hotel for over a month. By that time, my father, brother, and brother-in-law had obtained employment at a local shipyard and could start looking for another place to live.

To begin with, we moved into three flats on 401 1st Street, near the Bay Bridge. The new place was still located in the city's waterfront district and not a safe place to live. Still, it had to do until our financial position improved to the point where we could afford something better. My brother and sister-in-law had their second child, Alf, in December.

At about this time, Voss Landsgymnas notified me that I was accepted in the second year of study in the fall. I had started attending Mission High School, an institution with over 2,000 students. I found many in the same boat as me, recent immigrants from Europe with language difficulties. The problems I had experienced in Eureka's small community existed to a much lesser degree in San Francisco. The language difficulties were also beginning to fade fast.

I was not sure what to do. My parents left the decision to me. The minister at the Seamen's Church—whose name I have unfortunately forgotten—wisely argued I should face and overcome rather than avoiding a problem. I also received a letter from my grandfather in Norway (who I am named after) stating his conviction that I would have a better future with more opportunities in the U.S. I also knew my leaving would make things difficult for my parents and possibly destroy the family's plans and dreams. By early 1952, I had decided to remain in the U.S., although I held off canceling my appointment to Voss Landsgymnas until June.

The family's financial condition was improving steadily and, by 1953, we lived at three different addresses in San Francisco, in decent middle-class neighborhoods. Times were much better than when we initially arrived in the country and work was available for those who wanted it. Moreover, I was doing well in school. I did so well that in 1953 I won the Von Steuben Award given out each year by the California Scholarship Federation. Unfortunately, the gold-covered medal accompanying the award was stolen from my apartment in Germany eight years later. Except for English, I found my education in Norway had placed me one to two years ahead of my contemporaries at Mission High School.

I signed up for the Junior Reserve Officers Training Corps (JROTC) in school. We studied military subjects for five hours each week and wore uniforms one day a week. We also participated in parades and underwent training at local military installations. However, it was not my intention at that time to make the military a career.

The Korean War was winding down, but there were few indications it would end anytime soon. The draft was in force, and I would soon have to register (March 1954) and become subject to call up. Having taken JROTC would benefit me if drafted, which was as far as my thinking went at the time. The Korean War ended in a truce on 27 July 1953.

The family had grown by one additional member in August 1952 when my sister had a daughter, Bjørg. Also, my brother Ole joined us on the West Coast, so the whole family was now located in one place and I remember those months as happy ones. Everything seemed to be improving and the future looked promising.

I had maintained an A average during my last two years at Mission High School. I submitted my application for admittance to the University of California (UC) at Berkeley in late 1953. I was accepted and provided a scholarship by the California Scholarship Federation. It was a two-year scholarship, offering $300.00 for those two years. It might not seem much today when a university education can reach $70,000, but it was immensely beneficial. Classes were scheduled to begin in August 1954. In the meantime, I took some courses at nearby San Francisco State College, now San Francisco State University.

The whole family's time assembled at one location was short-lived and it would never happen again. Ole was the first to move. He went back to New York, where he had lived since 1945 and felt more at home. Shortly after that, in the summer of 1954, my sister-in-law Emma moved back to Norway with her two children. Arthur remained in the U.S. for another six months and then he returned to Norway. Their stated plans were to stay in Norway for about a year and return before their residence permits expired. However, as we will see later, those plans were forced to change.

Three of my best friends from Mission High School entered UC with me. Two were second-generation Japanese Americans, David Yamakawa (valedictorian at

Mission in 1954) and his sister Patricia. They were two of the most intelligent individuals I have ever met. David ended up as a prominent lawyer in San Francisco like his father before him, but he died in the early 1990s. My other friend was Serge Demyanenko, who was the salutatorian at Mission in 1954.

Along with his mother and father, Serge had come to the U.S. as a refugee from Germany in 1949. His father had been a junior officer in the Imperial Russian Army and had escaped to Turkey after the revolution in 1917. He met Serge's mother in Paris, where he made his living as a portrait painter and where Serge was born. After the war started, they moved to Bremen, Germany, and Serge's father served with the Germans as an officer in an East Europeans' organization sympathetic to the Germans. He was lucky to find himself in the British Zone of Occupation at the end of the war and received permission to enter the U.S. I was happy that these friends entered UC at the same time I did.

I managed to pass all entrance examinations, except one. I failed the English language examination. However, my grades in the other subjects were high enough to compensate and I was told to take a remedial class in English in the first semester. It was affectionately referred to as the "bonehead" English course. Successfully passing this class would be the equivalent of passing the examination. With some hard study, I managed to get through the course.

UC was one of the largest and most respected universities in the U.S., where members of the Norwegian Royal Family have since studied. At the time of my attendance, it had a student population of well over 20,000. The transition from high school to university was rough. The leap in educational standards and expectations was considerable. I was now competing with the best. The increase in demands on abilities and time came as a shock.

It also reinforced my desire to strive to be the best at whatever I did, bordering on the fanatical. Combined with strong traits of individualism, it was influential in all decisions I made in both peace and war. It worked to my benefit most of the time, but not consistently.

When I entered the university, I had only vague ideas of what I wanted to do with my life. My initial plan was to join the U.S. Foreign Service to become a foreign service officer (FSO). I was encouraged by my counselors at the university to pursue this avenue, so I decided to major in history and political science.

Three-quarters of the subjects I selected or had selected for me dealt with history, political science, economics, and languages. The professors who taught these subjects were some of the best minds in their fields, both nationally and internationally.

Money was a constant source of worry and concern during my four years at the university. The two-year scholarship I had, while helpful, did not go far to meet the requirements of tuition, books, food, clothing, housing, and transportation. One semester, Serge and I lived in a student boarding house near the university. We figured we could use the time saved from driving back and forth to San Francisco to study and work. However, we soon found this way too expensive and reverted to living at home.

I signed up for the Senior Reserve Officer Training Corps (SROTC) to help with the expenses. This program provided me with $30 a month during the last two years. I also worked at the Bancroft Library for 28 hours a week—initially at 89 cents per hour. During the first summer vacation, I worked for Bethlehem Steel at their shipyard in San Francisco. The second summer, I worked for the Pinkerton Detective Agency. I could not work during the third summer since I attended the SROTC summer training at Fort Lewis, Washington.

My parents helped as much as they could with my expenses but in the end, I received $1,500 from my cousin Andrew Rolfsnes, who had a farm in Rhame, South Dakota, and a residence in Los Angeles. He insisted I continue my studies as I would be the first in the family in almost 200 years to have a university education. After entering the Army, I paid him back with interest, making my last payment to his daughter Clara after he died in 1963. I visited his grave in Rhame in 1995.

One of my jobs for the Pinkerton Detective Agency was as the driver for U.S. Senator Margaret Chase Smith (1897–1995), the first woman to serve in the House and Senate, and also a presidential candidate in 1964. She continued to serve in the U.S. Senate until 1973. She was in San Francisco to attend the Republican National Committee meetings in preparation for the 1956 convention (I was an alternate delegate to that convention). She impressed me as a very sharp, intelligent, and kind human being, and it was easy to see why she had become the first woman elected to the U.S. Senate.

Senator Smith knew about my studies at the university. She would often ask what I thought about various national and international issues while driving or at breakfasts she insisted I have with her at the hotel. At the end of my assignment, the senator gave me more tips than what Pinkerton paid me for the job. After she returned to Washington, she wrote me a friendly letter of thanks. She also sent Christmas cards for several years.

While many have characterized the 1950s as a happy decade with law and order, progress, and relatively free from the violence and disorder that prevailed in the following 10-year period, it was a decade of great upheaval. As a student, first in high school and then at university, I witnessed this as it affected both the domestic and foreign policy of the U.S.

On the international scene, it was a decade when old colonial empires crumbled before the new wave of nationalism, revolution, and civil wars. The decade was ushered in with U.S. forces deeply involved in a war in Asia, several crises, and interventions in various parts of the world, and a looming involvement in Southeast Asia at the close of the decade. The period saw the spread of nuclear weapons capabilities, which generated widespread fear at home and abroad. Finally, the end of the decade saw the beginning of the Space Age.

The period was one in which a second industrial revolution and new forms of mass communications transformed human existence circumstances. During the second half of the decade, the hydrogen bomb threat—so soon after Hiroshima and Nagasaki—became an unpleasant fact. This threat endangered the very foundation of American democracy. It was a time when perception, foresight, and wisdom were needed as never before. Instead, part of this period was a time of national paranoia.

Explanations had to be found for the loss of Eastern Europe, China, and Cuba, and the Soviet Union's quick acquisition of nuclear weapons. For the first time, weapons of mass destruction posed a direct threat to the American homeland. The old norms of life became threatened and it was a time ripe for demagoguery. Senator Joseph McCarthy (1908–1957) became the spokesperson for those who maintained that America had been betrayed from within, and enormous energies were expanded hunting for communists or communist sympathizers.

There was no storm of public outrage against McCarthy and his friends. Americans have always admired the stand-up guy, but few stood up in these years, instead trying to shelter themselves. Unfortunately, seeking shelter was most acute in those very circles that should have provided leadership but instead most abjectly capitulated to the witch-hunt and hysteria which characterized much of the 1950s.

Senator Smith was an exception. She was a voice of conscience for fellow Republicans when she spoke out against the anti-Communist witch-hunts of the 1950s. In widely hailed speeches two decades apart, she warned of the threat of extremism. Her 1950s declaration of conscience was a repudiation of McCarthy's smear tactics. Twenty years later, as the nation was in the middle of students protesting the Vietnam War, Senator Smith delivered a Senate speech updating her declaration. Extremists, fomenting divisions in American society, are forcing our people to make a narrow choice between anarchy and oppression, she said. But make no mistake, she continued, if that close choice were made, the American people would choose oppression.

I am sure Senator Smith would have the same feelings about the current political situation in the U.S. The racism I thought was nearly solved again reared its ugly head, proving that it was just below the skin of millions of whites. Racism was now superimposed on top of hatred for immigrants and religious groups, and other national minorities. Even gender intolerance crept into the mix.

In the early 1950s, a petition drafted by Madison's *The Capital Times* demonstrated the paranoia of the 1950s and Americans' unwillingness to embrace our past's noblest traditions. The petition consisted entirely of quotes from the Declaration of Independence and the Constitution's Bill of Rights. A reporter tested public reaction by stopping 112 people and asking them to sign the document. One hundred and eleven considered the sentiments taken verbatim from our two primary national documents positively subversive and refused to sign. Some even urged that the FBI be called to investigate what they considered provocative behavior.

At the same time, the 1950s were a period of contentment. The public was, in some respects, far more tolerant than their parents in the 1920s and 1930s were. It was a more humane, open, and liberal society than before. The worst racist terms and intolerance for minorities and ethnics had, it seemed, disappeared from American politics. The period saw the beginnings of many political and social movements that have since dominated American politics. The civil rights movement, for example, gathered steam during this time, eventually leading to the use of federal military force in the South to ensure compliance with the law. Despite rumblings of things to come in the 1960s, the Korean War briefly interrupted this widespread domestic contentment but, by 1954, the world again seemed at peace, jobs were plentiful, energy was cheap, and inflation was low or nonexistent.

This contrast between a society content with its situation, fearful of real or imaginary dangers, and unsure of its future is illustrated by the attitudes of the college class of 1958 (my graduating class). The views of graduates from major universities were encapsulated in articles written by *The Nation* dealing with domestic and foreign issues.

These articles reveal typical cynicism toward politics, helplessness concerning influencing events, materialism, and unwillingness to participate in social and political controversies. A sense that law and order in society were of equal or greater importance than individual justice was standard.

Of course, these are generalizations. While I was growing up, the description of the social and political conditions was too fleeting and inadequate but provided a framework and setting for the events that shaped my life and subsequent decades.

Since my major was history and political science, it was natural for me to show interest in what was transpiring in the country and participate locally. I was active in the debating society and traveled to other schools to engage in or monitor debates on domestic and foreign policies.

The Republican National Convention in 1956 was a somewhat relaxed affair, since it turned out to be only the formal setting for the re-nomination of President Dwight Eisenhower (1890–1969) and Vice President Richard Nixon. My status as an alternate was never activated so I did not participate in the process.

My plans underwent a significant change at the end of 1955. I inquired about taking the Foreign Service Entrance Examination in 1956. To my dismay, I received an answer from the Department of State that candidates for the Foreign Service Officers Corps must be citizens and have held citizenship status for 10 years. These rules had come into effect because of the McCarthy movement and were unknown by my faculty advisers and me. The letter from the State Department could offer no encouragement. There were no exemptions to the new regulations.

The news came not only as a complete surprise but also threw my plans into total disarray. Since I would not receive my citizenship papers until the summer of

1956, it meant I could not hope for an appointment as an FSO until 1966. I was very depressed and seriously considered ending my studies at the university.

Everyone I talked to argued against this option. Several people suggested I consider a career in teaching, but this had no appeal to me, and I did not feel myself cut out to be a teacher, something I would confirm in my mind over 25 years later. Furthermore, it was a bit late in my studies to consider a significant change without lengthening them beyond four years.

Fields I considered myself suitable for at this time, such as economics and the legal profession, would require additional work. I did not cherish the possibility of extending my studies beyond 1958, which would be my seventh year of school since arriving in the U.S. Instead, I was eager to get on with my life and start earning some money.

My friend David Yamakawa suggested a possibility I eventually accepted. He recommended I concentrate on becoming a Distinguished Military Graduate (DMG) and obtain a commission as an officer in the Regular Army (RA). Most graduates from the SROTC program received commissions as officers in the Reserves and spent only two years on active duty. David pointed out that I could spend seven years in the RA while waiting to become eligible for the Foreign Service. This option would provide me with valuable experience and the time spent in the Army would eventually count towards a federal retirement. It could lead to seniority within the Department of State and would not require a change in my studies' focus or a lengthier stay at university.

A couple of other factors also influenced my decision. First, I had received the Military Achievement Award, an award a person was eligible for only if he was in the top 10 percent of those students who received a grade of "A" in the military curriculum. Second, I had become interested in competitive marksmanship. The Department of Military Science and Tactics sponsored this program at the university. I did very well, culminating in being number one in the rifle category at the Hearst Trophy Reserve Officer Training Corps (ROTC) National Match held over 12–14 December 1956.[1] By spring of 1956, I had decided to continue my studies and concentrate on receiving a commission in the RA.

My social life during my university years was minimal. With an average of four to six hours of formal classroom studies each day, four to six hours working at the library, two hours commuting to and from the university, and several hours of studying and writing each evening, there was little time left for socializing.

I had met a girl, Marion Myrtle Swingle (1938–2012), in my high school French class in 1953 and we dated off and on, particularly after 1955. Our two families had also become friends. Marion graduated from high school as valedictorian of her class in 1956 and went to work for an automobile club. Everyone assumed we would get married once I had completed my university studies.

Our family presence in the U.S. had meanwhile decreased. I have already mentioned that my brother Arthur and his wife and children had returned to Norway. Those of us who remained assumed they would return the following year before their entry permits expired. My sister and brother-in-law, Birger, also began talking about returning to Norway. His parents were getting old and in poor health and he wanted to see them before it was too late.

Birger was also thinking about building an American-style motel in Norway with my financial assistance after graduating and working for a few years. These considerations led my sister and her family to return to Norway in the spring of 1957. Again, though, it was with the understanding they would return if things did not turn out as expected.

I believe other considerations were also at work in the failure of these two families to return to the U.S. The workplace in America is often a demanding experience. It is not that the work is more challenging, and Scandinavians' work ethics were highly regarded by most employers. Other conditions are different, however.

Employers tend to have more power than their counterparts do in Norway. Unions were weak and did not always have the best interests of their members as a high priority. Transportation to and from work could take several hours and, if he wished to stay continuously employed, a worker had to be willing to travel far away. For Arthur, Birger, and my father, this translated, at times, into traveling roundtrip distances of 1,000 kilometers or more and involved staying away from home under less than adequate conditions for weeks at a time. With its crowds, pollution, traffic congestion, fast pace, and a relatively high level of petty and severe crimes, life in the big city was something both families found hard to accept.

It has always been the case in the story of U.S. immigrants that the first generation has had a hard time both economically and emotionally. The road to success and prosperity can be rough and always requires hard work and sacrifices. Nevertheless, those who recognize the promise and opportunity of the U.S. in terms of individual freedom and financial rewards for hard work usually endure the early hardships for the sake of future generations. The differences in opportunities are evident to those from less fortunate societies and these people tend to remain. The differences were much less apparent to those who came from mid-20th century Norway and there was, for them, a tendency to focus on the negative aspects of their new country.

I believe my sister and brother were concerned their children would grow up in a fast-paced society with a relatively high crime rate, such as that found in the San Francisco Bay area of California. I believe these considerations were important in their decisions to leave and their eventual decision not to return.

My last year and a half at the university involved much hard work. I applied myself as hard as I could and there were many nights, particularly in preparation for the examinations at the end of each semester, when I did not sleep at all. The officers who taught at the military department had begun to monitor a few of us for selection as Distinguished Military Students, and I was aware of this.

At no time was this scrutiny more apparent than at the six-week summer training period at Fort Lewis, Washington, in 1957. This was the practical and physical part of the evaluation to determine if we would be nominated. The commanding general of the Sixth Army notified me on 21 October 1957 that I had been selected as a DMG. In turn, the DMG selection led to notification at the end of December that I had received one of the appointments in the RA. My friend, Serge, was also given a RA appointment. We both felt honored to be among those selected from a large field of candidates.[2]

The military graduation ceremonies, with both student regiments participating, took place on 29 May 1958. I was notified on 19 May that the U.S. Senate had routinely confirmed my presidential appointment as an RA officer. The selection was effective immediately upon the execution of the oath of office.

Serge and I took this oath on 13 June (oral and in a signed statement). This oath as an RA officer is unique because it is made to the law of the land, not to any person or institution. For me, it read:

> I, Henrik O. Lunde, having been appointed a 2nd Lieutenant in the Regular Army of the United States, do solemnly swear that I will support and defend the Constitution of the United States against all enemies, foreign and domestic; that I will bear true faith and allegiance to the same; that I take this obligation freely, without any mental reservation or purpose of evasion; and that I will well and faithfully discharge the duties of the office upon which I am about to enter so help me God.

Significantly, this oath of office emphasizes the protection of the Constitution as the first loyalty. It gives an officer a personal responsibility to uphold the laws outlined in the Constitution.

The oath prevents officers from taking refuge in any claim that they were only following orders if they should become involved in something not legal by either national law or the laws of warfare, which the country has signed and ratified. Therefore, an officer must only follow legal orders by this oath and the service's traditions.

13 June was a busy day. In addition to taking the oath of office, there was a civil graduation ceremony to attend. To my surprise and pride, I was the designated honor graduate in the Department of History. As usual, Serge and I participated in these ceremonies together.

A few years before, I had introduced Serge to the girl he later married. This meeting happened at a time when we commuted to university by car. A Korean girl named Katherine (Kathy) Chey and her brother, Pildong, replied to my notice on the bulletin board at Mission High School offering rides to UC and asked to ride with me. Serge would usually bring his car to the university.

Serge met Kathy and Pildong on their first or second trip with me. Serge took an immediate interest in Katherine. He suggested he park his car at my home, that I drive every day, and that he would help with expenses. I agreed.

Katherine was the daughter of a former finance minister in South Korea under President Syngman Rhee (1875–1965). Her father had since died and she was living with her mother and brother in San Francisco.

Serge and Kathy planned to marry as soon as he graduated. In late May, Serge told me he and Kathy had not found anyone to perform the marriage. He asked if I would talk to Pastor Schroeder of our Lutheran Church and ask if he would perform the ceremony. Pastor Schroeder agreed to marry Serge and Katherine.

The wedding took place in the Lutheran Church on the evening of 13 June, and Marion and I were their witnesses. I thought it was rather sad that neither family was in total attendance, thus publicly giving their blessings to two people who were very much in love. However, Serge told me in a letter on 11 April 2018 that this lack of attendance was prearranged. Neither he nor Katherine had made their marriage widely known, and they had not asked anyone—including their parents—to attend what they did not consider much of a ceremony, squeezed in at night just before the rehearsal for my wedding the following day. We have now passed Serge and Kathy's 65th wedding anniversary and that speaks volumes about their devotion to each other, in sharp contrast to my early matrimonial failures—the difference between love, infatuation, and friendship.

My situation had also rapidly reached a climax. I had immersed myself in studies for the final exams, and there was little rest or sleep, particularly in April and May. This was unfortunate since it was a time when some crucial personal decisions needed to be made.

Both Marion and I—mostly I—had begun to have second thoughts about our forthcoming marriage and felt that maybe we should delay it until my Fort Benning training was completed. The delay would involve a one-year postponement. We thought that our separation during this period would determine if our feelings for each other were appropriate for entering a marriage, a step we both considered crucial.

By the time we engaged in these discussions, the preparation for the June wedding was well underway. We both decided to seek advice from our parents first. They were supportive of the marriage and urged we proceed with our plans. We followed their recommendation but, in retrospect, I know we would both have benefited from a postponement and that our futures may well have been different. As on so many other occasions in my life, it demonstrated the value of following the initial instinct rather than rationalizing a solution that could be problematic.

The wedding took place on 14 June, the day after I graduated. The date was selected because both our families wanted me to wear my uniform. The marriage took place at the Lutheran Church, with Pastor Schroeder performing the ceremony. Marion and I had held our practice the previous night after Serge and Katherine were married. Serge was my best man, as was Marion's brother-in-law, Al Gibson, a San Francisco police officer.

The reception and dinner took place at an elegant restaurant in downtown San Francisco. I suspected someone would try to play tricks on us after the marriage and I felt I had made adequate secret plans with Serge's help, an unwise selection. He booked us into a motel in San Francisco under assumed names and he had agreed to prevent anyone from following us as we left the reception. After leaving the dinner, I drove around in circles to make sure we were not followed. Then, having satisfied ourselves we had outsmarted any potential pursuers, we drove to the motel. I left Marion in the car as I went to register.

When I returned to the car, it was empty, with a note on the windshield stating something to the effect that my bride was detained as a material witness to a misdemeanor (registering using an assumed name) and interference with law officers in the performance of their duties. I immediately recognized the involvement of my newly acquired brother-in-law and his friends in the police department. I had no idea where they had taken her and figured they would bring her back to the motel. I waited at the motel until about 0200 when I drove home. My parents had come back late from the reception and had just turned in.

With considerable embarrassment, I explained what had happened. My mother called Marion's home and learned she had been delivered there and that a continuation party was in progress. I decided not to join the party to avoid the ribbing I would undergo and went to bed.

Marion and I spent the following day packing for our trip to Fort Benning, Georgia, our first duty station. We took along only those things we knew we would need to set up light housekeeping and fit into the car. We left the rest of our stuff with our parents. We drove with Serge and Kathy in separate vehicles. It was sad to leave my parents behind, as they would now be alone. My father was approaching his 65th birthday, and his health problems from being exposed to mustard gas in World War I had worsened. My parents planned to stay in San Francisco until his Veteran and Social Security pensions were approved. They would then come and visit us in Georgia on their way to Norway.

We left San Francisco on 16 June 1958 after driving my father to catch his bus to Sausalito, where he now worked. Marion and I were full of anticipation and excitement about what lay ahead.

CHAPTER 3

A Time of Preparation: Fort Benning, 1958–1959

We arrived at Fort Benning on 24 June 1958 after a pleasant trip across the country. I signed in at the military post as soon as we arrived to prevent using leave, as only so many days were allowed for travel from the West Coast. As we drove through the gate at Fort Benning, the military police (MP) guard gave me the first salute of my career, and, following tradition, I forked over a silver dollar carried for just that occasion.

Marion and I spent the next couple of days locating a place to live off the post. Finally, we found a place in a development called Victory Apartments. It was small with one bedroom, one bath, a kitchen, and a living room, and very sparsely furnished. Serge and Katherine also found an apartment in the same complex.

My orders read to proceed from San Francisco to Fort Benning to attend the Basic Infantry Officer Course (BIOC). They further directed me to travel to Fort Dix, New Jersey, for transportation to Germany and assignment to an unspecified unit upon completing that course. However, I could anticipate that my job would be with an infantry unit, usually for duty at the company level. Most likely, I would not find out what unit I would be assigned to until I reported to the U.S. Army Overseas Replacement Center at Fort Dix.

Basic Infantry Officer Course

The BIOC was a 17-week course intended to give recently commissioned officers from West Point and the various universities the technical and professional training necessary to perform as a lieutenant in an infantry unit. The training was challenging and exciting, and time passed quickly.

Serge and I had always had a healthy and friendly sense of competition. This competition carried on during our stay at Fort Benning. The RA officers who attended the BIOC could elect to take airborne training, a one-month course, Ranger training, a two-month course, or Army Aviation training, a 29-week course. One could volunteer for one, two, or all three of these training courses. If anyone elected to take all three classes, Army Aviation flight training was to be taken last. There was a subtle message in this requirement. The Army did not want to waste a lot of money to train a pilot who could become injured during the more rigorous airborne and Ranger courses to the point where he might have to be released from the service.

Neither Serge nor I were particularly interested in aviation training. We considered helicopter pilots as just "drivers" of airborne vehicles, a technical ability that did not appeal to our macho image of an infantry officer. I changed my mind seven years later when I saw these pilots' skill and courage on the battlefield. Serge decided to attend both Ranger and airborne training, and his decision, more than anything else, caused me to choose likewise. Both of us also felt these courses would continue our preparation for leading troops in combat. The training could well save our lives or those of soldiers under our command.

Ranger Training

We completed the BIOC at the end of September and began Ranger training after a two-day break. This training consisted of three phases. The first phase of approximately three weeks took place at Fort Benning. It consisted of physical exercise, hand-to-hand combat, and preparation for and conduct of both reconnaissance and combat patrols. It was a grueling three weeks. The Ranger candidates had to finish a timed run of 7 miles in full combat gear to complete this phase and go on to the other two. They also had to demonstrate they could swim 100 yards fully dressed for combat.

The worst prerequisite for me was the swimming requirement.

I had not learned to swim in Norway, despite being wholly surrounded by water, and I hurriedly enrolled in a swimming course at the YMCA in Columbus, Georgia, as soon as I learned about the requirement. I would go there almost every night during the BIOC to take lessons. However, it was not enough to learn how to swim. We had to do the test fully clothed, with boots on, and with our weapons. I managed to get through the ordeal but halfway drowned in the process.

The timed run was also something that had me worried. I have never been a good runner. I collapsed from cramps on the final run while less than 200 meters from the finish line. I would not have made it if it had not been for two husky guys who saw my predicament, grabbed me under my arms, and virtually dragged me across the finish line. One of these was a black officer who had been a football player in college. Unfortunately, I have forgotten their names.

We also spent much time in patrol training and on how to conduct raids. One of the most frightening sessions came when we had to crawl on our bellies at night and cut our way through barbed wire while stationary machine guns fired long bursts of live ammunition about four feet over the ground. I could only hope that whoever secured those machine guns knew what he was doing. A soldier is supposed to suffer to become a Ranger and I can genuinely say I suffered during those three weeks at Fort Benning in heat that often exceeded 100 degrees Fahrenheit.

After Fort Benning, we traveled to Eglin Air Force Base in Florida for two weeks of jungle training in the thick swamps surrounding this 1,875 square kilometer base. It was not a survival school but a test. It was supposed to be an experience as close to actual combat as possible. Realism was built into every aspect of our training. We were expected to do this with little food, sleep, and shelter while making intelligent decisions about complex tactical and technical problems that we might encounter in wartime.

We were given little food during those two weeks and were expected to forage for ourselves. Snakes were killed and eaten. Plants we knew to be edible were collected. Still, the rations fell far short of what was needed to withstand the grueling physical and mental pressures. We were purposely deprived of sleep to see who could function and make decisions under these difficult circumstances. The lack of sleep got to the point where a person would start hallucinating, run into trees, or wander off zombie-like.

The Ranger candidates were paired in buddy teams and each man was expected to look after and take care of his buddy. I was paired with Second Lieutenant John W. Loffert (1934–2018), a West Point graduate. John was probably the best map reader and compass man in the class and was invariably appointed as compass man by a patrol leader. Since we worked in teams, I always became the point man for the unit when Loffert was compass man.

During the first week of the Florida phase, we made a night raid on Santa Rosa Island (an old fort) in the Gulf of Mexico. A Navy minesweeper brought us to a point about 2 kilometers offshore. We launched our rubber rafts from the minesweeper and started paddling for shore. About 100 meters from the beach, the lane-grader (officer instructor and umpire) pulled the rubber raft plug to simulate a hit by gunfire from shore. All of us had to exit the raft and start swimming for shore with our weapons and gear. I would probably not have made it had it not been for John, an excellent swimmer.

On one of the last night patrols in the swamps, I was, as usual, the point man. We arrived at a riverbank and, according to John's calculations, we should have reached the bank near a bend in the river. Unfortunately, I could not see a curve in the darkness and the patrol leader directed that I climb an old oak tree near the river to see if I could locate the bend and get a fix on our position. I discovered the curve, but I lost my footing and fell about 12–15 feet to the ground when climbing down from the tree. I landed on my left foot and felt something snap. Within a short time, my ankle had swollen to where I had to remove the boot. It also hurt like hell. The patrol leader decided I would be left behind and picked up later since I had difficulty keeping up. He should, according to procedures, have left John with me, but he did not.

I stayed behind and tried to make myself comfortable, only to be discovered by an "enemy" unit searching for the patrol. I was thrown into the back of a truck and moved to an interrogation center. I finally convinced my captors I had been injured and required medical attention.

The doctor who looked at the ankle decided I had probably chipped a bone or torn a ligament and wanted to send me to the hospital at Fort Benning. However, we had only two days left in Florida and I managed to convince the doctor to wrap my ankle and let me continue. I hoped the two-day rest at Fort Benning before we proceeded to the mountain phase at Dahlonega in northern Georgia would heal the injury.

We had many injuries during the three phases of training. Some ended up in the hospital; others were dropped from the course when it became apparent they could not keep up. There have been several fatalities over the years, and we had one—a foreign officer. We were conducting a confidence exercise called, appropriately, the "death slide." A wire was strung across a lake from the top of a tree on one side to the base of a tree on the other side. The Ranger candidates climbed the tree and were given pullies that hooked over the wire and would slide at ever-increasing speed towards the other side of the lake. We were instructed to keep our eye on a safety officer on the far side who would signal us when to release our grip on the pulley. By doing so, when he signaled, we would plunge harmlessly into the lake near the far bank. Unfortunately, the foreign officer apparently failed to understand the instructions. He released his hold on the pulley too late and was thrown against the tree. He reportedly died from his injuries.

There have been other accidents over the years. Although the course has been modified and adjusted since the late 1950s to include increased rations and more sleep, trainees are still killed. Two drowned in 1977, one in 1985, and four died in 1995. The latest accident was the worst in the history of the Ranger School.

I had to report to the doctor on our return to Fort Benning, and he told me there was no chance of me completing the course. I pleaded to be allowed to try. It was not an act of bravery. If I were dropped from the course at this time, I would probably be required to start from the beginning in a future class when my ankle had healed. I did not want to go through another five weeks of hell now that I was within a little less than four weeks of completing the course.

The doctor had planned to put a cast on my ankle, which would have prevented me from continuing. He finally gave in to my pleas and agreed to wrap the ankle instead and let me try to go on to the last phase. He stated that he expected to see me again in a couple of days.

I was still limping when I exited the truck at the Dahlonega camp two days later. As soon as I took my place in the formation, a wiry first lieutenant lane-grader walked over to me. He asked what was bothering me. I told him. He looked me straight in the eyes and told me I might as well get back on the truck for Benning since I would not make it through the course. I did not answer but remained in the formation. I later learned the lieutenant's name was Anthony B. Herbert, a legendary warrior from the Korean War, where he was allegedly the most decorated soldier. After touring Europe at President Harry Truman's (1884–1972) orders, he had left the Army and entered the University of Pittsburg. He graduated in 1956 and returned to the Army as a Reserve Officer. He was assigned to the Mountain Ranger Training Camp at Dahlonega after attending the BIOC.

The mountain training program in the area near Dahlonega again centered on patrols and raids. Here, however, we also learned the necessary skills of mountain climbing and rappelling. The sheer cliffs on which we worked were from 20 to 40 meters in height. It was a dangerous business. We also learned to evacuate casualties by rappelling them off cliffs. The climbing was the worst part for me with my bad leg. Our first climbs were supported climbs; we had safety lines to keep us from falling onto the rocks below. The next to last day at Dahlonega involved a free climb without a safety harness, and I worried about this the whole time I was there.

We continued the torturous physical conditioning and learned a wide variety of skills and techniques for mountain warfare. Again, as in Florida, we learned to live off the land and make the terrain work to our advantage. The instruction in hand-to-hand combat, survival, first aid, and river-crossing techniques continued at a more advanced level. Each class was headed by a senior tactical officer (TAC) who kept score sheets and decided who passed and who failed. For our class, it was Captain Coffee. He doubled as the commander of the course and its counselor. The lane-graders, such as Herbert, turned in grades for each student to the TAC. While I was there, the Mountain Camp commander at Dahlonega was Lieutenant Colonel Byerly, but we never met.[1]

On the first morning at the camp, I was told the TAC wanted to see me. He came right to the point.

There was a meeting of lane graders and staff of the Mountain Ranger Camp last evening, and there was unanimous agreement that, in your condition, you are not going to make it through this phase of training. We have your safety and the safety of the other candidates to consider. For these reasons, I am asking that you voluntarily withdraw from the class. We can have you back at Fort Benning this evening.

The leg had bothered me a lot during the night and I had half expected something like this to happen. I was standing at attention in front of his desk. I fixed my eyes on a poster of General Washington at Valley Forge on the wall behind his desk.

Sir, should I consider the request that I withdraw from the class an order?

No, lieutenant, it is not an order. I want you to decide for yourself. However, we do feel this is the best course of action. You have tried your best, and you have no reason to be ashamed. After a few weeks of rest and light duty at Fort Benning, you will be in an excellent position to repeat the course in early 1959.

The grueling experience of the past five weeks was fresh in my mind and I did not care to repeat that misery. My friends and acquaintances from BIOC were in this class and I would not know anyone in the next course. It would have been so much easier if the TAC had dismissed me from the class for medical reasons. I could not agree that somehow there would not be a stigma attached to a voluntary withdrawal. Anyone reading my records in the future would not know the circumstances surrounding my removal—only that I withdrew voluntarily. However, I felt it would be an evasion to mention the noticeable alternative of dismissal for medical reasons. They had thrown the ball into my court.

Sir, I do not intend to withdraw voluntarily.

I believe my answer was somewhat of a surprise to the TAC. He stared at me for what seemed a long time. Then he got up from the desk and walked over to the window.

I disagree with your decision but, as I stated earlier, it is yours to make. I will arrange for the medics to give your ankle heat treatments on nights in camp. If you should fail to keep up, I will not hesitate to terminate your stay in Dahlonega.

I saluted and headed for the door. As I was about to exit, the TAC gave me this final parting thought: *Lieutenant, do not expect to be treated differently from the other candidates because of your injury.*

He was sure right about the last statement. Tony Herbert was the senior mountain climbing instructor as well as lane grader for several of our patrols. At times, it seemed he went out of his way to make my life miserable. Twice, he made me a patrol leader in the middle of a problem during our combat patrol phase. Another time he found me using my M1 rifle as a crutch as we were descending a steep hillside. He locked my heels, chewed me out for five minutes, and told me that if I ever did that again, he would see to it that I was dropped from the class.

If he saw me resting during one of our occasional breaks, he would always find me something to do so I would not be able to relax. I concluded he had set out to break me, to make my life so miserable that I would ask to be dropped from the class. My reaction was to become even more determined to go on.

During the second week at Dahlonega, I came down with pneumonia on top of my other troubles. It was not a surprise—several candidates had been dropped already because of colds and respiratory problems that eventually led to pneumonia. The mountains in northern Georgia can be frigid in November and this was an unusually cold year. The water in our canteens sometimes froze while on night patrols, even though they were padded.

After becoming wet from hasty river crossings, exposure to the rain and snow was enough to bring on colds and pneumonia. In our case, our worn-out physical condition and general lack of sleep aggravated the problem. When the medics told me I was coming down with pneumonia, we had only one patrol remaining, but it was the big one. It involved a Blue Ridge power station raid in Tennessee, almost

80 kilometers through Dahlonega's mountains. The medics, who had come to know me rather well, did not want me to go, but I was adamant and asked them not to make it an issue. Tony Herbert was our lane grader. I do not know to this day how I managed those three days and nights, particularly with Tony paying close attention to everything I did or failed to do.

After arriving back in Dahlonega, we only had the free climb remaining, and then it was back to Fort Benning to clean and turn in our equipment. The night we came back from the long patrol, I received orders to report to the TAC. I figured this was the end. I limped into his office and reported as smartly as I could. First, he asked if I was ready for the climb the following day. I replied that I was.

He had a bunch of papers in front of him. He asked me to stand at ease and said he wanted to show me a report on my performance by my lane grader, Tony Herbert. I was prepared for the worst. To my great surprise and relief, it was an extraordinarily detailed and complimentary report on my activities while under Herbert's supervision. It ended with the following sentence: "In summary, this Ranger has more guts and determination than the rest of the class combined."[2] I was utterly at a loss for words. The TAC laughed at my evident surprise and said he would not have bet a nickel on my chances of making it this far two weeks ago. He was familiar with my records since he remarked he had spent some time at a Norwegian field hospital in Korea and had good memories from that experience. He dismissed me after adding his compliments to Herbert's.

I virtually walked on air from the TAC's office back to my bunk. I did not get much sleep that night, even though I was exhausted. I felt happy about what Herbert had written, particularly given who he was. I also had a great sense of pride at the TAC's comments. I felt that, for a moment, I had lived up to the best in my heritage. I was glad Herbert and the TAC were unaware that it was fear of having to repeat the Ranger training's misery, not guts, that kept me going.

I saw Tony Herbert only once after Ranger School—at Fort Leavenworth, Kansas, 11 years later. I was a major attending the Command and General Staff College (C&GSC) while Tony was a lieutenant colonel. After the relief of command as a battalion commander in the 173rd Airborne Brigade and given a bad efficiency report, he had come back from Vietnam. Herbert fought his relief and bad efficiency report by going on the offensive and filing charges against his superiors, accusing them of covering up U.S. war crimes. He was at Fort Leavenworth while awaiting the outcome of these investigations. He ran the physical fitness test for our class when I met him.

When we first met, I saluted and started to introduce myself. Tony interrupted me and said, *I know who the hell you are. And from what I have heard and read, I was not wrong about you either.*

We had several talks after that first meeting. Herbert could not discuss the investigation, but I realized he was a bitter man because of his experiences. He retired from the Army a short time later at the age of 41. Together with James T. Wooten, the national correspondent for *The New York Times*, he wrote a best-selling autobiography in 1973 titled *Soldier*.[3]

I got through the free climb without any problems, with Tony Herbert's compliments and the TAC's statement ringing in my ears. They took me to the Martin Army Hospital as soon as we arrived back at Fort Benning, and John Loffert was left with the task of cleaning my equipment and turning it in. I told him it was the proper punishment for causing me to be the point man so often, leading to the fall from the tree.

I was immediately admitted to the hospital and spent approximately three weeks recovering from pneumonia and my ankle injury. I was on a respirator off and on for the first week or so. I could not attend the class graduation ceremony, but the coveted Ranger tab with orders I had worked so hard for was brought to me at the hospital. Serge was selected as the messenger.

A fellow officer in the class, the late Colonel Norbert Grabowski, told me someone was planning to publish a story about this class since many of its graduates became well known or rose to a high rank within the military. He reminded me that Colin Powell, the chairman of the Joint Chiefs of Staff (JCS) during the Gulf War and later Secretary of State, was a class member. He was most likely a second lieutenant like the rest of the cadets. He may have been one of the two who hauled me over the finish line during the 7-mile run.

Airborne Training

I missed the airborne class for which I was scheduled because of my hospitalization. I was rescheduled for a course in January 1959. I had two weeks after release from the hospital before the class began, and I ran, with Marion following in the car, and exercised each day, trying to build up my strength so I would have no difficulty passing the required tests or keeping up on the morning runs.

Serge had completed the class before Christmas and he and Katherine departed for their first duty station at Fort Devens, Massachusetts, during the holidays. Although we were both infantry officers, we would never be stationed together during our careers, saying something about the Army's size and sizeable officers' corps. I only saw him twice after 1958, once in Germany in 1961 and the last time when he was at Fort Bragg for a short visit in 1966.

The airborne training started during the first week of January. It consisted of three phases. The first, which lasted about a week, involved the more technical details of parachuting, such as how the parachute is packed, how it deploys, how the aircraft is rigged for airdrop, and what to do in emergencies. The training would begin at about 0600 hours and last until about 1700.

Every morning of the first three weeks would begin with a rigid inspection of each paratrooper by veteran airborne NCOs. If the paratrooper's haircut or shave were not up to standards, if his brass belt-buckle or boots were not shined to the point where you could practically use them as mirrors, or if the uniform were not properly starched and crisp, it would result in punishment. The punishment took the form of so many pushups, pullups, or running in place for so many minutes while being screamed at by the NCOs.

I hate to think of how many pushups and pullups I performed during these three weeks. It was all part of making the trainee pay attention to every little detail and follow all instructions to the letter. Failure to do so could easily result in injury or the loss of life. The inspections preceded a period of calisthenics and a 5-mile run. The second phase, which also lasted about a week, consisted of practicing exiting a mock aircraft door, the proper body position after exiting and waiting for the parachute to deploy, and what seemed to be an endless period of rehearsing parachute landing falls (PLF). It later became evident to me why so much emphasis was placed on this aspect of parachuting. Most injuries I have witnessed over my many years of parachuting took place on landing. Most were due to the paratroopers failing to follow the correct procedures for a proper landing.

We also spent many hours in the suspended harness, what the trainees affectionately referred to as the "ball cruncher." Here, the trainees learned how to manipulate their parachutes in the air. Troops also learned how to avoid entanglement with other paratroopers and the procedures for guiding their fall towards a spot on the ground. Finally, they learned safety procedures for landing in trees, high-tension wires, or in water. It was the most agonizing period of this intense training.

We referred to the third week of training as the "tower week," when we began dropping from the 85 meter (250 feet) towers. We were hoisted to the top in a parachute. An automatic release system would free the paratrooper and his parachute when at the top of the tower. The descent gave the paratrooper a chance to control and maneuver his parachute and make a proper PLF. This training was also psychological in that it exposed the trainee to greater heights and gave him confidence in his parachute and his ability to control it. The tower was referred to as "the great separator." It was the first real test of courage and determination and there was a number in each class who found it impossible to master this phase, leading to their elimination from further training.[4]

The tower drops were under calm weather conditions to avoid having the trainee and his parachute blown into the tower, possibly causing injury or death. We also used the wind machine during this week of training. A paratrooper is not necessarily out of trouble just because he has returned safely to earth. A strong ground wind can drag a person over rocks and stumps and cause severe injury or death. Because of this possibility, a paratrooper had to master the quickest and most efficient method of collapsing his chute. These machines (large motor-driven propellers) could cause winds far higher than what was considered safe for parachute operations.

The fourth week consisted of actual parachute jumps from aircraft. The rigorous inspections, calisthenics, and runs were dispensed with to concentrate entirely on what we were doing. I was apprehensive on my first jump and I was worried about my last drop, about 25 years later, after hundreds of jumps under my belt.

I believe this is true for everyone and tests conducted at Fort Bragg in the early 1970s tend to confirm this belief. A person may become outwardly calmer and have more confidence in his equipment and his ability to overcome problems. However, the underlying feeling of tension and apprehension is still there as you exit an aircraft flying at a speed of 200 kilometers per hour.

Mass military parachute operations take place from relatively low altitudes. This is intended to have a unit arrive on the ground in a tight formation for ease in assembly. The actual parachute operation and the initial minutes on the ground are when an airborne group is most vulnerable to enemy action. It is not unusual for aircraft flying in tight and staggered formations to drop hundreds of paratroopers on a relatively small piece of ground. As paratroopers exit many aircraft at various altitudes as rapidly as possible, the congestion in the air is always a concern and often results in injuries.

Our senior NCO's last words kept running through my mind as I climbed aboard the aircraft for my first parachute jump on 2 February 1959: *It takes eight seconds to hit the ground without a chute! You count three of them away before you pull your reserve! It will take you one or two seconds to react to pull it! Then, it takes one or two seconds more for it to open! That is seven, which means you have one second to daydream up there, soldier—one second!* My first jump was from a C-123 aircraft. The parachute drop went off without a hitch, as did the following four also made from a C-123. After five jumps, we graduated and were authorized to wear the parachute badge and qualified for assignment to airborne units.

To Germany

My duties at Fort Benning were over with airborne training completion and I was ready to proceed to my next duty station. In January, I had been informed I would be assigned to the 2nd Battle Group, 6th Infantry Regiment, in Berlin. However, my departure was delayed while awaiting approval for concurrent travel for Marion. There was a policy in force that dependents were not authorized to accompany a service member to Europe unless government quarters were available.

Approval of this request was received in February. There would now be two people traveling instead of one, which caused the travel method to change. For once, the change was a positive one. It had been planned that I would travel by air or troop carrier to Europe, but since my wife would now accompany me, commercial travel was authorized from the U.S. Army Overseas Replacement Station at Fort Hamilton, New York. We were notified we would travel first class on the SS *United States*, the newest, largest, fastest, and most luxurious ocean-liner in service at the time.

Marion and I drove our car from Fort Benning to New York and turned it in at Fort Hamilton for shipment to Europe. We remained in New York for three days, staying at Hotel St. George. Most days were spent preparing for our trip or visiting tourist sites.

My parents had planned to visit us in Georgia over the holidays, but a work accident where my father lost most of a finger prevented them from joining us. However, their pensions were approved and they planned to leave for Norway later in the spring.

We departed New York on 6 March and arrived in Bremerhaven on 12 March after short stops in Le Havre and Southampton. We experienced some rough seas in the Atlantic, particularly on the third day. Nevertheless, the steaming time from New York to Le Havre was only four days, six hours, and 34 minutes and we were told that was a new record, with an average speed over 31 knots.

The time on the ship was an adventure. The accommodations and service were outstanding and beyond anything we had ever experienced. It was a far cry from the sparse third-class accommodations on MS *Gripsholm* almost eight years earlier. There were several military officers among the passengers and we were encouraged to wear our uniforms. The captain's formal dinner the night before we arrived in Le Havre allowed me to wear my dress uniform for the first time. The first-class passenger list read like pages from American and European social registers. Our table companions were The Honorable Frederick B. Lyon and his wife, Miss Dorothy Bellmore, and Mr. Jules H. Levee. The captain of the *United States* was Commodore John W. Anderson.

A military sedan picked us up at the dock in Bremerhaven and took us to a hotel where we stayed for the night. The next day, Friday 13 March, we took the military train from Bremerhaven to Berlin. The day and date did not fill us with superstitious feelings but, in retrospect, the tour in Berlin proved to be a difficult time for both Marion and me.

CHAPTER 4

Brink of Armageddon: Berlin, 1959–1961

Berlin is a beautiful city. However, in the late 1950s, it showed the visible scars of the ferocious bombing and ground fighting at the end of World War II. There were still large areas with bombed-out buildings that had not been repaired and reoccupied.

There were mountain-sized piles of rubble cleared from the thoroughfares and streets and left to be disposed of later. The area between the Soviet-occupied zone and those occupied by the three Western powers showed no rebuilding effort. Instead, blackened skeletons of buildings marked this no man's land and bore stark evidence of what war means in the modern age.

The once beautiful Kaiser Wilhelm Memorial Church at the end of Kurfürstendamm was left in deformed and burned-out condition as a memorial to the tens of thousands who died. The charred clock's hands showed the time when bombs wiped out over 4 square kilometers of the city in a single night on 18 November 1943. A new tower has now been built alongside the deformed skeleton. Unfortunately, little had been done to rebuild and repair the old governmental area to the east of the Brandenburg Gate and the Reichstag building was still a burned-out hulk.

The population of Berlin in the late 1950s was less than three million, slightly over half of what it had been at its earlier peak. Berlin was Germany's most bombed city and more than 150,000 civilians died there during the war. These losses were either because of the bombing or because of the battle for the city in 1945. The number of people who fled Berlin in the last few days has never been accurately estimated. A large number left after the war to seek work and a better future in West Germany.

The result of these losses and outflow of people, when combined with the millions of German soldiers who died during the war, was an unbalanced population where females outnumbered the males by a factor of at least three to one. It was a bachelor's paradise and a place where marriages could quickly end up on the rocks.

Berlin covers a vast area and, at times, a person can forget they are in one of the world's great metropolitan centers. Interlaced by rivers, canals, lakes, and forests, the city has a charming, country-like setting. The Havel and Großer Wannsee

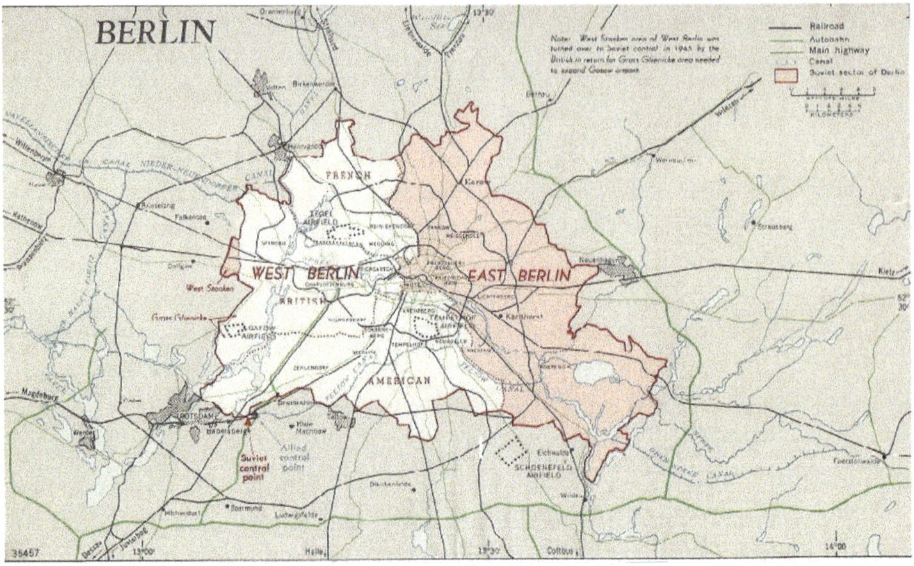

Map 1. Berlin Command map showing the four occupied zones in Berlin.

Lakes stretch for miles from the district of Pichelsdorf west of the city center in a southeastern direction. The Havel was a favorite weekend outing place for Berliners, as was the Grünewald, a large, forested area on its southern bank. Over one-fifth of the city's total size lay in parks and woodlands, lakes, canals, and streams.

Berlin was divided into four occupational sectors at the end of World War II. The largest sector, which included most of Berlin north and east of Potsdamer Platz, belonged to the Soviets. The second-largest sector belonged to the Americans and covered much of the central business district and the south and southwestern portions of the city. The British area was a pie-shaped area from Berlin's center to Kaldow, Gatow, and Spandau in the west. The northwest part of the city constituted the French area of occupation. Berlin was still an occupied territory, and the occupation troops and their dependents were not subject to local authorities or courts. A commandant who doubled as the military commander and chief political representative of his country ruled each sector. These four commandants would meet to resolve issues of common concern to the four powers or the citizens of their respective areas. This organization met only sporadically and never functioned as intended.

Despite the suffering they had so recently undergone, the Berliners impressed me with their friendliness, hard work, optimistic view of the future, and sound appreciation for democracy. The work carried out to rebuild the city from the rubble of 1945 was enormous and impressive. This work continued at an accelerated pace even though this area's future was far from certain. There were little or no ill feelings demonstrated against the Western occupiers and I came away with the impression that the population accepted as their responsibility what had happened to their lives and fortunes. Some of this friendliness was no doubt generated by the proximity of the Soviets, who they detested.

The division of the city separated many families, but travel back and forth was still relatively free, and those who lived in the western sectors had a chance to compare how their fellow citizens lived in the eastern area. This freedom of travel gave them an appreciation for democracy and the free enterprise system. It led to a continuous and accelerating exodus from East Berlin and from East Germany through East Berlin. Eventually, the freedom of travel became a problem for the Soviets and their puppets in East Germany and ultimately led to the erection of the Berlin Wall.

American troops in Berlin were quartered primarily in Lichterfelde in the southern part of the city. The primary combat elements consisted of two battle groups from the 6th Infantry Regiment, each comprised of approximately 1,500 troops. McNair Barracks served as home for these troops, while Andrews Barracks, a short distance away, served as quarters for the support troops. The old Air Ministry buildings on Clay Allee in the Dahlem district contained the American command's headquarters. Most dependent housing units and support facilities were in this affluent area of the city.

Platoon Leader

Marion and I were assigned furnished government quarters on Flannagan Strasse in Dahlem upon arriving in Berlin on 13 March 1959. We spent the next day signing for our quarters and buying some minor things we needed for housekeeping. On Sunday, we attended a reception for newly arrived officers hosted by Colonel Harold B. Ayers (1919–1989), the 2nd Battle Group commander. I was happy to meet one of my Ranger classmates at this reception, Second Lieutenant Norbert Dieter Grabowski (1936–2007). Norbert was born in Poland and had come to the U.S. as a refugee in the late 1940s. His family settled in New Orleans, Louisiana. Norbert's branch of service was the Transportation Corps but, like all RA officers assigned to a technical branch, he had to serve two years with one of the combat arm branches and, in his case, it was with the infantry. He had been assigned to Company C, 2nd Battle Group, while I joined Company D.

My first day of duty was Monday 16 March, my 23rd birthday. I reported to the Company Commander, Captain William G. Cash (1930–2016), who gave me one of the 48-men rifle platoons. The other officers in the company were Lieutenants Israel Nezvesky, William R. Whitley Jr., William Bailey, and Edward King. These officers were all first lieutenants and undoubtedly enjoyed having a second lieutenant assigned to carry out the more onerous extra duties.

My platoon sergeant was Master Sergeant Francis E. McHenry. It was up to him to take me under his wings and ensure I did not make too many mistakes in commanding the platoon. He was a World War II and Korean War veteran and I paid close attention to his advice as he guided me through those first crucial months.

My service in Company D lasted until the end of August 1959, a little short of six months. We spent much of that time training either in the Grünewald in Berlin or at the Wildflecken training area in West Germany. Live fire exercises in Berlin were limited to known-distance ranges, as we could not train with supporting weapons such as mortars, artillery, or armor due to the city's congested nature. For this training, we traveled to West Germany for at least a month each year. Tank and artillery units, of which few were in Berlin, would spend even more time in the west.

We spent much time on drills and ceremonies. Berlin was a visible station in the late 1950s and early 1960s and many VIPs would stop for visits. Parades and celebrations also took place on certain holidays. The purpose was more psychological than anything else. It was a reminder to the West Berliners, and our potential enemies in the east, that we, and our British and French allies, were in Berlin to stay.

The troops and officers were of an exceedingly high caliber. Only in later airborne assignments did I encounter soldiers of an equal or better quality. Both NCOs and officers underwent checks before posting to this very vulnerable station. Any severe infractions of rules or the way we behaved would result in the reassignment of the soldier or officer to a unit in West Germany.

There was a program in Berlin that called for junior officers of the three occupying western powers to spend some duty time with our allies. If it came to war, the partners would have to fight together and it was beneficial if we, at the company level, knew how our allies were armed, intended to fight, and what their strengths and weaknesses were.

When my turn as an exchange officer came, I spent a month with Company C, 1st Battalion, The Royal Scots. The battalion commander was Lieutenant Colonel McQueen. An officer from that company took my place in Company D for the same length of time. This exchange was a beneficial experience and resulted in friendships that endured for many years.

The stated reason for my assignment to the battle group S-3 (operations) Section on 31 August 1959 was to fill one of the two liaison officer positions. A liaison officer was primarily a wartime duty when the battle group commander could be required to send one to a higher or adjacent headquarters as a means of facilitating the exchange of information and instructions. There was little requirement for anyone to perform this function in peacetime since no exercises above the battle group level had ever occurred in anyone's memory. These two officers were primarily used to monitor the training.

My transfer to headquarters was for an entirely different reason. Every year the NATO countries would engage in the Le Clerc (named after a French general) marksmanship competition matches. The allied troops in Berlin were not NATO troops but were allowed to participate and Colonel Ayers had set his sights on winning this prestigious match. It had come to his attention that I had placed number one with a rifle in a national-level competition in 1956.

I was ordered, along with one other officer, to carry out Ayers's dream. The other officer, First Lieutenant H. Norman Schwarzkopf (1934–2012), was placed in charge of the team because he was two years senior to me. Norm was a West Pointer from the class of 1956 and an expert with the .45 caliber pistol. Neither of us cherished our assignment, but after fruitlessly expressing our misgivings, we set out to do our best.

The team consisted of three sections corresponding to the weapons we were required to fire during the matches. Each national team had to shoot three of the weapons generally carried by soldiers of his Army. In our case, this was the .45 caliber pistol, the M1 rifle, and the Browning Automatic Rifle (BAR). There were strict inspections of the weapons before each match for unlawful modifications. Norm Schwarzkopf took charge of the pistol and rifle teams and I received the BAR team.

A team of two fired the BAR. First, there was a timed firing exercise from 300 meters against stationary targets. Second, a run from the 300-meter range to the 200-meter range, followed by firing two magazines within a specified time. The same procedure took place from the 100-meter range. Soldiers were in full combat gear. The biggest problem was firing accurately within the prescribed time limit after each of the 100-meter dashes. The breathing rhythm had to be linked precisely to the short bursts and we were required to fire to stay within the time constraints. We practiced this for weeks, often under the watchful eyes of Colonel Ayers.

All went well at first. We had no trouble eliminating our sister unit, the 3rd Battle Group. Colonel Ayers was very complimentary in his remarks after my companion and I set a new match record with the BAR by coming in with a score of 386 out of a possible 400. Unfortunately, however, this was to be our only moment of glory. We were soundly defeated in the early stages of the elimination matches and had to watch another team represent our country. Colonel Ayers had difficulties concealing his disappointment at our poor performance that winter day in 1960.

After the matches, I asked Major Robert D. Glaser, the S-3, for an assignment to a rifle company. I had served less than six months at that level and felt this was insufficient. I had been routinely promoted to first lieutenant on 13 December 1959 and I wanted more service in an infantry rifle company before being considered for promotion to captain. I expected my consideration for promotion to captain in 1963 and the only place I could hope to get further experience was in Berlin, since I would likely leave the city in the summer of 1962. Glaser agreed and we both went to see Lieutenant Colonel Richard F. Wilkinson (1921–2010), the battle group deputy commander.

I was the only liaison officer assigned to the S-3 Section at this time and Major Glaser wanted a replacement. Schwarzkopf had been on temporary duty (TDY) with the Le Clerc team from the Combat Support Company. The decision assigned

Schwarzkopf to the S-3 Section as a liaison officer. I would go to Company C. This was particularly pleasing since Norbert Grabowski was in that unit. This change in assignments for Schwarzkopf and me took place on 26 April 1960.

I spent the next 16 months in Company C. The first commander I served for was Captain Vernon E. Staum (1930–2014), but it was only for a little over two months. Therefore, he was not required to write an Officer Efficiency Report (OER) but wrote a great one nevertheless. He was an excellent officer. I met him several times in the U.S. He was interested in my career and often talked to me about what I should or should not do.

For the next 14 months, I served under Captain Donald E. Rosenblum. He was also an excellent infantry officer, a graduate of the prestigious Citadel Military Academy in South Carolina. He had more influence on my career than any other officer I encountered during my tour of duty in Berlin. Rosenblum was a challenging but fair taskmaster and a person who was satisfied by anything less than perfection only if convinced the individual or unit concerned had given the task their best and maximum effort. He was a leader who could inspire and it was not surprising that his company excelled in every field. This outstanding record ranged from alerts and field-training exercises to repeated top scores in such areas as personnel records, arms room, and mess hall standards in annual Inspector General (IG) inspections.

One of my first duties in Company C was as commander of the security forces at Spandau Prison, where the war criminals from the Nuremberg Trials were incarcerated. By 1960, only three of the original seven inmates remained in this large facility in the British sector—Hitler's deputy Rudolf Hess (1894–1987), Hitler Youth leader Baldur von Schirach (1907–1974), and Armaments Minister Albert Speer (1905–1981).

The physical security of Spandau Prison was the responsibility of the occupying powers on a monthly rotating basis. First, the Soviets were in charge, then the Americans, the British, and finally the French. We posted guards in several towers within the prison compound and at the front gate. The military guards who were not on duty, and some personnel, were kept as a reserve in a nearby building. Nearly 100 troops were involved in this duty in one way or another.

The routine for the duties at Spandau Prison was in detailed protocols agreed to by the Big Four. The changing of responsibility for security from one nation to another occurred at a very formal ceremony in the prison's front courtyard. I marched my troops through the gate and took up a position directly opposite the formation of Soviet soldiers in the courtyard. The two formations remained facing each other until the prescribed time for the change of responsibility. At that time, the Soviet commander ordered his troops to present arms, and I gave my soldiers the same order. The Soviet commander then announced in Russian that he was ready to relinquish control of the prison. I would counter with a short-prescribed phrase in English that

I had dutifully memorized: "I, Lieutenant Lunde, in the name of the United States of America, am ready to accept responsibility for the security of Spandau Prison."

The two formations then marched off to the guard towers in a specified order. We stopped at each guard post, and I called out for a member of my command to assume his position; the Soviet guard, being relieved, fell in at the rear of the Soviet formation. We repeated this procedure at every guard post. The final guard post to be changed was at the gate. The two military formations again faced each other in the courtyard and I confirmed to the Soviet commander that the transfer of responsibility was correct. After an exchange of military courtesies, the Soviet detachment marched out of the compound. After a month, the same ceremony was performed again, with a British unit accepting responsibility from the Americans.

I remember that I had the Spandau security duty twice in 1960, but I am not sure. It was a somewhat routine duty and, when the novelty wore off, also dull. We sometimes questioned the need for so much security. There was virtually no chance the prisoners could escape. It appeared to us we were there primarily to prevent someone from the outside from entering, and this seemed somewhat far-fetched. However, there were recurring rumors of a possible raid to free the prisoners by such individuals as Colonel Otto Skorzeny (1908–1975), the famous German commando leader. He freed Benito Mussolini (1883–1945) in a daring raid towards the end of World War II. The soldiers pulled a two-hour tour of duty at their posts. I entered the prison to inspect the guards three times in 24 hours, although I could enter whenever I wished.

We were not allowed to enter the prison building unless asked by the directors' chairman. The chairmanship rotated so that an American was chairman when the U.S. was responsible for security. He was a civilian federal prison official, as were the unarmed interior guards.

In his Spandau diaries, Albert Speer expressed the prisoners' relief whenever the Western Allies took over security. They were afraid the Soviet guard force, after the East–West rift in the late 1940s, would take over the prison building by force and execute the inmates. We were instructed not to communicate with the prisoners without the permission of the directors.

I frequently observed the prisoners in rather lengthy and animated discussions with each other. They spent much time in the rear courtyard when I made my rounds and I would pass them at close quarters. Hess never acknowledged my presence. Von Schirach spent most of the time pacing back and forth in the yard and, if he noted me, it was with a stiff nod of the head. Speer spent most of his time working in what appeared to be a vegetable garden and he invariably expressed a friendly "Guten morgen" or "Guten tag, Herr Leutnant." It felt rather strange for me, who, just 15 years earlier, had been an unknown young boy in one of the countries occupied by Nazi Germany, to now have responsibility for the secure incarceration of some of the highest officials of that regime.

Personal Difficulties

My personal life underwent a significant change in 1960. Marion and I took a short trip to Norway in 1959 after she had made one trip by herself. We entered a partnership with my sister and brother-in-law to construct a motel in Voss. Before we obtained construction loans, the property had to be purchased, and this took all the money Marion and I could locate. We had also begun to repay my cousin, Andrew Rolfsnes, the loan he had given me while I was a UC student. My Army pay at the time was $187 per month before taxes and was only enough to meet recurring expenses. As mentioned earlier, we had not expected the motel project to be undertaken until I had worked for several years.

We again turned to Marion's parents for help to purchase the property. Our financial limit was at hand after that purchase. We were unable to provide any significant assistance after our initial purchase of the land except for a few $100 checks in times of dire need.

Marion decided she should get a job. She started working for an American intelligence agency in Berlin, which eventually led to a 30-year career in the State Department. We were not getting along well in our marriage and her job led to a situation where we seldom saw each other except on weekends when I did not have duties. Her work was primarily at night, while mine was mainly during the day. It was not often in those days that a wife worked, particularly an officer's wife.

In all military assignments in those days, there was a demanding social life, both official and private. The military was a society within a society with its separate laws, judicial system, and traditions. The social life in Berlin was more lively than usual. There were often invitations to social functions by British, French, and German authorities or officers.

When Marion and I moved into our apartment, there was an extra room with a separate entrance for a maid. We did not see any need for this until Marion began to work. The maid cleaned, made sure my uniforms were sent to and picked up from the cleaners, and off and on she did some cooking. She also worked for Captain Cash and his wife Dottie, who lived in the apartment above ours. This helped with expenses.

Most social events were in the evenings or on Saturday afternoons. This situation often made it impossible for Marion to attend. Of course, we could regret invitations, but not too often, to prevent receiving an unsociable label.

The lively social life with numerous parties, both official and private, involved much drinking, and the many temptations that characterized the Berlin tour did not help matters. The marriage was obviously on the slippery slope towards a break-up. I feel I was mostly to blame for this situation. I had not settled down to the point where I had accepted all the responsibilities of marriage. During these two crucial years of my life, some of my behavior can only be described as reckless, thoughtless, insensitive, and would have been detrimental to any marriage.

The fact that we had entered the marriage in 1958 with some misgivings, as already described, showed that the bonds at that time were not strong enough to weather my behavior and the kind of situation we faced in Berlin. By June 1960, we mutually decided a divorce was the best solution. Marion did not want to leave her job in Berlin, and our first action was to seek separate quarters. The application was approved quickly.

Usually, we would have sought a divorce in the U.S., but our finances did not allow for this, and we asked the Army for permission to seek a divorce in a German court. The German legal institutions did not have authority over Americans in Berlin, so a limited waiver was required and granted for this purpose. The fact that the divorce was on the grounds of incompatibility and not contested made it easier for the U.S. authorities to grant the waiver.

I was not sure we were doing the right thing and I spoke to a few of my closest friends about our problems. Most thought we were making the right decision. The exception was Norm Schwarzkopf, who—in his straightforward manner—stated that I was making a dumb-ass decision and that a divorce could be detrimental to my career in the Army. While I respected and admired his blunt advice, I did not follow it.

The German court granted us a divorce in November 1960. Marion and I parted as best of friends and we remained so until she died on 5 June 2012. She never remarried, although she was engaged in 1970. Her fiancé disappeared over Laos in late 1970 or early 1971.

In early 1961, an American named Robert L. Morton, who was working for an international investment company and who had become aware of our American-style motel in Norway, invited Marion and me to a party. There he introduced us to Kemmons Wilson, the chairman of the board of Holiday Inns of America, Inc., the largest motel chain in the United States. At that time the chain was considering the possibility of expanding operations overseas, and Mr Wilson asked if we'd be interesed in being involved. The suggestion was that if a survey by Morton about Norway's potential for motel operation was viewed positively by the board of Holiday Inns, they would then offer to purchase the motel already built for a percentage share by my brother-in-law and me in future Holiday Inns operations in Europe.

My brother-in-law would remain as manager of the motel he had built. After discussing with Birger and my sister, we decided to accept the offer tentatively. Morton's final report was a glowing description of Norway's possibilities, backed up by many statistics, however I felt uneasy about some of its conclusions and recommendations. I judged that the report contained some very questionable assumptions, and the statistics used were misleading. The cover letter accompanying the report stated that I had received a copy, but the inference was that I had given it my approval.

After discussion, I wrote to Mr. Wilson, assuring him that I had had no part in preparing the report. Although Mr. Morton's conclusions and recommendations were mainly valid, I felt that the rosy scenario and some statistics could be misleading. In the end, Holiday Inns did not look favorably upon the feasibility study. I do not know if my letter played any part in their decision. Despite the disappointment, I felt our action was correct and have never regretted it.

Company Executive Officer: Race and Ethnicity

The officers in Company C were an exceptional group of professionals. First Lieutenant John M. Kirk was the XO when I arrived. He was a harsh taskmaster who tolerated no slack. He left at the end of 1960 to take over his own company. First Lieutenant Stanley Z. White was the next most senior officer and commanded the weapons platoon. He was one of only two black officers in the battle group. My friend Norbert D. Grabowski had the 1st Platoon, First Lieutenant Claude L. Stults the 2nd Platoon, and Second Lieutenant David B. Browning Jr., the 4th Platoon. I was assigned the 3rd Platoon with Master Sergeant William Scott as my platoon sergeant.

Captain Rosenblum called me into his office around the time John Kirk left the company. He informed me he was appointing me as his new XO. He made the statement in such a manner as not to invite any comments.

Because of the situation, I felt compelled to point out that Stanley White was my senior, and Grabowski was also my senior by four days. Rosenblum answered that Grabowski was leaving for a job with the transportation corps as his two-year tour with the infantry was at an end. He further stated he felt I could handle an XO's duties better than White. He went on to say that he did not feel White had the requisite respect of the other officers and NCOs to handle the job. I expressed my belief that he would do an excellent job as an XO and that I was being placed in a very precarious position since he was my friend. I stated that, while I was flattered by the offer, such a move could be devastating to White's self-confidence. The whole unit would know immediately that the company commander demonstrated a lack of faith in this officer's abilities.

Rosenblum was annoyed at my protests and cut the conversation short by stating he had already decided. While U.S. Army regulations prevented him from entering the position I would be occupying in my files, it would be reflected in the annual OER. Rosenblum kept his promise, and the report submitted on 30 June 1961 states: "Subject officer has been serving in the capacity as the company XO. Since he was junior to another officer, no orders were ever made assigning him this duty." I knew that further objections would be useless and ended the conversation by asking Rosenblum to inform White before he learned about it from others. Rosenblum did so the same morning.

Lieutenant White was an officer of average ability with a happy-go-lucky attitude that, at times, could be interpreted as a frivolity by those who did not know him well. I do not think race played a role in this incident and I believe Rosenblum's decision would have been the same if Stanley had been white. However, sometimes appearances are as notable as reality. Every officer in the battle group would quickly know about Rosenblum's action and it would not pass unnoticed that White was one of only two black officers in that organization.

Captain Rosenblum was an outstanding troop leader and fair and honest. While I have absolutely no reason to question his motives, I believe, even today, that a different solution was available. It would not have been difficult to transfer Stanley to the battle group staff or another Berlin office. This solution would have avoided the unfair perception and spared him the inevitable embarrassment and loss of pride. I felt I was right in frankly telling Rosenblum what was on my mind. Having done so, I let the matter drop.

Although the military services, notably the Army, had taken the lead among national institutions to integrate its personnel and assure equal opportunity for all, vestiges of racial inequality were still present. Lieutenant White was a bachelor and occasionally dated German girls. He spoke German exceptionally well, better than any other officer in the battle group except Norbert Grabowski.

Stanley's dating of white girls often led to derogatory comments by his fellow officers when he was not present. He approached me in early 1961 and said he wanted my view on something. There was a formal battle group officers' party coming up at the Harnack House Officers' Club and Stanley planned to bring a date to that event. He asked what I thought about it. I knew he was talking about bringing a white girl. I asked him about the girl's background. The reason for this question was that the Officer's Guide stated that any officer escorting a pick-up or woman of ill repute to an official social function "should be viewed with scorn."

Stanley assured me the girl was not a pick-up and came from a reputable family in Steglitz. I then told him he was an officer in the U.S. Army and had as much right as anyone to bring a date to the social function. Nevertheless, I also told him he should look upon the situation realistically and expect some to comment adversely.

He asked how I thought Rosenblum would react. I told him I did not know, but my view was that Rosenblum was a straight shooter. I further opined that Rosenblum would never let personal feelings about an officer's private life influence his evaluation of that officer's ability to perform his duties. Stanley then asked me directly what I would do in a similar situation. I told him I would say to hell with everyone else and do what I thought was right. However, I should have been less direct in my advice, given the possible impact on his career.

Stanley showed up at the social function in the company of a nice-looking and well-dressed young German lady. There must have been at least 150 officers, wives, and guests at this formal function, and one could not avoid noticing the tension in the room as Stanley and his date entered. There was an evident effort by those present to move away from Stanley and his partner. They were left by themselves in the corner of the room.

It was an awkward situation. Lieutenant Claude Stults, his German date, and I finally separated ourselves from the group we were with, walked over to Stanley and his companion and struck up a conversation. Norbert Grabowski came over to join Stults and me. A couple of other officers subsequently joined us and Captain Rosenblum stopped by to say hello.

Stanley and the German woman were uncomfortable and they decided not to participate in the dinner that followed the reception. Claude, another officer, and I paid our respects to the battle group commander, Colonel John R. Deane (1919–2013), and requested permission to absent ourselves. We joined Stanley and his date for dinner at a German restaurant. It had been an uncomfortable situation, demonstrating that racial integration had its limits, even in the U.S. Army. No one commented to Claude or me about this affair after the reception.

Suspicions and prejudice were not limited to race. Travel into the Soviet sector of Berlin was relatively unrestricted before August 1961. Automobiles with plates that showed the occupants to be part of the occupation forces could pass without East Berlin police interference. Many Americans stationed in West Berlin traveled to East Berlin for one reason or another.

Norbert Grabowski and I may have done so more than most. We both spoke German, although I was far from fluent in the language. With an unofficial exchange rate of four East German marks for one West German mark, one could make good buys in East Berlin on certain products.

The last days of ferocious fighting in Berlin in 1945 had centered on the area around the Brandenburg Gate and the government district. I have always been interested in military history and spent a couple of afternoons walking around those areas—still heavily damaged—trying to retrace the fighting and imagine what it had been like for those who fought there. The fact that remnants of the *Nordland* Division, containing many Norwegian volunteers, were wiped out in the fighting for the center of Berlin influenced my interest.

I also made several shopping trips to East Berlin, primarily for books and paintings that were much more expensive in West Berlin. Classical phonograph records were also very reasonable, and I bought several of them. Finally, I would occasionally have dinner in East Berlin. The food and service were excellent and the prices reasonable. Budapest Restaurant was my favorite.

Marion and I made one of these shopping trips after we separated and had lunch at Budapest Restaurant, parking our car behind the building. A German couple who stated they had heard I was interested in books from the war later approached us. I said yes, certain types of books. The man described what they had: about 25 World War II books, pictures, maps, an officer's dagger, and minor items. He asked approximately $62 for the lot. I accompanied him outside and paid him. He did not want us to come to his place, which he said was nearby, but he would bring a couple of boxes containing the items and put them in our car. I gave him the key to the trunk and he returned within 45 minutes with the trunk key.

We unpacked the boxes at home, and they were as the seller had described, but they also included two flags—Nazi Party and German Navy flags. For the time being, I put the flags on the arm of the sofa. A few days later, I received a call from the MP saying they had received an anonymous telephone call stating that I was displaying a Nazi flag. Since I lived on the fourth floor, no one could see the flag and I assumed the report was from my maid, who had a key (the only other people who had access were Marion and the MP). The MP instructed me to pack the flags away. I put them back in the paper bag and locked them in a dresser drawer. I sold the flags and dagger at an auction in the U.S. To my amazement, they brought in more than two expensive pieces of Drexel furniture.

In late 1960, I received a summons through intelligence channels to report to a captain in the G-2 (Intelligence) section of Berlin Command. I lived in the same bachelor officer quarters (BOQ) as Norbert and discovered he had received a similar summons for an appointment one hour after mine. The summons did not indicate what it was all about and I agreed to wait for Norbert in the coffee shop after my interview.

I reported at the prescribed time and found myself being interrogated by a captain about my off-duty activities, centering on my visits to East Berlin. The questions were detailed, in some cases personal, and the fact I was not an American by birth kept creeping into the interrogation. I received no explanation as to why I was there.

I became angry but was careful not to be insubordinate.

After the captain, for the umpteenth time, referred to my foreign birth and some comment that I interpreted as questioning my loyalty, I'd had enough. I told him I was proud that I was an American by choice and not by chance and that I intended to answer no further questions until he told me what this was all about. He did not answer but indicated I could leave. Grabowski was waiting outside and could tell I was upset.

It was nearly an hour before Norbert showed up and he was furious. He was treated in the same manner as I but had not kept his temper as well. We concluded we should pursue the matter because of the challenge to our loyalties and our treatment as suspects. We saw Captain Rosenblum and requested an appointment with Colonel John Deane. Rosenblum agreed. We saw Deane and explained what had happened and how we felt about it. He listened intently, picked up the telephone, and requested an appointment to see Brigadier General Frederick O. Hartel, the Berlin troop commander.

The captain in question was shipped to an organization in West Germany within 48 hours. Both Norbert and I felt vindicated, but it also alerted us that our activities received more attention than others.

Captain Rosenblum left practically all the company's administrative duties to me, in addition to being assigned most of the extra responsibilities such as Mess Officer, Arms Control Officer, Training Officer, Pay Officer, etc. I also continued to be the commander of the 3rd Platoon. I authored most field training exercises (FTXs), both in Berlin and West Germany. I also wrote new standing operating procedures (SOPs) for the unit and coordinated clandestine visits by officers and NCOs to familiarize themselves with our main defense line in the city and the various fallback positions. This activity took place in civilian clothes and groups of three or four. Most of our defensive positions were in buildings (private and commercial) in the city's Steglitz district. We did not enter these buildings, but the tours familiarized the leaders with their initial positions in case of war and allowed them to pick locations for their units, particularly for their crew-served weapons.

We, in Berlin, had no illusions about our ability to withstand a Soviet assault and survive. We knew our ability to offer resistance, almost 200 kilometers from the nearest friendly forces, was not long, only a few days. We knew we would not survive and took a macabre and twisted sense of pride in this fact.

Khrushchev's threat in Vienna to sign a separate peace treaty with East Germany and thereby relinquish control of the access routes to the East Germans was a grave and ominous turn of events. According to Khrushchev, this action would nullify the rights the Soviet Union had guaranteed the Western Allies under the Yalta and Potsdam agreements. The Soviet threat in Vienna was too dangerous to ignore and President Kennedy used every means at his disposal to prepare the American public for what might be a collision of significant proportions between the Soviet Union and the U.S. over Berlin. The U.S. response was not limited to educating the public.

Draft calls increased significantly and the military forces were increased by more than 200,000, 76,500 reserves were called to the colors, and naval ships in mothballs were re-commissioned. These measures were intended to accomplish two main objectives. First, they alerted the American public and informed them that a showdown with the Soviet Union might be unavoidable. Second, the hopes were that the expected public support for its government, together with the military measures, were clear signals to the Soviets that the West would not back down in any confrontation.

Willy Brandt (1913–1999) was the mayor of West Berlin. He was an essential player in the events that unfolded in the city in the early 1960s. He and his wife occasionally attended some of the American social gatherings, particularly our Independence Day activities.

I first met them at one such event soon after I arrived in Berlin. They were part of the official receiving line through which most of us passed. As my turn came for introduction, he shook my hand, hesitated, looked closely at the name tag on my uniform, and then asked if perhaps there was a Norwegian background in my family. When I answered that I was born in Norway, he said *we must talk some more*, then turned and introduced me to his wife Rut in fluent Norwegian. I knew little about his background up to this point and he enjoyed my surprised reaction.

He and his wife approached me later in the evening and we had a more extended and enjoyable conversation, mainly in Norwegian. He would politely switch to English when others joined us. He explained how it was that he spoke Norwegian. He had spent some time as an officer in the Norwegian Army during World War II and married a Norwegian woman. I saw him a few more times during my stay in Berlin. He was always amiable and invariably greeted me with *Hello, Normann.*

I have already mentioned the steady flow of VIPs to Berlin. The influx of visitors increased as tensions sharpened, both before and after the erection of the wall. I was often involved in some ways with these visitors, either as an escort or briefer. For example, a group of Norwegian mayors visited the city in March 1962 and I gave them the standard presentation in Norwegian and served as their guide.

Earlier, I had served as an escort for Lieutenant General Bjørn Christophersen (1900–1985), the commander-in-chief of the Norwegian Army. This duty lasted more than a week, including visits to maneuvers in West Germany and visiting various NATO commanders. These visits and escort duties proved to be a valuable learning experience. In addition, they introduced me to contemporary political and military leaders from multiple countries and their views as the tensions over Berlin increased.

The atmosphere in Berlin was tense, but the people remained relatively calm. The strain was most visible on the communist side, where the exodus of people reached new heights. In the last month before the erection of the wall, more than 30,000 people crossed the border to freedom. That rate accelerated to where 22,000 crossed the border during the first 12 days of August 1961.

In the meantime, I had requested a one-year extension to my tour of duty in Berlin. Without an extension, I would return to the U.S. in the early summer of 1962. The request, if approved, would extend my tour there until the summer of 1963. There were a couple of reasons for my decision to lengthen my tour. First, Captain Rosenblum was eager to have me stay on as his XO and was constantly badgering me to put in my request.

The second, and probably more telling reason, was my conversations with personnel at the Department of the Army (DA). They indicated that if I returned to the States in 1962, I could expect to spend a two- to three-year tour of duty at some stateside post before being sent to the one-year Infantry Officer Career Course (IOCC) at Fort Benning. DA informed me that if I delayed my departure from

Germany, there was a 50/50 chance of going directly to the career course. Being an early graduate of that course would enhance my assignment possibilities. I eventually submitted a request for an extension and received quick approval.

This somewhat routine action significantly impacted my career and life but, as is usual in such cases, the decision's importance can only be seen clearly in retrospect.

Captain Rosenblum was disappointed when the extension approval did not translate into staying on as his XO. Shortly after the extension approval in mid-May 1961, Colonel Deane called me to his office. He offered me the command of the reconnaissance platoon. The assignment proposed was the most sought-after assignment for a lieutenant in the battle group, and I accepted without hesitation. Rosenblum knew this was a career-enhancing assignment and supported my decision. I assumed my new duties on 1 July 1961.

The reconnaissance platoon was the eyes and ears of the battle group commander. For administrative purposes, I was assigned to the combat support company, commanded by Captain Herman J. Vanbebber, but for all practical purposes, I worked directly for Colonel Deane through his S-3, Major Alexander M. Weyand (1928–2011). The platoon consisted of an infantry section, mounted in armored personnel carriers (APCs) or jeeps, an anti-tank section comprising 106mm recoilless rifles on jeeps, a 60mm mortar section, and a tank section with M48 Pattons. The tanks were at a separate location in Berlin and only attached on alerts or impending hostilities.

The reconnaissance platoon's regular mission was to act as a front or flank screen for the rest of the battle group. Expectations were that we would be the first to engage the enemy, and our mission was to delay his advance while the rest of the command occupied their defensive positions. For that reason, we had to be the first unit ready to roll during an alert. The NCOs and enlisted men assigned to this unit were the best in the command.

Norbert Grabowski and I had a three-week leave approved for the end of July. I asked Colonel Deane when he offered me the new job whether I should alter my plans. He said he saw no reason to do so, since I would have about a month to familiarize myself with the new duties and return well before the fall maneuvers. Norbert and I, therefore, proceeded with our plans and left for Norway around 1 August. Norbert and his future wife Ann stayed in Norway for about 10 days and then went to West Germany.

I was still at Voss in Norway on 13 August when the radio reported the East Germans were constructing a wall through the center of Berlin and that American forces worldwide were on alert. I immediately called my unit in Berlin. I found out a recall order for personnel on leave was in effect. I informed my headquarters that I expected to be in Berlin within 48 hours.

It was harder to say goodbye to my parents and the rest of the family this time. I did not believe the Western allies would acquiesce in the wall and anticipated this was the long-awaited flashpoint that would lead to war, a war I did not expect to survive. I quickly started to pack my things. My father came into my room. He said he wanted to tell me a couple of things but did not wish to alarm my mother.

This old soldier from World War I—who had also lived through World War II—knew what was at stake. He asked me not to take any unnecessary chances and that he hoped to see me again, but added that if that was not God's will, he wanted me to know he felt our cause in this otherwise crazy world was just.

Although nothing was said directly, I believe the rest of the family had also concluded that this probably was the beginning of the third world war in the 20th century. I tried to put on a cheerful face, but one of the last things I did was to give my 12-year-old niece, Solveig, my class ring for safekeeping until my return.

The Wall

I returned to Berlin early in the morning of 16 August. My unit was at Tempelhof Airfield from where it was running reconnaissance patrols along the east–west sector boundary. The reconnaissance unit from the 3rd Battle Group was also at Tempelhof together with both battle groups' forward headquarters. We operated from this location until the end of August.

When they erected the wall, the East Germans declared they would introduce strict controls along the East–West Berlin border. They backed up this declaration by moving tanks to the border and closing 68 of 80 crossing points. The 12 remaining were only open for official traffic and West Berliners who wished to enter East Berlin.

My fellow officers and I fully expected decisive action from the Western allies—at the very outset—to remove the wall. We felt that if we acted immediately in a persistent manner, there was a good chance war could be avoided. Action later could prove more difficult and riskier. We did not believe for one moment the Western allies would allow this barbed wire and concrete structure to become a permanent part of the landscape. The ringing inaugural speech delivered by President Kennedy only seven months earlier was still fresh in our minds:

> Let the word go forth from this time and place to friend and foe alike, that the torch has been passed to a new generation of Americans … Let every nation know, whether it wishes us well or ill, that we shall pay any price, bear any burden, meet any hardship, support any friend, oppose any foe to assure the survival and success of liberty. This much we pledge—and more.

President Kennedy ordered reinforcements for the U.S. garrison in West Berlin on 18 August and sent Vice-President Lyndon B. Johnson (1908–1973) and General Lucius Clay (1898–1978) on a fact-finding visit to Bonn and Berlin. General Clay ended up staying in Berlin as a personal representative of the president. The unit selected to reinforce the Berlin garrison was the 1st Battle Group, 18th Infantry, stationed near Mannheim, West Germany.

While not the primary unit escorting the 1/18th from Checkpoint Alpha (entry point to Berlin from West Germany), my group witnessed the wild ride to the reviewing area from the checkpoint. Tens of thousands of cheering Berliners lined the route into the city. At times, the convoy came to a halt as the crowd spilled from the sidewalks into the broad streets despite hundreds of West Berlin police efforts to keep the route clear. It was like a victory parade with the vehicles and soldiers showered with flowers.

We used the next couple of days to familiarize officers and NCOs with Berlin, especially in the wall area. The situation in the city was still explosive. The East German Interior Ministry announced on 22 August that Friedrichstrasse would be the only crossing point open to foreigners after midnight.

Thus, the famous Checkpoint Charlie came into existence. The announcement also added that no Germans or Berliners could use the Friedrichstrasse checkpoint. Berlin was physically divided and would remain so for more than a generation.

In the next two months, I spent most of the time making reconnaissance visits to East Berlin to assert our unrestricted access rights. The reconnaissance units of the two battle groups had the task of performing this mission on alternate weeks. During these missions, we worked directly for the G-2 of Berlin Command. The surveillance was in military sedans. The focus of most reconnaissance was on Soviet units in East Berlin. We tried to identify the units we observed and noted any unusual activities.

Although frequently altered, our reconnaissance route would bring us by the barracks of significant Soviet and East German units. The reconnaissance party consisted of a driver, a sergeant, and me. We wore uniforms, were unarmed, and had a radio for communications with our headquarters. Our allies ran similar missions, as did the Soviets to West Berlin. I had one incident—which could have turned severe—during my many trips to East Berlin.

This incident occurred after a patrol from our sister battle group was stopped and treated threateningly by East German police and a large crowd. The patrol was finally released after a Soviet patrol was halted in West Berlin and held until the U.S. vehicle and personnel could proceed.

My driver on the October day in question was on his first mission and not familiar with the area. We had completed more than half of our mission and drove around one of the last military installations on our route. I told the driver to take a left at the next intersection. He mistook the entrance to what looked like a Soviet motor-pool area for the crossing and made a left turn. The driver managed to stop and back up before entering the restricted site, but not before Soviet guards spotted our actions. They yelled and motioned for us to stop. I ordered the driver to continue and ignore the Soviet demands.

I tried to notify the headquarters about the incident but was unable to make contact. I decided to abort the rest of the reconnaissance mission and return to West Berlin. As we approached the downtown area, we noticed that an East German police vehicle followed us. We headed for the checkpoint by the most direct route when we found the road to our front blocked by two police vehicles. My nervous driver asked if he should try to bypass the two police vehicles. The street was relatively narrow and would have required that he drive on one of the sidewalks to get around the two cars. I told him no, and that he should park in the middle of the street with the engine running, the doors locked, and the windows rolled up. I also tried unsuccessfully to contact our headquarters by radio.

The East German police approached our vehicle and ordered us out. We ignored the order and remained in the car. I opened the window sufficiently to inform the police that we were on a legal mission to East Berlin. I also pointed out that their actions in impeding our passage were a violation of the Four Power Agreement. I informed them that we were not exiting our vehicle, and they should immediately summon a Soviet officer to the scene.

The police replied that we were on sovereign East German territory over which they had exclusive jurisdiction. Furthermore, we had illegally tried to enter a restricted area. A Soviet military vehicle had meanwhile pulled alongside the police vehicle parked behind us. There was a conference between the police and the occupants of the Soviet vehicle. The police officers who had talked to the occupants of the Soviet car signaled for the cars blocking our sedan to move. Similar incidents continued, but I was not involved.

The largest FTX held in Berlin was conducted during the period 16–20 October. For the first time, both battle groups participated, along with some elements from our allies. The exercise took place in the Grünewald.

The reconnaissance platoon received special praise after the exercise for outflanking the "enemy" successfully via the Havel Lake on a stormy night with some enthusiastic German police help. I asked Colonel Deane for permission since I was unsure if using Havel Lake was within the exercise rules. The only caution he gave me was not to drown. I took that as approval. After landing in the opponents' rear, we raided the "enemy's" (3rd Battle Group) headquarters and disrupted the maneuver, causing the umpires to call a temporary halt.

The 3rd Battle Group commander, Colonel Frederick C. Weyand (1916–2010), came over to me and said, *This is no way to treat a fellow alumnus*. We were familiar with each other's backgrounds. He was a Californian and a 1937 graduate of UC. The reconnaissance platoon received 10 minutes to get out of the area before the maneuver was resumed.

CHAPTER 5

Secret Assignment, Personal Problems, and Refocusing, 1961–1964

Detachment A

In late October 1961, Colonel Deane sent for me. He told me a request from an agency in Berlin had arrived, giving me a new assignment. This offer surprised me since I had expected to keep command of the reconnaissance platoon until completing my tour in Berlin. He stated further that the request came from a classified unit, that he knew little about it himself, and it was strictly voluntary. It sounded intriguing, but I was also a bit wary. I told Colonel Deane I would consider the assignment but needed more information before making an intelligent decision. He said he would set up an appointment with someone who could answer my questions.

Two days later, I received a summons to appear at the U.S. headquarters' military intelligence office. There I met Lieutenant Colonel Roman T. Piernick. He told me he commanded an Army unit with a clandestine wartime mission. He warned me that whatever information he provided should be immediately forgotten if I did not accept the assignment he was about to offer me. Furthermore, he assured me the DA would not consider the job a specialty. It would not lead to similar appointments in the future unless I wished and would not be detrimental to my career. Unfortunately, all these assurances proved wrong. It was probably one of the biggest mistakes I made when I accepted the assignment and went to work for this secretive officer of East European background. I remained in this assignment until the completion of my tour in Berlin.

I reported for my new duties on 26 October 1961. My unit within the organization consisted of 27 individuals. Virtually all were born and raised in Europe, primarily in Eastern Europe. They were the so-called Lodge Act people. This congressional act, sponsored by Senator Henry Cabot Lodge, provided a route to U.S. citizenship through military service. Many were refugees from Eastern Europe who had found themselves in displaced persons camps in West Germany or perhaps in a labor service battalion, working for the U.S. Some had escaped to the West immediately after World War II. Others were recent refugees from Eastern Europe. Most had seen service in the German Army during the war or some other military forces in Eastern Europe. They were recruited in the 1950s with the promise of eventual citizenship.

Typically, they were recruited in Germany, took basic military training at some stateside base, and received advanced training in whatever specialty their background indicated suitability for. They were then assigned to various stations worldwide. Many eventually joined the elite Special Forces (SF) and became the early backbone of that organization. For example, Detachment A was an SF organization, and we traveled to Bavaria to make parachute jumps.[1]

I found myself the youngest among this varied group of individuals. Some could barely speak English, but I soon grew to respect their immense talents and high degree of competence within their fields of expertise.

Detachment A consisted of a headquarters and three operational groups. I also doubled as the S-2 of the detachment. Two groups were to move out of the city in case of hostilities. One group would move to the north and one to the south. My group's mission was to stay in the city, go underground, and begin operating against the enemy after a period. We would do so by blowing bridges; blasting rail lines and canal locks; and ambushing convoys, couriers, and high-ranking military and political officials. This was generally aimed at creating an atmosphere of fear and uncertainty behind their lines.

We hoped that our activities would result in some valuable intelligence for our units fighting in Western Europe, lead to a partial disruption in the flow of men and equipment through Berlin to the West and diversion of valuable resources in hunting us down.

These 18 months of my career were exciting, challenging, and full of learning experiences. There are many fascinating aspects of this period about which I do not feel I should write. Although the unit's existence is no longer classified, and books and articles have been published about it, I still believe that information about our sources, doctrine, and some methods could be helpful to a potential future opponent.

Since we served in a classified unit, we wore civilian clothes and blended into urban Berlin. We used detailed documentation and cover stories that we learned and practiced in intricate details. When war was imminent, we would pick up a supply of European gold coins for use.

Our exercises were realistic operations in urban settings where we used covert means of communication and a strict cellular approach to plans and activities. We reconnoitered, planned, and executed mock attacks on real targets. Finally, we had weapons and supplies stashed at various locations throughout the city, but no single individual knew the place of more than one such site.

The intelligence community solicited the West Berlin police's help penetrating our organization and locating various individuals involved in our exercises without revealing who we were. These very realistic exercises would last for nearly a month at a time.

It attests to the professionalism of the organization that no one was apprehended or compromised during these operations. It gave us confidence in our ability to survive for at least a short period after a war started. We had no illusions the intelligence services of the Warsaw Pact signatories could not eventually track us down.

We also assumed they were already aware of our existence and our missions. Since we were to operate as guerrillas, we expected that, if captured, we would undergo severe interrogation and then be executed. However, we hoped our operations would damage the enemy enough to warrant this sacrifice.

The tension in Berlin reached a high point in late October 1961 and we all expected war to erupt at any moment. The crisis began with trouble between a U.S. official and East German border guards at Checkpoint Charlie and escalated to a tank standoff from 25–28 October.

The Soviets upheld an East German order requiring American officials to show identification before entering the eastern sector. American officials refused to accept the East German ruling and continued to enter the Soviet sector while refusing to show the identification demanded by East German police. There were two reasons for this. First, there was a long-standing agreement with the Soviets that an official license plate on the car was the only identification required. The second reason was the East German police authority at the border points, since the Western Powers did not recognize the East German government.

A series of meetings between the U.S. Commandant and his Soviet counterpart began on 25 October to avert hostilities. No traffic was permitted to cross while these discussions were in progress. Instead, American troops and tanks moved to Checkpoint Charlie to underscore U.S. readiness to defend free access to East Berlin.

The Soviets replied to our show of force on 26 October by positioning 33 tanks about a mile from the Friedrichstrasse checkpoint. Personnel carriers and jeeps accompanied the tanks and parked in an Unter den Linden's enclosure for the night. The following day, 10 of the 33 Soviet T-54 tanks formed up on Friedrichstrasse, facing the U.S. tanks on the other side of the sector boundary.

This political-military gamesmanship seemed rather silly to many of us stationed there, despite its high drama. We felt the Western allies had made a grievous mistake in not taking immediate resolute action when the East Germans built the wall. The crossing points were reduced from 80 to 12 and finally to one, which only allied personnel could use. We saw the issue as the incarceration of an entire people in blatant violation of the Yalta and Potsdam agreements.

These people's rights were obscured by our fiddling around at Checkpoint Charlie over minor issues having to do with only the rights of allied personnel and what constituted proper identification. The Soviets had every reason to be overjoyed at shifting the focus from the broader issue of the freedom of movement for millions of people and their rights to decide their destinies to a technical argument over the modalities involved in allied personnel crossing the sector boundaries.

In our view, we should have insisted on reopening all crossing points and used heavy equipment backed by military force to remove the barbed wire and concrete obstacles at these locations. The decision of war or peace would then be with the Warsaw Pact group, and we felt they would have backed down as they did later during the Cuban Missile Crisis. We felt that resolute action to uphold the sanctity of agreements and the fundamental rights of a whole people carried less risk of miscalculation than a similar effort in the future that could lead to war.

Many felt our failure to meet the situation with more firmness and resolution made a mockery of the now-familiar passage from Kennedy's inaugural address, quoted earlier. It may be that they, as I, forgot or overlooked another excerpt from the same speech: "Let us never negotiate out of fear. But let us never fear to negotiate." This passage is as important now as it was in the 1960s.

In his inaugural address, President Kennedy had filled most of us in the military with much hope. We interpreted it as a ringing call for action. His words gave the nation a sense of purpose and pride. The Germans seemed to share this affection for Kennedy. They spoke and acted as if he were also their leader. This feeling was particularly evident by the Berliners' wild reception when he visited the city in 1963.

The debacle at the Bay of Pigs somewhat tarnished the uplift to our morale by Kennedy's speech. He inherited this project from the previous Administration, and its planning was well advanced when he assumed the presidency. Unfortunately, he was also poorly served by some of the military and intelligence advice he received. But there were enough "red flags" and uncertainties about this operation, which placed the prestige of the U.S. on the line, to have caused a more experienced leader to have second thoughts about its wisdom.

The failure to act more firmly in Berlin in 1961 further eroded our once high-held hopes. These were later in no small measure restored because of the actions taken by President Kennedy to streamline the approach to America's defense, the adoption of the "flexible response" strategy, and his firm and statesmanlike handling of the Cuban Missile Crisis. The West Berliners saw the outcome of this 1962 crisis as a turning point in the Cold War and demonstrated strengthened American policy approval. It was virtually impossible to go to a German restaurant or nightclub without receiving offers of free drinks accompanied by compliments for the firm resolve our nation had demonstrated in the Cuban Missile Crisis.

The events at Checkpoint Charlie in Berlin were taking place as I left one job and assumed another. If war resulted from the military confrontation, I could not carry out my new assignment duties. I discussed this with Piernick on 27 October. American forces were on alert and he agreed I should report to my old unit, where I might be able to do some good. I was to return to take up my new assignment when the situation returned to normal.

I reported to the battle group that same day and spent the next few days assisting the staff in any way possible. The tense situation at the border had calmed down by 30 October, so I returned to my new assignment. We had several tense and dangerous flare-ups over access to East Berlin in the months that followed, but none had the same sense of anxiety and drama as in those early days of the wall.

With few exceptions, the remainder of my tour in Berlin was routine. The promotion to captain came in October 1962, almost a year earlier than expected. The promotion did not affect my Berlin duties, but it made it more likely that I could proceed directly from this assignment to the IOCC at Fort Benning.

Lieutenant Colonel Piernick disappeared in 1962. By that I mean, he suddenly, and without warning, ceased to be the commander of the unit and my superior. We were discouraged in our efforts to find out what had happened and I never saw or heard from him again. I do not know—to this day—what happened, and any guess on my part would be pure speculation. Captain Adam Klys (1935–2021) saw Piernick's name on a retirement list in 1964.

Piernick's replacement was Lieutenant Colonel Francis L. Mahan (1919–1995). Mahan wanted me to extend my tour past my four-year limit. I was reluctant to do this for a couple of reasons. First, I had an excellent opportunity to attend the IOCC ahead of my contemporaries with my recent promotion. Second, I was beginning to believe that any extension in this specialized and clandestine assignment would be detrimental to my career. The Office of Personnel Operations (OPO) at DA had already hinted that this could result. I was afraid damage had already occurred by taking me away from regular infantry duties for about 18 months. I expressed my reservations to Mahan but carefully avoided refusing his request. Mahan's OER carried double weight as it covered 18 months due to Piernick's disappearance.

Despite my misgivings, Mahan requested U.S. Army Europe (USAREUR) make an exception to their rules by keeping me in my present assignment for another year. I was very relieved when USAREUR denied the request since I was already selected to go to Fort Benning.

Lucky Avoidance of Problems

It was easy for a soldier to get into trouble with all the rules and regulations in Berlin, problems that could seriously jeopardize one's career. I had several near misses over the years, and one is discussed briefly in this segment.

Until I assumed my Detachment A position, I was permitted to drive my car through the East German zone to West Germany. This 200-kilometer drive was along a well-constructed four-lane autobahn. There was a strict speed limit of 90 kilometers per hour. A traveler leaving Berlin had his papers time-stamped at Checkpoint Alpha and again as he entered West Germany at the Helmstead checkpoint. Any discrepancy, which indicated the traveler had exceeded the speed limit, could result in severe sanctions. Furthermore, the fact that a traveler was forbidden to stop along the road meant he had to drive at a somewhat consistent slow speed over this primarily deserted stretch of autobahn. Instructions were to report any incidents promptly.

I left Berlin at about 0400 one day in 1961. I had not had much sleep and I dozed off for the first time as a driver. I woke up when the Mercedes 190SL hit the gravel on the side of the road, but not in time to avert sideswiping one of the large stone markers located at regular intervals along the autobahn. The car's front right side was damaged, but I was able to continue after pulling the bent metal away from the right front wheel.

The Soviet guard who checked my papers at Helmstead approached the driver's side and did not notice the damage. Nevertheless, I decided to inform the U.S. MP on the checkpoint's West German side in case a report was forthcoming.

I told the gruff-looking MP sergeant what had happened. He made no immediate comment. After walking around the car, he returned to the driver's side and handed me my papers. There were British, French, and West German police standing near the guardhouse in the middle of the road, but the car's right side was not visible to them. As he handed me the papers, the MP sergeant said in a voice loud enough to be heard by those who stood nearby, *Yes, sir, your right front tire is rather low, and I would have it tended to immediately if I were you.* After paying the nearest Mercedes repair shop several hundred marks, I was back on the road and heard nothing more about the incident.

Second Marriage and its Failure

I remarried in March 1962. I had dated a girl, Brigitte Rosemarie Schumann, off and on since early 1961 and regularly since the fall of 1961. Her stepfather, Herbert Ballstead, was a bank official in West Berlin. The Soviets captured him during the war and, since he was an officer, they kept him until 1956. Brigitte's mother, Gjertrud Ballstead, was the best chess player I ever met.

Because I'd had a previous marriage, I wanted a private civil ceremony, but Brigitte and her parents insisted on a military wedding with all the frills. I gave in to their wishes. If Brigitte's stepfather had his way, it would have been a fully fledged Prussian military wedding, and he kept introducing Prussian customs during the wedding preparations.

The wedding took place in the McNair Barracks Chapel and the reception was at the Harnack House Officers' Club. In old Prussian tradition, Brigitte came from her home to the chapel in a fancy carriage drawn by two white horses and our trip from the chapel to the reception took place in that conveyance. It was a "traffic stopper" and people applauded, cheered, and wished us well from the sidewalks as we passed.

My second marriage was even shorter than the first, but I did not feel I was the leading cause for the break-up. Whether it was love or infatuation, I was very much attracted to Brigitte, a beautiful girl. All went well until shortly before I departed Germany but, with the wisdom of hindsight, there had been indications of infidelity I should have noticed.

Brigitte worked part-time as an accountant for the American Thrift Shop in Berlin. I received 30 days' leave before our scheduled departure and wanted to spend most of that time with my family in Norway. All the paperwork for Brigitte's travel to the U.S. was complete, and all that remained for us to do was deliver our car and pack our hold baggage. My leave began around 23 May.

Brigitte said she had to stay in Berlin to close out the accounts for the month at the Thrift Shop and recommended I proceed to Norway by car to have as much time with my family as possible, and she would join me in a week by plane and train. I agreed and we also planned to turn in the car for shipment from Bremerhaven to the U.S. on our way back. I made the necessary reservations for the two of us to return to Berlin from Bremerhaven on the military train.

I talked with her several times by telephone from Norway. The last time was to ask her to bring my dress uniform since we received an invitation to the wedding of my cousin Magnhild Olsen and her family wanted me to attend in uniform.

I was not terribly worried when Brigitte did not show up on the train as scheduled. I figured she had missed a connection in Frankfurt or Oslo. To make sure she was on her way, I called our apartment in Berlin and received no answer.

I met every train for the next two days, but no Brigitte. By now, I was apprehensive. I occupied a sensitive position. There were instructions on what to do in cases where something like this happened. First, I called my friend Captain Adam Klys and his wife, Chris. Chris was a German national and knew my wife. At my request, they obtained keys to my apartment from the MP and went to investigate. They called back in a few hours and told me she was not in the apartment, that it looked like someone had left hurriedly, and that my dress uniform was still there.

My next step was to call my superior, Lieutenant Colonel Mahan, and inform him of the situation. He called back that evening and told me they had determined, after a quick preliminary investigation, that Brigitte had departed Berlin on schedule. Mahan agreed to get the authorities involved if she did not show up that night. She did not. Mahan said he would take care of informing the MP and intelligence agencies in Berlin and for me to do the same with the Norwegian police.

The next few days were a nightmarish period with little or no sleep. All kinds of thoughts raced through my mind. Brigitte might have been in an accident and needed help, been kidnapped by the East Germans to pressure me, or been subject to foul play, including murder. The Norwegian police, through INTERPOL, determined she had not boarded her plane in Frankfurt and she had not entered Norway.

I decided to return to Berlin. My sister and brother-in-law decided to come along. They were worried about my lack of sleep over the past week. I talked to Mahan on the morning of our departure, and he asked that I notify the Norwegian police that they should terminate their search. I asked why. The only thing he would say on the telephone was that he was trying to save me possible embarrassment and that we would talk when I returned.

I learned from military intelligence upon my return to Berlin that Brigitte was in Italy. She was in the company of another man, who they refused to identify. Later, I learned he was a married Air Force officer with four children who lived across the hallway in our apartment building. The information was a shock. The Air Force officer faced adultery charges in a military court. I do not know what happened, as I left Berlin that month, but it must have been devastating for his wife and four children.

Brigitte returned to Berlin in early July, and we met twice in the presence of her parents. I busied myself with packing and took the car to port for shipment. I made a quick flight to Norway since I had not had a chance to say the proper goodbyes and assure them I was okay.

I returned to Berlin two days before my departure. The last night in Berlin, I went to say goodbye to my parents-in-law, who were good people. Brigitte was there and said she would see me the next day. I assumed she planned to come to the train station. I had mixed feelings about that since I expected some of my friends to be there to see me off, but I did not say anything.

I departed Berlin for Bremerhaven on the military train to catch the boat back to the U.S. on 6 August. Some of my friends, including Adam and Chris Klys, came to see me off. Brigitte did not show up; I assumed she had changed her mind from the night before, possibly because of her parents' intervention.

Whereas I had traveled to Germany in luxury, the trip back was on a troopship, the navy ship (USNS) *General Maurice Rose*. The vessel, built in 1945, had a displacement of 17,000 gross tons. It was scheduled to bring over 2,000 troops and several hundred dependents back to the U.S. As I processed through Bremerhaven on 7 August, I was informed I was troop commander for the voyage. I was rather happy about this since it meant a trip full of work with little time to think about my situation.

The port authorities asked that I stay ashore, at or near the processing station, until all passengers had boarded. I gave my hand luggage to a soldier to take to my cabin. When my work was completed, it was time to board. I presented my papers to the security guard at the boarding station and he checked these against the passenger roster. All was in order and as I was about to leave, he said, *Sir, your wife checked in a couple of hours ago and is already on board.* I was stunned. In response to my questioning look, he referred to the paperwork on his clipboard and asked, *Her first name is Brigitte, is that correct?* I answered yes and proceeded to board the ship.

The ship sailed in less than two hours, and I knew there was a meeting between the ship's captain, certain ship personnel, and me in about 40 minutes. So,

I proceeded to my assigned cabin. There I found Brigitte. Her papers for entry to the U.S. had been approved between early March and May, as had her permission for concurrent travel.

During all that happened in July before my departure, I neglected to notify the processing center that there was a change in our status. Brigitte stated she had taken a plane from Berlin to Frankfurt, a train from Frankfurt to Bremerhaven, and arrived early morning. She said, crying, that she was sorry her actions might cause me problems and embarrassment. Brigitte told me that she realized our marriage was in ruins and she did not expect forgiveness.

She stated—I believe honestly—that she saw this as a once-in-a-lifetime opportunity for her to enter the U.S. She also said she did not intend to create any problems for me but would travel to "friends and relatives" in Chicago. Military intelligence had told me earlier that Brigitte had a police record because she ran away from home twice and had associated with unsavory people. These facts would probably have prevented her from entering the U.S. as an ordinary immigrant. It was on the ship I realized Brigitte used our marriage to reach the U.S.

There was little time left before the ship sailed, and even less before I had to be at the scheduled meeting. It was evident Brigitte did not love me—despite her statements to the contrary—and that she had used me for her own purposes. In short, the marriage had been a scam. Despite this, I believed she was a decent individual—even today, I think that after these many years.

Since we were married, her papers were in order, and she desired to go to the U.S., there was little I could do. Whatever I might try in that direction would probably prove fruitless and be very embarrassing, so I did not even get angry with Brigitte. I was too filled with sorrow and sadness for both of us.

The voyage was uneventful, except for encountering an intense storm—remnants of a hurricane—west of the English Channel. The ship had to slow to a crawl with the bow against the heavy seas for approximately 18 hours. The storm delayed our arrival in New York by two days.

There was much work involved with the troops. For example, the schedule of meals, sick calls, exercise periods on deck, etc., had to be coordinated daily with the Navy. In addition, a joint inspection of the troop quarters took place each morning following breakfast.

We also carried a couple dozen maximum-security prisoners. These were troops who had been tried by general courts-martial and given long sentences to be served at federal prisons in the U.S. For the most part, they were guilty of murder or rape. These prisoners were in a brig on a lower deck in the ship's bow section under an MP guard. I had to inspect this area twice every 24 hours. The brig's location in the bow section during the rough weather caused all prisoners to become seasick, and the air in that area was incredibly foul.

The ship traveled at a moderate speed for the last day and night. I believe this was on purpose, to arrive in the morning hours so all troops and passengers could disembark and continue their travels in daylight. My duties were over when personnel from Fort Hamilton arrived.

We spent two days in New York with my brother while waiting for them to unload our car. I then drove to Fort Benning and Brigitte left for Chicago by train. So that Brigitte would have enough money when she arrived in Chicago, I gave her half of the cash I had on hand.

I remember several contacts with Brigitte—directly or indirectly—in the next two or three years. I am sure there were others that I have forgotten, like the one mentioned by the wife of the first executive officer in my SF battalion.

Brigitte came to Columbus, Georgia, unexpectedly just before Christmas 1963, hoping we could make a go of our marriage. Unfortunately, too many things had happened for this to be possible and she soon returned to Chicago. I had obtained the services of a lawyer in Alabama after arriving at Fort Benning. I petitioned for a divorce in Georgia, but the petition could not be acted on until I satisfied the one-year residency requirement. The divorce became final in early December 1964. I helped her out with about $6,000 from 1963 to 1964, a major slice of my annual pay. I do not know where she is or what happened to her. I hope she is well and found happiness.

IOCC, Pathfinder School, and a Lasting Marriage

The IOCC was a one-year course for captains. Its purpose was to prepare officers for battalion-level command and staff assignments at the battalion, brigade, or division level.

I began my year at Fort Benning in a very depressed mood. I had concluded my divorce in 1960 and the one now pending had irreparably damaged my Army career. Because of this, I gave up any thoughts of entering the Foreign Service, for which I would otherwise have been eligible in 1966.

With my personal life in shambles, I concentrated all my efforts on my studies. I purchased a two-bedroom trailer and rented a lot in a trailer park in Columbus to have a place to live off post. Stanley White, now promoted to captain, showed up at Fort Benning in the fall of 1963 and could not find a place to live except in Columbus' slum areas. I offered to share my trailer with him until he found a place to live.

We received many harassing telephone calls, and the trailer had racial slurs scribbled on it a couple of times, but nothing serious happened. Stanley saw what was transpiring and offered to move out. I told him we should not give in to racial pranks.

I contacted the military housing authorities and asked them to make an extra effort to find Captain White quarters at Fort Benning to avoid a possible severe incident. This request energized the military authorities. They found an on-post place for him within a week.

Concentrating on training and studies paid off, as I was designated an honor graduate. I also received a very sought-after assignment to the 101st Airborne Division. Finally, I was offered the three-week Pathfinder course before proceeding to Fort Campbell, Kentucky.

The Pathfinder course's aims were to train personnel to operate behind enemy lines and establish drop or landing zones (LZs) for follow-up parachute assaults or air landing operations. It included training in creating and marking a drop zone (DZ) for both day and night operations.

The rigorous course—with me suffering from measles—included some night parachute operations from C-130 or de Havilland DHC-4 Caribou aircraft. We carried a heavy load of all equipment required to do the assigned mission.

My personal life underwent a profound change while at Fort Benning. I did not do much cooking while living in the trailer. Instead, I stopped at a restaurant named "BJ" to have breakfast on the way to Fort Benning and, after the training was over, I would have supper at that restaurant.

The evening after I graduated from the IOCC as an honor student, the female owner of BJ, Welma, closed the restaurant early for a surprise party for me arranged by her and the waitresses.

One of the waitresses I met at BJ was Florence Justina Little (born McEldowny in Brooklyn, New York). Florence had come through a messy divorce in 1961–1962 and had ended up with custody of her three children—Barbara, 10, David, 7, and Monica, 5. They lived in a trailer park in Columbus and she was trying to support them and herself on the meager wages and tips as a waitress.

Florence and I hit it off from the very beginning, no doubt influenced by our failed marriages. She'd had a short marriage in the mid-1940s to a soldier, but because she was not yet 18, her parents annulled it through the Catholic Church.

Florence and I dated regularly for nearly two years. I bought her a 1964 VW Beetle before leaving Fort Benning. I lived in a dilapidated BOQ at Fort Campbell for the first six months and I met Florence at Gadsden Lake in northern Alabama for one weekend each month. I would drive south from Fort Campbell and she would drive north from Columbus. These meetings went well until the fall of 1964, when she overturned her VW on the way to meet me. She was not hurt, but it scared me to the point where I asked her to move from Georgia to Clarksville, Tennessee, where I bought a four-bedroom rancher for about $11,000. She and the kids moved there before Christmas.

It was not without some misgivings that I took on a family of four, and it was a rocky marriage at times, but we both had our minds firmly set on making it work. Florence had been in a severe car accident in the late 1940s or early 1950s. This accident took place before seat belts were the norm and the impact sent her through the windshield. She had a severe concussion and many facial bones broken, including a shattered jaw. She spent months in hospitals undergoing reconstructive surgery.

Florence came down with bipolar disorder early in our marriage, and I believed it could be connected to the concussion she sustained in the accident. The condition got worse over the years despite medications, and she would have severe mood swings that at times became life-threatening to either herself or those around her. She was also left to care for the children while I spent years in Vietnam or other places away from home. Barbara moved out after graduating from high school.

Despite being rocky at times, the marriage in early 1965 lasted for 47 years, three months, and 10 days until she died in a botched routine stenting operation in the spring of 2012.

101st Airborne Division

My assignment to the 101st was for the express purpose of obtaining command at the company level, an unwritten "must" for an infantry officer's advancement. I would be eligible for consideration for promotion to major in a few years. The lack of command of a company would weigh heavily against my chances for an early selection. However, when I arrived in the division on 18 July 1964, my assignment was as the G-2 Plans Officer at the War Plans Division because of a priority need.

The 101st and its sister division, the 82nd Airborne Division, were among the U.S. Army's most elite units. The division's name and its "Screaming Eagle" shoulder patch were recognized instantly by the American public due to its well-known exploits in World War II, particularly its legendary defense of Bastogne during the German Ardennes Offensive in December 1944. An assignment to the division was a distinct honor for a young officer and eagerly sought. To make a mark among the high-quality officers assigned to this unit, a person had to perform exceptionally well.

The work in the War Plans Division was both exciting and challenging. This small staff's mission, which worked directly for the division commander, was to prepare war plans for employment in various world areas. The 101st was one of General Paul D. Adams's (1906–1987) Strategic Army Command. This status meant it had to be ready to move—almost anywhere in the world—on a one-hour notice in response to unanticipated contingencies.

The goal was for the division to respond to an alert by having the first combat elements of the Immediate Ready Force (reinforced company) in the air within 30 minutes after receiving the "go" message. Additionally, a reinforced battalion was required to be on its way within two hours after the alert order. These readiness requirements cut into the time available for training. Many of my associates and

I considered this lack of training critical in how our outfit would perform if called on to execute one of my office's many plans.

The War Plans Division's files already contained numerous contingency plans, but these needed frequent updating as new intelligence indicated revisions were in order. My small staff and I would read large numbers of political/military intelligence reports each day. Our responsibility was to analyze these reports, update our contingency files, and recommend changes to operational concepts if we felt this was required. We made these recommendations to the chief of the War Plans Division (a colonel), who, in turn, would bring the issues to the attention of the division commander, Major General Beverly Powell (1912–2011). Changes of this nature were frequent.

The War Plans Division continually monitored political and military developments within our primary responsibility area (the Middle East and Africa). We made recommendations for changes to plans through our chain of command. If a contingency plan was necessary, it required coordination with DA, Continental Army Command (CONARC), Third Army, 18th Airborne Corps, and appropriate Air Force and Navy headquarters. This coordination often required travel to these headquarters. The preparation of the actual plans was the responsibility of the division staff. When a plan was in the draft stage, we briefed the brigade commanders and their primary staff officers and tasked them to prepare supporting plans. This procedure was always a give-and-take process, with brigade commanders recommending changes to our draft plans. The modifications would often require certain aspects of the plan be re-coordinated with higher or supporting headquarters.

Two of the three contingency plans prepared during my assignment to the War Plans Division involved situations within our primary area, namely Cyprus and the Congo. The Cyprus mission was to prevent or limit hostilities between the Greeks and Turks, both NATO members. The Congo plan called for protecting American lives and property and that of our European allies in the chaotic and bloody situation in 1964. The plan required division units to parachute into the Stanleyville area to seize the airfield for use by follow-up elements. The activities of the Belgians and the French resulted in an improvement in conditions in the Congo. It also resulted in the cancellation—much to my relief—of my scheduled reconnaissance trip to establish communications and select a parachute landing zone.

The third plan involved follow-up support for the 82nd Airborne Division, whose orientation was Latin America and dealt with protecting American interests in the Dominican Republic, which had experienced an unstable existence since dictator Rafael Trujillo's assassination three years earlier.

All these activities involved much work and travel, but I enjoyed the job and its responsibilities. Somehow, I found time to attend the rigorous one-week Jumpmaster course that qualified a paratrooper for pre-jump inspection of other troopers and proper rigging and supervision of a planeload of troops during a jump. The course was necessary for company commanders and helpful in eventually receiving the coveted Master Parachute Badge. In parachuting, particularly in "mass" military jumps, a tiny mistake can result in losing lives. Therefore, it was not surprising the strict old airborne instructors would flunk anyone for missing even the most minor and well-hidden mistake in the pre-jump inspection of troops and aircraft. All checks involved specific time limits, and this was particularly difficult since most of the tests were at night without the benefit of lighting. The inspections of the aircraft to ensure proper rigging for airdrop were equally exacting. My earlier experience in the Pathfinder School was beneficial in successfully getting me through this course.

I had not forgotten that I had come to the division to obtain a command. I worked at this at every opportunity. I had come to know the three brigade commanders as part of my work in the War Plans Division and when Colonel James Simmons Timothy asked if I would like to join his staff, I accepted immediately. Timothy promised I would get command of the first company to become available in his brigade.

CHAPTER 6

1st Brigade, 101st Airborne Division

I reported to my new assignment as Assistant S-3 of the 1st Brigade on 7 December 1964. The brigade consisted of three airborne infantry battalions with their old regimental designations, each led by a lieutenant colonel—the 1/327 was commanded by James Wilson; the 2/327 by Edward Collins (1924–1984); and the 2/502 by Wilfrid Smith—and various supporting units.

Colonel James Simmons Timothy (1919–1994) was the brigade commander. Timothy was a West Pointer from the 1942 class and a Distinguished Service Cross (DSC) recipient from World War II. He was a calm and articulate officer and one of the most exceptional people I encountered in the Army. We soon developed an excellent working relationship that lasted through two tours in Vietnam. Our friendship continued until he died on 24 January 1994. He was what we call an Army "brat," his father having retired as a brigadier general of Engineers. The brigade sergeant major was Trinidad Prieto, according to Tim Swain.

Lieutenant Colonel Joseph Rogers (1924–2000) was the brigade XO and, as such, supervised the activities of the staff. My immediate superior, the brigade S-3, was Major David H. Hackworth. He joined the brigade after obtaining his undergraduate degree at Austin Peay College and attending the C&GSC at Fort Leavenworth, Kansas. He joined the brigade a few days before Christmas.

Dave Hackworth was a highly decorated officer from the Korean War, where he received a battlefield commission at the early age of 20. I had met him briefly in Berlin in 1961 when he was a company commander in the 1/18th Infantry as that unit reinforced the 6th Infantry after the erection of the wall. Dave eventually became America's most decorated living soldier, retired in 1971 after publicly criticizing our conduct of the war in Vietnam, and wrote a best-selling autobiography, *About Face*.

Dave and I developed an excellent working relationship from the very beginning. We had reached identical conclusions about the combat readiness of the 101st and had similar ideas about what actions were required to correct the shortcomings. We would invariably put in a 12–16-hour day in the field or at the office and then adjourn to the Officers' Club Annex, near my BOQ, for a few beers. We both had a great interest in military history. Our sessions at the club were an extension of our workday. Our talks focused primarily on military subjects, especially on what was needed to prepare our units for combat that we felt sure would eventually come. Events in Southeast Asia indicated an ultimate involvement of U.S. ground forces. The alleged attack by two North Vietnamese torpedo boats on two U.S. Navy destroyers in the Gulf of Tonkin in early August 1964 led to the Gulf of Tonkin Resolution passage by Congress with hardly any dissent. The resolution authorized the president to "take all necessary measures" to repel attacks against U.S. forces and "prevent further aggression." This blank check led to air attacks against North Vietnam. The People's Republic of China exploded its first atomic bomb in October and Nikita Khrushchev lost his job as Premier of the Soviet Union. These developments complicated the situation in Vietnam.

By the end of 1964, 23,300 U.S. personnel were in Vietnam in an advisory or combat support role. A VC mortar team penetrated Bien Hoa Air Base on 30 October 1964, killing five Americans. Material damage was severe, with five B-57's destroyed and 13 damaged. These losses were in addition to four other aircraft destroyed and eight severely damaged. On 24 December, the VC attacked Brinks Hotel, which housed American military personnel in Saigon, using a car bomb underneath the hotel. The bottom floor was destroyed, killing two Americans and wounding 60 Americans and Vietnamese. Most Americans were unconcerned about events in Vietnam. Polls published at the time indicated that almost two-thirds of Americans were paying "little or no attention" to Southeast Asia's happenings. However, most of us in the military had concluded we would soon find U.S. ground forces in Southeast Asia, barring a complete reversal of the two sides' policies.

The team that made up the brigade S-3 section was first class. The chief NCO was Sergeant Major Grady Jones, and his principal assistants were Master Sergeant Billy Sullivan and Staff Sergeant Curtis W. Herdner. These three tough airborne NCOs knew more about handling the flood of paperwork and reports than all of us combined. Captain Phil Stynes was the Chemical Officer, Captain Richard Meyer was the brigade Communications Officer, Captain John M. Sellers was the S-3 Air Officer, and Second Lieutenant Joel S. Stephenson monitored our training programs. The brigade Aviation Section was also under the supervision of the S-3 section. Captain Frederick G. Terry Jr. was the Aviation Section chief, with two additional pilots, Lieutenant Kulik and Chief Warrant Officer Wymer. Except for Captains Meyer and Terry, all these officers worked under my supervision, and I wrote their OERs. For Kulik and Wymer, I was the endorser.

As I remember, the brigade S-1 was Captain David Pinson. I do not recall if he accompanied us to Vietnam.

As on most staff, the S-2 and S-3 sections worked closely together. This was made easy as both sections occupied one floor of the building. Major Joseph E. Hicks (1925–2002) was the S-2. He had served in World War II and Korea, where he survived 69 days cut off behind enemy lines. Lieutenant Timothy (Tim) Swain was the Assistant S-2 and worked closely with me to develop the movement plan of the brigade to Vietnam and task organizing it.

Like the NCOs in the S-3 section, those in the S-2 section were superb. They were among the best I encountered in the Army. The senior NCOs were Master Sergeant L. C. Pennycuff from Jamestown, Tennessee, and Sergeant First Class Harry (Ike) Ikner from Columbus, Georgia. Ikner later received a field commission in Vietnam but became a casualty of the reduction in force (RIF), discussed later in this book, and reduced in rank to an NCO.

The job in the S-3 section was a seven-day-a-week job. We frequently spent 16 to 18 hours a day trying to keep abreast of the unbelievable number of requirements. Every third week one of the three battalions served as the division ready force. These readiness requirements prevented that battalion from participating in anything but classroom training. Parades and inspections consumed as much time in the 101st Airborne Division as I had experienced in the 6th Infantry Regiment's high-visibility environment in Berlin.

The Command Material Maintenance Inspections (CMMI) struck fear into even the most seasoned commanders since they could mean the end of an officer's career if his unit failed. The fear generated by these "spot checks" of equipment, logistics, and personnel procedures caused commanders to spend excessive time eliminating even the minutest discrepancies. Moreover, as pointed out by David Hackworth in his book *About Face*, the vehicles and equipment were, in some cases, in danger of being under-utilized due to over-maintenance or the fear their use would lead to malfunctions showing up on a CMMI spot check. In short, the readiness requirements, demands of peacetime soldiering, peculiarities associated with airborne duty such as parachute operations, and the never-ending pressure to keep equipment in top-notch condition cut mightily into the time available for training.

The first month after my assignment to the brigade was spent primarily getting ready for a series of extensive exercises scheduled for early 1965. These large-scale exercises effectively eliminated most of the remaining time allocated to training. These exercises' purposes—and the only benefit—were to test out-loading, communications, and staff procedures. The individual soldiers and small units became tools to test the staff's effectiveness rather than the reverse. These exercises' goals could be accomplished by command-post exercises, which would have required the involvement of only a few troops.

Lieutenant Colonel Henry (Hank) Everett Emerson (1925–2015), the G-3 of 82nd Airborne Division at this time, and later destined to become one of our most famous troop commanders in Vietnam, had a theory that explained why commanders favored these large-scale exercises. He believed the emphasis on large-scale exercises was because the officers now in charge were the ones who rose to ranks of lieutenant colonels or colonels overnight in World War II and therefore never had much experience at platoon and company level. Thus, it was natural for these officers to gravitate towards large-scale exercises, something they were familiar with. Dave Hackworth shared this belief.[1]

I believe there was also another reason. Small unit training lacked glamour and visibility. The large-scale exercises with U.S. Air Force participation were grand show-and-tell extravaganzas with much media and public attention. A commander likes to see himself and his unit favorably mentioned in the press. It further enhanced his career when superiors read those accounts. Large-scale exercises were ideal for this purpose. The results were staff highly proficient in airborne operations at battalion level and above, with troops having only those fundamentals of soldiering acquired in basic and airborne training. Time was not available to expand on these fundamentals or to integrate them effectively at the squad, platoon, and company levels.

The brigade participated in FTXs Silver Streak, Eagle Jump, Natchez Trace, three battalion operational readiness tests (ORTs), and two command post exercises between the first of the year and the end of April 1965.

I have awful memories of Eagle Jump. The DZ approach in C-130 Hercules aircraft was at a low altitude (treetop level) to avoid "enemy radar." The aircraft formation would begin a steep climb about 2 kilometers from the DZ to reach the right height for parachute operations (900–1250 feet or 300–450 meters). The air turbulence during the low-level approach was severe and many of the paratroopers became airsick. The air inside the aircraft was foul and the floor slippery from vomit, and I was relieved when the doors opened and the green light came on so I could exit into the cold night air.

The ORTs devised for the battalions were robust and realistic exercises designed to determine how combat-ready our units were and what needed attention to correct the deficiencies. The ORTs revealed what we had expected. The units performed well at the battalion level, but the platoons and squads performed poorly in two of the three battalions.

The troops were tough, highly motivated volunteers. The NCOs were among the best I had seen in the Army, dedicated professionals whose mission and troops' welfare came first. They were a proud bunch who usually went from one airborne assignment to the next in the four major airborne units we had worldwide. The junior officers were also the Army's best—virtually every one RA and either West Pointers or DMGs from the ROTC at the various colleges and universities. Their basic training had been augmented by airborne and, in some cases, Ranger training at Fort Benning. The combination of troops, NCOs, and junior officers had the making of a first-class fighting team. Unfortunately, the ORTs revealed, to almost everyone's satisfaction, that the lack of realistic small unit training kept this potentially first-class fighting team from functioning correctly.

With Colonel Timothy's total support, we set about trying to correct the most glaring deficiencies revealed during the ORTs. The brigade issued a training guidance paper that caused some hard feelings among the battalion commanders and staff. It appeared the brigade was assuming a too centralized role in the training, usurping some of the prerogatives usually left to the battalions.

Lieutenant Colonel Wilfrid Smith, commander of 2/502 Airborne Infantry, attended a briefing I gave on the new policy paper to battalion training officers. Smith lost his temper during the presentation. He questioned—openly and in no uncertain terms—the validity of our ORT findings, our solutions to the "so-called" training problems, and even challenged the authority for the issuance of the policy paper.

I took no issue with his verbal barrage and he finally stormed out of the session with the warning that he would take the whole issue up with the brigade commander. I do not know if Lieutenant Colonel Smith took the matter up with Colonel Timothy. If he did, I assume Timothy overruled him since I heard nothing further on the subject. However, this public display of defiance of the new brigade training policy served only to hamper us in overcoming the identified problems. After this incident, Hackworth personally took over the new training program's supervision to demonstrate its importance. I continued to devote my time primarily to our operational and contingency responsibilities. Unfortunately, it also led to bitter feelings between Hackworth and Smith, which followed us into combat.

Hackworth and I agreed that, although our primary area of contingency responsibility was in the Middle East and Africa, our most likely place to see combat soon was in Southeast Asia, in a counter-insurgency environment. If we were correct, it placed a higher premium on the combat readiness of the individual soldiers and units at the company level and below since most operations in such an environment were at those levels.

We convinced Rogers and Timothy that we would be remiss in our responsibilities if we did not alleviate this problem by providing training exercises emphasizing jungle and counter-insurgency conditions instead of the desert and conventional war environments.

I set about working up a large training exercise set in a counter-insurgency environment with Hackworth's blessings. We had the exercise in the final draft by the end of January and we briefed Timothy, who gave us the green light. Timothy overcame the initial reluctance of the division at training in a non-contingency environment. The exercise took place in Natchez Trace State Park in western Tennessee. We enlisted SF support from Fort Bragg, where I still had friends from my days in that elite unconventional warfare organization. We used the latest SF doctrine for insurgency operations and the considerable experience gained by SF personnel from their service in Vietnam.[2] I passionately believed guerrilla warfare did not invalidate the traditional principles of war; it only required changes in some methods to further these principles. The brigade scheduled the exercise for April 1965.

In the interim, on 2 March, I received orders from the DA directing that I report to Fort Bragg, North Carolina, on 17 July to attend the six-week Military Assistance Training Adviser course. After that, I was to proceed to Vietnam on about 1 November. My order was unwelcome news since I had still not had command at the company level. Moreover, a tour in Vietnam as an adviser would prevent me from having that all-important assignment before consideration for promotion.

Colonel Timothy appealed to DA in writing, trying to get my assignment delayed for a year since he planned to give me command of a company on 1 May. In his appeal, Timothy stated it would be a disservice to the Army and me to deny me the opportunity to command an infantry company since command assignments were not available in Vietnam. While noting my need for command, DA rejected the appeal with the dubious promise they would take care of my need for command when I returned from Vietnam. Shortly after that, Hackworth also received orders to go to Vietnam as an adviser to the Vietnamese Airborne Brigade.

When the Dominican Republic situation exploded in violence, Timothy pulled me out of the exercise and sent me to the 18th Airborne Corps Headquarters at Fort Bragg to coordinate our possible participation in that evolving crisis. President Johnson had already called in the Marines, and the 82nd Airborne Division received a warning order for deployment. While the 101st was a follow-up unit, the Marines and the 82nd presented enough force to bring the situation in the Dominican Republic under control and secure American interests. After only a few days at Fort Bragg, I was on my way back to Fort Campbell.

However, before arriving back in Kentucky, our brigade received orders for another deployment—to Vietnam. The classified orders called for the deployment of one reinforced brigade. Timothy's brigade received the mission. Our brigade's emphasis on counterinsurgency and jungle operations no doubt had some influence on the choice. The division ended the exercise in Natchez Trace and the troops were on their way back to Fort Campbell by the time I returned from Fort Bragg.

The tasks involved in moving a unit of approximately 5,000 soldiers with all their equipment, as secretly as possible, across the American continent and then over the world's largest ocean—a straight line distance of almost 20,000 kilometers—and into a hostile environment were staggering. The S-3 office had the overall responsibility and Major Hackworth put me in charge of the planning group. Sergeant Major Grady Jones was my principal assistant within the office. All assigned and earmarked units and all brigade staff elements supplied project officers for my planning group. We also had a free hand to draw on the expertise and talents within and outside the division.

Our move was to remain classified until the president made an official announcement. This was a severe obstacle to proper coordination. This restraint made telephone coordination exceedingly tricky and forced us to limit our contacts to essential offices. After the Department of Defense (DOD) eventually issued a code name for the operation to the Services, the coordination problem eased somewhat. Despite these difficulties, the plan to move the brigade to Vietnam was completed and coordinated in less than three weeks.

The brigade also required reorganization into a separate and self-sustained unit that could operate independently from the division and its logistics and personnel support organizations. We carried this out by drawing organizations from the division support structure and forming them into a support battalion. The division also augmented the brigade with artillery, engineer, military police, signal, and medical units. We increased the strength of the other units in the brigade to well above that authorized. This action allowed for the considerable number of personnel who were too close to the end of their enlistment. Many of these re-enlisted and became part of the deployment. The added strength would also allow for personnel attrition during and immediately following the deployment.

The plan called for the movement of several echelons of advanced parties to Vietnam to prepare for the unit's arrival, scheduled for late July or early August. The brigade's main body, and some of its supplies and equipment, moved to the West Coast by commercial air and rail transport. We shipped the heavier equipment and supplies from ports in the southern part of the country, such as New Orleans and Pensacola. The troops and their individual equipment were to proceed from the West Coast by ship to South Vietnam. It was already late May when the plan was complete (a document a foot thick). As related by Hackworth, the Infantry School at Fort Benning used it as a model.[3]

When alerted for deployment to South Vietnam, brigade personnel had instructions not to tell their families what was happening. However, this secrecy proved impossible to enforce and the local military community was soon fully aware of what was about to happen.

I had bought a house in Clarksville, Tennessee, in late October 1964 and had just married Florence. Since we had both been married before, we kept our plans quiet and had only a civil ceremony at the local Justice of the Peace in Clarksville office. We were not in a hurry to tell anyone, not even my friends in the Army.

In the last couple of weeks of May, we were so busy preparing plans for the move that I did not even have a chance to fill out the Army's dependency forms or obtain identification cards for Florence and the kids. I figured we would still have several weeks before anyone would leave for South Vietnam. While I would be among the first to go, I did not expect this to happen until late June or early July. Because of what happened, Florence had to complete the dependency forms and obtain identification cards with help from division personnel.

By luck, I managed to take out a life insurance policy on the evening of 2 June. One of the life insurance application questions was whether I had orders for deployment to an area where hostilities took place. A yes to this question would have made it impossible to obtain insurance. My earlier orders sending me to Vietnam as an adviser were canceled, and since the deployment we were preparing for was classified, I gave a no answer.

My statement caused some problems later since the insurance company claimed I had provided false information on my application. My later explanation that I could not violate the move's classified nature and the government's help in thousands of similar cases were enough to retain the policy and the little peace of mind it provided.

Lieutenant Colonel Rogers visited the planning group on Wednesday 2 June, and told the personnel to take the rest of the week off after working around the clock for three weeks.

A Hasty and Unexpected Trip

I decided to return to the brigade headquarters on Thursday 3 June, to check on a couple of annexes to the support battalion plan. I planned to stay only a couple of hours and then return home as Florence and I had decided to take the kids to a movie that had just come out—*Shenandoah* starring James Stewart.

Ready for my first cup of coffee, I arrived in my office on the second floor of 1st Brigade Headquarters at 0730 hours. Staff Sergeant Herdner told me the brigade commander wanted to see me. I found a notebook and headed for the colonel's office on the first floor. He was at his desk when I entered.

Timothy looked up and smiled as I entered. *Good morning, Herr Lunde, are you ready to travel on short notice?*

Yes, sir, I answered, not knowing what was in store for me.

Good, you, three others, and I will leave for South Vietnam from the local airport at 1130 hours this morning. The travel orders are being prepared and should be ready by 0900.

I guess I looked a little perplexed at the information he was giving me, and Timothy told me *I will brief you in detail, or at least as much as I know myself after we are on the plane. In the interim, with about three hours to go before you must be at the airport, I suggest you may want to go home and throw a few things together for the trip. We travel in civilian clothes. Any questions?* The only one that came to my mind at the time was, *How long will we be gone?* Timothy indicated he expected the trip to take about a week or 10 days but that I should prepare for a more extended stay if that became necessary.

I went back to my office to finish my cup of coffee. Second Lieutenant Stephenson brought in a stack of messages that had come in overnight. In the pile was a message from the DA directing the 101st Airborne Division to send a liaison team to Military Assistance Command Vietnam (MACV). Finally, things were beginning to make sense. I asked Herdner to check with the S-1 (Adjutant) to see when the orders would be ready. He came back and said they expected them to be ready in about

30 minutes. I decided to wait in my office until then, as this would save me from swinging by the headquarters on the way to the airport.

As I waited for the orders, I thought about what I needed to do in the three hours left before we had to be at the airport. Herdner shook me out of my thoughts when he brought in a thick packet of travel orders. The other officers in our small group had already departed the headquarters. It was their understanding that I would wait for the orders and bring their copies to the airport. I left the 1st Brigade Headquarters at 0930 hours, not realizing I would never again set foot in that building.

The drive home took about 20 minutes and when I got there, I had about an hour before having to be at the airport, a 15-minute drive. I had called Florence from the office, stating I would be home shortly, that she should start packing things I would need for a short TDY trip, and that I had to leave in a couple of hours. There was no time for any planning when I arrived home. Florence had already packed most of the things I thought I would need for what I believed would be a two-week trip. The kids had gone to school and I would not see them again for over a year.

Florence drove me to the airport, and we arrived a few minutes before 1100. On the way, I realized I had forgotten a copy of the brigade's Movement Plan to Vietnam. No one had said we should bring a copy but, back in the office, I had thought it a good idea to do so but had forgotten to bring it along. There was no time to go back to the office to get a copy, so I hoped that someone else in the group had brought a copy or that it would not be required.

The other officers in the party, Colonel Timothy, Lieutenant Colonel Kenneth G. Kuefler, the designated support battalion commander, Major Hackworth, and Captain Meyer, were already at the airport when Florence dropped me off. I said a quick goodbye to Florence, fully expecting to see her in a couple of weeks. I then proceeded to give the travel orders to the other officers. In the process, I noticed that my orders were different. The orders for the other four read for them to proceed to Vietnam and return within 20 days. My orders read to proceed to Vietnam and return within 60 days.

While waiting to board the aircraft, I asked Hackworth why my orders were different. He said it was only a precaution if someone had to remain behind for a while to help coordinate the move from the Vietnam end, but he did not expect that would be necessary. I could not help but think differently; I realized that when the 60 days were up, the brigade would be on its way to Vietnam. I had left a couple of copies of my orders with Florence and I could not help but worry that she would think I had tried to deceive her by not mentioning the long period my orders allowed.

We had to change planes in Chicago on the way to our point of departure in San Francisco. While waiting for our plane, I called my office at Fort Campbell and asked Captain Sellers to package two copies of the Brigade Movement Plan immediately and ship them to us at MACV by the most expeditious means. Getting my office to send copies proved to be a wise precaution since Timothy asked Hackworth, on the plane to San Francisco, if he could look at a copy of the plan. Hackworth was surprised. He looked at me, hoping I would have the proper reply. I ended this conversation by telling Timothy something to the effect that *Major Hackworth's dumb-ass assistant* forgot to bring them, but those plans were now on their way to Vietnam and should be there by the time we meet with the MACV staff. As it turned out, we did not need the plans until our third day in Vietnam and, by that time, we had four copies. My office had sent two copies by one means and two copies by another, thereby hoping we would at least have two by the time we needed them.

From San Francisco, we were to fly by Air France to Saigon via Hawaii and the Philippines. I remarked to Hackworth that I thought it ironic we were flying to Vietnam on the airline of a country that had met defeat in Vietnam a decade earlier. It seemed an inauspicious beginning.

We had several hours at the airport in San Francisco while waiting for our departure. I had dinner with Timothy and Kuefler, and afterwards I retired alone to a lounge to have a couple of drinks. I considered San Francisco my hometown and I had many old friends there, including an ex-wife and her parents. I toyed with the idea of calling some of them but realized it would only lead to questions I could not answer. Instead, I settled back to enjoy my drink and the beautiful sunset. I had an eerie feeling my life was about to change and that nothing would ever be the same again.

CHAPTER 7

A Command in Disarray

We arrived in Saigon on the Air France flight on 5 June 1965, after brief stops in Hawaii and the Philippines. I had never been to the Far East before and the sights, sounds, smells, and heat of this bustling Asian city made a deep impression. I became thoroughly familiar with this environment over the next decade.

Our assigned quarters were in a French-era hotel on the Saigon waterfront, called the "Majestic." This hotel was within a short walking distance from the center of the city. Although not airconditioned, it was comfortable, clean, and served delicious French food.

The next few days were hectic. The five of us split up to cover as much ground as possible. Colonel Timothy wanted to find out what problems U.S. units already in the country were experiencing and what lessons could benefit his brigade.

There were three major U.S. units in the country. First, the Third Marine Regiment had recently deployed from Okinawa to the northern part of South Vietnam—the Army of the Republic of Vietnam (ARVN) I Corps area—to defend Da Nang Airfield. Second, the U.S. Army's 173rd Airborne Brigade had also deployed from Okinawa to the ARVN III Corps area at Bien Hoa, north of Saigon in May. Third, the 5th Special Forces Group, which had arrived from Fort Bragg in October 1964, had its headquarters in the coastal city of Nha Trang in the ARVN II Corps area. Finally, the 1st Battalion, Royal Australian Regiment, was deploying into the III Corps area.

Until our arrival, the U.S. mission was to defend critical installations housing American personnel and equipment, such as Da Nang and Bien Hoa airfields, and leave offensive combat operations to the Vietnamese. This policy changed on 8 June when President Johnson authorized U.S. troops in direct combat if the ARVN requested assistance. A series of significant defeats suffered by ARVN units precipitated this substantial policy change.

The other four officers in our party devoted most of their time coordinating the brigade's movement with MACV and support organizations. At the same time, Colonel Timothy wanted me to spend as much time as possible with the 173rd Airborne Brigade to learn whatever I could from their experience. Accordingly,

I linked up with that unit on 7 June and went on a short operation with one of its companies the following day.

Our liaison team had an exit interview with the U.S. Commander in Vietnam, General William C. Westmoreland (1914–2005), on 9 June. During this interview, Westmoreland told Timothy it would be advisable to leave an officer behind to liaise between his headquarters and the brigade. My orders anticipated such an eventuality and the choice as to who would remain was clear. It would be a long time before I returned to the U.S. Timothy gave me detailed instructions on what he expected me to do while waiting for the brigade to arrive. These instructions were later expanded on in a handwritten letter of eight pages, dated 25 June 1965.

These numerous tasks—by my lonesome—were overwhelming. However, they represented only a small part of the many requests and directions I received in multiple letters and messages from Timothy, the support battalion commander, Hackworth, and other principal brigade staff officers over the next month. However, although I felt overwhelmed, I was also proud of the confidence displayed in me by Colonel Timothy.

His instructions gave some flavor of the thinking both in Saigon and the U.S. at that time. For example, the emphasis was already on traditional combat operations that officers like Timothy and his contemporaries had experienced in World War II and Korea rather than the many other essential elements of counter-insurgency operations. While our service schools taught our more junior officers that this conflict had other characteristics that needed consideration for success, these teachings had not taken hold—and seldom did—at the senior echelons in Vietnam.

The thinking in both Washington and at MACV in June 1965 was for a short U.S. involvement in Vietnam. Some people believed that somehow the mere presence of elite U.S. combat units with modern, sophisticated weapons and equipment would immediately reverse the trend and lead North Vietnam to abort its efforts to subjugate the South. This belief reflected an almost total lack of understanding of Vietnamese history and conditions, particularly since 1945.

Doctor Arthur M. Schlesinger and President John F. Kennedy had warned us not to carry the idea of American exceptionalism too far. Kennedy stated bluntly:

> We must face the fact that the United States is neither omnipotent nor omniscient—that we are only six percent of the world's population—that we cannot impose our will on the other ninety-four percent of mankind—that we cannot right every wrong or reverse each adversity—and that therefore there cannot be an American solution to every world problem.[1]

This caution is as pertinent today as it was at the time of the Vietnam War.

The feeling that this would be a relatively short affair was widespread. The reason Colonel Timothy believed we would be operating out of Vung Tau and Bien Hoa, for example, had to do with ideas explored by Brigadier General William Eugene DePuy's (1914–1992) J-3 at MACV. The 173rd was temporarily deployed to Vietnam (another indication of the quick war scenario prevailing in various quarters). The plan was to move that unit back into its strategic reserve location in Okinawa and have the 1st Brigade, 101st Airborne Division, assume its mission in Vietnam.

This exploration occurred when other units such as the 1st Infantry Division at Fort Riley, Kansas, and the 1st Air Cavalry Division at Fort Benning, were preparing for deployment to Vietnam. These deployments demonstrate the lack of clear outlooks or expectations compared with the plans of the J-3 in the previous paragraph.

MACV—as an organization—had no idea or plans for how long we would be involved in Vietnam. Nor had it any ideas what kind of forces would be required. The command was undergoing a turbulent period shifting from a slow-moving advisory role to a fast-phased combat headquarters.

I attended several planning sessions at J-3 as an observer during this period. I became entirely convinced no one knew where they were going, how they were to get there, or what would be required to accomplish whatever we were there to do.

It was tough to keep the brigade informed since even its destination changed virtually weekly. While some officers at MACV believed we should prepare for a long involvement, the consensus appeared that if everything went well in the coming months, there was a good chance our unit would return to the United States before the end of the year! I relayed this feeling to Timothy and cautioned him that I did not share this optimistic assessment.

On my way to Vietnam, I felt I was participating in events that would have significant consequences for my country and the world and decided to keep a written record of events and my feelings at various times. It was against the rules to keep a diary in a war zone. The loss or capture of such a document could prove especially useful to the enemy. It was also not very practical to try to keep a diary. We were always on the move and I spent most of my time in the field.

I decided to record the unclassified events and my feelings in letters I wrote to Florence. Eventually, this part of my correspondence amounted to 114 single-spaced typewritten pages. While these letters do not cover nearly all that transpired and go into few details, they provide a chronological record of events that serve, even now, to remind me of what happened on a given date and how I felt. I also kept my form of shorthand notes in numerous field notebooks. For example, on 13 June, I wrote to Florence that I believed the war would be long and that she should not listen to reports of an early return. This letter was in answer to newspaper articles she had read about the 1st Brigade returning by Christmas.

After Timothy and the rest of the liaison party departed on 10 June, I divided my time between General Westmoreland's headquarters in Saigon, the 173rd Airborne Brigade, and the newly arrived Australian unit.

The monsoon rains had started in the Saigon area and would last until September or October. Roads not hard surfaced became a quagmire of mud and rice paddies flooded.

I had an opportunity to spend two days in the northern part of South Vietnam, near Da Nang. The conditions were not much better for the U.S. Marines, although this area was in the dry season, with exceedingly high temperatures.

The Marine units were experiencing a high rate of heat casualties in one form or another. I concluded the problem resulted primarily from the burden they carried and the lack of adequate acclimatization. One lasting impression from Da Nang's visit was that loads carried by our soldiers needed reducing. The Marines had weapons, ammunition, supplies, rations, and all kinds of contingency equipment.

Soldiers weighed down with extraneous equipment and supplies become tired and worn out, are not alert, and not immediately prepared for and capable of engaging the enemy. Over the years, I grew increasingly obsessed with reducing the weight a soldier carried into battle in Vietnam. I was always searching for ways to do this without impairing his fighting capabilities. I will discuss this issue at more length in those sections dealing with my participation in the war as an infantry commander.

There was not much time for participating in operations with either the 173rd or the Australians. I had to be present at MACV almost daily in case someone needed to contact me. The distance from Saigon to Bien Hoa was 45 kilometers and took about an hour by jeep. Bien Hoa housed the headquarters and primary units of the 173rd. One battalion of that brigade and the Australian battalion was in Vung Tau on the coast. The road was unsafe for travel at night and not all that safe during daylight. On 24 June, while on the way back to Saigon, the jeep I was riding in had several shots fired at it from a nearby wooded area. There were no injuries in this incident.

I sent a message to Hackworth around 15 June requesting I be augmented with a few officers to help me carry out the many requests from the brigade and MACV. My message eventually led to the arrival of six officers.

Captains James R. Andonaegui, Theodore Roman, and Norman Schwarzkopf—friends from my Berlin days—had just arrived in Vietnam. We planned to have dinner together on 25 June. I had toyed with the idea of taking them to the "My Can," a floating Vietnamese restaurant not far from Hotel Majestic. Something led me to change my mind, possibly because the place was so popular that we needed reservations or had to wait long to be seated. Instead, we assembled at a club, I believe at the Brinks Hotel.

The three newly arrived officers were eager for my views of the situation and although I was a relative newcomer with less than four weeks in the country, I unloaded my frustrations. I do not remember their reactions, but I know at least two of them came to share my feelings as time passed. After we broke up, I stopped with Ted Roman for a couple of beers at the sidewalk café outside the Majestic.

A loud blast rocked the floating restaurant where I had initially planned to take my friends. We were located about 300 to 500 meters down the street from the restaurant. People had begun to stream ashore when I witnessed a second explosion.

The second explosion was probably a claymore-type device set to rake the boarding platform as people tried to get off the boat.

About 50 people died, nine of them Americans. South Vietnamese police and medical personnel quickly filled the area. Ted and I took our beers and moved to the restaurant on the fifth floor of the hotel. I also said thanks for not having taken my friends to that restaurant. Those who now proclaim that terrorism is a new phenomenon on the world scene would do well to keep this—and numerous similar events—in mind.

Six officers from the brigade reinforced my one-person liaison mission in Vietnam on 1 July. The group leader was Captain Terrence W. McClain, who had joined the brigade just before its deployment to Vietnam to augment the S-3 section and be my replacement when I eventually took command of the long-promised company. I had known Terry when he and I worked in the G-2 section in the division and I had recommended him as my replacement to Lieutenant Colonel Rogers and Major Hackworth.

Terry joined the 173rd Airborne Brigade headquarters as an observer, and the other five—lieutenants from our battalions—joined the units of the 173rd to participate in any scheduled operations. These newcomers relieved me of some work as I could now concentrate on my liaison duties at Westmoreland's headquarters and prepare for the brigade's arrival.

The J-3 section's confusion about where to locate our brigade continued during the first 10–12 days of July. The NVA regular units operating in South Vietnam significantly impacted the decision. Military estimates indicated that ARVN lost the equivalent of one battalion a week in pitched battles with the NVA. This kind of attrition could not continue for long and caused a re-evaluation of the earlier thinking about moving the 173rd back to Okinawa.

This, in turn, influenced the debate about where to locate our brigade. Pleiku, in the Central Highlands, and several points along the coast—Phan Thiet, Phan Rang, Cam Ranh Bay, Tuy Hoa, and Qui Nhon—were frequently mentioned. Time was getting short and we had to make definite plans for the brigade's reception, now underway by ship from the U.S. West Coast. I considered the two likeliest places in the country to be Cam Ranh Bay and Pleiku and made a quick reconnaissance of those places on 6–7 July.

Upon my return to Saigon, I recommended to the J-3 staff that Cam Ranh Bay, just south of Nha Trang, be selected as our initial location in Vietnam. I gave several reasons for my recommendation. First, the troops needed a period of adjustment and acclimatization. This relatively quiet area south of Nha Trang was well suited for that purpose. Here the brigade units could slowly begin to achieve familiarity with this war and the terrain without becoming engaged in large-scale operations against seasoned NVA regulars. Second, the brigade would be much easier to supply through the excellent anchorage in Cam Ranh Bay, where both the U.S. Air Force and Navy had plans for large-scale construction. Third, from Cam Ranh Bay, the brigade could quickly move to other parts of the country by air or sea. This last provision was important since Westmoreland was planning to use our unit as a strategic reserve. Brigadier General DePuy listened intently to my recommendation and said it would be considered.

Major Hackworth and a relatively sizeable advanced party arrived in Vietnam on 9 July. Every staff section was represented, but most were from the S-3 and S-2 sections, including Major Hicks, Master Sergeant Pennycuff, and Staff Sergeant Ikner. I do not recall seeing any S-1 and S-4 section officers, but Tim Swain wrote that a lieutenant from S-4 named Jim Pahris was in the party. I guessed Major Dexter had already moved to 2/502. In my view, S-1 and S-4 were underrepresented given their heavy chores when the brigade arrived.

The J-3 had informed me that MACV had selected an area for the brigade's initial location the previous afternoon. The place was near the Dong Ba Thin Special Forces Camp on Cam Ranh Bay's inland side. Accordingly, Hackworth and I, along with three others, traveled there via Nha Trang on 10 July. The camp was the home to 19 American advisers and about 200 Vietnamese soldiers, and the only secure connection to the outside world was by air.

At this time of the year, the heat in that area was terrible—often reaching 110 degrees Fahrenheit and the place swarmed with mosquitoes. The dry season had just begun in this area of the country. The rainy season would not start here until the end of September or the beginning of October. The countryside's topography was beautiful, from first-class beaches along the coast to a strip of jungle-covered lowlands with 700 to 1,200 meter high jungle-covered mountains in the background.

Cam Ranh Bay was considered a relatively safe area. We soon found out—in an incident related by Hackworth—the operative word in that phrase was "relatively."[2] Hackworth, Sergeant Major Grady Jones, and I had already inspected large portions of our new area by jeeps borrowed from the SF in Dong Ba Thin. One day, while we were looking at the western part of the perimeter we had planned for the brigade, an automatic weapon opened up on us. Instinctively, we unloaded the jeep, which continued at slow speed and ended up in a ditch. All was quiet after the first and only burst of automatic weapons fire. We spread out and searched the area but found no trace of the weapon's owner.

Colonel Timothy, the battalion commanders, and a large contingent of the main advanced party arrived in Nha Trang on 14 July. The pace of events now became very hectic as we prepared for the arrival of the brigade. The 35th Engineer Group was located on the Cam Ranh Peninsula. They arrived on 9 June to begin construction of an airfield and harbor facilities, eventually the most massive construction project in Vietnam. An infantry battalion from the 1st Infantry Division had also just arrived in the area to provide security.

In addition to the work associated with getting things ready for the troops' arrival, we had to brief many dignitaries. We briefed Secretary of Defense Robert McNamara (1916–2009), Chairman of the Joint Chiefs of Staff General Earle G. Wheeler (1908–1975), and General Westmoreland on 19 July. Our briefing was mostly limited to the plans for the reception of the brigade, but it also briefly addressed the initial operations to make the troops familiar with the climate and terrain.

Since Captain McClain had now assumed most of the duties of the Assistant S-3, I reminded Hackworth and Timothy about their promises that I would receive command of the first available company. Hackworth was reluctant to let me go because of the staff's workload, and Timothy was likewise opposed to immediately changing any of the company commanders. Timothy wanted to retain the old hands during the break-in period. He told me I would still get the first command to come open but that he did not plan to make any changes until November. I understood this, even though it was disappointing.

To prevent McClain and me from getting in each other's way, Hackworth temporarily reorganized the duties within the S-3 section. McClain would focus on getting ready for the brigade's arrival and the administrative functions of the S-3 section, while I would concentrate on planning future operations. As I saw it, I received the better end of the deal.

Our first parachute jump in Vietnam was on 21 July, an administrative jump designed to keep us qualified for the extra money paratroopers receive. A trooper had to make a minimum of one drop every 90 days to stay qualified. It was not until later in 1965 that we received an exemption from this requirement because of Vietnam duties.[3]

I took a seven-vehicle convoy by road from Dong Ba Thin to Nha Trang on 24 July. Travel in and out of our place was usually by air, and the 45 kilometers of road separating the two areas were not consider safe for travel. However, we needed to move some heavy equipment and supplies and we planned to use this road after the brigade's arrival. The trip was uneventful and soon became routine.

I stayed in Nha Trang to receive and process personnel who came in by air. These were troops who had remained behind in the U.S. to close out the brigade when it left by sea. Four planeloads came in on 25 July, carrying 155 soldiers.

The brigade troops arrived by ship (USNS *Eltinge*) on 29 July and landed on the Cam Ranh Peninsula. It was an exceedingly hectic day with many VIP visitors, including Ambassador Maxwell Taylor (1901–1987). He had commanded the 101st Airborne Division in World War II. In addition, General Westmoreland and about a dozen other dignitaries were present. The ship arrived in the middle of the afternoon. Except for a ceremonial landing, most of the troops remained on board until the following day.

Navy ships offshore fired in support of the soldiers when they landed. This bombardment was unnecessary and a public relations gimmick. The S-3 section was overruled when it opposed this silly idea. The whole operation had the characteristics of a staged event for the benefit of a significant media presence. We put out the word through our Vietnamese allies that we would be firing into an area. The area was already designated a "free-fire zone," but many local farmers and loggers appeared not to know or paid little attention to the warnings. Some did not get the word despite the additional warnings and two were wounded in the unnecessary bombardment.

Most of the troops landed on 30 July and moved into their designated areas. Although things appeared to be a mass of confusion for the next few days while we were trying to link up the troops with their equipment and supplies, there were no serious incidents. The soldiers went through the "jittery" period when, at night, whole sections of the perimeter would open fire on imaginary movements to their front or unusual jungle noises. It was a wonder no one was killed or wounded in these shadow-shooting incidents.

Over the next two weeks, the troops slowly became accustomed to the jungle and its noises, and the indiscriminate firing tapered off. However, we only had a few tents. Most of the soldiers had only a poncho for cover from the blazing sun. Our supply system could not keep up with the rapid build-up, and for the next three to four months, we all ate C-rations.

The advance party had made plans for small unit operations by the brigade near Cam Ranh Bay and the battalions quickly executed these. The purpose was primarily to acquaint the troops with the terrain and get them used to operating in the oppressive heat. They also allowed squad and platoon leaders to practice their operating procedures. Plans called for a gradual increase in operational scope and scale to battalion size by the beginning of September. The battalion staff handled the detailed planning and execution of these operations.

The S-3 section became increasingly involved in contingency planning for possible deployment to various parts of Vietnam. Hackworth and I made several reconnaissance trips to potential deployment areas. These included Duc My, about 100 kilometers north of Dong Ba Thin, Ban Me Thuot, a provincial capital about 320 kilometers inland, Tuy Hoa, Qui Nhon, Phan Thiet on the coast, and Pleiku, the largest town in the Vietnamese Highlands.

While waiting for the brigade, I flew to Saigon on 11 August to clear out where I had lived and bring my things back to Cam Ranh Bay. There was a ceremony to award Combat Infantry Badges on 12 August to seven troops. I was one of those seven. It was the first award of this kind to members of the 101st Airborne Division since World War II. General Westmoreland came to make the presentation, which I missed since I was not back from Saigon.

As stated earlier, we hoped the brigade would stay in the Cam Ranh Bay area for its shakedown period until late September, but events soon overtook our planning. Two weeks after the troops arrived, we received an alert to move north and secure a base at An Khe for the 1st Air Cavalry Division with 20,000 men and 420 helicopters.

The base location had to be secured, and the road—the famous Route 19—between the harbor city of Qui Nhon and the base at An Khe needed clearing and kept open. Route 19 was the road where *Groupement Mobile 100*, consisting of France's finest soldiers, was annihilated 11 years earlier. Some rusted vehicle skeletons from that unit were still visible, not far from Qui Nhon. Again, we had little time to plan this complex operation.

On 18 August, I flew to Qui Nhon to present our concept of operation. Several changes—contingent on approval by Colonel Timothy—were made to the concept at the conference. It speaks highly of the professional working relationship existing on the brigade staff before and during our deployment that a junior staff officer could make conditional adjustments to our concept and have them accepted by the rest of the staff and commander on my return. As it turned out, this was my last function on the brigade staff because one of the changes I proposed to our plan at the conference in Qui Nhon had a far-reaching effect on my life.

One of the issues raised at the meeting in Qui Nhon was the lack of mobile forces to secure Route 19 and provide escorts for the convoys of supplies and equipment for the 1st Air Cavalry Division from Qui Nhon to An Khe. The representatives from Task Force (TF) Alpha—the brigade's next higher headquarters—questioned our ability to accomplish this part of our mission with only one cavalry troop assigned to the brigade. At this time, I advanced the idea that we could form an additional cavalry troop by grouping the reconnaissance platoons of the three battalions under one command.

The provisional cavalry troop and our regular cavalry troop would operate under the brigade's direction, secure Route 19, and escort the convoys between Qui Nhon and An Khe. TF Alpha accepted this as a workable solution, and both Hackworth and Timothy approved the concept. The battalion commanders, on the other hand, opposed the idea as hard as they could. This reaction was natural and anticipated since no commander is willing to lose any of his units as he is about to go into battle. Timothy's support and the underlying logic of the idea finally won out.

As mentioned earlier, it did not look promising for me to obtain a command until November or December, and I did not look forward to spending another three to four months on the staff. A directive from MACV, which had recently arrived, gave me another incentive for leaving the brigade staff as quickly as possible. MACV was trying to solve the rotation problem by personnel who had arrived in the country simultaneously. This problem involved our unit. The MACV directive requested that the brigade Assistant S-3 (me), the battalion Assistant S-3s, and all reconnaissance platoon leaders be reassigned to MACV or other U.S. units in Vietnam to alleviate the simultaneous rotation problem. Rumors had it I would go to the 173rd Airborne Brigade. While this was an excellent unit, it would almost certainly mean that I would not get command of a company.

On the helicopter returning from the meeting at Qui Nhon to Cam Ranh Bay, I thought of a way to avoid leaving the brigade and, at the same time, get off the staff. I figured that if my superiors approved the idea of a provisional cavalry troop, there was a good chance they would allow me to command that unit. This thinking had not been a consideration when I proposed this solution to TF Alpha at Qui Nhon—an explanation that was never entirely accepted by my friends in the brigade. After receiving Timothy's approval for the unit's formation, I immediately asked Lieutenant Colonel Rogers to support my request for the new unit's command. While the unit was a temporary arrangement—for the operation's duration—it would keep me in the brigade while letting me off the staff.

In going directly to Rogers, I was circumventing Hackworth, my immediate superior. I decided this was worth the gamble since I had concluded Hackworth would not allow me to leave his staff unless ordered. To a certain extent, I blamed Hackworth for not supporting my repeated requests for command more forcefully. I no longer felt the initial reasons for retaining the old company commanders were valid and I believed the repeated promises given to me needed fulfillment. My relations with Hackworth had cooled somewhat during the past month, partly because of this issue, and I figured going around him this one time could not make matters much worse between us. We all knew the new unit would exist only for this operation's duration, and I made it clear to Rogers that I still expected to get command of the first rifle company to become available.

Rogers discussed the issue with Timothy, who quickly gave his approval. In the interim, I had told Hackworth what I had done, and although his initial reaction was anger, he eventually went along with the idea. After he cooled off, he even provided personnel and equipment from the brigade staff to operate my new headquarters.

Since the new unit was a provisional one without a table of organization and equipment (TO&E), the personnel assigned to its headquarters were on a TDY status from their parent units. This TDY status meant that, on paper, I was still carried as brigade assistant S-3 and, therefore, subject to reassignment if Saigon should so decide. However, I figured I would worry about one thing at a time and immersed myself in the task of organizing and readying my new unit for its role.

In my proposal at Qui Nhon, I had envisioned the two cavalry troops would work directly for the brigade, with no intermediate headquarters. However, Timothy thought it wise to have an intermediate command between the two cavalry troops and the brigade and tagged Major Mark Hansen, the XO of the 1st Battalion, 327th Airborne Infantry Regiment, for the task. Hansen organized a small TF headquarters and became my new commander.

CHAPTER 8

Provisional Cavalry Troop: Battle of An Ninh

I assumed command of my new unit on 21 August. I spent the rest of that day and the following day organizing the unit and briefing my subordinates. On 23 August, I made a helicopter reconnaissance of the unit's area of operations (AO). I tentatively selected an operating base about midway between Qui Nhon and An Khe Pass.

I wanted to land to take a closer look at the area, but as we passed over Route 19 and attempted to land, we received several bursts of automatic weapons fired from a village near the highway. The helicopter was a light observation craft with no armament, so we departed the area without further attempts to land. The pilot reported finding three bullet holes in the aircraft's rear section when we returned to Qui Nhon. There were no damages to any critical systems. However, the incident confirmed we should not be surprised to meet opposition in clearing and keeping Route 19 open.

My XO, Lieutenant Tim Swain from the brigade S-2 section, brought our nearly 200-man unit from Cam Ranh Bay to Nha Trang while I was on the aerial reconnaissance. I joined the unit in Nha Trang in the afternoon and we loaded on to Navy ships for the overnight trip to our new operational area. We arrived in Qui Nhon the following morning and went into an assembly area, pending operations.

Major Hansen briefed Captain Wilson, the commander of the A/2/17 Cavalry, and me.[1] The operation would start before daylight, with my unit leading the way and securing the 70-kilometer stretch of road between Qui Nhon and the bottom of An Khe Pass. At that location, Wilson's unit would pass through my unit and continue to open the rest of the road to An Khe, the 1st Air Cavalry Division's future site. An Khe was also the location of our brigade headquarters.

Hansen was a demanding but decent officer, having served in the Italian Theater of Operations at the end of World War II, and Korea. In my opinion, these experiences had conditioned his thinking, a fact that would affect our operations for the next month. He believed in firm centralized control in an operational environment that required a decentralized approach. The Vietnam War was at this time fought at the platoon and company level. Both Wilson and I had occasional disagreements with

Hansen over the next month. These disagreements dealt primarily with tactical operations and how best to bring the convoys from Qui Nhon to An Khe.

Hansen asked Wilson and me for our concept of operations. I explained that I wanted to leave the reconnaissance platoons' heavy weapons (primarily the 106mm recoilless rifles sections) behind and use my whole unit as mounted infantry. I explained I intended to outpost the high ground along the route with squad size elements while keeping about half of the unit in a central location as a mobile reserve.

Major Hansen immediately vetoed this concept, stating it was reckless and that I was asking for defeat in detail. I agreed there was a risk to our outposts, but I felt we could almost eliminate this risk by leaving them in one location for no longer than 12 hours. I stated the remaining risks were acceptable to provide adequate security for the many vehicles and personnel traveling on the road.

Hansen disagreed and ordered that we operate from Route 19 unless we came under attack. He further directed each troop to concentrate at a single location each night for maximum security. Wilson would spend the nights at An Khe while I would establish a base at the bottom of An Khe Pass where he also planned to locate his TF headquarters.

The arrangement Hansen directed required we launch an operation each morning to clear Route 19 of mines, booby traps, and ambushes. The convoys we escorted were on a tight schedule to maximize the use of the limited number of available vehicles. This procedure required we pick up the convoys in Qui Nhon, some 70 kilometers from our base, within one hour after daybreak. It forced my unit, if it were to perform its mission correctly, to begin the clearing operation long before daylight. Wilson had more time to clear his section of road since he picked up the convoys near his overnight location and delivered the empty trucks to us at the base of An Khe Pass shortly before noon when he also picked up the next loaded convoy from Qui Nhon. We then brought the empty trucks to Qui Nhon, trying to return to our night location before dark.

I decided to appeal Hansen's decisions in a one-on-one meeting shortly before midnight. He was annoyed at me coming to see him. Hansen denied my appeal for a change in operations, and our argument became heated at times. To this day, I do not know why I was not relieved. While Hansen and I disagreed on various operational issues, it never became quite as heated as that night.

We began the operation well before daylight on 25 August, and encountered some opposition in the early afternoon as we neared An Khe Pass. The unit's lead elements, checking the road for land mines, came under fire from two groups of huts on the south side of Route 19. The total number of grass and weed huts may have been 20–30, and from the amount of small arms fire, we estimated the enemy force opposing us at less than a platoon in size. The enemy fire was ineffective, mainly because the range at which they opened fire was over 300 meters.

I will digress for a moment to address a few of the stringent rules of engagement under which we operated—and the defensive posture they forced us into—in those initial weeks of our involvement in the war. For example, we could only use our weapons if we received fire, and then only if we had a specific and well-defined target. When you are belly-down on the ground and fired on in daylight, it is exceedingly difficult to determine the exact location of the incoming fire with any sense of accuracy. The use of smokeless powder makes it all but impossible to pinpoint an enemy weapon in daylight. Under these circumstances, it was tough to explain and defend this rule to troops who risked their lives. There were repeated denied appeals by commanders at the company level to modify the stringent rules of engagement.

To keep from suffering needless casualties and maintain unit morale while we tried to carry out our missions, those of us at company and platoon level—where this war took place—soon began to ignore the most senseless of these rules of engagement. The rules were either changed or disregarded as time passed. However, they were infuriating to those of us on the ground at this stage of the war.

The enemy force that opened fire on us that first day of our clearing operation began to withdraw as soon as we started to maneuver in their direction and tried to outflank them from the east. We had no casualties and found no enemy dead or wounded. The huts from which we received fire were deserted and had not been occupied for a long time. They did provide excellent cover and concealment for anyone firing at our convoys on Route 19, as had just been demonstrated. Since I was not allowed to outpost the area, I authorized the burning of the structures. This action caused another unpleasant confrontation with Hansen, but a more justified one from his side since I had violated one of the "rules."

We spent the next three weeks primarily on road security and escort duties. We would proceed to Qui Nhon each day with at least half the unit, pick up convoys ranging in size from 70 to 140 vehicles, and escort them to the bottom of An Khe Pass, where Wilson's group took over the security and brought them to An Khe. My unit would wait at the bottom of the pass and escort the empty vehicles back to Qui Nhon. This procedure left less than half the unit available for other tasks, and neither Wilson nor I liked it. We finally persuaded Major Hansen to change the procedure. One unit would escort the convoys from Qui Nhon to An Khe one day and the other would do the same the next day. This change in procedure allowed either group to stand down for a day or, as was usually the case, conduct small operations on either side of Route 19. This change directly increased the route's security and was a primary reason why Hansen approved the concept.

As soon as we adopted the new procedures, we began making enemy contact. The enemy we encountered consisted of small local guerrilla units and we fought numerous minor engagements in the period that followed. Unfortunately, we also began to suffer casualties. One sergeant sustained a leg wound, one trooper had a severe lower stomach wound, and a grenade wounded my RTO. Although I was next to him on the ground, I did not receive a scratch.

The most crucial action during this period took place on 3 September. We had been harassed the day before by snipers from the south side of Route 19 and I used two platoons, led by Lieutenants Glass and Burkhart, to search the area. We soon came under sustained enemy small-arms fire, and I received permission to bring the rest of my unit into the action, which lasted about three to four hours.

The enemy made a fighting withdrawal to higher ground about 2 kilometers from Route 19. First Lieutenant George Burkhart, from Murfreesboro, Tennessee, died during our pursuit up the slopes of the 800-foot hill, later called "Burkhart's Hill." He was the first officer from the 101st Airborne Division killed in combat in Vietnam. We estimated the strength of the enemy to be a company of local guerrillas. Most managed to slip away in the rough terrain. Our only consolation was that we might have frustrated a plan to prevent our use of Route 19. If it had not been for artillery support, our casualties would no doubt have been higher.[2]

This action almost led to another confrontation with Major Hansen. Although my provisional cavalry troop was the only unit involved in the fighting, Hansen repeatedly injected himself into our operation from his light observation helicopter (LOH). If he did not receive an immediate answer on the task force command net, he would switch his radio to my command net. Hansen interfered directly with my ability to communicate with my subordinates during the engagement a couple of times. For example, after we started maneuvering against the enemy, he complained—on my command net—that our pursuit was feeble and without vigor. I had to control myself by not telling him that Burkhart had just died, leading his men in this "weak" pursuit of the enemy.

I was also upset about my inability to use the whole force at my disposal. I had pointed out that the jeeps could not traverse the off-road areas and asked Hansen to disband the recoilless rifles and use the troops as infantry. Hansen vetoed my idea. During this engagement, the result was that 30-some troops were just off Route 19 with their jeeps and recoilless rifles and could not participate in the fighting.

That evening, I was still steaming about what had happened earlier and went to the task force command post (CP) to directly lodge my complaints to Hansen. His statements about the feebleness of our pursuit over the unit radio net when the troops were fighting and taking casualties had caused bitterness in the unit. I also intended to demand a free hand in organizing my unit for combat. I realized my actions would probably lead to my relief, but I felt I owed this to my men and my self-esteem.

I was in a hurry to get back to the CP area as it would soon become dark. I told Tim Swain, since he was the only Ranger in the outfit, to bring the troops back to our encampment while I took some of the recoilless sections so that I could quickly get back to confront Hansen. Unfortunately, I believe it became dark before Tim successfully reached our perimeter.

When I entered Major Hansen's tent, and before I had a chance to make a statement, Hansen volunteered that he had just talked to Timothy, who had congratulated us on the operation to which he wanted to add his thanks for a job well done. He also went on to express his regrets about the death of Burkhart. His attitude and statements took most of the wind out of my sails.

I nevertheless mentioned that his statement on my radio net that we had not conducted ourselves sufficiently aggressively had stung the troops and me. I also renewed my request to disband the recoilless rifle sections, pointing out he could not have missed seeing them sitting near Route 19, unable to participate in the engagement. He agreed I could leave the recoilless rifles in the base camp and use the personnel as infantry. He did not comment on my other statement, but he never again communicated on my command net. Finally, after he offered me a cup of coffee—another first—I figured he was beginning to mellow.

The keeping of statistics—one of the most exasperating aspects of the Vietnam War—was already beginning to make itself felt. Every headquarters was under intense pressure to show the results of operations, particularly when U.S. casualties were involved. Since the measuring devices of previous wars, such as terrain and towns captured, were inappropriate for our actions, the number of enemy soldiers killed and weapons seized became the standard measure of success or failure.

Because we seldom captured as many weapons as the number of enemies killed, it frequently led to questions about whether the person killed could have been an innocent civilian caught in the fighting. Innocent civilians were, of course, hurt at times in the struggle and suffered, as civilians have in all wars. We tried, as best we could, to minimize this, but it was not always easy. At this stage of the fighting, the enemy would go to extraordinary lengths to recover weapons lost on the battlefield because these were evidently in short supply. In the end, we who were engaged knew when the fallen were not innocent civilians.

Repeated requests for information by higher headquarters were highly annoying when trying to direct and control a unit in combat. Later I learned to ignore those requests. However, I finally lost my temper after many meaningless requests for information by the brigade S-3 section after the 3 September action. In this case, the questions had to do with the nationality of those killed. Somehow, they had received some nutty intelligence that there could be Chinese advisers with the unit we had engaged, and we received repeated queries about whether we were sure those killed were Vietnamese.

I had one of the dead enemy soldiers tied to the hood of my jeep. I told my driver to proceed to the brigade headquarters and deliver the body to either Major Hackworth or Captain McClain so they could decide for themselves what the answers were to their many ridiculous questions. Immediately after I had done this, I felt sorry and ashamed. A fallen enemy soldier—one who had given his life for his cause—deserved better and more dignified treatment. At least in spirit it was probably a violation of the Geneva Convention on treating fallen enemy soldiers.

When Hackworth wrote his best-seller, *About Face*, in 1989, he asked my permission to include this incident in his book. I asked him not to use it at that time as I was not incredibly proud of that event, resulting from built-up frustrations. He honored my request. I still regret my action, but I have also concluded that it requires an explanation since it did happen.

Still, the action I took resulted in a significant lessening in this type of harassment from the brigade. A few days later, a platoon I was accompanying received fire from a small group of huts on the north side of the river that parallels Route 19. The fire was not heavy but accurate. We returned the fire with our M16s, but this was ineffective.

The enemy force withdrew to the east into a small village where they continued to fire on us. I knew we would suffer casualties if we tried to cross the intervening open area without artillery support. I did not know if there were any civilians in the village, but I assumed some were present. As distasteful as it was, I called in artillery on the village and started moving the troops forward. The enemy disappeared as we approached the village. We found that the artillery fire had wounded a few civilians, and our medics tended to the injured.

Afterward, a couple of groups of civilians from other areas approached us under white flags. They were also hurt by artillery fire or airstrikes. We spent some time there and provided whatever help we could. I was particularly distressed to see a small boy who had lost a hand, probably several days earlier.

I received a visit from Colonel Timothy on 5 September, and we had a long talk before the memorial service for Burkhart. He stated I would get a company at the end of this operation, which he guessed would end in October. I talked to him again on 10 September and, at that time, he told me I would take command of A/2/502. He also informed me that Lieutenant Colonel Rogers was leaving to assume command of 1/327 from Lieutenant Colonel James Wilson, and that Hackworth would become Rogers's XO. He said he was thinking of assigning Hansen as Hackworth's replacement. Later in the day, Hackworth called to tell me about his upcoming assignment and that I would soon assume command of B/1/327. Thus, by the end of the day, I had been promised command of two companies and kept my fingers crossed that at least one promise would be honored.

Throughout the war, I continually tried to instill in my officers and NCOs the importance of flexibility, initiative, and improvisation. I wanted to teach them to expect the unexpected on the battlefield and encouraged them to deviate from plans to achieve their goals. Quick decisions and equally fast executions are the cornerstones of military success on a fluid battlefield. The goal is always to confuse, demoralize, and paralyze the enemy through unrelenting pressure.

Operation *Gibraltar*

By the middle of September 1965, the 1st Brigade had been in Vietnam for about six weeks. Our contacts with the enemy had only been minor skirmishes with local

VC units. We had not encountered any major VC or NVA units, but that was about to change and would result in the most significant U.S. engagement thus far in the war, Operation *Gibraltar.*

While I had no part in the planning or the fighting, I did monitor the brigade command net. Since this engagement was—I am sad to say—in many ways a classic example of how not to fight the Vietnam War, and since the unit I was assigned to command at the end of the operation took part, I concluded I should cover it.

I had been confused about what I found in the literature even before I began writing this book. To better understand the engagement, I made it a point of reading all the accounts I could find. I talked to some officers who were involved, including Timothy and Hackworth. I also discussed the battle with my officers and NCOs. Finally, I had access to friendly and enemy reports, both somewhat confusing. These conversations and references serve as the basis for my analysis of what went wrong.

The brigade staff had anticipated the 1st Air Cavalry Division would be entirely in place and assume security responsibility for the Qui Nhon and An Khe road by late September. This route continued to be of great importance since it served as the only link between the interior and the coast in this area. The 1st Brigade now had two battalions in this area, the 2/502nd at An Khe and the 2/327th at Qui Nhon. The brigade planned to use these battalions plus part of TF Hansen in offensive operations.

The operation began on 18 September. The Provisional Cavalry Troop had no part in Operation *Gibraltar* as it was still involved in escort duty on 17 and 18 September. Nevertheless, I knew the brigade had planned an operation. Hackworth stopped at my location near the bottom of An Khe Pass earlier in the month and he told me that, with the 1st Air Cavalry now virtually in place, the 1st Brigade was planning to begin large-scale operations. He asked me where I thought the best hunting grounds were, north or south of Route 19. I told him I believed there were higher chances of finding VC forces to the north of that route.

The military literature has been relatively quiet concerning this first significant engagement between the U.S. and main core enemy troops in the Vietnam War. Westmoreland and the press heralded it as a great victory when, in fact, that was an exaggeration. It was the first in a long series of engagements announced as "great victories." Hackworth wrote about it in *About Face.*[3] *Infantry Magazine*'s 1967 book *Infantry in Vietnam*, edited by Lieutenant Colonel Albert N. Garland,[4] covers it briefly, and Judge Mallon Faircloth wrote a small but excellent paperback titled *Behind the Names.*[5] I believe he wrote the account mainly because he lost his brother, Staff Sergeant Johnny Faircloth, at An Ninh. Mallon Faircloth was appointed U.S. Magistrate Judge for the U.S. District Court, Middle District of Georgia, in 1999. There were also a couple of short pieces in *The First Screaming Eagles in Viet Nam*. Finally, an article titled "101st Airborne vs. Viet Cong at An Ninh" by Colonel Thomas E. Faley, Jr. appeared in the August 1997 issue of *Vietnam Magazine* and a member of A/2/502nd wrote a book that included the action at An Ninh.

Judge Faircloth wrote:

> The battle at An Ninh has remained virtually a secret in our war histories. The few times it is found recounted at all, reveal a short and confused story, told in differing shades of truth to suit different personal and political agendas of the time. And after short consideration, it is deemed a good thing to forget.[6]

The performance of the troops was heroic in every respect. They gave an excellent account of themselves and were not to blame for the rather poor results. Instead, the blame rests with the senior officers who planned and conducted the operation.

After we were both retired, Hackworth explained to me that the original plan envisaged lifting the whole brigade (those units in the An Khe and Qui Nhon areas) into two LZs. One LZ was about 2,000 meters south of An Ninh, where 2/502 was to land, and one to the north of An Ninh, where 2/327, commanded by Lieutenant Colonel Edward Collins, would land. The northern unit would fan out and block An Ninh approaches from that direction. I do not know what TF Hansen's mission was, but it would probably reinforce the 2/327 cordon from the west.

Hackworth briefed the plan to the subordinate commanders in the early evening of 17 September after Colonel Timothy approved it. Both Faircloth and Hackworth agree this was the case but that Lieutenant Colonel Smith bypassed Hackworth and went to see Timothy around midnight. Smith persuaded Timothy to change the plan, primarily concerning 2/502. He wanted to undertake a strike operation and was given a free hand as to when, where, and how to initiate the assault with the 2/502.[7]

While I knew about Operation *Gibraltar*, I did not need to know any specifics since no role was planned for my unit. Nevertheless, after the operation got underway on 18 September, I turned a radio to the brigade command net to see what was going on. It soon became apparent that things were not going well, but I did not fully understand the chaotic radio traffic.

The forward brigade CP had moved into a location close to my CP. Eventually, I walked over but was careful not to get in the way of the hectic activities. After having looked at the maps, I asked who had picked those dumb LZs. All I got in return was a shrug of the shoulder, or *I do not know*.

I walked back to my unit, and my radio operator (RTO) told me that it appeared the situation had become worse during my absence. He related that someone on the brigade command net had reported they had suffered many killed. The troops from the 2/502 were pinned down by the massive fire and spread in small groups throughout the battlefield.

After seeing the command and control (C&C) helicopter land, I again walked back to the brigade CP, hoping to see Hackworth, but instead, I met Timothy, who looked distraught. Nevertheless, he smiled and asked for my thoughts, apparently believing I knew the plans. I said the radio traffic indicated that there were problems. Timothy—used to my understatements by now—said the 2/502 had taken heavy casualties and lost all rifle company commanders.

In his book, Hackworth wrote that the battalion commander, Lieutenant Colonel Wilfrid Smith, reported that 113 men had died.[8] If this is true, it was a significant exaggeration by an officer who had been on the ground a short time and was pinned down behind a rice paddy wall and, therefore, not in a position to give an accurate assessment.

I left Timothy pacing back and forth outside his tent. As I departed, he asked me to remain in a place where he could quickly get in touch with me. At the time, I did not know what he meant and walked back to my area.

It was not until several days later, as I talked to the troops in A/2/502 who had participated, that I learned how the operation had gone on the ground. However, the perspectives of the few who got into the battle area were limited to their immediate surroundings as they spent most of their time pinned down or trying to link up with friendly units spread all over the battlefield.

In my view, and based on what I learned later, the most significant problems with Operation *Gibraltar* were:

1. Heavy reliance on Vietnamese intelligence. Judge Faircloth mentions we relied on signal intelligence (radio intercepts). However, he also wrote that two platoon-sized patrols from 2/502 and 2/327 had found the NVA camp at An Ninh on 14 September and kept it under observation for 24 hours without being spotted. This was news to me.

2. Sharing our plans with the Vietnamese District headquarters. It may have been necessary to brief the South Vietnamese because a couple of their companies took part. If this was the reason, the detailed briefing of those companies should occur after departing their base.

3. One of the worst mistakes was the failure to provide adequate artillery support. I am not sure where the artillery was at the outset. The April 2012 article in *The First Screaming Eagles* has TF Hansen, consisting of A/2/17 Cavalry, one company from 2/327, 2/320 Artillery (commanded by Lieutenant Colonel William Francis Braun (1918–2012), and a platoon of tanks from 2/7 U.S. Marines.[9] I believe the artillery was not the whole battalion, but only those batteries that usually supported the two infantry battalions involved. TF Hansen and the artillery must have been along Route 19, south of the Song Con River, about midway between Qui Nhon and An Khe Pass.

I had been in the Song Con River Valley (also referred to by some as the Vinh Thanh Valley) several times during the past four weeks and had sent patrols into the area north of the river. The ground was very marshy and soft, but Hansen and the brigade planners did not know. The onset of the monsoon rains made the ground even worse for vehicles. As a result, the artillery became bogged down when it tried to move forward to take up positions to support the An Ninh action. Lieutenant Colonel Smith was aware he would have no artillery support initially but disregarded this danger, instead placing his reliance on air support.[10] The air support also quickly turned sour; see below.

4. The worst mistake was probably the selection of LZs too close to enemy positions. Faircloth wrote that nothing in the plan changed concerning the other forces because of Smith's midnight meeting with Colonel Timothy. However, when one major part of a plan changes at the last minute, those changes affect the whole operation. For example, changing the LZ location from one 2,000 meters from the target area to smaller LZs at the foot of the low ridge that constituted the target area changed the whole battle.

At 2,000 meters from the target area, the helicopters and troops would have been outside the effective direct fire range and the soldiers could have assembled and moved to contact in good order. As it turned out, the troops landed under heavy enemy fire. The losses in airlift capability because of downed helicopters affected all units. The airlift of 2/502 required four roundtrips by the 26 troop-carrying helicopters assigned to support the brigade. This piecemeal feeding of the battlefield (each lift requiring 20–30 minutes) gave the enemy ample time to adjust and meet each lift as it arrived. When the third lift was on the ground, all helicopters assigned to support Operation *Gibraltar* were either shot down or damaged to the point where they could not participate. Had the landings taken place as planned initially, 2/502 would also have been able to maneuver against the enemy flanks. In countering this, the VC would have to spread out and thin their lines. Landing too close enabled the enemy to concentrate their fire, thereby preventing the U.S. forces from maneuvering.

5. Failure of early air support on which Smith had relied. The air support did not materialize except for two A-1E Skyraiders early in the morning on 18 September. A light observation plane crashed in Qui Nhon Bay, killing both the pilot and the passenger. A quick check of the fuel revealed the Air Force fuel at Qui Nhon was contaminated. As a result, all aircraft were grounded until new fuel was available. That left 2/502 without air support for nearly two hours while MACV scrambled jets out of Bien Hoa—about 450 kilometers away—to fill the void.

Attempts to obtain support from the 1st Air Cavalry Division and its plentiful supply of helicopters failed initially. However, after Westmoreland's deputy, Lieutenant General John L. Throckmorton (1913–1986), intervened, the division sent many helicopters to the rescue. The evacuation of the wounded took place. The artillery was lifted to a location where it could support the operation, and 2/327 was lifted toward An Ninh but inserted on an LZ 5 kilometers from An Ninh instead of the one designated, only 2 kilometers from the target. The troops had to march through rice paddies and make a river crossing before they reached An Ninh on the morning of 19 September. Most of the enemy survivors had slipped away during the night.

The fighting at An Ninh consisted of squad and platoon battles fought with great courage by troops living up to their historic division's best tradition. Major Herbert Dexter, the S-3 of 2/502, with several SF tours in Vietnam under his belt, was the most senior officer killed. He led a courageous but futile charge against enemy positions early in the morning of 18 September. I knew him well from when we both worked on the brigade staff. He was the S-4 (Logistics) and helped coordinate the Natchez Trace exercise in April 1965.

Captain Robert Edward Rawls, the commander of C/2/502, was on the first lift and killed by an enemy machine gunner early in the morning. Captain Wilford Roe, who commanded B/2/502, was on the second lift and sustained a leg wound as enemy machine guns peppered his helicopter. He was unable to exit the chopper and was immediately evacuated to a hospital. Captain Gerald Landry was on the third lift with troops from A/2/502. The massive fire prevented a landing at the designated location, but he put down 1,000 meters away after sustaining several wounded, including himself, who were also immediately evacuated.

According to Hackworth, friendly losses were 13 killed and 40 wounded—12 of the latter from friendly fire.[11] The 2/502 moved back to its loading area on the morning of 20 September, and 2/237 remained behind to police the battlefield. The number of U.S. troops killed, as reported through channels, was described as light, while the number of dead enemies was 257, with only 21 weapons captured.

Such discrepancies in weapons captured versus enemies killed were invariably attributed to survivors carrying the weapons away or killed by airstrikes. Local VC units would attempt to retrieve their fallen weapons, but it was rarer among NVA units, which generally had an adequate supply of weapons and ammunition. How a fast-moving strike aircraft could come up with an accurate count of enemy killed is hard to understand. I grew ever more skeptical of these counts as the war progressed.

Some sources refer to them as VC. However, Hackworth wrote that the enemy unit was interlaced with regular North Vietnamese troops. I believe the 95th Battalion of the 2nd VC regiment was in transition and eventually became an NVA unit. We had several bloody encounters with that unit the following year in the Tuy Hoa area and, at that time, they wore full NVA uniforms, so the transition must have been completed.

At least one account refers to two VC battalions taking part in the An Ninh battle, the 95th and the 94th. Another report refers to the 95th and elements of the 94th.

A member of A/2/502 when I took over was Private First Class Peter S. Griffin, who later wrote *When You Hear the Bugle Call*. An excerpt dealing with An Ninh is on the internet. Griffin reports listening to "Hanoi Hanna" on a transistor radio a few days later, and she identified the VC unit confronting the 2/502 as the 95th Battalion, 2nd Viet Cong Regiment. The VC AA report confirms this information.[12] I have a copy in English of this report.

The average size of a VC battalion in this period of the war was around 350 troops. Their composition, organization, and armaments differed somewhat from those of NVA units. Suppose one battalion took part in the battle and we used the typical number of three wounded for each killed. In that case, the enemy casualty figures were highly exaggerated—257 killed plus about 750 wounded. That is much more than the average strength of a VC battalion and even more than the number of troops in two VC battalions.

Sudden Change of Command

If my recollection serves me right, Colonel Timothy sent a driver to fetch me at some time between 1000 and 1100 hours on 19 September. He greeted me with his usual *Herr Lunde*. Timothy went on to tell me I was finally getting the company I had often reminded him about over the past year. He said I would "go down" to take command of A/2/502.[13]

I guess I looked a bit perplexed since Timothy said, *I thought you would welcome the news?* I said I was overjoyed but a bit uncertain by what he meant by "going down." He told me the 1st Air Cavalry Division was now providing lift support and one of their helicopters would bring me to the battle area.

When Captain Landry was wounded, the command of the few dispersed troops of A/2/502 had passed to his XO, First Lieutenant Charlie Y. Talbott. I believed that flying into the battle area to assume command made no sense since it would only add to the confusion to have a brand-new officer take control. Talbott was an excellent officer and was assisted by a group of professional senior NCOs, some with two wars under their belt. Furthermore, other A/2/502 officers were probably on the ground.

I explained this to Timothy and he agreed with my reasoning. So, instead, I would go to the A/2/502 rear area. This area was further to the east off Route 19. There, I would take command of the company when it returned.

A person is always a little apprehensive when he takes over a new command, but he usually has some time to get ready, find out something about the unit, the NCOs, and the officers. This was not the case with my assumption of command. I knew nothing about A/2/502 except that it had just lost the popular commander who had brought it to Vietnam. How would they take to a stranger like me? The brigade S-3, Sergeant Major Grady Jones, tried to assure me that I would be well received by First Sergeant Theofilio Raymundo "Ray" Macias (1925–2008).

Since there was no longer any urgency, I returned to my unit to brief my subordinates on what had transpired. I asked that they have my mail forwarded and told my driver to load my few belongings and some extra maps of the operational area into the jeep. I then turned command of the Provisional Cavalry Troop over to my XO. I wanted to get my driver and RTO back to their unit before it turned dark, as the route was unsafe at night. They dropped me, the duffel bag, and maps off at the A/2/502 rear area around 1600 hours. I was surprised at the large number of troops in the rear area. It turned out most had not made it into the battle area, and the helicopters had brought them back to the starting point.

I introduced myself to the senior NCO but asked him not to tell Talbott or the first sergeant—I would do that myself. Next, I asked for a copy of the company's standard operating procedures to read while waiting. It had not changed significantly since the company left the U.S., and I made a mental note to update it soon. I also made a call to brigade to find out the status of Captain Landry.

It was now dark and after having a couple of canteen-cups of coffee and some C-rations, I settled into the driver's seat of one of the company jeeps, the one that happened to belong to the first sergeant. It was raining, so I pulled the poncho up to my neck and tried to sleep. There was a lot of air activity, distant detonations, artillery fire, and many parachute flares that kept the battlefield lit throughout the night.

I awoke to a loud and heavily accented voice, one that was to become familiar to me over the next nine months. The words were not precisely those of a formal introduction or a warm welcome. If my memory serves me right, it went something like this: *Soldier, who the f**k are you? Get the hell out of my f*****g jeep right now.* First Sergeant Macias must have seen my insignias as I stepped out of the jeep, and Talbott had walked up and recognized me, but neither knew that I was the new company commander.

I turned to Macias and introduced myself, saying *I am glad to meet you too.* Macias was embarrassed. I put my arm around the neck of the short and stocky Mexican American and said, *From now on, you are my guardian angel, and you have no idea how difficult that job is going to be.* This exchange was the beginning of a life-long friendship, and I could not have wished for a better first sergeant.

Being the first sergeant of an airborne outfit in combat was no easy job. Ray had to manage many tough, experienced, and strong-willed NCOs. He was also a disciplinarian, adviser, and confidant to upwards of 200 troops. Finally, he had to look after me—to make sure I did not make too many mistakes or make a fool of myself too often—and that may have been the most demanding of his tasks.

There was no opportunity to talk to the assembled troops as we had an alert order to move to Qui Nhon and from there to Cam Ranh Bay. I asked Macias to set up a brief meeting with the platoon sergeants and Talbott to arrange an informal meeting with the officers.

I kept my meetings short, introduced myself, and asked each to briefly describe his background and experience. I started by expressing my condolences over the losses they had sustained, mentioning that I knew Landry from Fort Campbell and Fort Benning, where he had been a member of my IOCC class and the Pathfinder Course. I told them his wounds were not life-threatening and that he would soon be back with the brigade. I also told them not to expect him back in the company as I would fight that tooth and nail since I had waited for this opportunity for 18 months. I was careful not to express any feelings about Operation *Gibraltar* except to compliment them on a tough job well done.[14]

The second short meeting was with the officers, of which there were only four—Lieutenants Talbott, Robert Lee, George VonDruska, and William Settlemire—all without combat experience except Operation *Gibraltar*. I went into more detail about my background with them, stating that I felt well prepared for the job. I asked for their help in running the company and said I did not plan to make any changes.

I did not meet the battalion commander for more than a week as he was whisked off to An Khe to brief General Westmoreland, and from there to Saigon to brief the U.S. Press Corps and receive a Silver Star.

The convoy to Qui Nhon was uneventful, as was the trip to Cam Ranh by LSTs (Landing Ship Tank), departing Qui Nhon before darkness on 22 September. We debarked at the southern end of Cam Ranh Peninsula late at night on 23 September. The rumors were that the battalion would stay in this area to rest and receive replacements for about three to four weeks.

The battalion headquarters, B/2/502, and C/2/502 remained on the Cam Ranh Peninsula while A/2/502 moved to a peninsula across Cam Ranh Bay's entrance named Cam Lao Peninsula. My troops could only reach the rest of the battalion on the Cam Ranh Peninsula by sea or air. There was a narrow neck connecting the Cam Lao Peninsula with the area south of Cam Ranh Bay. Since that neck constituted the only land avenue of approach for an enemy force, we set about to fortify it (sandbags and logs). The neck's narrowness allowed one platoon to occupy the position and the platoons rotated every 24 hours.

Cam Ranh Peninsula and the excellent deep-water harbor were bustling with activity caused by hundreds of troops and civilians, mainly engineers. In addition to constructing an airfield and harbor facilities, there was the ongoing construction of permanent barracks to house Air Force personnel. The airfield was not complete to a planned 10,000 foot runway, nor were the harbor facilities. Ships anchored in the bay and supplies came ashore by LSTs.

I had been in the 2/502 for more than a week without meeting the battalion commander. That changed on 27 September when a helicopter came to pick me up to meet with Lieutenant Colonel Smith. He did welcome me to the battalion but spoiled that by adding, *You are here not because I asked for you but because of the brigade commander's orders.* When I did not reply, he asked if I had worked with Hackworth to plan Operation *Gibraltar*. I assured him I was not involved in the planning, which he should have known, but it was another way to tie me to his archrival Hackworth. I thought to myself, *This is payback time*. I made no comments whatsoever about *Gibraltar*.

Smith said that Captain Thomas H. Taylor (1934–2017) would assume command of B/2/502, and Captain Robert C. Murphy (1939–2020) would take over C/2/502. I had briefly met Taylor in the SF in Germany and again before taking over the Provisional Cavalry Troop.

Bob Murphy was a long-time friend and a superb combat officer. With my help, he tried to join Detachment A in Berlin in 1962, but Lieutenant Colonel Piernick was looking for officers with language capabilities and Murphy did not fit into that category. Bob Murphy served in one of the other brigades at Fort Campbell when the 1st Brigade was alerted for Vietnam. He immediately came to see me asking for my help to get into our brigade. I introduced him to Hackworth and we both convinced Lieutenant Colonel Rogers to bring him to the brigade.

I was appointed to be the officer responsible for making an inventory of Captain Robert Edward Rawls's personal effects. I was also responsible for shipping those effects back to his wife, Joan, and staying in contact with her until all matters were settled.

It was an emotional task as I had met the Rawlses at one of the brigade social functions before leaving Fort Campbell. Bob and Joan had a large family. They had six children ranging in age from four months to nine years. In my initial letter to her, I offered whatever help I could give and we corresponded until well after my return from Vietnam in the summer of 1966. She took the news of her husband's loss in the fashion of a strong Army wife. I hope life has been good for her and her family.

The buildup of forces in Vietnam was so massive and rapid that the supplies were not keeping up. My troops' uniforms and boots were falling apart, but new ones were not arriving in the company. While inventorying and shipping Rawls's items in the rear area, I saw soldiers wearing brand-new jungle fatigues and jungle boots. I decided to bring this to the attention of Lieutenant Colonel Smith at the earliest opportunity.

That opportunity came in the afternoon of 29 September when Smith came for a visit. I had picked out four troops to be present when his helicopter landed. They were troops with torn fatigues and boots falling apart. However, the colonel had something entirely different on his mind and he was angry.

While in this rear area, someone had arranged for movie projectors with speakers and white sheets to show movies to the troops. The movie reels came from the battalion on a specific day, and we had them long enough to show all soldiers on a rotating basis. One day the supply sergeant returned from the Cam Ranh Peninsula with two reels. I figured it was either a bonus or a mistake, but I did not see the need to go to the trouble to send one back.

Smith did not take this matter as a minor slip-up. He told me that because of our action, the battalion headquarters company had to do without a movie. I told him it was a mistake, and whoever ran the battalion program was equally to blame. He did not take well to that answer and told me he wanted whoever was responsible punished. He then boarded the helicopter and did not return my salute as he left. The four troops witnessed this incident, but Smith left before I had a chance to show him the condition of their uniforms and boots.

The next day we were visited by the corps commander, Lieutenant General Stanley "Swede" Larsen (1915–2000) and Smith came along. To my amazement, Larsen recalled me as an honor graduate in the 1964 IOCC when he was assistant commandant of the Infantry School at Fort Benning.[15] The general was pleased with our defensive preparations and, as he was ready to leave, he asked if there was anything we needed. I told the general we were in dire need of jungle fatigues and jungle boots. He nodded and asked his aide-de-camp to make a note. Smith did not say anything then or later.

The officers and troops had eaten C-rations since they arrived in the country. Now, the Army added insult to injury by requiring the officers to pay for those meals. The amount was not large—$2.10 per day deducted from our pay each month. The payment would have been acceptable if we had hot meals, but for the government to impose the same amount for C-rations in a war zone was ludicrous. We finally got our first fresh meal in November at Suoi Tanh, about 15 kilometers south of Nha Trang.

A few words are necessary to describe our laundry service. The battalion handled it, apparently through a contractual arrangement with the Vietnamese. We would deliver a bundle to the battalion every week and each piece had to be marked. We were lucky to get the stuff back at all, and it was invariably someone else's laundry.

The uniform and boot problems were slow to improve. It all came to a crunch on 1 October when I received orders to provide a 44-man honor guard for some visiting dignitaries in October. The instructions said the troops should be dressed in starched jungle fatigues and new boots, properly bloused. I immediately replied that we did not have enough new uniforms to go around, did not have starch, and had far from the number of new boots required. My reply caused the order to be canceled.

That night I wrote Florence:

> It is hard to believe how the soldiers of the richest country in the world are living and treated. Maybe it is this way at the beginning of every war and that it will get better, but it is hard for the troops to understand.

Much of the "official" mail I received was from parents who had not heard from their sons, paternity suits, one letter from neighbors of one of my sergeants whose wife lived near Fort Campbell, informing me a man had moved in with her two months ago. Also, there was a continuous flow of letters of indebtedness. These needed answers within a specific time—I believe it was 48 hours. It usually fell to my XO to answer, but he was away, so I was stuck with the chore.

Five Korean officers visited the company on 10 October. Their company was to take over our security mission when we moved out. I also heard rumors that we would get a new battalion commander at the end of the month.

The Koreans were to take over on 14 October, but a last-minute postponement resulted in a 24-hour delay. In the meanwhile, the coastal rainy season had begun and our camp had turned into mud.

We moved to the Cam Ranh Peninsula on 15 October, and from there, we proceeded by truck to our new area the next day. We were dropped off on the main road and had to hack our way through the jungle to our destination. It was considered a relatively quiet area, but a force of 50 South Vietnamese with two American advisers was ambushed about 15 kilometers to the north of Nha Trang, and reports said they were all killed. The first thing on the list was to dig defensive positions—which invariably filled with water from all the rain—and we quickly switched to sandbag bunkers. With the news of enemy action to our north, the battalion reinforced the company with 50 men.

We received orders to provide 90 soldiers for the battalion headquarters' protection and a brigade installation the following day. That left me with about 120 troops. This bamboo jungle area was full of giant lizards, red ants, and scorpions. The clearing of the jungle for a battalion-size camp was a significant task. We were assigned about 500 South Vietnamese laborers for that job, but most of them were women.

The relations between Lieutenant Colonel Smith and I had not improved. He was a decent enough person, but he never fully adjusted from the norms of stateside assignments to one in a combat zone. He would stop my sentries and chew them out for not having their fatigues bloused or helmets fastened properly. Subsequently, I also received a lecture on the matter. He insisted that even those on jungle clearing details and patrols wear helmets. Wearing helmets on patrols is not too bright. It obstructs hearing, and branches snapping against the metal helmet (even when covered by cloth) are loud enough to give away our presence. My arguments against this policy got nowhere.

The Dong Ba Tinh Special Forces Camp was about 20-some kilometers to our south. A VC force attacked it on the night of 28 October. The garrison repelled the attack, but this indicated that VC forces were both to our south and north.

Towards the end of October—I believe on 27 October—Smith informed the company commanders at a meeting that a new MACV policy was in effect. It required that company commanders and platoon leaders rotate every four months. For me, that meant that my command time would end in December 1965, while Taylor and Murphy would have to give up their commands in February 1966. We all protested this order, but Smith said he would not appeal it since he agreed with it. We pointed out that this rapid rotation of company-grade officers would be hard on troop morale. Each new officer would not have time to gain experience, which would invariably result in increased casualties. Our arguments did not change Smith's mind.

A new XO arrived on 24 October. He was First Lieutenant Phil Mock. I had met him earlier and he impressed me as a dedicated individual. The second piece of good news was that Smith would be leaving at the end of the month and a new battalion commander would take over on 31 October.

CHAPTER 9

Phan Rang, Ben Cat, the Iron Triangle, and Tuy Hoa

There are times when events take place that shape a person's life. Unfortunately, the importance of these events is often not recognized until much later. The last day of October 1965 was such a day in my life.

That morning there had been a subtle change of command ceremony between the outgoing battalion commander, Lieutenant Colonel Smith, and the incoming battalion commander, Lieutenant Colonel Henry E. Emerson. After receiving a briefing by his staff, Emerson called a meeting with the company commanders, where the principal staff officers were also present. This meeting took place in a large battalion tent arranged with tables and chairs for dinner. The dinner served was a fancy B-ration meal cooked up by the battalion mess personnel, and it tasted good. After dinner, Emerson offered scotch and bourbon along with soft drinks and beer.

The actual meeting took place after the meal. The new battalion commander was tall (6'3") and slender with a serious demeanor and piercing eyes that focused sharply on the person he talked to. Emerson explained this would be a listening session for him. He wanted the company commanders' opinions on operations, focusing on what we needed and our wishes. He had someone from battalion S-1 keep notes at the meeting.

Over the past six weeks, I had made detailed notes of what I believed we were doing wrong. After waiting a few seconds for someone to speak up, I realized it was up to me to begin since I was the longest-serving company commander. I did not need my notes as I had committed all the items to memory much earlier. I faced Emerson, returned his stare, and began a monologue that lasted for more than 15 minutes. In short, what I said boiled down to the following points:

1. The company has done nothing for six weeks, and the time needed to rest and receive replacements has long passed.
2. We had not conducted any actual operations in that period, just sat around or served as a labor force for clearing jungles. I pointed out that this was detrimental to morale, which would become apparent when he talked to the troops.

3. We had gone on a few patrols, but the troops were loaded down with equipment and had to wear helmets—both detrimental to patrolling, fast movements, hearing, and successful engagements. The battalion spelled out the patrol routes and missions, and I believed that should be the company's job.
4. I pointed out that we were still lacking critical equipment—boots, fatigues, and especially radios. Each platoon had only one PRC-25 radio. The shortage left no radios for patrols.
5. I said that in equipment and behavior, we were operating on the old doctrines of linear warfare. I opined that all that had to change for us to succeed in this war without front lines. Although I was not present at An Ninh, I took the chance to let Emerson know that I believed we had made grievous mistakes that we must avoid in the future. I fully expected Lieutenant Colonel Smith had already given his views on An Ninh.
6. Finally, I pointed out that the enemy was as cunning and brave as the French Regular Army and the Foreign Legion had discovered more than a decade ago. We demonstrated our misplaced omnipotence by referring to the enemy as geeks and France's defeat as typical French, drawing a false short-term analogy to 1940. In my mind, the biggest mistake would be to underestimate the enemy.

When my monologue was over, Emerson kept looking at me as if expecting something more. He then turned to the note-taker and asked if he had taken down all my points.

The other rifle company commanders now gave their views. They focused their comments on the lack of operations, equipment, and far too extensive centralized control. Their comments reinforced some of my major points.

Emerson then outlined what we soon recognized as his operational philosophy. He intended to give the company commanders the most extensive latitude and use mission-type orders. Since this war was a platoon and company war, it was only fitting those leaders had full authority to conduct operations. He said he would show us complete loyalty and expected the same from us. To answer our point about the lack of operations, he assured us he would do his best to ensure we actively did what we came to do in Vietnam. The meeting did not break up until after 2200 hours.

This meeting was my first with this outstanding officer, highly decorated in the Korean War. He was a battlefield innovator and did not hesitate to think and act outside the box. As we all realized, one of his exceptional leadership qualities was that he did not micro-manage operations, but gave his company commanders a wide range in their operations. In return, he earned genuine respect and loyalty from his subordinates. In addition, he was always a loud voice for the battalion at higher headquarters.

As I returned to my tent that evening, I felt more optimistic. A short letter to Florence that night reflects my new optimism. However, I did not know at the time that this meeting would lead to a life-long friendship. Emerson died in early February 2015, but not before summoning my wife Truong and me to Marathon, Florida, for a final meeting. According to the nurse who accompanied him to Florida, we were the only two from his time in Vietnam so honored. He was obviously ill, and both of us knew it would be our last meeting. As I left, I turned around at the top of the stairs and gave this great soldier, now a lieutenant general, a final salute. Unfortunately, he died within a week, and I could not attend the Washington funeral due to my health problems.

After Emerson assumed command, there was a noticeable improvement in the areas the company commanders had discussed with him on 31 October. The supply situation improved, probably due to Emerson's prodding of Colonel Timothy and the brigade staff. The supply flow had also started to catch up with the rapid buildup of forces in Vietnam. The line troops received priorities for new uniforms and boots due to Emerson's actions.

Phan Rang

The change in the operational tempo was almost immediate. On the day after Emerson assumed command, the battalion was alerted for a move to Phan Rang in Ninh Thuan Province, on the coast about 140 kilometers south of Nha Trang. There we would establish our first semi-permanent base camp. It was a place from which we would stage operations in other Vietnam areas.

The rifle company commanders, commander of the battalion headquarters company, and Battery C/320th Artillery commander made an aerial and ground reconnaissance of the new area on 2 November. The three rifle company commanders walked the defense perimeter, selected their sectors' trace, and agreed to the points where the units would tie in. The headquarters company commander was primarily concerned with the battalion headquarters location and the motor pool area. The artillery captain selected the position for the artillery battery. We also contacted Air Force personnel who had just begun construction of an airfield and associated facilities.

The actual move did not take place until 5 November. The battalion moved in three TFs named after the three rifle company commanders. The first element was TF Lunde, consisting of my company, an artillery section, and several smaller combat support units.

The battalion did not have enough organic transportation to move everything simultaneously, so we borrowed vehicles from our brigade and the engineer brigade working on the airfield and harbor at Cam Ranh Bay. We brought everything along since Phan Rang was to be our new base area. That included everything scrounged from other units in Nha Trang and Cam Ranh to make our situation better. Emerson passed overhead several times in his LOH and noted we looked like a "mounted" mob going down the road.

We arrived at Phan Rang without incident. I pointed out where I wanted the company CP and took the platoon leaders and platoon sergeants on a tour of our section of the perimeter to show them where we tied in with adjacent companies and let the platoon leaders pick the location where the platoons tied in. They were also responsible for selecting crew-served weapon positions. Although we had no intelligence of enemy activities in the area, I prioritized preparing defensive positions and claymore mine placement. Eventually, the place would have barbed wire protection, but that would have to wait until the wire arrived. Emerson told us we would not spend much time in Phan Rang. That proved to be correct.

The new SOP, which First Lieutenant Mock had written, and I had approved, called for a sequential preparation of the camp. First on the list was the preparation of fighting positions along the perimeter. Only one platoon would occupy these positions every 24 hours, spread out so the whole company part of the perimeter ended up lightly occupied. Then, an attack would bring two more platoons into the line while one remained in a central location as a reserve. We practiced this periodically in the dark and during inclement weather.

Second on the list were the locations of various tents (squad-size tents for the troops and company headquarters and two-person tents for the officers and senior NCOs and an open area in the middle of the camp to serve as a place where the company could assemble. As soon as we selected their locations, we dug spider-holes around the tents before putting them up. Spider-holes were one of Emerson's innovations and used throughout my service with the company. It allowed for the quick digging of a one-person hole in the ground, large enough for one man to crouch in and have protection against mortar fire. Unfortunately, it did not work well in the jungle where roots made it virtually impossible to dig, nor did it work in the delta, where the water table was so high that holes immediately filled with water.

Third on the list was the erection of tents for the troops to have shelter when not in the line. The company command group was in two areas to prevent eliminating the whole command structure with a few well-placed mortar rounds. The XO and his group were in one area of the camp while I, the first sergeant, and the bulk of the communicators were in another location.

Emerson agreed we should keep Vietnamese civilians away from the camp. That included setting up an area outside the camp as a free-fire zone, announced to the district and province authorities. This designation served to prevent civilian loss of life. It also helped keep an enemy from approaching close enough to map our camp's layout, the fighting positions along the perimeter, and our indirect fire weapons location.

During this initial period, I convinced Emerson that we should leave our heavy weapons (mortars and recoilless rifles) and their heavy ammunition in the camp when on operations and make the weapons platoon a fourth rifle platoon. I had made this adjustment when I had the Provisional Cavalry Troop. It increased the rifle strength of the company while reducing the load troops had to carry. Nevertheless, the heavy weapons would accompany us to temporary operational areas in case they were needed. The 20 percent increase in rifle strength more than offset the lack of mortars and recoilless rifles, making the unit more mobile.[1]

During every move, it took a week to 10 days for the mail to catch up with us and the same was true for some of the supplies. I had warned Florence that she should expect these interruptions, but I could not alert her to the actual moves until we were in the new area, and she did not know our destination for obvious security reasons. So, I got into the habit of writing a letter almost every night. However, during a move, I would not post them until we were in our new area, and this served as an outline of what we did on any given date—a somewhat accurate chronology of events for the future.

Other elements of the brigade began moving into the Phan Rang area on 9 November and this, of course, caused much confusion as the Air Force was also moving units into the area.

Our time at our new camp in November 1965 was the most prolonged period we spent in a "base camp" during my command period. We were still receiving replacements—averaging one soldier per day. Unfortunately, we also lost many troops to malaria—29 according to my notes for October and November. Those evacuated troops, with few exceptions, failed to return to the unit.

We all knew we would soon become involved in significant engagements. The newspaper *Stars and Stripes* was delivered regularly to the unit and it was evident our casualties in Vietnam were going up every week. The week ending 17 November reportedly resulted in 85 Americans killed and 478 wounded. Total American losses had reached around 1,000 dead and over 5,000 wounded. Being aware of these losses while sitting in a relatively safe base camp affected the troops. It was essential to keep them active and their minds off what may be ahead.

We conducted nightly patrols in the area but made no enemy contact. We, and the other companies, were also assigned to occupy an outpost security line about 500 meters from the perimeter. We occupied this outer security line on a four- or five-day rotating basis.

Colonel Timothy had approved a policy that set the time in command for company commanders at four months to give as many officers as possible command experience. I was adamantly opposed to this policy and said so to Emerson. I also told him that to risk soldiers' lives to enhance officers' careers was not right. It was not proper for a company to have this many changes. I wanted to keep the command until it was my time to go back to the U.S. I felt the unit would benefit from me having enough time to gain experience and save lives.

All of us continued to try to keep troops active while in our camp at Phan Rang. We held classes, increased physical training, and had sports matches between companies. On 23 November, we had boxing matches with Company C, and my company won all five bouts. Captain Murphy promised revenge, but we moved out of the area before he had a chance.

Ever since we had been in the Cam Ranh area, I had encouraged the NCOs to scrounge materials to build an NCO club in the company area. We moved all the materials to Phan Rang. I told them they had to do the work themselves—no troop labor. They had the building ready at the end of the year.

Ben Cat and the Iron Triangle

There were increasing signs that our time at the base in Phan Rang was ending. On 21 November, Emerson sent me on a reconnaissance of the town of Phan Thiet. This coastal town is about 150 kilometers southwest of Phan Rang. It is almost due east of Saigon, on the South China Sea. However, we did not go there until April 1966.

On the evening of 28 November, we were alerted for a move to Bien Hoa Airfield, on the edge of "War Zone D." This was the operational area of the 1st Infantry Division ("Big Red One"). It had become involved in heavy fighting and ARVN had lost a big battle near Ben Cat in War Zone D, reportedly suffering 600 casualties. Our battalion moved to Cam Ranh by trucks since the airfield at Phan Rang was not yet operational.

The 2/502 and 1/327 moved to Bien Hoa and remained there until 3 December, waiting for deployment into War Zone D. Troops from C/2/502 accidentally fired a machine gun while at Bien Hoa. I do not recall if anyone was hurt. My company had a similar incident at Phan Rang involving a .45 caliber pistol, but it resulted in a minor flesh wound that did not require evacuation. These accidents were, for the most part, the result of improperly clearing the weapons involved. As a result, I ordered every squad leader to conduct classes in the proper clearing of weapons—.45 caliber pistols, M16 rifles, and the M60 machine gun. This training took place under the supervision of the platoon leader or platoon sergeant.

The troops at Bien Hoa received orders to move to Ben Cat on 3 December, but the move was to take place the following day. Ben Cat is about 40 kilometers northwest of Bien Hoa, just inside War Zone D. The move was by truck and A/2/502 was the first element. Shortly after arriving in Ben Cat, Emerson ordered his S-3, Major George Neroutsos, and me to conduct an aerial check of the area north of Ben Cat, where an enemy unit was reportedly operating. Emerson planned to deploy Companies A and B in that direction the next day. We did not spot any enemy troops, which led to the two companies' proposed operation's cancellation.

Instead, my company went on an operation a short distance northwest of Ben Cat. There was a brief firefight when we encountered some enemy troops at a watering point (creek). It was becoming dark and the situation to our front was uncertain. We sustained no casualties. The battalion ordered us back.

In the late afternoon of 5 December, my company had another accident when a soldier from the 3rd Platoon was clearing his pistol. The bullet went through one soldier's hand and into the side of a second soldier. Both were evacuated but rejoined the company after short hospital stays.

I'd had enough of these incidents! Since both accidents in my company involved .45 caliber pistols, which I did not find especially useful, I decided on drastic action by taking all pistols away from troops and officers and locking them in a large metal container. Unlike the M16 rifles, the pistols often became covered with rust after short operations of one to two days. I made sure that soldiers who had earlier carried only a pistol were issued M16 rifles. I did this without seeking approval from the battalion.

In the afternoon, the whole chain of command (the squad leader, Second Lieutenant George VonDruska, me, and Emerson) received orders to line up in front of Colonel Timothy's tent, where we received a well-deserved dressing down. After he had completed his reprimands, Timothy asked what we had done about it. Emerson was the first to answer by pointing out that two companies had received thorough instructions in weapons safety, and a repetition of those instructions would take place when we were back in a base area.

I then asked if I might speak. Timothy nodded. I explained I had withdrawn all .45 caliber pistols—the weapon causing most of my company's problems—locked them up in a metal container for the duration, and replaced them with M16 rifles. Timothy looked at me for a while, as did Emerson, who was not yet aware of what I had done. Then Timothy smiled and said, *Herr Lunde, I hope you do not experience problems with M16 rifles, machine guns, or M79 launchers; otherwise, we will have to engage the enemy with rocks and entrenching tools.*

The 1st Division was engaged in some heavy fighting, but we were not sent into the fray, although my company was alerted for possible deployment. A battalion from the 1st Division took heavy casualties based on initial reports that came down to the company—38 killed and 96 wounded. In the next few days, we were alerted several times, but these alerts were always canceled, either because of bad weather, lack of helicopter resources, or failure to get artillery within supporting range.

One thing about our operations out of Ben Cat has bothered me since I began writing this book. For example, it is obvious we were in the notorious "Iron Triangle." Still, there is no mention of this in my notes from briefings we received from the battalion, nor do I remember this fact being mentioned by Emerson and Timothy in our conversations. Lieutenant Colonel Perrine could also find no mention in the battalion and brigade papers in his possession.

The Iron Triangle was an area interlaced with tunnels and underground installations, some dating back to the 1880s when resistance to French occupation began. These underground installations gained increasing importance during the joint rule of Vietnam by the French Vichy Regime and the Japanese.[2]

While there are differences in the Iron Triangle maps, there is general agreement that it covered an area of 310 square kilometers in Binh Duong Province, running from 11 kilometers north of the province capital of Phu Cuong to about 12 kilometers north to Ben Cat. From there, it runs west-northwest for 16 kilometers to the town of Ben Suc and from where the third leg of the triangle runs back to 11 kilometers from Phu Cuong, a 21-kilometer portion. Two rivers border the whole area—the Thi Tinh River in the east and the Saigon River in the west.

The area we began operating in on 10 December by moving west from Ben Cat was the Iron Triangle, despite its lack of mention in my notes. The river we crossed was the Thi Thin running south near Ben Cat. We did not cross any other rivers or streams during the operation as we stopped short of the Saigon River but within its view.

The whole battalion took part in the operation that began on 10 December. I did not see the "Recondos" (2/502s Reconnaissance Platoon), and they may have stayed behind to secure the battalion base in Ben Cat. There were reports that about 800 enemy troops were in an extensive rubber plantation area to the west. Emerson decided to employ all three rifle companies. The plan called for A/2/502 to make the first crossing upstream from a bridge before daylight, then swing downstream when on the western side of the river to allow the other two companies to cross using the bridge.

The battalion would thereupon head westward into the rubber plantation where we believed the enemy force operated. The battalion would advance in an open formation with A/2/502 on the right, C/2/502 in the center, and B/2/502 on the left. The formation was to avoid ambushes and rapidly close the open formation when we made contact.

Emerson agreed to my suggestion to send a patrol ahead to scout the river's far bank to our west and proceed westward on the north side of the plantation area as far as possible while staying within range of the artillery. I chose Sergeant Gene Hawthorne's squad for the mission. Hawthorne, from Lupton, Arizona, was one of three Native American NCOs in my company; they all served with distinction, and two gave their lives, in addition to one from Alaska who died in August 1965. Hawthorne's squad numbered nine men,[3] and I told them to carry four basic ammunition loads since they may have to fend for themselves until help arrived. I also told Hawthorne to avoid engagements—his mission was to relay information to the company and battalion.

Hawthorne and his men crossed the river after dark on 9 December 1965. A good swimmer was sent over first to attach a rope to a tree on the far bank, which the

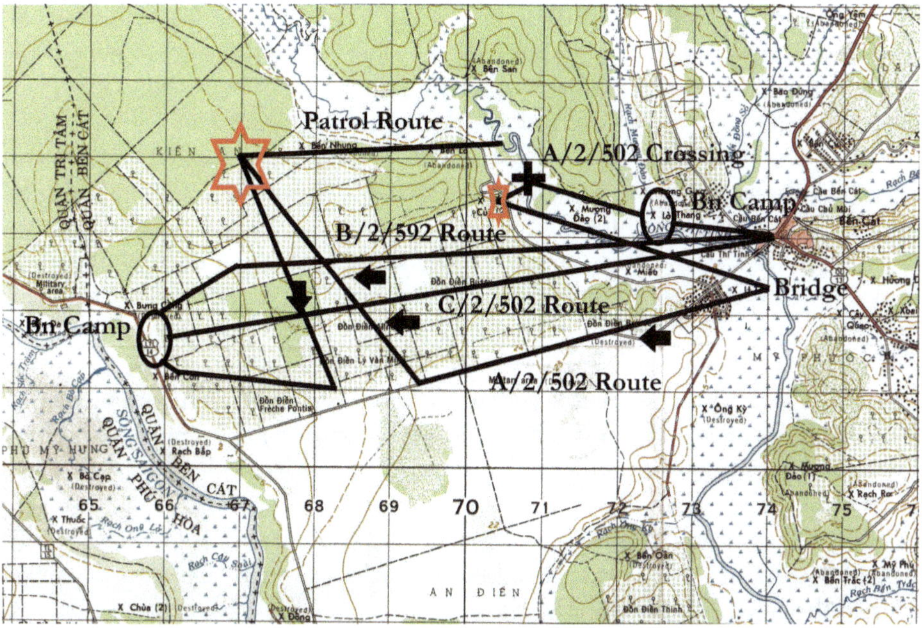

Map 2. This modified U.S. topographic map depicts the *Iron Triangle* operation on 10 December 1965. The red stars denote where A/2/502 had enemy contacts.

rest of the troops used to guide them. Hawthorne floated the equipment across the river in an improvised rubber raft made from air mattresses. After crossing without mishap, the patrol moved rapidly under cover of darkness to the planned location. They were careful to avoid all inhabited areas.

A/2/502 began crossing the river about seven hours after Hawthorne made it across (approximately 0200 hours on 10 December) but in a slightly different location. We also used ropes that good swimmers fastened to trees on the far shore and improvised rafts for our equipment. In a little over one hour, the company was on the far side of the river and ready to move south to the bridge.

As soon as we began moving, we encountered a cluster of booby traps. One soldier died of his wounds—his name was Specialist 4 Robert R. Bohler. The command group was behind the lead platoon when the first booby trap exploded, and I received word that the gravely wounded soldier wanted to see me. I hurried to his location, but he had gone into convulsions, vomited much blood, and could not speak. He died while I was kneeling next to him, and I never found out why he wanted to see me.[4]

A few minutes later, booby traps wounded four more soldiers, but the wounds were not life-threatening. I directed the company to halt since we could not see the tripwires in the dark and I felt sure we would continue to take casualties if we did not wait for daylight. After daylight, we found several additional traps that we detonated. I called Emerson and reported the situation and that I had halted the advance to avoid further casualties. I also told him that it was my opinion the other two companies could proceed across the bridge since there were no enemy troops along the river line. It seemed they were relying on improvised explosives. Emerson agreed, but later the S-3—Major George Neroutsos—informed me A/2/502 would become the battalion's left flank.

I do not know why this change took place as we were supposed to be the right flank company, and that is why I had sent the patrol to the north (right) side of the rubber plantation. I can only speculate about what led to this change. Emerson could have had second thoughts about his earlier agreement that I proceed in the direction of Hawthorne's patrol, or his staff could have convinced him that what he had told me involved taking an unwarranted risk. I do not know why the lead company (C/2/502) could not have sent a patrol across the bridge to confirm our observation.

A/2/502 started on a southerly course when the dead and wounded were evacuated around 0600 hours on 10 December. We switched to a westerly direction when we reached the wood line along the plantation's southern edge. In the process, we had covered the front of the two companies using the bridge. The plantation was dim and dismal, and it looked like it had not been in use for a long time. We did not know if it was part of the Michelin Plantation across the Saigon River to our west. We kept 500 meters from the wood line since it was an area with much concealment for an enemy and we wanted to be outside the effective range of his weapons. The result was that my company was about 5 kilometers from Hawthorne's patrol when it was attacked. If we had been on the right flank as initially planned, we would have been less than 1 kilometer from them when the engagement began.

We used the checkerboard concept as we moved. The checkerboard formation was one of Emerson's innovations, dating back to his days at the U.S. Army War College (USAWC). He based his idea on the checkerboard line formation inaugurated by Gustav Adolphus during the Thirty Years War. Emerson had discussed his concept with the company commanders. It involved staggering the platoons as they moved forward, allowing them to collapse the checkerboard to meet attacks on any of the checkers (platoons). The open-forested rubber plantation was the ideal terrain to try the concept. The concept was not useful in dense jungle areas where one platoon risked defeat before others could come to its aid because of movement difficulties. It also led to repeated sharp discussions between Emerson and me during this tour and the one that followed.

This operation lasted five days and resulted in two incidents that are worth mentioning. The first involved A/2/502, and the second involved B/2/502, commanded by Captain Thomas Taylor. Both events were well covered in

U.S. newspapers and the one involving B/2/502 is included in Tom Taylor's book, *Where Orange Blooms*.[5]

The first event dealt with the patrol we had sent out under the command of Sergeant Hawthorne. Here I have used Sergeant Robert B. Drake's newspaper statements. He was the assistant patrol leader. There are minor differences between my notes and Drake's statements since Drake was not privy to what transpired at company and battalion levels.

The patrol was in position before daybreak on 10 December without having been spotted by the enemy. However, after taking up their position, an enemy soldier stumbled on their location. He quickly disappeared into the jungle. A short time after that, the enemy launched their first assault on the patrol. The patrol drove the enemy back after killing six to eight enemy soldiers. The patrol did not sustain any casualties. At this time, I learned about the attack and informed Emerson I was pivoting the checkerboard advance 90 degrees to the right to go to the patrol's assistance. I asked the battalion to notify the other two companies that we would be crossing in front of their line of advance.

The second enemy assault resulted in one patrol member's wounding, causing Hawthorne to shift his position about 250 meters. The enemy was aware of the move as they attacked a third time, again causing the patrol to change its position. During this move, one soldier tripped a booby trap and was killed, and the explosion wounded Hawthorne in both arms. He bled profusely. The booby trap explosion also affected Hawthorne's eyesight to where he could only see a few meters ahead.

The company advanced rapidly in a very spread-out battle formation with three platoons forward and one in reserve and covered the distance in 50 minutes. I also instructed my artillery forward observer to talk with Hawthorne and help him use supporting artillery.

In the meantime, the enemy continued their assault on the patrol. The patrol drove back the fourth and fifth attacks, but two patrol members died. The enemy was unable to overrun those who were left. Hawthorne had lost much blood and was in and out of consciousness. He was able to adjust the artillery by listening to the sounds of the falling rounds.

The enemy withdrew from the area with the approach of the company. The battalion SJ states we linked up with the beleaguered patrol at 0925 hours, which sounds correct. Unfortunately, the patrol suffered three killed and three wounded—those killed were Specialist 4 Charles E. Boston, Sergeant James H. Lewis, and Specialist 4 Rudy M. Sagon.

We set up an extraction zone (EZ) for the evacuation helicopters. As Hawthorne was loaded on the helicopter, he reportedly remarked, *I am going in for a refill, and I will be back.*[6]

After the evacuation, we headed in a southwesterly direction to get back to our assigned axis of advance. We accomplished this by early afternoon. The whole battalion used one base area that night, within sight of the Saigon River.

General Westmoreland visited the battalion in Phan Rang twice in December 1965. On the first visit, he expressed his staff's amazement at the speed by which A/2/502 moved through enemy-infested terrain. I was also proud of my troops, particularly the beleaguered patrol. At this meeting with Westmoreland, I first heard him refer to our brigade as his "Strategic Reserve," a unit that could expect to be sent into action when other units were in trouble.

To understand the second incident, we must return to the time we spent in Phan Rang before moving to Ben Cat. Emerson wanted to do something that would set his battalion apart from the other two and fire up the troops' esprit de corps. So, at his own expense and with a $3.00 contribution from the recipient soldier, he ordered enough red hatchets to give to each soldier in the rifle companies and reconnaissance platoon.

I am sure Emerson was a bit annoyed at me passing on his offer. I told him I would rather have the troops carry extra ammunition and rations than those red hatchets. I also added that everyone in the company carried bayonets or machetes. The machetes were much more helpful in cutting through the thick bamboo jungle than the hatchets.[7]

I was present at Phan Rang when Emerson spoke to half of the battalion about the hatchets from the top of a jeep. He talked to the other half of his command in the afternoon, but I was not present. I never heard him suggest the hatchets be used in the way one soldier used his on this operation.

B/2/502, on the far right of the battalion line, had sporadic contacts with what may have been an enemy rear guard. Journalist Malcolm Browne, accompanying Tom Taylor's company, described this contact in the following manner:

> There was a flicker of movement, and suddenly it was there on the trail—an ugly black grenade with a wisp of smoke shooting from the wooden handle. It was there for only a split second. Chinese-type potato-masher grenades have short fuses. When it went, four Americans were hurt, one of them screaming in agony.
>
> The crash of the explosion left GIs stunned momentarily, but then some began firing, and others charged into the thick of the jungle, intent on getting the Vietcong who had thrown the grenade. He got only a few hundred feet before a GI found him …[8]

Taylor explains that a soldier killed him with a hatchet rather than capturing or shooting the wounded VC. Instead of dragging the body a couple of hundred feet through the jungle, the troops decided to cut off his head with a hatchet and brought it to where Emerson, Taylor, and the journalists were. Taylor explained his troops brought out the head for possible identification by ARVN! The reporters photographed both Emerson and Taylor, as well as the severed head.[9]

Journalists frequently accompanied Taylor's company, apparently because of his famous father. Both Murphy and I were happy not to have journalists with us on most operations.

There was a flurry of investigations after returning to Phan Rang. No charges against Emerson and Tom Taylor resulted. However, the hatchets disappeared, and the use of the nickname "Hatchet Battalion" quickly ceased.

The battalion sergeant major, Melvin C. Strawser, had words with Emerson about the hatchet incident and that afternoon he joined A/2/502 and asked to stay overnight with his friend Macias. After breakfast the following day, he was still with us, so I took him aside and told him I was sure the incident was as much to Emerson's dislike as it was for us. I recommended he return to battalion headquarters as his commander undoubtedly needed both support and advice. He left the company in the afternoon.

The next three days were devoted to searching through my AO. We found two company-size camps but were not able to destroy them because we lacked enough explosives. We rectified that shortcoming in the evening, and on the morning of 14 December, I set out with two platoons and the attached engineer squad to destroy the camps. Two platoons stayed behind in the company camp.

We destroyed the two camps and found a vast enemy ammo dump. The dump was abandoned as we approached after a sharp firefight with an enemy squad, resulting in no casualties to either side. My first inclination was to evacuate the contents, but the battalion informed me there was insufficient helicopter lift capability to accommodate the large stores. We did bring back eight of the most serviceable weapons. My attached engineers had the joyful task of rigging the ammo dump for destruction. The massive explosion blew down big trees in a large radius.

A/2/502 spent 15 December on a mission 15 kilometers to our north, providing road security for the 1/327th from our brigade and the 2/28th Infantry from the 1st Division as they moved out of War Zone D. It was a relatively uneventful day. We were ordered back to Ben Cat in the evening but since it was already dark, we delayed our return by foot until the following day, arriving at our destination in the afternoon.

We spent the remainder of 16 December preparing to move to Bien Hoa on the 17th. We arrived in Bien Hoa in the afternoon, but the aircraft that were to take us to Phan Rang did not leave until 20 December because of bad weather at our destination. We camped on the airfield between the runways and had little sleep because many aircraft took off and landed.

It had rained heavily in Phan Rang while we were away and the company area was a mud hole with tents filled with water. It took a lot of hard work to bring the camp back to some semblance of order.

We had a second visit by General Westmoreland a few days before Christmas. It was supposed to be an award presentation visit. Still, in my view, there must have been other reasons, since the supposed award ceremony was only a lieutenant colonel in the general's party handing me four presentation boxes—one Silver Star and four Bronze Stars—without accompanying paperwork. The lieutenant colonel tried to give them to me, but I asked him to place them on a table and told an individual from brigade S-1 to care for them. I never saw them again. As soon as he landed, Westmoreland, Emerson, Captain Taylor, and I believe Colonel Timothy adjourned to another tent. That leads me to think the reason for the visit was the hatchet incident and the imminent arrival of the Chief of Staff of the Army.

Emerson told me on 23 December that he was losing his S-3, Major George Neroutsos, in January and that he, Emerson, planned to make me his new S-3. The position called for an officer with a major's rank, and the offer was a big compliment.

I voiced strong objections at becoming the S-3, telling Emerson it was my firm conviction that I would be of more benefit as a company commander and would like to stay in that position until my rotation. Emerson also told me both he and Colonel Timothy considered A/2/502 the best company in the brigade. Emerson did not raise the subject of a new job until March when we were in the Tuy Hoa area.

After getting our camp back in shape, the NCOs completed their club. We had an opening ceremony to which we invited Emerson, Major Donald B. Schroeder, the battalion XO, and some battalion staff members. I donated several cases of beer for the occasion. We were the only unit to have a club for the NCOs, and they were proud of their accomplishments. Its completion coincided with a USO show featuring Eddie Fisher, and Emerson brought him to have a drink at the NCO club on a day when I was away.

The company continued its routine patrolling without enemy contact. Otherwise, nothing of importance happened aside from an overnight visit to the battalion on Christmas Eve and Christmas Day by the Army's Chief of Staff, General Harold Keith Johnson (1912–1983).

Many troops took advantage of the lull in operations to go on a few days of R&R (rest and recuperation) in Saigon. The resort town of Dalat was in the mountains about 100 kilometers west of Phan Rang. It reportedly had the most exceptional climate in the country because of its location. Captain Murphy had secured Emerson's permission to spend New Year's Eve there and he talked me into coming along on the helicopter, which flew routinely to that location.

It was not much of a New Year's celebration since the VC decided it was a good time to act against Dalat. The result was that Murphy and I spent most of the night on the hotel roof with our M16 rifles and a bottle of French champagne that Murphy grabbed as we headed upstairs. Emerson thought it wise to bring his two company commanders back the following day.

The battalion was alerted on 13 January 1966 for movement and I was among those who made a reconnaissance of the new area—Tuy Hoa in Phu Yen Province—which is located on the coast about 320 kilometers north from Phan Rang. The move was to take place on 15 January. The troops moved by air (C-130 aircraft) and the heavy equipment by sea.

The 1st Brigade operated in the Tuy Hoa area until early April 1966. We participated in two named operations, *Van Buren* (15 January to 25 February 1966) and *Harrison* (26 February to 25 March 1966).[10] The brigade's mission in these two operations was to protect the Tuy Hoa area's rice harvest. This area was a rich rice-growing region and the assumption was that, as in past years, the communists would attempt to disrupt the harvest. We expected that, for the first time, regular NVA units would take part in the fighting. Intelligence stated we should anticipate encountering the 95th NVA Regiment besides well-trained local VC forces consisting of several battalion and company-size units.

The ARVN units in the area were primarily engaged in the static defense of critical installations and population centers. Korean (ROK) units had operated in the Tuy Hoa area since before the turn of the year. However, their furthest westward operations had been limited to a line about 10 kilometers from the Tuy Hoa Airfield, where they had their base and artillery support.

By the time my company arrived in Tuy Hoa on 15 January 1966, the men had only participated in the fighting at Ben Cat, and some in Operation *Gibraltar*. This limited combat experience was not enough to make them seasoned veterans, and about half of my company consisted of new replacements with little or no combat experience. While at Phan Rang, the company had increased in strength to 247—despite losses—and more troops were still arriving.

Most of our veteran troops had come to respect our foe's cunning, dedication, and professional fighting abilities. By the time I left Vietnam at the end of my first tour of duty, my conviction was that we were up against one of the world's best light infantry forces. A combination of mistakes on our part and highly disciplined and professional fighting by our enemy would cost us heavily in the days ahead. But, on the other hand, the lessons we learned the hard way near Tuy Hoa would lead to the saving of many lives in the future. The experience we gained paid off well in our finest hours, when, as Hackworth relates in his book, in the bamboo jungle at Bu Gia Map near the Cambodian border, we turned a potential disaster into the very model of how to fight this war.[11]

The 2/502nd was moved initially to an area about 30 kilometers south of Tuy Hoa to relieve two Vietnamese airborne battalions. The plans were to conduct a night operation the first evening of our arrival, but higher headquarters canceled it. I felt good about this change since I was not eager to operate at night on the boulder-strewn jungle hillside rising steeply to about 700 meters above the plain.

We moved to a new location a few kilometers north of Tuy Hoa Airfield on 17 January 1966 and established a temporary base. From there, we conducted operations along the coast north of Tuy Hoa, as far as nearly 45 kilometers from our base. Our furthest northward move brought us to the coastal villages of Phu Thuong and Tan Hoa (1) in the district of Tuy An. Again, we encountered only small VC units that sniped at us from a distance.

The population in the villages consisted of women, children, and older men. We assumed the younger men were with the VC in the hills. We also believed the VC

Map 3. Modified U.S. topographic map showing the villages of Tan Hoa (1) and Phu Thuong north of Tuy Hoa.

would avoid killing their own families and not attack the village. Instead, the VC continually harassed those companies which camped in the open country.

There was only one incident at Phu Thuong. The episode involved the South Vietnamese Navy's coastal patrol, referred to as the "Junk Fleet," since the boats looked like flat bottom Chinese junks. They were unaware of our presence and mistook us for VC. They opened fire on us with what we judged to be 37mm and 75mm guns. I ordered my troops to take cover and not return fire since they were out of range of our machine guns and displayed large South Vietnamese flags. I reported the incident to the battalion. Our operation was kept from the Vietnamese to prevent its compromise. They immediately notified the South Vietnamese in Tuy Hoa, and the firing ceased in about 10 minutes. We had no casualties and returned to the battalion.

A VC force about 5 kilometers north of the battalion base surrounded a patrol from B/2/502. The patrol was extracted but left a PRC-25 radio behind in the ensuing confusion. Emerson told me to recover the radio. When I asked why Captain Taylor did not receive the mission since it was his radio, Emerson said that Tom had a fever that could be malaria. When I asked if the rest of Company B's officers also suffered from that illness, Emerson told me not to give him a hard time.

I left half the company at the base and took two platoons to search the engagement area. We encountered a force of about 40 VC, but they quickly withdrew as we approached. We did not locate the radio and had no casualties. On our way back to the battalion, we surrounded a village flying a VC flag. We arrested eight suspects and hauled down the flag. We planned to keep the flag as a souvenir, but, since Emerson was interested in it, the squad that hauled it down presented it to the battalion commander. On our way to the battalion, we also found the badly decomposed bodies of two Korean soldiers.

Our northern operations ended on 26 January, the same day that Colonel Timothy turned over command of the brigade to Brigadier General Willard Pearson (1915–1996), who had arrived from Fort Campbell. We spent the next four days securing the Tuy Hoa Airfield. While we had sustained no casualties on the operation, we also had few results to show: two VC killed and one captured, plus eight detainees.

Other elements of the 1st Brigade also moved into the Tuy Hoa area at the end of January and beginning of February 1966. Emerson told the company commanders we would soon launch an operation into the rice-growing regions to the west. He issued a verbal order on 1 February.

CHAPTER 10

Searching for and Finding the 95th NVA Regiment

A/2/502 moved by helicopters from Tuy Hoa Airfield around noon on 2 February 1966 and arrived at the Korean positions, about 10 kilometers to the west, shortly after 1300 hours. We noted much damage to the surrounding villages. Company A's mission was to secure Hill 51 for the battalion. Unfortunately, the two other companies lost their airlift at the last minute, and Lieutenant Colonel Emerson did not want us to push on alone to Hill 51.

I explained the situation to the Korean battalion commander, and he assigned us an empty area to the left front of his southern flank where we could stay for the night. A Korean captain and two NCOs accompanied small advance parties from the platoons and the command group to look at the area, which turned out to be a partially destroyed village. The inhabitants of the village were almost entirely older men, women, and children. There were several unburied corpses in and around the village. As we walked through the area, we came upon a small girl who could not have been more than seven years old. She was burned and suffering from exposure and malnutrition. The girl was crying and clinging to the corpse of a woman, presumably her mother. Judging from the stench in the area, the woman had probably been dead for at least a day. As we approached, the Korean captain said something to one of his NCOs, who started toward the girl shouting and gesturing for her to leave.

I told the Korean, *Tell your men to leave the girl alone; we will take care of her.*

The captain failed to give any instructions to his NCO, who was now next to the girl. He was yelling at her and lifting his weapon as if to strike. The girl responded by increased crying and clinging more tightly to the dead woman. I heard bolts pulled back and rounds chambered by troops in my party. I turned around and told them to take it easy.

Get your NCO out of here NOW, I told the Korean captain.

The captain replied, *This is our AO.* I answered, *Not any longer. Your battalion commander assigned this area to us, and I respectfully suggest that you get your men out of here before someone is hurt.*

The Korean captain gave me a hateful look, glanced back at my troops, then shrugged his shoulders, said something in Korean to his two NCOs, and departed.

The company medics tended to the girl, who was very scared when first approached. They gave her first aid, water, and food. She was later placed on a helicopter and taken to the brigade aid station. Eventually, she ended up in a local Catholic Orphanage supported by our brigade.

The few civilians left in the village began to appear when it became evident we meant them no harm. Our medics treated several who were either sick or wounded. I told my interpreter to explain to villagers that the dead—for health reasons—required burial and offered our assistance. They declined our help but buried their dead outside the village before nightfall.

We did not know how the civilians were killed but assumed the Koreans destroyed the huts to provide better observation and fields of fire. The number of artillery impact craters indicated the Koreans shelled the area heavily before occupying it.

My troops were visibly upset, and I feared an incident could occur between my forces and the Koreans in this tense atmosphere. I asked Emerson—without going into details—for permission to proceed to Hill 51. He told me to remain where we were and keep a lid on the situation.[1]

After the company moved into the village, I proceeded to the Korean CP to report we were in our designated location. I also requested permission to send early warning outposts to our south and east. The Korean operations officer curtly denied my request. *Tell your troops to keep their heads down tonight. Too much movement may make our troops nervous and trigger-happy*, he said as I was about to leave. I recognized the comment for what it was—a poorly camouflaged threat. I answered: *If that is the case, we have a mutual problem; any fire received will result in return fire. Make sure you tell your troops*. I saluted and left, thinking this was a hell of a way for allies to cooperate.

My soldiers had occupied their positions and, as the sun was setting, I took a break to consume my favorite C-ration—a can of cold franks and beans. It also gave me a chance to reflect on the operation. Things had failed to go according to plan from the very beginning. The helicopters that moved the company to the Korean positions were several hours late. After delivering my unit, they were committed to another operation, leaving the other two companies from 2/502 near Tuy Hoa. The revised plan called for these units to proceed to Hill 51 by foot at first light on 3 February. As a result, instead of securing Hill 51 as planned, we found ourselves spending the night among our rather unfriendly allies.

I had an uneasy feeling that night. I felt the lull in large scale fighting was about to end. As was so often the case in Vietnam, we did not know when and how this would happen, but I felt confident we were in good shape to handle whatever was in store for us. Except for a small detachment left behind on the airfield to manage resupply and process newly assigned personnel, I had my entire company in the field. That evening, the field strength was 281, including 23 attachments and two interpreters, considerably above the authorized strength. A large influx of personnel in late December and early January 1966 to replace losses we had suffered the previous four months was the reason for this over-strength status. A detachment from the battalion communications platoon also accompanied A/2/502. Their task was to establish communications on Hill 51 before the battalion headquarters arrived.

The organization of the company was a command group and four rifle platoons. As explained earlier, we had created the fourth rifle platoon from the weapons platoon since the previous five months had demonstrated little or no use for the mortars or recoilless rifles. These weapons and their ammunition were too cumbersome for the type of operations we were conducting. Therefore, we left them in the rear area near Tuy Hoa.

Despite my fears of a firefight with our allies and the ensuing debacle this would cause at higher headquarters, the evening and night passed without incidents. After my meal, I spent over three hours walking around our perimeter, talking to the troops while consuming several tin cans of coffee offered along the way. Those gung-ho volunteer airborne troops appeared unusually somber and subdued that night. I believe most shared my feeling that we would soon find ourselves locked in deadly combat with an enemy we knew to be well prepared. The troops had received a detailed briefing on what to expect, so I tried to keep my conversations light and on subjects not connected with our operation. This was easy since I knew almost all my troops by name, except some newly assigned.

On my perimeter tour, I found two newly assigned troops smoking under a poncho. I had a strict policy against smoking between sunset and sunrise while on operations and meticulously adhered to this policy myself. A lit cigarette is visible for up to a kilometer or more, revealing the position of the smoker and his fellow soldiers. Lighting a cigarette in the dark can temporarily ruin a person's night vision. Doing so under a poncho leaves the smoker in a position of not observing what is going on around him, actions that can prove deadly. After giving the troops a stinging chewing out, I left further disciplinary measures to their immediate superiors.

We started our move to Hill 51 before first light on 3 February 1966. All was uneventful until we reached a cluster of huts about 300 meters to the east of our objective as dawn broke. The 2nd Platoon, commanded by Lieutenant Frankie Wallace from Alabama, was in the lead.[2] The point squad from that unit came under small arms fire from Hill 51 at about 0600 hours. After moving forward to assess the situation, Frankie concluded his platoon could handle the problem without assistance. Nevertheless, I ordered the 3rd Platoon, commanded by First Lieutenant James Schoonover,[3] to move up on the right flank of the 2nd Platoon and be prepared to assist. I joined the 2nd Platoon with my RTOs and the artillery forward observer, First Lieutenant Thomas Clements.

We continued to receive sporadic fire from Hill 51. The enemy was firing their weapons at their maximum effective range, causing no casualties. I agreed with Frankie's estimate that only a few local, lightly armed VC confronted us. The 2nd Platoon began its attack after placing heavy small arms and M79 fire on the hill. The troops reached the crest of the hill at 0645 hours without sustaining any casualties. The enemy vanished and we saw no evidence they had suffered losses.

We consolidated our positions on Hill 51 by 0800 hours. Troops from the 4th Platoon detonated a booby trap. Two men were wounded and evacuated. The battalion command group arrived by helicopter in the late morning and the other two companies showed up in the early afternoon. On the way, B/2/502 and the Recondos encountered a VC force. Several men from the two units received minor wounds in the ensuing skirmish.

An enemy patrol passed within 300 meters of Hill 51 around 1100 hours, apparently unaware we had occupied the place. We fired at them but inflicted no losses, a fact that caused Emerson to comment despairingly on our marksmanship abilities or lack thereof.

The rest of the day was uneventful. We established four outposts to the south and west of Hill 51 and I sent a combat patrol from the 3rd Platoon (14 men) to check the base of the mountains on the south side of the valley with orders to return in the afternoon of 4 February. The patrol's objective was about 2,000 meters from Hill 51.

The relatively peaceful day allowed us to observe and study the area we would operate in from our vantage point on Hill 51.[4] This hill, with an elevation of 51 meters above sea level and therefore referred to as Hill 51, was located on the north side of the entrance to the Song Banh Lai Valley and was the first dominant terrain as one enters from the direction of Tuy Hoa, more than 20 kilometers to the east. The valley runs from east to west. The bottom of the valley was flat rice-land and varied in width from about 500 meters to over 2 kilometers. The area was the location of numerous villages, some abandoned by their inhabitants in early 1966.

The Song Banh Lai River meanders through this valley and intersects with the Soui Ba Den River coming out of the southern mountains. The river was fordable in some places but with difficulty. The ridges on the valley's north side rose 250 meters and the southern mountains to 900 meters. The hills were steep, covered with boulders the size of large buildings and dense triple-canopy jungle. Movements in these mountains were complicated, as we found out over the next two months. The valley is about 15 kilometers long and had an offshoot that ran about 5 kilometers in a southwesterly direction. This appendage was 9 kilometers west of Hill 51.

Intelligence reports received at the battalion on 3 February gave additional evidence that large formations of regular NVA units were present in the area west of Tuy Hoa.

The evening passed without enemy contact. The quietness was only disturbed by the fact that one soldier was wounded by the discharge of his M16. He claimed he was cleaning it when it went off, sending a bullet through his foot. It was the only incident during my first tour in Vietnam where I had a lingering suspicion the wound could have been self-inflicted to avoid the dangers that lay ahead. Despite the odds against an accident happening the way the individual described it, I found it difficult to believe a person would voluntarily inflict so much pain and suffering on himself. We classified the wound as an accident and evacuated the soldier to the brigade aid station along with casualties from one of our outposts.

Our outposts to the west received sniper fire during the night of 3/4 February. The sniping appeared to come from Ngoc Lam's direction, a large village more than a kilometer to the west of Hill 51. Another outpost, commanded by Sergeant Richard C. Youngbear, a Native American, came under attack. The outpost had three wounded, and Youngbear died. We evacuated all before daylight.[5]

I decided to send the 2nd Platoon to check the area in the morning. Frankie Wallace's orders were to make a thorough search of Ngoc Lam, push on across the Song Bai Lai River to the village of My Thanh (2), about 2 kilometers further to the southwest, and leave an ambush patrol near Ngoc Lam when he withdrew to Hill 51 in the evening. The 2nd Platoon left on its mission at about 0900 hours on 4 February.

Ngoc Lam and My Thanh (2)

I observed Ngoc Lam's search through binoculars from Hill 51 when, at about 1100 hours on 4 February, I noted movements in the tree line that parallels the Song Bai Lai River (the river runs in a south–north direction at this point). I counted about 50 enemy troops moving south. They were clad in the gray field uniforms of the NVA and wore helmets. I immediately notified Wallace, instructing him to cease searching Ngoc Lam village and close, as rapidly as possible, on the north end of the wood-line where it joins with the dense vegetation at the bottom of the ridge. I hoped this would prevent an enemy retreat to the northern hills. In addition, I told Frankie I would join him with the rest of the company as quickly as possible.

The combat patrol from the 3rd Platoon, sent south the previous day, now reported its location at the base of the mountains, about 1500 meters to the southeast of the enemy sighting. A member of the patrol had just set off a mine or tripped a booby trap. The explosion severely wounded the patrol leader, Staff Sergeant Carlos L. Burges,[6] and a sergeant from Pennsylvania whose name Burges believed was Nathaniel Franklin, but he was unsure.[7] The location of the patrol presented us with an opportunity while the wounded troopers introduced a problem. The patrol would be ideally located to block the enemy's southward movement if we moved it a short distance to the northwest. Simultaneously, we had two severely wounded soldiers requiring medevac and they could not be moved more than necessary.

Time was also critical. If the patrol moved to an open area to secure an EZ to air-evacuate the soldiers, the opportunity to prevent the enemy unit from reaching the southern mountain would probably be lost. Since the area was considered "hot" (under enemy fire), we were not confident helicopters would land. I had to earn my pay by making a quick decision, knowing I may come to regret it.

I instructed the patrol to leave two men with the wounded soldiers and immediately move the rest of the unit about 500 meters to the northwest and set up to block the enemy's route to the southern mountains, their obvious objective. Establishing a blocking position was a dangerous assignment for a unit of only 10 men. However, I expected to close with the enemy with the company within the hour and told the patrol to make liberal use of artillery if pressed. I also asked the patrol leader to explain the necessity of our actions to his patrol.

The company moved out at 1120 hours and I briefed the platoon leaders as we walked. Near Ngoc Lam, we heard heavy firing from our right front and Wallace reported he was in contact with the enemy. I deployed the rest of the company with the 3rd Platoon on the left, 1st Platoon on the right, and 4th Platoon in reserve.

The engagement that followed was the first against the 95th NVA Regiment, followed in rapid succession by three other encounters. Two of these involved A/2/502.

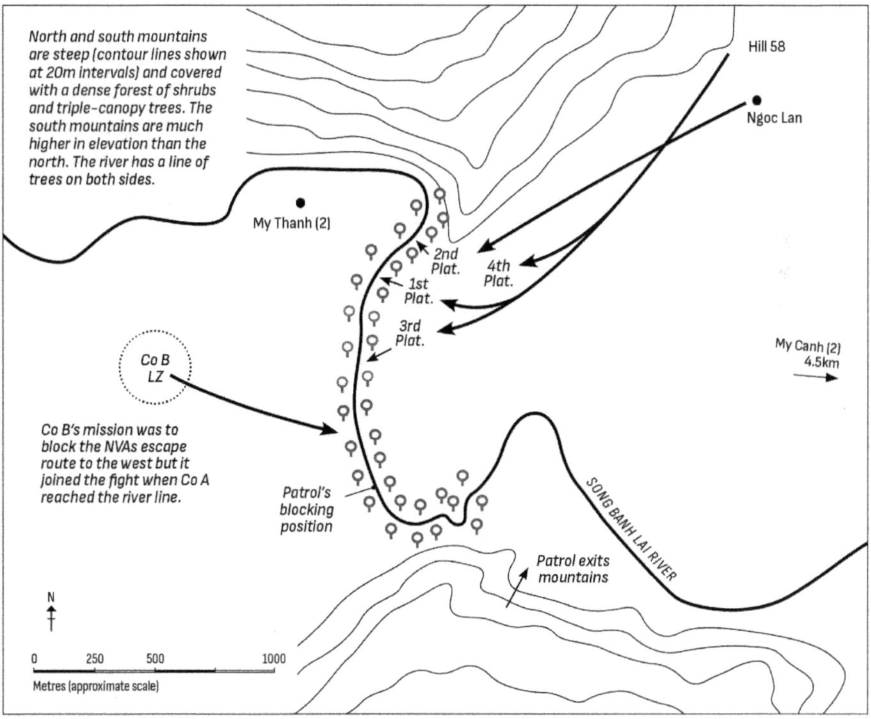

Battle Sketch 4. Battle sketch of the fighting along the Song Banh Lai River, 4 February 1966.

I was confident we had the enemy force, estimated at company strength, boxed in from three directions but realized the NVA commander had several possibilities for escaping our cordon. The enemy could slip back into the northern hills before we could seal off the wood-line at the base of those hills. On the other hand, if the enemy commander knew a lightly armed force of only 10 men held up his southward progress, he could elect to overrun that force and reach the southern mountains.

The enemy force could also escape to the west even though the river presented an obstacle, as did 500 meters of open rice fields on its west bank. I explained my concerns to Emerson. He had already anticipated the problem and said he would airlift B/2/502 into blocking positions west of the river as soon as the airlift was available.

In the meantime, I hoped heavy small arms and artillery fire would make it difficult for the enemy to disengage and withdraw to the west. I also expected the enemy commander was sufficiently confused about our dispositions and strength not to attempt a major attack on the weak blocking force to the south. It seemed most likely to me the enemy would try to slip back into the northern hills.[8]

However, it soon became apparent that the enemy's initial choice after finding his route to the south blocked was to stand and fight. The enemy commander may have hoped he could hold us at bay until dark when it would be easier for him to slip out to the west or into the mountains on either side of the valley. My troops had to cross about 200 meters of relatively open fields before reaching the NVA positions, which gave the enemy a significant advantage. I hoped the 2nd Platoon would be able to work itself along or through the dense vegetation at the base of the hills and come in on the enemy's left flank, thereby avoiding the apparent costs a frontal approach would entail.

I considered the enemy's decision to stand and fight illogical unless he had additional forces nearby. I hoped the enemy now engaged by the 2nd Platoon was the southward moving NVA unit's rear element. If not, we may have taken on more than we could handle. We had to press on, but I asked Wallace to keep a sharp eye on his right flank if we were up against more than just one company of NVA regulars. I also directed the acting commander of the 4th Platoon to be prepared to move to the northwest, behind the 2nd Platoon.

Evidence that the enemy commander had elected to fight became clear when the advance of the 2nd Platoon was stopped dead in its tracks by heavy fire. My hope of being able to close with the enemy without sustaining heavy losses seemed to evaporate. I considered the 2nd Platoon to be my most robust unit. Although he had recently returned from an extended TDY, Wallace had shown great promise. This action was, however, his first major operation. The company's momentum was in danger of collapsing and the only chance I had of regaining it was to get the 2nd Platoon moving. I called Wallace on the radio.

Hunter 2, this is Hunter 6, what is your situation?

This is Hunter 2, two-thirds of my unit is pinned down in the open less than 75 yards from the enemy wood-line by several automatic weapons. I am not sure about casualties, but I believe we have several wounded.

This is Hunter 6, Frank, you must get into the wood-line to seal it off; otherwise, the enemy is sure to escape to the north. If our other units must make a frontal attack, we will suffer many casualties. Your unit holds the key to this damn situation.

This is Hunter 2, I do not know if we can gain the wood-line with all the fire we are receiving.

This is Hunter 6, you must make that wood-line and use the vegetation's concealment and cover on your right flank. Lay down a heavy volume of covering fire to allow those pinned down to move. Use artillery. Frank, get out there, kick some ass, and get your troops off their butts. I want that wood-line sealed as soon as possible.

After my conversation with Wallace, the command group started moving towards the 2nd Platoon. A few minutes later, Wallace called to ask the artillery to drop smoke and white phosphorus (WP) on the wood-line to his front and stated his troops were ready to move forward. Within less than a minute, a shaken operator came on the radio:

He is dead.

This is Hunter 6, who has been killed?

This is Hunter 2 Golf (Golf was the addition to the radio call sign to indicate it was the RTO, not the platoon leader). *Wallace—he was cut down as soon as we started forward. We are receiving a lot of fire.*

The news that Lieutenant Wallace had died while trying to lead his men forward filled me with indescribable anguish and remorse that he may have died because of my rather harsh demands. I also felt guilty for not being at that critical point of the engagement. It was of little consolation that this excellent officer died in the best tradition of a proud unit. He was posthumously recommended for a DSC.[9]

The 2nd Platoon's advance stopped because of enemy fire, and within a few minutes Schoonover reported heavy enemy fire had pinned his unit down. Things were beginning to get complicated and my temper was short. The battalion staff exasperated me by continually asking for situation updates. I finally told them to get the hell off the radio and let us get on with our job. I instructed my senior communicator, Sergeant Donald H. McFann, who was on the battalion command net, not to answer any calls unless they were from Emerson.

We continued to the 2nd Platoon, as I worried about the effect Wallace's death might have had on his troops. One squad leader had died, and two more were wounded. However, the Platoon Sergeant, Sergeant First Class Robert Jack, who had assumed command when Wallace died, had the situation under control. Jack was an old hand, having served in Korea and distinguished himself at An Ninh the previous year.

We had to dodge some enemy fire before joining Jack near the northern flank of his line. He was in the process of shifting his troops to their right to obtain cover and concealment at the base of the hills.

If your platoon fails to take that wood-line, the rest of the company may suffer many casualties. Your unit is the only one with some cover available, and you must get your men moving, I told him.

Jack replied, *Captain, I know that, but it is crazy to approach the wood-line directly. We need time to shift our positions.*

I agreed he had to get his troops away from the open area but told him we did not have much time as I suspected the enemy would soon escape to the north. Jack understood the urgency of the situation and stated, in his usually calm and unruffled manner, *We will do our best, sir.* Although our attack had lost its momentum, and I feared the enemy would escape, I felt better after talking with this steady trooper.

As we were about to leave the area, I noted an open map-case on the ground next to Lieutenant Wallace's body. In answer to my question, a couple of troops related that the lieutenant was carrying it when killed. I had never liked those Infantry School gadgets. They looked good on training exercises, but in combat they were cumbersome and a dead giveaway as to who was the commander, even at a considerable distance. I always preferred a tightly folded map to stick in the side pockets of my jungle fatigues or tuck inside the shirt. We went through more maps that way, but maps were not items in short supply. I do not know whether carrying that obvious map case contributed in any way to Frankie's death, but I was not about to take any further chances, so I put out an order that night that map cases were to stay at the base on future operations.

From the 2nd Platoon, the command group proceeded south, and I asked Sergeant First Class Samuel G. Taylor, the acting commander of the 1st Platoon, to support the 2nd Platoon with fire in its maneuver. Taylor was another old hand, had served in Korea and been with the company since it arrived in Vietnam. Then we went to check on the situation in the 3rd Platoon area.

A gap had developed between the 3rd and 1st Platoons and as we tried to cross it, we came under intense small arms fire from the wood-line, about 180 meters to the west. We were quickly pinned down. The grass was too high for us to return effective fire and we came under renewed fire every time we tried to move.

This operation is probably the one when an incident related by Colonel David Johnson in an unpublished book he wrote for his grandchildren took place. He gave me a copy.[10] Dave was the S-1 of 2/502 after having served earlier as XO of B/2/502. He describes the somewhat unorthodox procedures for awards recommendations, since Emerson wanted every act of bravery recognized. The witness statements were sometimes written in pencil on the backs of C-ration boxes and turned over to the S-1 section for processing. An incident described by Dave in his book[11] must have taken place on 4 February 1966 and involved one of my RTOs, probably Specialist 4 Michael Ellis.

> One I remember was written for CPT Lunde by his Radio Operator, who was alongside him during a firefight. He states that "CPT Lunde, with complete disregard for his own safety (and mine), dashed across a clearing while under heavy fire to assist one of his platoons which had become pinned down." The RTO obviously wanted us to know that CPT Lunde's brave act involved him as well—just keeping up with his CO.

Master Sergeant Macias, behind the 1st Platoon, saw our predicament and decided to do something about it. He yelled to us, *I will try to draw the fire away from you. Be ready to move.* I did not have the foggiest idea of what he was talking about and was about to tell him when I looked back and, in disbelief, saw this stocky Mexican American running parallel to the front line on top of a rice-paddy wall. Fire from several enemy weapons was kicking up dirt all around Macias. I watched this spectacle for a couple of seconds. Then I ran with my troops to cover behind a mound on the left flank of the 1st Platoon. Miraculously, Macias was unhurt. I recommended my crusty senior sergeant for an award after the operation.

We had been unable to contact Schoonover for the past 10–15 minutes and I needed to assure myself he knew the patrol's location to his left front so his men would not fire on it. I had to get across the gap that had developed between the two platoons. As I believed the command group's radio antennae would only draw enemy fire, I left the RTOs behind and managed to cross the open area by a combination of crawling and running. I alerted the squad leader on the right flank of the 3rd Platoon to the patrol location and asked him to pass that information quickly to Schoonover. I managed to rejoin the command group without drawing fire.

However, as luck would have it, Emerson had tried to call, and I had my ass chewed for separating myself from my RTOs. He was right. Gallantly leading from the front is a great troop motivator but in so doing, a commander puts his whole command in danger of becoming leaderless, resulting in a catastrophe. There are plenty of historical examples of such calamities. A leader's place in battle is where he can best control the action. Only when all resources used in a set course of action are insufficient, and when the outcome is uncertain, should a leader become personally involved in fighting to tip the scale in his favor. It is a difficult principle to live up to and I repeated the same mistake within a week, but never after that.

Heavy artillery fire continued to fall on the enemy wood-line, and Emerson informed me that B/2/502 was loading on helicopters for its assault. The artillery fire reduced the intensity of the enemy fire, and Sergeant First Class Taylor, seeing an opportunity to cross the open space separating his unit from the enemy, boldly took the initiative and ordered his platoon to attack. At the same time, he called for the artillery fire to shift. He was successful, thereby splitting the enemy force into two parts. The whole company could now resume the attack and we cleared the wood-line after some sharp close-quarter fighting. B/2/502 had landed to the west and was closing on the river line. The engagement was over by 1430 hours.

Our casualties in the engagement amounted to two killed and eight wounded.[12] Staff Sergeant Burges and Sergeant Franklin (?), as stated in an earlier endnote, are not mentioned in the MR, but I have added them to the total number of wounded.

We concluded that the enemy unit was severely mauled. Statistics on enemy casualties are nearly always misleading and often meaningless. In Vietnam, the body count had become a way of gauging who was winning and by what margin. Unfortunately, this measuring device lent itself to distortions by padded counts that make one's unit and oneself look good in the eyes of senior commanders at each echelon of command.

I saw numerous enemy dead in the wood-line and near the riverbank, the majority killed by artillery fire or cluster bombs. A consolidated count from the platoons indicated that at least 23 enemy soldiers had died in the engagement. We also captured two severely wounded NVA soldiers. They could provide much-needed intelligence information. Unfortunately, within a short period, I had to report to the battalion S-3, Major Arthur Taylor, that the prisoners had died from their wounds, increasing the number of enemy dead to 25.[13]

Emotions in War

To control or direct the emotions of soldiers in battle is a significant challenge to effective leadership. Fear is a natural ingredient of war, but anxiety must be under control. A person who claims they have not experienced fear in combat is either lying or has never experienced combat. Alleviation of fear is through realistic training, confidence in oneself and one's leaders, devotion to fellow soldiers, pride in the unit, and discipline built on fairness and respect.

The emotion of hate has no place on the battlefield, despite what Hollywood movies portray. It interferes with a soldier's logical reasoning process, leads to loss of self-control, self-respect, and pride in the unit. Hate is ruinous to discipline and morale. I told my troops our opponents were soldiers—like ourselves—who had a job to do. Our solemn duty required us to treat fallen enemy soldiers, and those we captured, with respect per the laws of war and civilized behavior. I told my troops to fight like tigers but conduct themselves with honor. A quote from the Prussian political philosopher Friedrich Nietzsche made a deep impression on me in my early life: "Whoever fights monsters should see to it that in the process he does not become a monster."[14] I let my troops know that anyone not willing to follow the enunciated rules would be transferred. Correct and kind treatment of an NVA prisoner saved my unit from almost certain annihilation later in the war.

Land warfare is gruesome enough without allowing the elements of hate and malice to run rampant. I am not saying those elements were never present in my unit. They are practically impossible to eliminate in an environment where friends are killed or maimed or soldiers exposed to—or taught about—enemy atrocities. I am proud to say that these elements were kept on a tight rein by a group of exceptionally fine professional NCOs and officers.

After policing the battlefield and evacuating our casualties, we began our return to Hill 51. A nearby herd of water buffalo had become restless because of all the noise and activity, and as the 2nd Platoon passed their location, one of those large animals charged a group of four men from the 1st Squad. One soldier, unable to get out of the way in time, suffered a broken arm. The other soldiers killed the buffalo. The platoon leader later labeled the buffalo "enemy" and recommended the soldier for a Purple Heart. Major Donald Schroeder, the battalion XO—a tough hombre who had been a rodeo rider in Wyoming—returned the recommendation with the notation that anyone dumb enough to tangle with a water buffalo should be transferred to a leg outfit (non-airborne unit).

After the fighting ended, the first thing I did was check to make sure the wounded soldiers from the patrol had evacuated. They survived their ordeal, but their wounds were so severe they ended up as amputees and never rejoined the company. I have not had contact with the soldier who triggered the booby trap, but Burges, now a retired master sergeant or sergeant major, told me at the 2006 reunion in Atlanta that he had survived.

Meeting Carlos Burges at the reunion was an emotional event. He saw me as I entered the hotel lobby and came over, and we gave each other a firm hug. He had an artificial leg, but it did not seem to hamper him much, or it did not show. I asked him to sit down with me on one of the sofas in the lobby and I began the conversation by apologizing for delaying his evacuation in 1966. He stopped me and said there was no need for an apology. He was aware of the situation and told me I had done the right thing. This meeting with Burges lifted a stone from my conscience. I had breakfast with him the following morning.

Correspondence with Next of Kin

I had a final duty to attend to after returning to Hill 51—write letters to the nearest relative of those killed.[15] Writing these letters was a sad duty, especially when I may have come to know or learn about an individual's family. As time passed, I avoided seeking information about a soldier's family and private life unless he brought such information to my attention. I spent considerable time personalizing each letter. By rules, they began with the chilling phrase: *It is with deep sorrow and regrets that I must report to you that your son (or husband) (rank and name) died in action on this date in the service of his country.*

The letters would usually contain, at a minimum, a brief description of the circumstances of the soldier's death. In addition, the letters gave the name of the person appointed on orders to inventory and forward his personal effects if known. Finally, the unit's condolences and an offer of further assistance should also be in the letter.

The next of kin often accepted this offer eagerly. They wanted, typically, to know more about the soldier's last day alive, any last words he may have spoken, and whether he suffered at the end. In answering these requests, I would sometimes have the soldier's best friend, who may have been with him at the time of his death, write a personal note attached to my reply. Still, I was not always truthful in the information I gave about how a soldier died. He may have died in great agony, but I saw no purpose in telling this to his family and usually stated that he died quickly and with little pain or suffering.

Several next of kin wrote to me and requested permission to give copies of the letters I wrote to their local newspaper. I felt good about these requests and always gave consent.

Having delivered the letters to the battalion S-1 section, I consoled myself with the fact the company had performed exceedingly well and we were lucky in having experienced so few casualties. However, I was somewhat concerned about the number of killed, wounded, and malaria casualties since we left Tuy Hoa. It was only the third day of what looked like a lengthy operation, but the company's MR strength remained at over 220 because of a continuous flow of replacements.[16] Both Emerson and Brigadier General Pearson expressed their compliments for the company's success along the Song Banh Lai Riverbanks.

My Canh (2)

The night of 4/5 February and the following day was uneventful with no enemy contacts. We sent out two patrols on the evening of 5 February to observe the Song Banh Lai River line in the vicinity of the engagement on 4 February. One patrol encountered an enemy force of unknown size early the following morning. The night action resulted in two of our men receiving minor wounds that did not require evacuation. Enemy losses, as was typical in these types of engagements, were unknown. A/2/502 became brigade reserve at noon on 6 February.

The other companies of 2/502 and the Recondo unit also had patrols operating in an arc extending from southwest to southeast of Hill 51. The companies began working in this area on 6 February.

A platoon from B/2/502 made the first contact with the enemy shortly after midnight on 5/6 February. A squad checked My Canh village but ran into a minefield and had two wounded. My Canh (2), about 5 kilometers east of Hill 51, was part of a cluster of villages in the area. It appears some Recondos joined the platoon during the night or in the early morning of 6 February.

The contact by B/2/502 was the beginning of a very bloody battle. Although A/2/502 was not involved, Lieutenant Colonel Perrine suggested I cover it and provided me copies of the one-paragraph battalion AA report and the brigade SJ for that period. Some overly complicated and unexplained shifting of forces took place. Emerson received command of the battlefield at first since he had the only troops in the area. This designation resulted in the first of several adjustments to the AOs of 2/502 and 1/327. What was involved in this and the other modifications that followed is difficult to determine because the overlays did not accompany the brigade SJ. I did write a segment about My Canh action, but realized it consisted of too much speculation. In addition, I had no notes, and the reports are virtually useless without overlays.

Furthermore, we would still not know why the decisions were made now that all principal participants have died. Therefore, the reasons for the decisions must have been based on conversations between Brigadier General Pearson, Emerson, and Lieutenant Colonel Rogers, commanding officer of 1/327, and not recorded anywhere in writing.

Two additional platoons from B/2/502 arrived on the battlefield piecemeal—one by foot and one by air—on 6 February. C/2/502 (minus) was inserted by air after A/2/502 replaced it as brigade reserve at noon on 6 February. It is curious that C/2/502 deployed with only two platoons.[17] B/1/327 and the Tiger Force (1/327 Reconnaissance Platoon) arrived in the AO on the afternoon of 6 February.

Two boundary changes took place on 6 February. At 1630 hours, Emerson received operational control of all ground forces. Shortly after that, the SJ indicates—without explanation—that 2/502 would disengage in the morning of 7 February, and C/2/502 (minus) would be under the operational control of 1/327. The brigade approved the plan for the next day at 2020 hours, which included another boundary change. It must have involved giving Major Hackworth the command in the battle area.

Since I could not understand the shifting plans and forces, I decided not to write about My Canh (2) except for this short overview. The shifting plans and units, as well as the execution, seriously violated age-old military principles. Nothing known to me has been written about this operation, clarifying what transpired. It was the costliest operation in casualties while I was in the brigade—30 were killed, and nearly 50 were wounded.[18] The reasons for not committing additional forces to block the 95th NVA battalion from retreating into the southern mountains remain unexplained.[19] An over-strength A/2/502 sat on Hill 51 doing practically nothing, and 1/327 had two other companies.

There was no lack of personal bravery (one Medal of Honor and two Distinguished Service Crosses), but common sense and proper use of age-old military principles were lacking. Within a few days, I exhibited a similar disregard for military principles.

While I have been transparent about my mistakes, I find no transparency in what I have read about My Canh (2).

Operations 5–7 February and Officer Replacements

A/2/502 spent the time that TF Hackworth was fighting at or near My Canh (2) in relative tranquility on Hill 51. We had patrols to the south and west, and one soldier is listed on the 5 February MR as evacuated with a shrapnel leg wound from a mine. The soldier's name was Private First Class James E. Wilson.

On 7 February, a combat patrol from the 1st Platoon searching the mountains to the south set off a mine or booby trap. A sharp, close quarter's engagement followed. Several soldiers were wounded, two of them seriously, and evacuated. The enemy also suffered several killed in this encounter and we captured some weapons.[20]

The fact that we had on two occasions run into mines or booby traps along the base of the southern mountains caused me to order an end to all night movements in that area. However, I wondered what these improvised explosives protected.

Two new officers assigned in early February played critical roles in future operations.[21] First, I gave First Lieutenant Karl Beach command of the 2nd Platoon. He served in that capacity until I made him my XO later during the Tuy Hoa operation. He was my third XO and performed with distinction in that job until the end of my tour. He was a company commander in the battalion I was assigned to as XO in the 9th Infantry Division. The second officer was Second Lieutenant William Otto III. I assigned him to the 1st Platoon, which had been without an officer for some time. Bill proved to be an outstanding combat leader.

Lieutenant William Settlemire Jr., commander of the 4th Platoon, returned from a well-deserved R&R. He was the only officer in the company who had deployed with the company to Vietnam. He had never liked the M16 rifle and traded something for an M1 carbine while in the rear area.

I had not tolerated anyone carrying non-issue weapons in the past. There were valid reasons for this policy. First, non-authorized arms create an ammunition supply problem. Second, after some time in combat, soldiers become accustomed to the sounds of various weapons. Using non-authorized weapons when authorized weapons are available only serves to increase confusion on the battlefield.

I could not make an exception for Bill Settlemire and I told him to get rid of the carbine. He did not protest but remarked he would have no use for it after the next operation. I felt Bill had spent too much time at the company level and had arranged a relatively safer job on the battalion staff. The fact that Bill was an only child also influenced my decision. I assumed his comment was about his programmed transfer and paid no further attention to it at the time.

CHAPTER 11

Days of Flawed Decisions

The following two relatively long chapters deal with three days of fighting—8–10 February 1966. There are several reasons for this lengthy treatment. First, they deal with two fights with the 95th NVA Regiment. Second, they involve intricate and sensitive issues that had not emerged before. Thirdly, as mentioned in the previous chapter, I made some serious operational mistakes, and they must be fully covered. Finally, they deal with difficulties I had with two of my officers, mentioned in the introduction. I will now tell my side of events after all these years and include their versions as promised. The first officer's side is partially explained in the text and expanded in note 2 of this chapter. The problem with the second officer also begins in this chapter. I have included his version of events, using references to his draft article. This occurrence is the only case of this type of problem during my three tours in Vietnam.

Leave No Man Behind

In the morning of 8 February, with the operation at the hamlet of My Canh (2) winding down, I secured permission to send a platoon size force to the west while the company was still brigade reserve. Accordingly, First Lieutenant Jim Schoonover's 3rd Platoon departed on his mission around 0900 hours. The instructions I gave Jim called for his platoon to proceed west through the valley for approximately 7–8 kilometers and set up in ambush positions for the night.

The mission of the 3rd Platoon represented the furthest westward penetration of the valley. The battalion was planning future operations in this area. A recent U.S. Army Vietnam directive—reportedly brought about by the fact that 2/502 was outside the range of supporting artillery at An Ninh—stipulated that no force larger than a platoon could proceed outside the reach of artillery. The destination, given the 3rd Platoon, placed it about 2 kilometers outside the range of artillery.

The 3rd Platoon came under small arms and automatic weapons fire shortly before darkness from its front and left flank while crossing an open area about 2 kilometers from its destination. Schoonover ordered a withdrawal to cover on the northern side of the open area. However, the lead squad was heavily engaged and had difficulties withdrawing into the wood-line. The squad leader, Staff Sergeant Carlos Betancourt-Mojica, and his point man, Specialist 4 Sylvester Jackson, Jr., were reported killed in action.

It was rapidly getting dark, and Schoonover told me he intended to hold up in his present position for the night. At this time, I learned the two KIAs remained behind in the open area when the platoon withdrew. I told Jim to make every effort to retrieve the two fallen soldiers.

I reported to the battalion that we had two MIAs. Un-retrieved KIAs should be listed missing until their bodies were recovered, even in cases where there were eyewitnesses. Still, I told the battalion we were sure they were dead, knew their location, and would try to retrieve them under cover of darkness.

I will digress a moment to discuss this issue. The 1st Brigade was one of the most elite units in the U.S. Army and it was a well-known policy that no member of the brigade, whether wounded or killed, should ever be abandoned. We were proud of having maintained a perfect record in this regard. This practice had important morale implications since every soldier knew his comrades would never leave him. It was also crucial for the next of kin since no one wants to go through the agony and despair of having one of their own classified as MIA. However, this policy had to be weighed against the illogical requirement to risk additional losses when it was known that those we were trying to recover were dead.

After a relatively short period, Schoonover came on the radio and wanted to talk to me.

This is Hunter 3, I see no point in risking additional casualties trying to recover dead men.

This is Hunter 6, I assume someone checked the two men and can verify they are dead.

There was a considerable pause before Jim came back on the radio. I guessed he was checking the answer to my question with some of his men.

This is Hunter 3, no one physically checked the two men, and we cannot swear that they are dead. However, I feel sure they are dead. They were seen falling and failed to answer calls by other members of their unit.

This is Hunter 6, based on your earlier reports, I informed higher that we had two un-retrieved KIAs. Now you tell me you cannot swear they are dead. Jim, this is unacceptable. We must do everything possible to recover them or at least confirm that they are dead. I want you to do that as soon as possible. Keep in mind that the enemy may use the two soldiers as bait, so proceed cautiously. Keep me informed.

This is Hunter 3, understand, will comply.

I did not change my report to the battalion. First, I believed Jim was correct in assuming the two men were dead, but we had to find out for sure. Second, a revised report would, at this stage, only complicate matters and lead the battalion to wonder what the hell was going on in my company.

Jim had joined the company on 9 December 1965, after we returned from Ben Cat but before we moved from Phan Rang to Tuy Hoa. He impressed me as a serious, sensitive, and capable officer. I thought he could demonstrate a bit more self-confidence than I had observed, but I figured that would come with time as he became more familiar with his job and men.

A lack of trust or respect could prove critical in a tight situation when Jim might have to demand instant risk-taking and possible sacrifices. While I had found no faults with Jim's performance on our operations since he joined the company, and personally liked him, his platoon was not the strongest.

It appears there were problems in the 3rd Platoon on its first night out, as mentioned in a telephone conversation I had recently with one of my former soldiers from Alabama, Private First Class Larry Greenhill, a member of the 3rd Platoon. Larry also told me that Sergeant Hawthorne had returned from the hospital and rejoined the platoon by the time of this action. As mentioned in endnote 3, Chapter 10, Schoonover had been the leader of this platoon back at Fort Campbell. This could have caused familiarity to develop between him and his NCOs. This is my speculation based on what Larry related.

About 30 minutes after his call for permission to scrap the mission to recover the two men, Jim called again.

This is Hunter 3, I do not see any logic in the task assigned to us. Request we be relieved of the mission.

While I suspected that some of Jim's NCOs were behind these calls, the information that they had not attempted to recover the two fallen soldiers or verify they had died was more than enough to trigger my short temper.

This is Hunter 6, I do not give a rat's ass whether you see any logic in the task I gave you, but you better damn well do it, and immediately. When you tell me "will comply," I expect you to do just that. If not, I will find someone who can. Now, do what you are told, and do not give me any more crap.

This is Hunter 3, roger.

I was so angry that my hand holding the radio handset was shaking. I looked around at those present. No one uttered a word and got busy doing something.[1] Finally, I got up and took a walk to cool off. I walked past the battalion S-3 tent, and Major Taylor told me he was about to release a LOH used by the battalion earlier. He said the aircraft still had enough fuel left for a short flight before going back to Tuy Hoa if I wanted to use it. The pilot was in the S-3 tent, so I asked if we could take a close look at the area to see if we could find the two killed soldiers.

We climbed aboard the two-seater and, although it was now dark, made two or three low passes (30–50 feet) over the area where the action had taken place. We received no fire, saw no movements on the ground, did not find the two soldiers, and returned to Hill 51 after a 15-minute flight.

Schoonover sent out a squad about two hours after dark to try to locate the two soldiers. They came under fire before reaching the two bodies and withdrew. One soldier was wounded and required evacuation.

The 3rd Platoon continued to report sporadic fire from an enemy force estimated by Jim to be of company size. I was a bit skeptical about this estimate's accuracy as I felt the enemy would have pressed the attack more aggressively if he were that strong. I also thought it strange that the observation helicopter had not drawn any fire despite passing over the open area at an exceptionally low altitude.

Nevertheless, based on Jim's estimate, I went to see Lieutenant Colonel Emerson and requested the company be relieved of the brigade reserve mission so that the whole company could move out to join the 3rd Platoon. Brigade denied this request around midnight. Brigadier General Pearson also called and asked for an update on the situation. He stressed the importance of recovering the two soldiers. I requested a delay in any MIA notification until we could clear up the problem in the morning. He agreed we should wait with the report until recovering the soldiers.

I had calmed down from my earlier anger and called Schoonover to tell him he could remain in his present location, which I believed was still on the west side of the river and that we would try to join him in the morning. I asked him to take advantage of any opportunity to retrieve the fallen soldiers if he thought he could do so without undue risk of further casualties. Jim must have felt my instructions were somewhat muddled—and maybe they were—because he asked that I clarify whether I wanted him to make another try to recover the soldiers. I was beginning to become annoyed again.

This is Hunter 6, look, use your damn common sense. If you feel there is a chance of recovering the two soldiers, take it. However, if you think you will suffer additional casualties in so doing, wait until we join you. You are the man on the ground, and it is your call to make. Jim said he understood.

At approximately 0130 hours on 9 February, Schoonover withdrew his platoon to the river's northeast side. I was informed about the withdrawal after it took place and immediately passed this information to the battalion. It was paramount that all friendly units' exact location was known to prevent casualties from friendly fire. I did not mention I had not authorized the withdrawal.

I was very troubled by Jim Schoonover's actions and discussed the issue with Major Don Schroeder over a beer.

Schroeder felt I had shown enough patience and recommended I replace Schoonover at the end of the operation. I also asked First Lieutenant Philip Mock, my XO, for his views. Phil, a West Point classmate and good friend of Schoonover, reminded me that I had told Jim about being the man on the ground in my last radio conversation. He suggested Jim could easily have read more into that statement than was intended. Phil agreed that Jim should have informed us before, not after, he withdrew, but felt this was insufficient for him to lose his command. Phil asked for an opportunity to discuss the issue with Schoonover at the end of the operation before I took any action.[2]

Lieutenant Colonel Emerson called on the landline at about 0300 hours. He had been told about the withdrawal of the 3rd Platoon and wanted to know what the hell I was doing. I explained the platoon had received sniper fire throughout the night. The new position was better suited to ward off a possible enemy attack by a force the platoon leader estimated to be a company in size. Emerson was not impressed. *Look, Hank, we are here to close with the f*****g enemy, not to run away when we have. I want to talk to you about this in the morning.*

I could not blame Emerson for his reaction to the situation, but I was also very annoyed with the battalion and brigade. They demanded I do something about a problem 6 kilometers away while keeping my hands tied by refusing to release us from the brigade reserve mission.

I called battalion operations on the landline and asked the duty officer to put Major Taylor on the telephone. The duty officer explained the major was asleep. I told him I did not care if he were in a coma, I wanted to talk to him. When he came on the phone, I unloaded my frustrations. I told him the old man (Emerson) and Pearson were both on my ass while their staff was creating senseless obstacles by refusing to release us from a mission that was stupid in this kind of war. Major Taylor patiently explained he had no authority to change my mission as I well knew. I suggested he find someone who had the authority, as I did not intend to be burned continually for something I could do little about from Hill 51.

After a night without sleep, I saw Emerson at breakfast around 0600, with Captain Murphy, now back from My Canh (2). Murphy opined that it was good to see my tail in the hot seat for a change. I told Bob that I was in no mood for his silliness.[3] Emerson did not mention anything about our previous conversation when he joined Murphy and me, leading me to believe that Don Schroeder and Art Taylor had talked to him.

Company A was released from the brigade reserve mission at 0800 hours on 9 February. C/2/502 became the brigade reserve. Shortly after that, Emerson accepted my plan to take my company into the Song Banh Lai Valley, recover the two missing soldiers, and proceed further into the valley. Artillery would be displaced to cover our advance. The company did not have a specific mission other than searching the valley and attempt to reestablish contact with the 95th NVA Regiment. The lack of a specific mission was fine with me, as it gave us maximum flexibility. Emerson established no limit of advance, but he mentioned he planned to set up a battalion forward operating base near the western end of the valley and expected to see me there in the evening. Tom Taylor received orders to reinforce or exploit if we made enemy contact.

I split the company into two groups. The 2nd Platoon and the alternate command group, under Phil Mock, departed on foot at 1030 hours to link up with the 3rd Platoon and then proceed to the area of the two missing soldiers from the northeast. The rest of the company (command group, 1st Platoon, and the 4th Platoon) made a helicopter assault at 1100 hours into an LZ to the southeast of Schoonover's position. The plan called for the two elements to approach the missing soldiers' area from two directions—my group from the east and Phil's from the north or northeast. This scheme would allow half of the company to maneuver and take any enemy force, confronting the other half, in the flank.

One of those amusing and embarrassing incidents that will always remain in my memory occurred near our LZ. The maps we had were not always accurate. I had made it a policy that my artillery forward observer, First Lieutenant Tom Clements,[4] always knew exactly where we were so he could call accurate artillery fire immediately. As we set out from the LZ, I discussed our location with Tom, and it turned out we disagreed about our exact location by almost 400 meters. I felt confident I could read a map better than someone from the artillery could.

I bet Tom two cases of beer because I was sure I was right. The only way to determine who was right was to call for an artillery marking round. I told Tom to call it on his coordinates as I did not want the round too close.

He did. The round landed with an ear-piercing screech in the middle of the command group, not more than 10 feet from Tom and me. My reputation as a navigator suffered considerably among the command group members sprawled in the muddy rice field. I paid the bet after the operation. I never again challenged Tom's ability to read a map.

At about noon, Phil Mock linked up with the 3rd Platoon and started moving his force towards the two missing soldiers' location. At about the same time, we linked up with the patrol from the 1st Platoon sent out on 5/6 February, and I did not notice any wounded troops. We continued towards the location of the two missing soldiers.

I had several worries. The first had to do with a possible enemy ambush as we approached our destination. We tried to alleviate this danger by keeping our point element well in advance and the rest in a more spread-out formation than usual. My second worry was that the enemy could have booby-trapped or mutilated the two soldiers. Such actions could create the element of hate we had tried to avoid. Finally—and most important—there was the possibility we would not find the two soldiers and would therefore not conclusively know if they were dead or alive.

My group reached our destination about 1300 hours and Phil's two platoons a few minutes later. We had no enemy contact as we approached our goal and located the two bodies almost immediately, plus a damaged M16 rifle. We found the two soldiers in a bomb crater covered with dirt by the enemy. Macias used the engineers to recover the bodies, and some soldiers, including Larry Greenhill, helped. It was a rather slow operation because we feared booby traps. To my relief, the bodies were not booby-trapped or mutilated. Major Taylor evacuated the fallen soldiers around 1340 hours.

Violations of Basic Military Principles

The company continued westward at 1400 hours with Beach's platoon in the lead. I decided to leave the 3rd Platoon behind to establish a patrol base. The primary reason for leaving the 3rd Platoon behind was Macias's conversations with Sergeant First Class Albert T. Ledford, the 3rd Platoon Sergeant when Macias visited, and spent some time with, that platoon. Macias and the platoon sergeant had concluded that some of its members were a little unsettled by the previous night's experience. Both Macias and Ledford felt the unit would benefit from a night of relative rest. In my mind, it also confirmed the lack of strong leadership in the platoon.

In retrospect, the reason for leaving the 3rd Platoon at the entrance to the side valley had insufficient validity to warrant reducing my combat power by nearly 25 percent. Moreover, I had allowed myself to violate a cardinal principle of military tactics—not to split the command when faced by possible superior enemy forces.

I made a series of violations of age-old military principles that day. One such principle was not to feed the battlefield piecemeal. Another was my failure to factor into my plan what the enemy might do and be ready to counter it—always be prepared to tackle the unexpected. Probably the most crucial principle violated was never to do what the enemy wishes us to do. In short, I underestimated the enemy, was not prepared for all eventualities, and played into the enemy's hands by going against him in a piecemeal fashion in terrain with which he was thoroughly familiar.

Ironically, I made these mistakes two to three days after I was critical of TF Hackworth for making similar mistakes. It is inexplicable.

The valley we were at the entrance to split into two spurs about 2,500 meters to our west. One led northwest to the future forward battalion CP in the vicinity of the abandoned hamlet of Lac Sanh. The other led in a southwesterly direction. The more I looked at the map and the terrain we passed through, the more convinced I became that we were not likely to find an enemy force between our location and the place selected for the new forward battalion CP. The area was sparsely vegetated and without running water. Experience taught us the enemy usually established their camps with adequate cover, running water, and quick withdrawal routes.

The valley spur running southwesterly where the valley split had vegetation and water since the Song Banh Lai River, coming out of the southern mountains, ran through it. Therefore, I considered it more likely we would find the enemy in that location. I discussed this with Major Taylor when he arrived to evacuate the two KIAs and asked that he secure Emerson's permission for my company to search the

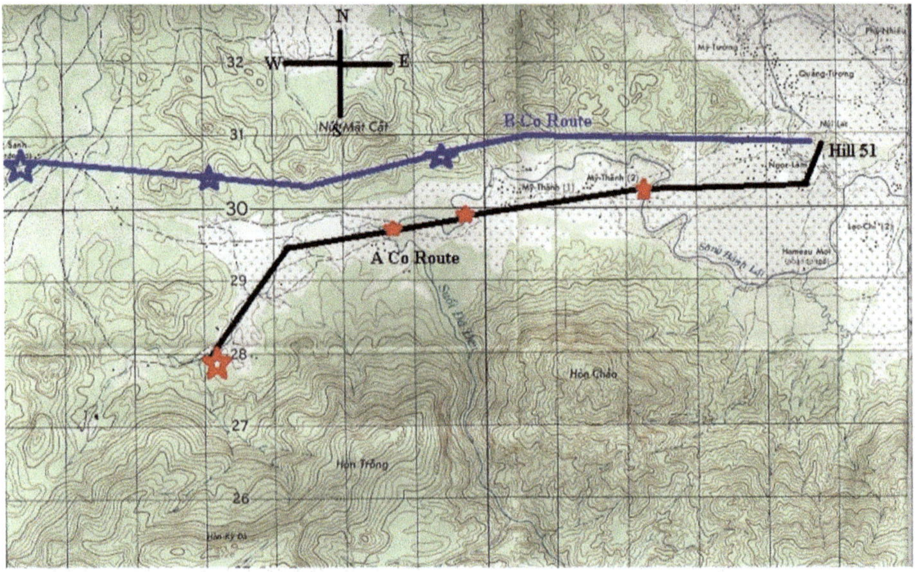

Map 5. Modified U.S. topographic map of our engagements with elements of the 95th NVA Regiment 4–11 February. The easterly red star is about 2 kilometers west of our action on 4 February. The second red star denotes the action of the 3rd Platoon on 8 February. The third read star is the approximate location where Staff Sergeant Reda was wounded, and the last red star is the location of our engagement on 9/10 February. The route of B/2/502 is marked in blue, and the second star from the east is the company's night position. The western blue star is the location of the battalion forward CP.

southwest spur where the valley split and not return to the battalion base until the following day. Emerson agreed to my request and ordered B/2/502 to move west on the other side of the valley and then take the northwest spur.

A couple of days after the action that was about to begin, I had the opportunity to visit and observe the battle area where the enemy commander may have been during the fighting. He had an excellent view of the valley and was probably overjoyed seeing me split my command and then remove my rear protection before we disengaged. Unfortunately, I played into his hands. The only benefit of my mistakes was that I would never repeat them later during this or subsequent tours. However, it was a costly lesson.

The company was well spread out and moving slowly into the side valley. We had covered only a few hundred meters from where we left the 3rd Platoon when our lead element received sniper fire from the southwest. One soldier, Staff Sergeant Michael Reda, the weapons squad leader of the 2nd Platoon, was shot through the stomach. Although he belittled his wound, Reda required immediate evacuation. I ordered Beach's platoon to continue its move in a southwesterly direction to flush out any snipers and provide security for the rest of the company, which I halted. In doing so, I exacerbated my previous mistakes by allowing a unit of about 50 troops to proceed into the valley, leaving the main body behind. Despite my reasons for these decisions, I was inviting trouble by feeding the battle area piecemeal.

For some time, I had contemplated having the officers and NCOs remove their insignias of rank. By looking at the number of casualties we were suffering in these two groups in relation to overall losses, it had become evident we were making it too easy for the enemy to identify and eliminate the leaders in the company. Squad and platoon leaders must, in any case, expose themselves more than their men must—it comes with the territory. Nevertheless, it did not make sense to make the enemy's job easier. The wounding of Staff Sergeant Reda—with very visible chevrons on his sleeves—was the proverbial straw that broke the camel's back, and I passed the word that all symbols of rank were to be removed or made invisible that night.

Initially, there was some grumbling and resistance to this policy among the NCOs. Their main objection was that the insignias were necessary for the soldiers to identify their leaders. My response was that if their soldiers needed insignias to identify their leaders, it was time for new leaders. The value of the removal or suppression of emblems soon became evident to all.

It was now around 1445 hours, and I had decided to continue into the valley for about 3 kilometers before establishing night positions. Since we had initially planned to be at the new battalion forward base by nightfall, we had only brought enough rations for one day. It now appeared we would be out for at least two days. I figured we could save time by receiving resupply at the same time as we evacuated Reda. Most of the resupply could be broken down and distributed on location and we would only have to carry the rations for the 2nd Platoon forward in bulk. The 3rd Platoon could also pick up its resupply from this location since the LZ was only a few hundred meters from its patrol base. The plan was good, but the enemy failed to cooperate.

While waiting for the evacuation helicopter and our resupply, we heard firing from the southwest. Beach came on the radio to report his platoon had encountered a suspected enemy squad dug in at the base of a hillside. The time was about 1510 hours. A quick check of the coordinates given by Beach made me realize this aggressive officer had covered almost 2,500 meters and was near the location tentatively selected for the company's night position. I sensed an opportunity to corner a small enemy unit and immediately aborted the resupply mission.

I gave Lieutenants Settlemire and Otto a quick briefing and we started for the sounds of the firing within five minutes of receiving Beach's report. I left First Lieutenant Phil Mock and the first sergeant behind with their RTOs, the engineers, four medics, the 4.2-inch mortar forward observer team, a Vietnamese interpreter, and the wounded sergeant. Phil and his group were to join us as soon as Reda was evacuated.

Phil Mock wrote an article about the upcoming action while at the IOCC at Fort Benning.[5] The article has me initially leaving the 1st Platoon under William Otto and the 4th Platoon commanded by Karl Beach to secure the evacuation site for Reda.

Phil is mixing up some of the units and their leaders (they are correct in Garland's book).[6] Second Lieutenant Otto commanded the 1st Platoon, First Lieutenant Karl Beach commanded the 2nd Platoon, and Bill Settlemire commanded the 4th Platoon. Phil Mock also wrote that the 4th Platoon strength was only 20 men. While I do not know the strength of that platoon on 9 February, that figure seems much lower than it should be, given the company's over-strength status as late as 8 February, referenced earlier. I assume that virtually the whole platoon was in the field and they had not taken any casualties so far.

With Otto's platoon in the lead, we reached a creek line (the Song Banh Lai River) about 500 meters behind Beach's location around 1545 hours. There was much firing coming from the direction of the 2nd Platoon. Beach had deployed and tried to outflank the enemy from the south, but the enemy's fire intensity increased, and the platoon was quickly unable to move. We had already suffered casualties, and I regretted leaving the extra medics with Phil as part of his LZ security force.

I told Lieutenants Otto and Settlemire to remain near the creek line with their units as I moved forward with the command group to join Beach to get a better picture of the situation. However, the command group ran into heavy enemy fire about 100 meters short of Beach's location. Most of the enemy fire came from our right front and flank. With Otto and Settlemire monitoring, Beach briefed me by radio on his situation and his troops' location using distances from pre-selected map reference points. His calm and business-like manner while under heavy fire impressed me. I requested tactical air support and told Tom Clements to begin delivering artillery fire on the enemy positions.

Emerson called and recommended using CS gas (potent riot control agent) dispensed from an aircraft, the first use of gas in Vietnam. The required equipment had just arrived in the brigade. It was not a good idea to give this innovation its first test during a battle. However, I was ready to try anything, and Emerson informed me we could expect the CS ship within 20 minutes. It arrived at about 1720 hours. Emerson asked me for an estimate of the enemy's strength. I replied that any estimate at this time would be pure guesswork. He said he was halting B/2/502 and holding it in readiness in case we needed help.

I tried to formulate a plan of action. The 1st and 4th Platoons were still about 400 meters to my rear, and I realized all too well that we had about two hours of daylight remaining. A night engagement in the dense triple-canopy jungle on the enemy's turf at the base of the mountain was something we had to avoid. I directed Otto to swing his platoon to the south and come up on the right flank of the 2nd Platoon.

Settlemire informed me his platoon did not have their protective masks. That did not bother me. We had never needed the gas masks before and they only added to the weight the troops had to carry. After a few days of operations in our environment, they became soaked in water and mud and practically useless.

I preferred the troops carried a few extra hand grenades or additional M16 ammunition instead. I told Bill Settlemire to bring his soldiers to the north side of the creek and spread them out in the tree line that paralleled it, about 400 meters north of my location. He was assigned the mission to protect the company rear and told to join the attack—only if I called for him—after the CS gas had dispersed sufficiently.

In the meantime, we continued to employ all available artillery. Point-detonating fuses caused no damage as most exploded in the dense jungle canopy high over the enemy positions. We, therefore, requested a delayed fuse since it was apparent the enemy was well entrenched. Even the delayed-fuse shells failed to silence the enemy fire, but they allowed the troops some freedom of movement to readjust their positions, especially after mixing in a few salvos of smoke and WP.

We had identified at least two enemy machine guns and, from their distinctive high rate of fire, we judged them to be MG42s. I, consequently, figured at least one enemy platoon confronted us. I checked my estimate with Karl Beach, who agreed. I informed Emerson accordingly. This estimate was drastically revised before the night was over.

We lifted the artillery fire at 1700 hours to allow helicopter gunships to make several passes at the enemy positions. The gunships came in low from the north. They delivered their ordnance of rockets and machine-gun fire while practically on top of us. They appeared to be right on target.

At 1715 hours, a Forward Air Controller (FAC) in a light, fixed-wing aircraft reported on station. These Air Force officers served as the communications link between the Air Force fighter-bombers and us. Like most Army medevac helicopter pilots, FACs impressed me with their enthusiasm and courage throughout the war. In their vulnerable and slow-moving aircraft, they would crisscross the battle area at tree-top level and usually received a steady stream of ground fire because the enemy was aware of the meaning of their presence over the battlefield. Also, this FAC had supported us in previous operations. He contacted me on the battalion command net.

Hunter, this is your knight in shining armor. I see you have managed to get yourselves in trouble again. Where do you want me, on this net or yours?

This is Hunter, talk to me on my net. I wanted him on the company command frequency so the platoons could monitor the conversation.

Within a few seconds, he was on my command net. He was flying in a lazy circle, obviously making himself familiar with the area.

I have two fast-moving birds from the big city. They will be here in 05 and do not have much time. They have cold beers and hooch girls waiting at home.

The FAC told us that two fighter-bombers out of Bien Hoa Air Base would be overhead in five minutes and would not be able to stay on station long because they were low on fuel.

This is Hunter 6, we have a whole bunch of bad guys in the wood-line at the base of the hills 500 meters to the south of the creek. I will have my forward element pop a smoke, you identify, and we will give you directions.

We did not provide the color of the smoke we intended to throw since the enemy could be monitoring the transmission and throw an identical color to confuse the FAC. Instead, I asked Karl to mark his front with a smoke grenade and give the FAC the necessary directions.

I see red smoke; now, where do you want the strike?

This is Hunter 2, red is correct. In the wood-line directly south of the smoke.

The FAC fired a white smoke rocket at the wood-line specified by Karl to mark the fighter-bombers' target.

Is that where you want it?

This is Hunter 2, right on the mark and 50 meters on either side.

Roger, we are inbound. Keep your butts down.

Within less than a minute, two F-4Cs thundered in at a low level from the east. They banked sharply to the north after releasing their bombs. Each aircraft dropped two 250 pounders, and we could clearly see them plummet towards the wood-line. The explosions shook the ground and sent clouds of smoke and debris into the air. It appeared the explosions were about 50 meters inside the wood-line.

The FAC was back on the radio. *How was that?*

This is Hunter 6, it looked well from here. At least you made their ears ring.

The FAC approached our position from the east, cut his engine, came over us at the height of no more than 50–75 feet, restarted his engine, and roared off in a steep climb.

The FAC stated, *I noticed much activity and movement in the tree line to your north and northwest, which runs from the creek south to the target area. Do you have any of your folks in that area?*

This is Hunter 6, yes, but we always appreciate you passing on whatever you see.

I believed the FAC's sighting was the 1st Platoon moving forward on the right flank of the 2nd. I did not bother to say anything to either Otto or Beach because I figured they had monitored the FAC conversation since it had taken place on the company command net. Based on my assumption that the FAC had seen members of the 1st Platoon moving forward, I took no further precautions—another regrettable mistake.

The article written by Captain Philip Mock about this action is limited in its perspective. A segment of Albert N. Garland's book *Infantry in Vietnam* is based on Mock's article, but it is abbreviated.[7] An August 1966 article in *Army Digest* also deals with this engagement.[8] Finally, it was covered by *Army Times* on 9 March 1966 in an article titled "PFC Sweats Long Night After Hell Opens Up: Fear Turns to Numbness in Total Darkness."

There are several inaccuracies in Phil's account. Phil was not present at the engagement site until shortly before we began our disengagement, and he was therefore not privy to all decisions and the reasons for them.

The 1st Platoon joined the fight about 1715 hours. In coming up on the right flank of the 2nd Platoon, it ran into heavy small arms and automatic weapons fire on both sides of the creek. This fighting confirmed the FAC sighting involved enemy movements to our right front, but I believed the 1st Platoon now had these troops engaged. I should also have remembered the FAC had mentioned movements on our right flank, to our northwest. We did revise the earlier estimate on enemy strength and I told Emerson we might be up against an enemy company

I was increasingly concerned about the amount of daylight left and our ability to take the enemy positions before nightfall with the available forces. Accordingly, I told Emerson I intended to have the 3rd Platoon join us.

Before I could take any action, the CS aircraft arrived. My failure to act at once on my decision, or immediately after the CS drop, was, in retrospect, another error. The first CS drop took place around 1730 hours, according to my notes. The battalion SJ states that three CS drops occurred at 1720 hours, but I only recall two.[9] Because of the apparent worry of ground fire, the first drop was from a height of about 800 feet. This height caused the canisters to open and the gas to disperse long before reaching the ground without affecting our opponents.

I told the pilot that if he did not have enough balls to make the drop from treetop level, he might as well return to his safe and comfortable surroundings at the Tuy Hoa Airfield and let us use our artillery. He ignored my needling comment and prepared to make a second drop. The second drop was from a height of 300 or more feet, and it appeared to land in the middle of the enemy positions in enough quantities where it should have had some effect.

I ordered the two platoons to take advantage of the CS drop and attack. We also resumed the artillery fire. The troops started advancing on the enemy positions by fire and maneuver and entered the wood-line. Tom Clements shifted the artillery fire when the lead troops were about 100 meters from where the shells were falling. The CS gas was not effective and the soldiers soon discarded the gas masks. It was the first and last time I used CS gas in Vietnam.

Phil Mock, who was not yet present, was overly impressed with the CS drop. He wrote, "that a light aircraft had answered CPT Lunde's request for an aerial gas attack … and it and supporting fires broke the back of the stalwart defense" (Mock, pp. 4–5). The CS drop did not break the back of the defense. My troops and I judged it a total failure.

Since the command group had not received fire for a while, we tried to move forward to join the 2nd Platoon. I told the men in my group that I would cross the clearing first and they were to join me when I was safely across. We did not know a gap existed between the two platoons, and several enemy positions covering the clearing had not been eliminated or engaged. I headed straight towards these positions and was, of course, taken under fire and pinned down about 50–60 meters from my RTOs, ruining my ability to control the company and violating Emerson's warning a few days earlier.

My first thought was disbelief at this happening to me again. My second thought was probably a faint hope Emerson would not find out about my predicament. I had no cover except that provided by the dry furrowed ground that had once been a rice paddy. Every time I tried to move, I was sprayed with dirt and sand kicked up by the impact of bullets from rapid-fire machine guns.

I fired one magazine in the direction of the enemy positions without any noticeable effect. However, when I tried to reverse the magazine (two magazines taped together so that when one was empty, I could remove it and insert the other end of the makeshift double magazine), the rifle jammed. The jam was caused by dirt collected in the bottom magazine as I crawled on the ground. I never again taped two magazines together, nor would I allow my troops to do so.

Despite covering fire from my command group, it took me about 20 minutes to extract from the clearing. In the end, the only damage I sustained was the loss of one of my two canteens, blown off my belt by an enemy bullet. While I was pinned down in the field, Specialist 4 Michael W. Ellis and Tom Clements did an outstanding job bringing helicopter gunship strikes to support the attacking platoons.

Sergeant McFann, my communications chief, had kept up a steady fire on the enemy positions that had pinned me down and informed Beach and Otto about these positions' location so they could engage them. I was back with the command group shortly before 1800 hours, fully aware my dumb actions had cost us about half an hour of precious daylight.

The 1st and 2nd Platoons, although their interior flanks had lost contact with each other as they tried to work their way through what turned out to be an enemy encampment, were still meeting stiff resistance.

As soon as I rejoined the command group, I did what I should have done an hour earlier. I called Jim Schoonover, whose platoon was still at the valley entrance, and asked if he could join us before darkness. Jim estimated it would take 15–20 minutes to assemble his men and another 30–45 minutes before he could reach us. I concluded that his answer meant he could not reach us before dark and told him to keep his platoon assembled at his location and remain there until daylight.

Specialist 4 Ellis, to my dismay, had briefed Emerson fully about my earlier predicament in the clearing.

This is Gunfighter,[10] *what the f**k are you doing down there, Hank?* Emerson was not long on proper radio procedures.

This is Hunter, we are trying to clear this enemy encampment before dark.

This is Gunfighter, that is not what I mean. Your job is to command the company, not being a rifleman playing hide and seek with enemy machine guns. I want you to stay with your radio operators. If necessary, hold their hands, but I do not want to call again and find you unavailable.

This is Hunter, roger, over. Emerson was correct; there was no excuse for my actions.

This is Gunfighter, how long before you will have that place cleared out?

This is Hunter, it sounds like the firing is tapering off somewhat in my 2nd element's area, but heavy firing is still coming from the other side of my line. I was hoping to have the area cleared before dark, but I do not know if that is possible. I have decided not to bring Hunter 3 to my location since they could not make it before dark. I am a little puzzled why the enemy has not already broken off the fight, something they could easily do in the rough terrain on the side of these hills.

This is Gunfighter, do not allow them to break contact! There was anxiety in his voice at the prospect of letting the enemy get away. *I can have Taylor swing up in your direction, if necessary.*

This is Hunter, there is no way Taylor could make it here before darkness since he is further away than Hunter 3, and I do not see any advantage in diverting Tom currently.

This is Gunfighter, Schroeder has brought Murphy's element and the Recondos to our new location. I will leave Taylor where he is, for the time being, to see how your situation develops.

It would soon be dark. I was concerned the attacking platoons—both under new leaders on their first operation—would inflict casualties on each other in the enemy encampment. It was already getting dark due to the dense jungle cover. As far as I could tell, the two units had lost contact. They were heading towards each other at an angle—one from the northeast and the other from the northwest. Beach believed there was still a chance of clearing the encampment before it became dark, but Otto disagreed and stated it was already becoming a bit hairy in the twilight. The heaviest firing was coming from where the 1st Platoon had entered the wood-line.

We still had not committed the 4th Platoon, but the critical element was no longer a lack of combat power forward but the fact that we ran out of daylight. It was not a good idea to send additional forces into the middle of a fight in the dark when the engaged units were separated and their leaders were unsure about their flanks' location. Using Settlemire's platoon would also leave our rear uncovered.

I decided the best course of action was to break off the engagement. Breaking contact was disappointing since I did not have much hope of finding the enemy in the morning. I planned to pull back to the Song Banh Lai River (really a shallow creek at this point), where I had left the 4th Platoon, keep the enemy encampment under harassing artillery fire, destroy it in the morning, and then try to re-establish contact with the enemy. Now came the hard part, telling Emerson about my decision.

This is Gunfighter, Hank, I am not at all happy at the way things have turned out.

Emerson's reaction was milder than I had expected.

This is Hunter, neither am I, but I believe the enemy is in the process of withdrawing, and it would be virtually impossible to try to maintain contact in the dark in this broken terrain. The part of the statement about an enemy withdrawal was not precisely correct. Except for diminished firing in the 2nd Platoon area, I had no information that the enemy was breaking contact, but I believed it to be true. I figured it made no difference, but the info might appease Emerson's annoyance. The part about the near impossibility of conducting night operations on a jungle hillside covered by building-size rocks was right.

In his contribution to *Infantry in Vietnam*, Mock wrote that the two platoons gained the enemy trenches, that all action stopped. He further claims that after the enemy did not reappear after some 15 minutes, I decided the battle was over and ordered the two platoons down off the hill to consolidate in a relatively clear area at its base (Mock, p. 5).

This statement is, unfortunately, wildly inaccurate and misleading. First, the platoons were not on a hill but at the bottom of a mountainside. The top of the mountain to the north was over 900 meters above our location. The mountain to our west had a height of 204 meters. If we were on a hill from which we had driven the enemy, I certainly would have stayed on that hill since it would have been a more defensible position. The terrain to the rear of the enemy encampment was a very steep, boulder-strewn jungle hillside. It would have been sheer folly to establish defensive positions against an enemy who held the higher ground. There would have been no fields of fire, the enemy could lob or roll grenades in our direction, and he could easily move, covered and concealed, to within close-quarter combat distance of our positions.

The enemy force had by no means been destroyed or otherwise eliminated, and we sent no such report to the battalion. My decision to disengage was because we could not clear the enemy positions before dark. We were likely to suffer unnecessary casualties from friendly fire in the darkness. I did not want a night engagement under conditions favorable to an enemy who knew the ground thoroughly.

The main problems remaining were how to disengage the two platoons, effect a withdrawal to the selected night location, set up in a perimeter, evacuate our casualties, and try to receive resupply before darkness. So far, we had suffered one killed and seven wounded, three of them requiring evacuation. I instructed Beach and Otto to disengage and move their units to where I had left the 4th Platoon. I also asked they meet me at my place as soon as possible for further instructions.

My primary concern was that the enemy might follow the withdrawing units. Tom Clements kept artillery fire on the enemy positions during our withdrawal and mixed in smoke rounds to alleviate this potential problem. However, employing artillery was complicated because neither Beach nor Otto knew where their troops were in the broken terrain. As it turned out, the enemy did not press the withdrawing units. All contact with the enemy ended around 1820 hours.

I had a quick meeting with Lieutenants Beach, Otto, and Settlemire and pointed out where I wanted to set up that night and assigned sectors of the proposed perimeter to each platoon. I ordered the platoon leaders to move their troops to the selected location as quickly as possible to establish a perimeter before dark.

Lieutenant Phil Mock also joined us. I instructed him to set up an evacuation and resupply zone as quickly as possible. Phil suggested an open area to the southeast of the company positions and I agreed. I instructed Otto and Beach to bring any wounded requiring evacuation to that location and troops to carry the resupply back to their platoons. Phil then left.

Beach, Otto, and Settlemire remained at my place for a few minutes. I told them the battalion had moved its forward CP with C/2/502 and Recondos into an area at the western end of the valley. I also gave them the location of B/2/502. Furthermore, I noted that Schoonover had orders to link up with us after the first light in the morning. I informed them we would meet in the new company perimeter to discuss and plan the next day's operation at 2100 hours. The three platoon leaders then departed to join their units.

Phil Mock described this meeting place as "a jungle of radio antennae."[11] This exaggerated statement had nothing to do with what was about to transpire. There were undoubtedly several radio antennae at my location, but it had been our policy for several months that the platoon leaders leave their radios and RTOs with their platoons when reporting to my location. This policy was part of our SOP. Its intent was not to reduce the number of antennae at my CP. Instead, it enabled the platoon leaders to pass instructions to their platoons while still at my location. It also allowed me to communicate with the platoons should an emergency arise while the leaders were going to or from their platoons. We modified this policy as we acquired more PRC-25 radios.

I doubt a violation of the policy in force at the time would have escaped my notice. Therefore, I believe the only RTOs at my location were those who always accompanied me: the battalion net operator, the company net operator, and the artillery fire net operator. Phil undoubtedly brought the same number of radios from the alternate command group.

Phil Mock made another observation to Garland although he could not judge the troops from the forward platoons, which were in the process of disengaging. These were the only two units that had been in the middle of heavy fighting. The only other soldiers Phil had seen up to then were his group and the 4th Platoon, and they had not participated in the fight.

Phil stated there was a feeling of relaxation among those present, including the troops. This is, unfortunately, something that tends to happen after a battle, particularly with new soldiers. They are happy and relieved to be out of immediate danger and eager to talk to friends about their experiences. It is one way of reducing the pent-up emotions after a fight. Of course, we were always on guard against this condition, but the troops from the two forward platoons were so busy they had not had time to relax at this stage.

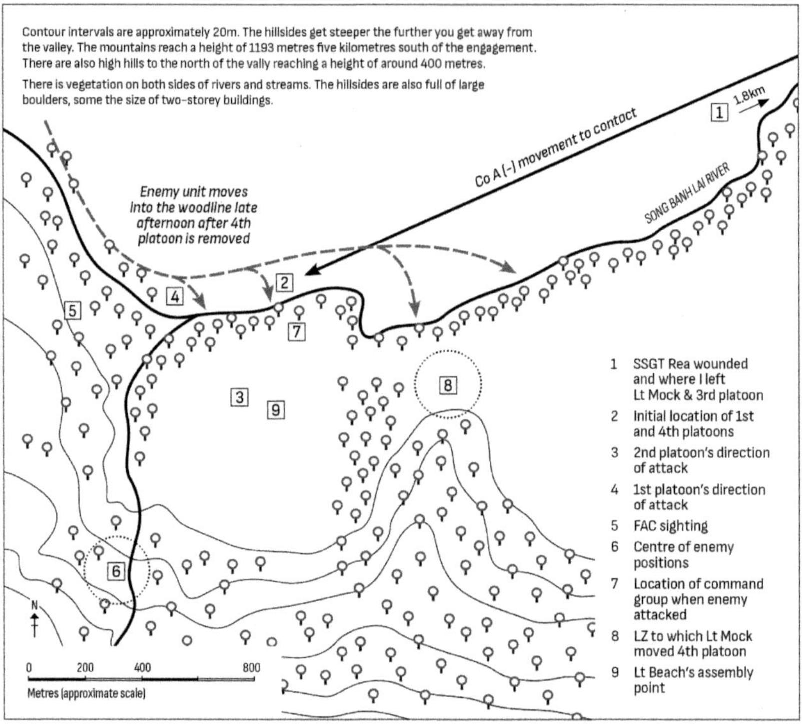

Battle Sketch 6. My battle sketch of the 9/10 February engagement including the night ambush.

CHAPTER 12

Ambush: A Night of Terror

After briefing the platoon leaders, I called Lieutenant Colonel Emerson and told him we had successfully disengaged and gave him the day's results as we knew them. He told me he had allowed B/2/502 to continue westward but expected they would soon go into night positions.

Having talked to Emerson, I headed for the new company location, accompanied by my command group. As we proceeded towards the tree line paralleling the creek to the 4th Platoon site, I talked to Phil on the radio and asked what was holding up the evacuation and resupply flights. I also gave Jim Schoonover a quick update and spoke briefly to Tom Taylor. He confirmed he was going into night positions about 2 kilometers west of his previous location.

The 2nd Platoon had begun to cross the clearing and was heading towards the creek line. The lead elements were about 100 meters to my left rear as we headed north. The 1st Platoon had begun to exit the woods to my left (west). The troops were moving to the creek line on an angle with our approach. A small group of 1st Platoon personnel was about to cross our path, apparently heading for the LZ to receive resupply. The time was about 1845 hours and it was quickly becoming very dark. First Lieutenant Mock has an earlier time—1830—for the ambush (Mock, p. 7). Specialist 5 Francis Faulkner's article "Battle Diary: Long Night near Tuy Hoa" has the earliest time for the ambush, writing that it took place at 1630 hours.[1] The battalion SJ notes only that the battalion lost contact with A/2/502 at 1910 hours.[2]

I could hear First Sergeant Macias, to my right, yelling for the troops to spread out. The most terrifying night of my life was about to begin.

About 20–30 meters from the creek, the wood-line to our front erupted in a sheet of flames. One of my soldiers, Private First Class William C. Fowler, described those first moments as "The gates of hell were opened."[3] The shock was indescribable. The initial bursts, a mixture of small arms and machine-gun fire, came from a 300-meter section of the wood-line along the creek. It was professionally aimed at the rear of our formations, at the troops furthest from the wood-line. No doubt the enemy commander assumed he could later eliminate those of us who were close to the wood-line.

This tactic by the enemy saved the command group from immediate annihilation since we could hit the ground. However, the flat ground did not offer much protection.

There was mass confusion in the first horrific seconds, with cries for medics coming from our rear and left. The 1st Platoon on our left was already returning a steady stream of fire against the wood-line. Some of the troops in the 2nd Platoon were also returning fire. This did not make us very comfortable, caught in the middle of grazing fire. Tracers lit up the night all around us, interspersed with the brilliant flashes from exploding hand grenades and incoming mortar rounds. The mortar fire gave me the chilling realization that we had underestimated the size of the enemy force opposing us.

The radio on the battalion command net, carried by Sergeant McFann, was damaged. Specialist 4 Ellis, who now carried the company net radio, was on the ground to my left. I turned to Ellis and told him to *Get Settlemire on the radio and find out what the hell happened to his platoon. They are supposed to be in the wood-line to our front.* But, before he could relay the message, a call came in from Phil Mock saying his troops, including the 4th Platoon, were heavily engaged on our right.

First Lieutenant Phil Mock wrote that he tried to find me after the evacuation of Staff Sergeant Reda by traveling "through alternate patches of murky swamp and dense jungle vegetation when he stumbled into the Weapons Platoon."[4] I saw no "murky swamps" in the battle area, as he shows in his sketches.

Mock's first battle sketch shows that he and his group had not come the same way as the 2nd Platoon and the company. They had moved through the jungle hillside, which undoubtedly is why it took him so long to reach us. We had approached the battle area by the flat and open valley, keeping a safe distance away from the wood lines. The company covered the distance in 35 minutes, and the 2nd platoon had done so in 40–45 minutes.

Phil could easily have contacted me or my RTO by radio. Mock relates, furthermore, that he had a quick conference with First Lieutenant Settlemire. He then moved the 4th Platoon and his detachment "down the left fork of a streambed to a position about 200 yards behind the two engaged rifle platoons. … The Weapons Platoon and the engineer squad held that position" while he moved "forward" with the medics to meet me.[5]

Mock's move was away from my location and the scene of the fighting! In its original position, the 4th Platoon was about 400 meters to the northeast of the fight. The eastward move would place the platoon about 700 meters away from its original position and almost 1,000 meters from the fighting platoons, not 200 meters. The move of the 4th Platoon left the company's rear unprotected. The fact that Mock's group ended up in the creek bed at a considerable distance (see later) to my right after the fighting began supports my conclusion that the move was about 700 meters in an eastward direction.

Phil also wrote that when we met, I ordered him "and Bill Settlemire" to coordinate the medevac, resupply, and join the company. Then he wrote that I preceded the rifle platoons back down the "hill" to meet him and Settlemire again about 50 yards west of the 4th Platoon position, and this is "when all hell broke loose" (Mock p. 5). What he means here is unclear. We were not on a hill, and I did not tell Settlemire to assist with the evacuation or resupply. I did not meet either Mock or Settlemire after the meeting with them and the other platoon leaders, and they were not in my vicinity when the enemy launched their attack.

Phil also wrote that the enemy caught us in a crossfire from three sides. We only received fire from the north, from the wood-line along the creek. There was much fire against that wood-line from the south and southwest, but this was friendly (Mock, p. 6). Phil may have the compass direction wrong as he does on his sketches attached to the article. For example, he has the Song Banh Lai River flowing towards the north when it flowed in an easterly direction, turning slightly northeast before it exited the valley where it again turned east. The scale used for Phil's sketches is also wrong—the distances are more significant.

Soldiers can become confused and mixed up under combat stress, and it is often difficult to piece together an accurate picture of what happened. On page nine of his book, *About Face*, Hackworth wrote that in battle, a soldier's perception is only as broad as his battle sights. He continues that five soldiers near each other will tell different stories of what happened, even within hours.

My recollection of what happened is quite different from what Phil wrote. Notes I made in my field notebook on the evening of 10 February support my memory. Phil provides no exact time for some of his critical actions, and this exacerbates the problem. When was Staff Sergeant Reda evacuated, when did his group start to join the company, when did he move the 4th Platoon, when did he leave the creek, and finally, when did he reach the rendezvous location on the knoll?

Until his article, I was almost sure Phil had moved the 4th Platoon after meeting me, when I ordered him to set up an LZ. The differences between Phil's account and my recollections are devastating. In my view, it is impossible to square the situation on the ground with Phil's sequence of events. Based on his writing, I now believe Phil moved the 4th Platoon before meeting me at the so-called "veritable jungle of radio antennae". The facts he relates about when he moved the 4th Platoon—without my permission or knowledge—amounted to an intolerable interference in operations.

I directed Phil to set up a medevac and resupply LZ and then join the company. I told Settlemire to assume responsibility for a portion of the company perimeter we were about to establish.

Phil claims Settlemire was with him when all hell broke loose. This claim is probably correct. Settlemire had stayed behind with Otto and Beach when Phil left to set up the LZ, and as we broke up, he had started back with me, and I assumed he was heading for his platoon.

Settlemire was no longer with the command group when the firing started, indicating he knew where his troops were. He managed to rejoin some of them early in the fighting but died in the process. The most persuasive evidence that Phil Mock had failed to let me, or the other platoon leaders, know what he had done with the 4th Platoon is that two platoons and the command group—as the point element—would not have headed for the wood-line if we knew that the 4th Platoon was no longer there.

The relocation of the 4th Platoon was the deadliest mistake of the operation. It allowed a daring and professional enemy commander to move some of his forces to envelop our company and attack us from behind at our most vulnerable moment.

When I talked to Second Lieutenant Otto after the operation, he was sure the enemy had not shifted troops confronting either his or Beach's platoons, as it would have been virtually impossible for him not to notice such movement. He believed the unit that struck our rear came from further up the valley to our west. I agreed with this assessment.

I had not explicitly told Phil who was to provide LZ security, but he had been my XO for three months and knew what our SOP said; in fact, he was the author. The alternate command group, the attached engineers, and the 4.2-inch mortar forward observer section provided security for medevac and resupply when delivered outside the company perimeter. Sometimes, the medics who were not deployed with the platoons were also used for security. If he needed additional security, Phil should have requested extra forces from me.

The platoons were responsible for bringing their casualties to the evacuation site. In resupply, platoon personnel helped break down the supplies and brought them to their respective units. These were also available as extra security. Phil worked directly with the platoon leaders in arranging this, or more often, Macias would do so by working with the platoon sergeants.

I had strong words with Phil about this action after the operation. Still, at that time, I did not know what I learned years later, including the past two years, as Lieutenant Colonel Perrine provided me with excerpts from the battalion SJ, battalion AA report, the Faulkner article, and the *Army Times* articles dealing with this action. Phil never told me he had moved the 4th Platoon away from the fighting scene and its security mission. If he had, I would have questioned his sanity and probably relieved him of his duties. Instead, with what I knew at the time of the engagement, I considered his action a grave and unfortunate mistake and severe breaches of our SOP and let him know my feelings about the incident.

I did not press the matter. I had made a whole series of deadly mistakes myself and, in the final analysis, I was responsible for all the company did or failed to do. These two days had not been my best.

After I received a copy of Garland's book (I believe from Sergeant First Class Jack) in late 1969, I was encouraged by some members of 2/502 to write a correction to the information in that book. I told them I had considered doing so but had rejected the idea since some might interpret it as self-serving and an attempt to shift the blame for what happened that night to a subordinate. However, the events of that period are now far enough in the past for me to present my version of events as I remember them, supported by other information not available to me before I began this work.

The 1st Platoon was engaged in furious combat on our left, with at least one squad pinned down in the open. The small group I assumed was heading for the LZ had become intermingled with the command group. The left flank of the 1st Platoon attacked and managed to reach the creek to the west of our location. Part of the 2nd Platoon was pinned down in the open to our rear. A few 2nd Platoon members were located near the command group. The bulk of the 2nd Platoon was behind a slightly elevated piece of ground—which I shall refer to as a knoll—about 200 meters south of our location. Phil's group also had their hands full, as indicated by heavy firing to our right.

Except for the left flank of the 1st Platoon reaching the creek line, minimal movement had taken place since the enemy's surprise attack. In those early moments, the moves were by men crawling to the nearest depression to escape the storm of grazing fire. The opening volley and the scramble to find some cover dispersed the units. It was virtually impossible to gain control in the black of night. Men stayed where they were, hugging protection and waiting for some directions.

Since it was impossible to employ artillery in this mass confusion, I had First Lieutenant Tom Clements turn his radio to the battalion command frequency. The only person we could reach was Tom Taylor. I told him we were in trouble and requested he forward the report to Emerson, who was on the ground at the new battalion forward CP location. I cautioned Tom not to move to our position in the dark. That could be precisely what the NVA wanted him to do. This call must have taken place shortly after 1900 hours.[6]

We were receiving hand grenades from the wood-line, an unbelievable number of hand grenades. The enemy was using potato-masher grenades, and some of these were of poor quality and did not explode. One hit my left leg and bounced in the direction of Specialist 4 Ellis without exploding. However, more than enough of them detonated. The enemy commander must have decided to eliminate the company's close-in elements pinned down in the initial furious salvos.

It was now fully dark and the area looked like the mass night firepower demonstrations at Fort Benning. Gun flashes, tracers, and explosions were everywhere. We had still not seen an enemy, only gun flashes from the whole length of the tree line. Occasionally, an M79 grenade fired by our men would explode and briefly light up a small portion of the creek line.

The gun flashes and explosions played hell with our night vision. Flat on the ground, we also could not see each other.

I asked Ellis to try to contact the platoon leaders. He was unable to contact Otto and Beach but managed to reach the 4th Platoon. He handed me the handset and I talked to the acting platoon sergeant. I told him to bring his platoon into the woods along the creek and begin working on the enemy's left flank. If that was not possible, I instructed him to bring everyone into the grove of trees west of the proposed LZ and link up with First Lieutenant Beach. I asked him to give Mock this information.

Specialist 4 Ellis was bringing M16 fire on some of the enemy positions. He carried—by my direction—a disproportionate amount of tracer rounds in his magazines. The reason was that this would help us mark targets for the platoons. Ellis's fire resulted in increased incoming fire at the command group. One trooper had an arm wound and bled profusely before we were able to stop it. A soldier from the 1st Platoon, who had become intermingled with the command group, was unconscious from a mortar round concussion and we thought he was dead.

A hand grenade landed a few feet away from me and the explosion caused me to blackout for a few seconds. When I came to, I felt a warm and sticky substance on my face and neck. I could tell it was blood by touching it and then licking my fingers. The bleeding appeared to come from my ears.

Time seems to stand still when you are in a situation full of danger and terror. You lose track of how much time has passed and it all seems unreal. Thoughts of despair raced through my mind as I figured we were about to be defeated in detail and overrun. I had an overwhelming feeling of guilt for those in my command killed. The situation at that time looked like an unmitigated disaster.

I had to force all those thoughts from my mind and focus instead on rectifying the situation. My immediate concerns were the safety of the command group and regaining effective control of the company. The command group and the troops intermingled with it were on the ground in an area smaller than a basketball court. Slowly, my thought process emerged from the terror and despair around us. I do not know how long this period of agonizing self-doubt lasted. It felt like an eternity, but it was probably a matter of minutes.

It was obviously up to me as the commander to decide what to do and make the first move. It was also evident we could not remain where we were, within hand-grenade range of the wood-line and entirely immobilized by many automatic weapons. It was not possible to withdraw across the open field swept by enemy and friendly grazing fire.[7]

The only thing I knew was that if we remained where we were or withdrew, we would probably all end up dead. The only other option was to go forward and close with the enemy. I knew our chances of making it were poor, but we should at least try to take some of our opponents with us if we were to die. The element of surprise was in our favor, as I was sure the enemy would not expect us to attack.

If we lived to talk about this fight, the story would sound better if we aggressively attacked rather than tried to slither away. However, it was not a courageous decision, but one born out of a pure survival instinct. It was—as I saw it then and now—the only course of action that gave us a chance to live.

I waited for a momentary lull in the massive fire directed at the wood-line by the 2nd Platoon to avoid having my troops mowed down by the friendly fire. I did not know how many soldiers were still in my immediate vicinity or, for that matter, how many could or would follow me in this desperate dash, but I yelled over my shoulder that we were going for the enemy wood-line and for everyone to fire as they moved.

The next few minutes were a blurry nightmare. As I ran for the wood-line, firing my M16 straight ahead, a nearby explosion sent some small fragments into my upper right side and torso—wounds I would take considerable ribbing about in the future. Fortunately, I hardly noticed the shrapnel at the time—the last small fragment that worked itself to the surface was removed by doctors in the 1990s.

Glances over my shoulders confirmed I was not alone. Shadowy figures firing their weapons were following me on the right and left. We reached the wood-line and tumbled into the creek in the middle of a group of NVA soldiers who, I am sure, were just as shocked to see us as we were. The next few moments were chaotic and it is hopeless to reconstruct what happened.

It is near impossible for anyone who has not experienced close-quarter combat in the pitch-black of night to understand its sheer confusion, fear, and horror. It is equally difficult for a participant to explain or describe. We managed to clear a small section of the creek bed, but two more soldiers were lightly wounded. The artillery forward observer radio was also sporadically inoperable, probably because of water exposure. There were enemy bodies in the creek. We did not know how many, nor did we care at the time.

I managed to contact Phil Mock by radio after we set up in the creek bed. He reported he was also in the creek bed to our right with his group. That included the engineers and the 4th Platoon. I was worried troops firing up and down the creek might inflict casualties on each other.

This is 6, I need to find out how close you are to my group. I want you to call out my name as loud as you can.

They were safe from our fire if I could not hear his call above the other battlefield noises. Phil did what I asked.

This is 5, I do not think much of your idea. My calls resulted in a rain of grenades. I will get back to you after we sort things out. I had not heard Phil's calls, which confirmed in my mind that he was outside the range of our weapons, but I was still unable to contact Beach and Otto on the radio.[8]

The enemy was also obviously in a state of confusion. Their commander had undoubtedly hoped that, after catching most of us in the open, we would try to withdraw, thereby enabling him to inflict heavy casualties. The enemy commander had no doubt planned to follow up such withdrawal with an attack of his own.

Instead of making a withdrawal, we had attacked at several points and become intermingled with his forces. The command group had split his command in two near the center of his line. Elements of Otto's platoon and Phil Mock's group had entered the creek bed at or near his right and left flanks, respectively. I suspected the enemy commander found himself losing control of a situation unfolding in an unexpected manner.

For those of us in the command group, the creek bed had become untenable because of enemy fire and hand grenades. We both preferred to use hand grenades in this kind of close-in fighting since they did not give away the user's position. They also produced more terror than rifle fire since, although you could hear them land, it was difficult to see where they ended up in the dark. We crawled out of the creek and onto the banks—six on the south bank and Tom Clements, his RTO, and two soldiers on the north bank.

I took stock of the situation and the troops I had with me. There were 10 of us. Five of these had wounds, and we only had one fully operational radio. We were still receiving heavy fire, most appearing to be friendly. I told my men not to return fire from the south or southwest as those were our units' locations. The only immediate precaution we could take was to find ground depressions and stay low.

I used our last operational radio to try to contact my subordinates. This call took place shortly after 2100 hours.[9] I was able to reach Mock and made the first contact with Otto since the firing had begun. Mock stated his group was still in the creek bed with NVA soldiers all around. He recommended I bring the 3rd Platoon forward and divert B/2/502 to our aid.

Otto stated his unit had cleared about 75 meters of the creek to our west. He was still missing about 40 percent of his troops. He believed most of them were with the 2nd Platoon. I told him that four of his people were with the command group. After 10 minutes, I was able to communicate with Karl Beach. He said he could account for about 65 or 70 percent of his troops. He had some personnel from the 1st Platoon but did not know how many. He had collected his troops in a tight perimeter on the small knoll mentioned earlier. I described our location as best I could and cautioned both Otto and Beach not to fire in our direction unless they had specific targets or came under attack. These directions resulted in a significant reduction in incoming small arms fire. Beach recommended all try to reach his location on the knoll.

After considering the situation, I made several decisions and communicated these to my subordinates shortly after 2115 hours. First, I decided not to bring up the 3rd Platoon or ask that B/2/502 come to our assistance. I assumed that many of our small groups of troops were without radios. To bring the two units forward in the dark was to invite a collision with some of these groups. Also, I felt sure the enemy was in the area in strength and we had to assume they knew the location of possible reinforcements. It was a favorite NVA tactic to heavily pressure one unit and then ambush the relieving force. The enemy commander had already demonstrated considerable daring and aggressiveness, and I did not want to expose a relieving force to another ambush.[10]

There is an SJ entry on 092140 February that has me confused. It states that the 2nd Platoon was trying to locate me without success. I had just talked to First Lieutenant Beach about 30 minutes earlier, described our location, and he said nothing about searching for us.

I now believed we could hold our own until daylight, at which time I expected the enemy to have broken contact. I did not want to illuminate the battlefield, as it would be more advantageous to the enemy than us by making it more difficult for personnel to make it back to their units under cover of darkness. Second, I ordered all groups to concentrate at Beach's location.

The knoll was about 200 meters from the surrounding wood-lines (not 50 meters as Phil states), and the enemy could place effective small arms fire on it without exposing themselves. On the other hand, the cleared areas around the knoll provided first-class killing zones for any ground attack. To alleviate the danger of mortar and small arms fire from the wood-line, I told Karl to prioritize digging in, using the quick "spider-hole" technique, unless the ground was too hard.

I was beginning to feel more confident that if we could re-assemble significant portions of the company, we could defeat an enemy attack across the open ground. The knowledge there were no reinforcements headed in our direction could make the enemy commander attempt such an assault before daylight. An enemy surprise attack against the knoll from the north was problematic since he had to assume those of us along the creek line would alert the rest of the company of such an attack. What had looked like an utter disaster a short while ago began to appear manageable and even held out the possibility we could inflict heavy casualties on the enemy if he tried an attack. Although I had no firm information on our losses, I felt they must have been substantial.

I told both Otto and Mock not to leave anyone behind when moving to Beach's location. I felt sure this caution was unnecessary, but my earlier experience with the 3rd Platoon was still fresh in my mind. However, Sergeant Bear's three initial searches show that Phil Mock's group completely ignored this warning.

The enemy had pinpointed our location because of the noise I made on the radio, despite keeping my voice as low as possible. We again started receiving fire from automatic weapons and incoming grenades. Fragments from one grenade hit the right side of my neck. Although painful, this wound presented no immediate danger since it had not severed any major arteries. We replied to the enemy fire mostly with grenades whenever we felt we had a target. Except when clearing the creek bed, we had still not seen the enemy. I became concerned about the amount of ammunition we had left and told my people to conserve and fire only when they had specific targets.

Intermittent exchanges of gunfire and grenades continued for the next two hours. Two soldiers from the 1st Platoon joined our group at about 2300 hours, one with a minor wound. Two more soldiers from our original group also received minor injuries. This fact made it, in my view, virtually impossible to try to get back to the designated company rendezvous point in one trip since two of our wounded were unable to walk on their own.

In any case, I was in no hurry to leave as I felt we were serving our unit best in our present location, right in the middle of the enemy line. I felt our presence in that location presented the enemy commander with severe communication and coordination problems. We could also pour flanking fire into an enemy attack against the knoll. The enemy commander had demonstrated he was a true professional and I was relying on him not to try to overrun our group. To do so would be a waste of resources and reveal his intentions. I assumed he was after bigger fish and figured he could quickly dispose of us if he were successful in taking the knoll.

One enemy automatic weapon to our west—believed to be a light machine gun—was especially troublesome. It took us more than half an hour to silence it since it was outside hand-grenade range.

At about 0100 hours, we heard movements in our direction in the creek bed from our west. Since our last remaining radio was now inoperable—probably because of battery failure—we could not contact the 1st Platoon to determine if anyone from that unit had managed to get as far east as our location. I doubted what we heard were troops from the 1st Platoon. The firing from the direction of their previous position had only been intermittent since midnight, and I believed Otto would have taken advantage of the lull to move his unit to Karl Beach's location. Nevertheless, we could not take the chance of killing our people. Our small group was entirely out of hand grenades and we were dangerously low on M16 ammunition.

I decided to take two men with me into the creek and wait for whoever was approaching. The two soldiers' names are not in my notes, but I remember that they were the Artillery Reconnaissance Sergeant Miser and Specialist 4 Ellis, but I am unsure about this. It was even darker in the creek than on the bank because of the dense foliage. One man went to the far side of the stream while his companion and I waited on the near side. We could hear movement coming towards us, and when they were about 15–20 feet away, we heard them whisper in Vietnamese. This was the indication we had waited for, and my two companions opened fire on the group. I did not fire because one of the soldiers who accompanied me managed to get in my way. Although I did not know it at the time, this proved fortunate within less than a minute. If I had fired, I might not have inserted a new magazine in the weapon while in the creek bed.

The muzzle flashes from the M16 lit up the creek bed briefly and I could see the lead enemy soldier and the silhouettes of several others behind him. Most of them managed to escape on the north side of the creek. Clements and his companions then engaged them. Several NVA soldiers must have been killed or wounded in that hail of bullets. It was over in less than 20 seconds and we received no return fire.

We did not linger in the creek bed for fear of enemy grenades. We had lost our night vision temporarily due to the muzzle flashes. As we were in the process of crawling back onto the south bank, flares began to light up the sky, and the night virtually turned to daylight.[11] I looked back up the creek and saw an enemy soldier about 30–40 feet away on the opposite bank. He had his AK-47 lifted and pointed in our direction. Some troops on the bank had come forward to help the rest of us out of the creek. We presented a compact target for automatic fire. Again, it seemed that time stood still and what happened took an eternity. It probably took no more than a few seconds.

The enemy soldier seemed unsure of what to do. At first, he partially lowered his weapon and then raised it again. The others in our group had not yet seen him. I must have turned quickly in his direction and fired without raising my weapon to my shoulder to aim. The first rounds hit his right leg and practically tore it off. Other bullets hit his mid-section and chest, and these set off grenades or ammunition he was carrying. The result was a series of explosions, which tore him entirely apart. It all seemed to happen in slow motion, as it does in my dreams, except in my dreams there are no sounds.

One of the soldiers from the 1st Platoon—with a minor wound—who had joined us earlier that night must have thought all this activity meant we were about to be overrun and decided to take his chances by escape and evasion. He was lucky to make it back to the 2nd Platoon position, where he allegedly reported the NVA had destroyed the whole command group.

The flares that started illuminating the battlefield caused an increase in small arms fire. I could see no movement at or near the knoll designated as the assembly point, nor was any fire coming from that location. There was only sporadic firing around us and most of that came from places where we assumed isolated groups of friendly troops were.

Without communications, we were not aware of what was happening to the rest of the company. Since firing after midnight was light and sporadic, I believed most troops from the 1st Platoon had made it to Beach's location. The enemy's most opportune time to try to assault that position had passed, and I concluded the movements we heard around our area were evidence they were in the process of withdrawing.

We spotted flashing red lights to our south several times after midnight, indicating the 2nd Platoon guided troops to its location. We used McFann's flashlight to try to draw attention to ourselves but without success.

Mock wrote in his article that he saw our flashing light after he "radioed the commanding officer's operator with instructions to blink a flashlight equipped with a red filter three times to the south." Despite this observation, Phil wrote, "Sergeant Bear made three fruitless searches."[12] I do not remember any calls from Mock after 2115 hours, and after 0100 hours we only had one radio on the south bank that only operated sporadically for a minute or two each time.

Concerning the "three fruitless searches," Specialist 5 Faulkner and the *Army Times* article explain them in detail in their story about Private First Class Norris Maultie Jr., who spent a terrifying night surrounded by NVA troops. There were, in fact, four searches, but only the last involved looking for the command group. The first three searches were in the area vacated by Mock and his group.[13] Mock and his men were still in the creek at 2115 hours. They must have departed shortly afterward without notifying the command group its eastern flank was now open.

The first three searches by Sergeant Bear's squad (3rd Squad, 2nd Platoon) were in the area vacated by Lieutenant Mock. On the first search, they found one dead soldier on the bank of the creek.

They brought the body back to the knoll and returned for a second search, which located another body in the same area. This soldier was initially with Norris. Again, they took the body to the knoll. Finally, at midnight, Bear's men found a wounded engineer on the third search and brought him to safety. The withdrawal appears to have been overly hasty and disorganized because of the abandonment of two KIAs, one wounded engineer, and Norris in that retreat. Mock, or possibly Macias, who appeared to have been in his group, must have realized this when they reached the knoll, and they sent Bear and his men to search for them. But why did Mock find it necessary to write that the searches were for the command group when the first three were in the area he had abandoned?

I am sure we could have made it back to the 2nd Platoon after 2300 hours. However, it would have been difficult to bring along those with serious injuries, and we would not leave them. I could also have made it back by myself, but leaving my group was the wrong thing to do under the circumstances.

I knew from the flashing red lights that Karl was at the company rendezvous point, although we had not seen any movements when flares lit up the battlefield. They were doing the right thing by staying low and not revealing their positions. I also hoped Otto had joined Beach. They were perfectly capable of handling any problems. I felt the situation was well in hand compared to what it was earlier. We were giving our wounded as much treatment as they could receive at Beach's location. I decided to wait for daylight.

Around 0230 hours, there was some heavy firing to the west. We believed it came from where the 1st Platoon had entered the creek the previous evening. It lasted for about a minute and sounded like M16 fire, but we could not be sure.

At about 0245 hours, we again heard movement towards us from the west. We had collected the ammunition from those most wounded and redistributed it, but it still left less than two magazines per man.

The movement toward our position this time was along the southern bank of the creek. We estimated that at least 8–10 people were moving in our direction. Again, there was a possibility the group was friendly, particularly since they were approaching our area along the south bank. However, the recent resurgence in firing to our west left us uneasy. I passed the word for no one to open fire before I did. It was not until the group was about 20–30 feet from our location that we determined they were friendly troops by the shape of their helmets and load-bearing equipment. We blinked the red-filtered flashlight in their direction. It turned out to be Sergeant Donald Bear and his squad. Faulkner and the *Army Times* article confirm this was the fourth search but that it took place on the creek's north bank and that the search found four men. While First Lieutenant Clements and his three men were on the north bank, seven additional troops were on the south bank.

With Sergeant Bear and his men's help, we could bring our casualties back to the 2nd Platoon location in one trip by 0310 hours. Mock and most of the 4th Platoon had made it to the 2nd Platoon location, as had Otto and the 1st Platoon. We were still missing some men, and two squads were out searching for them. The last missing troops were located well after daylight.

The SJ gives a fluctuating number of missing soldiers. These numbers indicate some confusion on the knoll. Mock's report at 092235 February mentions 90 troops on the knoll with only 8–10 missing. Our strength in the field was about 180 plus attachments. The 3rd Platoon with about 50 was still at the valley entrance, so where are the rest? Sixteen minutes later—092301 February—90 are still present on the knoll with 10–11 missing. The revised number of missing in the journal at 092345 has the figure rising to 12. By 100050, there were only four missing, and this dropped to one at 100055, five minutes later. In addition to the discrepancy between missing and present in the field, all reports excluded 11 in the command group. Maybe they did not consider us missing. Furthermore, we still had personnel missing when I came to the knoll at 0310 hours. I was later told the battalion staff was confused. I believe those on the knoll may have failed to count the dead and wounded.

I was utterly exhausted and sat down to eat a can of cold C-rations while Macias brought me up to date on the company's situation. He told me who had been killed and severely wounded and who were still missing. There were five dead—Sergeants John D. Bowman III and W. Cooley, Privates First Class J. M. Mincey and J. P. Price, and First Lieutenant William D. Settlemire. Macias did not have a count of the wounded but said he would find out.

A medic put a dressing on my neck wound. My left shoulder was in pain and I had no feeling in my left arm. I figured I had hit the ground too hard and too often in the past 18 hours—a right-handed man tends to hit the ground with the left shoulder to be ready to fire his weapon. The medic fixed a sling for the arm.

I was worn out from two nights without sleep and relief at being safe with the company from the ordeal in the creek, and it finally got to me. The last I remember is Macias asking if I wanted to go and see the dead and wounded. I told him yes, in a couple of minutes. I woke up to the sounds of incoming helicopters. I felt terrible about falling asleep, as I had wanted to visit both the fallen and talk to the wounded.

Emerson was the first to land at our location. I had half expected a reprimand but, in his typical fashion, he lavished praise on the company. In the presence of the troops, Emerson also stated he had recommended me for a Silver Star for the 4 March action and was submitting a DSC proposal for the fighting just concluded. To this day, I believe I did nothing except what a company commander should do in those circumstances. Furthermore, I had not even done that well during the previous two days. The mistakes I made from the outset by not heeding well-established military principles and the problems this caused during the fighting should be evident to all readers. There was no doubt in my mind the enemy had dealt us a setback despite gallant and heroic conduct by our troops and our enormous air and artillery superiority. That was the conclusion then and now.[14]

I briefed Emerson on our status and then discussed the plans for the day. I guess I looked ragged with bandages on my neck, arm in a sling, and wearing muddy, bloody, and torn jungle fatigues. Emerson insisted on taking me to the brigade aid station, but I was adamant about staying with the company.

As it appeared I was losing the argument, I took him aside, pointing out that I believed it would be good for unit morale if I stayed. He bought that and relented.

We evacuated 11 wounded soldiers, but 17 walking wounded refused evacuation. We located the last missing troops during Emerson's visit. Medevac and resupply helicopters were also arriving.[15]

There are 14 wounded listed on the 9 February MR.[16] My notes show 11 wounded evacuated on 10 February, but no names. Staff Sergeant Reda, evacuated before the main engagement began, is also on the MR. The other two could be casualties we sustained on the way to the battalion CP. The two soldiers evacuated from the battalion CP location on 10/11 February were soldiers who had initially decided to stay with the company. They were in so much pain that I had them evacuated, but they may not be on the MR, or they are listed, but those wounded on the way to the battalion CP are not listed. I do not know which scenario is right—only that there should be two additional soldiers evacuated.

As stated already, most of the soldiers with minor wounds decided to remain with the company and received treatment from the company medics. There was, unfortunately, one problem with this. Those who refused evacuation were not counted as wounded and therefore not eligible for a Purple Heart.[17] It made me proud, however, that they opted to stay with their unit

I estimated we could complete the enemy encampment search by 1000 hours when discussing future activities with Emerson. However, the chaplain that Emerson had left behind (Father (Major) William J. Barragy) asked my permission to hold a memorial service.[18] The service took longer than expected, and we therefore failed to destroy the enemy camp until around 1100 hours. With that task completed, I recommended we continue in a westerly direction and try to re-establish contact with what, in our judgment, had been significant elements of the 95th NVA Regiment.[19] I suggested we proceed west for about 4 kilometers and then turn southwest through what seemed to be a likely valley where the enemy might withdraw.

Emerson agreed with the concept but could only permit us to proceed westward for 4 kilometers and then turn north to the battalion forward CP because we lacked adequate artillery coverage to enter the other valley. He said he would try to displace an artillery battery to cover the valley in question but was not optimistic since another operation would start northwest of Tuy Hoa.

The enemy encampment search turned up numerous documents, clothing, and about 28,000 rounds of AK-47 ammunition. We also found some very severely damaged weapons at the campsite. The battlefield's sweep was disappointing, as we found only 17 NVA bodies and 17 individual weapons, plus two machine guns and one rocket-propelled grenade (RPG).

The enemy had made an orderly withdrawal and had no doubt taken their wounded along. We found about a dozen freshly dug graves on the west side of the enemy encampment. The battalion S-2 instructed us to open the graves. I became angry and told the S-2 I would not turn my troops into gravediggers unless ordered by Emerson as we had other more important things to do. I never heard from Emerson, but an unidentified station came on the air with the comment, *Watch your blood pressure, Hunter 6*. The voice was that of Bob Murphy.

The company started moving west through the valley at 1100 hours with the 1st Platoon in the lead. We encountered a suspected enemy squad where the valley divided, one branch running southwest and one north. A short firefight ensued. Only the lead platoon was involved. Two enemy soldiers died in this skirmish and their weapons were seized. We suffered four wounded. The contact strengthened my view that we would be likely to locate the enemy in the southwest valley. However, my request to move in that direction was denied because we lacked artillery support.

The company did not make any further contacts on its way to the battalion forward CP. We arrived there about 1600 hours on 10 February. Major Schroeder had killed a water buffalo earlier in the day and we received a feast of steaks. It was the toughest steak I ever ate.

After this meal, Schroeder and I had a private meeting where we discussed Lieutenant Mock. Schroeder observed that to spare Emerson from sanctioning Phil

Mock's relief, whose father was an active-duty lieutenant general, he could arrange Mock and Schoonover's transfer at the end of the operation. I told Don this was acceptable. I did not want to destroy their careers, especially not Jim Schoonover's; I just wanted them out of my company since they had lost my confidence and trust. If I had known what I know now, I might have given a different answer to Don's proposal. Schroeder kept his promise. The two officers left quickly.

I also talked to Macias about finding another job within the battalion for Sergeant First Class Ledford, platoon sergeant of the 3rd Platoon. This request was acted on, as described in the next chapter in endnote 3.

On 11 February, I took my company back to an area about 2 kilometers west of the 9/10 February action. We established a company patrol base from which we sent patrols into the mountains to the south and southwest to regain contact with the enemy. We had scattered contacts with small enemy units for the next four days but no significant engagements. These contacts resulted in three enemies killed, but not without losses, as we evacuated three of our wounded. Unfortunately, I have not found these listed on any readable MR.

In one of these minor engagements, we captured three small horses. I planned to turn them loose, but Emerson—always an innovator searching for fresh ideas—directed me to keep them as pack animals. We had many amusing incidents with these horses—known as "Macias's Cavalry." Once a Korean unit stole them. I guess they were going to kill and eat them. When my men went to reclaim them, it almost resulted in a firefight. We even brought them on helicopter assaults after the medics gave them shots to calm them down. It was always amusing to watch the expressions on helicopter pilots' faces as we led three horses, acting as if they had just consumed a bottle of vodka, up to the aircraft. They also allowed Macias and some of the troops to star in a couple of prime-time TV newscasts.

I recollect that Macias—with my tacit approval—turned them loose on our last operation north of Tuy Hoa. Macias remembers they ended up as dinners for the Koreans while I told Emerson that he lost them.

I became ill on 14 February. The neck wound had become infected—I was running a high fever, unable to keep food down, and had periods of hallucination. As my condition became worse, Macias sent word to Emerson on 16 February, who ordered me to report immediately to the brigade aid station. My evacuation is mentioned on the 22 February MR, six days after it occurred!

CHAPTER 13

Operations, 17 February–4 April 1966

AWOL from the Hospital

This chapter deals with two operations. First, it covers the activities of A/2/502 near Dong Tre from 26 February to 9 March 1966. Second, it includes the mountain operations of A/2/502 in the Tuy Hoa area from 9 March to 4 April. First, however, the chapter starts with my hospitalization on 16 February.

I arrived at the brigade aid station around 1600 hours on 16 February 1966. My neck wound had swollen to the size of a tomato. I received treatment for it and my injured shoulder, and went through the usual tests. By the following morning, I was still running a high fever, fluctuating between 101 and 104 despite having my wound lanced, cleaned out, and given antibiotics. After ruling out malaria, they decided to evacuate me to a facility that was better equipped. That was the 85th Evacuation Hospital in Qui Nhon. This move worried me because the 85th was often a stopover while awaiting evacuation to Japan.

I was evacuated by air to the 85th in Qui Nhon on 19 February, my temperature measuring 104 degrees. I was sick and had a miserable night (19/20 February), my temperature increasing to 105 degrees. I could tell my doctors and nurses were worried because they continuously looked after me throughout the night.

I went through more malaria tests and several tests for other known diseases for the next few days. The fact that I received different medicines almost every day indicated they did not know the cause of my fever. On the following nights (21 and 22 February), my temperature also reached 105, so they immersed me in water.

They began a new medication on 23 February. I do not know its name, but it gave me a chance to get some sleep, and the fever began to go down.

One doctor told me on 24 February that if I continued to improve, I would probably be allowed to go back to my unit the next day. However, on the 25th, a higher-ranking doctor told me they would evacuate me to Japan to determine what caused my fever even though I felt better. It was labeled a fever of unknown origin.

I felt very depressed at that news since I thought for sure I would lose my company. Captain Patrick Canary (his radio call sign was, of course, *Yellow Bird*), the battalion

S-3 Air showed up in an L-19. He brought my mail and a message from Lieutenant Colonel Emerson stating that since it looked like I would be away for some time, another captain would be assigned to my company as an operation was to begin on 26 February. Pat also told me that Schoonover and Mock were no longer in the company. That left Beach and Otto the only officers with combat experience, since the new company commander would come from staff.

I decided I had to do something to get out of the hospital that day. Captain Canary was to return with the L-19, which was waiting at the airfield. I saw that aircraft as my only chance to rejoin the company before the next operation, so I told Canary I would take the L-19 back to Tuy Hoa, and since it only had room for one passenger, I would send the aircraft back the next day to pick him up. I knew Pat had a friend on the hospital staff and would probably not object to spending an extra day there.

Canary's main worry was what Emerson would say. I told him not to worry; I would tell Emerson I pulled rank and took the aircraft. I did not wait for the afternoon doctor's visit but changed quickly into my jungle fatigues, grabbed the medicine sitting on my nightstand that had helped, and headed for the airfield.

I was back in Tuy Hoa by 1600 hours. Emerson was happy to see me and immediately canceled the planned change of command of the company. I explained to Emerson I had left the hospital without being discharged and confiscated Canary's L-19 to return to Tuy Hoa. I had already arranged for that aircraft to pick up Canary the following day.

Seventeen years ago, Emerson wrote:

> He [me] was once wounded and refused evacuation until his wound became infected. After a brief stay at a field hospital and before healing, he went AWOL from the hospital and made his way back to his company. That one act says more about the quality of Hank Lunde than he would ever say about himself.[1]

The hospital did raise a fuss and threatened to act. Emerson and Brigadier General Pearson told me to forget their threats, but the incident caused other problems over the years. I had come to Vietnam on TDY orders at the beginning of June 1965 and had, therefore, not brought my medical and dental records. I figured they would arrive with the brigade. They did not. For that reason, the brigade aid station had to create a temporary medical file on 16 February 1966, and it accompanied me to the evacuation hospital. These temporary records were never returned, even after returning to the U.S. and despite numerous requests by my new unit, the Airborne, Electronic, and Special Warfare Board at Fort Bragg and the Test and Evaluation Command (TECOM) to Vietnam through Medical Command. The only record found by the Medical Command was a log from the brigade aid station, showing my treatment there before I evacuated to the 85th Evacuation Hospital.

Operations near Dong Tre

Intelligence reports claimed that a large NVA force was assembling inland from the SF camp at Dong Tre (Trung Luong Valley), about 40 kilometers northwest of Tuy Hoa. That is where the next battalion operation took place. The battalion mission was to engage the NVA force and provide protection for the SF camp.

The operation began on 26 February. A/2/502 was the last to be inserted, with a strength of 169 troops plus attachments, according to my notes. The only thing unusual about the landing was that the helicopters did not set down, and the soldiers had to exit while the choppers were 6–10 feet above the ground. Unfortunately, exiting at this height caused two soldiers to sprain their ankles. Since they had difficulty walking, we sent them back on a helicopter in the afternoon.

A/2/502 was initially in reserve, pending the arrival of two Civilian Irregular Defense Group (CIDG) companies from Dong Tre, with SF advisers. Those companies would be under my operational control for the duration of the operation. However, they did not join us until 1 March. The battalion did not make any contact on 26 February or the following day.

We proceeded northwest into the eastern part of the Trung Luong Valley on 28 February. While it was rough going, we had no contacts, but several Vietnamese were detained and turned over to the two companies of CIDG when they joined us.

The company spent the night of 28 February/1 March on a mountaintop overlooking the Trung Luong Valley. It was a mosquito-infested area and the troops did not get much sleep. This location is where the 2/327th fought a battle with the NVA in 1967, involving significant 1st Air Cavalry Division elements. This bloody engagement is covered in Brigadier General S. L. A. Marshall's book *Vietnam: Three Battles*.[2]

My company searched the southern bank of the river that runs through the valley for the next few days, as far west as 11 kilometers. We were not permitted to cross to the north side of the river. After descending the mountain ridge, we linked up with the two CIDG companies. Again, we had no enemy contact.

On 3 March, helicopters moved us to an area about 40 kilometers north of Tuy Hoa in the afternoon. A/2/502 was initially in reserve around the battalion CP. The rest did not last long since Emerson sent us on foot to the northwest. The company moved in three columns during darkness on 4 March, and that afternoon we set up in three mutually supporting camps. The camps were moved again after dark to confuse any enemies that might be observing us.

We continued westward the next day—5 March—for another 5 kilometers. One column ran into a small VC force, killing four and capturing two. That night we killed an additional VC and caught five suspects. I assembled the company that night to be ready for helicopter extraction the following morning. My troops did not sustain any casualties in the two skirmishes.

We moved to Tuy Hoa Airfield at about noon on 6 March and became brigade reserve. One prisoner we brought back jumped out of the helicopter on the way. The prisoner undoubtedly died in the 1,500-foot drop.

I received permission to conduct an informal company-level investigation rather than having it done at battalion or brigade. Some troops who had been on the helicopter—Staff Sergeant Laguana and his squad—were not happy about this investigation. They asked Macias to bring their feelings to my attention. I told Macias, who was also worried about my safety, to let those involved know that I would withdraw from the investigation if they did not think I could be impartial and turn it back to the battalion. I also asked him to tell Laguana that I was greatly disappointed by his behavior and lack of moral courage in not bringing his gripes directly to me. On the other hand, if they preferred to keep it at the company level, I did not want to hear any more malarkey, and for Macias to pass that on also.

I questioned the troops, who had been on the helicopter, and the two pilots, and there were no discrepancies in their stories. I felt terrible about the incident and issued orders to secure all prisoners moved by helicopter inside the aircraft in the future. I believe this precaution became a brigade policy.[3]

Lieutenant Colonel Emerson told me during the Dong Tre operation that he would be assigned as Director of Instruction at Fort Benning after his tour in Vietnam. He wanted to know if I would accompany him and offered to write a letter to Major General Robert H. York (1913–1988). I held off giving an immediate answer since I was expecting to receive orders soon for my next assignment and I wanted to see what they had in mind for me. Emerson ended up going to the Pentagon so, for once, I had made the right decision.

Tuy Hoa

We remained in the dunes near Tuy Hoa until 9 March. I was sick two nights while there and had severe vomiting, but otherwise felt fine. Brigadier General John R. Deane, who had commanded my battle group in Berlin as a colonel, visited us. He was now the Chief of Staff of II Field Force. We had a long talk and brought each other up to date on some of the other officers who had served in Berlin.

Emerson traveled to Thailand for R&R on 9 March. Captain Murphy became the aide-de-camp to some general about the same time. Captain Taylor was already selected to go to Hong Kong as a liaison officer to the British. Taylor's XO, First Lieutenant Lou Sill, became commander of B/2/502, and Captain Pat Canary took over after Bob Murphy. I do not remember seeing Major Arthur Taylor after I returned from the hospital, so he may also have left, and that explains why Emerson offered me the S-3 position later in the month.

A/2/502 was alerted on 8 March to move 25 kilometers north from the Tuy Hoa Airfield to provide security for two artillery batteries and conduct patrolling activities to the south and west. C/2/502 received this mission, but since it had a new commander, A/2/502 got the task, although we remained brigade reserve.

I received a call from Brigadier General Pearson on 10 March, stating he had a mission for me. I was to take half the company on a helicopter assault and cross-country approach to a peninsula where we had been in early January. There were reports of a company of VC on that peninsula. I do not know the nature of this intelligence. Signal Intelligence (SIGINT) may have been the source for which company commanders did not have the required security clearance.

As the war progressed, I became more and more skeptical of these reports since most of them turned out to be dry holes. I guessed the NVA and VC were aware of our SIGINT capability and left a radio on some mountaintop that came on periodically, causing us many unsuccessful operations in the 101st Airborne Division and 9th Infantry Division in 1968.

I went on the operation early on 10 March to about 20 kilometers north of the artillery we were securing. I told the general I was skeptical about the intelligence report since no VC commander would be caught dead on that narrow peninsula, an easily sealed place, leaving him with his back to the sea.

We did not find the VC company and were back at the artillery location by 1900 hours. However, we did run into a VC squad on our return. We sustained two wounded in the ensuing firefight, and two others received injuries in the rough terrain we traversed. We received sniper fire all the way back to the artillery position but could not close with the elusive enemy. We felt sure we killed four VC but captured only one weapon.

We received orders, already on 11 March, for another operation southwest of Tuy Hoa to begin after midnight on 13 March. We were relieved of our brigade reserve mission, which was given to C/2/502. The first part of the operation was a night helicopter assault at the base of a 750-meter mountain. Then we had to climb up the boulder-strewn hillside to the top—hillsides that we knew from previous experience contained numerous mines and booby traps. Two of the helicopters carrying the company had a near mid-air collision in the dark. Again, I believe we were chasing some SIGINT reports.

There was a night B-52 drop on the top of the ridge further west early on 14 March. It took place at about 0500 hours. By that time, my company was back from the mountaintop after finding nothing, seeing no enemy, and suffering no casualties from booby traps.

A/2/502 became brigade reserve while B/2/502 and C/2/502 checked the results of the B-52 strike. As I recall, they found nothing at the strike site except blown-down trees and large craters.

Emerson returned from his R&R in Bangkok on 15 March. He showed me an engagement ring he had purchased for a lady friend who was a military widow. Florence and I had met both at a dinner at Pinehurst, NC, in 1967. They also visited

Florence at our home in Fayetteville in 1969 after Emerson had returned to duty from the wounds he sustained in September 1968. Nothing came of the engagement.

Emerson again brought up the subject of making me his S-3. He said I had been in command of a company longer than any other officer in the brigade. He and Brigadier General Pearson were concerned I would be killed if I continued as a company commander due to my aggressive behavior. I told him my demise was possible, but I felt I might save others with all I had learned over the past months. Moreover, I was still looking for a last big fight in the next two months before it was my time to rotate back to the U.S. He dropped the subject with the statement that I should take R&R to recharge my batteries.

I do not remember who the S-3 for the remainder of our time in Tuy Hoa was, our operations at Phan Thiet, or on the Cambodian border. I know Captain Ron Brown was assigned to the S-3 section at Phan Thiet and remained in that position until 18 May. However, he was not the S-3 since he was a junior captain. Many majors were eager for such a key position.

The next day—16 March 1966—was my 30th birthday. I sat on a knoll near my CP, feeling sorry for myself, thinking there were better places I could have spent the birthday. However, there were a couple of packages from the U.S. and my family in Norway. I shared these with the troops.[4] In the end, the birthday turned out to be one I would never forget.

Macias and the other NCOs had two cakes made up in the brigade rear area and they brought them out on a resupply helicopter. Macias and the platoon sergeants brought the cakes up to the CP. There was enough for every man in the company to have a slice. They also brought several cases of beer.

Before I could enjoy the cake and beer, the battalion S-4, Captain Cain Bridgeman, called. He was in a jam, as he was trying to bring resupplies to the other two companies that were exploiting the B-52 strike. The request, based on my familiarity with that treacherous terrain, was a dangerous mission. The resupply of the first company came off without a hitch despite high winds. For the second company, we could not land and had to lower the supplies. A strong wind gust took the helicopter down between the trees, and the pilot notified us he did not think he could get out. He tried and succeeded, but the rotor blades hit and cut the trees' upper limbs in the process. Later in March, my company lost a helicopter under similar circumstances in the strong, shifting, gusty winds near the top of the mountains.

When I returned to the company, I sat down with the NCOs to consume the cakes and very depleted beer supply. I also gave thanks for not having ended my birthday on the boulder-strewn mountainside.

The next day two generals visited us. One may have been Major General York, as I recall meeting him while at Tuy Hoa. The other was Pearson. He brought up the subject of me leaving the company. He must have talked to Emerson and stated

I had done everything in Vietnam except being severely wounded or killed. He said he had a responsibility to the service to pull me out of the field to "preserve me."

I figured that, since the general had become involved and he used those words, my chances of staying in the company had just taken a sharp downturn. I had to quickly muster up someone of higher rank on my side somehow. I had heard Pearson was a religious man, so I told him a divine power had kept me protected thus far and I would like to put my experience to use in another encounter with the NVA. He just nodded and went on to another subject. I admit I was not entirely confident my response would do the trick, but the fact is I remained with A/2/502 until my tour in Vietnam ended.

My company went on an operation in the lowlands southeast of Tuy Hoa on 19 March. We expected the operation to last one day, but instead it lasted 10 days, not ending until 30 March. We engaged a VC force, estimated at 30 troops, on 20 March. We did not suffer any casualties, and the enemy withdrew as I sent one platoon to flank them. We found one enemy KIA.

The following day I was ordered to take two platoons and ascend a 750-meter mountain. I protested my company's use, but Emerson replied I came from a country full of mountains and was, therefore, the most qualified. I replied that Norway was mountainous but had no snipers or booby traps that I knew about. Emerson laughed but let the order stand.

As I was returning from the battalion, my RTO mentioned the troops would not be happy. I assembled the two platoons and gave them the news. There was a lot of groaning in the ranks, and one soldier spoke up: *Sir, why couldn't you have been born in a flat country?*

I told them, *It is what it is, and you should consider it a high compliment that higher headquarters has so much faith in you that you always receive the worst and most dangerous tasks.*

It became dark before we reached the top, and we (70 men) camped for the night on the hillside because booby traps made it too dangerous to proceed in the dark. We also received word from the battalion S-2 that 500 to 600 NVA troops were located about 800 meters from our location. These were allegedly remnants of the 4th and 5th battalions of the 95th Regiment. We did not get much sleep that night. I kept hoping the information came from a wildly inaccurate SIGINT report.

There were no enemy activities against us during the night. When we cautiously checked the location where the enemy was supposed to be, we discovered they had departed or had never been there. This fact was good news since two platoons were no match for the size of the force reported.

A resupply helicopter bringing us supplies crashed due to the shifting and robust wind. There were no casualties. We left 10 troops to guard the downed aircraft until a heavy-lift helicopter arrived to recover the wreck. We also sent

10 men to escort the crew down the mountain after they expressed no burning desires to accompany us.

Since I had only 50 troops on the mountainside, I ordered Karl Beach, my new XO, to bring the rest of the company to join us. Karl reminded me the rest of the company had security duty for the battalion headquarters. I asked him to tell the battalion S-3 or Emerson to use the clerks, cooks, and communicators for that task. Karl probably found a more polite way to get the troops released, but my RTOs found the conversation enjoyable. We did not expect them to arrive until the morning of the 22nd. We continued up the mountains with my remaining 50 troops. Just before darkness, we found an empty enemy camp and stayed there for the night. We had a minor skirmish with three enemy soldiers, but they managed to get away, and neither side suffered any casualties.

We resumed our ascent at first light on 22 March. The going was slow in the rugged terrain full of boulders the size of buildings. We also had to be on the lookout for the numerous booby traps. We had only moved a couple of hundred meters when we encountered five VC. That small enemy force was able to hold us up for four hours as my troops climbed a cliff, trying to flank them in the rough terrain. When we finally were able to get around them, they quickly withdrew, leaving one killed behind.

The 20 troops I had sent to guard the downed helicopter and escort the crew down the mountain re-joined us shortly after midday. The rest of the company also showed up a couple of hours later, bringing our force to about 140. We had another brief engagement before the day was over and killed one VC. The company received another resupply just before dark. Unfortunately, it dropped through the jungle, resulting in the ruin of a large portion.

We stayed on the mountaintop on 23 March. We had a panoramic view of Tuy Hoa and the valleys leading west and northwest from that city from an opening in the jungle foliage, but the foliage otherwise obscured our view. Our patrols had three engagements with small groups of VCs on 23 March. We could not tell if we inflicted any casualties, but suffered none ourselves. Lieutenant Colonel Emerson had ordered another company to assist us, but they ran into a minefield, which resulted in two of their soldiers killed and nine wounded. That company, A/2/327, temporarily attached to 2/502, was recalled.[5]

We received orders to proceed 5 kilometers south to a helicopter EZ on 24 March 1966. The terrain was exceedingly rough, and we only made it about halfway before dark. There were no enemy contacts. We started again on the 25th. When we reached the designated EZ, it was too small for our use. We also received resupply through the trees. Emerson had sent a few cases of beer, but they were destroyed when they hit rocks. There were many glum faces at chow that night.[6]

I had trouble matching the coordinates given in the battalion AA report covering the period from the end of Operation *van Buren* on 25 February to the end of

Lunde, my home until 1951. (Personal collection)

My parents' wedding in 1922. The picture was taken on my maternal grandparents' farm. My mother is wearing her family's crown. (Personal collection)

My father in Norwegian uniform, 1912. (Personal collection)

My father in U.S. uniform, 1917. (Personal collection)

Lieutenant Colonel Hackworth. He is wearing General Staff insignia and only one Distinguished Service Cross, so it must have been taken while he was at the Pentagon when I received it in 1968 or 1969.

Brigadier General James Simmons Timothy in 1971 or 1972 before he retired. (Tim Swain)

Serge Demyanenko and I at UC in 1958. (Personal collection)

Ranger field platoon at the bottom of the Dahlonega cliffs—I am in the last row, number 31. Sent to me annotated by a Ranger classmate, name forgotten.

My platoon leaders and I on Burkhart Hill off Route 19 on 3 September 1965. (Tim Swain)

First Lieutenant Tim Swain on Route 19 in 1965. (Tim Swain)

Most of the A/2/502 assembled in the sand dunes at Tuy Hoa in late February 1966. Thirty to forty troops are absent. (Larry Greenhill)

From right to left: Sergeant McFann, Master Sergeant Macias, and I in front of the company command post in Phan Rang, Christmas, December 1965. (Personal collection)

Memorial service in the sand dune at Tuy Hoa for nine or ten troops who were killed fighting the 95th NVA Regiment. (Larry Greenhill)

Major David (Skip) Perrine in Vietnam in the summer of 1967. He was indispensable in this manuscript's successful completion. (David Perrine)

Bu Gia Map Campaign May 1966. Breakdown of resupply and mail (ammunition and food had already been distributed) on 10 May 1966. Sergeant First Class Robert Jack is at far left. The two tall individuals in the background are Lieutenants Otto and Clements. (Associated Press)

A soldier, I believe Sergeant First Class Jack, moving cautiously toward the wounded and captured NVA sergeant on 10 May 1966. (Associated Press)

Bu Gia Map campaign. Private First Class A. T. Howell tending to the NVA sergeant's wounds while the prisoner is questioned by my interpreter (partially hidden) on 10 May 1966. (Associated Press)

Bu Gia Map campaign. Staff Sergeant Laguana bringing a captured weapon on 10 May 1966 after he confirmed the prisoner's statement of a large NVA force 800 meters to the west. (Associated Press)

Bu Gia Map campaign. Two of the Montagnard scouts we armed with captured weapons on 10 May 1966. (Associated Press)

Bu Gia Map battle. First Lieutenant Clements checking the damage NVA machine gunners had caused to our command post grove area. (Associated Press)

Battle of Bu Gia Map. First Platoon moving to contact and spreading into a skirmish formation. This photo is a good example of the lack of visibility. (Associated Press)

Bu Gia Map battle. The evacuation of a casualty. (Associated Press)

Award ceremony at Fort Bragg in 1967. (Personal collection)

Airborne Test Division in 1967.The tall officer in the center of the front row is Lieutenant Colonel Luttrell. On his right is the civilian engineer. I am on Luttrell's left. Major Ezzard and Captain Andersen are to my left and Chief Warrant Officer Miller, the chief of the testing facility, is on the far right of the front row. (Personal collection)

Colonel John Geraci minutes before I picked him up in my C&C helicopter when he was shot down. (Army photo)

Results of heavy fighting in the Vietnamese Highlands in 1969. (ARVN photo)

Saying farewell to the II Corps ARVN Commander. (ARVN photo)

Major General Henry E. Emerson in late 1973. (Army photo)

In Iran with U.S. and Iranian officers in 1973. I am in the left forefront. (Personal collection)

My first trip to Hanoi with my guide, allegedly a former interrogator of U.S. prisoners. (Personal collection)

The negotiations division with two officers and one Vietnamese national not present. I am in the first row flanked by Technical Sergeant Brown and Major Thomas, Captain Scanlon is at the far right. In the second row are Nguyen Thi Mai at the far left, Barbara Kavulia in the center, and Nguyen Thi Ban to the right. (Army photo)

Negotiations in Hanoi February–March 1974 for the return of the remains of those who died in captivity. From left to right is Mr. Tan, the chief interpreter, me, and Captain Scanlon, my legal advisor. (Army photo)

The other side of the negotiating table. (Army photo)

DRV and PRG chiefs from their delegations at Gia Lam Airport for the DIC transfer ceremony. Colonel Tu is second from the right, and his deputy Lieutenant Colonel Bao is at the far left. I do not recall the names of the other two. (Army photo)

Some of the 23 boxes of remains and headstones of those who died in captivity. (Army photo)

The Defense Assistant Office compound on 30 April 1975 after military demolition teams destroyed the building. (Army photo)

Receiving a Legion of Merit from Brigadier General Robert L. Schweitzer at SHAPE on 15 June 1979. (Army photo)

Major General Dewitt C. Smith, Jr, twice Commandant of the U.S. Army War College. 1976 Yearbook.

Operation *Harrison* on 242400 March. The next operation was *Austin II*, and the battalion AA report for that operation did not begin until 111850 April, issued on 18 May 1966. There is, therefore, a period of about 18 days when there are no AA reports. Eleven days of operations by A/2/502 occurred in this period. Furthermore, some of the coordinates given during the last part of Operation *Harrison* are off the map sheet I have. These mountain operations took place about 3–8 kilometers southeast of My Canh (2).

On the morning of the 26th, Emerson ordered us to proceed back to the northeast for 3,000 meters to an NVA/VC hospital's supposed location. *Here we go again, chasing a SIGINT report*, I thought.

We had covered the 3 kilometers by 1700 hours when the point element spotted seven VC and heard many voices further away. It was late in the day, and I had no idea what confronted us.

Therefore, we retrograded about 200 meters and set up a perimeter. I sent three combat patrols out to the northeast to scout and attempt to surround the enemy in the darkness.

That evening I was informed that B/2/502 had a sharp encounter with a VC force on the other side of the valley, resulting in 12 VC killed. Company B suffered three KIA and 16 wounded. Friendly artillery fire caused most of the casualties, and the rest was due to enemy snipers.

Our three patrols found the enemy, set up blocking positions on three sides, and stayed overnight. The rest of the company moved forward to complete the encirclement before first light in the morning. As I viewed the enemy positions through binoculars, it had an ordinary enemy camp's appearance without any distinctive markings. I saw about 20 VC.

I was not sure what to do initially. Attacking a medical facility was a breach of the laws of land warfare. On the other hand, the facility was not displaying the required markings. I decided not to seek advice from my superiors and I determined to take the camp.

I asked all units to let the VC open fire first in case they opted not to resist. A few of my men and I showed ourselves and made enough noise to ensure the enemy would hear, and we received immediate enemy fire. The VC unit was completely surprised, still engaged in eating their breakfast. In the engagement that followed, they offered a short but determined resistance. Ten VC died, and six were captured, including three women who were nurses. The company had no casualties.

We scoured the enemy medical facility and found many medical supplies, which—by my orders—we left and did not destroy. We set up a defensive perimeter on high ground near the facility and sent patrols to give early warning if an enemy force should approach. We decided to keep the prisoners at our location overnight.

There were no enemy contacts during the night, and after the first light on 28 March, I sent Karl Beach and 10 soldiers to bring the prisoners down from the mountains. Beach delivered them to the battalion, which later turned them over to South Vietnamese authorities.

The rest of the company remained in the same position on the mountain. We sent out several patrols, and one of those patrols encountered a small VC force, apparently heading for the hospital location. We killed two VCs and captured two. The patrol did not suffer any casualties.

We started our return to the battalion on 29 March and reached our destination before dark. The troops were tired after the 10-day operation in the mountains. I tried to reduce the route by taking a shortcut but ended up having to cross a swamp full of leeches; my extra effort was not appreciated.

A/2/502 became the brigade reserve on 30 March. Emerson visited the company and told me he was sending me on R&R to Saigon, and he did not want any arguments.

The time in reserve was short. The brigade wanted my company to make one more ascent of the mountains. We started on 31 March, and after an exhausting search that failed to result in any contact with the enemy, we returned to the battalion on 4 April and moved to Tuy Hoa Airfield by trucks.

I felt good about the results of more than five weeks of operations since I left the hospital. We had conducted continuous operations, inflicted sizable losses on the enemy, and did not have anyone killed.

Problems and Solutions

Communications had been a problem that dogged us ever since arriving in Vietnam. Unfortunately, the TO&E was not adjusted to correct the need for additional PRC-25 radios at the company level. We received the replacement for our losses in radios on 9/10 February, but that still left us short.

Our supply personnel came up with a solution that was not strictly legal, but served to save lives and better use the radios rather than leaving them sitting in a storage facility. I was aware of their plans but told them to keep me out of their activities. Whenever a helicopter we used crashed, they (the supply personnel) reported a lost radio, or in the more significant engagements or river crossing, they did likewise. We acquired some extra batteries in the same manner. I called an end to their activities after we had obtained four additional radios. We had enough to provide communications for one patrol from each platoon in Phan Thiet and on the Cambodian border.

We also came up with an innovation to further reduce the weight carried by the soldiers and put it to use during the last two excursions into the mountains. It was relatively simple. We obtained sacks of rice from the brigade supply organizations, supplemented with thousands of small powder soup packets of various flavors. Each trooper carried two socks full of rice tied to his belt and several soup packets in his gear. All that was needed to make an energy-rich and tasty meal was a canteen cup of boiled water. While this innovation did not eliminate the need for C-rations, it reduced resupply frequency by helicopter, always a dead giveaway to our location.

The brigade's policy was to turn in all enemy weapons. We faithfully did so until after our operations at Ben Cat, when more and more of these weapons were discovered among the brigade's support personnel. Some of my scroungers—mostly young NCOs—had persuaded me not to turn in all weapons captured, but to use some for trading with support personnel for things we might need, like extra radios and batteries. They also made fine presentation pieces for deserving soldiers departing the unit. This use was particularly true for a cache of Soviet sniper rifles in their original containers discovered in the lowlands in mid-March. The only mention I found in the battalion AA report was the capture of 12 foreign weapons.

If my recollection can be trusted, there were four containers of sniper rifles, with six in each box. My troops may have kept half and reported the other half. Commanders at every echelon knew this situation existed, but it was not officially condoned. For this reason, the number of weapons seized was, in many cases, understated. Despite this, Donald Schroeder wrote later that the ratio of weapons captured to enemies killed by A/2/502 was the highest in the battalion and probably the highest in the brigade.

CHAPTER 14

Phan Thiet and Bu Prang

I started my R&R on 4 April 1966 but only got as far as Phan Rang when I learned that Saigon was off-limits to R&R personnel because of a curfew due to riots and unrest. I planned to head back to the battalion on 6 April but received word that 2/502 would soon be on its way to Phan Thiet, which I had reconnoitered in November 1965. Consequently, I headed for Phan Thiet early on the morning of 8 April. The 1/327th also deployed to Phan Thiet, as did many brigade units, including two artillery batteries, a company of engineers, and later A/2/17 Cavalry. 2/327 Infantry remained in Tuy Hoa to participate in Operation *Fillmore*.

Phan Thiet, in Binh Thuan Province, was a charming coastal city almost due east of Saigon, astride the II and III Corps' boundaries. It was the country's largest producer of fish sauce. To this day, I do not know for sure why we came to Phan Thiet, a quiet area that had not seen much fighting. According to the 1st Brigade AA report, intelligence believed a threat was developing in the mountainous region to the north. However, our operations took place in the lowlands west and northwest of Phan Thiet, and we never operated in the mountains.

The battalion was located on the airfield south of the city, downwind from the fish sauce factory's nauseating stench. It got to the point that troops were eager to get into the interior to escape the foul smell.

Operations for A/2/502 began with a warning order on 11 April 1966. We were ordered to an area 35–40 kilometers northwest of Phan Thiet. On the evening of the 11th, I sent a squad-size patrol under Staff Sergeant Jose Laguana to secure an LZ for the rest of the company to make a night assault the following morning. As was often the case, the planned assault was canceled because of bad weather and rescheduled as a daytime assault on 13 April. The attack took place at 0900 hours without opposition.

The company started immediately in a northwest direction through a heavily wooded valley. On the way, we had one soldier wounded by a punji stake.[1] We found a small enemy base camp that looked like it had not seen any use for a long time.

The heat was unbearable, and we suffered some heat casualties, among them a newly assigned lieutenant who passed out. Two new officers joined A/2/502, either during the Tuy Hoa operation or when we moved to Phan Thiet. As I recall, they were Lieutenants Ron Odom and Robert Vaughn. Captain Ron Brown from the battalion staff also accompanied us on this first operation out of Phan Thiet. Lieutenant Colonel Emerson was eying him as my possible replacement and wanted him to go along with the company and give him my opinion at the end of the operation.

We continued up the same valley on 14 April, but the going was much faster. We reached our objective on the bank of a river at 1300 hours after two minor VC encounters. We found another enemy camp at the edge of the river, recently evacuated as the campfires were still warm. We set out ambushes all around our position and had three patrols further away. One man fell into the river and floated downstream until another soldier dived into the river and brought him to safety. The trooper who risked his life to save his comrade received a Soldier's Medal.

On the 15th, we set out early in the morning and covered more than 10 kilometers before we stopped. We had problems finding water. The company had one minor contact with a small VC force. While maneuvering to close with the enemy, one soldier received a wound from another punji stake.

We got new directions from the battalion at 0900 on 16 April but did not start our move until 1900 hours to avoid the worst of the sweltering heat. We moved during darkness until 0100 hours on the 17th, when we stopped for a few hours rest after covering 11 kilometers. Despite having waited for dark, it was a tortuous move in the heat, with several troops suffering heat exhaustion. We had, luckily, no enemy contacts.

We received orders for extraction on 18 April, but the designated EZ was unusable and we had to move another 3 kilometers before finding a suitable site. We were subjected to sniper fire as we extracted but had no casualties. We were back on the airfield at 1900 hours.

We received an alert on 20 April for an operation about 30 kilometers north of the airfield. I immediately sent a strong combat patrol consisting of 14 men under Staff Sergeant Laguana into the new area. The patrol got into a firefight, believed they killed four to six VC, but the body count confirmed only one along with his weapon. I received statements from participants, some via Lieutenant Colonel Perrine, about this patrol action, including Private First Class Clifford Rosseau. Rosseau had been with the company since its arrival in Vietnam. These inputs were helpful.

As soon as Laguana's troops made contact, Emerson and I headed in their direction in his C&C helicopter. Emerson talked briefly with Laguana but could not understand him. I did a little better since I was used to his accent and knew he was more difficult to comprehend when excited. He reported he was in contact with the enemy and that the patrol had suffered casualties.

It was planned for the company to make a night helicopter assault, but now I requested Emerson's permission for an earlier daytime assault. Since he was sitting across from me in the helicopter, I received approval immediately. I then called Karl Beach, asking him to prepare the company for a 1330 hours takeoff, and told him I was on my way back. Emerson called his S-3 to task an airlift company. I instructed Laguana to maintain contact with the enemy and bring any casualties to our planned LZ by 1400 hours. I also told him I would not reinforce him but swing around his eastern flank to trap forces confronting his patrol.

We did not receive any fire on the LZ; Laguana's people had brought two KIAs for the helicopter to take back to the Phan Thiet Airfield. The KIAs were Specialist 4s Famous L. Lane and George. J. Skapinsky.

Immediately upon landing, the company set out on an east-northeast heading. We had gone less than 1 kilometer when we encountered a force of about 40 VC. We killed 10 without suffering any losses. The VC made a rapid withdrawal towards the north. We did not pursue them because there was not much daylight remaining. The company established a perimeter, and we pulled Laguana and his troops into it for a well-deserved rest.

Laguana's unit was highly decorated because of the earlier action. Specialist 4 Lane received a DSC. Additionally, Staff Sergeant Laguana, Sergeant Nealy Jackson and Specialist 4 George J. Skapinsky received Silver Stars.

We started moving south on 21 April and were subjected to long-range sniper fire all day. While we found and destroyed an enemy camp, we had three wounded but could not close with the enemy snipers. We winched the casualties up to a helicopter.

We continued our southward move on 22 April, again under continual sniper fire. We had one soldier, Specialist 4 William DeLoach, severely wounded as the femoral artery was severed. It was tough for the medics to stop the bleeding even with a surgeon's help via radio. The surgeon told the medics not to move the wounded soldier by helicopter until the bleeding stopped. With the bleeding controlled, DeLoach was air evacuated.

The wounding of DeLoach happened in the vicinity of a small uninhabited enemy village. We also found some rice and the rusted hulk of a 1952 pickup truck.[2] We destroyed them before we departed. I also dropped one squad behind the company with orders to stay concealed and covered. The squad would move on my orders to a new location, thereby remaining 400–500 meters behind the company as it moved south. We hoped this might reduce sniper activity.[3]

Dropping a squad back worked well, and we received no further sniper fire during the operation. We were ordered to extract in the early morning of 24 April. The extraction, which began at 0800 hours, went well, and we were back on the airfield by 0900 hours. A/2/502 became brigade reserve.

Emerson had asked me to be on the first extraction lift as he wanted to talk to me. We were alerted for movement to the Cambodian border area, and Emerson asked me to stay past my scheduled rotation date to continue as company commander for that operation. I told him I was more than willing.

He then asked me about Ronald Brown, a West Pointer with some rough edges who reportedly had several brushes with the military justice system. He impressed me as a quick-thinking and aggressive officer. I gave Ron Brown a positive recommendation to Emerson. Ron allegedly resigned from the Army in early 1968, although he was on the promotion list to major, just published. I do not know what caused this abrupt action, and I have not met or talked with him since 1966.

In anticipation of a future change of command, Brown and I traveled to Phan Rang on 27 April to inventory the company property. Additionally, we had a chance to get a good meal and several drinks at the brigade club, adjacent to my company area.

After building their club in late 1965, the NCOs had some materials left and decided to make an Honor Roll sign in the middle of our camp. It was removed at the end of the Tuy Hoa operations because there was insufficient space for the names of all killed and wounded. When Ron and I were there in late April, the rear party was still in the process of making the sign bigger and the lettering smaller. They completed the alterations by late May 1966.

Our stay in Phan Rang was very brief. Shortly after arriving, I received a call from Emerson ordering us back to Phan Thiet as quickly as possible the next day, the 28th, to meet the timetable for moving to the Cambodian border. Karl Beach had the company ready to move by noon on 28 April.

In late spring 1966, Saigon's command became concerned over the NVA troop buildup rate along the Cambodian border. With the monsoon about to begin in that area, the increase posed a significant threat against the Vietnamese Central Highlands. Force levels were too low to protect this long and rugged border. The North Vietnamese and Cambodians denied any buildup and Washington scorned the idea for apparently political reasons.[4]

The most recent intelligence indicated a significant infiltration of NVA troops in the II and III Corps' Tactical Zones. It was the mission of the 1st Brigade to deter or stop this infiltration. The brigade started arriving by air at Nhon Co from Phan Thiet on 1 May 1966[5] (2/327 did not move to Nhon Co but continued its operations in the Tuy Hoa area). The brigade headquarters and 1/327 remained at Nhon Co, while 2/502 (minus) moved to Bu Prang's vicinity by helicopter on 1 May. C/2/502 remained in Nhon Co as brigade reserve until 6 or 7 May.[6]

The 2/502 had a tragic mishap on 4 May. A CH-47 helicopter bringing supplies, newly assigned personnel, and hospital returnees, primarily to Companies A and C, crashed due to mechanical failure before reaching Nhon Co. Six of those killed were from my company: Staff Sergeants Gene Hawthorne[7] and John A. Brown, and Privates First Class Robert L. Clark, Roger L. Berg, Roger C. Colette, and R. A. Fenton. The two staff sergeants were hospital returnees, but the four privates were newly assigned troops. Another five were from C/2/502, three from the battalion Headquarters and Headquarter Company (HHC), and the two pilots.

The distance from Nhon Co to Bu Prang is about 40 kilometers, and Bu Prang is approximately 50 kilometers from Bu Gia Map. Bu Prang is also about 20 kilometers from the Cambodian border. Bu Prang was the location of a district headquarters, and its only protection was one CIDG company. South Vietnamese intelligence concluded the NVA had targeted Bu Prang for elimination. A minor probe against the place had taken place in mid-April.[8]

The 2/502 (minus) operated in the Bu Prang area until 5 May 1966 with negative results. While the battalion AA report implies the location of A/2/502 was Bu Prang, this is not correct.[9] As soon as we arrived at Bu Prang, A/2/502 moved about 10 kilometers west towards the Cambodian border. The other battalion units remained in a central location near Bu Prang and conducted local reconnaissance. The move of A/2/502 had to do with planned operations in the direction of the border.

We tried penetrating the jungle to the Cambodian border during the night of 2/3 May, but it was virtually impenetrable. There were no trails, no evidence of humans having been there, but thousands of leeches dropped from the trees like rain. It was an unpleasant experience and we returned to our company base late in the afternoon of 3 May. Plans were to return to the battalion location on 4 May.

We managed to establish excellent relations with the local Montagnard tribe. These mountain tribes had supported our SF until their withdrawal from the border area earlier in 1965. Their support was not because they loved Americans but because they detested the Vietnamese. We made the initial contact after we returned from our failed attempt to reach the border. A more significant meeting took place the next day.

The Montagnard tribal chief, dressed in a French uniform with French medals, arrived at the company base on an elephant on the morning of 4 May. Other elephants brought large jars of rice wine and food. I felt it would be an insult not to accept their gifts, so I sat down with the chief next to a large jar of wine, with plenty of flies, insects, and other critters swimming around in it. I drank a full canteen cup, taking extra care to avoid the additional meat floating around. I did so without any ill after-effects. I invited some of my troops to partake, but they declined, seeing what was in the jar. Most consumed the fruit the Montagnards had brought though.

We had not found any invasion trails in our unsuccessful push westward towards the Cambodian border. The Montagnards told us we would not find any invasion trails in the Bu Prang area. They stated the invasion routes were further south, which would place them somewhere near the border between II and III Corps' Tactical Zones. I passed all information to Emerson.[10]

The company was getting ready to return to the battalion base. When I asked the chief if he would accompany us to meet the battalion commander near Bu Prang, I received a blunt refusal. He did not want to go anywhere near the

District Headquarters at Bu Prang. He also appeared uneasy talking to me through my Vietnamese interpreter. His attitude changed when I attempted to use my very broken French, which I had not used since my school days. After this awkward conversation, I accepted the chief's offer to provide porters. He and his entourage thereupon departed. Before he left, I asked how he would find us if we moved south from Bu Prang to a more promising area. He assured me, *We will find you*. They did find us, joining the company on 6 May.

In the meantime, the South Vietnamese District Chief had appeared at the battalion CP. He was there to make sure we did not provide the tribe with any arms and ammunition. Despite the South Vietnamese protests to Emerson, the Montagnards provided us 26 young men to accompany us as porters, under the leadership of a Montagnard, a former NCO in the French Army. The number of Montagnards was increased to around 33. While some were attached to the Recondos, the Montagnards allowed A/2/502 to carry more ammunition and rations, extending the time we could remain in the field without resupply.

Because of our lack of success in the Bu Prang area and the information provided by the Montagnards, Emerson secured permission to move his battalion southwestward to the Bu Gia Map area, just inside the III Corps Tactical Zone. A/2/502 had moved to join the rest of the battalion in the afternoon of 4 May. The new operation was planned for 5 May, but inclement weather forced a 24-hour postponement. Accordingly, Emerson issued a fragmentary verbal order (frag order) on the evening of 5 May.

CHAPTER 15

The Bu Gia Map Campaign, 6–10 May

Bu Gia Map was the location of a U.S. Special Forces camp abandoned in 1965. They had torn down all structures, but the place still had an airstrip overgrown with grass and cratered in some places. Recon by Lieutenant Colonel Emerson of the area in an L-19 on 5 May drew ground fire from the airstrip's northern side.

According to one entry in the battalion AA report, the original plan was to insert the Recondos on 5 May, as called for in the frag order, and for them to proceed directly to the airstrip and secure it.[1]

The postponement of the operation from 5 to 6 May resulted in the insertion of the Recondos at 0900 hours on 6 May.[2] However, they became engaged with a small enemy force and had one wounded soldier who needed evacuation; this delay explains why they had not secured the LZ before A/2/502 landed.

A/2/502 was to make the initial assault directly on the airstrip around 1130 hours on 6 May. The battalion AA report states the landing occurred at 1145 hours on 6 May, but my notes indicate it took place 15 minutes earlier. Twenty helicopters were available for the assault. B/2/502 was on the second lift, and the battalion CP and C/2/502, coming from Nhon Co, were on the third.

This uncertainty is the first of many with battalion and brigade AA reports' clarity and accuracy. It was a fluid and arduous campaign, but the battalion AA report was delayed until a week after the operation terminated. I had left Vietnam by that time and the brigade AA report was not issued until 5 June, three weeks after the campaign ended. There are also problems with the date on which the operation began. Some sources have it starting on or about 7 May.[3] I do not remember who the S-3 was at this time—nor do others I have contacted—as there appears to have been a change in late March. The turbulence in the S-3 section was evident during the Phan Thiet operation and throughout the Cambodian border area activities.

The helicopters that brought us to Bu Gia Map could not carry seven personnel as planned because of the elevation. Consequently, one A/2/502 platoon remained behind in the Bu Prang area to come along with B/2/502 on the second lift.

The lack of security of the airfield had me worried. I made several calls by radio on the morning of 6 May to the Recondos without receiving answers. I finally called the battalion S-3 just before liftoff, as mentioned in the battalion AA report. I wanted to use helicopter gunships if the airfield was not secured. Battalion denied this request, but I was assured the airstrip would be secure before our insertion.

We also worried that the SF could have mined or booby-trapped the area around the airfield before they departed. Someone had contacted the SF, but they could not assure us the place was clear of mines. Our main worries were mines, booby traps, and the fact that Lieutenant Colonel Emerson's L-19 received ground fire the previous day.

We made the assault at about 1130 hours, according to my notes. There was no opposition, and we did not encounter any mines or booby traps as we landed. Furthermore, we did not see any Recondos. The battalion AA report states the Recondos secured the airfield at 1200 hours after A/2/502 had landed.

The Bu Gia Map operation story is covered primarily in Brigadier General (Retired) S. L. A. Marshall's book *Battles in the Monsoon*. It is also covered in books by David Hackworth and Thomas Taylor,[4] articles in *Harper's Magazine*, in *Newsweek*, and various other magazines (i.e., *Stag*), and numerous newspaper accounts. I have again relied on my notes.[5] I also used all reports from the battalion and brigade and six participant statements for the *Special Study* cited in endnote 3. Finally, I looked at a manuscript written by a British lady named Kim Coleman.

What emerges from these sources is an assortment of errors by individuals who were not present. Since Emerson gave me operational control of all ground forces in the battle area early on 10 May, I have taken issue with some writings. My operational control of the ground forces continued until the pursuit reached the Cambodian border on 14 May. Marshall (1900–1977) did not interview me as I had already departed Vietnam and, in fact, I never met him but had read many of his books.

First, my account differs significantly from that presented by Marshall. I am certainly not accusing the late general of deliberate distortion or misrepresentation. I believe he relied on the information he received. Marshall used the "troop after-action report interview method," which is helpful if done correctly. The interviews must be numerous and cover all ranks to spot inconsistencies. According to letters I received after returning to the U.S., Marshall interviewed only a few troops from A/2/502.[6]

Second, I am unaware whether those interviewed had a chance to review what Marshall wrote before it went to the publisher. If he wished, Marshall could also have contacted me at the Airborne Test Division at Fort Bragg for an interview before publishing his book. Having written several books and numerous articles on military history since I retired, I know the importance of accurate sources.

The correctness of Marshall's many verbatim quotes also gives me pause. Usually, quoted statements are from interviews between the writer and the person named. I am quoted numerous times in the book without even having met Marshall or spoken to him, and this makes me wonder if some of the other "interviews" are from sources other than the person quoted. If the quotes are from statements by a third individual, they should be so labeled. Finally, the interviewer must ensure the truthfulness of those interviewed and spot whether it is a skewed story to suit various personal or career agendas, as Judge Faircloth concluded about An Ninh.

Emerson also became concerned about the lack of accuracy of what Marshall had written.[7] The difference in the battalion and brigade AA reports and the various inputs to the 22nd Military History Detachment's *Battle of Bu Gia Map Special Study* mentioned above makes it exceedingly difficult to develop a coherent story.

Terrain

The terrain in the Bu Gia Map area was different from anything we had encountered in Vietnam. To understand the campaign, one needs to have an appreciation for the terrain. The areas to the south and southeast of Bu Gia Map Airstrip were relatively clear and open compared to the west and north.

To the north, west, and southwest, one quickly encounters a prehistoric jungle of tall trees—some with a height of over 120 feet—with triple canopies. There was a secondary and virtual impenetrable growth of thick bamboo at ground level between the tall trees. Hacking through these bamboo thickets to clear enough for a single file was exhausting work, wore out our machetes, and made it necessary to change the lead element every 15–20 minutes.

Determining one's exact location on the map was exceedingly difficult throughout the operation. The ground consisted of rolling hills, but the dense ground vegetation reduced visibility to only a few meters and prevented us from fixing the low hills shown on the maps. The maps themselves were inaccurate. Some cleared areas with clusters of huts shown on the map did not exist. Some of the streams, particularly the intermittent ones, also did not exist. These gullies probably became streams during the height of the monsoon season.

We seldom saw the sky. The temperature and vegetation created a greenhouse effect with high humidity and scorching heat. The visibility was so limited we could have passed within a few meters of an invasion trail without knowing it. Locating these paths from the air was virtually impossible because of the dense vegetation.

Searching for the NVA

The battalion AA report has A/2/502 beginning its operation immediately after landing on 6 May. This is not correct. We moved into a holding area about 800 meters northwest of the airstrip while waiting for the last platoon to arrive on the second lift. The reason for establishing the assembly area in this location was that, in the 5 May frag order, Emerson had planned to send A/2/502 in a northwest direction. There must have been a last-minute meeting between Emerson and me (not in my notes) where he changed my company's course to the west-southwest. This change probably had to do with the supporting artillery's location, which he did not know when issuing the frag order. If we headed northwest, we would quickly run out of artillery coverage.[8]

We began our operation shortly after 1400 hours on 6 May 1966, by which time all those scheduled to join us had arrived.

According to the battalion AA report, the B/2/502 lift, carrying my last platoon, arrived at 1332 hours. It made no sense for us to spend a night near the airstrip, so B/2/502 deployed into the more open area to the south, while C/2/502 remained on the airfield as a reserve.

The company had no encounters with the enemy until about 071430 May, when we encountered about 15 VC. This encounter is not in my field notes but in the battalion AA report, the battalion SJ, and Lieutenant John D. Mooneyham's statement for the *Special Study*. He is identified as the weapons platoon leader of A/2/502 and must, therefore, have been a very recent replacement since I do not remember him and his name is not in my field notes. Subsequently, the *Special Study* notes he became Company A's XO. His assignment as XO must have been after Beach's rotation to the U.S. in mid-June.

When I returned from the hospital on 25 February 1966, I only had two officers in the company. When I later made Karl Beach my XO, only one platoon had an officer, the 1st Platoon commanded by William Otto. I recollect that I received two officer replacements at the end of the Tuy Hoa operation or while in Phan Thiet. Mooneyham was not one of those. They were Lieutenants Bob Vaughn and Ron Odom since they are mentioned in my notes.

There are several discrepancies between my brief field notes and what Mooneyham wrote. He has us arriving at Bu Gia Map on 7 May while we came on 6 May. John gives the time of the first enemy encounter after dark on 7 May. Mooneyham reported that we suffered two KIAs in this initial encounter. He also mentions that "SGT Bare" was wounded. We did not have anyone named Bare, but he probably referred to Sergeant Donald Bear, who was in the 2nd Platoon.[9]

The battalion AA report states the encounter took place in the early afternoon on 7 May. The battalion SJ also reports this daytime skirmish at 1430 hours on 7 May, in which one soldier was severely wounded in the thigh and stomach and evacuated at 1535 hours. The injured soldier was Private First Class Philip P. Jenkins, who later died from his wounds. Therefore, Mooneyham's report of two killed must be a reference to happenings on 8 May.

It looks like Mooneyham has my company moving in multiple columns, with multiple night positions. We did not move in multiple columns, as I had already told Lieutenant Colonel Emerson before we departed that I would not checkerboard in this terrain. I reiterated this in the sharp radio conversation we had in the early morning of 8 May. However, we did send out security to our flanks. We also did not use multiple night positions, but again we had all-around protection. On the night of 6/7 May, the battalion SJ has A/2/502 in multiple night locations—some separated by up to 2,800 meters! That is something I would never do in this type of terrain.

We had a change in direction early on 8 May. This change resulted from a radio conversation I had with Emerson, also related by Marshall. Emerson wanted me to continue west while I wished to go south since that gave us a better opportunity to interdict any east–west trails used by the NVA. This observation was a point repeatedly stressed by the attached Montagnards. In French, the Montagnard leader bluntly stated it was not too smart to look for east–west trails by moving westerly. Furthermore, since leaving the airfield, the area seemed virtually uninhabited, with no water or anything resembling a trail. The only exceptions were three small villages west of the Bu Gia Map airstrip, which we avoided on 6/7 May.

Emerson also wanted A/2/502 to use the checkerboard concept that he said was used by B/2/502. I told him the terrain we were moving through was unsuitable for checkerboard operations. The bamboo forest at ground level was too thick to allow one platoon to come to another platoon's timely assistance. I mentioned that any comparison to what B/2/502 was doing (Emerson had needled me by saying First Lieutenant Sill could show me how to checkerboard) made no sense as that company was in the more open area to the south.

Emerson realized I was becoming annoyed and laughed, saying I should follow my instincts if I felt so strongly about going south and not using the checkerboard concept. After this conversation, I immediately turned the company south; that change is on the map opposite. S. L. A. Marshall is correct in noting that the whole operation "pivoted on this hard-kidding conversation."[10]

This change in direction is not in the battalion reports, but that does not surprise me. Emerson was his own operations officer, often giving subordinates instructions and not telling his S-3 until much later. This tendency was probably in play on 8 May. I was Emerson's brigade S-3 in 1968 and learned to live with this frustrating and at times dangerous practice.

A look at the small engagements' coordinates on the 8th makes it evident we were heading directly south. It appears the battalion S-3 had learned about the route change by noon since we received a new Tactical Area of Responsibility (TAOR) at 081320 May after we had our first two engagements with the NVA.

My notes have the morning engagements about 500 meters further north than shown on the map opposite. The first encounter at 080730 May was with five NVA soldiers and resulted in one enemy soldier being killed and the capture of his AK-47. The second encounter at 080955 May was with an enemy sniper a little further to the east. It resulted in the killing of the sniper and the capture of his Soviet sniper

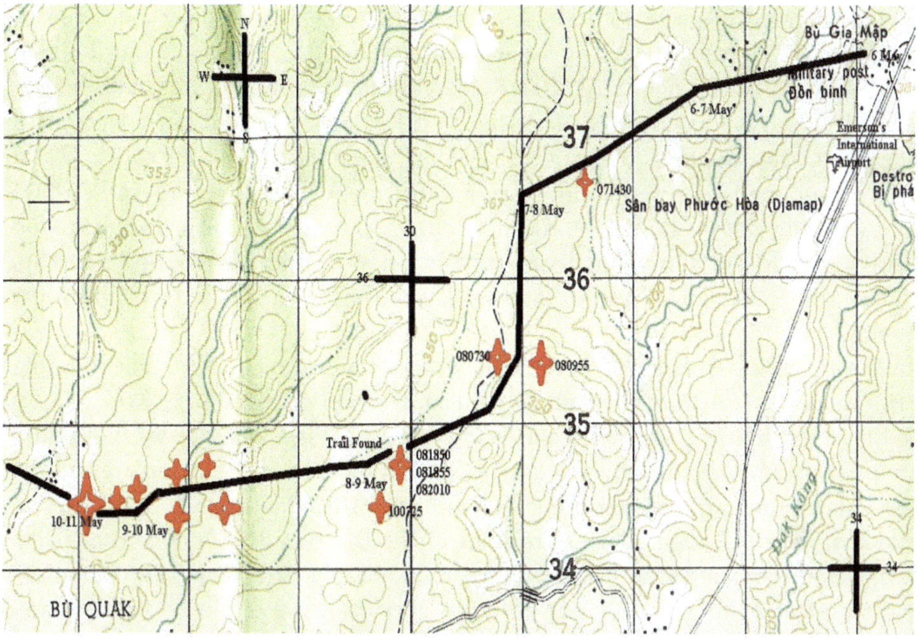

Map 7. Modified U.S. topographic map of the route followed 6–10 May 1966 with engagements, marked with red stars, according to either the battalion AA report or the battalion staff journal.

rifle. The battalion AA report also states we found two tons of oats at 1420 hours that we subsequently destroyed. Unfortunately, I do not recall that incident.

The route my company followed takes a southwestward turn in the afternoon on 8 May. The reason for this turn was to stay within our assigned TAOR. This change led to a series of evening/night engagements noted on the map. The engagement at 081855 May in the battalion AA report (081800 May in the SJ) ensued when a flank patrol encountered a sniper. The sniper wounded one U.S. soldier who later died at Nhon Co. Another sniper killed a second U.S. soldier soon after that; both casualties evacuated simultaneously.

My notes fail to mention the loss of the two soldiers, and Lieutenant Colonel Perrine called this serious omission to my attention. The names of the soldiers were Specialist 4 Robert L. McCaig and Private First Class Stephen J. Steriti. Perrine told me these names are also on the Vietnam Memorial Wall, together with Private First Class Philip P. Jenkins. I recognize the name Steriti but not McCaig or Jenkins (killed on 7 May). They are not on the 31 January 1966 roster, indicating they joined the company after that date. While not mentioned in my field notes, the last letter I sent to Florence on 18 May states we lost three soldiers on our way to the battle area. General Marshall makes no mention that anyone from A/2/502 was killed on 7 or 8 May, but we suffered fatalities.

The other engagements in the evening of 8 May were an encounter with 12 NVA soldiers at 082010 May who fled, leaving behind one killed, an AK-47, plus a bunch of equipment; and a fight with 10–15 NVA resulting in one NVA soldier killed, later identified as a member of the 141st NVA Regiment. In addition, we captured one AK-47 and an RPG.

We continued in a west-southwest direction on 9 May. My notes indicate we intersected an east–west invasion trail at about 1500 hours. I informed the battalion that we had found a broad and well-used invasion trail not marked on the map, and we were proceeding west on that trail. Accordingly, I requested an adjustment in our TAOR.[11]

As soon as we headed west on the trail, we encountered one NVA soldier heading east. The lead element of the company killed him and captured his AK-47.

Emerson called on the radio and wanted to know if I was sure we had found an invasion trail. I told him I was convinced and that the engagements we had the previous evening and this morning had all been with NVA soldiers. I also said to him that we had fought eight skirmishes in the last two days and, at times, had struggled through a virtually impassable bamboo jungle. The troops were exhausted and we planned to go into night positions as soon as we found a suitable place. I added that my instincts told me the troops should rest before continuing west on the trail since we could be near something big given the increased number of contacts.

I told Emerson the NVA could be aware of our presence but asked that helicopters keep away from our position in case they did not know our exact location. I also informed him we needed a resupply of ammunition but felt we should wait. Emerson replied that my instincts on 8 May had proven correct and asked if I thought he should begin concentrating forces to support A/2/502's advance. I asked him not to do that until we had further evidence to support our beliefs.

We only proceeded west on the trail for a few hundred meters on 9 May until we reached a slight rise in the terrain where we stopped and set up a perimeter. On our way to the night position, we encountered an additional four NVA soldiers moving east in a leisurely manner. We killed all and captured their weapons. Lieutenant Otto sent one of his best squads—under Staff Sergeant Jose Laguana—further west along the trail to act as our western security. That evening I reverted to my previous habit of keeping rather detailed field notes—maybe another instinct.

The enemy was apparently not yet aware of our presence since Laguana's squad encountered more NVA soldiers that evening and killed all before the enemy had time to un-sling their weapons and return fire. We killed eight and recovered their weapons. Some NVA soldiers we did not see could have turned around and reported our presence. While this was not likely, we had to proceed on the assumption some had escaped. The fact that we continued to encounter similar leisurely groups the following morning indicates otherwise.

Marshall makes some negative remarks about the troops' marksmanship in A/2/502, stating, "it was nothing to write home about."[12] I do not know where he gets this from and I respectfully disagree. As far as we knew, all enemy soldiers we met were killed by single shots or short bursts so quickly that most could not return fire. By the morning of 10 May, we had an impressive number of captured weapons. I do not know how the marksmanship could have been any better. Since leaving the Bu Gia Map airstrip, A/2/502 had killed 24 enemy soldiers and captured 25 weapons.

The most important encounter was with an NVA patrol of eight soldiers at about 0940 hours on 10 May.[13] Our troops killed five. The NVA sergeant, who led the patrol, was wounded and captured. Two slipped away in the dense jungle.

Although the command group was behind the 1st Platoon, I was on the engagement scene within two minutes. While pictures show only a wound to the prisoner's right thigh, I recollect that he had wounds in both legs. He had surrendered his weapon and grenades before I arrived on the scene. While the event is now in the distant past, it was of great importance in the lives of those present on the ground—keeping many of us from becoming names on that black marble wall—that I think my vivid memory of that day is trustworthy about what happened.

As I remember, those present in the prisoner's vicinity when I arrived included Lieutenant Otto, Sergeant First Class Robert Jack, Staff Sergeant Laguana, and Private First Class A. T. Howell, a company medic. In addition, my two RTOs, Sergeant McFann and Specialist 4 Ellis, my interpreter, the artillery forward observer First Lieutenant Tom Clements with his RTO, and Henri Huét were also present. Huét was a former French paratrooper who now worked for Associated Press as a photographer/reporter. He accompanied A/2/502 during the Bu Gia Map operations.[14]

Howell[15] was already bandaging the NVA sergeant's wounds when I reached the scene. I told my interpreter to inform the prisoner that the war was over for him, that he was my responsibility, and should follow my orders. I stressed to the prisoner that he would be treated humanely and not hurt. I also told him he would be evacuated by helicopter later today. I then asked the interpreter to find out if there was anything the prisoner needed. He asked for water and a cigarette. We gave him water, and one soldier—I believe it was Sergeant First Class Jack—gave him a cigarette and stuck the rest of the pack along with matches into the prisoner's breast pocket.

I then questioned the NVA prisoner through the interpreter. I asked him about his unit's identity, what he was doing in the area, and what other NVA forces were in the vicinity. To my great surprise, the prisoner told us he was from the 3rd Battalion, 141st NVA Regiment, on a reconnaissance mission. His battalion was in fortified positions a short distance to our west. He also related that another two battalions of the same regiment were a little further to the west. When I tried to get him to be more specific about the other two battalions' location, he told us he believed they were 30–40 minutes' march away from his battalion. The brigade AA report has a vastly different story about how we captured this NVA NCO.[16]

After questioning the prisoner, my first action was to ask for Laguana to see me. Laguana was one of two or three squad leaders I relied on for challenging missions. I informed him this could be the most crucial mission I had ever given him. He was to scout forward, avoid becoming engaged, keep radio silence, and report on the prisoner's story's accuracy. He departed on his mission shortly before 1000 hours. As usual, this superb soldier successfully carried out his mission, confirming a large enemy force in positions about 800 meters to our west. As I recall, he became embroiled in a short firefight on his way back and captured two weapons.

At about 1020 hours, I called Emerson and gave him a complete report over the radio. He directed us to stay in our location, that he would send reinforcements, and for me to send a patrol forward to check the prisoner's information. I told him I had already done that and expected confirmation within the hour. Emerson also told me I would have operational control of all ground units, including the reinforcements, effective immediately and to guide the reinforcements to our location.[17]

Since the enemy was now aware of our location, I called for helicopters to bring the prisoner back to the battalion and bring resupplies for the company. I requested two days of rations and a triple basic load of ammunition. The resupply took place around 1115 hours. We hoisted the prisoner up through the jungle. The resupply was also lowered through the trees, like my XO Karl Beach the following day. The stories that Emerson landed at my position to pick up the prisoner are just not correct.[18] The weather was rainy, visibility poor, and there were no LZs in our vicinity.

Laguana returned about the same time the resupply was delivered, and I called Emerson to confirm a large enemy force were in prepared positions as the prisoner had told us. He told me I would have a reinforced cavalry troop (A/2/17 Cavalry) and Captain Ronald Brown's composite TF under my command.

General Marshall makes the damaging claim that "a National Police interpreter went to work on him [the prisoner], and he sang like a canary." The inference in the five words "went to work on him" is obvious and unfortunate.[19] I do not know why Marshall felt it necessary to include this statement; maybe he was given erroneous information. I can swear that we treated the prisoner well while under company control. He had given all the tactical information we needed while in the hands of the company. Laguana had confirmed that information. Furthermore, I had my regular interpreter, who was not from the squad of National Police mentioned by Marshall on page 228 of his book.

The most robust rebuttal of Marshall's claim came from Henri Huét, who filed his story on 12 May under the headline "Kindness to Enemy Save GIs from Trap." The story appeared in American and world newspapers.[20] Huét concluded our kindness to a captured soldier saved the unit from possible annihilation and resulted in a classic and successful engagement.

Preparations for the upcoming battle were now in full swing. We distributed the resupply down to the individual soldiers. I also decided to arm the Montagnards using captured weapons and embedded these native soldiers among U.S. platoons to ensure they would not be mistaken for NVA.

The most crucial element in the plan was getting the reinforcements in place before dark. I told the reinforcing units our location and how to get there and that I would give all future orders. I also asked the reinforcing commanders to speed their march, as did Emerson. Marshall's description of the maneuvers on 10 May after the NVA sergeant's capture is not entirely accurate, nor is his supporting sketch map.[21] I made a sketch map, on page 199, showing the assembly of reinforcements.

Captain George Hamilton, commanding A/2/17 Cavalry, was told to travel as light and as fast as possible.[22] Consequently, Marshall wrote, "they shucked most of their ammunition, spare canteens and whatever else could be discarded."[23] I seriously doubt Hamilton would have discarded a single round of ammunition, knowing he was going against an NVA regiment.

Marshall also mentions that Hamilton had a hard time even after finding the trail because he brought along "wheeled machine guns."[24] The trail was wide enough to allow for those contraptions, but they would have been useless the following day as the cavalrymen hacked their way through a jungle. I do not recall seeing any wheeled machineguns when we linked up with Hamilton, nor did I see any on my walks around the perimeter.

Had I seen any, I would have told Hamilton to detach them so the troops using the trail could have used them in the upcoming engagement. However, he did have two platoons from C/2/502 attached, giving him a force of well over 250 soldiers, based on his report.

TF Brown, consisting of the Recondos, one platoon from C/2/502, and an Apache Platoon with two U.S. advisers, had difficulties penetrating the jungle to the designated assembly area.[25] Neither Ron nor I were sure about TF Brown's location. It appears from the report Captain Brown submitted to the *Special Study* that Ron had the direction of the trail I was on wrong. Ron believed his TF had passed my company on its south, but I did not think so based on the distance he told me they had traveled. When Ron informed me that his TF was hacking his way westward, I instructed him to turn north until he intersected the trail and then turned west. If not, there was a good possibility they would not reach our location before dark.

Marshall wrote that I wanted to charge the enemy battalion and put words that I never uttered in my mouth. In fact, I considered them insulting. It is not the way I talk. He wrote that I told Emerson, "Let me charge them! I have got them on my hip. Do not let them get away. Turn me loose!"[26]

I had commanded a company-size unit for almost 10 months and had become highly respectful of the enemy's proficiency based on numerous actions before Bu Gia Map. The statements Marshall attributes to me make me look naïve and inexperienced. Let us not forget the NVA had two more battalions they could quickly deploy, and they could have been in the process of doing so already. Under these circumstances, it would be reckless to launch an attack without reinforcements.

I did have a very frank radio conversation with Emerson during the afternoon. It dealt with his order to turn my company around and go to Brown's assistance. Brown was under attack to our east, near the trail. Marshall wrote that Emerson ordered me to keep covering fire to my front for a while before withdrawing my company to go to Brown's assistance.[27] Again, Marshall has the facts wrong.

I received no such order from Emerson. He was aware of the situation on the ground and knew we were not in contact with the enemy—we had halted, as ordered, about 800 meters to the east of the enemy location. Laguana returned from observing the enemy position, and I was about to send out another patrol to find out what the enemy was doing. To follow the order related by Marshall would require A/2/502 to move forward and engage the enemy, since visibility in the jungle was limited to less than 30 feet. Such a move would have led to a decisive engagement, just what Emerson and I did not want to occur until reinforcements were in place.

Still, I was irked by the order to turn my company around to go to Brown's assistance. I could not understand why the two TFs coming up behind me, consisting of over 450 troops[28] could not overcome what had to be a much smaller force (estimated by Captain Brown to be an NVA recon company) than the more imposing forces facing A/2/502.

The collision between TF Brown and the NVA company near the east–west trail was intensive. Part of the problem was that Brown had his TF moving in a checkerboard formation, and it was difficult and time-consuming to assemble it in the thick jungle. TF Brown repelled the NVA unit but not without suffering casualties. The Recondo platoon sergeant L. N. Koontz was wounded—shot through the thigh. Sergeant Schiavoni was also wounded, and Sergeant Peppers was killed. A total of six men were injured, including a news reporter accompanying TF Brown. In his report, Brown wrote that the enemy suffered 23 killed by body count but that a later prisoner report placed the enemy death toll at 70.[29]

Marshall notes Brown reached the trail and became engaged with enemy troops at 1430 hours and that A/2/502 did not reach Brown's location until 1800 hours. At 1800 hours, the jungle was already dark.[30] My notes have our linkup with Brown shortly before 1600 hours, and this is roughly the time reported by Captain Hamilton, who wrote that his unit reached TF Brown at approximately 1530 hours.[31]

Marshall also claims that Captain Hamilton's cavalry troop had passed Brown's location and was on the trail between Brown and me as Brown brought in gunship support. The cavalry must have been to the east of Brown—otherwise, we would have encountered them on that trail as we moved to assist Brown.

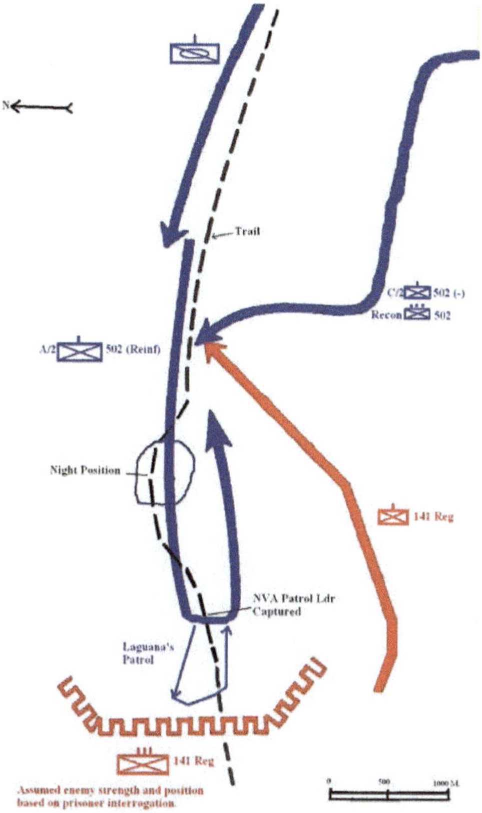

Battle Sketch 8. My sketch of the concentration of forces.

Marshall reports that Emerson was overhead and directing supporting fires for TF Brown. He notes that some of the rockets and machine-gun fire from the helicopters hit Hamilton's column, or at least the bamboo splinters from that strike did. This helicopter strike resulted in six cavalrymen wounded by flying bamboo splinters.[32] I was aware of the helicopter strike, but Hamilton did not mention having six wounded. This action also shows that Marshall is wrong about Hamilton being on the trail between Brown and me.

As far as my alleged complaint that Emerson had cost me my last chance to corner a large enemy force is concerned, that conversation dealt with the fact we no longer had visual contact with the enemy. I believed the enemy had two courses of action now that he knew we were fully aware of his presence and were bringing in reinforcements. If the enemy regimental commander were as aggressive and daring as the one we encountered in the Tuy Hoa area in February, he could launch a full-scale attack on our perimeter with the whole regiment during the night or at first light.

The weather conditions with low cloud cover and rain favored such action since it would be tough for us to use air support.[33]

I believed that if the enemy commander were cautious, he would probably slip back towards the border. I anticipated he would adopt this course of action. I told Emerson I did not expect to find the enemy in their former positions in the morning and we had lost our best chance to corner a large enemy unit, always a difficult task. Emerson believed it was equally likely the enemy would remain in their positions—events proved him correct.

Marshall also infers that I ordered all forces to take up night positions where Brown had his previous action. This is inaccurate. Captain Brown reported the enemy confronting his TF broke all contact as TF Hamilton and A/2/502 approached from different directions. Therefore, we could safely evacuate the wounded by winching them to a helicopter hovering above the jungle. When completed, we still had some time before darkness.

Having passed up and down the trail twice in one day, we had noticed more than halfway west on the trail to our former position that there was as suitable a place as could be found for a night perimeter. It was also near a bend in the trail, which I intended to use in the morning. As soon as we linked up with Brown and Hamilton, I sent a strong security force from A/2/502 west to scout and secured the new perimeter. I briefed Hamilton and Brown on their designated portions in that perimeter. That is where we spent the night.[34]

It is difficult to tell where the battalion AA report has us located. It gives a seven-digit location (YU 2172248), probably a typing error since the north-south coordinates would place it about 6 kilometers west of the battle area. Later they give YU 273348 for our night location. That was our location when we left to go to Brown's assistance. Our night location was about 1,000 meters to the east. The SJ gives A/2/502's location at 2150 hours at coordinates that are not wholly readable on my copy. However, it appears to be YU 298333, which is too far to the east, but on the third line below that entry, A/2/502's location in the SJ is YU 267315, near where we captured the NVA sergeant. We consistently reported our location to the battalion and supporting artillery to prevent friendly fire injuries and to be able to deliver artillery fire rapidly. I do not understand the different coordinates given by higher echelons.

CHAPTER 16

Battle of Bu Gia Map and Pursuit

Battle Plan

According to Marshall, Lieutenant Colonel Emerson forwarded the plan for the next day's action to us.[1] This is wrong. Having received operational control of all ground forces early that morning, those of us on the ground prepared the plan and forwarded it to Emerson for approval. Hackworth also wrote that this was the case.[2]

After a walk around the perimeter, Brown, Hamilton, Clements, and I formulated a plan for the next day in the early part of the night. During this meeting, Brown raised the issue of Emerson's role in the upcoming fighting and whether he might intervene in the operation. I told them Emerson was fully aware that to have two officers lead a battle could lead to a catastrophe. He had given me the authority to plan and execute the battle together with responsibility for failure. While confident that he would refrain from intervening, I asked them to keep their radios on my command frequency, and I would answer all calls from Emerson. I told them the command line was Brown and Hamilton in that order if something happened to me.

I had experienced the terrain to our west and we agreed we should conduct a right envelopment around the enemy's left flank with part of our force while the rest of the command approached the enemy frontally. Hamilton's cavalry, with two attached platoons from C/2/502, as well as some Montagnards, was the enveloping force. One of the platoons from C/2/502 was transferred to TF Brown at Hamilton's suggestion to strengthen the units in direct contact with the main enemy.

The choice of a right rather than a left envelopment was primarily due to the trail configuration near our night position and the direction of that trail on the other side of the battle site. The trail made a sharp northward bend just west of our night position but turned west about 500 meters from our perimeter. Thus, the envelopment units needed to penetrate the jungle northward from that bend for a relatively short distance before turning west to get north of the enemy flank.

A recon by Laguana and another by Sergeant Wilmer Nelson from the same platoon earlier in the day suggested the trail we were on ran through the enemy positions and they felt it then made a slight northward turn. This turn made sense from a map study since it would connect to a series of ridgelines leading to the Cambodian border. Therefore, it was essential to cut the trail as quickly as possible to prevent reinforcements from reaching the 3/141 NVA Regiment.

Since the cavalry had to travel the farthest in challenging jungle terrain, we agreed they start their northward move at first light. The other two units would give the cavalry a 90-minute head start before beginning a slow westward movement. A/2/502 would lead with most of the attached Montagnards scouting its advance. On contact, these scouts were to withdraw and become part of their assigned platoons.[3]

TF Brown, now consisting of the Recondos, two platoons from C/2/502, and the Apache scout platoon, was to follow A/2/502 in the westward movement on the trail and then swing south at a designated point so that it ended up positioned on my left rear when we reached the enemy positions. We expected the NVA to be in their usual U-shaped ambush position. We envisioned TF Brown's position would be east of the southern part of the "U." TF Brown was to be the reserve and, at the same time, engage the southern part of the enemy position.

I had sent Laguana and his squad forward after darkness to keep the enemy position under observation. I told him not to get embroiled in a fight even if the enemy came awfully close to his place. If they came too close to his position, I told Laguana to dispose of them silently. I also told him to keep total radio silence and break that silence only if the enemy made a significant shift in their positions or brought up reinforcements. Laguana and his men would rejoin the company as we approached the enemy line.

The company was to go into line formation after we linked up with Laguana's patrol. My platoon's and TF Brown's orders were simple: engage the enemy with fire, fix them in their positions, but not attempt a frontal assault until the cavalry broke into the enemy rear.[4]

We sent the maneuver/attack plan to Lieutenant Colonel Emerson via radio, using coded map reference points. It was quickly approved. Thereupon, I sent Brown and Hamilton back to brief their respective units, telling them they would receive the fire support plan later. I said to them that it was not feasible to assemble the troops for a briefing, but I asked them to convey some specific information down the chain of command:

1. We are going against well-trained and possible superior NVA forces in prepared positions.
2. We have a front-line strength of 628 seasoned and best-trained troops in the U.S. Army, and we are preparing a massive fire support plan, the like of which you have never seen.
3. We will not go against enemy strength but use a maneuver to pry them out of their prepared positions.

4. Be alert tonight as the enemy might try a spoiling attack or bring up the rest of the regiment.
5. Finally, paraphrasing something I had read and had stuck in my mind, great challenges often produce exceptional solutions. I expect you to deliver a great victory that will become part of our unit's proud history.

After a canteen cup of coffee and another walk around the perimeter, Lieutenant Clements and I sat down to prepare a fire support plan for the morning. It took most of the night, interrupted only by a meeting with Lieutenant Otto, who asked to see me on a personal matter.

Bill Otto and I got more coffee and sat down on a log. Bill told me his marriage was on the rocks and described a letter he had received from his wife as a "Dear John" letter. I assumed it had arrived in the resupply/mail drop earlier in the day. He had the letter with him, but I did not ask to read it. Bill was distraught but not to the point where I worried about him. I told him I would arrange for him to travel back to the U.S. on emergency leave as soon as this operation was over and for him to proceed on the basis that the matter would resolve itself to everyone's satisfaction. I told him jokingly that he and I could end up on the same flight.

That night, I had much on my mind, as 628 troops (plus 26 Montagnards) under my command were getting ready to engage the 141st NVA Regiment. I finally had the significant engagement I had often mentioned to Emerson and Pearson as a reason for wanting to stay in command of the company until the end of my tour. My mind was wholly absorbed in ensuring that it was a success. However, that is no excuse for doing nothing about Lieutenant Otto's situation.

I could have pulled Bill up to my headquarters and turned the platoon to his competent platoon sergeant. I would surely have benefitted from this since I had no staff, not even a complete company headquarters. I had left Master Sergeant Macias and Lieutenant Karl Beach in Nhon Co. Pulling Bill up to my headquarters just hours before a battle would undoubtedly have raised questions in his platoon but may have saved the life of an outstanding officer with a bright future. It is one of those disturbing what-if questions I must live with for the rest of my life.

Clements and I got back to the fire support plan after Otto headed back to his platoon. We agreed there would be no artillery marking rounds. After we double-checked the coordinates, Clements prepared, labeled, and marked artillery concentrations and sent them to the artillery headquarters via radio. Ensuring the many coordinates were correct was time-consuming work. Clements suggested we aim the initial salvos—planned for 0930 hours—at what we believed to be the enemy rear to ensure our troops' safety. I agreed with his suggestion since I was eager to hit the enemy headquarters early in the engagement, thereby complicating the enemy's command and control. After the battle started, we moved the barrages from two artillery batteries eastward as close to our line as possible. We requested that each volley include WP and smoke rounds.

Having completed the fire support plan, I called Captains Brown and Hamilton to send runners to pick up copies. Clements briefed our platoon leaders and I told the task force commanders he could explain the plan to them if necessary.

The Battle

The battle took place over 8 kilometers from the southern end of the Bu Gia Map Airstrip. All units departed the night position at the planned times. TF Brown and A/2/502 were at the line of contact minutes after the artillery began the bombardment.

We had requested a FAC be on station by 0930 hours. I did not want the FAC earlier than 0930 since it could tip off the enemy about what to expect. The FAC appeared at the designated time after we had started shelling the enemy positions with artillery. As Clements and I had expected, the FAC requested we lift the artillery fire so he could bring in strike aircraft. We told the FAC we would not stop the artillery bombardment, thereby allowing the enemy to adjust their positions or launch counterattacks. We also reminded the FAC that the Air Force manual allowed for simultaneous airstrikes on targets engaged by artillery. There was a pause before he came back on the radio. He undoubtedly conferred with his superiors. He asked for the artillery position coordinates. Lieutenant Clements had those ready and gave them to the FAC.

Getting the Air Force to deliver their ordnance on a target without lifting the artillery fire was a first for me and the brigade.[5] It worked perfectly. The air support started soon after the troops were in their designated positions.

The Commander's Analysis part of the brigade AA report (paragraph 15a) states, "Suitable techniques must be developed to permit simultaneous employment of close air support and artillery." I had no idea where this came from until October 2019 when Perrine sent me a 1st Brigade document dated 27 May 1966 titled *Informal After Action Critique, Operation Austin 6*. It includes input from 2/502, with comments from that organization about close air support. The paragraph reads:

> Suitable techniques must be developed to permit simultaneous employment of close air support and artillery. Every effort is made to utilize close air support as soon as it arrives on station. Close air support aircraft will not strike while artillery is firing. When the cease fire is given to the artillery, there is usually a lull while the FAC identifies and marks the target. This lull has been used by the enemy to police the dead, wounded, and equipment from the battlefield. Likewise, there is usually a lull following an air strike before artillery can again be brought to bear.[6]

The battle plan we sent to Emerson on the evening of 10 May only included the maneuver and timing part of the battle. If Marshall came up with his battle sketch based on the plan we submitted to the battalion on 10 May, the battalion staff did not get that right. We completed the fire support plan around 0400 hours on 11 May, but I do not recall if we forwarded it to the battalion. We may not have since going through the complicated procedure of sending a fire support plan to the battalion by radio was a waste of the little time we had left before the movement to contact started. Furthermore, there was no need to do so since Clements dealt directly with the 320th Artillery.[7] The air support portion of the plan was not part of the fire support plan because it was not arranged until around 0930 hours on the 11th since we were not confident the Air Force would accommodate our wishes. I am sure we did not tell battalion as we were rather busy by that time.

The rain had stopped, but it was still heavily overcast, and Emerson, although overhead in his C&C helicopter, could not see anything on the ground. We had warned him to stay clear of the airstrikes and artillery fire, and he was well to the north of the battlefield. I do not recall if I told him the artillery and airstrike were going on simultaneously. Emerson called me on the radio and wanted to know if we were still in contact with the enemy. The command group was in a bamboo grove about 50 meters behind my two left flank platoons' junctions. Before I could answer, enemy machine guns fired a few long bursts in our direction. Sharp bamboo sticks torn off by enemy machine-gun slugs flew in all directions. One tore the handset out of my right hand, and the noise must have sounded deafening to Emerson on the other end. Another twig hit my ring finger and broke it at the second joint.[8] Emerson wondered what had happened, and I told him we were under heavy fire.

Emerson worried about the enveloping force (TF Hamilton), which he felt had fallen behind schedule in hacking its way through the bamboo forest. He wanted Hamilton to throw a smoke grenade. I reminded him the whole battlefield was shrouded in white smoke, and to use any other color would not work since he was colorblind.

It was not until around 1200 hours that we got a fix on the position of the cavalry. We judged they were about 600 meters to the northeast of our right flank. I figured it would be another 60–90 minutes before Hamilton would be able to make the planned left turn to attack the enemy rear. I passed the word to the units to begin conserving ammunition. Through an extraordinary effort, Hamilton and his men made it to the turning point in less than 45 minutes.

General Marshall's description of the attack and envelopment actions are misleading both in his text and sketch (p. 256 of his book). A/2/502 is not shown, but C/2/502 is. C/2/502 was Emerson's reserve back on the airstrip. TF Brown is depicted peeling off to the right and left before reaching our battle position, another inaccuracy. The enemy was deployed in a linear formation, and their line overlapped both our flanks. Our left and right flanks had to shift to the south and north, respectively, to prevent the enemy from enveloping the company.

I called Brown and asked for his help since I expected the enemy would try to press our flanks back and inward, placing us in a box. According to his report for the

Special Study, Brown sent one platoon from C/2/502 to tie in with my left flank, and the one C/2/502 platoon transferred to him earlier in the day from TF Hamilton to tie in with my right flank. He ordered both platoons to curve their flanks eastward to keep the enemy from getting behind us. He also suggested he move the rest of his TF northward behind Company A's line, from where he could better react to an enemy counterattack. I agreed with Ron's suggestion. The overlapping caused me to order the 4th Platoon, which I had initially planned to keep as a reserve, to take up positions on my right flank. This shuffling of forces began around 1015 hours, according to my notes.

The flank threats took longer to materialize than expected. The enemy move against our left flank took place shortly before 1050 hours. It was somewhat disorganized and less robust than expected, probably because of the massive artillery fire and airstrikes. We had little difficulty driving the attackers back after a short but sharp firefight, but it could have turned out differently if Brown had not moved a platoon to tie in with our left flank.

The enemy move against our right flank—about 15 minutes after hitting the left flank—was equally desultory and driven back without any heavy fighting.

Marshall wrote that the company was in column formation along the trail when the enemy counterattacked.[9] His statement is wrong and contrary to my notes and Captain Brown's report for the *Special Study*. As soon as we linked up with Staff Sergeant Laguana's patrol around 0900 hours, the company spread into a skirmish line, and all units were at the line of contact and engaged around 0930 hours. The attack on our left flank did not take place until more than an hour later, and we estimated it to be a company-size attack.

Marshall wrote further that Brown personally led the attacks against both enemy flanking attempts. This statement is again contrary to Brown's notes for the *Special Study*. Marshall was unaware we had changed the task forces' composition by moving a second C/2/502 platoon from Hamilton to Brown. There was, therefore, no need for Brown to "cartwheel" his platoon, as claimed by Marshall.[10] Nor was it possible for him to do so in the thick vegetation behind our line.

Kim Coleman, in her manuscript, takes this wrong information from Marshall a step further. She has Brown leading two counterattacks, almost 1,000 meters apart in a dense bamboo jungle within 15 minutes of each other. Coleman claims Brown charged an enemy machine-gun position, killing three NVA soldiers. Then he fought his way through an NVA encirclement. These actions resulted in him receiving a DSC. My friend Ron was an aggressive and courageous officer, but he never claimed to have done what Kim Coleman describes at Bu Gia Map. She seemingly has Bu Gia Map confused with Dak To the following month, where Brown did receive a DSC.[11]

Marshall mentions a lonely and confused soldier guarding the trail behind my CP, facing east. Initially, there were several soldiers in that area. After sending the

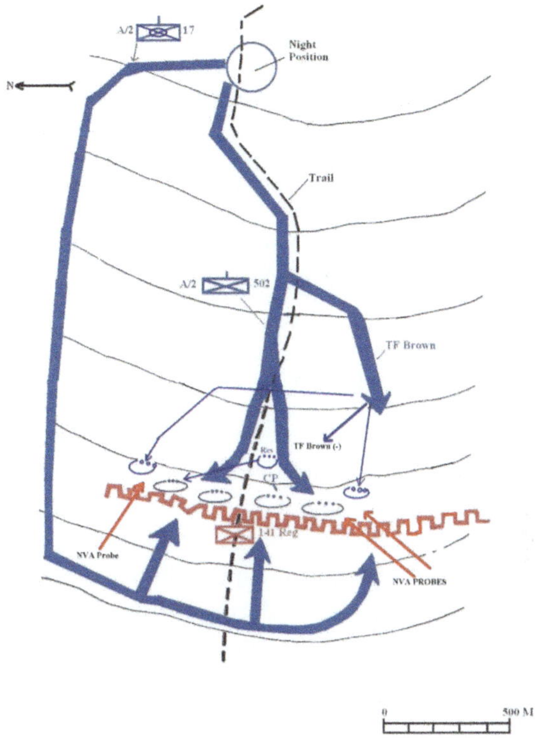

Battle Sketch 9. My battle sketch was submitted, in the form of a pen drawing, on 18 May. It shows deployment and initial adjustments.

4th Platoon to the right flank, Lieutenant Otto peeled off a fireteam of four or five men to act as CP security. I was grateful he took this action on his initiative. The experience from 9/10 February was fresh in our minds, and we did not want a repeat. When Brown moved the rest of his TF behind our line, I sent the fire team back to its platoon.

It may be of some interest to see what the brigade AA report had to say about the engagement when we dropped an enormous number of explosives on the enemy to our front and repelled counterattacks. There is virtually no similarity between the brigade Combat Operation AA Report for Operation *Austin 6*'s description of the battle and the situation on the ground. Keep in mind that this report was issued 5 June, and what happened should then be well known from battalion reports and from individuals who participated.

In one part, the brigade describes the battle of Bu Gia Map as follows:[12]

> 111050 May A/2/502 engaged reinforced VC platoon at YU 261349. The engagement continued through the afternoon. Enemy forces increased during the battle to an estimated two companies. The enemy was dug in, and communications wire had been laid in the position. The enemy force

> was enveloped by A/2/17 Cav from its rear. Airstrikes and 1500 rounds of artillery were called upon the enemy trapped between our forces. At 1600 the enemy broke contact and withdrew northwest (probably along a trail vic YU 255245, YU 240355, YU 180390). Results: 51 VC KIA (BC), 59 VC KIA (est), 15 VC KBA (est), captured three MG and nine individual weapons.[13]

The brigade report is even internally inconsistent. The forces we met were NVA, not VC. In paragraph 11 b (3) in the same report under Operations, it says:[14]

> During the early morning hours, 11 May 1966, 2/502 began receiving sniper fire while conducting search and destroy operations west of Bu Gia Map. This contact developed into a battle with two-company NVA force. Elements of 2/502 Inf and A/2/17 Cav surrounded this force, directed artillery and Tac Air into the area, and was able to decimate an entire NVA Battalion, as confirmed by body count and later POW interrogation. Two batteries of 2/320 Artillery fired 2,000 rounds in support of 2/502 Inf during the engagement.

The various parts of the brigade report were obviously prepared by different people and inadequately reviewed before publication. It is up to the operation section or the XO to check the entire report before publication in my operational experience. My conclusion is that this was not the case in the 1st Brigade in late spring 1966. It is also a reminder that what AA reports contain should not always be treated as gospel.

I did not witness Lieutenant Otto's death. However, later conversations with Sergeants Soto and Drake confirmed an enemy machine gun cut him down. I do not recall Otto telling me over the radio that he would bring me a machine gun, as reported by Marshall. TF Brown and A/2/502 were the fixing forces, and these units were not to attack until the cavalry had attacked the enemy rear. If I had known that Otto intended to move forward to capture a machine gun, I would have reacted quickly to the quote by Marshall.

According to my notes, the cavalry broke into the enemy rear a few minutes before 1300 hours, which was the signal for TF Brown and A/2/502 to attack frontally. The fighting was over about 45 minutes later. TF Brown covered the area south of the trail in the battlefield's sweep as they advanced while A/2/502 cleared the area north of the east–west trail. The space between our line and the enemy position was a pulverized jungle. The airstrikes and 2,000 rounds from two artillery batteries[15] had not only brought down the bamboo forest but large triple-canopy trees. It took some time for our troops to work their way forward through this twisted mass of fallen jungle growth. Dead NVA troops, battered bodies, and plenty of ghastly-looking body parts littered the ground.[16] No enemy troops surrendered.

An immediate pursuit of the enemy was impossible since the artillery needed to displace to cover our advance to the west. The companies also needed a resupply. Nevertheless, the delay was a welcome respite for troops worn out from the previous days' activities. Both TF Brown and Hamilton's cavalry troop remained under my operational control during the pursuit. The battalion AA report states Hamilton's unit was extracted on 13 May and reverted to brigade control. The extraction took place on 14 May after we reached the border. The platoons from C/2/502 also remained attached. The battalion AA report shows that they stayed with the units to which they were assigned, which is also my recollection. The original TF stayed intact for the next three days due to the uncertainty about what the rest of the 141st NVA Regiment was doing.

After going into a defensive perimeter at the top of the ridge, I met Captains Brown and Hamilton, along with Lieutenant Clements, and we spent much of the night preparing for the pursuit. Before we started planning, I thanked the two task force commanders for their loyal support and the plan's superb execution.

We agreed that A/2/502 would lead the pursuit, followed by Hamilton and Brown, in that order. However, we did not know what the terrain looked like to our west or the trail's exact location. Therefore, we had Clements pre-plan artillery barrages along the route where we expected the trail to run.

Brown and I also discussed his encounter with the NVA Recon Company on 10 May. We both agreed this company did not come from the 3/141st. Instead, we concluded it came from a higher echelon with the mission to scout the route ahead of the 141st Regiment.

The number of killed in A/2/502 was relatively small considering the hours of heavy fighting: Private First Class Andrew C. Evans, Lieutenant William F. Otto, and Specialist 4 W. M. Taylor. I recollect we had seven wounded, but I cannot be sure because I do not have MRs from this operation. Hamilton reported the cavalry troop had five KIA and five wounded. I will address this later. TF Brown had no soldiers killed or wounded on 11 May.

Interrupted Pursuit

None of my sources except Hackworth mention an incident on 12 May that irritated me more than any other during this operation. I have not found it mentioned by Brigadier General Marshall. All reports from battalion and brigade are silent on this subject. However, it is mentioned indirectly in the battalion AA report, which notes an urgent request from A/2/502 for a large supply of explosives.

The three task forces started their northwestward pursuit of the enemy at first light on the morning of 12 May. Still, they did not get far before A/2/502 was recalled to an area northwest of the engagement to clear an LZ, collect captured weapons and equipment in stacks, and wait for VIPs. I left TF Brown and TF Hamilton at the location we had reached as I moved back with my company to meet the VIPs. Hackworth took note of this incident and wrote, "Lunde and his people received the dubious honor to clearing an LZ in the shattered jungle … an eight-hour job, but it was that kind of war."[17] The orders also required us to bring some deserving troops to the LZ. The VIPs were Dan Rather, a CBS TV crew, and Lieutenant Colonel Emerson.

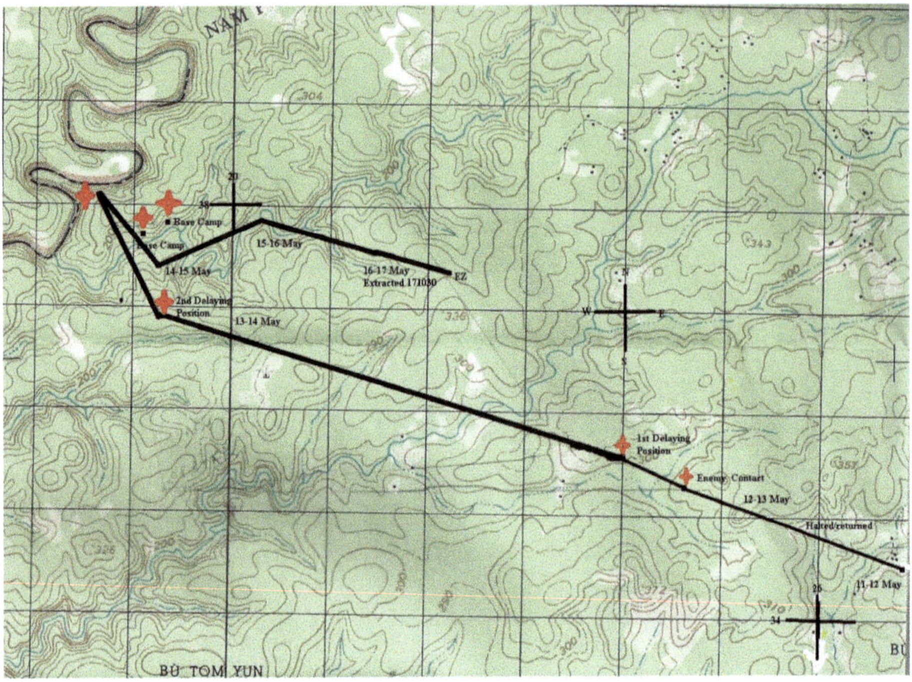

Map 10. This modified U.S. topographic map shows the approximate route of the pursuit with red stars marking enemy encounters. However, the invasion trail followed ridgelines and may not coincide precisely with the above route that the battalion reports show.

There is also a warning in the 1st Brigade AA report that an immediate pursuit must occur after a battle. I agree, and that would have taken place if higher headquarters had not sent the CBS TV crew, requiring A/2/502 to spend most of the day preparing an LZ in the jungle. I find it inconceivable that Brigadier General Pearson at Nhon Co did not know about this visit and the full-day delay cost in the pursuit.

I started introducing the few troops brought forward. Unfortunately, my annoyance and frustration at the interrupted pursuit and lack of sleep for almost 90 hours caused me to forget the names of a couple of soldiers who had been with me for months.

After that embarrassing incident, I unloaded some of my frustrations, but Dan Rather signaled the camera crew to turn off the camera before I got far. The Administration in Washington claimed we were not facing any infiltration through Laos and Cambodia. I told Rather the troops we had just fought—the 141st NVA Regiment—had come through Cambodia, that we were in pursuit when called back to meet him. Dan Rather asked if I objected to him quoting me. I told him I did not. As far as I know, he never quoted me.[18]

After the "guests" left, the pursuing force started northwest again but had to stop in a little over an hour because it was becoming dark. TF Brown had one minor enemy contact while waiting for A/2/502 to rejoin the two task forces.[19] We all felt pessimistic about the possibility of catching any NVA survivors as two days had passed since the battle. Nevertheless, there was a slim chance because we expected the enemy to bring many wounded along, slowing their withdrawal. Furthermore, Brown, Hamilton, and I felt the 3/141st Regiment had been practically wiped out, and the regimental commander could have sent new forces to help extricate the survivors.

B-52s from Guam carpet-bombed the ridgelines after midnight on 13 May, but most of the strike was to the north of the ridgeline we were following.[20] I saw only one large crater on our way to the border. Unfortunately, the battalion AA report is scarce on information regarding the pursuit, and my copy of the battalion SJ is virtually unreadable. What follows is, therefore, primarily based on my notes and memory.

Marshall wrote that the companies used the checkerboard concept as they moved west, and that the terrain was more open and flatter.[21] The straight-line distance from the battle area to the border was over 10 kilometers. We moved north-northwest in the beginning and then switched northwest. The slight directional change is not evident on the map opposite, which is based on the battalion reports. This small change in direction and the rough terrain lengthened the distance we traveled and my guess is that the actual ground covered was closer to 15 kilometers.

We did not checkerboard. The country we passed through was more rugged than what we had experienced before. It was not flat but full of sharp and narrow ridgelines and deep ravines until we reached the high ground overlooking the Prek Dak Huot River—the Cambodian border. The ruggedness is evident from the map. Its vertical contour interval is 20 meters (66 feet).

We encountered two NVA delaying positions during our pursuit. The first consisted of an NVA force of nine troops who fought to the last man. The NVA lieutenant who commanded this rearguard action was among the dead. A plastic envelope he carried contained letters from his parents or wife and some pictures and an unfinished letter we assumed was to his family based on the conclusion of our interpreter. We did not turn these over to intelligence as we saw nothing of military value. Instead, I kept them until I made my first trip to Hanoi in 1973, at which time I turned everything over to one of my North Vietnamese counterparts, Lieutenant Colonel Bao, for delivery to the lieutenant's family. I included a brief description of the action, along with the statement that he and his troops died gallantly protecting their regiment. I added my condolences to the family of a brave officer.

The narrowness of the ridgeline we were on precluded maneuver except by platoon-sized units. I had a quick meeting with Captains Brown and Hamilton, and we all agreed we needed to spread out. Therefore, I directed Brown to take his

Recondos and all C/2/502 platoons and descend the north side of the ridgeline into the valley and then turn west while searching the valley, generally keeping abreast of our progress on the ridgeline. There are several notations in the battalion AA report referencing the Recondos and C/2/502 platoons' activities, mainly finding abandoned enemy camps.

A/2/502 and A/2/17 Cav continued along the ridgeline in the direction of the border. The second delaying position we encountered was more challenging to approach, and several of the defenders slipped away, leaving four dead behind. We suffered no casualties in these two engagements but captured 13 weapons.

We reached the steep hills above the Prek Dak Huot River early on 14 May. We had strict orders not to violate Cambodian territory. I received a radio call from Captain Tom Taylor. He was apparently assigned to the brigade staff, as related in his book.[22] He reminded me not to cross into Cambodia.

I had already talked to Emerson and told him about an elongated island with some vegetation that divided the river into two channels. This island did not show on our maps. I asked if we should consider that island a part of Vietnam and fire on the NVA troops assembling there pending crossing the second channel. Emerson told me to use my judgment but not to create an international incident. On the far side of the river, NVA troops were leisurely loading on trucks.

I told First Lieutenant Clements to bring artillery on our side of the river and the island. We learned the difficulties in bringing artillery on a steep hillside facing away from the artillery positions. Some of the artillery shells exploded in treetops over our heads. A bunch of hot shrapnel fell among our troops, and two soldiers with wounds required evacuation. This evacuation may have coincided with the departure of the Cavalry Troop since we had reached the border without meeting a large enemy force and the task force was dissolved.

Clements soon had the problem of artillery shells exploding in the treetops solved, and we brought massive salvos on the Vietnamese side of the river and the island. Later, some of our troops crossed to the island and searched it. It was not possible to avoid thinking about what difference the many hours we wasted preparing for Dan Rather's visit could have made. We found a further 13 bodies on our side of the river and six on the island. We also found 29 very severely damaged weapons or parts of weapons. Artillery shells that fell while the company descended the steep hillside to the river appeared to have killed all the enemy soldiers we found.

We had planned to spend the next few days searching north along the Prek Dak Hout River. Battalion denied this plan since we would be outside the artillery fan. For the next three days, we, therefore, moved generally east-southeast, changing course every day. We had no enemy contacts. The only unusual thing that happened was when we stopped for the night on 14/15 May. The battalion S-4 must not have been aware of the task force's dissolution since the meals delivered were for all three original units. The Montagnards turned in their weapons and left for their tribe that night. I thanked them for their help and gave them the extra meals we had received. A/2/502 was extracted by helicopter late on 17 May and then moved to Nhon Co. The battalion AA report has our extraction date on the 16th, and that we were brought first to Bu Gia Map airstrip and then to Nhon Co the next day. I believe this is a mistake. Lieutenant Mooneyham's report also has 17 May as the helicopter's extraction date and that we moved to Bu Gia Map, where we at once loaded on Caribou aircraft for Nhon Co.

Confusion About Friendly Losses

I could not develop an exact friendly KIA number by using the battalion AA report, the brigade AA report, and the *Special Study* by the 22nd Military History Detachment. The figure for the whole operation in the Bu Gia Map operation was nine KIA according to the brigade 5 June AA report, seven KIA according to the 24 May battalion AA report, and eight KIA according to the *Special Study*. These figures do not include the helicopter loss on 4 May. One of those killed was from TF Brown on 10 May; six were from A/2/502 on 7, 8, and 11 May; five were from A/2/17 Cavalry on 11 May. These numbers make a total of 12 killed and are higher than reported by the sources.

While I initially assumed the difference in all three sources could be poor reporting, further research by Lieutenant Colonel Perrine cleared up most of these discrepancies. First, it showed that Captain George Hamilton's input to the 22nd Military History Detachment on 27 October 1966 had a difficult mistake to explain. Hamilton wrote that A/2/17 Cavalry suffered five killed and five wounded during the operation. Perrine's research revealed that A/2/17 Cavalry suffered none killed and only two injured. These numbers bring the friendly KIAs reported in the battalion AA report in line with our count in the above paragraph. It is still two less than the brigade showed, but this may be due to other brigade units (i.e., 1/327) having casualties. The *Special Study* by the 22nd History Detachment must have realized the mistake in Hamilton's input, and that should have brought their count to seven, but they report eight killed. When and how that one additional soldier died is unknown to me. These reports also show that A/2/502 had the preponderance of KIAs—six of the seven named.

Confusion About Enemy Casualties

When it comes to the enemy forces we engaged, their composition, and their losses during the Bu Gia Map Operation, we run into a confusing picture in the sources. Neither the AA reports, personal interviews, nor the *Special Study* prepared by the 22nd Military History Detachment is even close to an agreement.

It appears from later intelligence reports that the 141st NVA Regiment was part of a division-size force consisting of two more regiments and that they were heading for War Zone Delta, north of Saigon. The various units also had code names, making it difficult to identify them. One thing is clear: this was a significant movement of NVA troops into South Vietnam from Cambodia. We had met the spearhead of this force. Prisoner interrogation also showed that the NVA was plagued with malaria and other diseases, and that morale was low. Some units had lost half their strength. One should be careful in accepting what prisoners tell their captors—often, they paint a picture of their units in the starkest of terms. According to the sergeant we captured on 10 May, the companies' strength in his battalion was around 120. The troops we met did not display low morale and were not suffering from malaria or other diseases to the extent concluded from prisoner interrogations.

Lieutenant John D. Mooneyham, who placed the NVA body count at 37, gave the lowest number of NVA killed by far. He is obviously speaking only about the narrow area between his platoon and the low ridge previously held by the enemy. I included Mooneyham's count in the partial report I made to the battalion as we moved through the battle area. The command group moved forward with the 1st Platoon over ground littered with enemy dead. A combined count from the platoons gave an enemy body count of 101. I reported this to Emerson, cautioning that this figure would undoubtedly rise significantly when counts from TFs Hamilton and Brown were received. A/2/502 amended its count the following day (12 May) when we discovered an additional 16 bodies not included in the original count, and are in the battalion AA report. To that number, you must add the 24 we killed on 8–10 May on our approach to the battlefield, the 32 dead NVA soldiers we found in the pursuit, and Brown's report of 23 killed by body count on 10 May.

The *Special Study* places the number of enemies killed at 93. Why this number is much lower than the combined number reported by those who provided inputs is unknown. However, it should at least equal the total reported by the contributors. The brigade AA report gives the number of enemies killed by body count at 101 (obviously based on the initial count I submitted on 11 May) plus 148 estimated. Captain Brown's report gives a body count of 180 for his battlefield area—south of the trail—and Captain Hamilton's count was 103 for his area—top of the enemy ridgeline. The battalion AA report gives an enemy body count of 95 plus 100 estimated. This number is what is listed in one part of the report. In another part of the report (page A-1-1), the total enemy killed by body count is 551. This last number must include the casualties inflicted during the whole operation. Hackworth and Marshall wrote, respectively, the number of NVA killed was over 450 and 400.[23]

A recent article in *Screaming Eagle* magazine (Volume 17, Number 1, January 2015) is equally confusing. This writing is a two-page extract from *The History of the*

2/17 Cavalry 1916–1976 sent by Lieutenant Colonel Perrine. The two pages dealt with Operation *Austin 6* at Nhon Co in May 1966. The article has A/2/17 Cavalry occupying a blocking position behind the enemy forces, not striking them from the rear. The body count given is 106 enemies KIA, approximately the same as Hamilton's count for his battlefield area. The article also reports that only 50 NVA soldiers from the 3/141st NVA Regiment escaped the B-52 strike on our route of advance based on the report from a prisoner we captured. My comment on this statement is that we did not capture prisoners on our way to the border, as far as I know. Furthermore, we encountered only one large crater from the B-52 strike, as most bombs appear to have fallen to the north and east of our advance. The article confirms my recollection that A/2/17 was extracted on 14 May.

I have given all these organizational body counts and estimates to illustrate how poor and open to manipulation the body count is as a measurement of success on the battlefield and to differences that can creep in at various command levels. In the final analysis, no matter what the NVA losses were, they suffered a devastating defeat. We destroyed or decimated at least five companies of NVA when we include the recon company that grappled with TF Brown on 10 May. It was the most successful operation since the brigade arrived in Vietnam, and the report from the 320th Artillery concurs. We had accomplished this with relatively light casualties. Our success illustrates the value of fire and maneuver, a concept not used often in later battles in Vietnam, starting within a month.

Completing My First Tour in Vietnam

After a briefing by First Sergeant Macias, I sat down to write letters to the families of those who had died,[24] but Macias convinced me not to do it this time as he pointed out I had enough on my plate for the next two days. I followed his advice and left most of them for my XO to write. First, however, I felt I should write a letter to Bill Otto's wife.

She answered in a four-page handwritten letter dated 31 May. Her letter reached me when I reported to Fort Bragg. It was a sad letter and she seemed to blame herself. I limited my answer to stating Bill had always talked well about his family. If anything, the widow's letter increased my feeling of sorrow and guilt for not having acted differently that night.

Having written the letter, Macias and I set down to make a list of those who should receive awards for making our victory possible. We consulted the platoon sergeants in preparing the list. We recommended 20-some soldiers for awards. Unfortunately, too much time has passed for me to match incidents to names.

Macias and a company medic wanted me to go to the brigade aid station to have my finger looked at and thereby qualify for another Purple Heart. I refused and pointed out that since we arrived in Bu Prang, I had lost 12 soldiers and had a higher number of wounded, and it would be unseemly for me to get a Purple Heart for a broken finger. However, the finger splint had only been changed once since 11 May and was very dirty, so I asked the medic to change it.

Some NCOs came by to give me a tapestry made in a shop in Nhon Co titled "The Last Sixteen." It contained the names of the NCOs who had been with me from the beginning and were still around. This treasured framed tapestry hangs in my study. I also received other gifts and memorabilia from the company of emotional value, including an inscribed Soviet sniper rifle. But these had to be shipped, either because they did not fit into my duffel bag or the papers for bringing them to the U.S. were not ready in time. I asked Captain Brown to send them to me. Brown informed me in a letter that he had mailed the other gifts, but he had lost the receipt. The end of the story is that I never received them.

Before going to bed on 17 May, I wrote a short letter to Florence, because the last I had written was on 4 May at Bu Prang. I knew she must be apprehensive because of her many letters and newspaper and TV coverage of our activities in the intervening period. I told her to expect me home no later than 10 June as we had already discussed that I would stop a couple of days in California to meet some of my school friends. We had planned that she would meet me on the West Coast. I told her I would call from the first stop on U.S. soil.

I received some depressing news when I arrived at Nhon Co. Orders for my next assignment had arrived—the U.S. Army Nuclear Arsenal at Edgewood Proving Grounds in Maryland. I had no desire to go there, and Brigadier General Pearson appealed it to Major General Delk M. Oden (1911–1997), Chief of Personnel in Washington, and Lieutenant General John A. Heintges (1912–1977), the deputy at MACV.

My last day in command of the company was 18 May 1966. Before Captain Ron Brown assumed command, First Sergeant Macias assembled the company for me to say a few words. I had not had much time to think about the significance of this day, but I had very mixed feelings about leaving. The company had been my home for the better part of a year. The troops were my family and we had gone through much together. As I walked down the lines of young, tough, but tired paratroopers, I was sad to note that only a small number of soldiers who had started with me the previous summer were still around. Some had caught malaria or other diseases and were sent back to the U.S. Some of the many wounded left the company and never returned. However, all too many of my family had made the ultimate sacrifice.

I was also struck by the reality that my time as a commander of a company in combat—the greatest of all jobs for an infantryman—had concluded. The thoughts about my friends and the knowledge I would never again lead a company in combat played with my emotions. What I hoped to be a few eloquent words of thanks and advice became quick thanks and good-bye instead, since I was afraid trying to say what was in my heart would make me completely choked up.

In 2004, Colonel Landry and I traveled to Fort Campbell to be inducted as Distinguished Members of the Regiment. Some current troops from our old command were present, as was Command Sergeant Major (Retired) Macias. I reminded the company's current members of the brave soldiers who stood formation far away and long ago. I told them I wanted to finish the talk I had failed to give in 1966.

The brigade held a farewell dinner for me on the evening of 18 May. Those present included Brigadier General Pearson, Lieutenant Colonel Emerson, and Lieutenant Colonel Donald Rosenblum, my company commander in Berlin. He had just arrived in the brigade to take over one of the battalions. Majors Hackworth and Schroeder were among the others who attended. Pearson gave a short speech reciting a laundry list of information that he must have received from the brigade Public Information Section. This information included the number of enemies killed and weapons captured while I commanded A/2/502 and the awards I had received, or for which I'd been recommended. The statistics on enemies killed and weapons seized are much lower than the actual figures. The numbers are even lower than the results of our most recent campaign. The statistics cited were the same as in the July–August 1966 issue of *The Screaming Eagle* by the 101st Airborne Division Association.[25] Pearson ended his short speech with these very meaningful words, "Captain Lunde is the type of commander under whom I would like my own son to serve in combat." Emerson mentioned that a second DSC recommendation should be added to my awards as he had prepared one for the operation concluded the previous day.

I considered it strange there was no mention of the last operation, the most successful since the brigade arrived in Vietnam, by anyone at the dinner. Three of those present knew I had command on the ground (Emerson, Schroeder, and Hackworth). It was not a daily occurrence in Vietnam that a captain was the ground commander of 600-some troops, which alone warranted a comment. Pearson and Rosenblum may not have known I was the ground commander. I received no invite to make any comments—the first time at a going-away event that this happened—I did not know why.[26] Maybe the senior officers were ashamed to admit the most successful operation since the brigade arrived in Vietnam was brought about by three captains.

However, I was more dismayed and depressed because Emerson did not recognize the troops' performance and sacrifice; they had been most instrumental in bringing him victory while suffering the most fatalities. He could have done this by only walking about 100 feet to my company area to express his gratitude. Despite this and his failure to mention that I was the ground commander in the Battle of Bu Gia Map in the DSC recommendation or the OER and difficulties in the 9th Infantry Division, we remained friends.

The following morning (19 May), I departed on an aircraft for Phan Rang to begin out-processing and then head to Saigon for a flight back to the U.S. I had not been in Phan Rang for more than an hour when I received a call from Emerson. General Westmoreland had requested Emerson brief a joint session of the Vietnamese War College and the Vietnamese General Staff College on the operation concluded on 17 May. He also asked Emerson to bring me and an outstanding NCO from Company B, Platoon Sergeant Robert B. Wightman. Emerson picked me up in Phan Rang and brought me to Dalat, where these military colleges were.

It began with Emerson giving an overview of the operation, emphasizing that the checkerboard concept was the key to our success. The mention of the checkerboard required a 15-minute explanation since the audience did not know what Emerson was talking about. I was supposed to briefly describe what happened after finding the infiltration trail on 9 May, including reinforcements, battle, and pursuit, but Emerson covered my part of the briefing. I do not believe this was accidental. He may have feared I would mention I was the ground commander.

I left Phan Rang for Saigon late on 22 May after completing my out-processing. I visited Saigon's Associated Press office, where I picked up a thick envelope Henri Huét had told me would be waiting for me if he was away from Saigon. It contained many pictures from the operation on the Cambodian border. The most precious things he gave me were copies of a collection of interviews with my troops about the officers and senior NCOs in A/2/502 and the war in general. The names of those interviewed were redacted or removed. The 1993 flood heavily damaged these interviews. I left Saigon on 24 May.

Meanwhile, the 1st Brigade moved to Dak To/Toumorong in Kontum Province, where heavy fighting took place with many losses. Six of my military family were among the 48 killed in 2/502, 1/327, and 1/5 Cavalry. I refer to these events as the mountain battles, which continued through 1967. I discuss them in more detail in the next chapter.

CHAPTER 17

Airborne Test Division: The War in 1967

My flight back to the U.S. stopped in the Philippines, Guam, and Hawaii on the way to Travis Air Force Base in California, where we arrived on 28 May. I had called Florence from Hawaii, and she told me she did not feel she could meet me on the West Coast with the kids leaving for Alaska.

Two days of processing and briefings at Travis gave me a flavor of events on the home front. I had left the country with a vast majority of the people supporting our efforts in Vietnam. Now, a significant element of the population had turned against the war and the soldiers who fought it. The starkest evidence of this change was the fact that the buses taking us to San Francisco Airport had their windows painted to prevent anyone along the route from seeing they carried troops.

We traveled in buses to San Francisco after processing on 30 May. I got off downtown near the bus terminal. I wished to see some of my friends from Mission High School and UC and say hello to my ex-wife and parents. I had dinner with them and some others they had invited the first night. The second night Marion and I had dinner with David Yamakawa. Some of my high school friends met me for brunch on the third day. I do not recall all who attended, but I feel sure Don Ramos and Joseph Young were there. My former mother-in-law took me to San Francisco International Airport on the evening of 1 June for a flight to Nashville, Tennessee, via Denver, Colorado.

I arrived in Nashville on 2 June 1966. Florence was there to pick me up. I wore jungle fatigues, as did most troops who were on the same aircraft. I saw Florence from a distance and waited for her. She walked right past me and went to the aircraft arrival gate, looking for me. After turning around, she finally saw me when I raised my hand. I had lost much weight while in Vietnam; my face looked gaunt, drawn, and much sunburned. When I processed through Travis, my weight was 117 lbs. compared to the 164 lbs. I weighed when I left in 1965.

After we found my duffel bag, we drove home but not before stopping at a Dairy Queen for a cheeseburger and milkshake, my first since returning. In the afternoon, I watched the news from Vietnam with Florence. Afterward, we discussed what we needed to do in the coming weeks. I had not received a change in orders, but I hoped the letter from Brigadier General Pearson and the support of General Westmoreland's deputy would result in a change of assignment.

I signed in temporarily at Fort Campbell, pending a change in my assignment to prevent using up accrued leave. We wanted to do as much as possible in the next two weeks. I had more than the maximum leave accrued and would lose 45 days if I did not use some at the end of the year. Therefore, I received 45 days' leave before reporting to my new duty station when I signed out from Fort Campbell.

We spent the next two weeks preparing for a move, not knowing where our new station would be. We alerted the transportation office at Fort Campbell that there would be a move in July and requested boxes to begin packing the smaller items. Florence also contacted a realtor to list our home for sale, effective 1 July, and gave the realtor keys to the house so his agency could show it to prospective buyers. We told him to notify the transportation office at Fort Campbell if the home sold before we returned from leave so they could pick up our shipment and place it in temporary storage. While we had contacted the Post Office to hold our mail, we told the realtor to keep any mail delivered by the Post Office despite the hold request until we returned.[1]

In out processing, I received the medical and dental records that had not followed me to Vietnam. As I was ready to leave, the woman asked, *Do you not want these?* and held up a fat gray folder that contained my personnel records. I had not realized my personnel records had also not gone to Vietnam with the brigade. I showed her my personnel file from Vietnam and asked her how I should handle the two files. She said the admin office at the new station should combine them into one file. The end of the story was that we left all records at the personnel office with the understanding we would pick them up after our leave before I reported to my new assignment.

Florence and I drove to Long Island, New York, on 22–23 June, where she would stay with her sister and mother until I returned from my trip to Norway. I spent two days at McGuire Air Force Base in New Jersey, waiting to see if I could get space available on a military aircraft. I was unsuccessful and decided to take a flight from Kennedy Airport. I left New York on 26 June and arrived in Bergen, Norway, the following day.

My parents were there to meet me. My sister, her husband, my brother Arthur, and his wife were also there. We stayed at Hotel Hordaland one night and headed to Voss with my parents on 28 June.

It had been three years since I was last in Norway, and much had happened in my life and the lives of my parents. My father was hospitalized three times for heart problems. They lived in Rolfsnes at the northern end of the island of Bømlo, where they lived until they purchased Lunde in 1925. There were no hospitals on the island, the nearest one being on the island of Stord, and it was only a regional hospital. It took about three hours for an ambulance to pick him up and take him to the local hospital.

My siblings were worried our parents' lives were in jeopardy by living in the somewhat isolated area of Rolfsnes. My sister and my brother Ole asked me to encourage our parents to move closer to a major hospital. I discussed this with my parents at length, and they agreed to sell their home in Rolfsnes and begin looking for a new home next year. They were able to find a buyer and eventually found a new home in Os but had to wait for the sale of their current house.

My parents were worried about paying the difference in the old and new home's cost, but I assured them I would help if they had temporary monetary difficulties. When I visited Norway before deploying to Vietnam in 1968, they were in their new home. I believed my father felt the end was approaching and he was now worried about my mother being able to manage if he was no longer around. In a conversation we had when my mother was not present, I assured him I would help.

My parents insisted the first thing on the list after we arrived in Voss was to go to a professional photoshop to have a picture taken of us, with me in uniform.

I had not been at Voss long before the word got around that I was in the country, and I began receiving requests for interviews. My father's service in the U.S. Army in France in World War I made the story more newsworthy. Before meeting with anyone, I contacted the U.S. Embassy and asked for their advice. They encouraged me to hold all newspaper, magazine, radio, and TV interviews offered.[2]

The first interview was with the local newspaper *Hordaland*. More interviews followed quickly by *Bergens Tidende*, the major newspaper in western Norway, and news magazine *Aktuell*. The 13 July story in *Bergens Tidende* was a lead article of two pages. The interviewer and article writer for *Bergens Tidende* was Olav Kjelsvik. In addition to their photographs, I provided several of those given to me by Henri Huét.

The article in *Aktuell*—written by Odd Harald Røst—appeared on 30 July, after I departed Norway. There was another article in the same issue about U.S. pilots shot down and captured over North Vietnam. I do not think this was a pure coincidence.

My father and I received invitations to appear in Bergen for television and radio interviews after the 13 July interview with the *Bergens Tidende*. The Norwegian Broadcasting System (NRK) sent a seaplane to pick us up on the lake at Voss and brought us to Bergen. It was our first seaplane ride. The plane landed in choppy waves in the fjord and taxied to the inner harbor where a car waited.

The TV interview lasted about 10 minutes and aired on the evening news. The radio interview was longer.[3] It aired at the end of the week in a program that dealt with human-interest stories that had taken place during the previous week.[4]

I told all interviewers that I did not want to discuss political issues since those were not within my professional field of expertise. Most honored my wishes, except for Odd Harald Røst and the photographer Aage Storløkken.

The *Aktuell* reporters were decidedly critical of the Johnson Administration's policies, but I did not allow myself to become involved in a political discussion. They then asked me about casualties, saying the Pentagon seldom announced how many Americans had fallen in Vietnam. I took issue with that statement, telling them the Pentagon issued casualty figures weekly and that those numbers could be trusted.

They then asked about relative enemy casualties, and I gave them the night engagement results on 9/10 February 1966 near Tuy Hoa, where we had five killed, and the enemy suffered at least 17 killed. I also gave them the count of the battle of Bu Gia Map, where we suffered six dead, and the enemy dead numbered around 450. They asked how many of these were innocent civilians? I told them none since the battle took place deep in a jungle where there were no civilians. They said to me without hesitation that the ratio I mentioned was unbelievable and wrote in the article that these numbers needed a pinch of salt ("en klype salt"). The article also characterized me personally as "cold and unemotional."

The Norwegians have shown generous support and admiration for the U.S. throughout history. There were in Norway, as in all western European countries, a small number of communist supporters. However, they had little or no influence on the government. Then there were also those—primarily students—who were active against the war in Vietnam. I received a couple of postcards that we could label "hate mail." Still, they were mild compared to the offensive ones my family and I received in the U.S. during the Vietnam years.

U.S. Army, Airborne, Electronics, and Special Warfare Board

I returned from Norway in mid-July 1966 and picked up Florence in New York. We proceeded to the Nuclear Arsenal at Edgewood Proving Grounds in Maryland since I had not received a change in orders. We arrived at the arsenal on the afternoon of 16 July, a Saturday, and the in-processing office was not open. There was a sign-in log at one of the windows, but a handwritten sign in large red letters told me not to sign in but contact the duty officer for instructions. He brought a stack of orders that changed my posting to Fort Bragg for assignment to the U.S. Army Airborne, Electronics and Special Warfare Board (USAAESWB), a U.S. Army Test and Evaluation Command (USATECOM) facility.

I was satisfied with the change since it was an airborne assignment and kept me from working at an unknown job at Edgewood Nuclear Arsenal. I had returned from Europe the night before and was tired, so we checked into a nearby motel and decided to drive to Clarksville, Tennessee, early the following day.

We arrived in Clarksville after dark on 17 July. Since the Fort Campbell transportation office had picked up our furniture and placed it in temporary storage, we had to stay at a nearby motel after retrieving Florence's car, which we had parked in the garage. The next day, we drove to the transportation office, giving them a copy of my new orders and asking them to ship our things to Fort Bragg. We also contacted the realtor, who told us he had a good prospect for our home's sale. Our last stop was at the 101st Personnel Office to pick up the records we had asked them to keep until we returned from leave.

David and Monica returned from Alaska on 19 July, so Florence and I drove both cars to Nashville and stayed at a motel near the airport. The kids arrived so late that we spent another night at that motel, leaving the following day with Florence and Monica driving to Columbus, Georgia, to pick up Barbara. David and I drove directly to Fort Bragg, where we stayed at the post guest house.

I signed in at the USAAESWB on 22 July, stating I would report for duty on 25 July, a Monday. In the meantime, I contacted Fort Bragg housing authorities. We were assigned on-post quarters, held a joint inspection of the four-bedroom rancher, signed the inspection forms, and received the keys.

I also stopped at the transportation office. They needed the address where our household goods should be delivered. David and I camped that night in the empty new home. Florence, Barbara, and Monica joined us on the afternoon of 24 July.

I reported for duty at the USAAESWB on 25 July 1966 but had to return home the following day as our household goods from Fort Campbell had arrived. Therefore, my first full day of duty was 27 July when I met the board president, Colonel James M. S. Strickland, the support staff, and Chief Warrant Officer Jack Miller. The latter's people worked in a hangar at Pope Air Force Base adjacent to Fort Bragg. The parachute rigging detail was in that facility. I ended up spending almost half my time there, where much of the testing took place.

The Airborne Test Division usually consisted of two branches—the Aircraft Branch and the Equipment Branch. Due to a shortage of officers during the Vietnam buildup, the two branches were combined. With the influx of officers who had completed their first tour in Vietnam, the Airborne Test Division was again re-established into two branches. The re-establishment of the two branches took place shortly after my arrival, and I became Chief of the Equipment Branch since my promotion to major was imminent. Lieutenant Colonel Robert E. Luttrell (1928–2007) was the chief of the Aircraft Branch and, at times, doubled as Chief of the Airborne Test Division.[5] I eventually had eight officers assigned:

Captain (promoted to major in 1967) Richard D. Ezzard had reported on 1 May 1966, almost two months before my arrival. He became my deputy.

Major Roy D. Martin (1930–2012) arrived on 3 January 1967 from the 1st Air Cavalry Division.

Captain Arne Andersen, a Norwegian American, arrived on 16 April 1967, after an extended hospital stay from serious wounds received during his first tour in Vietnam. His parents lived in the same community in Norway as my parents. He returned to Vietnam for a second tour about the same time I did.

Captain Carroll M. Coomer arrived on 24 November 1966.

Captain James T. Dowdy arrived on 16 February 1967.

First Lieutenant David A. Remenaric came on 2 August 1967.

Second Lieutenant Juan Perez arrived on 28 April 1967.

Second Lieutenant Richard P. Thompson arrived on 15 September 1967.

The Airborne Test Division assignment was unique and the people I worked with were first class. Most officers stayed in contact with me for much of my career.

Colonel Strickland and his wife departed in May 1967, and the new president, Colonel Karlton Warmbrod, took over on 1 June 1967. As I recall, the Stricklands left for an assignment in the Caribbean. They had a white German Shepherd named Sheila. Unfortunately, they could not take a dog to their new duty station, so Florence and I were happy to give her a new home.

A new deputy board president reported on 27 July 1967. His name was Colonel Henry T. Agee. He was still there when I departed. The same is true for the later Chief of the Airborne Test division, Lieutenant Colonel Luttrell, who arrived on 30 October 1967. He eventually took over the Airborne Test Division from Lieutenant Colonel Charles W. Eckels a month after I departed, according to TECOM.

The board also had an Operations Branch and an Admin Branch. The Adjutant was, for most of my time at the Board, Lieutenant Colonel Guy Peterson. Two of his assistants, Captain Walter N. Mott and Chief Warrant Officer Owens, signed my travel orders. They also handled most requests sent out to various commands to locate my missing temporary medical records.

There were also slots for liaison officers from the other services, major commands, and allied countries. Most of these positions were unfilled while I was on the Board.

A period of reorganization and rationalization in the U.S. Army had begun after President Kennedy took office. The Pentagon "Whiz Kids" working for Secretary of Defense Robert McNamara intended to reform the military. The reforms dealt primarily with a restructuring of major military commands.

Another critical target of changes addressed the test and evaluation of new equipment. The reorganization made the newly formed USATECOM, located at Aberdeen Proving Ground in Maryland, subordinate to Army Materiel Command. User testing remained the top priority, with a secondary priority of participating in technical testing directed by TECOM. Troop testing and recommendations to developing agencies were another, but lesser, priority. Despite this lower priority label, troop testing and recommendations to developing agencies ended up accounting for much of the travels of test officers.

The Airborne Test Division itself has a complicated history.[6] USATECOM was our immediate superior during the Vietnam era. Recommendations by an Army committee required TECOM to rationalize and centralize testing. To emphasize the importance of the testing process, the Airborne and Electronics Board moved from CONARC to TECOM in 1962. The same was true for the other Army boards. Recognizing the new importance of special warfare, the old Airborne and Electronics Board became the testing service for SF and the name of the board altered in January 1962 to Airborne, Electronics, and Special Warfare Board.

The special warfare assignment increased the workload, but the responsibilities we had in that area lacked specificity. My contacts with the electronics part of the board were sporadic. I was not familiar with what they were doing, except I believe they were developing a computerized artillery fire direction system. This system never reached the point where testing for airdrop or air landing occurred while I was in the Airborne Test Division.

Since the U.S. was in the middle of a bitter war in Vietnam, it was logical that our testing and evaluation focus was primarily on items needed in Vietnam. The primary source I have used for TECOM states that over 90 percent of the tests conducted between 1962 and 1967 fell into this category.[7]

However, many old Qualitative Material Requirements submitted to various laboratories were not acted on (some of these dated back to World War II) and these made their appearance now and then. The Army no longer needed most, or the specifications were outdated. With the agreement of TECOM, we rejected most without testing. We tested a few—a cargo net and a gantry for field rigging materials for airdrop—and rejected them.

There were numerous items tested and the workload was heavy. I had to step in at times to perform tests, although I was a branch chief. The Equipment Branch was involved in over 100 projects during my time at the board.

Some projects required only two or three days of testing. However, writing the reports and their review by the board president (or his deputy), the civilian engineer, the branch chiefs, and the testing officer invariably took several days. The reviewers accepted the report as written or, if additional testing was necessary, the reports were re-written before the board president signed and forwarded them to TECOM.

Requests to perform tests, which involved the Equipment Branch, came to us from the Operations Branch. Major Ezzard or I would then designate a project officer. I had a wall-size laminated board in my office, listing the project officers on one axis and their assigned projects on the other. Projects handled solely by the Equipment Branch were typically assigned to a junior officer. They were usually less complicated tests. Majors and senior captains were stuck with complex projects, including those involving another branch or outside agencies. Consequently, when looking at the number of tasks assigned to lieutenants, they seemed to be overworked.

In March or April 1967, there was a retirement/award ceremony by an 82nd Airborne Division brigade. Pictures from the award ceremony appeared in the *Fayetteville Observer* and *Paraglide*, the Fort Bragg newspaper. I received six combat awards.[8] A few of my former NCOs from Fort Campbell attended the ceremony, as did Captain Adam Klys and his family.

The Airborne Test Division's work involved much travel, leading Florence to comment to the board president at a social function that she saw me almost as rarely as when I was in Vietnam. She was right. The workload was heavy throughout my time at the Board, and all test officers traveled a lot to coordinate various projects. Luttrell and I probably held the record, as we were required to accompany the Board president or his deputy to various meetings since we had more detailed knowledge of the issues.

Special instructions in our travel orders always read: *Due to the type of activities being conducted at the location indicated above, it will possibly require further TDY to destination unknown at this time.* I could go into any travel office to have them re-direct my travel to a destination other than that spelled out in the original order. I frequently traveled to various laboratories and proving grounds from Massachusetts in the east to Arizona and Utah in the west.

The scope of the Equipment Branch work was broad. Examples of projects tested for air transport and airdrop demonstrate this. These tests involved writing rigging instructions and tie-down procedures. We tested the XM8 Automatic Chemical Agent Alarm System, the TOW Missile System, numerous heavy pieces of engineer equipment, the M715 1 3/4-ton truck, sophisticated communications systems, the XM166/67 Atomic Demolition Charge, the Chaparral Weapons System, and survival kits. We also assisted the Aircraft Branch in many of their projects. Among these were the test and rejection of a ballistically deployed reserve parachute, developing a new release system for heavy airdrop loads, and the airdrop of the M551 Sheridan.

The most substantial project assigned to the Equipment Branch while I was there was related to our Vietnam efforts, involving personnel from the Equipment Branch, the Rigging Facility, and Pope Air Force Base people. It was an extremely high-priority project brought about by the NVA siege of the U.S. Marine base at Khe Sanh in northwestern Quang Tri Province. It became one of the most controversial battles in Vietnam. Khe Sanh was the western anchor of a series of strong points. The siege began before the Tet Offensive attacks in other parts of South Vietnam and may have been a major diversion just before the countrywide offensive.

General Westmoreland had submitted a proposal to Washington for an invasion of Laos to cut the Ho Chi Minh Trail. He wanted to use the upgraded Khe Sanh base as a launching pad for that operation.[9] The upgrade, which started in 1967, involved committing the heavily reinforced U.S. 26th Marine Regiment and an ARVN Ranger Battalion to Khe Sanh, totally over 6,000 troops.

There was fear in Washington that Khe Sanh could become another Dien Bien Phu.[10] According to Colonel Summers, President Johnson was so concerned that he required a written guarantee from the JCS that the Marines could and would hold Khe Sanh.[11]

The NVA and the U.S. used considerable resources in the battles that followed. Estimates are that the NVA committed 15,000–20,000 regulars with substantial additional reserves within striking distance. The U.S. resorted to massive airstrikes and resupply, which undoubtedly distracted from the efforts in other parts of South Vietnam.[12]

The resupply effort was what involved the Equipment Branch of the Airborne Test Division. Both the U.S. Army and the U.S. Air Force had experimented with low-altitude delivery systems. The Army effort had begun with the Quartermaster School and was referred to as LOLEX (Low-Level Extraction System), using a parachute to extract the load from an aircraft flying close to the ground. The Air Force had tested its system at Eglin Air Force Base in Florida. They called their system LAPES (Low Altitude Parachute Extraction System), and, as with LOLEX, the C-130 would fly a few feet above ground at a slow speed when delivering the load. This ability was crucial as Khe Sanh was under continuous mortar and artillery bombardment, preventing safe landings.

Pope Air Force Base and our Equipment Branch launched an intensive effort to test LAPES and develop tie-down procedures. I placed one of my best officers, Captain James Dowdy, in charge of this project.[13] The tie-down procedures were complicated as they covered a whole range of equipment and supplies needed in Vietnam. After much experimentation and some failures, we also developed methods for delivering large bladders of fuel or water to the besieged Marines. The tests were started on a Saturday and completed the following Friday. One hundred copies of the Rigging Procedure Manual were dispatched to the Philippines and Vietnam four days later. The magnitude of this achievement is easier to understand by the fact that under normal conditions and circumstances, it would have required several months to complete the project.

The LAPES rigging procedures were so extensive and complicated that we found it necessary to send Captain Dowdy and a team to Clark Air Force Base in the Philippines to train the Air Force personnel responsible for delivering the supplies to Khe Sanh.[14] It worked out well, and as far as I know, LAPES became a standard delivery system.

The War in Vietnam: 1967

The war in Vietnam was almost a daily subject of discussion by the officers assigned to the USAAESWB. We were surprised at the low level of fighting in areas of Vietnam familiar to us. Most accepted the news from the Administration in Washington and from Saigon, which was full of optimism. The majority felt the NVA had lost the South Vietnamese population's support, as indicated by the pacification program reports. That was why the fighting had shifted to Quang Tri Province and the border region near Cambodia or Laos.

Other board officers who had recently returned from field duties in Vietnam and I were more skeptical. We noted the U.S. casualties in the war had reached 6,664 KIAs by the end of 1966, and it looked to us that this would more than double by the end of 1967—it reached 16,021.[15]

The optimists pointed out that U.S. troop strength in Vietnam had increased by around 100,000 during 1967, and with more troops in harm's way, it was natural that losses would increase. Their point was valid but was not a complete explanation for the rapid casualty increase.

As I listened to or read battlefield reports in 1967, I became troubled with our strategic and tactical conduct of the war. I will illustrate why I felt that way by describing the battle of Dak To (Operation *MacArthur*), an area that became familiar to me in 1969.[16] The operation was one of a series of mountain battles in late 1966 and reached a crescendo during the second half of 1967. These hilltop battles took place in the north and northwest provinces of South Vietnam, close to the Laotian, Cambodian, and North Vietnamese borders, where the NVA could quickly bring in supplies or seek quick refuge.

The battle of Dak To took place from 3–23 November 1967. U.S. forces involved in the campaign numbered about 16,000, consisting of two brigades from the 4th Infantry Division plus the 173rd Airborne Brigade. The overall commander was Major General William R. Peers (1914–1984), commander of the 4th Division. Brigadier General Leo H. Schweiter (1917–1972) commanded the 173rd Airborne Brigade.[17] ARVN forces also participated.

The NVA forces consisted of four regiments with a total strength of around 6,000 troops. Their hill positions had bunkers and interlocking trenches built over the previous months, and it was against these that U.S. and ARVN troops launched their attacks. The battle became one of the bloodiest of the Vietnam War.

To me, in 1969, the terrain in the Dak To area looked like an assortment of what we had experienced during 1965/66 in the mountains around Tuy Hoa and the jungle on the Cambodian border, with steep hillsides, triple canopy jungles, and secondary growth of thick bamboo. There were no natural LZs and the area did not readily lend itself to maneuver. It was evident the NVA had established themselves on these hilltops to draw the U.S. troops into frontal assaults.

The battle began with the shelling of the SF camp and airstrip at Dak To from Hill 875. This camp was also a forward operating base for the highly classified SOG (Study and Observation Group) for operations against the Ho Chi Minh Trail. Colonel Jonathan Ladd, the SF commander in Vietnam, flew into Dak To evaluate the situation.

In a quote from a New York Times opinion article in 2017 by the Pulitzer Prize-winning reporter Neil Sheehan, Colonel Ladd tried unsuccessfully to convince Major General Peers not to move against the entrenched hill positions. He allegedly told Peers, *For God's sake General, don't send our people in there. That is what the bastards want us to do. They will butcher our people. If they want to fight us, let them come down here where we can kill them.*[18]

The U.S. and ARVN troops tried to dislodge the NVA in assaults against well-prepared positions on hilltops for about three weeks. There was no lack of heroism: three members of the 173rd Airborne Brigade received the Medal of Honor posthumously. The battered NVA units withdrew into Cambodia towards the end of November. The 173rd Airborne Brigade had sustained such heavy losses it was considered combat ineffective.

It had been a costly three weeks. The U.S. had lost 361 KIA, 15 MIA, 1,441 WIA, and lost 43 aircraft, while the South Vietnamese forces suffered 73 KIA, 18 MIA, and 290 WIA. MACV estimated the NVA suffered between 1,000 and 1,400 casualties. While the U.S. eventually gained temporary control of the battlefields, these battles were indeed pyrrhic victories—victories achieved at too high a cost to the victor. Moreover, while maneuver in this terrain was exceedingly difficult, it seemed to me some of the vastly superior U.S. and ARVN forces could have cut the NVA supply and withdrawal routes.

These hilltop battles near sanctuaries were, in retrospect, probably intended to draw U.S. and ARVN forces away from the populated areas of South Vietnam in preparation for the Tet Offensive in 1968. If so, they succeeded as half of all U.S. maneuver battalions were in the border regions when the NVA and VC began their offensive.

The news from the American military and civilian leadership in Vietnam and the opinions by the Administration in Washington were overly optimistic about the war, noting that we were winning, as the following quotes from 1967 indicate. On 15 November 1967, Westmoreland visited Washington and stated, "I have never been more encouraged in my four years in Vietnam."[19] Ambassador Ellsworth Bunker (1894–1984) in Saigon echoed Westmoreland's sentiment by saying in Washington on 19 November 1967, "We are at the point now not only of being able to continue, but to accelerate the rate of progress."[20] Even Commander-in-Chief, Pacific (CINCPAC) in Honolulu, Admiral Ulysses Simpson Grant Sharp Jr. (1906–2001), chimed in on 21 November 1967 with "We are winning … It is pretty obvious that all the enemy can do is resort to guerrilla tactics …"[21] Saigon's American leaders misunderstood the enemy intentions and truthful and accurate flow of information from the battlefield to civilian authorities in Washington failed.

It would be a mistake not to mention U.S. Defense Secretary Robert S. McNamara. I only met him once, at a briefing on 19 July 1965, before the main body of the 1st Brigade arrived in Vietnam. That was the extent of my knowledge about a critical individual in our efforts in Vietnam.

My readings later revealed we had some things in common. McNamara was born in San Francisco, a city I also considered my home. Like General Frederick C. Weyand, McNamara attended UC at Berkeley, where he majored in economics, graduating in 1937, the same year as General Weyand.[22]

McNamara was a strong Kennedy supporter but also early and avid supporter of the war in Vietnam, as demonstrated by his numerous statements. He supported the continued escalation and increases in troop levels. Despite his utterance on 12 July 1967, "some more troops will be needed," some doubts appear to have crept in. As far as the bombing was concerned, he favored bombing the infiltration routes but balked at an increase in Hanoi's bombing or other North Vietnam areas. He had concluded these bombings did little to help the situation in South Vietnam. On

25 August 1967, he noted we had struck 1,900 targets in North Vietnam, but he concludes that enemy operations in the South had not stopped by increasing air bombardment of the North, such as bombing the ports and mining the harbors.[23]

His book *In Retrospect* was followed four years later by another book, after several meetings with key individuals from victorious North Vietnam. It concludes both countries had misread each other's intentions, a poor excuse for the death of more than 3 million people.[24]

As mentioned earlier, we had a poor understanding of North Vietnamese history and motivations. Policymakers failed to factor this into their policies.[25] If one does not know one's opponent thoroughly, one should not enter an elective war.

Nevertheless, we continue to do so. We should never forget Sun Tzu's warning about patience spans, and he was not speaking about democracies, which did not exist at the time of his writings. Democracies have much shorter patience spans than a centralized government such as that in North Vietnam. General Giap (1911–2013) and others clearly counted on this short patience span in the Tet Offensive.

Early Unenthusiastic Peace Attempts

I would be remiss in not mentioning something about the early attempts at a peaceful settlement beginning in 1965. Peace negotiations began to have significant effects on the ground during my second tour in Vietnam, as did domestic problems, some of which were caused by our short patience span.

It remains an enigma to many why President Johnson did not concentrate on the Great Society programs. He had won a convincing electoral victory over Barry Goldwater (1909–1998) in 1964, leaving him with supermajorities in both the Senate and House. What did Johnson hope to gain by hurling the U.S. military strength into Vietnam? This action took place despite the recent French defeat and our fight with the Chinese in Korea that ended in a draw. It was also contrary to the long-standing warnings against becoming involved in a land war in Asia. The decision must have been for fear that the political opposition would pounce on a do-nothing policy and disrupt the Great Society programs.

The Secretary-General of the UN, Charles de Gaulle (1890–1970) in France, and a few Americans not in the Administration, recommended the negotiated route. They were not acted on as we were only prepared to negotiate from strength after defeating the VC and convincing the North of the impossibility of prevailing. This was the same illusion of victory, de Gaulle told U.S. Undersecretary of State George Ball (1909–1994) that had drawn France into trouble in Vietnam, "a hopeless place to fight," and a "rotten country" where the U.S. could not win despite its vast resources.[26]

While we had sent peace feelers to North Vietnam in 1965, the North Vietnamese viewed those, for the most part, as ultimatums rather than serious proposals to negotiate. In a major policy speech at Johns Hopkins University on 7 April 1965, President Johnson offered a vast economic assistance program for Vietnam, amounting to one billion dollars in which North Vietnam would share. Johnson declared he was ready for further discussions, but the North Vietnamese interpreted that as meaning negotiations after conceding defeat. Still, they did respond to President Johnson's peace feeler in 1965, and it is interesting to see what their demands were and compare them to the terms of the 1973 Paris Peace Accords. Hanoi announced four preconditions to President Johnson's overture the following day.[27]

1. Withdrawal of all U.S. forces.
2. No foreign alliances or the introduction of foreign troops by either side.
3. South Vietnam's acceptance of the Viet Cong program.
4. The reunification of the country without outside interference.

Let us look at what we obtained in the Paris Peace Accords after eight years of fighting:

1. All U.S. forces, except 50 personnel, were to leave Vietnam within 60 days—by 27 March 1973.
2. North Vietnam (DRV) could keep about 123,000 troops in the south, a unilateral concession to the DRV by President Nixon.
3. The VC (PRG) would likewise control the areas they occupied.
4. Step by step, reunification of Vietnam by peaceful means.
5. Replacement aid to South Vietnam by the U.S. was limited to a one-to-one replacement.

It appears to me the North Vietnamese reply to President Johnson's 1965 overture is no worse than what we agreed to in 1973. It may be better if we interpret their statements as announced principles for starting negotiations, not their end demands. It could have served as a basis for further talks.

However, the U.S. authorities believed the North would become more reasonable after a taste of U.S. military might, but, unfortunately, this approach did not work, and in the end, what was unacceptable in 1965 became acceptable in 1973 after almost 60,000 U.S. troops were killed, over 300,000 wounded, and roughly 1,600 missing.

The Study of War

The study of our profession has never been a substantial part of the education of our officers. American military writers have produced extensive literature dealing with war, but it addresses almost exclusively military history, techniques, weapons, and logistics. My writings have followed the same pattern as they focus on military history. Part of the problem is that the reading public shies away from our profession's intricate features, military theories, strategy, and tactics. Such books are challenging to sell because of their perplexing nature and the public yearning for more action-packed accounts. This situation is unfortunate, as pointed out by some prominent writers on the military and society in the 20th century including Walter Millis (1899–1968) and Samuel P. Huntington (1927–2008).[28]

Millis illustrates the woeful lack of U.S. military writers who address military strategy or theory by mentioning a book edited by Edward Mead Earle (1894–1954) during World War II, *The Makers of Modern Strategy*. Only two of the 34 individuals included in the book are Americans—Alexander Hamilton (1755 or 1757–1804) and Alfred Thayer Mahan (1840–1914).[29]

Short-term military analogies are another fallacy that plagued our involvement in Vietnam, and I frequently refer to this problem in the book. Winston Churchill sounded a strong warning against the use of short-term analogies by noting that these are often incorrect.[30] Our Vietnam involvement policies were full of short-term metaphors—the worldwide communist conspiracies, the "loss" of China, and communist-led insurrections from Europe to Southeast Asia. In doing so, we failed to consider the unique nature of the Vietnam problem. Even our Founders alerted us to national councils "warped by strong passion or momentary interest."[31]

We were obsessed with the so-called domino theory, holding that if South Vietnam fell to communism, the other countries in Southeast Asia would quickly follow. However, this theory was incorrect if the North Vietnamese driving force was nationalism rather than communism. While Cambodia and Laos came under Hanoi's influence and sway after our withdrawal, the North Vietnamese left them to their own devices after a few years of severe turbulence in Cambodia. It appears that Hanoi preferred not to become permanently involved if these two states posed no threats to Vietnam.

The theories of warfare presented by Sun Tzu almost 2,600 years ago, hold that "No country has ever profited from protracted warfare."[32] We became involved in Vietnam without heeding the above warning and without knowing our society and that of our enemy, a sure recipe for failure, according to Sun Tzu.[33] General of the Army Douglas MacArthur (1880–1964) sounded a similar warning when he said it is fatal to enter a war without the will to win. We would also be wise to heed another piece of advice by Sun Tzu that may become crucial in this century, concluding that a country that engages in constant warfare will eventually succumb. There are numerous historical examples of great powers on the verge of decline resorting to small wars on an increased tempo to arrest the slide, only to exacerbate it. The Duke of Wellington echoed Sun Tzu when he allegedly stated that great powers do not fight small wars.

Most of our senior leaders naturally relied on their experiences from World War II and Korea, supplemented by the expertise of allies who had battled insurrections in their own countries. This view clouded the difference we experienced in Vietnam. John F. Kennedy warned us against negotiating out of fear, but that is what we did when President Lyndon B. Johnson decided to deal seriously in 1968. In addition, the anti-war movement and racial unrest had become major domestic problems that directly affected the patience span.

Volunteering for My Second Tour in Vietnam

Beginning in August and lasting until November 1967, I received many calls from Colonel Emerson, now serving in the Pentagon. Our conversations' substance was that he would take over a brigade in the 9th Infantry Division in the Delta area of Vietnam in the late spring of 1968, and he wanted to bring some of those who had served with him in the 101st Airborne Division. He mentioned that Lieutenant Colonel Hackworth, who also served in the Pentagon, and Lieutenant Colonel Donald Schroeder had agreed to join him. Still, Hackworth did not arrive in Vietnam until early 1969 after I had left the 9th Division. Emerson said he wanted to make me his S-3 and asked me to convince some of my former NCOs to join him.

I told Emerson I was flattered by the offer, but since there were no command slots for majors, I would instead join a volunteer outfit such as the 101st or the 173rd Airborne Brigade. I told him I did not think any NCOs would volunteer to serve in a non-airborne assignment, specifically the 9th Division, which did not have a good reputation. I did call a few, but the answers were as I had anticipated. Three company-grade officers from 2/502 went: Captains Karl Beach, David Johnson, and Robert Kaszer (1936–2012) from C/2/502.

Florence and I had, in the meantime, discussed my options. Even if I said no to Emerson, it was apparent I would go to Vietnam at the end of 1968 and would face the same problem of not getting a command position.

In the fourth call, Emerson acknowledged my desires and said that if I came, the S-3 assignment would only be for a couple of months. He would discuss the issue with the incoming 9th Division commander, Major General Julian J. Ewell (1915–2009). Emerson proposed to convince Ewell to create a "Raider Unit" of about 300 men to operate in the Plain of Reeds along the Cambodian border and interdict NVA infiltration into the built-up areas of the Delta.

Such a unit was precisely what I had in mind, since the only U.S. forces along the border were SF-led irregular ARVN units along with one weak ARVN division. Increasing the force level along the border made it more difficult for the NVA to reach the built-up areas of the Delta, where dislodging them could result in many civilian casualties. I gave Florence, who had answered Emerson's call and remained on the telephone extension, a thumbs-up sign. Florence always said what she meant, regardless of who they were. She broke into the conversation and explained to Emerson that I had always been very loyal to him but did not want to go to Vietnam to shuffle papers and be devastated by a broken promise. Emerson, taken a little aback by Florence's frankness, said he was very aware of what she told him.

Both Florence and, I assumed, Emerson would raise the subject with Major General Ewell before I volunteered for Vietnam. Ewell was then Chief of Staff of the U.S. Army Combat Developments Command at Fort Belvoir, Virginia, only a short distance from the Pentagon. Getting Ewell's approval should, therefore, have been quick and easy to obtain. We were mistaken.

I received a letter from Major General Ewell, dated 6 November 1967, asking that I join the 9th Infantry Division. The letter did not mention anything about my assignment except noting that I was to join Emerson's brigade. However, the letter goes on to state:

> If your assignment to the 9th could be managed, I would be willing to put you in a responsible job which would do the unit and yourself the most good. I am particularly interested in getting a G-2 who would have the ability to get down below the surface and come up with real gut information.

I received the letter at my office on 9 November and brought it home to show Florence. Her immediate reaction was *Ewell is trying to steal you away from Emerson by offering you a job calling for a lieutenant colonel,* a grade higher than an S-3. Ewell's letter had also raised red flags for me, but I had not thought about it the way my wife did. I did not intend to accept a job outside my primary specialty, especially an intelligence job. I was still worried about what damage my SF specialty might have done to my career. I needed to talk to Emerson before answering, but I could not reach him until 14 November.

In the meantime, I received a brief handwritten note from Lieutenant General Frederick Weyand who now commanded II Field Force in Vietnam. Somehow, he had found out I was returning to Vietnam and wanted to know if I would join his command. I always liked Weyand but going to a corps headquarters without knowing what I would be doing did not appeal to me. I wanted to be as close to the troops as possible and this would take me in the opposite direction.

Emerson told me, when I finally reached him, not to worry about what Ewell had written. He reiterated that I was coming to Vietnam to be his S-3, pending the "Raider Unit's" formation. That sounded to Florence and me as if Emerson had already received Ewell's blessing to create a "Raider Unit."

I did not tell Emerson about Weyand's note. I answered Weyand and politely explained I had already agreed to go to the 9th Infantry Division with Colonel Emerson. On the same day, 16 November, I also answered Ewell without referring to the G-2 offer; I relied on Emerson to address that issue.

I put in my formal request for voluntary assignment to the 9th Infantry Division on Friday, 1 December, based on the assumption Emerson had received Ewell's approval.

Florence and I had already purchased off-post quarters, anticipating a move since we had to give up our post quarters. We bought a home in the Cottonade development in Fayetteville, adjacent to Fort Bragg. Captain Andersen and his wife Judith also lived on the same street in that development. We did not have much furniture, so we needed to buy enough to furnish the new home, including appliances.

After making a quick visit to Norway, I departed the Fayetteville Airport on 31 May to return to Vietnam. I felt very pessimistic about the situation in the U.S. What I confronted at my destination did not help. Florence was more worried than ever.

CHAPTER 18

Arrival in Vietnam and Assignment as Brigade S-3

The pivotal year in our involvement in Vietnam was 1968, both in the field and on the home front. The U.S. troop level in Vietnam had grown to over 536,000 in 1968.[1]

The unreal optimism that characterized 1967 continued in early 1968. On 1 January 1968, Westmoreland stated from Saigon:

> Through careful exploitation of the enemy's vulnerabilities and application of our superior fire power and mobility we should expect our gains of 1967 to be increased manifold in 1968 ... Our forces have been able to detect impending major offensives and to mount spoiling attacks.[2]

Robert W. Komer (1922–2000), the Civilian Administrator of the American Pacification Program, stated on 24 January 1968, "Eleven and a half million people of South Vietnam's seventeen and a half million population now live in secure or use reasonably secure areas."[3]

A few commanders took a more sober and cautious attitude. U.S. troops in the Capital Zone consisted of only 14 maneuver battalions in early January as II Field Force had moved most towards the Cambodian border. Lieutenant General Weyand became concerned and suspicious when his troops near the Cambodian border failed to encounter any substantial enemy forces. He saw Westmoreland and requested permission to reinforce the Capital Zone. Although more concerned about Quang Tri Province, Westmoreland agreed, and Lieutenant General Weyand increased the Capital Zone forces to 27 battalions.

All optimism began to crash because of the Tet Offensive, which started on 31 January 1968.[4] The NVA buildup for the offensive was a masterful deception. The U.S. failure to detect or recognize it was one of our military history's most severe intelligence failures. It became evident that the border battles' primary goal was to make the U.S. and ARVN withdraw combat units away from the populated areas.

Westmoreland still viewed the 1968 Tet Offensive as a deceptive effort on the part of the NVA/VC based on the following statement he made in Saigon on 1 February 1968: "In my opinion, this is a diversionary effort to take attention away from the Northern part of the country."[5]

Westmoreland's views undoubtedly influenced President Johnson, as he made the following statement on 2 February:

> We have known for some time that the enemy planned this offensive ... The ability to do what they have done has been anticipated, prepared for, and met. The stated purposes of the general uprising have failed ... as a military movement, it has been a failure ... I do not believe that they will achieve a psychological victory.[6]

Two days later, Johnson wrote, "I don't want any damned Dienbienphu [sic],"[7] referring to the ghostly threat that Khe Sanh could share the same fate as the French in the epic battle of Dien Bien Phu in 1953–1954 that for all practical purposes spelled the end to the French War against the Viet Minh. Thus, President Johnson's two statements echoed Westmorland's announcement, including the latter's fear that the offensive was only a diversion, and the real threat was in the northern part of the country.

The well-coordinated enemy offensive struck 36 of the 44 provincial capitals and 64 of the 242 district capitals, and about 50 villages. Five of the six autonomous cities were also hit, including Saigon and Huê.[8] While most of the attacks took place in the early morning hours of 31 January 1968, fighting in the Vietnamese Central Highlands had begun the day before. The attacks on some sites in the III and IV Corps' areas occurred on 1 February, and Dalat in the II Corps area occurred on 2 February. It would have been strange for an offensive planned this way. The reasons for this staggering were probably coordination difficulties and problems getting the attacking forces in place.[9]

Carl Schuster wrote that the staggering was due to a one-day postponement in the NVA plans from 30 to 31 January. I have not seen this mentioned by other writers I referenced. If true, it does not explain the above-noted delays in the II and III Corps' areas. Schuster also suggests Hanoi's plan worked because the North Vietnamese enjoyed superior knowledge of their opponents, a statement which I wholeheartedly support. He also gives most of the credit for planning the attack to Party General Secretary Le Duan (1907–1986), who had gained much power in the infighting at Hanoi's highest levels.[10] In my informal discussions with North Vietnamese officers in 1973 and 1974, they failed to mention the pivotal role of Le Duan. They were undoubtedly reluctant to admit to any political infighting.

In Saigon, the enemy penetrated to the very gates of the heavily defended U.S. Embassy. We can only speculate what would have happened if Weyand had not succeeded in increasing Saigon's force level from 14 to 27 battalions. Some other cities, such as the old Imperial Capital of Huê, were only fully liberated after 39 days of ferocious fighting. The fighting in Huê was one of the war's bloodiest battles and the most intense urban combat in American history.[11]

While the NVA and VC were eventually driven back with heavy losses, they had achieved a decisive political/psychological victory that sent shockwaves through the

American political system. It made President Johnson's statement on 2 February a futile attempt to put what had happened in the best light. Some writers have concluded the 1968 Tet Offensive aimed to create a general uprising in South Vietnam, but I disagree. The leadership in North Vietnam, both political and military (often they were the same), were thoroughly familiar with South Vietnamese conditions and were sufficiently pragmatic to conclude an uprising with about 600,000 allied troops in the country and the 820,000 South Vietnamese forces were unrealistic.

The North Vietnamese had laid out what amounted to a blueprint for the 1968 Tet Offensive in September 1967. They identified that the offensive's primary goal was to exploit the U.S. unwillingness to fight a protracted war. They hoped the assault would increase opposition to the war in the U.S. and cause growing pressure on the U.S. leadership.[12] These were the main objectives of the offensive. If the attacks created unrest in South Vietnam, it was only a byproduct for which the North Vietnamese did not plan.

The 1968 Tet Offensive certainly fueled the growing anti-war movement. Many concluded the country had been lied to by both Westmoreland's headquarters and the Johnson Administration. Millions from the so-called silent majority began to give support to the anti-war movement. The most revered TV news anchor, Walter Cronkite (1916–2009), concluded that the Vietnam war was unwinnable in a broadcast on 27 February 1968. He made this conclusion after the all-time high U.S. casualties for the week of 10–17 February became known: 543 killed and 2,547 wounded.

General Westmoreland continued his optimistic, and unrealistic, view about the situation in Vietnam. On 7 April 1968, he stated while visiting Washington, that "militarily we have never been in a better relative position in South Vietnam," and on 9 June, he said from Saigon, "The enemy has been defeated at every turn."[13]

Washington quickly rejected a request from General Westmoreland for roughly an additional 206,000 troops. He was later removed from his assignment to become Army Chief of Staff and replaced in Vietnam by General Creighton Abrams (1914–1974).

The depletion of the strategic reserves had reached the point where we were in danger of not meeting our other obligations in Asia, Europe, and the Middle East. Furthermore, we did not have enough forces to deal with the unrest in the U.S. It would take a mobilization to rectify this situation, and such a move was politically unrealistic.[14] However, new troop units were still arriving in Vietnam. As a result, a brigade from the 82nd Airborne Division and one from the 5th Mechanized Infantry Division was deployed to I Corps. In a televised speech to the nation on 31 March 1968—following a two-day meeting of the Senior Advisory Group on Vietnam—President Johnson announced he was de-escalating the Vietnam War and seeking a negotiated settlement.[15] The negotiations announced by President Johnson were born out of fears generated mainly by the domestic situation. We had reached a point in the public patience span that it was the only thing to do. At the end of his speech, President Johnson stunned the world by announcing he would not run for re-election later that year, throwing the Democratic Party into chaos. These events show that the 1968 Tet Offensive had achieved what I believe was its goal.

The anti-war movement received a significant boost when racial riots broke out after Doctor Martin Luther King Jr.'s assassination on 4 April 1968. The fury of riots that broke out in about 100 cities and towns in the U.S. reportedly claimed 45 lives, caused 2,500 injuries, and led to over 15,000 arrests. Federal and National Guard troops were deployed to Washington, D.C., to protect the Pentagon and other Federal installations and quell the arson and looting in the capital.

Thousands of National Guard troops and 500 Maryland State Police tried to stop the riot and arson in Baltimore on 6 April. When this proved insufficient to control the riots, about 5,000 Federal troops from the 18th Airborne Corps arrived on 7 April, and a Light Infantry Brigade from Fort Benning joined them on 9 April. I was still at Fort Bragg when these happenings took place. I viewed burning towns and U.S. troops with fixed bayonets patrolling some cities with dismay and worry. It seemed like the fabric of society was unraveling.

The political unrest continued with Robert Kennedy's assassination, a Democratic presidential candidate, on 5 June, as I was landing in Vietnam. All this unrest contributed to a comfortable victory by Richard Nixon in November 1968, who had promised to begin withdrawal from Vietnam.

Initial Impressions on Arrival in Vietnam

Processing on the West Coast was quick and orderly, and I boarded the flight for Vietnam. After 18 ½ hours of flight, with a 30-minute stop in Honolulu and a 45-minute stop at Clark Air Force Base in the Philippines, I landed at Bien Hoa Air Base at 0700 hours on 3 June (Saigon time). Buses took us the short distance to Long Binh.

It was the beginning of a year which I came to view as my worst in Vietnam. My pessimistic outlook resulted from what I witnessed in the U.S. and what confronted me in Vietnam. I became convinced we were on the road to losing the war. My negative attitude received much strengthening as time passed by personal tragedies.

We spent almost all the first day processing. Many of the troops who had arrived on my flight ended up having their orders changed by U.S. Army Vietnam (USARV), but there were no changes for the six of us who were second tour volunteers. We completed processing by 1600 hours. I stopped at the officers' club for a meal and a couple of drinks after the staff informed me transport to the 9th Division would not be available until the following day.

Those of us assigned to the 9th Division traveled to Bear Cat, about 50 kilometers southeast of Saigon. Bear Cat was the 9th Division rear area as well as its main headquarters. We arrived around noon and spent the rest of the day processing. As expected, my assignment was as S-3 of the 1st Brigade and Colonel Emerson had sent a message that he would pick me up the next day. While an excellent job that most infantry majors would give anything to have, I was hoping it was only a temporary stop for me on the way to take over the "Raider Unit" Emerson had promised.

This was the beginning of a year when my whole outlook on the war in Vietnam underwent a fundamental shift. My feelings are evident in the second of two letters I wrote to Florence on 4 June 1968:

> I have had a sinking feeling ever since I arrived here that this is not going to be a good tour. As we flew over Cam Ranh Bay, I could hardly believe my eyes at the extent of buildup since I left here two years ago. The same is true for Bien Hoa, Long Binh, and the area here at Bear Cat. It seems we have firmly settled in for the long haul. The troops I have seen appear undisciplined with low morale, the poorest I have seen in my years on active duty. In talking to officers, NCOs, and enlisted troops at Long Binh and here at Bear Cat, I get the feeling that the war is not going well. It appears we have become locked into base camps, and large logistic complexes and operations have become routine and predictable, very much like the French before us towards the end of their war. If what I hear and see is true, I am very pessimistic about our efforts and where they will lead. We may have over 500,000 troops in the country, but I believe less than one out of every ten are out doing any fighting from looking at the crowded rear areas and base camps. At this rate, and if nothing changes, this whole mess can only end up one way—us losing. Of course, we can drag it out for a few years, but that will only make everything here and on the home front more difficult and the inevitable sacrifices more senseless. I hope I am wrong and that getting down to a fighting unit will give me a different perspective on the situation.

S-3, 1st Brigade, 9th Division

Colonel Emerson picked me up at Bear Cat in his C&C helicopter on the morning of 5 June. The first thing he said was, *Hank, what the hell is going on in the U.S?* Emerson was referring to the riots and burning after the assassination of Martin Luther King, Jr. and the news that had just broken about the murder of Robert Kennedy. He wanted to know if fringe elements caused the disruptions. I told him no, we were no longer dealing with fringe elements but with a large segment of the American public as far as our involvement in Vietnam was concerned. His only comment was that it did not bode well for our Vietnam mission, if I were right.

Emerson and I first flew to a hospital where we visited wounded troops from the brigade. After that, we flew to the division CP, where we had lunch. This lunch was my first meeting with Major General Julian J. Ewell. The 9th Division had two Assistant Division Commanders (ADCs). If my recollection is correct, Brigadier General Elvy B. Roberts was (ADC-A) and assumed that position on 1 June 1968. The second ADC (ADC-B) was Brigadier General William A. Knowlton (1920–2008). He was replaced by Brigadier General James S. Timothy on 16 July. The Division Chief of Staff was an engineer colonel named Ira Hunt.

At lunch, I was again surprised at the changes since 1966. Most of the troops wore clean and starched jungle fatigues. The mess hall had white linen tablecloths, and the meal was served on porcelain tableware by soldiers assigned to the division CP. Neither Emerson nor Ewell said anything during lunch about my assignment.

After lunch, Emerson and I headed to the brigade CP at Ap Dong, inland from Dong Tam. It was in an abandoned French rubber plantation. The buildings were dilapidated—full of giant rats—and the place looked ready to collapse in a moderate wind. I learned that the brigade S-3, who I was replacing—Major Day—would leave on or about 11 June.

We spent much of 7 June planning future operations. The brigade had only two company-size operations underway, but we made no enemy contacts. I spent the afternoon with Emerson on his C&C helicopter. I had difficulty orienting myself on the map because the ground was flat and full of rivers and irrigation canals. We flushed some VC from a village. Since we did not have any troops available, we set our helicopter down and captured one VC who was quite willing to surrender.

On the evening of 7 June, I was sent to the 3rd Brigade—commanded by Colonel George C. Benson (1923–2007)—whose operational headquarters were on Saigon's southern outskirts. The reason for this was classified at the time and involved one of the two significant changes that were to take place in the next few weeks.

One involved moving the main headquarters of the division from Bear Cat to the new base camp at Dong Tam. This move was scheduled for completion by 25 July. There were two reasons for this move. First, it would place the division headquarters in the heart of its operational area. Second, the Royal Thai Army Volunteer Force, arriving in Vietnam, was initially stationed at Bear Cat. The division would still have its rear area at Bear Cat.

The second significant change was a switch of operational areas between the 1st and 3rd Brigades, to become effective on 23 June. The 3rd Brigade, with two maneuver battalions, would relocate from Tan An (its headquarters) to Dong Tam to facilitate its transition to a Riverine Force. First Brigade, with three infantry battalions and one mechanized battalion, would operate in Long An Province, including covering Saigon from the south.[16] This substitution of Areas of Operation (AOs) involved moving the 1st Brigade CP from Ap Dong to Tan An. To ease this change of operational areas, the S-3 of the 3rd and 1st Brigades would switch places for two weeks, which is why I joined the 3rd Brigade's forward CP on the outskirts of Saigon.

My first trip to the 3rd Brigade was to introduce myself to Colonel Benson and become familiar with the area. I expected to return to the 1st Brigade on 8 June. However, my return was delayed because the 1st Brigade became involved in a sizable engagement (discussed in Division Report 20 August, pp. 17–18) and there were no helicopter assets available.

I rejoined Emerson at Ap Dong on the afternoon of 9 June. I was with Emerson on his C&C helicopter all day on the 10th, but we did not make any enemy contacts.

The previous day's battlefield was swept on 9 June, resulting in a 67 VC KIA body count, but we captured only 14 weapons.

General Ewell visited our brigade late on 9 June. I had heard nothing about the promise back in the U.S. for a "Raider Unit", and during a break, I surfaced that subject with the Division Commander. He did not acknowledge any earlier promise and said neither yes nor no when I mentioned the issue. His only answer was that it would depend on the situation later. I concluded from this short conversation that the prospects of getting command of a "Raider Unit" were not promising. That night I wrote to Florence that she was right in late November 1967 that we should not count on the promise.

I told Emerson about my conversation with Ewell. He just shook his head. I told him I still wanted to get as close to troops as possible. Emerson said he would continue trying to convince Ewell to form a "Raider Unit." However, I had come to believe he had not talked to Ewell about it, at least not in the U.S., based on Ewell's failure to acknowledge a promise.

If it were not possible to form a "Raider Unit," Emerson mentioned that both Lieutenant Colonels Hackworth and Schroeder had asked for me as XO, but Hackworth would not arrive before the end of the year while Schroeder would come in late June. Since Ewell had mentioned an assignment as a G-2 in his letter I received in the States, I concluded it would be wise for me to quickly join a battalion. I informed Emerson that Don Schroeder's XO's job was acceptable if a "Raider Unit" was not approved.

The following two days were quiet as far as enemy contacts were concerned, and I spent them in the C&C helicopter with Emerson. We crisscrossed the Delta without coming up with anything. On both days, we returned after dark and I had to do all the chores I should have done while on the helicopter with Emerson. In addition, my sleep was interrupted two or three times every night to deal with the panic that resulted from minor contacts.

On 13 June, I was back at the 3rd Brigade CP at Xom Can Mat and I told my wife that I would remain there indefinitely but could not yet tell her why. We had a mortar attack—28 rounds—soon after I arrived but suffered no casualties.

The 3rd Brigade was responsible for the defense of Saigon from the south. As the operations officer, I was responsible for planning and conducting the city's security. I told Florence that Colonel Benson and I would be blamed if the defenses failed in this politically sensitive area. Benson was away for most of the afternoon on 15 June and we got involved in a substantial engagement before he returned.

The operational area of the 3rd Brigade looked much like the area around Ap Dong. The only difference I could detect was that the area in which the 3rd Brigade operated was more densely populated, and the irrigation canals were fewer but greater.

The primary ARVN unit in the region was the 25th Division, headquartered in Duc Hue District in Hau Nghia Province. Before 1968, it was considered one of the

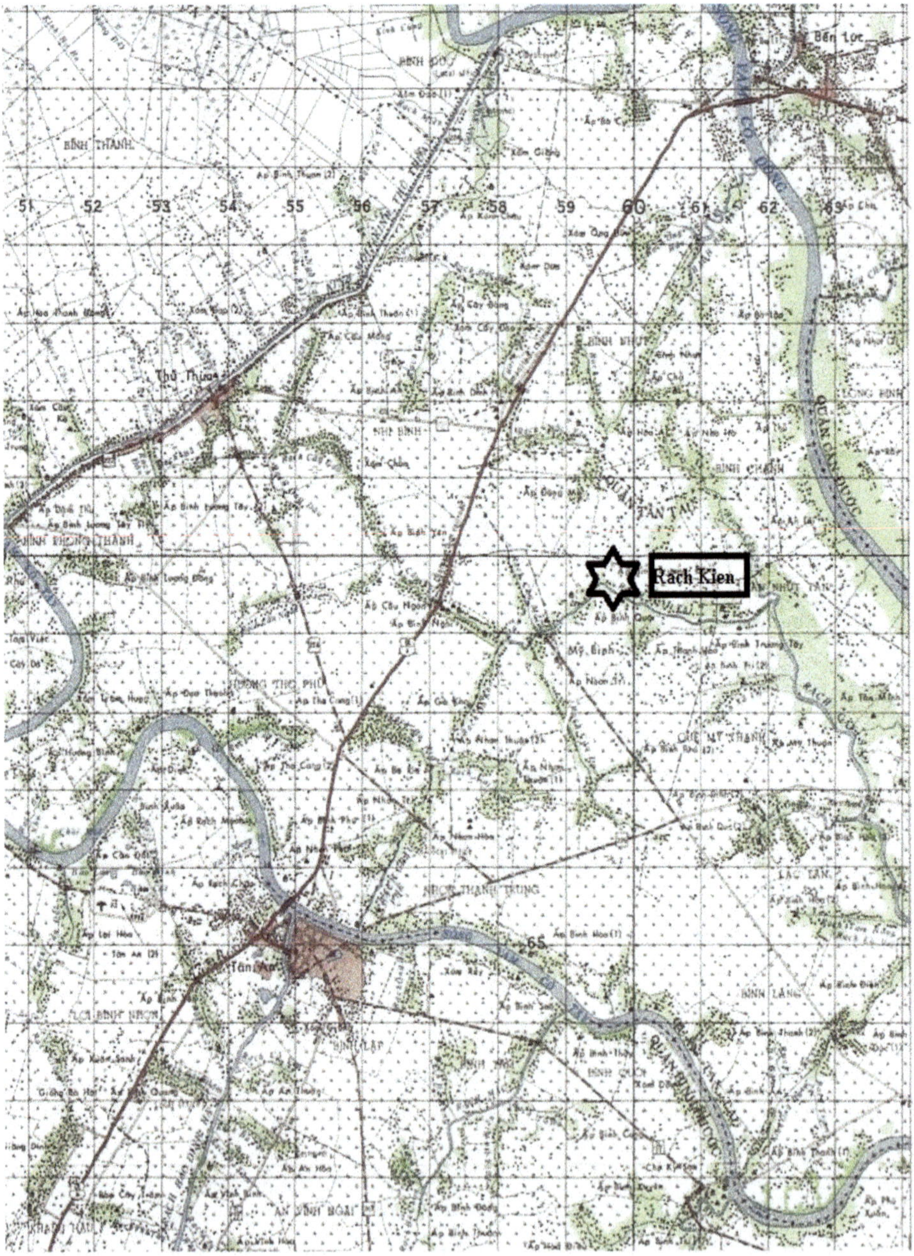

Map 11. This modified U.S. map shows most of the brigade area of operations as of 23 June 1968 and illustrates the importance of Route 4 for the Delta Region.

weakest divisions in ARVN. That improved in 1968 when its leadership changed. It served as a barrier to Cambodia's significant enemy infiltration route around the Parrot's Beak to Saigon.[17]

The 25th ARVN Division had three regiments. The 46th Independent Regiment was located at Can Giuoc in Long An Province, but it was a weak and ineffective force barely able to provide security for its immediate surroundings let alone handling the 1500 square kilometer area of Long An Province south of Saigon. I am not sure about the locations of the other two regiments, the 49th and 50th. There was one regiment near Ben Luc south of Saigon, but I do not know which one. Both units may have been in this area, or one could have remained in Hau Nghia Province.

Four rockets were fired into Saigon from our area during the night of 15/16 June. This attack was much smaller than usual, but USARV was not satisfied unless the fire stopped entirely, and that was virtually impossible to achieve.

The deputy commander of the 199th Light Infantry Brigade arrived with his staff about noon on 20 June, and I briefed them. The plans were that they would be stationed somewhere in the Saigon area. The rainy season had started and it had a severe impact on our communications. The 3rd Brigade days were so hectic I rarely had time to eat until after dark.

We had not received mortar fire since the first night after my arrival and Saigon had not received rocket attacks from the south for about four days. Still, I believed the VC could have fired rockets at the city from our area any time they wanted. There was just no way to stop them if they were willing to pay the price. Ten rockets from the north landed in Saigon on 19 June, killing eight civilians and wounding 22. My stay with the 3rd Brigade ended on 23 June, and I joined the 1st Brigade at its new headquarters in Tan An.

1st Brigade's AO, Task Organization, and Enemy Forces

The Long An province capital was Tan An on Route 4, about 30 kilometers southwest of Saigon. Route 4 was the road that connected the Delta Region to Saigon and was of immense importance. The 1st Brigade's primary AO was Long An Province as of 23 June, and we became responsible for Saigon's southern outskirts. Long An Province stretches for about 20 kilometers south of Tan An, giving it 50 kilometers in length. We were responsible for the area south of the Van Co Dong River, about 8 kilometers from Saigon's outskirts. We were also responsible for the southern approaches to the Ben Luc bridge spanning the river, while ARVN units were responsible for the northern approaches. This split responsibility bothered me and, with Emerson's permission, I sent a complaint to the 9th Division G-3, listing our objections.

The 1st Brigade was a large organization. We usually had three battalions attached while I was the S-3 but reinforced for large operations with battalions from the other two brigades. The organization of the brigade often changed as other forces were attached or detached. This task organization continued to the company level.

I will mention the battalions that were usually attached while I was S-3:

1. 2/39 Infantry battalion. It was assigned to the 1st Brigade most of the time I was in the 9th Division. Its location was at Bear Cat, but it moved to Rach Kien around 23 July as part of the AO reorganization, not Tan An, as some sources claim. It moved to Dong Tam in November 1968.
2. 6/31 Infantry Battalion. It was attached to the 1st Brigade from July 1968 to January 1970. Its location frequently changed: Bear Cat, Tan An, Nha Be, Dong Tam, and Ben Luc.
3. 2/47 Infantry Battalion (Mechanized) became part of the 1st Brigade in May 1968. Its assignments changed frequently, and in late 1968 it became part of the 3rd Brigade. When I was there, it was part of the 1st Brigade, and its location was Bear Cat or Dong Tam.

We also had one engineer company (minus) from the 15th Engineer Battalion, and four towed artillery batteries—three from the 4th Artillery and one from the 11th Artillery (all had four guns except for one, which had only two guns). The headquarters, 2nd Battalion, 4th Artillery, were located at Tan An. In addition, there were usually one or two airlift companies supporting the 1st Brigade.

I was amazed when I first visited the Tactical Operations Center (TOC) in Tan An, which was my responsibility. I believe 57 personnel were assigned to the S-3 section. Some of these were from the S-2 section and a couple liaison officers. Before the 1st Brigade of the 101st Airborne Division deployed to Vietnam, we had 19 individuals in the S-3 and S-2 sections combined. I am sure that was augmented when we arrived in Vietnam but, as far as I know, not to the number found in the 1st Brigade, 9th Division.

I commented on this to Emerson. He explained the brigade was so loaded down with reporting requirements that additional personnel were required. I soon found out he was right as we had some officers, NCOs, and enlisted troops whose primary function was to keep up on a myriad of statistical reports. As an example, it was not enough to report who had been killed or wounded and the nature of the wound. A somewhat detailed description of both the situation and the cause of the injuries was needed. We had to identify the weapon causing the wounds—mortar fire, mines, small arms, booby traps, snipers, etc. The injuries also needed to be described in detail—where the individual was wounded (leg, arm, head, back, chest, stomach, etc.). Details about what the individual was doing when he was injured were also reported—in a defensive action, on patrol, performing convoy duties, reinforcing another unit, etc.[18] These reports came up from the battalions daily and we consolidated them before we forwarded them to the division. The division would invariably have questions, so we had to contact the battalions for answers.

One type of report we did not have to make was AA reports. Those were made by the battalions and consolidated by the division.

There were no NVA units in our AO, only local and main force VC units. Some of these units may have had NVA fillers, but I did not see any NVA soldiers during my Delta tour. Intelligence identified six VC battalions in Long An Province. They were all viewed as combat ineffective or only marginally combat effective, with strengths averaging between 150 and 300.[19] Enemy units could also come to Long An Province from bordering provinces like Kien Tuong, Dien Tuong, and Hau Nghia.

The 9th Infantry Division lost two battalion commanders in July. The first was Lieutenant Colonel Frederick F. Van Deusen, commander of 2/47th Mechanized Infantry. His helicopter was shot down and fell into the Vam Co Tay River near Tan An on 3 July 1968.[20] Van Deusen was General Westmoreland's brother-in-law. The death took place only a few hours after General Westmoreland was sworn in as Army Chief of Staff. The second battalion commander, Lieutenant Colonel William Edward Berzinec, who commanded the 4/39th Infantry, was killed on 30 July 1968. He stepped on a mine and died instantly.

The Long An Province Headquarters was also in Tan An. It had a Province Prisoner Interrogation Center situated less than 100 meters from our TOC. It was about to be transformed into a joint interrogation center with U.S. troop participation. I did not think we should have anything to do with that center since the South Vietnamese were not known for their strict adherence to prisoner treatment rules. I told Emerson a joint interrogation center would only cause problems in IG inspections and our relations with the ARVN. After a couple of sometimes heated discussions, he said he would have Lieutenant Colonel Franklin Hart, his XO, talk to ARVN to see if the plan could be canceled. I am not sure what happened since I left the brigade staff before they decided.[21]

Emerson was much more hands-on in operations in the 9th Division than what I had observed when he was a battalion commander. Consequently, he did not give his subordinates the same freedom of action he had given his company commanders in 2/502, except for possibly two battalion commanders—Lieutenant Colonels Donald Schroeder and James Lindsey.

Emerson's trailer, his living quarters, was located less than 50 meters from the TOC. He had communications personnel install a radio in his trailer, giving him the ability to monitor the radio traffic on the brigade command net. This radio caused a situation where Emerson reacted to the slightest contact by one of our battalions. It led to a telephone call to the TOC. Emerson wanted to know what was going on and what we were doing about it. These events could happen several times during the night, and the TOC, of course, gave me a call if I had gone to my hut to get some sleep. I told Emerson I would take the radio from his trailer because it demonstrated a lack of faith in the battalion commanders and me. He did not argue, and when he went to Thailand for R&R, I removed the radio from his trailer.

Operational Concepts and Innovations

Emerson was still insisting on checkerboard operations. This concept brought him much fame in the 2/502, but it caused disagreements between us in 1966. Except for the Ben Cat operations in 1965 and the open areas around Tuy Hoa, I never conducted checkerboard operations because I considered the concept dangerous in terrain difficult to navigate. Emerson was fully aware of this fact.

I also considered the terrain in the lower Delta unsuitable for checkerboard operations. I pointed this out to Emerson when we landed to pick up a prisoner on 7 June. The rice paddies were at flood stage, although it was not high tide. I was immediately submerged in water up to my waist when I stepped into a nearby rice paddy. When I stepped into one of the nearby irrigation canals, the water reached up to my armpits, and I had difficulties maintaining my equilibrium. I did this to show Emerson that a soldier could not move quickly in this area, which is key to his checkerboard concept's success. I know I failed to convince him.

To add insult to injury, at the end of July, he asked me to brief the Secretary of the Army, who I believe was Stanley R. Resor (1917–2012), on the checkerboard concept. There was no way I could get out of this chore, but I asked Emerson to chime in if the secretary should pose a question about something I could not truthfully answer. The briefing tent was full of troops. I began by mentioning that Colonel Emerson had developed this concept when he was a USAWC student and put it into practice when he commanded the 2/502 two years earlier. The secretary asked how the concept was working in the Delta. I paused and looked at Emerson, who did not take the cue until I finally answered that Colonel Emerson had been here over three months, while I was a relative newcomer, and it would be better if he responded to that question.

As developed by the Swedes and Dutch in the 17th century, the checkerboard concept was not designed for Emerson's goal. Its intended use was for Central Europe's open fields, with the "checkers" constituting reinforced battalion-sized combined-arms units (pikes, muskets, and at times cavalry), not platoons. They were not intended to find the enemy but to break his main line in a steady advance, while pouring continuous fire at the enemy formations, or to break up enemy counterattacks. The other reinforced battalion "checkers" were often used to attack the flanks of enemy units engaged by other "checkers." They were never used in sizes less than a battalion and not in areas of reduced visibility. I describe the concept in detail in a book I wrote in 2014.[22]

A technique developed jointly by General Electric and the U.S. Army Chemical Corps was called Personnel Detectors. We named them "People Sniffers" because of their design to pick up human sweat and urine readings. This technology, first introduced to Vietnam in 1967, proved not especially useful because troops carried the sniffers, and the enemy could easily detect the noise it made. By 1968, an airborne version was developed and used in the 9th Division mounted on helicopters (mostly LOHs). While a considerable improvement, the densely populated Delta area resulted in very many false readings. The NVA and VC also came up with countermeasures. One such measure used by the enemy was to fill buckets with mud and urine, hang them in trees, and leave the area.

The encirclement was very troop-intensive since the places to cordon off were often substantial. There was also the danger the VC could elect to launch an attack at night on one part of the encirclement with considerable local superiority. A substantial reserve force was required to avoid this danger.

To make the encirclements and infiltration interdiction more effective, we came up with a low-technology solution. By flying over the Plain of Reeds early in the morning before the sun had a chance to evaporate the dew, the path taken by an enemy force was easily visible from the air. By 1000 hours, the sun had evaporated the moisture, and the track was no longer visible. If the trail led to a wooded area but did not reappear on the other side of the woods, it was a sure indication an enemy force was in that wooded area. If the area was small enough, one of the battalions would be alerted and given a quick mission.

The battalions had become used to operating only in daylight while searching for the enemy. After discussing the issue with Emerson, we decided to try operating at night and blocking the likely infiltration routes we identified. We were ready to begin these operations by mid-July.

The named operations in the 9th Division were often overlapping and of long duration. This procedure was different from the 101st in 1965–1966 except for Operation *Fillmore*, conducted by 2/327, while the other battalions conducted Operation *Austin*. The 9th Division's Operation *Enterprise*, which lasted from 13 February 1967 to 11 March 1968, involved several large engagements and hundreds of lesser contacts. The *People's Road* operation took place from 17 March to 30 July 1968. It was a security/repair operation of Route 4, which my notes indicate resulted in 28 U.S. KIAs and 205 WIA, many from units other than the 1st Brigade. Operation *Kudzu* was also a security operation in the Dong Tam area from 1 May to 20 November 1968. Then there was Operation *Quyet Chin*, which began on 17 July 1968 and lasted until 4 March 1969. It was a recon in force operation involving both the 9th Division and ARVN forces. It became part of Operation *Speedy Express*, which began on 11 December 1968. *Speedy Express* was one of the most controversial Vietnam War operations and is discussed in the next chapter.

Operations After 23 June 1968

The changes in the AOs for the 1st and 3rd Brigade became effective on 23 June, the day I returned to the 1st Brigade Main CP. It was a hectic day as the battalions moved into their new areas. In the process, we became embroiled in a fight with a VC battalion and soon we had three of our battalions involved in trying to surround the enemy. Unfortunately, the encirclement was unsuccessful. Most of the enemy forces escaped during the night (23/24 June) through an area left uncovered by the encirclement. As we searched the battlefield in the morning, we found only four dead and captured two. Our losses were three killed and 17 wounded. I spent the whole day on the helicopter with Emerson until 0200 hours on the 24th.

Lieutenant General Weyand visited Tan An early on 23 June. The 9th Infantry Division was part of the U.S. II Field Force, which Weyand commanded. II Field Force headquarters were in Long Binh, and it was responsible for 11 Provinces around Saigon.

After meeting Colonel Emerson, Weyand came over to me and shook my hand, calling me his "captor." Emerson did not know what Weyand was talking about until Weyand told him about the reconnaissance platoon incident in Berlin in the early 1960s. Neither Weyand nor I mentioned anything about the note he had sent me in November 1967.

Weyand's main reason for coming to Tan An was to visit his commands to express his appreciation before turning over command of the corps to Lieutenant General Walter T. Kerwin Jr. (1917–2008) in early August 1968. Emerson and I were not aware of this change. We explained the initial brigade effort was directed toward cleaning out the area to the south of Saigon, preventing further movement towards the capital in our AO, protecting Route 4, and providing convoy escort. Although the pacification effort was still necessary, it had taken a back seat to operations against enemy forces south of Saigon. We realized that before an area could be labeled "pacified," we must eliminate all major enemy units. Weyand stated that his other troops around Saigon were in a similar posture. This conversation is the essence of our meeting with General Weyand.

I was with Emerson in his C&C helicopter on 24 June when tracer rounds started whipping past our aircraft on both sides. Emerson asked me what I believed was happening. We flew at 1,500 to 2,000 feet above the ground, so I told him a .50 caliber machine gun was most likely firing on us. The pilot came on the intercom and confirmed our suspicions. Emerson asked the pilot if we could get out of the enemy range while staying in the area. The pilot said that was only possible if we increased our altitude to over 6,000 feet or descended to treetop levels where it would be more difficult for the enemy gunner to see us. Emerson elected to go to treetop level, and the aircraft made a very steep spiral descent, and the firing stopped as we neared the ground. We lost one helicopter in this operation, but I am unsure what our other losses were as my notes are unreadable.

Two APCs from the 2/47 Infantry (Mechanized) were hit and disabled in early fighting on 25 June. Colonel Emerson and I were in the air near the action in the

C&C helicopter. Two door-gunners with M60 machine guns were on the aircraft, along with Emerson's RTO, my RTO, and an Air Force captain, the brigade's liaison officer.

Emerson wanted to land to see what help we could give. I asked the pilots to set the helicopter down outside the effective range of small arms, keeping the disabled APCs between us and the wood line. When we set the aircraft down, it was almost 400 meters from the APCs with one door gun facing in their direction.

I exited the helicopter with my RTO, and Emerson unbuckled his seat belt, intending to join us. I told him this was not a task for a 6' 3"-tall brigade commander but more suited for us short guys. With Emerson's approval, we dismounted the door gun facing away from the APCs so it could give us covering fire, if necessary. The Air Force liaison officer (I cannot recall his name) offered to help, and I accepted. When he exited the helicopter, he drew his handgun. I looked at him in disbelief, told him to put that thing away, and asked Emerson's RTO to hand the captain his M16. I asked him if he knew how to use it, and he answered yes. Emerson said he would call for medevac helicopters as he was sure we would soon need them.

The three of us spread out and began to run and crawl towards the APCs. An FAC was overhead and he called to tell us he would fire smoke rockets at the woods to obscure what we were doing. He already knew the location of friendly troops. The FAC was Major Thomas R. Bevivino, and he used a radio call sign that I still remember—*Tamale 12.* Bevivino brought in airstrikes and crisscrossed the area at treetop level. He remained in our area while we tried to reach the crews of the APCs. Some of them had managed to reach the wood-line.

My RTO, the Air Force liaison officer, and I reached the APC personnel and started dragging the two wounded to a safe distance in case the smoking vehicles exploded. We received sporadic enemy fire, but it was inaccurate due to the smoke laid down by the FAC. We also did not have to use our weapons. Unfortunately, one of the APCs burst into flames a short time after dragging the two soldiers away. The medevac helicopters were now on station, so we evacuated the two men from the APC.

I told Emerson I planned to recommend the two Air Force officers and my RTOs for awards. He immediately agreed, and I wrote up the recommendations that night. My RTO's award recommendation was reduced to a Bronze Star, and I believe the division also lowered the two Air Force officers' awards. The S-1 also said Emerson had submitted an award recommendation for me. However, because he felt there were too many recommendations for a small operation, Ira Hunt denied it, and Emerson received a DSC, which included this operation.

By 26 June, we had been in continual action for four days and I slept for only four hours during those 90 hours. I was supposed to attend a dinner with Colonel Emerson at the quarters of the Province Chief on the evening of 26 June but decided not to participate and instead get some sleep.

We became involved in another sizeable multi-battalion engagement on 27 June—it lasted two days. We believed we had an enemy battalion encircled. However, there was a hole in the cordon's northern part, which I pointed out to Emerson. He did not think the enemy would move in that direction, and since he only had one company in the brigade reserve, he believed this was insufficient to seal the hole. I reminded him the enemy battalion was probably the same one we had battled on two previous occasions. Each time they had slipped through an unprotected area of the encirclement. Given our artillery and air superiority, I told him that one company was more than enough to act as a blocking force. He did not act on my recommendation until it was too late, and the enemy battalion slipped through the hole that night. The following day Emerson graciously explained to the battalion commanders that he had been wrong and that I had been right.

The first night operation took place on 15/16 July. It was the most significant and bloodiest encounter while I was the S-3. It lasted from early on 15 July until the afternoon on the 16th. The initial contact was by 2/39 Infantry, the organization I would join about three weeks later, and, if my recollection is correct, it resulted from a people sniffer reading. The engagement took place in a place called the Rats' Nest, about 24 kilometers southwest of Saigon along a tributary stream of the Vam Co Dong River. As the battle progressed, we inserted additional units, including the 2/60 Infantry, part of the 5/60 Mechanized Infantry Battalion, 4/39 Infantry Battalion, and a company from the Riverine Force.

It was a successful encirclement but shows how troop intensive these operations were, even when the cordon's southern portion did not need much coverage as the river prevented a VC escape to the south. Enemy losses were 77 killed, but friendly casualties were also steep—nine dead and 26 wounded. Weapons captured included 10 individual weapons, two machine guns, and four 60mm mortars. The low number of weapons seized in such a destructive engagement caused me to question the accuracy of VC killed.

Colonel Emerson traveled to Saigon on 18 July to receive a DSC from Secretary of Defense Clark Clifford (1906–1998). I believe the award covered actions from 23 June to 2 July. The following day, Emerson traveled to Bangkok for a short R&R, returning on 23 July. While he was away, the oil storage facility at Nha Be near Saigon endured a mortar attack from our area. About 145,000 gallons of fuel were lost.

We had a two-battalion engagement on 23 July. One chopper was shot down, and when another helicopter tried to land to help, the enemy fired on it and two soldiers on that helicopter died, and another was wounded. As already mentioned, my notes from this period are mostly unreadable. Therefore, I do not know what other losses we sustained or the damage we may have inflicted on the enemy. The 9th Division Reports seldom give detailed results.

It was towards the end of this period that the VC destroyed the Ben Luc Bridge. I vividly remember having to wake up Colonel Emerson to give him the bad news.

I had often complained about the split responsibility for that bridge and Emerson had agreed I write a letter to the division G-3. I did this about three weeks before its destruction.

Emerson and I flew to Saigon,[23] where I witnessed a severe verbal exchange between him, General Ewell, and the Saigon brass. During this argument, Emerson told Ewell we had warned the division about this problem. When Ewell said he knew nothing about any warning, I pulled out a copy of my letter to his G-3 much earlier and handed it to Emerson. We had never received an answer. As we waited in the hallway, Emerson noted we could both be relieved. We were not, and I was proud of Emerson for taking on his superiors on the brigade's behalf. The engineers built a temporary pontoon bridge across the river and had it in operation, as I remember, within 48 hours.

Another substantial engagement began at night on 4 August. The VC suffered 45 killed, but I have no information on our losses because of my sparse readable notes. Large-scale enemy activity had, in fact, shown a steady decline.

It was now past the date I was promised an assignment to 2/39 as XO to Lieutenant Colonel Donald Schroeder, who had arrived in late June. Emerson was waiting for my replacement. I commented to Florence that Emerson was hard to work for as a staff officer, particularly S-3, since he was his own operations officer. I told her our frequent disagreements probably made Emerson happy to see me go so that he could get a replacement more attuned to his thinking.

My assignment to the 2/39 took place on 6 August. I turned in the efficiency reports on some of my officers to Lieutenant Colonel Hart, said goodbye to the people in the TOC, and told Captain Stephens, my Assistant S-3, that he would be the acting S-3 until a new major was assigned. Emerson had asked me to join him for lunch in his trailer.

I apologized to the colonel for having given him such a hard time during my tenure as S-3. He said that was nonsense—he admired me for giving my honest opinions. He then expressed his regrets for not making good on his promise of a "Raider Unit" to operate in the Plain of Reeds; he had personally become convinced such a force was needed over the past few months.

Maybe it was meant to be that way, Emerson continued, because the troops in the 9th Division were not top-notch like those we had in the 2/502. He said my demonstrated behavior in the field might have led to my death and he did not want to be the one to have to explain that to Florence.

I had planned to travel to Rach Kien in the afternoon mail helicopter, but Emerson insisted I use his C&C helicopter.

CHAPTER 19

Battalion Executive Officer

The 2/39 Infantry was in the district town of Rach Kien, about 7 kilometers northeast of Tan An as the crow flies, but much longer over unsecured roads (see map in the previous chapter, page 242). The district was a center of insurgency going back to the French occupation of Vietnam. Whether we call them communists or nationalists is semantics—the bottom line is they were opposed to all foreigners.

The 2/39th had suffered more casualties than any other battalion in the 9th Infantry Division during the May–July 1968 period—54 killed and 142 wounded.[1] There was a sharp drop in large-scale operations from August onward and that decline continued during my tour in the 2/39th.

The 2/39th was co-located with the Rach Kien District Headquarters. Captain Ninh-Tuy-Ton was the district chief, and I paid him a courtesy visit on my first full day at Rach Kien. We occupied the southwest end of the compound while the Vietnamese district troops occupied the other end. Our troops lived in dilapidated huts or lean-tos, the worst I had seen in Vietnam, but the ARVN and 9th Division would not let us improve these places despite repeated requests. Moreover, the district troops were responsible for defending the perimeter in their area, and we in our portion of the town; this split responsibility gave us ongoing problems.

As I remember, there was only one gate into the compound and one road between that gate and the district headquarters and the district troops' location. Our headquarters' location was next to the entrance to the compound. As a result, there was a steady traffic of ARVN military personnel and civilians past our area.

An article titled "Former home of VC now houses 2d-39th" paints a rosy picture of Rach Kien District. Specialist 5 Wayne Campbell, apparently a division staff writer, wrote it. The article is dated 6 November 1968 and could have been part of *Octofoil*, the 9th Division magazine, but I am unsure.[2]

The following information and quotes are from that article. Campbell wrote that the population of Rach Kien was 1,700 when the 9th Division arrived. He notes that MACV Advisory Team 86, with Major Robert W. Black from Carlisle, Pennsylvania, in command, completed many projects. Black was a colonel and faculty member at the Army War College when I was a student.

> Some of the projects completed by the team included three bridges, seven new schools, two dispensaries, two markets and the repairing and building of 20 kilometers of road. … They also built sidewalks, 112 prefabricated houses. … In addition, under the command of Lieutenant Colonel Donald B. Schroeder, 39, of Las Vegas, Nev., the battalion has knocked down numerous old buildings and replaced them with new ones.

I did not see any evidence of these projects, and neither did David Johnson when I asked him in late 2018. If they completed the projects, it was not in the village of Rach Kien. As far as knocking down buildings, the VC did that, not us. We repaired some buildings damaged by their attacks, but we did not build new ones—we were not permitted by ARVN and the division. I have no idea where the 112 prefabricated buildings were—I did not see any.

Lieutenant Colonel Donald Schroeder, who met me on the helicopter pad when I arrived on 6 August, gave me a warm welcome. He had arranged for me to meet some of the officers at dinner in a combination officers' mess hall and club. The meeting involved most of the officers except those from the company with Rach Kien's security duties.

The organization of the 2/39th was under a different TO&E than the 2/502. This TO&E resulted from the work of the U.S. Army Combat Development Command at Fort Belvoir, Virginia. They were attempting to come up with light battalions suitable for the environment in Vietnam. A whole series of organizational structures under TO&E 7-15E covered all types of infantry battalions. For those desiring more detailed information, I suggest a publication written by Virgil Ney.[3]

There were several variations of these organizational structures, with the numbers of rifle companies ranging from three to five. As I recall, we had four rifle companies and a large HHC containing the various combat support elements. These included the following platoons: communications, support, maintenance, medical, heavy mortar, and anti-tank. Other versions of the TO&E have these elements in a combat support company. The fourth rifle company in 2/39 was Company D.

Interestingly, the Combat Development Command documents discuss reducing soldiers' load and making the weapons platoon a rifle platoon. This was a subject I was obsessed with during my first tour and led me to make the weapons platoon into a rifle platoon. It appears that some commanders (at which level I do not know) opted to make the weapon platoons into small rifle platoons by leaving their heavy weapons in the rear areas. Others pooled the weapon platoons and made them into a small company called Security Company. These organizational changes were undoubtedly in response to many complaints and recommendations from the field by officers who had reached the same conclusions I had.

These modifications were already made in 2/39 when I arrived. The assigned strength of the 2/39 was roughly 800 troops. I believe the TO&E called for 818.

Dave Johnson wrote that the companies' authorized strength was over 150 soldiers, but we never had more than 100 to 120 assigned and rarely had 90 available to go on operations.[4] The numbers Dave has for "assigned" and "operationally available" tallies well with my memory. The low number of operationally available troops was primarily due to the constant leg and foot problems from operating in flooded rice paddies and irrigation canals.

As I recall, we did not have a designated security company in 2/39, but there was a Company E briefly mentioned in some sources. If I am right, according to the TO&E, that was the weapons platoons' location and possibly the reconnaissance platoon. I make no mention of a Company E in my notes. If there had been five rifle companies, that would account for 750 of the battalion 818 authorized strength and leave only 68 slots for the large HHC and staff. I conclude that Company E was the security company referenced in the TO&E unless I learn something different. I was the endorser for all company XOs and platoon leaders. There is no mention of anyone from Company E, as they received their ratings from their parent organization's commander.

The first week I was in Rach Kien, there were no operations, which allowed me to become familiar with the unit and my staff. Therefore, I asked the battalion sergeant major to meet with the senior NCOs—platoon sergeants and company first sergeants. I told them this would be a listening session for me and that they should feel free to bring to my attention any subjects in areas that warranted improvements, both now and in the future. The meeting lasted about two hours.

The average ages of the NCOs were much different from those in 2/502. Platoon sergeants (E-7) were mostly in their mid-20s, and some were on their first tour in Vietnam. Sergeants (E-5) and staff sergeants (E-6) were unusually young, around 20 years old, and most had experienced little or no combat before assignment to the battalion. The average age of the junior enlisted personnel in the battalion was 19. The 9th Division had an NCO academy at Bear Cat that produced young NCOs from candidates submitted by the battalions. The companies' lieutenants were recent graduates from the Officer Training Course (OTC) at Fort Benning. Dave Johnson mentions some were in poor physical shape and that there were only a few from ROTC and none from West Point.[5]

I also met the rifle company commanders. I recommended to Schroeder that he write their OERs to maintain a solid commander to commander relationship. He balked at this recommendation and said even if he did what I suggested, he wanted me to write the reports, and he would sign them. He would also let the company commanders know that I was the writer, thereby virtually placing me in the command chain. In the end, I wrote and signed the reports on three rifle company commanders. I may have written one for the other company commander for Don's signature, which may be why I did not keep a copy.

Since they worked under my direct supervision, the most protracted meeting was with the principal and special staff officers—S-1, S-2, S-3, S-4, the chaplain, and the surgeon. I also included the headquarters company commander in this group.

Captain David C. Johnson from the 2/502 was the battalion S-1, having arrived on 21 June 1968. I believed he kept that position until I departed, but Dave wrote that he took over Company B when Captain Beach left on 27 October.[6] Dave is the best staff officer I have ever known, and Don Schroeder felt the same way. Therefore, it surprises me that Don and I would have let him leave the S-1 position less than three weeks before moving to Dong Tam and six weeks before facing the USARV IG inspection. However, Dave undoubtedly knows when he assumed command and was wounded during the night of 28/29 December, something a person never forgets.

I do not know how we obtained the highest score without Captains Johnson and Dent since my personnel and logistics record-keeping knowledge was abysmal. I have a vague memory of Dave being present for the IG inspection, so maybe he was in that half of the battalion Schroeder sent back to Dong Tam on 1 December to help prepare for the IG. I do not know who took over as S-1, but it may have been First Lieutenant Skolnick, whom I talked with by telephone several times from Pleiku (see next chapter).

First Lieutenant Anthony E. Burris was the battalion S-2 and assigned to that position on 26 June. He left the battalion on 26 October, and his replacement was First Lieutenant James L. Noles, who remained S-2 until I left.

I also had two S-3s while in the 2/39th. Major James A. Musselman was S-3 when I arrived, having worked in that position since 17 April. He left on 24 October to become brigade S-3. James had a successful career, retiring as a major general. Major Robert D. Yearout replaced Musselman on 25 October, and he may have still been there when I departed since I had to prepare an OER on him, either before I left Dong Tam or as an exigent at Pleiku. Dave Johnson believes he was given a new position or transferred by Don Schroeder.

Captain Norman M. Dent was S-4 when I arrived, assigned to the battalion on 26 June. He left on 18 October for Fort Benning, and his replacement was Captain James L. Redmond. Redmond remained the S-4 until I departed.

Captain Gary F. Vote came to the battalion on 1 August. After turning down an offer to command a rifle company, he was appointed commander of HHC and was still there when I left the division.

I was the OER rater for two battalion chaplains—Captain William B. Kirby Jr., battalion chaplain from 16 July to 27 September 1968, and Captain Edward B. Rogers, who replaced Kirby and was still chaplain when I left for Pleiku.

I was also the rater for two surgeons who were assigned to the battalion while I was there. Captain Gerald F. Nieters was the surgeon from 15 July to 16 September. Captain Carl R. Wirth arrived on 30 August, giving us two surgeons for two weeks. Wirth was still there when I departed.

The tour in 2/39 was the first time I had written reports on surgeons and chaplains, and to make sure I did not unintentionally hurt them, I sat down with Captains

Kirby and Nieters to find out what their branches were looking for to further their careers and what could be detrimental to their future.

Additionally, I ended up being the rater for all rifle company commanders. Captain Charles A. Hardin was commander of A/2/39 from 24 June to 28 August, and Captain Robert L. Anderson replaced him on 29 August and was still there when I left for Pleiku. Captain Karl L. Beach commanded B/2/39 from 6 May to 27 October. Captain Jesse L. Johnson, who had earned a DSC in operations 23–24 July (mentioned briefly in the previous chapter), commanded C/2/39. Jesse was a special operations commander for Norm Schwarzkopf in the Gulf War and retired as a colonel. Captain Joseph W. Hudson was commander of D/2/39 from 6 May until 1 December. For one company commander, I prepared the report for Schroeder's signature. There was a mutual dislike between this officer and me, and he may have requested Don sign his OER.

Finally, I was the OER endorser for the officers in the various staff sections and the XOs and platoon leaders in the companies. These reports amounted to much writing over the months, mostly at night. Statistical reports and summaries were as numerous as those at brigade headquarters. The difference for me was that I had an entire staff that took care of them. I had to sign some reports, but the appropriate staff officer signed the most. I was also the Special Court-Martial Officer; I took that job very seriously, ensuring all soldiers received a fair hearing. This job occasionally led to arguments with the company commander who had brought the charges.

Our TOC was close to the compound's main gate, near the end of our part. I had my office next to the TOC. A door led to the TOC from my office, while another door led to Lieutenant Colonel Schroeder and my sleeping quarters. Behind our quarters was a stockade for troops who had been court-martialed and were awaiting transfer to Bear Cat's confinement facilities. We never had to resort to such measures in 2/502. The mess/club was across the street from the TOC.

The battalion was not supposed to be the ready battalion on 12 August and Schroeder was in Saigon, where he visited wounded troops and attended to personal matters. The 2/60 Infantry, commanded by Lieutenant Colonel James J. Lindsay, made the initial contact, and I received a call from Emerson to "saddle up" the battalion for an attempted encirclement.[7] We made a helicopter assault, and by early afternoon, we became heavily engaged with three of our companies pinned in the rice paddies by heavy enemy fire. I landed with C/2/39 and managed to get pinned down almost immediately. We remained pinned down until about 1600 hours when the tide came in and forced us to retire under cover of smoke to drier ground.

Schroeder joined us on the ground around 1700 hours, as the action was beginning to wind down. While the more substantial encirclement Emerson had hoped for failed because of lack of troops, we had been partially successful in our area by trapping one VC company. Friendly losses were three killed and 22 wounded; one killed and 10 wounded were from 2/39. The two battalions reportedly killed 66 VC, captured 29 enemy weapons, and detained 25 unarmed suspects.[8]

Both Dave Johnson and I had our integrities tested in the 9th Division, involving the two issues high on the division's priority list—body count and awards. Awards had a high priority, demonstrated by 11,399 of all kinds being awarded in one three-month period.[9] While Dave Johnson's problem involved enemy body count, it was after I left the 9th Division. Dave covers this issue well in his book, referenced earlier. I believe many officers were struggling with these problems in the 9th Division.

For me, the integrity challenge dealt with decorations and started soon after an operation on 18 August. There was an unwritten rule in the 9th Division that all battalion commanders receive a DSC, a high award for personal bravery. I believe this award should be reserved primarily for troops that do the fighting and often lose their lives or for company-grade officers who likewise distinguish themselves. We only had three such awards in A/2/502 and all were posthumous. I passionately believe that dictating beforehand who should receive such distinction is highly inappropriate.

When the battalion took to the field on 18 August, the sergeant major and I stayed behind to make sure no one was refusing to deploy.[10] This chore had become a routine duty for the sergeant major, Captain Dave Johnson, and me and often turned into dangerous confrontations between armed soldiers and us. Dave describes one such incident on pp. 61–62 of his book, which I had forgotten. "One black soldier from C Company actually threatened a Major (our XO) with a piece of 2x4 lumber saying, 'This is not my war, white man—you fight it, not me.'" We placed the soldier under arrest, and I had to remove myself from the proceedings since I was the accuser. It also led to words between Captain Jesse Johnson and me. I am not sure how the incident ended. There were no such confrontations on 18 August.

As soon as the last troop helicopter had left, the sergeant major and I boarded our helicopter with our RTOs and headed for the battle area. I called Schroeder, told him the remainder of the battalion was on its way and that the alternate command group was airborne. I asked him where he wanted us. It was SOP not to have the primary and alternate command groups in the same location. Splitting the command groups was to avoid a well-directed mortar round, leaving the battalion leaderless. Don gave me coordinates that were about 1,500 meters from the main action. I figured I had failed to copy the coordinates correctly and read them back to him. He said they were correct.

We landed where instructed, on a small peninsula about 1,300 meters northeast of the battalions nearest flank. Neither the sergeant major nor I had any idea why we were there. The peninsula had some mud huts shaped like igloos. When we landed, we received no fire and released the helicopter to make it available for other battalion elements. We had not been there long before we began receiving sniper fire from the northeast, from across a nearby canal. We figured the snipers were using bolt-action rifles, which had a more extended range than our M16 because our return fire was ineffective. We took shelter behind one of the "igloos" and waited to see if the enemy would move within range. They did not, but fired in our direction every time we stuck our heads up.

Schroeder arrived in his C&C helicopter in the late afternoon. We warned the pilot we were receiving sporadic sniper fire from our northeast and threw a white smoke grenade where he should land. When he arrived, Schroeder told me the operation was winding down as the enemy broke contact.

Don set up his radio on the northeast side of the nearest "igloo," although both the sergeant major and I told him that would expose him to the snipers. He ignored our warning and sat down in full view of the snipers' location. There was a large puddle of water at his location, and the snipers soon zeroed in on his position. Rounds splashed into the water all around, but he stayed on the radio, ignoring the incoming fire. I went around to where he was located and asked if he had a death wish since it was only a matter of time before a round hit him. The others in our party gave him as much covering fire as possible, and I asked the helicopter pilot to move the aircraft slightly so that one door gunner could place machine-gun fire on the snipers' area.

Schroeder finally completed his radio calls, got back in his helicopter, and told us he would send an aircraft to pick us up when the action to our southwest was over. I could not understand why he had come to tell us that—he could easily have done so over the radio. Ground combat was new to Don, except for commanding a task force for a few days at Phan Thiet in 1966 and one or two operations before I became his XO. Later, I concluded—unsupported by facts—that Emerson had told him he would be recommended for a DSC on this operation and for him to ensure that some senior NCOs and I were around so we would be able to write the recommendation. No award is worth such unnecessary risk.

It was almost dark when a helicopter came to pick us up, receiving enemy fire on its approach. We were back at Rach Kien shortly after dark, and most of the battalion had extracted. The engagement resulted in 64 enemy soldiers killed and 14 detainees brought back to the battalion. We captured only six weapons.[11] If my memory is correct, our losses were only three soldiers with minor wounds.

Emerson called me on the landline that had just been installed and told me that he wanted a DSC recommendation for Schroeder for the action just completed. I said I was not where the fighting took place but would do as he directed, although I felt sure there would be more substantial operations in the future. He rejected my statement about future activities.

I completed the DSC recommendation on the 19th, with supporting statements from some present on the peninsula. However, we considered this an improper action for a DSC recommendation, despite stretching the truth considerably.

Donald Schroeder was a fine officer. His performance as XO of 2/502 in 1965–1966 was outstanding. In the Delta, he took a battalion with poor morale and other problems and eventually made it the best in the division. There was no doubt in my mind he would end up with stars on his collar.

There were no contacts on the 19th and 20th, but Rach Kien received mortar/rocket fire on 21 August. There was only minor damage, but three troops were wounded and evacuated. That night a rocket attack on the camp killed one soldier and left another injured. A portion of our base burned down.

Emerson arrived in Rach Kien in the late afternoon on 21 August. I believe he stopped at the club first to have a drink with Donald Schroeder. Emerson was not there long before coming to my office. I could tell he was angry. My mood was not the best since I had just received a letter from my sister-in-law dated 7 August, explaining there had been a fire in our home on the night of 4/5 August. Florence had received burns and was evacuated to a burn center in Texas. My mother-in-law, Mary McEldowny, would stay with the kids until Florence returned. I had also received a letter from Norway telling me that my father was in a Bergen hospital with severe heart problems.

Colonel Emerson threw a package containing the DSC recommendation on my desk, saying this will not fly, what it provides does not justify a DSC. Then, as calmly as I could, I reminded him of our conversation on 18 August. I had then pointed out that the operation that day—with a highly exaggerated body count, only six weapons captured, and only a few of our own lightly wounded—was not ideal for a DSC recommendation. Furthermore, neither I nor the sergeant major was present at the engagement area, but a kilometer and a half away.

Emerson said he wanted Don to receive a DSC and for me to spruce it up. I asked him what he meant by that—did he want me to use more colorful language or invent things I had not witnessed. I said I knew what damage could be done to a DSC recommendation when the most crucial information is left out. I assured him nothing had been left out from our vantage point but embellished.

Emerson grew visibly angrier, as I am sure he recognized my comments about omissions as a reference to Bu Gia Map. My DSC recommendation for that battle failed to mention I had been the ground commander of the most successful operation since the brigade's arrival in Vietnam. Our argument developed into the most severe I had with Emerson over the many years we knew each other.

It was not in line with Emerson's personality, and I concluded he was under pressure. I was also under pressure from the events involving my wife and father. The intense conversation refreshed in my mind his broken promises to Florence and me that brought me into the 9th Division and the unfortunate and disappointing closing events of my first tour in Vietnam.

As he was leaving, he said he wanted the new DSC recommendation for Don on his desk at 0900 in the morning. I saluted and said, "Yes, sir."

The door to the TOC had been partially open and Major Musselman had overheard some of our heated conversation. After Emerson left, Jim came into my office and offered his help. Initially, I turned down his offer. I told him there was no way to get Schroeder a DSC for the action on the 18th without lying, and there was no point in the two of us doing so.[12] As he continued to offer his assistance, I eventually agreed. He said he would provide a handwritten statement supporting the recommendation, arrange for a typist to be available, and for an air courier to leave at 0800 hours in the morning for Tan An with the re-rewritten recommendation.

We spent much of the night preparing the papers, consulting DSC regulations and what the 9th Division had to say on the subject, focusing on what the recommendation should contain. One thing it should contain was the result of the engagement. I purposely left that out because reporting 64 enemies killed with only six weapons captured could be viewed as highly unsatisfactory and counterproductive. We also re-read the battalion AA report for 18 October. Lieutenant Colonel Schroeder came back from the club and was ready to go to bed. He wanted to know what we were doing. I told him we were working on matters dealing with the AA report and a request for information by Emerson.

After we rewrote the DSC recommendation, I asked the typist to hang around for a while longer. I began writing my resignation and I wanted that delivered to Emerson along with the award recommendation. Unfortunately, we were interrupted by VC shelling our camp and the subsequent fire, which was destructive. The typist and I resumed our work around 0430 hours and completed it in time for the courier's departure.

I felt bad about not telling Schroeder about my resignation, but it was difficult to do without mentioning his award recommendation problems. Nevertheless, I finally told him about my resignation over a cup of coffee around 0730 hours on 22 August, apologizing for not telling him earlier.

Don was shocked at the news and wanted to know if he had done something to cause this action. I told him no. He said this was devastating news since both he and Emerson felt it was inevitable that I would be a future leader of our country's military. He said I already had one early promotion under my belt and he felt confident that I would have another one when the list for lieutenant colonel came out in 1969. Finally, he said, *I need you here to help me shape up this battalion.* I told Don I would not leave him, so I had asked for my resignation to become effective on 1 July 1969.

I am sure Schroeder called Emerson immediately since I received a call from Emerson around 0930 hours. He was very agitated, and some time passed before I could say a word. Emerson started with the statement, *What the hell is going on, Hank?* He continued, *I know you were highly disappointed in not getting the promised command, and for that, I am deeply sorry.* Colonel Emerson mentioned he was heading to Australia for a few days' R&R and would talk to the general again when he returned. He also said he planned to tear up my resignation and probably violate all kinds of rules and regulations by doing so. He said I was the best combat leader he had ever known, as he had many times before and after.

He did not mention the bitter conversation over Don's DSC recommendation, but it could not have escaped his attention that both documents were delivered simultaneously. He ended his call by saying that a leave would be authorized to look after the home front. This statement further reinforced my conclusion that Emerson had talked to Schroeder, since only he and Dave Johnson knew about those problems. Before he hung up, I asked Emerson not to raise the "Raider Unit" subject with General Ewell, as I was satisfied serving for Donald Schroeder.[13]

The 22 August conversation was my last with Colonel Emerson before enemy fire brought down his helicopter around 1700 hours on 26 August. There were seven people on board, and the aircraft started burning when it hit the ground. Colonel Ira Hunt was on the helicopter, and he managed to cut Emerson's seat belt and get him out of the aircraft. Two soldiers on the helicopter died and most of the others received burns or lesser injuries. Emerson was brought to the 24th Medical Evacuation Hospital north of Saigon, but he did not stay there long. Finally, he was evacuated, via Japan, to Walter Reed Hospital in Washington.

Most of the battalion went out on operations on 27 August, and by luck we captured two prisoners, only one carrying a weapon. I guess the Lord was looking out for me again since Rach Kien endured the heaviest rocket attack to date while I was in the field. My office took a direct hit, sending shrapnel in all directions, including into a stack of letters, tearing them up rather severely.

Operations continued on a much-reduced scale, as reflected in the 9th Division Operational Report's statistical tables. While the number of contacts remained high, the number of engagements with battalion-size enemy forces had declined significantly after July, and that decline continued. Most actions were now against smaller groups of local VC forces.

There were split opinions on the reasons. Some believed the VC forces had taken such a severe beating they avoided large-scale encounters with U.S. forces. Others suspected the VC were consolidating and refitting their forces for renewed large-scale activities. This trend continued until we moved to Dong Tam. I believe the second explanation is more on point. The two country-wide VC offensives in 1969 validate this view.

Enemy shelling of Rach Kien continued. Most caused only material damage, but some resulted in casualties—dead and wounded. One shelling, accompanied by a ground probe, will always remain in my mind as an example of the difference between my first and second tours in Vietnam.

The ground probe damaged two of our guard towers. The soldiers (two in each) from one tower made it through the wire, and only one was slightly wounded. We heard nothing from the occupants of the second tower across an irrigation canal.

Most troops had assembled in the rectangular area near the southeastern part of our compound. I asked for a couple of volunteers to go with me to check out the tower across the canal. No one volunteered. Karl Beach's company was nearest to the irrigation canal, and as I walked down the line, I gave them a contemptuous look. If I had asked for volunteers in A/2/502, the whole company would probably have stepped forward.

Captain Norman Dent, the S-4, eventually spoke up, and he volunteered to accompany me. We crossed the canal bridge and worked our way through the wire. As we approached the tower, which looked undamaged, Dent found one of the occupants hiding in the underbrush. He did not know what had happened to his companion, and I asked Dent to remain on the ground giving cover while I scaled the tower. I found the occupant crouching in a corner with the radio at his side. He was not wounded.

I picked up the radio and called the TOC. The TOC operator gave Schroeder the handset when he realized it was the second in command on the radio. Schroeder asked where I was. I explained to him that both occupants of the tower were unharmed, and the company providing these guards should be tasked to provide replacements as the troops there now were in no condition to continue their duties. I also told him we needed to talk when Dent and I returned.

Dent and I reported to the TOC and explained to Schroeder what had happened. He was outraged and said the incident was why he wanted me to be the OER rater for company commanders, thereby putting me in the chain of command. I told him that would only be a bandage solution and not solve the real problems of lack of discipline, esprit de corps, and training of the more than 800 so-called troops inherited from his predecessor.

This incident was the beginning of a long and sustained effort to get the battalion in shape. When the troops were not on operations, we started a training program, a beautification program, cleaning out the worst rat holes occupied by our soldiers and building bunkers where the troops could take shelter.

Furthermore, we needed to ensure that the officers and NCOs lived and ate their meals with the troops. Dent and I both pointed out that our perimeter security needed strengthening with patrols. We needed to limit the compound's access by Vietnamese civilians, as we were sure the camp was mapped by civilians or by unfriendly ARVN troops. Finally, I gave the surgeon orders to make it his priority to develop a solution to the severe leg/foot problems, which had resulted in the battalion being practically combat ineffective when Lieutenant Colonel Schroeder assumed command.

We took some steps immediately. I was particularly concerned that officers and senior NCOs were not living with the troops when not on operations. It is in this kind of environment that morale problems arise. Soldiers are sitting around thinking about the last fight and the next one, but no one in authority is present to hear or discuss their concerns. This situation was instrumental in causing a flurry of refusals to go to the field and kept our stockade filled. Since I was the Special Court-Martial Officer, I had concluded from my interviews with the accused and their superiors that this was a significant problem. We did not want the club occupied by officers at all hours drinking and playing cards when they should be with their troops. Therefore, we established new operating hours for the club. I had always felt that with the proper leadership, training, and support, draftees perform as well as volunteers.

These changes led to confrontations with the district chief and his subordinates. The plentiful supply of materials we requested to fix the troops' living quarters and the bunkers led to clashes between Colonel Ira Hunt and Schroeder. Schroeder grew to dislike Hunt intensely, almost as much as Hackworth did after he arrived. Some projects, such as improving the places where our troops lived, were only partially implemented, and requests to send patrols outside the perimeter received a flat denial. Other changes did not bear fruit until the end of our time in Rach Kien. But it was unavoidable not to notice the improvement in troop morale, almost from day to day. It was instrumental in leading the next brigade commander to label our battalion the best in the division.

I commanded the battalion on a couple of occasions when Schroeder was absent. Such was the case on 10–12 September, when we became heavily engaged with a VC battalion. The action had started when the 3/17th Air Cavalry received heavy small arms and automatic weapons fire near our planned AO. Since other battalions had operations underway in other areas of the province, our airlift capability was severely limited, forcing us to feed the battle area piecemeal, one company at a time.

Upon landing, D/2/39 and C/2/39 became heavily engaged with VC forces fighting from a system of well-fortified bunkers. My C&C helicopter (LOH) was subject to a stream of fire from machine guns as I made passes over the battlefield to find enemy positions and direct artillery fire. I made numerous landings to brief the company commanders on my observations.

The rest of the battalion was on the ground by late afternoon, along with one company from the 2/60th Infantry. As it turned dark, I landed to join the most heavily engaged company and stayed there during the night. Unfortunately, we were unable to seal the enemy positions because we lacked enough forces on the ground. As a result, the enemy broke contact during the night. A battlefield search the following day revealed we had killed 35 enemy soldiers and found 26 individual and crew-served weapons. We also captured five VC prisoners, four that were armed.

On 13 September, we had some senior visitors—General Abrams and Admiral McCain Jr. (1911–1981), Commander-in-Chief, Pacific. As usual, other VIPs from division and corps came with them, as did Colonel Ira Hunt, who took temporary command of the 1st Brigade after Emerson. The visit was short, lasting only 20 minutes.

I received a telegram from the Norwegian Red Cross through the U.S. Red Cross on 17 September, stating that my presence was required since my father was on his death bed, with the doctors having no hope for a recovery. Schroeder immediately arranged for me to take emergency leave so I could reach my father while he was still alive. It allowed me 30 days, like all emergency leaves, but I told Schroeder I would try to return in two weeks. However, he doubted this was possible because of the long roundtrip flights.

I wrote a letter to Florence on 17 September telling her I would leave Vietnam within a few hours for a flight to McGuire Air Force Base in New Jersey and to Germany. I told her I did not know if I would have a chance to stop in Fayetteville but for her to close one bank account since I only had $200 as I departed Vietnam. I said I would talk to her on the telephone when I reached the U.S.

After talking to Florence by telephone from Hawaii, our plans changed. She had never met my parents and expressed a desire to do so. She said she felt well enough and that Barbara, now almost 18, could take care of David and Monica for a short time. She would also ask Judith Andersen, who lived nearby on the same street, to watch things. We decided to do that, and I changed my route from San Francisco to Fayetteville rather than McGuire.

Florence did not have a valid passport, which usually took two weeks, but we hoped this problem could be solved. Before leaving North Carolina, we called the State Department and explained the situation. They understood and said the passport would be available for pickup that night. When we arrived to pick it up, all was in order, and we continued to New York as we had already purchased two roundtrip tickets for a direct flight to Bergen from Kennedy Airport. The plane departed on the evening of 20 September.

We visited my father three times in the hospital, starting on 22 September. He was weak, had lost a lot of weight, and was suffering from bedsores. I set up an appointment to talk to the doctors on 24 September. I asked them to explain what was wrong. Both doctors stated his condition was terminal as his internal organs had stopped functioning properly. I explained I was stationed in Vietnam and would have to return in a couple of days. I told them I would be in Vietnam until the end of May 1969 and asked if they thought he would be alive until then. They said he would be lucky to survive until Christmas. I asked them to do something about the bedsores and they assured me they would take care of that problem. They also said they planned to send him home soon since there was nothing more they could do at the hospital. My father had also expressed a desire to spend the end at home. Local doctors and nurses would look after him every day and give him pain medicines.

We visited him for the last time on 25 September. Florence and I were scheduled to travel from Bergen to New York on the morning of 26 September. It was tough saying goodbye to my father, knowing I would never see him again. I told him we were leaving in the morning, and he thanked Florence for coming to see him. To me, he said he believed I had found a good wife. As we left, the old soldier smiled, waved, and told me to be careful in Vietnam.

The flight back to the U.S. was uneventful and we landed in New York late on 26 September. Mary Torres and her husband Ed picked us up at the airport and we spent the night at their home.

Florence and I began our return trip to Fayetteville on 27 September and arrived late that evening. There was a letter from Don Schroeder waiting for me. He informed me the battalion would move to Dong Tam soon and that it had been selected as the one battalion in the division to stand a USARV IG inspection scheduled for 6–10 December. Don asked if I would return by 20 October. I wrote him a short message saying I would probably be in Rach Kien before the note.

Florence and I spent 28 September selling about half of our investments at a steep loss and arranged for the proceeds to be deposited in a Fort Bragg bank. The government only paid for the emergency travel to the U.S. home address; the overseas part was at our expense. This travel had taken care of a good deal of our available cash, and we realized another visit to Norway might be necessary if my father died. Monetary assistance for my mother, as I had promised my father, would also become necessary.

We took out a line of credit, and I applied for a Diners' Club credit card. Finally, we had to complete the insurance paperwork to receive reimbursement for the house fire's repairs.

I explained the incident with Colonel Emerson to Florence. She thoroughly approved of what I had done. She told me I had helped make him shine in 1965–1966 and he had not shown any friendship or appreciation by not mentioning my crucial role at Bu Gia Map in the DSC recommendation or the OER. Then he broke a promise made to both of us. She concluded he was consumed by looking after his career. She said if he did not tear up the resignation, we would do fine independently. Being a deeply religious person, she also said we should forgive and forget what had happened. I agreed with the forgiving part but forgetting was more difficult.

Having done all these necessary chores, Florence took me to the airport on 29 September to fly to San Francisco. I caught an aircraft to Vietnam from Travis Air Force Base. That flight left in the afternoon of 30 September, stopping in Hawaii and Okinawa, and I was back in Rach Kien at 1800 hours on 2 October. I reminded Don I had 24 hours left of my promise to return in two weeks and that I would go to bed after a couple of drinks. He reminded me the Vietnam date was 3 October, but he would nevertheless buy the drinks.

Schroeder briefed me on what had happened during my two-week absence, including a new brigade commander's arrival to replace Hunt. This change in command took place around 26 September. His name was Colonel John P. Geraci, but I did not meet him until early November. Schroeder said there had been no enemy action to speak of, but the compound's occasional shelling continued. In addition, his relations with Ira Hunt, the division, and the Vietnamese had worsened, and he was furious at Hunt.

There was a postponement in the move to Dong Tam to late November. This date change meant we would lose many officers and NCOs before the movement and the USARV IG inspection. We would lose all principal staff officers, the communication officer, the S-3 Air, and the supply officer. Captain Beach, who had B/2/39, was departing on 27 October for a job as Major General Ewell's aide and then to the U.S. as he was involved in a branch transfer. Captain Hudson, who commanded D/2/39, was leaving on 1 December. Several key NCOs were also departing. The losses of officers and NCOs in the S-4 section and communications were very detrimental to our move. All personnel losses would adversely affect the future USARV IG inspection, only six weeks away.

Schroeder said there was another reason for the note he had sent me in late September. He was experiencing family problems and that could require one long or two shorter trips to Hawaii. Don reminded me I had commanded over 600 troops at Bu Gia Map without a staff. Therefore, he was utterly comfortable leaving the battalion in my hands. I thought to myself that Don should have ensured that statement was in the 1966 OER. He did not explain the nature of the family problem until we were both at Dong Tam.

Schroeder began his leave on 24 October. He said he expected to be back on or before 7 November. The date of the move to Dong Tam now changed from late November to 12 November. Operationally all was quiet, which allowed me to select officers and NCOs to overlap with those scheduled to leave before Dong Tam's move.

We had an operation on 27 October, and one airmobile company was attached. It was not a significant encounter. The AA report states we killed 33 VC and detained two unarmed Vietnamese, but we captured only eight weapons, which led me to question the enemy casualty figures. Our losses were two soldiers with minor wounds.

There was a full-scale mortar, rocket, and ground attack on Rach Kien at 0150 hours on 28 October which lasted for 30 minutes. The attackers were driven back before penetrating the barbed-wire barrier, but there was much damage to buildings, perimeter towers, and quite a few casualties—22 wounded. Twelve of the injured were from the HHC. One who was hurt died from his injuries. We evacuated all severely wounded soldiers. The 10 with no life-threatening injuries received treatment at the battalion aid station. The enemy left some weapons and equipment behind as they withdrew under cover of darkness, including five 107mm rockets, one RPG B40 rocket launcher, and three 60mm mortars.

Ira Hunt and one ADC visited Rach Kien after daylight on the day of the attack. Hunt started reprimanding me and wanted to know what we planned to do. I answered: *If the prohibition on sending out early warning patrols remains in effect, and we are not allowed to restrict access to the compound and there are no materials to build bunkers for the troops, these attacks will likely continue and cause casualties.* Hunt became angry to the point of losing his self-control. He jabbed my chest repeatedly with his finger and told me, *Major, if you do not shape up or there is another attack on the camp, you can kiss your career goodbye.*

The ADC, standing behind Hunt, rolled his eyes.

As the "guests" were about to leave, I asked if they wanted to visit some wounded soldiers. Hunt gave me a curt no, but the brigadier general said he would like to see some if they were close. Captain Wirth, the surgeon, who stood nearby, said that the battalion aid station was less than 100 meters away and offered to take him there. They were gone for about 15 minutes, and the brigadier general shook my hand before he left. Hunt had already boarded the helicopter.

The following day I received a call from the division G-4 telling me that many supplies and equipment for building bunkers and digging slit trenches around the troop quarters would arrive the next day. He also said that Hunt wanted the bunkers completed in 72 hours, earning him the name "72-hour bunker Hunt" among the troops. Most of the supplies we received were useless without engineer equipment and personnel for building bunkers and digging trenches. Using troop labor, we managed to build eight bunkers, but we needed many more. Although the ground was hard as a rock, we dug shallow slit trenches in part of the camp. The work took place when there were no operations.

On 5 November, I was ordered to Dong Tam to brief General Ewell on the upcoming move. I had still not met the new brigade commander. That all changed on 7 November when our unit was the standby battalion if another force needed assistance. Schroeder had returned but had gone to Dong Tam, probably to receive his DSC, but I am unsure. Schroeder asked me to keep an eye on operations in case our assistance was needed.

I was crisscrossing the area in the battalion C&C helicopter when a distress call came in from the new brigade commander. His helicopter had crashed, probably from enemy action. It had burned and one soldier had a minor wound. I was about 3 or 4 kilometers away and immediately headed for the site. The brigade C&C aircraft was in a small jungle clearance with barely enough open space to land.

I told Colonel Geraci I would bring him and some of his key people out and send a chopper to pick up the rest. He looked at me and said: *No, Major, that is not how we will do it. I will take your chopper and my people and send a helicopter back to pick you up.* I replied he should not count on me to pick him up in the future. Geraci replied: *I do not believe that. Your commander told me you are a square head [Norwegian] and a snake-eater [Special Forces] and that in the 101st, you were always looking to get in harm's way.* I did not answer, but as he began to board my helicopter, I asked what he wanted us to do with his wreck. He told me to destroy it if a heavy-lift helicopter had not picked it up. As he lifted off, he gave us a big grin and waved.

We ended up throwing a bunch of fragmentation and thermite grenades into the damaged helicopter to ensure nothing useful was left for the enemy. We did this when the aircraft picking us up reported it was 15 minutes from our location. We had already made sure the door guns were beyond repair.

When we found Geraci and his troops, their weapons were soaked in water and mud, apparently because they jumped from the helicopter. I planned to ask them to clean their guns to keep them from jamming or exploding when they tried to fire them. However, I decided not to push my luck too far. Despite being sore, I took a liking to the new brigade commander. Schroeder could not stop laughing when I told him the story.[14]

The move to Dong Tam began on 12 November. We used 90 2 ½-ton trucks coming mostly from division resources. The vehicles made two trips. A few broke down on the way, and it was good that a tow/maintenance truck accompanied each serial. The total distance was about 100 kilometers. The sergeant major and I led the last serial of four vehicles from Rach Kien, and by the time we reached Dong Tam, it was already dark. Schroeder said we should have stopped in Tan An rather than risk driving in the dark over unsecured roads. I told him we did not visit Tan An, fearing that Colonel Geraci would confiscate our vehicles and make us walk.

The first bad news I received after arriving in Dong Tam was that I would be leaving the battalion on 6 December to become the division G-5. The G-5 was responsible for civic action programs and coordination with Vietnamese authorities. It was a job I did not want under any circumstances; Schroeder succeeded in getting the assignment canceled.

The battalion's combat elements moved into an operational area near Cai Be, 40 kilometers west of Dong Tam. Schroeder and I agreed to a division of labor that would allow him to run operations in the Cai Be area while I stayed in Dong Tam to prepare for the inspections. The battalion had a large and successful operation on 30 November, and half the rifle strength of the force returned to Dong Tam on 1 December to help us prepare for the USARV IG inspection.

Schroeder and I shared quarters at Dong Tam, as we had at Rach Kien. We had several long conversations where I learned what had necessitated his frequent absences and a relatively extended stay in Hawaii. He had marriage problems, was depressed, and said he planned to leave the Army after completing his Vietnam tour. He told me that Major General Ewell wanted to make him the division G-3, but he had turned it down since he did not want to work on a staff run by Ira Hunt. I argued against his plans to leave the Army, telling him we were all convinced he would see rapid promotions to general officer.

I also asked Schroeder not to be reckless during the remainder of his tour as a battalion commander in a war heading south. Don told me that if anything happened to him, there were things in his footlocker that he asked me to remove and not send back to the U.S. He also gave me the name and address of a person I should notify if something happened to him. I promised I would.

I received daily calls from Colonel Hunt from 4 December onward, threatening me with dire consequences if the division did not come out on top. I also had regular contacts with Colonel Geraci. He asked me how many R&Rs I had taken during my two tours in Vietnam. I told him none. He said that figured and ordered me to take one after the USARV IG inspection. The orders were for a week in Singapore.

Brigadier General Timothy also came to see me on 5 December about a briefly mentioned subject in mid-November. He said he was leaving to take over the MACV Advisory Team to II ARVN Corps in Pleiku at the end of December and requested that I join him and become the deputy G-3 adviser. I immediately accepted, and orders were issued, giving me a reporting date of 24 December.

The story of my tour with the 9th Infantry Division would not be complete without briefly mentioning Operation *Speedy Express*, which began on 11 December 1968 and lasted until 11 May 1969. It took place in Kien Hoa, Vinh Binh, and Go Cong Provinces in the Lower Delta. Colonel Emerson and I had crisscrossed this area when the brigade was in Ap Dong before moving to Tan An on 23 June.

The objectives of *Speedy Express* were to interdict enemy lines of communication and eliminate base areas. Elements of the 2/39 were operating in Dinh Tuong Province southwest of Long An when the operation began. All four 1st Brigade maneuver battalions participated in this operation, along with elements of the 2nd Brigade, about 8,000 troops, and a massive amount of artillery and air support.

Operation *Speedy Express* became one of the most controversial operations in Vietnam. The claim was that the 9th Division had killed 10,899 VC but captured only 748 weapons. The total number of U.S. KIA was 242.[15] I voiced my skepticism about the body count accuracy in the 9th Division earlier in this chapter. However, my complaints pale compared to what happened during *Speedy Express*—45 enemies apparently killed for every U.S. soldier who died and only 748 weapons captured.[16]

I agree with the media's conclusions that the 9th Division was obsessed with body count when I was there, but never as bad as during Operation *Speedy Express*. Conversations with Brigadier General Timothy and Colonel Hackworth confirmed my conclusions about *Speedy Express*.

Hackworth mentioned that Ewell and Hunt had a driving desire to increase the number of VC killed and weapons captured since the ratio was the lowest in Vietnam. As commander of the 4/39 Infantry during the operation, he confirmed that innocent civilians were slaughtered. He also wrote that Major General Julian Ewell earned the nickname "Butcher of the Delta" by members of 4/39. Colonel Geraci left the 9th Division in late February 1969, when his wife died, and, therefore, I do not know his views.

A person who is a reader of modern military history could not have failed to note one historical lesson of modern war—ill-treatment of, or atrocities against, the civilian population are counterproductive in the end. This historical lesson must not have made an impression on Ewell and Hunt, or they chose to ignore it.

When I reported for my assignment as Chief of Negotiations for the U.S. Delegation, FPJMT in 1973, I noted the areas controlled by the communists according to the Paris Peace Accord. It included most of the border areas, a large segment of the Central Highlands, and significant portions of the I Corps. The area where Operation *Speedy Express* took place was mainly VC-controlled. There is no proof that *Speedy Express* caused this, but it fits the historical pattern.

An alleged internal DOD IG report, classified, reportedly concluded that 5,000 to 7,000 of those killed were innocent civilians. It is difficult to understand that Ewell was promoted to lieutenant general and held several positions before retiring and that Ira Hunt retired as a major general.

Our battalion received the highest score on the USARV IG inspection. However, this achievement resulted from at least 30,000–40,000 hours of troop labor, a sad comment on our warped priorities in Vietnam. Except for writing many OERs, my job in the 9th Division was at an end. Schroeder put me in for a Legion of Merit, but Hunt rejected it.[17] Schroeder told Geraci who said he would take the matter up with Ewell.

I planned to visit the battalion after my R&R to pick up my footlocker. Schroeder also told me that the officers and NCOs were planning a party for me at that time. I left Dong Tam for Saigon on 16 December 1968.

CHAPTER 20

Deputy G-3 Adviser, II ARVN Corps

I left Saigon on the morning of 17 December for the two-hour flight to Singapore. I spent most of the morning in Singapore, clearing the airport and attending a briefing. I checked into my hotel at about 1400 hours. I was exhausted, went to bed in my air-conditioned room, and slept for 14 hours.

I spent 18 and 19 December buying two suits, a few shirts, shoes, and gifts for Florence and the kids. I also booked a ferry trip from Singapore to the island of Sumatra in Indonesia for the evening of 20 December, planning to return on 21 December for my flight back to Vietnam on 22 December.

All these plans came to a screeching halt on Saturday morning, 20 December. I received a message asking me to report immediately to the U.S. Embassy and that a car would pick me up in 30 minutes. I met the military attaché at the embassy. I believe he was a U.S. Navy captain, but I cannot be sure since he wore civilian clothes.

He gave me a message that had come in overnight, which stated: *Father dead—mother seriously ill.* One of the attaché's assistants came into the office and told me that arrangements were made for a 39-day emergency leave, departing on a KLM flight early in the morning. Tickets to Norway would be purchased as soon as the orders and naval fund citation were ready. I would also receive maximum advance pay.

I asked the attaché if they had telephone communications to Vietnam, and he said yes, both secure and insecure. I told him I needed to talk to General Timothy and that insecure was fine. He told me Timothy had already called and left a callback number. Timothy came on the telephone almost immediately and expressed his condolences. He had received a copy of the notification. I told him the U.S. Embassy had arranged for me to depart on a 39-day emergency leave in the morning. Timothy said, *Hank, take all the emergency leave you need. If you do not, you may spend the rest of your life regretting that decision. You will have your job whenever you return.* He also told me he was heading to France to spend the holidays with his family.

I headed back to the hotel and an embassy representative delivered the orders and the advance payment that afternoon. An embassy car would pick me up at the hotel about an hour before the plane departed. I also received a call from the military attaché, stating that I should contact the U.S. Embassy in Oslo and arrange return transportation. Those instructions were also in my emergency leave papers. The naval detachment in Singapore was ordered to issue emergency leave orders by their headquarters in the Philippines but failed to do so. Instead of regular leave orders, I received a one-page letter authorizing me to proceed on 39-day emergency leave for Norway. "Upon completion of authorized leave, you are directed to report to the American Embassy, Oslo, Norway, for return transportation to your permanent unit in Vietnam."[1]

I contacted the tailor shop where I had purchased the suits and shirts. Unfortunately, they were not ready, but they promised to send them to the U.S. as soon as they were. I wrote a short note to Lieutenant Colonel Schroeder (enclosing a copy of my leave letter), and he answered on 26 December, sending it to the Norwegian address. The battalion had planned to send flowers, but they would not have reached their destination in time since they did not have my address in Norway until he received my note. Don mentioned he had turned down, for a second time, the offer to serve as the G-3 of the division. He did not know what would happen and sounded a bit depressed. Although he still hoped to see me in Dong Tam, Schroeder offered to send my footlocker to Pleiku. He also told me I was selected to attend the C&GSC in 1969. I knew about that from Florence, who had seen my name in the *Army Times*.

I also called Florence. My family in Norway had already notified her. She suggested we meet in Norway and make the same arrangements for the kids as in September.

A Trouble-Filled Emergency Leave

The KLM flight departed on Sunday 21 December, and I settled into my coach class seat to get some sleep since I had not slept all night. The aircraft had some empty seats, but I figured we would probably get additional passengers at our refueling stop.

We had been in the air for about 20 minutes when one of the Dutch flight attendants came back to where I was seated; she said they had some empty seats in first class and I could have one of those. I gathered my things and moved to first class, where I remained until we landed in Amsterdam. The crew was exceedingly helpful, friendly, and talkative, and I almost wished I were back in coach class, where I could get some sleep. The flight attendants, who knew why I was heading to Norway, were full of questions. I believe they knew virtually everything about my life before we reached our refueling stop. The refueling stop, according to my recollection, was either Beirut or Rome. I realized they were trying to keep my mind away from the reason for my trip.

The stewardesses noted I wore shorts and a short-sleeve shirt. They told me Oslo's temperature on 22 December—the day of my scheduled arrival—was predicted to be minus 20 degrees Celsius (-4 degrees Fahrenheit). They suggested I buy an overcoat in Amsterdam since I had nearly a two-hour wait before boarding the SAS flight to Fornebu Airport near Oslo.

Things did not exactly work out as the flight attendants had predicted and I noticed this when we were over an hour late in departing our refueling stop. By the time we landed in Amsterdam, the SAS flight to Oslo was only 20 minutes from departure, and I had to rush to the SAS gate.

I was also treated well by the SAS crew. They told me I had to disembark at Fornebu and go to the ticket counter to validate my ticket to Bergen. The problem was that we had to disembark on the tarmac some distance from the terminal building and re-embark in the same manner. One of the flight attendants gave me an SAS stewardess cape to put on while I was on the open, windswept tarmac. We were one hour late when we arrived at Flesland Airport in Bergen.

Florence, who had arrived from New York that morning, was there to meet me along with a few members of my family. Florence burst out laughing when she saw me in a stewardess cape and wanted to know who I had disrobed. We returned the cape to SAS.

I borrowed some appropriate clothing from my brother-in-law for the funeral on 23 December in sub-zero temperatures. The church was full of people—relatives and friends.

Since I suspected the U.S. Embassy in Oslo was not open during the holidays, I waited to call until after the funeral to tell them I was in the country on emergency leave from Vietnam. I explained that the U.S. Embassy in Singapore and my orders instructed me to call the military attaché at the embassy in Oslo for transportation assistance when I was ready to return to Vietnam. The embassy said they would be happy to help and told me they would let Chief Lucas know. He was apparently in the naval section.

My mother was not in good shape from her ordeal after my father returned from the hospital. Although she received much help from my sister, she had to hire two nurses to look after my father and give him medicines, including pain shots—one for care during the day and one for night care—and a person to help her cook and clean the home. Despite this, her doctor sent her to convalesce in Voss when she was nearing a physical and emotional breakdown.

The Norwegian government paid a third of the nurses' and housekeeper's cost, but the remainder was twice the amount she received in Norwegian government retirement benefits. We knew this, and Florence had sent her a few hundred-dollar checks in November and December. Since my mother was a Norwegian citizen, the U.S. Social Security payments had temporarily stopped when my father died, as had the veteran benefits. My mother was worried about her ability to continue living in her home with the bills for the mortgage, utilities, insurance, and other essential living expenses.

I called the U.S. Embassy in Oslo on the morning of 26 December, and I was lucky to reach the person in charge of entitlement benefits. I told him we needed the forms to apply for widow benefits from the Social Security Administration (SSA) and the Veterans Administration. He promised to mail them immediately. I asked him how long he thought it would take before the payments started. He answered that I knew the bureaucracy as well as he did, but he guessed it would probably take several months, and this was not something I could easily handle from Vietnam. The forms arrived on 27 December. I filled them out, had my mother sign them, and mailed them back to the embassy on 29 December since the 28th was a Sunday.

In the meantime, Florence and I had an appointment with my mother's doctor, Doctor Sørli. We asked him what he thought about us bringing my mother to the U.S. to live with my wife until I returned from Vietnam. The doctor did not believe that was a good idea until she was eligible for U.S. government medical assistance. He suggested that a better solution was to find someone in the family to live with her in her own home until she was well. He stressed that she should not be alone in her condition.

Florence and I spent Sunday discussing what we should do. We ended up calling both Anna and Arthur since they had unmarried daughters who were 18 and 19, respectively, and asked them if one could stay with my mother until I returned from Vietnam. My siblings answered the same day, and both had reasons why this was not possible—Solveig was to begin a secretarial school, and Gunnlaug was to marry in a few months.

Florence and I continued our discussions most of the night after getting over our initial disappointment. In the end, Florence suggested that we travel back to the U.S., take the kids out of school, and she and the kids move to Norway for four-plus months, by which time I would be back from Vietnam and could pick them up. I told her that would cost us a fortune and cause language difficulties for the kids in school. She reminded me of the promise we had made my father. She also repeated what General Timothy had told me about a week ago. As far as money was concerned, it would not cost her much more to live in Norway for a few months than in the U.S. Furthermore, we could put our Cottonade home up for rent, and we would not have the bills for living there. By breakfast on Monday, we had made our decision and told my mother. She was happy to have someone living with her. It may not have been necessary in retrospect, and both Anna and Arthur told us so, but it gave us peace of mind.

Having decided, we returned to the U.S. on 30 December. We spent the following days preparing to move our furniture into storage and ready the house for listing by a realtor. We took Monica and David out of school on 6 January 1969. Barbara was to be married in Fayetteville in the summer, and we left her our VW.

The family flew to Norway on 9 January. We arranged for the kids to start school in Norway. I called the U.S. Embassy on 16 January and told them I was ready to return to Vietnam and needed travel instructions. I talked to the military attaché. He told me the next weekly embassy flight to Germany left on 20 January and asked if I could make that flight. I told him yes.

The attaché informed me that, for continued travel from Germany, I should use a DOD charter flight that flew between Germany and Vietnam. He explained these flights provided leave transportation for troops who had families in Germany. He also said the day I reported to the embassy for return transportation to Vietnam was when I returned to duty. Accordingly, I sent a letter to Brigadier General Timothy stating I hoped to be in Pleiku before my leave expired on 1 February unless further difficulties arose.

Everything looked well organized and I reported to the U.S. Embassy in Oslo on the morning of 20 January. It was, in fact, the beginning of a nightmarish story. First, with apologies for failing to notify me by telephone, I was told the 20 January flight to Germany was canceled. Chief Lucas also informed me the embassy could not write a transportation request (TR), but I should report directly to the 7420th Support Squadron at Villa Høvdde near Fornebu Airfield on 29 January. They would take care of me.

Rather than spending over a week in an expensive Oslo hotel, I returned to Bergen and reported to Fornebu Airport on 29 January. A Mr. Tanga informed me the embassy could not give me a TR because the letter from Singapore contained only a cost identification code, not a fund citation. I asked what I could do about it. He answered that only the unit to which I belonged in Vietnam could do that. I explained I was between assignments when I went on emergency leave. Mr. Tanga said he could wire the 9th Division for a fund citation, but I should not expect an answer for about 10 days based on his experience. The other option was to take the 2 February embassy flight since Frankfurt's Aerial Port of Embarkation could solve my problem. I called the embassy and told them I had complied fully with Singapore's instructions and was unwilling and unable to pay for my transportation back to Vietnam. I told them I was disappointed they had not informed me about these problems on 16 January, when I still had time to do something about them.

The trip to Germany was in a two-engine propeller-driven aircraft—a C-47. On the way, the identify friend or foe (IFF) on the plane failed, and the pilots had to land at Aalborg, Denmark, to have it fixed since an aircraft could not enter German airspace without it. They expected to solve the problem by morning, and I stayed at the same hotel as the crew.

After checking in, I went to my room to get some sleep. While at Aalborg, I called my wife and asked her to contact the U.S. Embassy and have them send a message to Pleiku explaining my difficulties. She called back and said she had talked to Chief Lucas, who said he would send the message. Thus, it became part of the package General Timothy sent to USARV.

After fixing the IFF problem, we continued our flight to Frankfurt on the morning of 3 February. I proceeded to the Army Liaison at the Aerial Port of Embarkation. A Specialist 5 Davidson looked at my orders and stated he could book me on a direct Pan Am flight to Saigon on the morning of 5 February as there were several empty seats. He asked me to be at the civilian airport at 1000 hours in uniform and further stated that I had to pick up a TR at the Frankfurt Transportation Office. He booked me on the flight and arranged for billets at the transit BOQ.

I went immediately to the transportation office, but the German national who prepared TRs had left for the day, and the NCO on duty asked me to leave my papers and pick them up the following morning.

When I reported back early the following day, the German national told me they could not write out a TR because my emergency leave papers did not have a fund citation, and they could not provide one. I argued with the German national for a while about his interpretation of the rules. Finally, I told him that USAREUR and USARV belonged to the same army, and all that should be required was to make an AUTOVON (Automatic Voice Network) call to the 9th Division or the Advisory Team at Pleiku to get a fund citation. That would only take a few minutes, but he just shook his head.

While at the transportation office, I made several telephone calls to USAREUR headquarters, talking to the personnel office, transportation office, finance office, and even the IG without success. Transportation told me they would be willing to put me on the direct flight to Saigon if I signed a statement saying I would reimburse the U.S. government fully. I believe they quoted me a total price of $876. I asked if they required similar payments from soldiers traveling that route on simple leave. They said no. I told them I would be willing to sign a statement reimbursing the government for the difference in cost of sending me from Frankfurt to Saigon instead of the price from the U.S. to Saigon. Both finance and transportation told me that this was not acceptable.

I again asked them to call my unit in Vietnam, but they refused. They did offer to send a message to the 9th Division for a fund citation. They estimated they would receive an answer before the next direct flight to Saigon left on 13 February and surely before the 20 February flight. I told Transportation to send the message, but I pointed out I was no longer a member of the 9th Division but had become a member of the II Corps Advisory Team on 24 December 1969. I requested they provide a copy of the message to that organization. They ignored my recommendation.

I stated that since my instructions read to report to the embassy in Oslo for return transport, I was unwilling to pay my way back to Vietnam and asked what else I could do. They told me I could try to get back to the U.S. space available. I informed the transportation office that I would go to the airport and try to get space available. If they received an answer to their message from Vietnam before I could get space available, I would take the direct flight.

I had no faith in USAREUR transportation living up to their promises, and I, therefore, decided to concentrate on getting a space-available flight from Wiesbaden. The distance from Frankfurt Airport to the Army airport in the Wiesbaden area was about 35 kilometers. To be close to the aircraft departure point, I checked out of the transit BOQ and checked into a hotel near Wiesbaden Airport. I was going to pay using my credit card but could not find it.[2]

I immediately called the Diners' Club office in Germany to report the card as lost or stolen. There was no answer, so I sent a telegram leaving a callback telephone number. I also called the transportation office since that was the only place I had left any papers, but they could not find the card.

I received a call the following morning from Diners' Club saying that any use of the card after my notification was their responsibility. They also told me a new card would be issued, but not to expect it until two or three weeks had passed.

My problems continued after I arrived in Wiesbaden. There were 18 soldiers or dependents on the space-available waiting list, and most of those were in category 1A while I was assigned the lower category 1B. Only three of the 18 had left by the end of the second day.

I learned from Air Force personnel that a Lockheed C-121 (or C-124) propeller-driven transport was departing Wiesbaden at 0400 hours on 6 February for Dover, Delaware, with a 24-hour crew rest at either Morón Air Force Base in Spain or the Azores. There were seats available, so I decided to get on that plane.

My only alternative to using the Air Force aircraft was to take a commercial flight to New York from Frankfurt. Unfortunately, I could not do that because I only had $300.00 in cash. If I had known what troubles were ahead when I left Bergen, I would have taken a commercial flight from there to New York.

I was boiling mad at the treatment by USAREUR of emergency leave personnel and started keeping detailed notes on what had happened, intending to file a complaint through USARV when I returned. However, I saw no valid reasons why they could not have received a fund citation via a telephone call.

I arrived at Dover Air Force Base on the morning of 8 February and caught a flight to McGuire, where I arrived about 1400 hours on the same day. It looked like my troubles would continue for a while since they would not recognize the Navy Cost Identification Code. I told them I could care less what in hell they did, but I was going to call or travel to the Pentagon to explain the rotten treatment I had received since I left Norway. I asked them to write their names on paper for use in my call to the Pentagon. That energized the bureaucrats who said they would put me on a flight to Vietnam on 9 February. The paperwork was ready at 1700 hours. This flight would depart at 1315 hours on 9 February. Unfortunately, a severe snowstorm hit the New Jersey area during the night of the 8th and the day of the 9th. This prevented any landings or takeoffs from McGuire. I spent two nights in an old BOQ without heat or light. The flight, which finally left at 1600 hours on

10 February, stopped in Anchorage, Alaska, then Japan, and we arrived in Bien Hoa at 0330 on 12 February.

There was a flight leaving for Pleiku around 1300 hours. I used the extra time to arrange to take the embassy flight back to Europe in May, an alternative I had just discovered. I also called Pleiku, talking to the Chief of Staff of the Advisory Team, telling him I would arrive in Pleiku in the afternoon. He told me that the deputy operations position was still open for me and that Timothy, who had become worried, eagerly awaited my return.

II ARVN Corps

I met Timothy for dinner on the day I arrived in Pleiku and I was surprised to find that Lieutenant Colonel Hackworth was there on a visit. I believed Timothy was trying to bring Hackworth to Pleiku to reconstitute the old team from the 1st Brigade, 101st, where Hackworth was the S-3, and I was the Assistant S-3. However, Hackworth was taking over the 4/39 Infantry in the 9th Division. Lieutenant Colonel Franklin Hart, who had been the XO of the 1st Brigade, 9th Division, when I was there, had later taken over the 4/39, and Hackworth took over from him. Hart would become the operations adviser to the II Vietnamese Corps.

I briefed Timothy about the problems I had encountered in returning to Vietnam and told him I intended to write a complaint through channels about the USAREUR transportation office's actions. He agreed and said he would prepare a cover memorandum when I had the document ready. He said the complaint and his cover memorandum might prevent others from receiving the same rotten treatment as I had. I had kept detailed notes, and the memo was prepared and sent to MACV within a week.[3]

It was during this dinner I learned that Lieutenant Colonel Donald Schroeder was dead.[4] He was supposed to turn over command of the battalion on Monday, 17 February, but died five days short of that event. He had tried to capture a VC running towards a wood line, but Don died as he was hit by a volley of automatic enemy fire from the woods.

I also learned Captain David Johnson had left for the U.S. He had stepped on a mine on the night of 28/29 December 1968 and was severely wounded.[5] All officers from 2/502 who had served with me in 2/39 had now either departed or died.

All travels from September 1968 to February 1969 had been very costly, and there were more expenses to come, as I had to travel to Norway to pick up the family and bring them back to the U.S. The maximum advance pay they had given me in Singapore also required repayment in six months. That meant large deductions each month until I had repaid the advance. They had started this withholding in January 1969.

The next four months were also challenging for Florence. She could not speak Norwegian, but it helped that most of my family knew some English. The kids picked up Norwegian quickly and were happy in Norway. David became a good skier, having a fourth-place finish in a competition with Norwegian kids his age. I also learned my sister and brother-in-law were planning to sell the motel. We hoped to receive what was due to us when that happened. Whatever we received, Marion, my first wife, was entitled to more than half.

II ARVN was by far the largest corps area in Vietnam, covering about a third of the country (see map on page 280). It also had the most soldiers assigned.

This area included the Central Highlands, stretching from the northern border of Kontum Province to just north of Saigon in the south. Along the coast, it covered the area from the north boundary of Binh Dinh Province in the north to past Phan Thiet in the south. These were areas well known to me from my first tour in Vietnam. In the west, the corps boundary ran along the Cambodian and Laotian borders. When I arrived in Pleiku, the troop strength of II Corps was about 175,000. There were also numerous U.S. units operating both along the coast and in the Central Highlands.

Melvin Laird (1922–2016), the Secretary of Defense in the Nixon Administration, announced the beginning of the war's "Vietnamization" in March 1969, meaning that ARVN would begin assuming responsibility for more of the fighting. This policy aimed to make it possible to start withdrawing U.S. troops as President Nixon had promised during the 1968 campaign.

Despite this policy, U.S. military strength in the country continued to grow, reaching a new peak at 543,400 on 30 April 1969. The number of U.S. killed in action as of 31 December 1969 stood at 40,024.[6] Almost 20,000 more would die before the withdrawal was complete.

The Paris Peace Talks opened on 25 January 1969 between the U.S., South Vietnam, North Vietnam, and the VC. However, the talks led nowhere for a long time, and the U.S. negotiator, Henry Cabot Lodge (1902–1985) quit in disgust.

Meanwhile, the VC continued their attacks. In an offensive starting on 23 February 1969, they attacked 110 targets throughout the country, followed in August by attacks against 150 targets. The VC suffered heavy losses in both offensives. These attacks confirmed my earlier conclusion that the lull in enemy activity in the Delta in the last few months of 1968 was due to a VC withdrawal to build up their units' strength for future operations.

U.S. troop withdrawals had not begun while I was there, but two brigades (1st and 2nd) from the 9th Division returned to the U.S. as I was reporting to my new duty station in July 1969. Three months later, there was an announcement that 35,000 more troops would come home. Thus, by the end of 1969, 115,000 U.S. troops had withdrawn. The South Vietnamese had also begun the agreed increase in strength of the ARVN by 500,000.

Map 12. MACV map depicting the four ARVN corps plus the Capital Special Zone.

The withdrawal's impacts on U.S. troops were predictable. Morale and discipline took a sharp drop among draftees. No one wanted to be the last to die in a losing war.

The massive anti-war demonstrations in the U.S. also affected morale. However, the worst problems caused by the withdrawal did not appear until after my departure. Drug use had not presented a significant problem before but became widespread during the withdrawal period. An estimated 60,000 U.S. troops used or experimented with drugs. Some medical facilities were busier in treating overdose cases than battle injuries. Fragging incidents[7] in 1970 rose to over 200, and racial friction—reflecting what was going on in the U.S.—became a problem.

Our withdrawal had a more immediate effect on our Vietnamese allies. They would eventually find themselves facing the enemy alone. I visited a Vietnamese division that had not performed well in April. The troops were sullen and the officers were correct but not friendly.

General Timothy wanted Franklin Hart to focus on dealings with MACV and U.S. units in the II Corps area while I devoted most of my time with ARVN units along the borders. Consequently, I spent 17–22 February visiting the units accompanied by a Vietnamese lieutenant colonel from the corps staff. Hart and I tried to arrange our schedule so that one of us would always be at II Corps headquarters.

An officer from the 2/39 arrived in Pleiku on 23 February, bringing mail that had come for me, some OERs that Lieutenant Colonel Schroeder had not completed before he died, and my footlocker. The battalion S-1 had also shown forethought in sending me the Army regulations covering exigent or atypical OERs.

I could only write reports on those who were in the battalion before my reassignment on 24 December. Lieutenant Colonel Robert A. Sullivan, who took over the battalion after Schroeder, would handle the reports on officers assigned after 24 December 1968. The lieutenant from 2/39 had to stay overnight since it took me longer than expected to complete the OERs.

I also learned from First Lieutenant Robert J. Skolnick (2/39) on 28 January that Colonel Geraci had resubmitted my Legion of Merit recommendation, but nothing had yet come back from the division. Later, Skolnick sent a copy of the proposed citation to the Advisory Team since Geraci had traveled to the U.S. after his wife died, and Skolnick did not think he would come back. He never returned to Vietnam. Ira Hunt was again in command of the brigade.

The days at Pleiku were somewhat routine but involved an immense amount of paperwork. Daily briefings were also attended—both internal team briefings and the II Corps intelligence and operational presentations. The average workday began at 0630 after breakfast, and I seldom left my office before 2300 hours. From March until my departure, both Hart and I often worked around the clock.

Then there were visits to the field when anything important happened. For example, I visited the area north of Kontum and Dak To—about 80 kilometers north of Pleiku—on 26 February. The VC had attacked a large village in that area with 7,000 inhabitants. Much of the town burned and about 3,000 civilians became homeless. Reports claimed that 53 Vietnamese died. We did not see anyone when we flew over and the road through the village looked deserted as we landed—no people in sight. The whole situation was somewhat eerie, so we departed the area.

The enemy began shelling Pleiku on 23 February with rockets and mortars. It was part of their nationwide activities mentioned earlier. These attacks became routine as time passed and we learned to live with the situation. The rockets had a more extended range than the mortars, carried a more substantial explosive charge, but had poor accuracy. The mortars were fired from locations closer to Pleiku and were more accurate. The ARVN replied to these attacks with counter-battery fire but were slow in their response. It was also lax in patrolling the mortar belt around the city and base.

I received a welcome packet from C&GSC in early March. My reporting date was 11–12 August. If I wanted an earlier reporting date, I had to apply. They also informed me there would be 1,248 students and post housing was by seniority. My number was 824 and they wrote that an officer with a number higher than 700 should assume they would live in local civilian communities. As it appeared I would report there in late June, I applied for permission.

In early March, I found out a special OER had been prepared by Brigadier General Timothy. There was a rule, which I did not know about, that allowed special OERs for promotion boards before their meeting to come up with the following promotion list. Timothy wanted to make sure it would arrive in Washington before the lieutenant colonel selection board meeting, so he sent the report to MACV by courier and from there to Washington.

Captain Arne Andersen, who served with me in the Airborne Test Division, arrived in Pleiku for a visit on 8 March. The advisery team had to prepare a situational assessment for the U.S. Secretary of Defense on the morning of 9 March. I ended up working all night until 0530 hours. Arne stayed in my room, but we did not have much time to talk because of my work. We had a mortar attack that caused no problems except for leaving many small craters in our compound.

Heavy fighting broke out throughout the II Corps area on 20 March. For us, in Pleiku, it resulted in several days of work around the clock. The enemy did not attack Pleiku itself except by rockets and mortars, but none landed in our compound. That changed on 28 March. A night rocket attack resulted in six U.S. personnel wounded, and three of our vehicles destroyed.

General Timothy called me to his office on 2 April. He asked if I had made any special plans for assignments after C&GSC. I told him I had not made any plans that far in the future but knew the Army had considered giving me further schooling to get an advanced degree, but that was before I volunteered for Vietnam. He asked if I would be interested in coming to Fort Benning to work for him since it appeared he would be assigned there as deputy commander in late 1969. I immediately answered yes, and he said he would write to the DA. He also told me he would be leaving Pleiku on 17 April for a 30-day leave in France to visit his family.

C&GSC also gave me an early reporting date—23 June. On 9 April, I learned I would leave Saigon on 15 May on the embassy flight. I had to report to Saigon two days early for processing and to get visas for India and Pakistan. This early reporting date allowed me to request Army transportation to pick up our furniture from storage on 2 June and send it to Fort Leavenworth for temporary storage. I also arranged to ship my footlocker to Fort Leavenworth. The personnel office in Pleiku said I should depart for Saigon on 11 May.

There was a U.S. award ceremony on 4 May, where I received another Bronze Star. In the afternoon, the lieutenant general commanding II Corps[8] awarded me a Vietnamese Staff Service Medal, 1st Class. One picture was taken in front of the corps situation map. The advisery team's Chief of Staff asked me not to display it for one year since it contained some battle information. The Corps Commander told me they had also planned to award me a Cross of Gallantry with gold star. However, since he had just returned from visiting some corps units, the diploma and paperwork were not ready. Nevertheless, he assured me they would mail the award.

I was surprised on 5 May. My pay was reduced, not only for repayment of the advance but also for travel from Singapore to Norway. These deductions left me with zero pay as I was leaving the country. The embassy in Singapore had told me I should not be charged for the airfare since it would have cost the government more to send me back to the U.S. via the Pacific. I sat down immediately to appeal to the finance center, although I felt sure I would end up losing. The Pleiku team's finance personnel recommended I delay sending the appeal until I could do so through the finance officer at Fort Leavenworth.

My replacement arrived on 3 May and I turned my duties over to him on 9 May. There was a departure party for me on 4 May by the troops and officers in the G-3 section, but the Advisory Team's official one was on 9 May. I received a crossbow and some other gifts that I now had to bring on the plane since my hold baggage had already shipped. The Advisory Team arranged a special flight for me to Saigon on 11 May. I departed Saigon on the U.S. Embassy flight on 15 May and arrived in Europe on 17 May after stops in India and Pakistan. The stop in India was an overnight stop. After that, I had to disembark in Spain, catch a military flight to Frankfurt, and take a commercial flight to Bergen via Oslo.

I spent about two weeks in Norway resting and doing some fishing. I found out the motel had sold, and Anna and Birger were in the process of temporarily moving in with my mother while they looked for a place to live in Os. The motel's sales profits had to be reinvested in another business within a specified time to avoid very steep taxes. My sister and brother-in-law were examining the possibilities of building a small shopping center. Since I received my part in cash, little remained after taxes, but it somewhat eased the financial pressure we were under after our travels in 1968–1969.

My mother was still not receiving her U.S. Social Security and veteran benefits, and I put that problem on top of my list when I arrived at Fort Leavenworth. After returning to the U.S., I began sending Marion's part of what I had received from Birger. We had already repaid her parents what we borrowed while in Berlin. She was understandably extremely disappointed at the tiny return on our over 12-year investment.

I received two letters from Pleiku while in Norway. One was from my assistant in the G-3 advisery group, Captain Joe Beranek, with some photographs. He reported it had been quiet in II Corps after I departed, but this changed as he wrote the letter (21 May). The VC near Ben Het virtually annihilated a mixed force of SF and ARVN. Before I left Pleiku, the Hamburger Hill battle had begun in the western A Shau Valley in Thua Thien Province on 10 May 1969.

Forces from the 101st Airborne Division, supported by an ARVN battalion, captured the summit at a steep price. U.S. troops withdrew from Hamburger Hill on 5 June. This withdrawal caused an uproar in the U.S., resulting in a directive from Washington prohibiting such large-scale battles in the future.

The second letter was from Timothy, apologizing for missing my departure as he had just returned to Vietnam. He wrote that he looked forward to working with me again.

The family and I departed Bergen for New York on 4 June 1969. We stopped in New York to pick up our car and spend three days with Florence's mother and sister. We left for Fayetteville, NC, on 7 June, arriving there on 8 June. We checked on our home, which was occupied by a general and his wife. After closing our accounts in the Fort Bragg banks and confirming our furniture had shipped to our new duty station, Florence, the kids, Sheila, and I headed for Kansas.

CHAPTER 21

Schooling and Battalion Command

We arrived in Kansas City late on 20 May, a Friday. The Fort Leavenworth offices had closed for the weekend, so we checked into a motel with the kids and the dog.

I reported to the personnel office at Fort Leavenworth around 1300 hours on 23 June. They sent me to a processing center they had established for incoming students in a nearby building. My assignment was to help process incoming students at that center after the assignment of quarters and delivery of our furniture.

The processing center had a couple of manila envelopes they had opened. They told me that one of them had arrived in February with a note "hold for Major Lunde" while the other had come in early June. They had opened both in case they contained something of an urgent nature.

The one dated in February was from Colonel Geraci and had some papers apparently about an award and a handwritten note saying he might have an assignment to offer me and would call at the end of the year. I did not take the time to look at the papers since I had to report to the housing office before closing. I have no idea why Geraci sent the documents to Fort Leavenworth when I was in Pleiku and had frequent contacts with the 2/39th in that period.

The second envelope was from the Advisory Team at Pleiku, sent in early June. It contained the promised diploma from the commanding general of II Corps for the Vietnamese Cross of Gallantry, but no medal, probably because it was a second award. The envelope also had two of the exigent OERs I had prepared in February asking for additional information. The processing center asked if I wanted a ceremony for the awards. I told them no but asked them to place anything in my personnel file that belonged there.

I reported to the housing office before it closed. I had to fill out another bunch of papers for our assigned quarters on N. 38th Street in Kansas City, Kansas. Our home for the next 10 months was a lovely two-story townhouse in a row of townhouses. We could not move in because our furniture stored in Fayetteville had not arrived, even though Fort Bragg had let us know it was on its way to Leavenworth. The housing officials said I should contact the transportation office.

Transportation confirmed the household goods were on their way, but there was much damage because the storage facility had flooded. They told me the Army would reimburse us for that damage after deductions for age. They would determine after the furniture arrived what was repairable. They expected the shipment to arrive on Monday, 30 June.

The damage to our household goods was extensive. The transportation officials declared most of the furniture irreparable and hauled those items away. Civilian contract personnel repaired a few worthwhile things. It was the worst damage we had sustained in a move and we had to buy a lot of new furniture in Kansas City. The relatively tiny sum we received after deduction for age did not help us much. There were reportedly Army regulations for disastrous losses to household goods while in Army hands, but we did not know about them, and no one volunteered that information. We had to live in the motel for two additional weeks while the mess was resolved.

I devoted much of my time while waiting to report for work by addressing my mother's problems with her Social Security and veteran benefits. The U.S. Embassy in Oslo had sent her a stack of papers that needed completion. It was now about eight months since my father died, and my mother had not received any of her entitlement, not even a burial allowance, and she was getting the run-around wherever she turned.

Florence and I regularly sent her checks during this period, although she had an account to draw on. Knowing how government bureaucracy worked, I complained to the very top in the SSA and the VA. They promised to investigate the matter and return my call within a week. Unfortunately, I received no callback and wrote a letter to one of the two U.S. Senators from Kansas, James B. Pearson (1920–2009), asking for his help and giving the names of those in the government I had already talked to without results. This action broke the logjam and my mother began receiving her benefits in late August, and all by late October.

The students began arriving in large numbers in late July and the processing center requested my help on 21 July. The *Apollo 11* Moon landing took place on 20 July, and President Nixon declared 21 July a government holiday, so I began my work on 22 July.

The course began on 15 August. The round-trip drive from our residence to Fort Leavenworth was 110 kilometers. This long commute in winter when the roads were frozen and covered with snow took a long time. So, after school began, I arranged with other students who lived in the same area to start a carpool.

The college and post, overlooking the wide Missouri River, had an illustrious history going back to the early 1800s when it was a gateway to the west. The college came into existence in 1881 as an Infantry and Cavalry School.

C&GSC was a 10-month mid-level officer's course for lieutenant colonels and majors, preparing them for battalion command or staff assignments at the division and corps level. It was the last school where students received grades for their performance and a class standing at the end of the course. There were also some officers from the other services, interagency personnel, and foreign nationals.[1]

C&GSC involved strenuous competitive work. The tests and briefings required much preparation and there were times when I worked all night, mainly towards the end of the course in 1970.

The commandant while I was there was Major General John Hancock Hay (1917–1995), who was also the post commander and had served in World War II. In Vietnam, he commanded the 1st Infantry Division. Then, as a lieutenant general, he commanded the 18th Airborne Corps until his retirement in 1973. The deputy commandant was Brigadier General Frank Butner Clay. Frank had a distinguished military heritage. He was the son of General Lucius D. Clay Sr., who I mentioned when I wrote about my tour in Berlin. Frank B. Clay retired as a major general.

I was notified at the end of August that I was on the promotion list to lieutenant colonel. I was below the zone (earlier than usual), which meant I could gain more seniority over my contemporaries. Usually, a list is exhausted within a year. However, this one took exceedingly long because of the reduction in the size of the Army. It took more than 3 ½ years before the list was exhausted.

My mother came for a visit in November. We had sent her money for the tickets, although her worries about managing to keep her home had subsided after receiving her pensions. Ole and I met her at the airport in New York. I drove her to Iowa in late November to meet some relatives. Ole arrived from New York shortly before Christmas and left a few days after the New Year, taking our mother with him to return to Norway.

The Army wanted me to attend a university to get an advanced degree in an interdisciplinary field. We received a wide choice of schools but quickly narrowed the list to Stanford University in California and Syracuse University (SU) in New York. They were both prestigious institutions, but I knew Florence preferred upstate New York since it would bring her close to her family for the first time.

I received a call from Colonel Geraci in late April 1970, who told me he had taken command of the Ranger School at Fort Benning. He wanted me to take command of the Ranger Mountain Camp in Dahlonega. I told him I felt honored by his offer, and if I had received his call two months earlier, I would have gladly accepted. However, I explained the Army now said it was too late to change my assignment.

SU asked that I report early to attend school during the summer semester after receiving my UC transcript, where I was the honor graduate in the history department. My SU assignment was for two years to get my master's degree. Still, I believe SU was planning for me to obtain a PhD in the time allotted.

C&GSC allowed me to end my attendance on Monday 11 May, to meet SU's request. The packers arrived to pack our belongings on 12 May. We had our quarters inspected on 14 May and left C&GSC on 15 May. We drove to Fayetteville in two days. The drive from Fayetteville to Syracuse took four days because I became sick on the way. We arrived at our destination on 23 May.

The immediate problem facing us was finding a place to live. We had written to several realtors before we left Fort Leavenworth. Syracuse and Buffalo are the largest cities in upstate New York, with populations of 143,000 and 257,000 respectively. I do not think these numbers changed much since I was there in 1970–1971 because of migrations to the Sunbelt States.

We were lucky to find a house within four days. It was a four-bedroom rancher in Baldwinsville's village on the Seneca River, 40 kilometers from the university. The Seneca River empties into Lake Ontario and the place was ideal for boating. We received our furniture at the end of May. I first met with my academic advisers from the economics, political science, and history departments on Friday 5 June. They recommended I begin my studies on 29 June and they would prepare a list of subjects they suggested I take.

Our economic situation was still shaky, so Florence decided to take a job at a store 10 kilometers from our home. It became necessary to buy a used car—a red 1965 VW—since there was no bus service. She began working on 1 July on an eight-hour shift, which started at 1pm and ended at 9pm.

My brother Ole visited us at the end of June and the beginning of July. I have never had much luck with boats, but since we both loved the water, we ended up buying a very used 35-foot cabin cruiser. The vessel had two gasoline engines and was not well suited for fishing, but Ole and his friend Bernard Sivertsen wanted to try. The plans were that I would use the boat while living near Syracuse. At the end of that period, Ole and Bernard would bring the vessel through the Erie Canal's lock system to the Hudson River and from there to eastern Long Island.

My classes at SU began on 29 June. The plans they had laid out for me were ambitious, and I could tell from just looking at the subjects that the work would be hard to cope with. I was particularly concerned about courses in statistics and advanced statistics. I informed them I had no prior knowledge of those subjects. They told me I needed those courses—statistical analysis was in fashion. A woman in the economics department gave the statistics classes, and she graciously offered to help me after class in her home if I needed it. I did need it and took advantage of her offer several times.

Most instructions occurred at the Maxwell School. Maxwell is a leading post-graduate school and provides a robust master's (MA) degree program, and a similar PhD program for candidates with a strong cross-disciplinary interest.

I received a detailed program for the summer months. The plans for the following semesters were in outline only. I was also encouraged to use the summer months in 1971. I voiced my doubts about my ability to cope with the ambitious workload laid out for me since I had been away from strictly academic studies for 13 years. My fellow graduate students were much younger and mostly fresh from undergraduate studies.

They answered that they had discussed this after they received my transcript from UC and records from the DA. These documents showed I was an honor graduate at UC and the Infantry Career Course and placed in the top 10 percent recently at the C&GSC.[2] These and my two years of combat in Vietnam were firm indications I was a highly motivated individual. Further, they noted that while I had come to SU to get an MA degree, my assignment was for two years, more than the time required for an MA based on my records. The advisers suggested I use the extra time to satisfy major requirements for a PhD in a cross-disciplinary field. They also noted I had a good command of several languages, which would serve me well. Finally, they pointed out my experience, and the fact that I would not teach undergraduates as most other graduate students did would add to my available time.

I was unsure about what to do. I did not want to work extremely hard to find out the DA would not support my desire to obtain a PhD. Although I was not familiar with SU and DA's contractual agreement, it did not escape my attention that SU probably had a financial interest in my pursuit of a PhD.

Florence encouraged me to try, saying she and the kids would do some of the chores I had done to give me more time to cope with increasing schoolwork. She also recommended I call DA to find out what their thoughts were.

I followed my wife's advice and called the OPO at DA. The person I talked to did not deal with postgraduate studies but would leave detailed notes for that person, who would call me back if the Army had any problems. He did confirm I would remain at Syracuse until late spring 1972. Unfortunately, I never received a return call from OPO, giving me a false sense of optimism.

We had worried when we came to SU about student riots and demonstrations following the shootings at Kent State University while we were at C&GSC. I had no bad experiences with the students, but a few of the professors were anti-military. As best I could, I avoided classes given by those professors, and I avoided all demonstrations.

There was much drug use in the local school system in Baldwinsville. Both Florence and I worried about David and Monica. We required them to be home before dark unless we went with them. The other school kids were not under similar restrictions, which caused some resentment against them in school. It was mainly against Monica and us as parents. Vandals painted large vulgar writings on our white home in black lettering—primarily anti-military words. We had to repaint the whole side of the house.

The fall semester began on 16 September 1970 and the workload suddenly doubled. I had my first introduction to computers; they were for use in the late afternoon or evening, by appointment. They were large floor-to-ceiling IBM mainframe punch-card machines and students paid for their use. I used them primarily for my economic courses.

Florence required a stomach operation, which took place on 12 November. My mother arrived from Norway before Florence's hospital stay, and she remained with us until January 1971. This helped while Florence was hospitalized and recovering.

We lived in the so-called Snow Belt, most of the snow that fell was lake-effect snow, and there was much throughout the winter. The weather turned cold, with several nights of frost in early October, and the first snowfall was on 14 October. We had freezing temperatures every night from early October and severe snowfall began at the end of the month. We had a 700-foot driveway and keeping it relatively free of snow involved much work. We finally decided to keep the VW parked at the corner of the county road near the end of our driveway. We left the Oldsmobile in the garage and I used the VW to get to the university after Florence became ill and had to give up her job for the winter.

I did well in school during the fall semester, despite the weather. Besides reading and writing, the History Department gave me many foreign books (primarily German) to read and prepare summary reports on. These reports could be up to 25 typewritten pages, and then I had to discuss them with the professor with expertise in the area. I also wrote five long articles (about 100 manuscript pages each), one in 1970 and four in 1971. These dealt with political/military and economic subjects and they counted considerably in the evaluation by the various department.

My brother Ole and his friend Bernard Sivertsen arrived on 21 May 1971 to take our boat to New York. They did not have a car to get to the marina. Florence was back at her job and needed the VW. Our neighbor John Hourihan offered them the use of his dock within walking distance from our home. We then moved the boat from the marina to John's dock. Bernard put in about a week's work installing a new toilet to meet revised Coast Guard requirements and serviced the engines.

At around 2230 hours on 24 June, the night before its scheduled departure for New York, we received a call from John Hourihan reporting that our boat was sinking after a large barge rammed it, destroying his dock. This accident began a lengthy court case that did not end until 1976 when I left Washington.

David and Monica left in early July for their annual visit to their biological father. They never returned, although their stay with their biological father was short-lived. They discovered the conditions they had hoped for did not exist. I guess they rebelled against the restriction Florence and I had placed on their activities.

It was a severe blow to Florence. She gave up her job permanently. We made a short visit to Norway in late July to get her away from the house. My mother came back with us to stay with Florence for the rest of my university tour.

The studies at SU proceeded well. I completed all five extensive articles and Professor Bishop, who had become my primary adviser, picked out two of the extended studies he felt were suitable for a PhD thesis.

In the summer of 1971, I received a letter from Brigadier General Timothy telling me the job he had hoped for had not materialized and that he planned to retire in 1972. I believe his assignment to the 9th Division had hurt his chances of further advancement.

In late June 1971—about one year after assignment to Syracuse—I received reassignment orders. Since this came as a great surprise, I called OPO at once.

I had a frank conversation with the assignment officer, whose name I believe was Lieutenant Colonel Lester E. Bennett, an infantry officer in the Assignment Section of the Infantry Branch at OPO, who later sent me a couple of memos.

I asked what the heck was going on. I told Bennett that in discussion with another assignment officer on 8 June 1970, I learned I would be at Syracuse until the spring of 1972. At that time, I had asked if the Army had any objections to me getting a PhD if I could within the allotted time. I told Lieutenant Colonel Bennett the officer who took the call said he saw no problems in me pursuing a PhD and that he would give the postgraduate assignment officer notes of the call and notify me if there were any problems. I had not received any calls from OPO and had made plans accordingly. I had worked extremely hard for a year based on erroneous information. I explained that my PhD classwork was nearly over. All that remained was to appear before a committee for my thesis's oral defense in early 1972.

I believe Bennett was a bit stunned by my irritation. Assignment officers are usually accorded great deference and respect because of their influence on an officer's career. I should have waited to calm down before making the call.

Bennett told me that my assignment, based on Army priority, was to the U.S. Army Combat Development Command, Institute of Land Combat in Alexandria, Virginia. The orders, dated 28 June 1971, arrived two days after my talk to Bennett, with a reporting date of 20 January 1972. A memo from Bennett came the same day.

After further consideration, I concluded the assignment offered was good for an infantry officer's career and decided to accept it. Two days later, after I had completely calmed down, I received a call from a colonel at OPO explaining my assignment was due to Army priorities and that I might be given time in the future to attend an oral defense of my extra work. I apologized for being abrupt with Bennett, but my sudden reassignment, without warning, had upset me. I told him I would gladly accept the assignment to the Institute of Land Combat.

I told Professor Bishop the Army was terminating my stay at Syracuse on short notice. He said the Army decision was shameful. He intended to write to the Army Personnel Branch's postgraduate section, stating it was not beneficial to the Army or me to terminate my studies in this manner. However, I doubt he wrote or sent such a letter. The report from SU, signed by William D. Coplin, Director of the International Relations Program, only noted I was one of the best students they ever had from the Armed Forces.

At the end of August, I received a welcome letter from Major Benjamin F. Ellis Jr. at the Directorate of Environments Concepts and Force Design Group at the U.S. Army Combat Developments Command. He was my sponsor. He wrote that no government quarters were available and that the average home cost in a good neighborhood would run to about $350,000. This information was worrisome to Florence and me since we were still struggling financially.

A few days before receiving the welcome letter, I received a memo from Bennett dated 20 August 1971. That memo stated my assignment was changed to accommodate Brigadier General Emerson's request, redirecting me to the JFK Center, Fort Bragg, North Carolina. He further wrote that my position was according to a valid Army Educational Requirements Board position to utilize my master's degree training. I had not talked to Emerson for a couple of years, and he had never asked for me in the past unless we had previously discussed the assignment, but he kept an eye on my career. Furthermore, he expressed surprise when we finally met at Fort Bragg in 1972. The admin office at the Center could find no record of a request by Emerson. Therefore, I concluded Emerson had not asked for me and that it was the assignment officer's way to get even for my earlier call.

The 20 August memo also stated my orders would be amended within a few days. However, I did not hear anything from DA until 21 September, when I received orders canceling my earlier posting to the Combat Development Command. The following day I received orders from the First U.S. Army at Fort Meade, Maryland, assigning me to U.S. Army Institute for Military Assistance (USAIMA)—a spruced-up Military Assistance Training Adviser that I was selected to attend in 1965. I received 15 days' leave, with a reporting date of 20 January 1972.

Florence and I had to cancel our house lease early, losing our deposit in the process, and arrange for the shipment of the household goods to Fort Bragg. My mother was still with us, and we drove two cars to Fort Bragg in mid-December 1971, stopping first at Florence's relatives in New York. Florence and my mother drove the Oldsmobile and I drove the VW, which was on its last legs.

We arrived in Fayetteville shortly before Christmas and ended up spending the holidays at a motel. After the Fort Bragg housing office informed us no government quarters were available, we began looking for a place to live. We also spent the period between Christmas and New Year buying more furniture because the Army payment of what we lost in 1969, after adjustment for age, forced us to buy mostly cheap furniture in Kansas City. My mother helped pick out most of what we needed in Fayetteville.

3rd Battalion, 5th Special Forces Group

I reported to USAIMA on Monday, 10 January. I asked what they planned for me after I had completed the course. They told me they did not know.

I then called OPO on 11 January and asked them the same question. They explained that, due to the new DA rotation policy that required troops to stay at one post for four years, my assignment would probably be Deputy Commander of the 4th Psychological Operations Group (Airborne). While there was nothing I could do, this information had a direct impact on our housing needs. I started the USAIMA course on 17 January.

We had rented a house in the Summerhill development just off post because the one we owned in Cottonade was still under lease. We did not particularly like the Summerhill house, but we learned a more substantial and newer home next door would soon be for sale as the woman who lived there was going to Germany to join her husband. We bought the new house on 21 January and moved our things from the rental home next door. We had to get help to move the furniture and postponed that chore until the end of February.

A welcoming ceremony for newly assigned personnel in the John F. Kennedy Special Warfare Center took place in an auditorium on Monday 24 January 1972. About 80–100 officers and senior NCOs were present, and I found myself a seat in the rear of the hall. The Center commanding general was Brigadier General Henry Emerson. This encounter was my first meeting with Emerson since 1969, when I returned from Vietnam. Emerson was then commander of the 18th Airborne Corps Support Command.

Emerson was unaware I was now at Fort Bragg, which reinforced my suspicion he had not asked for me. He spotted me during the first five minutes of his briefing. He stopped in the middle of his speech and asked, *Is that you, Hank? Please stand up so I can introduce the best combat commander I have ever known.* After that awkward event, Emerson asked me what I was doing at the Center. I told him I was attending a USAIMA course. He told me to go to his office and wait for him.

Emerson showed up after 20 minutes. He apologized for the delay as he had visited the personnel office to check on my promotion date. It should take place in early February. He also told me a battalion commander in the 5th Special Forces Group was due to leave at the end of January. Then he finally came around to asking me if I was willing to take that command. I told him yes.[3] He said his office would change my orders and stop my attendance at the USAIMA course.

Emerson called Colonel Jay B. Durst (1928–2002), commander of the 5th Group, who arrived, and Emerson introduced us. Emerson told Durst that he had found him a new battalion commander and went into a long pitch about my background. Emerson and Durst agreed I would assume command of the 3rd Battalion, 5th Special Forces Group, on Monday 31 January. That was 14 days before my projected promotion to lieutenant colonel.

After a simple flag exchange on the morning of 31 January, there was a pass-in review parade by the battalion in the afternoon. Briefings by my new staff and company commanders occupied the next few days. I also found out what two years of school had done to my physical fitness when I tried to make a 5-mile morning run with Captain Dolighan.

Florence and I hosted a party on 25 February. It doubled as an introductory event and a promotion party. The event was held at the Fort Bragg main officers' club. We had sent out 104 invitations and I recall that about 150 attended.

We moved the furniture into our home on 26–27 February. We planned to use movers arranged for by our son-in-law David Coffman but my XO at the time, Captain Dolighan,[4] had already organized the staff officers to help us over the two-day weekend. Florence and I provided lunch and a few cases of beer. By Sunday evening, 27 February, we were living in our new home.

While the country was still involved in a war in Southeast Asia, the assignment as commander of 3/5 Special Forces was routine peacetime duty. However, there were issues directly or indirectly related to the Vietnam War and its effects.

The Organization, Mission, and Doctrine

There were significant differences between an infantry battalion and an SF battalion. An infantry battalion was at least twice as large in terms of soldiers assigned, and the vast majority of these were enlisted troops. The soldiers in SF battalions were all NCOs and officers, older and with more experience. Their level of proficiency was much higher than soldiers in infantry battalions.

An SF group was usually part of a Unified Command. When I served in the 5th Group, its orientation was the Middle East, Persian Gulf, and Central Asia. The 5th was one of two groups headquartered at Fort Bragg in 1972.[5] The other group was the 7th Special Forces Group, which had South America and Central America as its orientation area.[6]

An SF battalion was typically part of a Theater of Operations or one of its significant portions. A battalion could deploy all its companies and their subordinate operational detachments (ODs). However, in lengthy operations the battalion could elect to deploy one or two of its companies into an area on a rotating basis. At the same time, the rest of the unit remained at its home station.

The SF were undergoing reorganization in this period. The old C and B teams were now named battalions and companies, respectively. The A teams were now called ODs, but their structure and mission did not change. I arrived at Fort Bragg as these changes were going into effect. Since the changes were mostly in terminology, they had little impact.

The 1970s was a decade of a significant decline in the SF due to the U.S. Army's reorientation from Southeast Asia to Europe. A study written by Lieutenant Colonel Corson L. Hilton at the USAWC in 1991 spells out the decline in SF and the resurgence in the 1980s. Since I left Fort Bragg, the changes that have taken place are too extensive to explain in this work. I refer those who desire more information to the Hilton book or even more recent studies.[7]

The total strength of my battalion, in all grades, was 303 on the day I assumed command. The battalion consisted of a headquarters element of about 35 officers and NCOs plus three companies. Each company comprised a headquarters element and four ODs of 12 men each.

The companies called for an officer with the rank of major as commander. The company commander was assisted by an operations officer with the rank of captain or lieutenant. If the officer strength allowed, a lieutenant handled supplies. There were also several NCOs in the headquarters element.

The ODs consisted of 12 men with a captain in command and a lieutenant as XO. Later, warrant officers became XOs instead of lieutenants, but this happened after my time at Fort Bragg. Each company had four ODs, but this number was very flexible, depending on the mission and the area they operated in. Each company could have six or seven ODs instead of four that we had at Fort Bragg.

I am not sure of the number of officers assigned to the battalion during my tenure as commander since I did not keep any rosters from that assignment. However, I was the rater, endorser, or reviewer for all officers assigned. Since I kept copies of all reports until recently, it shows that there were 61 officers assigned. I believe the TO&E called for 57 officers, so we must have had a few extra not filling an authorized position.

Doctrine and missions were hot subjects during my whole tour of duty. I did not endear myself to the old SF officers and NCOs by arguing for a shift in mission from a heavy emphasis on unconventional warfare (UW) to direct action. I made this recommendation because the old Lodge Act people, prevalent in the 10th Special Forces Group in the 1950s and 1960s, had retired or were getting ready to do so. Few new members were proficient in languages. UW requires a high degree of language proficiency to give SF some freedom of movement and survivability behind enemy lines. Direct action was part of the SF mission but had a relatively low priority, while a need for a robust capability in this area had risen. I alerted my superiors that direct action could pass to the Ranger battalions if we did not prioritize it.

My cautionary predictions did not come true while I was in the SF. Instead, they began to become a reality in the 1974–1984 period. First, the 75th Ranger Regiment, with two battalions, was activated, followed later by a third battalion. These became the primary direct-action force in the U.S. Army.

Reduction in Force

I begin this segment with a paraphrased quote from Rudyard Kipling: "It's Tommy this, and Tommy that, and Chuck him out, the brute! But it is 'Savior of his country' when the guns begin to shoot."

The decline in the Army's size from 1,570,000 at the end of 1968 to 810,000 in 1972 had a devastating impact on officers and created havoc in the NCO ranks. This reduction in force (RIF) was the worst drawdown of forces since the demobilization following World War II, and this time the reduction hit the Army much harder than the other services. Most of the SF officers were reserve officers. They suffered the most in a RIF situation like we experienced while I was at Fort Bragg.

RA officers had more protection under the law, and this gave them a significant advantage.

Based on the number of appeals I wrote or processed, I guess the careers of almost half of the officers in the battalion were in jeopardy. As soon as I arrived, I encouraged my officers to submit requests seeking appointments in the RA, verbally and in writing. Many did not heed the warning or decided a release from service was inevitable, and they made their plans accordingly. Many of those released transferred to reserve units. Those who appealed received a reprieve, but in most cases, their appeals resulted in rejection. A small number of officers who applied for an appointment in the RA were successful, like my battalion XO, but it took a long time of living on the brink. While I do not know how many we lost of those who wanted to remain in the Army, I feel comfortable guessing 15–20 percent.

New Efficiency Reports

Closely related to the RIF were the new OERs introduced by General Abrams, the Army Chief of Staff, in a message referred to as the "pull up your socks" message. He had concluded that OERs had become inflated during the Vietnam War and wanted this rectified. The reports used in Vietnam were a combination of a written statement and placing the officer in relation to others of the same grade in the unit. For example, if 15 captains were serving the same rater, he had to identify where the rated officer was placed among the 15. I liked that part of the system because it kept the evaluator honest, and the rated officer knew how his rating compared to the other 14. Unfortunately, this positive aspect of the old report was replaced by a much more subjective evaluation; in short, many did not see it as an improvement.

Since many of my officers faced a possible release from the Army, I gave all those I felt should be retained high marks. This OER would be the last report these officers received before the Army decided to keep them or kick them out.

The new report also affected me directly. The first report as a battalion commander was by Colonel Jay B. Durst, a West Pointer from Pennsylvania. His evaluation covered the period 24 January to 16 June 1972. He gave me maximum as all my raters had over the past decade or more and continued during my next assignment to Vietnam, the Pentagon, and Supreme Headquarters Allied Powers Europe (SHAPE). Emerson did likewise, and both recommended promotion to general officer.

The last OER was by Colonel Earl L. Keesling (1925–2001), a West Pointer from Indiana, who gave me an average score and did not recommend early promotion or special monitoring for general officers' advancement. I did not have an endorser since Brigadier General Michael D. Healy (1926–2018), the new center commander, had not been there long enough to rate me. That meant Keesling's report carried double weight.

I confronted Colonel Keesling about the report; he said it was not his intention to hurt my career and he would try to get the report back from the Center. He should have discussed the OER with me before forwarding it, as many raters did. Within two days, he called, telling me he could not recall the report. Instead, he offered to write a letter to the DA and I accepted because the OER was high enough where an appeal was inappropriate. Despite his promise, he never sent the letter.

I disagreed with Keesling's headquarters on several issues, such as mandating that officers show up at church in uniform on Sundays (passed to the battalions verbally by his XO since it was an illegal order). I told my officers that no one can order you to go to church, but the order to wear a uniform if you go is legal. We also disagreed on readiness reporting, those parts which were not subjective, such as the number of troops on TDY and those who did not participate in military occupational specialty (MOS) training. We had a relatively large number of these since the Gabriel Demonstration Team was part of my battalion. Notwithstanding the differences mentioned above, Keesling never expressed any dissatisfaction with me or the battalion. Keesling had no background in SF, never visited my battalion in garrison, training, or exercises. On the other hand, Colonel Durst was a frequent visitor to our training, and Brigadier General Emerson also visited us several times.

After an avalanche of commendations from communities where we trained, Colonel Keesling wrote a letter complimenting me and the battalion on 20 November 1972. I will quote three sentences from the operative paragraph of the letter that is in my possession:

> The outstanding performance of your command comes as no surprise. These accolades only add to the already esteemed reputation of the 3rd Battalion. Through your able leadership, the 3rd Battalion has become a bulwark of Special Forces professionalism and expertise.

Emerson, now commanding the 2nd Infantry Division in Korea, found out about the report from my XO, Major Passailaigue, and Florence after I left. My battalion staff had prepared extensive information on the performance of the battalion compared to the other two. Emerson answered Major Passailaigue and wrote to Florence and me at my new assignment in Vietnam. In this letter, Emerson informed me a report had hurt Keesling while a battalion commander in Vietnam, and he may have become bitter.

Since Emerson had been my endorser for 10 of the 12 months covered by the report, he prepared a letter to DA expressing his surprise and dismay at the OER submitted by Keesling. He stated I had one of the two best battalions of the 10 under his command and was the best of the six SF battalion commanders. He recommended early promotion and expressed his conviction that I should become a general officer.

Training and Exercises

Training was, for me, the number one priority, and exercises were ways to test our proficiency. I had a sign behind my desk that read More Sweat on the Training Field Equals Less Blood on the Battlefield. I believed in that statement.

We conducted most MOS training (such as demolition, medical, hand-to-hand, etc.) on the sprawling Fort Bragg reservation. In preparation for the new OERs, I had the staff come up with statistics on exercises. Each company conducted at least three full-scale training exercises while I was there, each lasting two or three weeks. Comparing these to the training and exercises by the other two battalions showed the 3rd Battalion spent 12 percent more time in the field than the other two units combined.[8] We also had two countrywide communications exercises, run from Dugway, Utah, and Fort Carson, Colorado.

Our month-long exercise by a reinforced company in Iran was also a great test of our communication capabilities. Our equipment and competency in this area made it virtually impossible for an opponent to intercept and read our messages.

We also did our winter training as a battalion near Fort Missoula, Montana. We operated at a place called the Snow Bowl and in the surrounding mountains. The reason for picking Missoula was that it had a lot of snow. Furthermore, it was easier to coordinate because Emerson owned a ranch north of Helena and was Montana Adjutant General John J. Womack's friend. A reconnaissance platoon from the Marines at Camp Lejeune, North Carolina, received permission to come along. As with most of our troops, they had never operated in deep snow.

After arriving in Missoula and looking at the terrain I had up to then only seen in summer, I regretted not choosing a less challenging area. I am sure the rough area kept the soldiers from learning much about winter training or survival.

We selected many of the training and exercise sites because of our limited training budget. To reduce expenses, we worked closely with the U.S. Air Force. They needed training time in moving troops, equipment, and parachute operations. Both the Air Force and we benefitted from these arrangements. For us, it kept the budget from exhaustion before the end of the fiscal year. Overseas exercise in our orientation area, like the one in Iran in 1972, came from a separate budget.

The exercise in Iran required a coordination visit in June 1972, with a brief stop at the SF in Germany. The group included Lieutenant Colonel Charles Dixon from 2/5 SF. The personnel from 3/5 SF comprised, besides me, Captain Michael J. Matteson, A/3/5 SF, Captain John P. Grace, S-4 3/5, Captain Jack D. Crabtree, S-3 3/5, Captain Milton Jones, Commo Officer 3/5, and Sergeant Major Howland, 3/5.

The reinforced company spent about a month in Iran training and exercising with the Iranian Airborne and SF. My counterpart was Colonel Ali-Akbar Yazdejerdi, commander of the 1st Iranian Special Forces Brigade. We also worked closely with Colonel Nasser Boroumand, Lieutenant Colonels Mohassen Jami and Fereydoun Kian, and Major Parviz Jahanbani. I was there for only two weeks, from 14 August to 4 September. We all received the Imperial Iranian Airborne Wings.

I left Iran to participate in another company exercise in the U.S. and left my XO, Major Edward Passailaigue (1932–2014), in charge during the remainder of the training. After returning to the U.S., I needed to report on my military/political impressions of Mohammed Reza Shah's reign.

I wrote a three-page report for the Center intelligence officer with a copy going to the 5th Group S-2. I described the opulence in Tehran, especially in the affluent northern part of the city. Major Edward Passailaigue and I visited the Shah's impressive office at the officers' club. We also attended dinner with our counterparts in their lavish homes in the northern suburb. I contrasted this with what I saw beginning within less than 70 kilometers from the capital. I wrote that this area did not appear to have changed much since Alexander the Great marched through it. Instead, the people looked destitute and suspicious. In my conclusion, I predicted this schism between the luxury of the ruling classes in the large cities and the total deprivation in the countryside resulted in the country being vulnerable to a bloody uprising. I do not know what happened to my report. Since it did not agree with the U.S. government's general view of Iran, I believe it ended up in the classified trash. Over five years passed before my prediction came true.

It was not only in training and exercises that the 3/5th Special Forces excelled. We were continually at the top in the IG inspections as well as in maintenance inspections. We participated in community improvement programs in the Fayetteville area, and in places, we conducted exercises. We often took troops from the 95th Civil Affairs Group at Fort Bragg along on the training for this very purpose. We received many letters of appreciation for our work in community relations. The troops spent much time working with youths and minorities. The battalion also led all annual fund drives. When it looked like we would come in second in one of them, I made an extra contribution of $250 to bring our battalion back on top.

My mother, my brother Ole, and my 19-year-old niece Bjørg Bryn came for a visit between Christmas and New Year 1972. Ole returned to New York after the holidays. My mother stayed until late March, and Florence brought her to the DZ to witness our parachute jump as we returned from Missoula. Bjørg, who was a U.S. citizen, remained in the U.S. for most of the year. She had met a helicopter pilot from Minnesota named David Westling. When I received orders to move, they took a motorcycle trip to Arizona and Minnesota to meet David's family. After that, she returned to Norway. She and David were later married.

I learned in January 1973 that my next assignment was as Deputy Commander of the 4th Psychological Operations Group when my command time was over. This news was after I received verbal confirmation that my alternate specialty had been changed to Foreign Area Officer with West Europe as the specialty area. I had anticipated this would happen. I received written orders making this specialty effective in May 1975. Since we could now look forward to another two to three years at Fort Bragg, we listed the Cottonade home for sale as it was now empty, leased the Summerhill home to Major Passailaigue, and bought a larger and newer one at 2515 Mirror Lake Drive in an upscale neighborhood in Fayetteville.[9]

There were numerous social functions in the first half of 1973 as Florence and I neared our departure. The Army's custom was that officers and wives call on their commanding officer on New Year's Day and we had such an event at our home in the late morning. There was a party at the officers' club for the 3/5th Special Forces officers and wives on 31 March.

The officers in the battalion had scheduled a Dining-In at the officers' club for 30 April. A Dining-In is the most formal social event with a long history. There had not been one in the 5th Special Forces Group in anyone's memory. Wives did not partake, and officers wore formal evening Mess Uniforms or Dress Blues with bow ties. There was a Drum and Bugle Corps present, and all traditional sequence of events spelled out.

Passailaigue, who came from a military family, planned and made all arrangements. Every officer, except a duty officer, attended. We invited Colonel Keesling, Major General Emerson, and Brigadier General Michael D. Healey. Keesling and Healey sent their regrets, but Emerson, newly promoted, was still at Fort Bragg pending the assumption of command of the Center by Healey on 1 May, and did attend.

Florence's Illnesses

The doctors admitted Florence to the Womack Army Hospital at Fort Bragg in late March as her problems with bipolar disorder had reached a point where it was life-threatening. One event could have caused severe injuries or worse. I did not report the incident as she could have had problems with the law or ended up spending a long time hospitalized. She also asked me not to mention it to the doctors. Only Barbara and her husband David knew what had happened until David and Monica were informed many years later. Florence and I believed that the kids' departure might have caused a resurgence in the bipolar problems she had not suffered from for several years.

Florence was also troubled with severe nerve pain (fibromyalgia) and constant migraine headaches. She was doing better after a few days in the hospital. She had some new medicines prescribed and given instructions on how to handle migraines. The hospital discharged her after one week.

It was a lousy half-year for both of us. We had no one to discuss our problems with or give us advice. I was depressed about my wife's illness, by the derailment of my career in the infantry, and my upcoming assignment. I began drinking too much, and this period was the closest I ever came to being an alcoholic, but it only lasted for a few months. Florence and I continued to discuss our problems, and we agreed to try a trial separation.

Florence was hospitalized again on 7 May. We were at a lawyer's office to discuss the trial separation. Florence excused herself and went out into the hallway to drink from a water fountain when she collapsed. The lawyer and his secretary said I should not be overly concerned since it appeared to be a fake event, and in their view, Florence did not want a separation, and this was her way to stop it. I could not take any risks and immediately brought her to Womack Army Hospital. They changed some of the medicines they had given her in March but concluded that she also had spinal spurs in the neck area, and she received a neck cast to wear when discharged.

New "Urgent" Assignment

By early May, I still had not received written orders for my new assignment. All this changed in May. I had driven to Virginia for a visit to one of my companies on 15 May; I believe the company was either Major William R. Hale's or Major Hugh Bell Sproul's. The troops were training young cadets from a military academy. I arrived in the area by evening and stayed at a motel.

The following day—16 May—I drove to the training site early in the morning. While I was en route to the company, the battalion headquarters had received a call from DA requesting I return the telephone call as soon as possible. Major Passailaigue called the company I was on my way to visit and left the DA callback number.

I was informed about Passailaigue's call as soon as I arrived at the company's training site, but I decided first to have breakfast with some cadets and my troops. The company commander reminded me when breakfast was over about the DA call, suggesting I call since it had some urgency.

I went to the nearest telephone and called the number Passailaigue had given the company commander. I explained to the woman who answered that I was returning a call my command had received earlier in the day. Lieutenant Colonel Andrew J. Miller, Jr., came on the phone.

After a couple of minutes of small talk, he asked me if I was familiar with the Paris Peace Accord. I told him all I knew was from TV and newspaper reports. He then said the treaty required all U.S. troops to leave Vietnam this spring and that this withdrawal might already be in its final stages. Only a small Defense Assistance Office (DAO) and a delegation to monitor the Paris Accord's implementation would remain. After a pause, I asked what all this had to do with me.

Miller stated that I was selected to serve as the chief of the negotiations division of the delegation. He also explained the reason for the call was to get me to volunteer for the assignment. Since I had already served two tours in Vietnam, DA policy was not to order me back. He also stated the appointment was a high priority.

I asked Andrew if I were the only lieutenant colonel in the Army who could undertake this assignment. I also told him I was very suspicious of offers labeled "high priority" since such appointments had turned out to be anything but a top priority over the past few years. Miller laughed and said this one was an undeniably "high priority." He said the Defense Department, the State Department, and CINCPAC were all involved. Assistant secretaries at the DOD and State had received a stack of records of candidates. This illustrious group selected me.

I reminded Miller I had over two months left in my command assignment, and I did not want that messed up. He answered that I would get full credit from DA for the command assignment if I left before my command time was over. He knew about my projected appointment to the 4th Psychological Group and astutely recognized it was an assignment I did not want.

I finally told him I needed to talk to my wife, who was in the hospital. He said he understood, but he had orders to get an immediate reply. I believed him and said I would return to Fort Bragg at once, and if my wife's condition had improved and the doctors were optimistic, I would accept the assignment. If our answer was no, I told him I would call within 48 hours—a truly short time given all we had wasted over the past 10 years or more in Vietnam.

At the end of the conversation, he mentioned it could be possible to have my wife move to Thailand or the Philippines, where excellent U.S. medical facilities were available. It would be easier for me to visit her. He was trying hard for a yes answer.

I briefed the company commander on the call, telling him I had received a short deadline to accept or decline the assignment. I asked him to explain the situation to the academy officials, the cadets, and troops, as I had to head back to Fort Bragg immediately.

I called the hospital and they said my wife's condition had improved, and there was a possibility the doctors would discharge her after the next day's morning visit. I also called Major Passailaigue and briefed him. I told him I would see him at 0700 in the morning.

I started the 500-kilometer return trip around 1500 hours and was back at Fort Bragg after darkness. I arrived at the battalion around 0615 in the morning and talked to Major Passailaigue and my staff officers. Passailaigue's appointment in the RA looked like it would be approved, and he was delighted. He and the staff were also happy about the assignment offered me as they knew how I felt about the 4th Psychological Operations Group.

I then walked to the 5th Special Forces Group headquarters to brief Colonel Keesling. His only comment was that I had managed to wriggle my way out of another Fort Bragg assignment. I told him the assignment offer came as a total surprise, as Florence and I had accepted we would be at Fort Bragg for possibly another three years, which was our reason for buying a new home. He knew Florence was in the hospital, but he did not ask how she was doing.

I then drove to the hospital to visit Florence. She looked better, and the doctors had told her she could come home that afternoon. I only told Florence we were offered a new assignment and needed to discuss it after her release. The administrators told me I could pick up my wife any time after 1600 hours.

Florence and I spent most of the night discussing our assignment. Her first reaction was, *Oh, my God, not again.* I told her I would not volunteer this time unless she agreed. We decided to call DA the following day and let Florence talk to Lieutenant Colonel Miller.

We called at about 0800 in the morning (17 May). Miller assumed I was calling to reject the assignment. I told him that was not the case, but it could help ease my wife's concerns and worries if he explained the job to her. He talked to Florence for about 20 minutes as good as any used car salesman, or assignment officers as we called them. At the end of their conversation, she asked him if he could delay my appointment for a while to give us a chance to straighten out our lives. He promised to do his best, but I needed to volunteer for Vietnam, still a war zone. I did this the following morning when Florence accompanied me to the battalion where Passailaigue and our good friend Captain Kim E. Kendle, the S-1, tried to cheer Florence. Kendle had been our good friend and helper throughout our assignment, and he told Florence to give him a call if there were any problems after I left.

The May, June, and early July social events became a single event—a lūʻau with all battalion members and their families attending. It was a large gathering of over 600. Florence and I received many gifts at this event that I still have, including a green SF blazer.

Miller called on 21 May to acknowledge receipt of my volunteer statement. He said I should have my orders by the end of the month, terminating my assignment at Fort Bragg on June 30, one month early. The delegation in Saigon had kept my position open since its inception, and this explains why the framed gift I received when I departed had me starting my assignment at the end of March. While not able to delay my Saigon reporting date, he pointed out the orders authorized a 30-day leave, which should give us enough time to take care of personal matters before departing.

I told Miller I was on orders to lead a coordination group to Germany and Iran on 5 June 1973 and return within 12 days. The group consisted of four officers from my battalion.[10] I asked that these facts be taken into consideration.

Florence had another short hospitalization on 5 July but returned home the following day. I asked Barbara and her husband to keep a close eye on Florence while I was away. Our Cottonade home also sold on 12 July, removing that unnecessary drag on our finances.

Florence took me to my flight from Fayetteville Airport to Washington in the late afternoon of Wednesday 25 July, as she had done many times before. We were both depressed. My flight to San Francisco left Thursday morning, and there were several hours' wait at San Francisco International Airport. Passailaigue, who had been in Montana on a short leave, surprised me by showing up at the airport to wish me well in Vietnam.

CHAPTER 22

Chief of Negotiation, U.S. Delegation Four Party Joint Military Team (USDFPJMT)

Pan American Flight 841 was late departing San Francisco and spent several hours in Hawaii for a plane change. It also stopped briefly in Guam and Manila.

I had told the DA there was no doubt in my mind that the Agreement to End the War and Restoring Peace to Vietnam (hereafter referred to as the Paris Peace Accord) did not mean an end to the North Vietnamese determination to conquer the South. I felt sure I might witness the inevitable fall of South Vietnam. The newspaper I picked up in San Francisco and the one I bought in Honolulu tended to confirm my feelings, as one paper talked about the loss of one ARVN battalion in heavy fighting. The other article discussed numerous peace violations, numbers of which were steadily climbing.

We had withdrawn entirely from South Vietnam, while the treaty we had recently signed allowed the North Vietnamese to keep about 123,000 troops in South Vietnam and control the territories they had captured. This fact does not appear anywhere in the Paris Peace Accord but had long been a blockage in the Paris negotiations. The Democratic Republic of Vietnam (DRV) never admitted to having forces in South Vietnam. President Nixon made a significant and damaging unilateral concession to North Vietnam on 8 May 1972 when he announced he would accept a cease-fire in place as a precondition for U.S. withdrawal. In other words, the U.S. agreed to a total withdrawal without requiring the other side to do the same, thereby ignoring the DRV's presence. It is easy to reach an agreement when you cave to an opponent's claims, known to be blatantly false by the whole world.

I kept asking myself why I was chosen for this job since I had spent two years fighting them on the battlefield. I felt that DA must also be convinced of the indisputable end in Vietnam since they had more up-to-date information than I had. I was not concerned for my safety, but I had a gnawing feeling of a future debacle and that I was one of those who might receive blame for inevitable failure.

As it appeared the arrival time in Saigon would be delayed by four to six hours because of the long stop in Hawaii, I sent a message to my new organization to let them know I would be late. Somehow, we made up the lost time, and we arrived at Tan Son Nhut airport in Saigon close to the scheduled time on Friday 27 July (Vietnam time).

We had to disembark on the tarmac, and I did not see anyone from the delegation. However, I did see a group of Vietnamese officials off to the side, holding up a sign reading "Trung Tà Lunde." Trung Tà is Vietnamese for a lieutenant colonel. I walked over to them, introduced myself, and presented my official passport. They explained I did not need to enter the terminal since they would take care of those formalities. They also said they would bring my luggage and place it in the sedan, waiting to take me to the delegation, only a short distance away.

When I arrived in Vietnam in 1965, the MACV headquarters was at 137 Pasteur Street in downtown Saigon, not far from the U.S. Embassy. As the U.S. force level in Vietnam grew, there was a need for a larger facility. In July 1966, shortly after I departed from my first tour in Vietnam, construction started on a new facility adjacent to Tan Son Nhut Airport. It was situated close to the ARVN Joint General Staff Compound. The price tag was $28,000,000, $229,000,000 in today's money. I am not sure when it was completed and occupied. The building was in use in the summer of 1968 when Colonel Emerson and I visited the place in late July after the VC destroyed the Ben Luc Bridge. I believe its completion date was before I left in 1969. This huge structure was referred to as "Pentagon East."

FPJMT's Mission and Other Players

I was somewhat familiar with the mission and organization of the FPJMT before I arrived. I had received an unclassified information packet about a week before I departed the U.S. The U.S. Delegation to the FPJMT was a follow-on organization of the U.S. Delegation to the Four Party Joint Military Commission (FPJMC), set up by the Paris Peace Accords.

The FPJMC existed for only 60 days from the signing of the Paris Peace Accords, coinciding with the time specified in the treaty for the withdrawal of all foreign forces. The primary function of the FPJMC was to receive the captured military and civilians held by the DRV and the Provisional Revolutionary Government (PRG). The FPJMT would carry on the task of the short-lived FPJMC.

The FPJMT derived its mission from the Paris Peace Accords, specifically from Chapter III, Article 8 (b) of that document.

It reads:

> The parties shall help each other to get information about those military personnel and foreign civilians of the parties missing in action, to determine the location and take care of graves of the dead so as to facilitate the exhumation and repatriation of the remains, and to take any such other measures as may be required to get information about those still considered missing in action.

There was also a two-party team named Two-Party Joint Military Commission (TPJMC), established by the Paris Peace Accords, and it began its work at the same time as the FPJMC and continued its existence after the FPJMC ceased to exist. The members of this commission were the two South Vietnamese parties (Republic of Vietnam (RVN) and PRG). They would handle the return of Vietnamese people captured and detained in South Vietnam. The exchange of Vietnamese civilian personnel lists of imprisoned personnel was to occur within 15 days of the cease-fire. The TPJMC continued to have a location at La Celle-Saint-Cloud on the western outskirts of Paris.

The Paris Peace Accords also set up an International Control Commission (ICC), like the one established by the Geneva Conference in 1954, ending French involvement in Vietnam, except that the membership was increased from three to four nations and was labeled International Commission for Control and Supervision (ICCS). The three countries in the ICC—Canada, India, and Poland—became members of the ICCS. The first country to decline to participate in the ICCS was India, and Indonesia replaced it, and the new fourth member was Hungary. Canada withdrew in 1973, just after I arrived, and Iran replaced Canada. The ICCS headquarters were near Tan Son Nhut Airport.

The word "control" in the title of this commission is a misnomer and inaccurate. It had no power to control anything. As far as I know, only the delegates from the DRV and PRG used this commission to lodge complaints about breaches of privileges and immunities, which were the same as agreed to by the FPJMC. These complaints went either to the U.S. Embassy, and then to the U.S. FPJMT Delegation, but they were sent directly to the U.S. Delegation in most cases. I was not involved in these issues unless they became agenda items for our weekly negotiation sessions. ICCS members often traveled to Hanoi on our liaison flights, probably for discussions with the DRV. Senior members of FPJMT also received invitations to social events given by the commission or its members.

The regular reporting channel for the team was through the Defense Assistance Office (DAO), then through the U.S. Support Activity Group in Thailand, to CINCPAC and the JCS. Policy guidance and instructions came from the U.S. Department of State through the U.S. Embassy in Saigon. The delegation could conduct direct coordination with the Joint Casualty Resolution Center (JCRC), responsible for recovering the remains of those labeled as missing. The FPJMT was also responsible for negotiating entry rights for U.S. search operations in areas we believed to be the location of the remains of those who died in captivity or were killed in action.

The Paris Peace Accords limited the number of U.S. military members in South Vietnam to 50 assigned to the DAO. The military personnel assigned to the FPJMT were beside the 50 limitations. The composition of each delegation settled earlier remained virtually constant while I was at the FPJMT.

Organization of the USDFPJMT

The U.S. Delegation to the FPJMT was a small joint organization consisting of a total of 45 U.S. personnel. The simple organizational chart below shows the team's organization and the number of individuals in each division, broken down into military personnel, U.S. civilians, and Vietnamese nationals. The number in all categories fluctuated while I was a member of the team. I will briefly describe the functions of the various divisions, concentrating on the negotiations division.

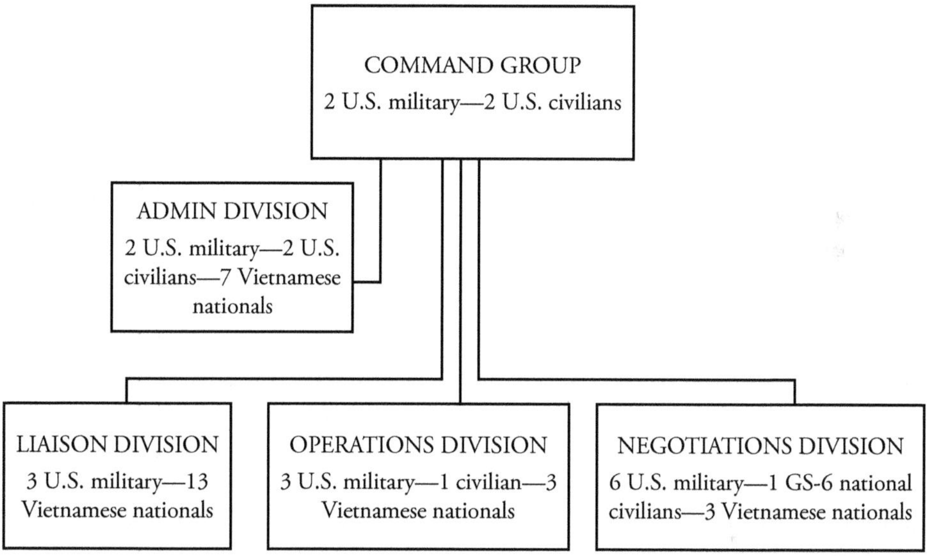

The command group consisted of the delegation chief, an Army colonel, William W. Tombaugh (1927–2002). The deputy chief was an Air Force lieutenant colonel, Gerald R. Edwards. The U.S. civilians were a GS-7 named Jacqueline F. Partridge, a secretary and stenographer, and a GS-5 clerk-typist named Candy Singletary.

An Army lieutenant colonel, John M. Fitzgerald II (1934–2006), ran the administrative division. The division was responsible for administrative and logistic support functions within the delegation, military and personnel management, and the delegation yearbook preparation.

An Army lieutenant colonel named Thomas R. Schornak was chief of the operations division. Schornak was a major when I arrived and was promoted while at the delegation. This division's primary function was to contact and assist the JCRC at the Nakhon Phanom (NKP) Royal Thai Air Force Base in Thailand to exhume KIAs. While I was at the delegation, Brigadier General Robert Charles Kingston (1928–2007) was in command of the JCRC. I only visited NKP once, and I dealt with Lieutenant Colonel Charles A. Beckwith (1929–1994), who I recall had the team responsible for recovering remains in South Vietnam. Colonel Sully H. De Fontaine (1927–2019) was also with the JCRC. I had met both these famous SF officers, Beckwith and De Fontaine, earlier.

Unfortunately, it turned out there were few requirements for recovering MIA remains, and I recollect that the operations division's primary function was organizing the liaison flights to Hanoi. The Operations Division's secondary roles included keeping MIA folders and a consolidated list of information we had provided to the DRV/PRG on these individuals, communications support, and the preparation of emergency action plans, like the evacuation of the U.S. Delegation and civilians.

The chief of the liaison division was a Navy commander, George P. Fitzgibbons. In addition, there were two other U.S. nationals. Also, there were five Vietnamese interpreters—some males and some females. In addition to providing interpreters, this division was responsible for liaison with the other delegations and the negotiations facility's upkeep, located at Camp Davis in the Tan Son Nhut area.

The negotiations division, which I took over, had five U.S. officers assigned. Marine Corps Major Richard C. Rich was my deputy. My senior staff officer was Major John T. Thomas, Jr., promoted to lieutenant colonel before my departure. There was also an Army captain named Stuart A. Herrington assigned. He was a counter-intelligence officer and was absent most of the time. Another Army captain was also assigned whose name was Jerome W. Scanlon Jr. (1940–2011). He was a lawyer with a specialty in international law. Jerome was promoted to major shortly before his departure in 1974. My admin assistant was an Air Force technical sergeant named Russell H. Brown. I wrote a report on Army Staff Sergeant William P. Craighead on 2 November 1973, listed as administrative supervisor. Most likely, Craighead departed in November and his replacement was Technical Sergeant Brown. I had one U.S. GS-6, Barbara Jean Kavulia, and she was my secretary/stenographer and the only secretary in the division with a security clearance. There were three Vietnamese nationals: Nguyen Thi Bich Loc, a public affairs writer; a secretary named Nguyen Thi Mai; and a clerk typist, Nguyen Thi Ban, whose family we sponsored in 1975.

Among the division's responsibilities was developing the FPJMT agenda, special studies when required, and keeping records of each plenary and special negotiating session. Each meeting's reports were by message to a long list of military addressees and various embassies worldwide. Message preparation was a time-consuming chore and often took much of the evening and night following important plenary sessions. The negotiations division was also responsible for continuous liaison with the U.S. Embassy's Political/Military Affairs Section in Saigon and the primary point of contact for the embassy's press office and its clearance of press releases. In addition, the negotiations division was responsible for developing alternate negotiation strategies and getting them approved. Because of these broad functions, we were also responsible for compiling the delegation history.

There were seven sedans and drivers. Three were for the negotiations division, two for the operations division, one for the admin division, and one for the liaison division. Following the Arab–Israeli War, the oil embargo resulted in all vehicles, except one for each division, being under admin division's management. I eventually received one of these back because of the negotiations division personnel's frequent trips to the U.S. Embassy. I believe RVN was not one of the countries embargoed since I did not witness any shortages in the local economy.

Major Paul L. Miles, who had been a member of the U.S. military delegation to the Paris negotiations, and after that, a member of FPMT's forerunner, the FPJMC, was still in the USDFPJMT awaiting reassignment when I arrived; we had a two-week overlap. He was a West Point graduate with a distinguished resume, studying at Oxford University as a Rhodes Scholar, and earned a master's degree in modern history. He retired as a colonel in 1990 and completed his PhD at Princeton. Then he went on to be a lecturer at Princeton.[1]

Graham Anderson Martin (1912–1990) was the U.S. Ambassador to Vietnam while I was stationed in the U.S. Delegation to the FPJMT. In his earlier years, Martin had worked as a reporter. When we entered World War II, he volunteered for the Army and became an intelligence officer, eventually becoming a colonel in the reserves. He began his diplomatic career in 1947.

Ambassador Martin arrived in Saigon on 21 June 1973, about a month before my arrival. He came to Saigon from Thailand, where he was the U.S. Ambassador. Before that, Martin was ambassador to Italy.

He had an adopted nephew, Glenn Dill Mann, who was a lieutenant in the Marines. Lieutenant Mann died in action near Chu Lai in Vietnam in 1965. Some officials at the embassy considered Ambassador Martin's hatred for the North Vietnamese to stem from this tragedy. I am not sure that was correct.

Graham Martin was a dedicated conservative. His service in Saigon was controversial, particularly during the final month before the fall of South Vietnam, but he had been a controversial figure before, particularly as ambassador to Italy.[2]

I seldom contacted Ambassador Martin, except for an introduction when I accompanied Colonel Tombaugh to the embassy. We met a couple of times in 1974, but most meetings were with his deputies.

The First Few Days

It was close to lunchtime when I arrived at the DAO building, previously known as "Pentagon East." Since it was 27 July in Vietnam, a Friday, few people were present except for Colonel Tombaugh.

Tombaugh then took me to a restaurant for lunch in what was known as the DAO Command Mess Compound, just across from the main road leading to "Pentagon East." The DAO compound was the home to 45 two-bedroom trailers, a chapel, and a building housing a restaurant, bar, and a small movie theater.

During lunch, I met a Vietnamese woman, nicknamed "Tiger," who oversaw the restaurant. I also met the Vietnamese woman who controlled all trailers and the maids who took care of them. Her name was Nguyen Thi Truong, nicknamed "June," who would have a far-reaching and significant impact on my life.

Tombaugh noted I was probably exhausted after two days of travel. They had booked me into the Brinks Hotel in downtown Saigon where Lieutenant Colonel Edwards lived. It was a temporary arrangement until a trailer was available. Tombaugh had arranged for my driver, Le Van Dien, to take me there, and he would also pick me up and bring me back to the delegation when I was ready to return. Tombaugh stated he would discuss my job when I was well-rested.

Dien delivered me and my duffel bag to the Brinks, dropping me off at around 1500 hours. The drive to the hotel was 45 minutes in heavy traffic. I asked him to pick me up at 0600 hours on Monday. After meeting Edwards, who had arrived earlier in July, we decided to travel back and forth together, using my sedan and driver.

The quarters at Brinks were on the third floor, in Suite 307C. The suite, which I described to Florence in a 5 August letter, consisted of four bedrooms, two baths, two sitting rooms, and a kitchen. The suite was for four individuals, but I had it all to myself after Edwards moved out on 3 August.

There was an Autovon[3] telephone in the suite, and I had a Motorola two-way radio for when I was not in my room. When I moved to a trailer, I had similar communication capabilities. We were also authorized to use the Autovon telephone to make calls to our families, first contacting the nearest military base to our homes and then have the operator connect using routine priority. However, the government imposed minimal use in emergencies (such as the Arab–Israeli War in October 1973) and regular calls were not allowed. There was also a safe in case I brought classified materials to my quarters.

There were no other military personnel, except Edwards, staying at the hotel at the time, but there were several U.S. civilian contractors. There was a large restaurant and bar on the third floor, often frequented by Americans who were not residents of the hotel. Edwards and I would have breakfast at this restaurant before our drive to the delegation but eat lunch and dinner at the command mess before returning to the hotel in the late afternoon.

In a second letter to Florence on 5 August, I described Saigon's conditions:

> They are more deplorable than they were before. There are many people out of work, poverty is everywhere, and crime is rising daily. It is dangerous to be out on the streets at night, and there is midnight to 0500-hour curfew.

I had a meeting with Tombaugh on Monday and he briefed me on what had happened in negotiations—which amounted to nothing. He and I then drove to the U.S. Embassy, where I briefly met the U.S. Ambassador and deputies. I spent the rest of the day in briefings by Major Miles and the negotiations division officers. I also met my secretarial staff.

Negotiations in 1973

Nothing of importance had happened before my arrival. The meetings ended in early June because of difficulties getting the other side to accept new safety regulations for the Hanoi liaison flight, which had a mishap when a briefcase carried by a DRV officer caught fire. It was seemingly rigged for destruction in case someone other than the owner tried to open it. This security mechanism was sensitive to altitude and started to burn as the C-130 gained altitude. The Air Force crew opened the rear ramp to get rid of the smoke which had filled the aircraft.

To keep from boring the reader, I will focus only on the critical twice-weekly meetings with the DRV, PRG, and RVN Delegations. I will address the leading trends and events I consider essential, both official and personal.

There was an unfounded optimism in the U.S. Delegation that the negotiations would proceed quickly and easily, based on the experience of the FPJMC that brought back the prisoners held by our former enemies.

Captain Scanlon, my legal adviser, and I were more pessimistic. We believed that getting the communists to account for our missing, leading to the exhumation and return of the remains to the U.S., would be exceedingly difficult. So far, the negotiations had concentrated on modalities and confirming the procedures inherited from the FPJMC.

Scanlon and I felt we would run into a hornet nest when we demanded an accounting of our missing. We also thought that every communist document and statement should be studied in-depth to determine any options for the U.S. Delegation. This procedure was also recommended by Major Paul Miles, who stressed that the other side was talented and determined.

There are four Geneva conventions from 1949 for the protection of war victims. Two of them deal with the Treatment of Prisoners of War and Civilian Persons in war time. The U.S. was one of the original signatories in 1949, and it entered into force on 2 February 1956 after ratification by the Senate the previous year. The RVN accepted all four conventions in 1953 before the 1954 partition and reaffirmed their decision in March 1967. The DRV officially acceded to all four conventions in June 1957. The PRG claimed the conflict was a civil war, and international law did not apply. However, the Geneva Convention states that specific minimum rules cover armed conflict not of an international character.

The optimists, including Colonel Tombaugh in the beginning, countered by saying that all prisoners we took we turned over to the ARVN. We explained that turning them over to another power did not absolve our responsibility under international law. Also, there was no way we could account for enemy dead since they were left on the battlefield or buried in mass graves, mostly unmarked. We were not concerned that the DRV would raise such demands, since they denied having troops in South Vietnam, but the PRG might, despite their statement that international law did not apply.

By the end of 1973, Tombaugh had concluded that the first months of the U.S. Delegation to the FPJMT had been too reactionary and overly optimistic.[4] He became a supporter of his negotiations division's position as described above, including an in-depth study of our counterparts' behavior—in short, what made them tick.

I accompanied Tombaugh as an observer to the negotiating session on 1 August, the first meeting of the four powers since early June. I met the DRV and PRG representatives but did not take part in the proceedings. The liaison flights to Hanoi resumed on 3 August, but I decided to stay in Saigon to review all that had transpired in negotiations between 27 March and my arrival.

In addition to the negotiation sessions called for in the Paris Peace Accords—twice weekly on Tuesdays and Thursdays—we also had meetings with the RVN Delegation to discuss strategy, usually before each plenary session. These were nearly as frustrating as the session with the DRV and PRG. We had another four-power all-day meeting on 7 August, but it became bogged down in a discussion of exhumation and moving remains to military cemeteries.

It was natural for other countries not involved in the FPJMT to use our organization as a venue for obtaining information on their missing. This process had begun well before my arrival. These countries fell into two categories: those who had fought with us (Korea, Thailand, Australia, the Philippines) and those who were not involved in the war.

Requests for assistance would usually arrive from those countries' embassies directly to the U.S. Delegation to the FPJMT or through the ICCS. We always cooperated in this effort by forwarding all the information we received to the other three delegations, requesting assistance. My memory is that there were at least 86 personnel in both categories, but there may have been more. In the second category, we provided names of civilians from the following countries: France (15); UK (30); Austria (one); Japan (nine); Canada (two); Switzerland (one); Federal Republic of Germany (two MIA and three who died in captivity (DIC)). All these requests were unsuccessful. The answer from the DRV/PRG was invariably that it was not within the scope of the FPJMT and that these countries should deal directly with the DRV/PRG. Dealing directly with these two entities would constitute de facto recognition.

Early Problems from Agent Orange

I came down with severe sores on my face, arms, and legs in early August. Since there were only a couple of military medics at DAO, I went to the 7th Adventist Hospital in Saigon for treatment since an arrangement existed with DAO. The many tests they conducted failed to reveal a cause, but they suggested it could be cellulitis, and

I received medicines for strengthening the immune system and antibiotics. These medical problems eventually became part of my medical records.

The 7th Adventist treatments did not help. Tombaugh eventually sent me to the U.S. Army hospital in Bangkok and then to the U.S. Air Force hospital at Clark Air Force Base in the Philippines. The Bangkok hospital had limited staff, as it was in a drawdown leading to a complete closing in 1976. The doctors at Clark in late November (21–23 November) did not change the diagnosis from the Adventist Hospital. These sores have flared up occasionally over the past 48 years, and treatments for every possible cause failed. These flare-ups were mainly of short durations until 2015 when they became permanent after my open-heart surgery.

Doctor Ivanovich, advertised as an expert in chloracne at the Cleveland Clinic, said the early diagnosis of cellulitis was utterly wrong. He concluded, by process of elimination, that they were probably chemical sores caused by Agent Orange, which was unknown when I received treatments in Southeast Asia.

When Lieutenant Colonel Edwards moved out of the Brinks on 3 August, I began driving myself to save Dien, my driver, from getting up at around 0400 hours to pick up the sedan at the command mess and then proceed to the Brinks. The morning and evening traffic was chaotic as thousands of rickshaws, mopeds, motorcycles, and small trucks darted in and out of the traffic as if there were no rules. However, all went well.[5]

I moved into a trailer in the command mess compound on 27 August. The trailer was located about 30 feet from the backdoor to the command mess building. The trailer was extensive: a beautiful kitchen, large living room, large bath, and two bedrooms, one set up as a study with a desk and a soft chair. The trailer had two air conditioning units so it stayed cool even on the hottest days.

In late August, I learned about rumors that I would move from the negotiations division to the operations division because of my operational background and that Schornak would take over the negotiations division. Schornak was a competent officer, but I had explicit orders for the negotiations division. This rumor was related to me by Lieutenant Colonel Fitzgerald, and I do not think Tombaugh knew about it. I immediately told Fitzgerald I had one of the three positions in the delegation designated as key, approved by State, DOD, and CINCPAC. I informed Fitzgerald I would contact Lieutenant Colonel Miller in the OPO at once, requesting release from the FPJMT if any such action occurred. I never heard anything further about this matter.

First Visit to Hanoi

I traveled to Hanoi on 31 August as the senior officer from the U.S. Delegation. My senior staff officer, Major John T. Thomas, and the civilian Vietnamese interpreter Nguyen Van Chu accompanied me. There were six members from the

DRV Delegation and three members each from the RVN and PRG Delegations. Ten members from the ICCS came along—three Hungarians and seven Poles—25 passengers in all.

I had talked to Colonel Tombaugh well before the trip and shown him the items we had captured from the body of a DRV lieutenant who died in the first NVA delaying position on our way to the Cambodian border on 13 May 1966. I told him I intended to turn them over to the North Vietnamese on my first trip to Hanoi. My secretarial staff translated my description of the event and my other comments and condolences into Vietnamese.

Tombaugh agreed to my plan and said we could also use that fact in one of our plenary sessions. I disagreed, stating it may affect our opponents more if we treated it as a private matter and refrained from bringing it up in our negotiations since the DRV never admitted having troops in the south. Furthermore, treating it as a private matter between soldiers would earn more respect from our opponents. Moreover, we did not have to clear it with the U.S. Embassy. Finally, I said that the DRV could construe the lack of linkage as a goodwill measure that could, over time, elicit a similar reply from them. However, I did not have high confidence that it would. Tombaugh agreed.

The flight to Hanoi took three and a half hours. I purposely sat next to Lieutenant Colonel Nguyen Duc Bao, one of the deputies of the DRV Delegation. Using my interpreter, I asked Lieutenant Colonel Bao for a personal favor. I explained I had some personal effects of a DRV lieutenant who had shown extraordinary heroism that should be recognized and asked him if he would forward them to the lieutenant's family. Bao initially appeared very skeptical. I told him this was a private soldier to soldier matter, and I assured him that these items' return would go unmentioned in our negotiations. After that statement, he accepted the plastic envelope and placed it in his briefcase.

After landing at Gia Lam Airport, we received some refreshments in the terminal before we drove into Hanoi. We were taken on a tour of an old temple and then to a French-era hotel for lunch. Curious people gathered wherever we went and all displayed a friendly attitude at the sight of their former enemies in uniform. Our guide was a DRV lieutenant who, according to an RVN officer, had been a former interrogator of U.S. prisoners. The only bomb damage we saw was at the airport, a railroad yard, and the bridge we used to get across the river to Hanoi. In a letter on 1 September, I mentioned to Florence that it was a far cry from the destroyed European cities after World War II.

Back at the airport, we had a chance to purchase souvenirs at a makeshift shop with two display cases. Most items for sale were from the metal of downed U.S. aircraft. They also had some wood carvings, and I purchased a couple. The bill came to about six U.S. dollars. They did not take South Vietnamese money but readily accepted U.S. currency. I gave the young girl behind the display case a $20 bill. She apologized profusely for not having paper change, dug into a box of change behind the counter, and gave me a handful. As I walked over to a chair, I realized that most of what she had given me was pre-1920 coins and a considerable number from the 1800s. All were virtually uncirculated. I had been a coin and stamp collector since 1952.

Realizing what the young girl had given me, I went back to the counter and bought a few small carvings. I gave her another $20 bill saying I had forgotten to buy anything for my mother and sister in Europe. This time she gave me over $15 in similar change. The next time I was in Hanoi, the old change boxes, apparently obtained from Hanoi banks, had disappeared.[6]

Florence's Visit to Vietnam

The U.S. Embassy in Saigon initiated a policy that encouraged officers, particularly senior officers, to bring their wives to Saigon. This policy was viewed as a confidence measure for the South Vietnamese to show them our conviction that they could provide for our families' safety. Most officers declined since they had children in schools in the U.S., and some wives were employed. Most of the very senior officers who did not have these chores to worry about decided to bring their wives.

Florence was eager to come as she said that her health was good. I initiated the paperwork from the Vietnam end and purchased the reduced-price tickets through the Army. The visas were valid for 90 days and renewable.

I began to have second thoughts about the wisdom of bringing Florence to Vietnam for two reasons. One reason dealt with Vietnam's situation: the DRV and PRG had stepped up their Paris Peace Accords breaches. Another reason was her statement that her health was good despite being evacuated to Brooke Army Medical Center in Fort Sam Houston in Texas in early October for an operation. Although she said it was a routine operation, I suspected it was more severe than she admitted. The procedure she described could have been handled in any nearby Army medical facility, such as Womack Army Hospital at Fort Bragg.

She was air evacuated to Fort Sam Houston for surgery on 3 October. She was in that hospital for over three weeks before she was taken back to North Carolina. Before that event, she had sold our Mirror Lake home for a hefty 30 percent profit after less than one year of ownership, and moved in with her daughter Barbara.

After the discharge from Brooke Medical Center, Florence stated she still wanted to come. She arrived in Vietnam on 8 December 1973 and was given VIP treatment at the South Vietnamese airport. As soon as she stepped off the plane, they welcomed her to Vietnam and handed her a large flower bouquet. They also took care of her paperwork and fetched her luggage. The next evening the people in the delegation gave Florence a welcome party at a villa. There she had a chance to meet the military and civilian members, including Vietnamese nationals.

Florence established an excellent relationship with the Vietnamese ladies in the command mess compound and the delegation. This superb relationship was especially true for Truong Thi Nguyen, the person in charge of the trailers and maids, who Florence treated as a favorite sister.

Florence was interested in importing things from Vietnam to the U.S. However, I had some reservations as I felt South Vietnam would eventually succumb to North Vietnam military pressure, eliminating our supply source. Florence replied that if that happened, we could switch our purchases to Thailand. In the end, we entered a partnership with Truong Thi Nguyen. She bought a used pickup truck and began purchasing items from RVN-controlled areas around Saigon and the city.

I accompanied Truong on a few of the shopping trips north of Saigon on weekends after Florence went back to the U.S. in March 1974. It was a bit scary, so I asked Truong to concentrate in or immediately around Saigon. We started placing the items in the trailer but soon ran out of space, and Truong took what she bought to her large home in Saigon.

With our help, Truong opened a convertible account in Vietnam, obtained an export license, and arranged with Bekins Moving Company to pick up the items and ship them to Charleston, South Carolina. We would send money to Truong for the items plus 10 percent and shipment costs, and she would continue with the purchases. Truong sent the first of four large shipments on 17 January 1974. By the middle of July, two additional loads of about 12,000 lbs. each were on their way to the U.S. Some other U.S. officers, both in the delegation and DAO, became interested in what we were doing, and Truong entered similar export agreements with them. Unfortunately, these activities also resulted in some feelings of envy in the delegation and DAO.

Anonymous calls to Florence began in December 1973. We never found out who made those calls, but we suspected it came from the receptionist in the DAO building. These calls upset Florence, as did the lack of proper medical services despite Lieutenant Colonel Miller's earlier assurances at DA.

Florence had a couple of nasty falls and signs of bipolar disorder returned. Her illnesses were taking place concurrently with unmistakable signs of a DRV buildup of forces in South Vietnam. An article in *Time* magazine titled "Assessing a Murderous Cease-Fire" appeared on 31 December 1973. This article reported that the DRV presence in South Vietnam had grown to over 170,000 troops with 600 tanks and tracked vehicles. Florence asked if this was true. I could not tell her that our intelligence services considered these figures too low. I told her I believed the report, but DRV needed a more massive buildup for a general offensive.

Florence left Vietnam in mid-March. She needed to return to Fayetteville to rent a store and prepare it for opening. She also had to arrange for the arrival of the first shipment, anticipated in early May.

Sporadic Boycotts: End to Search and Recovery Operations

The Communist delegations had a different view of the mission of the FPJMT. We viewed our mission as a humanitarian one that had little to do with the rest of the Paris Peace Accords. The DRV/PRG Delegations considered all portions of the peace document linked. It would have benefited our work if the Paris Peace Accords had clarified this issue. While never saying so, the RVN Delegation had no interest in a speedy resolution of the MIA issue since they feared that this would end the U.S. presence in Vietnam.

Therefore, we were not surprised that the DRV and PRG continually tried to link the various articles in the Paris Peace Accords, including Article 21. In that article, we had made a promise "that in pursuance of its traditional policy, the United States will contribute to healing the wounds of war and to the postwar reconstruction of the Democratic Republic of Viet-Nam and throughout Indochina." Our failure to act on Article 21 allowed the DRV to label it a breach of the Peace Accords. Because of their linkage interpretation, they used this and other provisions of the Paris Peace Accords—like our alleged failure to remove all mines from their ports—as a pretext for not acting on the MIA issue.

There were several DRV/PRG walkouts in the latter part of 1973. The reasons for these walkouts were standard charges of U.S. and RVN violations of the Peace Accords. The DRV/PRG charge centered around us using Article 8(b) of the Peace Accords to maintain a presence in Vietnam.

The euphoria in the U.S. at getting the prisoners back had subsided, and it was time to shift the emphasis to the MIA issue. The negotiations division convinced Tombaugh to begin a series of press releases highlighting the DRV's and PRG's refusal to live up to the humanitarian problem of accounting for our dead and missing. We hoped that continuing to highlight this issue would bring pressure from U.S. legislators and make the MIA search of interest to the rest of the world. Therefore, we expanded on the DRV/PRG refusal to account for the missing to include several countries, both allied with us and others that had not been involved in the war.

The war was also becoming more intense. The Communists launched a massive rocket attack on Bien Hoa Airbase on 7 November, about 40 kilometers from the FPJMT location. Three RVN individuals died, and 22 were wounded. The attack destroyed three F-5s. The following day, the RVN launched a 50-plane air attack on Loc Ninh, the southern headquarters of the PRG.

The rocket and air attacks were taking place simultaneously with the DRV launching an offensive to open a route along South Vietnam's eastern border from Quang Duc Province to Loc Ninh. The DRV troops overran the outposts of Bu Bong and Bu Prang and claimed they had eliminated three RVN battalions. I could not help thinking about the fate of the Montagnards, who had supported us in

1966 during the Bu Gia Map Campaign. Observers interpreted the attacks described above as the opening of a new phase in the expected offensive.

On 15 December 1973, PRG troops attacked a search/recovery team from the JCRC less than 20 kilometers southwest of Saigon, in Gia Dinh Province. This attack led to the death of the U.S. team leader, Captain Richard Reese, one RVN soldier, the wounding of several U.S. and RVN soldiers, and the destruction of one of three helicopters involved. The U.S. troops were unarmed, wore FPJMT armbands, and the helicopters were also correctly marked.

Colonel Tombaugh read a blistering statement at the 18 December plenary session. It ended with Tombaugh throwing Captain Reese's blood-stained jacket on the conference table as he stated in conclusion, "The treachery of your act lays bare your utter disregard for human life." Thereupon, the U.S. and RVN Delegations walked out.

The PRG later refused to accept responsibility for the incident claiming they had not approved the search. However, they had received notification from the U.S. Delegation but had provided no answer to that notification. As a result, it became evident to the U.S. Delegation that this brought an end to search and recovery operations in RVN-controlled areas.

Repatriation of Those Who Died in Captivity

The first indications that the DRV may be prepared to return the remains of those who had DIC in North Vietnam began to appear in early December 1973. There were lengthy discussions in the delegation of why the DRV had chosen this time to return the DICs. Some Vietnamese considered it a recognition of my earlier gesture in giving information on one of theirs killed in 1966. I rejected this belief because I felt the DRV was too pragmatic for such a gesture. Our frequent press releases may have played a part. The political turmoil in the U.S. and our problems in the Middle East may also have played a role. However, the likeliest reason appeared to be an attempt to drive a wedge between us and the RVN.

The DIC issue came up during the 11 December 1973 plenary session, the day after we provided the DRV with our concept of proceeding. Nothing further happened until a private meeting between the U.S. and DRV representatives on 8 February 1974. Events now began to advance rapidly. A second private meeting on 11 February led us to submit a revised proposal for repatriation to the DRV on 14 February. The DRV wanted all future negotiations in Hanoi, with the first meeting scheduled for 15 February.

I was designated to head the negotiating delegation to Hanoi. This meeting was the most significant event since our prisoners' return, and I do not know to this day for sure why I was selected instead of the delegation chief, Colonel Tombaugh. The lack of operations division participation was also strange, as was the lack of senior staff officers from my division. Vietnamese in the delegation opined that the DRV might have asked for me to recognize my earlier delivery of papers on one of their officers and kept the promise not to mention it during our negotiations. While possible, I did not believe this was the case. I later concluded, with little proof, that the delegation officers felt the DRV offer was a trap and expected the negotiations to fail and that Scanlon and I were expendable.

As soon as we received the DRV request, we called the U.S. Embassy for instructions. Instructions, allegedly from Ambassador Martin, told us to bring back the captives' remains but not agree to anything that would put the U.S. in an unfavorable light. I asked for clarification on which of the two had priority. The final embassy instruction was to use my best judgment, a standard cover your ass statement familiar to me by now.

The delegation that proceeded to Hanoi with me on 15 February consisted of Captain Scanlon and Nguyen Khanh Tan, the senior interpreter from the liaison division. A U.S. photographer from the delegation accompanied us to take both still photos and videos of the negotiations. Another officer who accompanied us to Hanoi was Marine Corps Colonel Ralph D. Wallace, assigned to the JCRC and designated as liaison officer to Hanoi. He never received country clearance but would be the officer accepting the remains when returned. He had no part in the negotiations.

The negotiations dealt mainly with the plan we had transmitted to the DRV on 14 February. The DRV Delegation said they needed additional time to review that document but foresaw no significant problems. They said they would provide us folders and personal effects of the DIC personnel during the next meeting, which they predicted would be longer. The liaison flight returned to Saigon shortly before darkness. Scanlon, who had taken notes at the meeting, had to prepare the message, and I met with Tombaugh and the other division chiefs in his trailer.

The main subject discussed was whether I believed the return of DICs was a genuine offer or whether we would run into problems. The DRV officials had told us there would be press in attendance for the actual transfer ceremony, but I also said that the offer appeared genuine.

The second meeting with the DRV representatives took place on 22 February. I had the same team, and again Colonel Wallace attended as an observer.[7] It was a much longer meeting since it involved receiving the personal items carried by those who DIC, determining the cause of death, etc. The protocol for the turnover ceremony also needed approval from both sides.

Most of the problems encountered were minor ones. We spent some time questioning the death certificates, especially about what medical care they had given the prisoners who died. We told them there would be two C-130 aircraft on the day of repatriation. One was the routine liaison flight from Saigon. The second one would arrive from JCRC in Thailand to take the remains back to that country. I also informed them that the highest-ranking U.S. officer would be Brigadier General

Kingston and that Colonel Wallace would sign the required documents for the remains. We asked to see a copy of those documents to ensure they were proper, without the usual propaganda statements. A DRV delegate went to Hanoi to fetch copies, and we received those after lunch.

There were two items they failed to accept. First, we had 24 remains on our list, but they had only 23 on theirs. They explained that the 24th individual had never been captured but had died from injuries and was therefore not in the DIC category. We argued about this for a while, pointing out it was absurd and uncooperative not to return his remains simultaneously. Finally, after it became evident that they would not accommodate our demands, I dropped the subject under protest.

The second issue had to do with the repatriation ceremony. I pointed out that it was customary to drape the caskets in our flag. They steadfastly refused the display of a U.S. flag on DRV territory. I had not expected they would agree and had already thought of a way to get around this subject. Finally, the DRV representatives noted this was a bilateral event between the U.S. and the DRV, and they did not want the presence of the RVN Delegation. My only comment to this statement was that I assumed the PRG Delegation would also not be present. We took their silence as an indication that the PRG would probably attend.

Delegation documents note two repatriation flights—one on 6 March bringing back 12 remains and one on 13 March bringing back 11. This statement conflicts with my memory and the boxes of photographs with remains and headstones. It was important for the DRV to do it all in one day to maximize the publicity. It turned out that a vast number of media representatives from around the world attended the ceremony. An article in the *New York Times* on 14 March 1974 supports my recollection.

Finally, the DRV representatives asked if we were satisfied with the arrangements. I told them the provisions were acceptable to me personally, but the final decision on these measures was "above my paygrade, and you are probably in the same situation." This statement elicited considerable laughter and affirmation. They did ask for an early reply as they were planning to announce the repatriation to the world on 4 March, and it would take some time for the various news agencies to respond and travel to North Vietnam. This fact also supports my memory that we repatriated all remains on 13 March since it was virtually impossible for the DRV to get the world's press corps to Hanoi on a two-day notice.

After returning to Saigon late on 22 February, we had another meeting in Colonel Tombaugh's trailer with key individuals, including Brigadier General Kingston. Scanlon was again stuck preparing a message but was told not to send it until we had completed our trailer session and had a meeting Colonel Tombaugh and I had planned with the U.S. Embassy in the morning.

I told those in the trailer meeting that I viewed the Hanoi negotiations as a success. The only serious issue I saw was the DRV's refusal to repatriate the remains of the 24th individual on our list since DRV did not consider him DIC, despite our official protest. I also told them DRV did not want an RVN presence and that this could give the U.S. Embassy a problem, despite no mention of it in our instructions. Finally, I told them to expect a large gathering of the world press during the actual repatriation ceremony. Wallace supported my observations.

There were no problems at the U.S. Embassy, and we received clearance for our message. The U.S. Delegation sent two letters to the DRV Delegation on 28 February. One was a summary of the agreement negotiated on 22 February. The second message was a request to repatriate two DIC remains we believed were located at the Van Dien Cemetery in Hanoi based on a previous gravesite visit.

We requested an earlier departure time for the liaison flight on 13 March, and the chief of the DRV Delegation, Colonel Nguyen Don Tu, agreed. He accompanied us on the aircraft. I wanted to assure myself there had not been any changes to our approved plans for the ceremony. Tu, sitting next to me on the flight, astutely concluded this was the reason for the early takeoff. I confirmed his conclusion that this was my reason. He noted that my action showed a lack of trust in him. I answered that he had my confidence, but I would be remiss in my duties not to verify the arrangements. My translator that day was a female[8] from the liaison division. The senior translator present during the negotiations accompanied Brigadier General Kingston and Colonel Wallace. This was another way to ensure the documents they signed were per the negotiated agreement.

The arrangements for the transfer of remains took place in the manner we expected. I found myself a seat behind the table set up for the signing of documentation. I had never seen such a large assemblage of media representatives from around the world. I saw no U.S. press attendance.

The caskets containing the remains were carried aboard the aircraft by U.S. military personnel through an honor guard of officers. The C-130 was parked with the rear of the plane facing the crowded part of the airfield. Its ramp was down and, in the full view of the assembled press corps, U.S. flags, brought by JCRC, were used to cover the caskets on the aircraft.

While waiting to board the return flight, Colonel Tu remarked I had not followed the agreed-upon protocol for the transfer of remains exactly. I replied I had followed the protocol to the letter, but possibly not to his intent. He answered me in French, stating he understood and that I was a creative officer. I wanted to avoid further conversations along this line, especially in French, where I risked making a serious misstatement, so I replied in English that *Your compliment sounds like you are trying to recruit me into the NVA.* Colonel Tu and the others, privy to our conversation, burst out laughing.

Instead of leading to further cooperation, the repatriation of DICs spelled the end of all meaningful work in the FPJMT. The RVN viewed the MIA issue as the only reason for our limited presence in Vietnam and they feared that any early resolution of that problem would result in our complete withdrawal. It is difficult to blame them for this view.

The FPJMT quickly became embroiled in a controversy over privileges and immunities. It was not entirely new since that issue was part of the difficulties that had begun in mid-April 1973 and lasted until my arrival. The Hanoi liaison flights' temporary suspension, until the DRV accepted new safety regulations after the briefcase incident discussed earlier, was seen by the communists as violating their privileges and immunities.

It may be appropriate to summarize this issue because it became the pretext to end all meaningful cooperation. The Paris Peace Accords addressed privileges and immunities in Articles 16 and 17 of the Paris Accords, but only in broad and somewhat vague terms. The expectation was that the short-lived FPJMC would develop specifics and that these would also become applicable to its follow-up organization, the FPJMT. The intentions of the privileges and immunities developed by the FPJMC were to be similar in spirit to those generally accorded to a diplomatic entity in foreign countries. The FPJMT formally adopted the 11 points of privileges and immunities developed by FPJMC in a written agreement on 3 May 1973.

All delegations operated with these privileges and immunities until the spring of 1974. The U.S. assumed responsibility for providing a weekly liaison flight to Hanoi for the DRV and PRG Delegations and the ICCS. However, most of the privileges and immunities had to be provided by the host country, the RVN. The RVN unilaterally granted some privileges and immunities not expressly discussed in the FPJMC but within the spirit of the objective to give the delegations limited diplomatic status. These rights, although unilaterally granted, were formally addressed in the FPJMT and accepted. Among the most controversial privileges granted by the RVN was the PRG's right to hold weekly press conferences and use of the telephone system in the Saigon/Gia Dinh area.

In mid-April 1974, the RVN canceled the PRG press conferences, claiming they had become a propaganda tool. The RVN also wanted to close access to the Saigon telephone system and provide direct service to the ICCS, FPJMT, and TPJMC for DRV and PRG Delegations. The RVN suspended the Saigon/Loc Ninh (the PRG headquarters) flights pending written safety guarantees. These RVN actions led to a walkout by the DRV and PRG Delegations on 30 May 1974 and the subsequent boycott.

The RVN notified the DRV and PRG Delegations on 7 June that the issue of privileges and immunities would revert to the situation as it existed before mid-April. This change came about because of much quiet work with the RVN behind the scenes. We had to be careful because the U.S. Embassy would not tolerate any pressure on the RVN, and the latter had indirect access to the U.S. Embassy. Three days later, RVN offered to carry out its commitment for the Saigon/Loc Ninh coordination helicopter flight, provided the PRG accepted aircraft safety and security arrangements the RVN had proposed.

At the 13 June plenary session, the DRV/PRG demanded the discussion of a written agreement that virtually granted full diplomatic privileges and immunities to both Communist delegations. The U.S. and RVN suggested this be discussed at the deputy level while the chiefs concentrated on the immediate and concrete implementation of Article 8(b).

The DRV/PRG, at the 18 June session, raised their demands by requesting U.S./RVN compliance with their position without discussion. When the U.S. and RVN refused, the PRG and DRV walked out of the meeting. On 22 and 23 June, Hanoi authorities canceled DRV/PRG participation in future FPJMT plenary sessions *sine die* (indefinitely) until we met their demands. Among these were the weekly press conferences of the PRG and access to the standard user telephone system of the Saigon/Gia Dinh area.

Other actions by the RVN infuriated the two Communist delegations, but you will not find them mentioned in any official documents. For example, the RVN cut off newspaper delivery and other media access, periodically shut off the electricity to Camp Davis, and suspended vehicular maintenance. They also reduced medical support, and it took the intervention of the U.S. Delegation and the ICCS to get Colonel Nguyen Don Tu to a hospital when he became sick.[9] These actions were contrary to the Paris Accords' spirit, but Ambassador Martin seemingly accepted this based on his strident press releases.

The U.S. Embassy became problematic to coordinate our efforts with beginning in 1974. On 20 April 1974, I wrote a memorandum to the U.S. Embassy, pointing out that U.S. Delegation FPJMT had 11 relevant documents dealing with our negotiation efforts awaiting a reply. No responses had been received either verbally or in writing. This situation was a notable change from 1973 and hampered our work.

The work of the TPJMC in La Celle-Saint-Cloud, France, also reached an impasse after the communists overran the Tong Le Chan base on the border of Bin Long and Tay Ninh Provinces, 15 kilometers southwest of An Loc. The garrison had held out for 411 days before the defenses collapsed. RVN gave notice on 16 April 1974 that it was suspending its participation in the TPJCM and the La Celle-Saint-Cloud Consultative Conference.

The negotiations division prepared a memorandum for Colonel Tombaugh's signature, giving our analysis of the RVN suspension of its participation in the La Celle-Saint-Cloud Consultative Conference and TPJMC. We concluded that it was further evidence that the RVN believed in a forthcoming general offensive.

The Communists were also hardening their stand on providing interviews with U.S. legislators. On 2 July, Colonel Nguyen Don Tu rejected a meeting with Representative Gillespie V. Montgomery from Mississippi (1920–2006), dealing with MIAs in Laos. Montgomery had already received a rebuff from Tu on 30 June but asked him to reconsider. Tu's answer was the same since Montgomery planned to visit Vientiane, Laos, to raise the subject. This statement aligned with the DRV policy of not recognizing any FPJMT responsibilities for Laos and Cambodia. On 3 July, David Rossiter, a staff member of the Senate Appropriations Committee, requested a meeting with the PRG Delegation on 5 July to discuss MIA Resolution's status with me as his escort. The request was rejected on 4 July by the PRG Delegation since "the situation at the present time is improper."

During this final boycott of the FPJMT, we continued to attend in case the Communist delegations returned. However, after the last DRV/PRG demands, Colonel Tombaugh and I stopped attending. Still, two of my staff officers continued to be present on a rotating base until mid-July, when all the old staff officers had departed.

Beginning in April 1974 and continuing until July, I received informal inquiries from the U.S. Embassy about the possibility of extending my tour in Vietnam. I call these informal inquires because they were not in writing but via telephone. I concluded they did not wish these inquiries communicated to the rest of the delegation. I told them I would do whatever the DOD directed me to do. Still, I wanted assurances that my wife could accompany me at the government's expense and receive assurances of adequate medical support.

When these unofficial inquiries began, I had not received orders for my next assignment. Still, I had a good indication of what it would be from a letter I had received from Washington.

I had written to OPO on 28 February since I was due for an assignment to the General Staff and wanted to avoid that at all costs, asking instead for an appointment to Fort Benning or Fort Bragg. I received an answer on 12 March from the person who had worked so hard to get me to volunteer for my third tour in Vietnam, Lieutenant Colonel Andrew J. Miller, Jr.

Miller informed me that my old friend Colonel Rosenblum had reviewed my file and selected me as Lieutenant Colonel Harry G. Summers's (1932–1999) replacement.[10] Sometimes, having a good friend in a critical position can be a problem. Miller also pointed out that the latest Senior Service College (SSC) selection board showed that 80 percent of those selected had DA/DOD staff experience in addition to extraordinarily successful battalion command. He noted that my General Staff credentials were still untested, but an outstanding performance in that position should make me a shoo-in for SSC. The letter continued:

> We feel, and DCSOPS agrees, that you are the man for the job to which you will be assigned. … We at Infantry Branch understand your desires and preferences, but we feel that your best chances for advancement are in the area we have you programmed.[11]

I also received a letter from Harry Summers confirming his selection as my replacement. He pointed out that he was given a 30-day leave between stations and could not give me an arrival date.

I received the above letters before the embassy's first inquiry. At their request, I provided copies to the Political/Military Section. They also asked me to give them any future documents dealing with my assignment. Consequently, I gave them copies of the orders I received on 4 June and a welcome letter from Major General Cleland (1925–2017). In his letter, he noted that FSO Harry B. Glazer was my sponsor and deputy in the new assignment. These letters and orders spelled an end to the embassy's attempts to have me stay in Saigon.

Colonel Tombaugh and all principal staff officers of the U.S. Delegation departed in early July. Colonel Tombaugh turned the delegation over to me on 7 July and accredited me as deputy chief when Colonel Madison arrived until my departure. I remained for nearly another month to provide continuity and help Colonel Madison, the new delegation chief. I believe he arrived on 19 July.

July 1974 was a hectic period with people departing and others arriving. We still attended the weekly plenary sessions in case the other side changed their minds. They did not, and 18 July was the last time our delegation showed up at the meeting place since all my officers had departed and Colonel Madison had taken over.

As it appeared that my replacement, Harry Summers, would not arrive before my departure, Barbara Kavulia and the others on my secretarial staff recommended I prepare an audiotape passing on to my replacement our experience up to the time of my leaving. The tape was unclassified, but I also made one marked "sensitive" as it dealt with our relations with the RVN Delegation and the U.S. Embassy.

I also encouraged the Vietnamese nationals to be ready on a moment's notice to leave Saigon since I expected the Communists would be able to launch their final offensive within less than a year. I gave Truong Thi Nguyen the same warning and asked her to pass it on to the other Vietnamese in the command mess compound that she trusted without mentioning that it came from me.

Cleland stated in his welcome letter that he expected to see me on the morning of 15 August. This reporting date would leave Florence and me less than a week to find a place to live and move from Fayetteville, NC, to Washington, virtually an impossible timetable. I explained this in a telephone conversation with FSO Harry B. Glazer, who agreed and said he would bring this matter to Major General Cleland's attention. As a result, my new reporting date became 3 September.

A short pamphlet titled *History of the United States Delegation, Four Party Joint Military Team 31 March 1973–30 April 1975* was seemingly prepared after the delegation returned to the U.S. since it included its withdrawal from Vietnam. The dates showing departure for the original team and the replacements' arrival differ from my notes and memory. The pamphlet has Summers's arrival on 16 July 1974, while my memory has his appearance after my departure, but I could be wrong. The fact that I prepared the audio tapes in late July supports my memory. My wife Truong, who handled the assignments of trailers, also remembers Summers arriving after my departure

The last event worth mentioning was the receipt of my OER for my tour of duty with the FPJMT. Tombaugh was the rater, and he gave me the maximum with the recommendation that I was general officer material and should receive early attendance at a Senior Service College. The endorser was U.S. Air Force Brigadier General Ralph Maglione, Deputy Defense Attaché, whose rating virtually mirrors Tombaugh's writings. The reviewer was Major General John E. Murray (1918–2008), the Defense Attaché. The two-page report signed by Josiah W. Bennett, Minister-Counselor for Political Affairs at the U.S. Embassy in Saigon, surprised me most. He worked directly for Ambassador Martin. Such a letter was not required, but he asked that it be attached to my OER. He wrote that there was unanimous agreement that Lieutenant Colonel Lunde was the ablest of an excellent team. He concluded that I should receive preferential consideration for high-level command and staff positions within the U.S. Army.

I left Saigon for my flight back to the U.S. via Hong Kong and Hawaii on the morning of 31 July. I did not receive any VIP treatment from the South Vietnamese. I had told my secretarial staff and Truong Thi Nguyen not to show up. After I gave Dien all my cooking utensils and other items from the trailer I had purchased, he took me to the airport. As I waited to board the aircraft, I had an intense sensation that I would never see Vietnam again.

CHAPTER 23

Pentagon and U.S. Army War College

I am not sure about the route back to the U.S., but my memory is that the Saigon flight flew to Hong Kong and Japan after that. There I remember having a plane change for the flight to Honolulu. Here, I stopped a couple of hours to meet with some intelligence analysts. The analysts already had up-to-date intelligence from the DAO.

Their questions had nothing to do with negotiations but dealt with my views on when to expect the NVA offensive. They were primarily concerned about how the NVA would factor in the rainy season. To the latter question, I answered I did not believe the NVA was concerned about the rainy season as they had demonstrated in the 1968 Tet Offensive, which struck targets in all areas of the country virtually simultaneously. Now, without having to worry about U.S. airpower, the weather was of even less concern.

I told them their guess was as good as mine when it came to the offensive's timing. Major NVA units were already in position. A supply route along the RVN side of the Laotian–Cambodian border was close to completion by eliminating border outposts, except for extending it eastward. The pre-positioning of huge forward supply dumps indicated it would be a one-phase offensive. That part still needed to be completed. I told them I believed the NVA offensive would take place within months, not years.

After 10 years, the assignment to FPJMT was my last wartime duty. The jobs that followed constituted routine peacetime duties, and I will cover them all in two chapters.

Pentagon, 1974–1975

I arrived on the West Coast, and from San Francisco, I flew to Fayetteville where I met Florence. We went out to eat and spent the night at our Fayetteville store, where we discussed what to do and when. I had arrived there on 7 August, and President Nixon announced his resignation effective at midnight on 8 August. His vice president, Gerald Ford (1913–2006), assumed the presidency on 9 August.

My assignment was as chief of the Southeast Asia Branch of the Political/Military Division of the Pentagon, a small interagency establishment. My deputy was State Department FSO Harry B. Glazer (1923–2014). The rest of the personnel in the Southeast Asian desk were civilians or Army individuals. My assignment turned out to be relatively short, but I did not know that at the time, as the policy still called for military personnel to serve four years at each post.

As mentioned in the previous chapter, Glazer had talked to the brass in the Pentagon to get my reporting date changed from 15 August to 3 September to give us time to find a place to live and have our household goods moved from storage in North Carolina to Washington. Harry had also contacted Florence and given her much information on the real estate market (shockingly pricey). Florence and I drove to Washington and found a furnished apartment on the top floor of a high-rise called "Sundown Apartments" as a temporary place to live. We rented it monthly while trying to find a more suitable location.

Shortly after that, Florence spent more than two weeks at Walter Reed Hospital for an operation. They removed spurs in her neck and fused two vertebrae, also in the neck. The legal case resulting from our cabin cruiser's loss in 1971 also came on the docket, and I had to make a two-day trip to upstate New York on 28 August 1974. My brother Ole and Bernard Sivertsen received orders to appear in court. These summonses dealt with their claim for tools and personal property on the sunken boat. Neither my brother nor Sivertsen showed up, and we, therefore, had to drop that part of the claim. The insurance company asked that we leave our petition open to help them in their request for reimbursement. The case was not settled until our departure for Belgium in 1976, and we received no compensation.

After my return from upstate New York, I began working in the Political/Military Division in the Pentagon. Colonel Arthur E. Dewey was the chief of the division. This division was part of the Strategy and Security Directorate headed by Major General John L. Gerrity for the short time I was there. He was born in New Mexico in 1925, graduated from West Point in 1947, and retired in 1979. All directorates and divisions were part of DCSOPS (Deputy Chief of Staff for Operations and Plans).

Colonel Dewey was one of the most intelligent officers I met in the Army. His great empathy was his strongest leadership trait. These two indispensable qualities—intelligence and compassion—go a long way to explain his unusual career, both before and after I met him. He graduated from West Point in 1956 as an officer in the Army Corps of Engineers and later received his master's degree from Princeton University. He deployed to Vietnam from Fort Benning as a helicopter pilot in 1965, when I left for my first tour in Vietnam. Arthur was named one of the White House Fellows in 1968. In 1970, he commanded an aviation battalion in Vietnam. On his return to the U.S., he spent a year as Director of the President's Commission of White House Fellowship.

In addition to attending the C&GSC, he was selected to attend the USAWC in 1972 but did his studies at the Graduate Institute of International Studies in Geneva. After leaving the Political/Military Division in 1975, shortly after I did, he served as Senior Military Fellow at the Council of Foreign Relations. He later became a Defense Planner in the U.S. Mission to NATO. Dewey retired from the Army in 1981 and accepted a position as Deputy Assistant Secretary of State in the Bureau for Refugee Programs and became heavily involved with Africa and the Middle East, leading to an appointment as Deputy UN High Commissioner for Refugees in Geneva. President George W. Bush nominated Dewey to be Assistant Secretary of State for Population, Refugees, and Migration, which he held from 2002 until his retirement in 2005.

I no longer have much information about the people who worked for me during the relatively short time I had the Southeast Asia Branch in the Political/Military Division. There were about 20 personnel in the division when I was there. I no longer recall their names, except for FSO Glazer, Major Robert L. Helvey, whose wife Janet struggled with cancer, and a civilian named Irving M. Zimmerman. Janet Helvey died in October 1975 while I was at the War College.

The Southeast Asia Branch's workload was heavy, and it usually resulted in 10-hour days plus another two hours' commute in heavy traffic. The emphasis was on the military assistance programs to five countries—Burma, Thailand, Laos, Cambodia, and South Vietnam. We monitored those countries' political and military situations and sent any significant changes and recommendations up the command chain. The work became even more hectic in 1975 as the U.S. position in that part of the world collapsed.

Florence and I moved out of Sundown Apartments in late October after finding a three-bedroom house for rent on York Road in Alexandria, Virginia, not far from the apartments. We were only able to rent it for one year, and that turned out to be a blessing as my time at the Pentagon was cut short despite the four-year rule per assignment initiated before I left Fort Bragg in 1973. Our household goods had arrived from Fort Bragg's storage and we were moved in by 17 November. It was hard work since Florence was still helping her sister Mary with the store on Long Island.

The store in North Carolina was not going well, and we decided to close it and bring what we had there to Washington since I was contacted by Air Force Brigadier General Floyd H. Trogdon (1924–2019). He had lived in the command mess compound in Saigon. Trogdon learned from Tiger that Truong had sent several shipments of Vietnamese merchandise to North Carolina. Trogdon's wife wanted to open a McLean, Fairfax County, business, where they lived after he retired in 1974. McLean is a very upscale neighborhood and the home to diplomats, businesspeople, Congress members, and high-ranking officials due to its proximity to Washington, D.C., and the CIA. They wanted to buy all we had in North Carolina if they could pay for it in installments. We agreed that I would start delivering the merchandise to him after closing the store in North Carolina and bringing the inventory to Washington.

I drove to North Carolina on Friday, 29 November. I rented a large truck and loaded the North Carolina inventory—about 15,000 lbs.—and drove back to Alexandria, Virginia, towing the car. I spent Sunday offloading the stock and placing it in the basement. I was utterly exhausted after this trip. The following week we began delivering carloads of merchandise to General Trogdon.

Since arriving in Washington, the best news was on 20 December 1974 when I received selection notification to a Senior Service College. At first, it looked like I would attend the National War College in Washington since the military was still trying to save money by reducing the frequency of permanent changes of station (PCS). I received a letter from the military personnel center on 17 January 1975 asking if I would agree to attend the National War College. While this would keep me in Washington, possibly leading to another assignment in the summer of 1976, I answered yes, but let them know that I would be away until mid-February. The USAWC in Carlisle was my alternative.

The reason for my absence was due to a short visit to my family in Norway. Colonel Dewey had found out I had not been home in about six years, and he demonstrated his empathy by directing me to take a three-week leave to visit my family. Florence came along. I spent two weeks in Norway and then returned to Washington. Florence stayed for a few additional days as my mother had decided to go to the U.S., but her papers were not ready when I left. She stayed with us until early May 1975.

I received a letter from the OPO dated 26 February 1975 stating that their efforts to reduce PCS costs had collapsed and that I would attend the USAWC. Again, this change was good news, and on 12 March, I received a welcome letter from the Commandant, Major General DeWitt C. Smith (1920–2005).

Smith, like Colonel Dewey, had an unusual career. He was a graduate of the University of Maryland. When World War II broke out, he joined the Canadian Army as a private soldier, allegedly using an assumed name so his father would not find him. However, his father found him and brought him back to be drafted into the U.S. Army in 1942 as a private soldier. He was later commissioned as a second lieutenant and served continuously in combat (in General Patton's command) until that war ended. He also served in the Korean War and commanded a brigade in the 1st Infantry Division in Vietnam.

General Smith was Commandant of the USAWC two times—1974–1977 and 1978–1980. After arriving at the USAWC, I grew to like and respect Smith. He had a keen interest in societal problems. Additionally, he was very concerned about the military's proper role in a democracy and he had a better knowledge of history than most.

As the fall of South Vietnam, Cambodia, and Laos approached, the Southeast Asia Branch's work became very hectic. As a result, I spent many nights in my office, getting some sleep on a cot.

The Southeast Asia Branch became heavily involved with the evacuation of Vietnamese nationals, who had worked for the Americans and faced an uncertain future if not evacuated. A U.S. Air Force brigadier in the Philippines was allegedly the individual who took personal responsibility for arranging their evacuation. The evacuation had to take place quietly while Ambassador Martin was in Vietnam, and there was also an attempt to keep the Philippine government from becoming involved. The evacuees were, therefore, sent on to Guam as quickly as possible.

The U.S. also decided to bring out orphans from Vietnam. The first C-5 aircraft leaving Saigon crashed northwest of the city in early April. Half of the passengers were orphans, and the rest were American civilians. My former secretary, Barbara Kavulia, was on the aircraft and died along with many others.

The evacuation of the orphans continued. Most were brought out by military aircraft, but some came by charter flights arranged by civilian organizations. One night in late April or early May, I was at my residence when the Pentagon duty officer called and said a chartered aircraft carrying orphans was coming to California. I asked him what that had to do with me. He said I was the highest-ranking officer from DCSOPS he had been able to locate since it was a weekend. He also said some members of Congress from California had asked for Army assistance. I told him to try to find a flag officer and pass the problem to him. About 20 minutes later, the duty officer called back, telling me he had again been unsuccessful in finding a flag officer. However, he added that some arrangements were needed since the orphan flight would soon arrive in California.

Earlier, I had listened to a speech by President Ford where he stated the government would provide all assistance possible for the orphans. He was probably referring to those arriving via military aircraft and not chartered civilian planes. However, the principle was the same, so, therefore, I issued instructions to U.S. Army Forces Command (FORSCOM) to take all necessary actions to meet the incoming orphan aircraft. These instructions included transportation, medical assistance, and other help. In addition, I directed FORSCOM to deal directly with the local authorities and congressional representatives in the area. A congressman from California called and I told him what instructions I had given FORSCOM and gave him contact information for that command. Then I informed the Pentagon duty officer, describing what I had done.

I arrived at my office early the following day, briefed Colonel Dewey, and read a complimentary newspaper article about the Army's assistance to an unscheduled orphan flight in California. I wore all my ribbons on the uniform that morning, figuring it might help as I had more combat decorations than some generals.

Very soon after I arrived at the Pentagon, I was summoned to the Vice Chief of Staff of the Army's (VCSA) office. Four-star General Walter T. Kerwin Jr., briefly mentioned in chapter 18, was VCSA when the incident I described above happened. He was from Pennsylvania and a graduate of West Point in 1939 as an artillery officer. He served in World War II and Vietnam. As typical for such summons, I believe Colonel Dewey and some supervisors from intervening staff in the Pentagon accompanied me. We all ended up in General Kerwin's office.

Kerwin was reading a newspaper but finally looked up and asked, with a serious demeanor, who was responsible for committing the Army to refugee assistance. I stepped forward, saluted smartly, and told him I had given the tasking. He then asked me directly who had given me that authority. I told him no one had given me such authority, but after the duty officer twice could not locate a flag officer, I used my initiative to task FORSCOM. I also pointed out I had received calls from Congressional legislators from California, as had the Pentagon duty officer.

General Kerwin looked at me for what seemed to be a long time. Finally, he noted with a slight grin that this was probably the first time Bernie (General Bernard W. Rogers 1921–2008, FORSCOM Commander) had received a tasking from a lieutenant colonel.[1] As we were exiting his office, he asked how long I would be at the Pentagon. I answered that I was supposed to report to the USAWC in July as a student. He asked me to say hello to Dee, which I assumed was DeWitt Smith's nickname among his contemporaries.

By early April, it had become evident the NVA would soon overrun South Vietnam. Colonel Tombaugh visited Washington in mid-April and asked me to join him at a nearby hotel for dinner. He was trying to assure that the Vietnamese nationals from the FPJMT who chose to evacuate had sponsors when they arrived in the U.S. and asked if I would help. I promised him that I would and that we would sponsor Truong Thi Nguyen from the command mess, and we also planned to sponsor my secretary Nguyen Thi Ban and her family. That would be six Vietnamese nationals and all we had room for in our three-bedroom home.

I watched the panicky evacuation of Saigon and Da Nang on television. It was a sad ending to our decade-long involvement. It was unavoidable not to think about the troops under my command who had given their lives.

My mother had returned to Norway in early May after we took her on a quick trip to Carlisle, Pennsylvania, so she could see our next duty station. Truong Thi Nguyen arrived on 19 May, and we made a second trip to Carlisle. We learned we would have to live on the local economy since I was the second youngest in the class, and there were post quarters for only more senior students.

We took another trip to Pennsylvania on Memorial Day, and we found a place to live in the small town of Mount Holly Springs, about 15 kilometers south of the USAWC. It was a four-bedroom home owned by a college professor, leaving on a one-year sabbatical to Italy.

Nguyen Thi Ban, 28 years old, her husband, 30, Ban's sister and brother, aged 22 and 18 respectively, and their mother, who was 51, arrived on 29 May. Florence and Truong took them shopping for more suitable shoes and clothing for Washington. I took two days off the following week, trying to find Ban and her family work and a place to live. We found them a home in a Maryland suburb of Washington. We also found a job for Ban at the University of Maryland, for her husband at a bank, and one for Ban's sister. They moved out on 15 June after obtaining driver's licenses for three of them and buying a used car.

We emptied the Long Island store and brought the inventory to Washington. General Trogdon picked up the last load of ceramic and porcelain, plus much of the merchandise from the Long Island store.

The Transportation Corps packed our household goods on 10 July, picked them up on 11 July, and delivered them to Pennsylvania on 13 July. I signed out from the Pentagon on 14 July and turned the branch over to Major Helvey until my replacement arrived. I left the Pentagon after receiving a copy of my perfect OERs from Colonel Dewey and Major General Gerrity, recommending early promotion.

Towards the end of my assignment in the Pentagon, Florence and I received an invitation to Major General Henry Emerson's wedding. He was awaiting promotion to lieutenant general. This invitation was a surprise. The wedding took place on 7 June 1975; his wife was a New York socialite he had met while a cadet at West Point. Her name was Joan Woodside. Unfortunately, Florence and I could not attend as we were getting ready to head for the USAWC and fully involved with settling Vietnamese refugees. I also had to give a briefing at the Special Warfare Center at Fort Bragg on the fall of South Vietnam.

I did attend Emerson's bachelor party, but I did not remain long since I knew few there. Most were general officers or relatives of Joan. I asked to be excused long before the end of the gathering. Emerson walked me to the door. He noted I was unusually solemn and asked me what I thought about his upcoming marriage. I told him I wished them well but noted it would take considerable efforts on his part—now almost 52—to adjust and that I did not know how his wife would react to Army life. He mentioned his upcoming promotion and what he referred to as an unwritten rule that four-star generals be married. I did not say anything but thought it was a weak reason for getting married. The marriage did not work and only lasted about six months.

U.S. Army War College (USAWC), 1975–1976

Carlisle Barracks is a small base (about 2 square kilometers) adjacent to the town of Carlisle and was the USAWC location. Carlisle is about 30 kilometers west of Harrisburg, the capital of Pennsylvania. Carlisle Barracks is the oldest active military base, and most sources reported its establishment in 1776.[2] Before that, it was an encampment for troops taking part in the French and Indian War (Seven Years' War in Europe).

The town of Carlisle became a significant gateway to the Alleghenies and further west. Small forts, known as "Burgs," are located along this route, separated by the distance wagons usually travel in a day. Shippensburg and Chambersburg were the first ones west of Carlisle.

Buildings were constructed at Carlisle Barracks during the Revolutionary War to serve as military depots. The Hessian Powder Magazine, now the Hessian Guardhouse Museum, was built in 1777. Carlisle barracks became a staging area for federal troops in the Whiskey Rebellion in the early 1790s. It was shelled and burned by the Confederate cavalry in 1863.

With Carlisle Barracks no longer needed as a depot, control passed from the War Department to the Department of Interior in 1879 to serve as a school for Native American children (Carlisle Indian Industrial School), beginning its operation in late 1879 and operated until 1918. It was an attempt to integrate the Native American children into American Society. However, it is equally valid to label them political hostages to ensure peaceful behavior by the tribes from which they came. Inside the back gate to Carlisle Barracks is a well-kept graveyard for Native Americans who died at the school.

The U.S. Army reclaimed Carlisle Barracks in 1918. They established a General Hospital as a rehabilitation center for 4,000 soldiers returning from France. A Medical Field Service School was established in 1920 and developed various innovations based on WWI lessons. The Medical Field Service School moved to Fort Sam Huston in Texas in 1946, and until 1951 six Army schools were located at Carlisle Barracks.

The USAWC moved to Carlisle Barracks in 1951. It was established in 1903 and had been in Washington before its move, except for one year at Fort Leavenworth. The Strategic Studies Institute and the Military History Institute were added in the 1950s and 1960s, respectively.

The USAWC prepared selected officers for high command or top staff positions. Over the years, many Army graduates eventually became generals or served in senior policy positions. Major General Smith's welcoming letter outlined the functions of the USAWC. He did it so well that I have chosen to borrow a portion of a paragraph from that letter.

> Your studies will be designed to do two principal things. First, to stimulate your inquiry into the conduct of national security affairs in a dynamic world through an examination of national and international elements of power, their impact on the strategic considerations which affect our national security, and the military policies and programs which evolve. Secondly, to enhance your professional development by providing the added knowledge, perception, and skills which you will need for the challenging tasks which lie ahead.

I signed in at the USAWC on 28 July. The classes were to begin on 4 August. Since the first days were for administrative processing, I asked for, and received, two days' delay in starting the school for travel to New York to meet my sister Anna and brother-in-law Birger who were arriving for a visit. We picked them up, along with my brother Ole, on 4 August and returned to Pennsylvania that evening. I began attending college on 6 August.

The class consisted predominately of Army officers (188), primarily lieutenant colonels, while a number were colonels. All branches of the Army were represented. There were also 16 from the other services and eight from other government agencies. The source of commission for the vast majority was the ROTC (117), followed by Officer Candidate School (OCS) (47) and Service Academies (32). Most had college degrees and had attended the C&GSC or equivalent.

Most instructions took place in seminar groups consisting of about 24 students, while formal lectures took place in a large auditorium (Bliss Hall), large enough for students, spouses, and staff. Wives were encouraged to attend unclassified lectures.

While there were student evaluation reports, they contained no numerical grading and no class standings. Each student was required to write on national or international security issues, and travel was authorized. I wrote an article on North Sea oil, which required a trip to England, Belgium, and Norway in early spring 1976. An unclassified version of it was published in *Parameter* in 1976, the War College periodical. As far as I know, it was the only student paper that made it to the journal. I also wrote an article on the deterrence of conventional Soviet aggression, which the War College labeled outstanding and suitable for publication in *Parameters* or *Military Review*.

When I arrived at the USAWC, I was designated seminar group leader and was briefed on my duties, which lasted until the New York field trip, after which another student took over. The one-week field trip to New York was to have the students visit the U.N., meet with leaders of major corporations, and receive a briefing by the New York Police Department on law enforcement problems in this large metropolitan area. Wives were encouraged to accompany students and participate in the activities.

Another field trip took place in the spring, this time to Washington. The purpose was to meet with legislators and various government departments to learn about their work and problems. There were no wives on this trip since some of the sessions were classified.

I received a request in January 1976 from Senator Edward Kennedy (1932–2009), who wanted to see me. I took a day off from my studies to drive to his office in the U.S. Senate. He wanted to discuss the subject of MIAs in Vietnam. I briefly shook his hand as he headed for a meeting or a vote on the Senate floor. I ended up talking to his staff. Their interest cooled when I stated I did not believe any prisoners were left alive in Vietnam. The fact they had announced this to the world repeatedly made it highly unlikely they would abruptly change their minds even if there were some that they had not returned to us.

I was admitted to Carlisle Hospital in mid-January with stomach pains. They evacuated me to Walter Reed in Washington. It was determined to be a stomach ulcer and the beginning of problems that would plague me until my retirement. I was at Walter Reed for about 10 days before returning.

There were more social gatherings at the War College than in any other of my assignments. They ranged from small intimate dinners or lunches to large formal parties such as the Infantry Ball, Marine Ball, Artillery Ball, etc. These large formal celebrations required evening dress uniforms while the dinners and lunches were in civilian clothes. These activities averaged two per week. We attended many of these social activities but regretted some because of Florence's medical conditions.

There was also mandatory attendance for military or civilian officials' visits that we might have known or involved with our secondary specialty. In addition, we usually attended the luncheons following their speech to the class.

During my family's visit, Florence had a bad fall and ended up in the hospital for more than three weeks. She had a back fracture and had to wear a back and neck brace until December. Florence's mother arrived and spent several months with us after my family visitors left. She came back around Christmas and stayed for another six weeks.

Shortly after our arrival, Truong received her driver's license in July, passing the driving test on her first attempt. We purchased a slightly used 1974 Chevrolet Vega that she used to commute to Joan Lee Beauty Culture School in Carlisle, from which she graduated in May 1976. Her instructors said she was the best student they'd had in a long time.

It appeared my next station would be in Europe after graduation. I was hoping it would be with troops, preferably as a deputy brigade commander.

General Alexander Haig (1923–2010) and his wife, Patricia (nee Fox), visited the USAWC in late 1975 or early 1976. There was a small intimate dinner at the commandant's quarters, and Florence and I attended along with six or seven others who had some connection to General Haig. I had never met the general before. I assumed my inclusion was because I was due to be stationed in Europe. The conversation during dinner and the cocktail period that followed was wide-ranging.

Eventually, it came around to Haig's classmates from West Point, including Henry Emerson and his recent marriage. This discussion allowed General Smith to drag me into the conversation as he mentioned I had served with Emerson three times. I told them that Emerson was an outstanding leader of troops in combat, the best I had ever observed. Haig then asked me about Emerson's recent marriage and the possibility it would last. I told him I wished it would be successful, but it would be difficult to manage since Emerson had been a bachelor for 52 years.

Since I worked at Haig's headquarters for three years, it is appropriate to briefly describe his career up to the time I met him, using public sources. The segment on Haig here and in the next chapter is also beneficial for anyone unfamiliar with his career. This description is in no way all-inclusive. Haig was a very influential and controversial national figure in the last half of the 20th century and had already become well known in the U.S.

Haig was born in Bala Cynwyd, an affluent suburb of Philadelphia.[3] His first attempt to enter West Point failed (one teacher allegedly commented: "Al is definitely not West Point material"). He was eventually admitted under a congressional appointment in 1944, arranged by his uncle. Haig was in the lower half of his class in 1947, the same class as Lieutenant General Henry Emerson, and was considered unlikely to be the first in the class to make general, according to a former assistant superintendent.

When looking at Haig's career, it is evident that he was a hugely ambitious officer who took advantage of every opportunity to advance his career. He married Patricia Fox, the daughter of Lieutenant General Alonzo Patrick Fox (1895–1984), Deputy Chief of Staff to General of the Army Douglas MacArthur (1880–1964). In 1950, he became General Fox's aide. Later, he became an aide to MacArthur's Chief of Staff, General Edward Almond (1892–1979).

In their obituaries (on the internet), the *Guardian* and U.S. news state that Haig's brief combat was controversial both in Korea, where he served on staff, and Vietnam. His citations did not always square with the conditions described on the ground. His service in Vietnam was as commander of a battalion in the 1st Infantry Division, and later, after promotion to colonel, he commanded a brigade in that division.

Between his service in Korea and Vietnam, he spent a short time at West Point and served in an armored battalion in Germany. After promotion to major, he joined the European Command Headquarters, where he became deeply involved in NATO's cost-sharing issue. Returning to the U.S., he received his master's degree at Georgetown University in Washington, D.C.

By this time, Haig became increasingly involved with the political side of national security. After obtaining his advanced degree, he came to the Pentagon, where his father-in-law now served. In 1963, Haig became a military assistant to Army Secretary Stephen Ailes (1912–2001). When Cyrus Vance (1917–2002), Ailes's predecessor, became deputy to Defense Secretary Robert McNamara, Haig also moved to the DOD. He attended the USAWC in 1965–1966.

When he returned from Vietnam, he went to West Point to be a commander of a regiment of the Corps of Cadets under Brigadier General Bernard W. Rogers, who had also served in the 1st Infantry Division.

In 1969, Haig became an assistant to National Security Adviser Henry Kissinger. In 1970, he became deputy assistant to the president for national security affairs. He was promoted to brigadier general in 1969 and major general in 1972. In January 1973, he became VCSA, skipping lieutenant general. In making this appointment, President Nixon passed over 240 generals senior to Haig.

General Haig served only four months as VCSA when he moved to the White House, becoming President Nixon's Chief of Staff. Haig allegedly worked out various options for securing a pardon for Nixon by his successor, President Gerald Ford. He oversaw the transition between Nixon and Ford. In his book *Haig: The General's Progress*, Haig's friend and biographer Roger Morris maintained that when Ford pardoned Nixon, he, in effect, also pardoned Haig.

Ford appointed Donald Rumsfeld as his Chief of Staff, and Haig became Supreme Allied Commander Europe (SACEUR) and commander-in-chief of the U.S. Command Europe in 1974, serving in that position until 1979. His involvement in the political scene had not ended as will become apparent.

To my chagrin, I received orders for SHAPE in late February 1976. However, since my article on North Sea oil was incomplete, it had no influence. And I do not believe my meeting with Haig at the War College caused this assignment. The most likely explanation is that General Smith recommended me to Haig, but that is only speculation.

My projected arrival date at SHAPE was 26 May. Furthermore, I received a letter from the officer I would replace in early March, where he briefed me on some of the peculiarities involved in an assignment to Belgium. His name was Lieutenant Colonel Otto R. Schultz, an Air Defense officer.

We still had many framed paintings and temple rubbings from Vietnam and Cambodia. Truong was able to sell them all in installments to a Washington store shortly before departing the War College.

We purchased a Mercury Marquis to take to Europe and brought it to New York for shipment to Rotterdam, about 30 days before our departure. Florence and Truong followed in the Vega to get all of us back. We also sold the Vega to a professor at the War College, again on installments, but kept it until we were ready to leave.

We also took a quick trip to North Carolina to purchase two houses we planned to rent out. They were in the Cottonade and Summerhill areas.

My orders for SHAPE, dated 19 March 1976, changed my reporting date to 7 July. Major General Smith wished to see me on 7 June 1976. The primary purpose was to provide me with a copy of my student evaluation signed by his assistant, Brigadier General Edward B. Atkeson, a graduate of the Staunton Military Academy in Virginia. DeWitt C. Smith added a paragraph in pen where he stated I was one of the classes outstanding student officers and had high potential as a leader and strategist.

We drove to New York on 16 July in a rental car. Ed Torres, who now had a limousine service, took us to JFK airport the following day. We were unable to catch the scheduled flight because Truong's visa for Belgium lacked a stamp. The U.S. Army had designated her a household member, but we had not informed the Belgian Embassy, only hand-carried the document, and that now needed a stamp. We booked a flight for the following day, drove to the Belgian Consulate, obtained the stamp, drove back to the airport, notified SHAPE about the delay, and stayed in a nearby motel for the night.

CHAPTER 24

SHAPE, USAWC, and Retirement

SHAPE, 1976–1979

We arrived in Brussels on 18 July 1976 and there was a sedan there to pick us up. The vehicle took us to a hotel in the town of Mons. This town is a one-hour drive south of Brussels and less than three hours from Paris. We were to live in this hotel for up to 60 days.

The Army personnel center at SHAPE had told us we would live on the local economy because we had our full allotment of furnishings and household goods, and there were three of us. It would be some time before the housing authorities could find suitable quarters. The hotel we lived at was excellent, and they served delicious French food—all paid for by a Temporary Living Allowance, which was more than adequate. I also took a train to Rotterdam to pick up our car.

I was offered leave between stations but elected not to take it. Instead, I requested two weeks' leave while staying at the hotel to visit Norway and another two weeks in December to spend the first Christmas with my family.

We used the first couple of weeks at Mons for administrative matters, such as getting ID cards for all three, having our driver licenses approved by the Belgians, and opening a Belgian checking account for paying local bills. Truong was officially designated as a member of the household by NATO in September. We also elected to have our mail forwarded to SHAPE and prioritized new address notifications to all those who owed us money in the U.S.

My assignment was as a staff officer in the Policy Section. I signed into the headquarters on 20 July and met Colonel Brumham, the British section chief. The Plans and Policy Branch, the next layer in the military hierarchy, was headed by a U.S. brigadier general, which I will discuss later.

Having taken care of most administrative matters, we were ready for our leave since hotel living was getting old fast. However, before we could begin our vacation, we drove to Brussels to get a visa for Truong's trip to Norway, which started on 23 July. We had to do that each time we visited Norway since Truong still only had a green card. However, it was just a formality that was easy to overcome.

After a relaxing visit to Norway, we returned to our hotel hideout in Mons on Sunday 3 August. I contacted the housing office the following day, and they told me our household goods had arrived and were in temporary storage waiting for us to sign for our quarters.

We ended up with a large home. I believe this was the home used previously by our sponsor, Lieutenant Colonel Otto R. Schultz, and his wife, Sally. They and their four children had lived there since they arrived at SHAPE from Germany. He was to depart for Carlisle, and I believe he may have left by the time we returned from Norway.

The home was in the village of Chièvres, across the road from an old fighter airfield. The Germans built this airfield when they occupied Belgium in 1914. It was subsequently taken over by the Belgian Air Force. We saw no activity on that field when we were there. Chièvres was near the U.S. Post Exchange and Commissary, and the drive to SHAPE was only 20 minutes.

The home was large, with a circular driveway and a separate garage. It had five bedrooms on the second floor with two bathrooms, one bathroom on the bottom floor, a large living room, and a formal dining room. The living and dining rooms had fireplaces. There was a second living room or den on the first floor and a kitchen. In short, it was our most substantial home up to then. I recollect the monthly rent was about 14,000 Belgian Francs. The cost would fluctuate with the dollar-BF exchange rate but remained in the range of $360 to $450 monthly for the time we were there.

We were completely moved in by late August, but there was some damage to our household goods and many things on the packing list were missing. We did not get all this settled until the late summer of 1977. We drove to a PX in Germany to obtain curtains for the large windows and chandeliers for the downstairs. We also purchased wardrobes because of the lack of closets in the bedrooms. We bought a new car from a dealership in Mons—a Mazda 818—delivered on 7 November because it was too difficult to get parts for the Mercury.

My niece Bjørg was the first in my family to come for a visit on 29 August. She stayed with us for a couple of weeks before we drove her to join her spouse in Kitzingen, Germany. The ferries from Norway came to Amsterdam in the Netherlands, so it took a full day or more to pick up and bring relatives to our place. Anna and Birger visited twice, as did my mother. All of Anna's children visited, some multiple times. Besides this, Florence, Truong, and I made three trips to Norway. The one at the end of 1976 was for only seven days. When we returned, Truong learned her mother in Vietnam had died. Her father had died a year before she left Vietnam.

Even though I had an opportunity to spend time with my family, I disliked my time at SHAPE. It was not because the work was hard or complicated; on the contrary, I felt I was wasting my time and abilities. The stomach problems resulting in my hospitalization at Walter Reed in Washington while at Carlisle returned, and

I was hospitalized twice at the SHAPE hospital for bleeding ulcers. Ulcers were considered to be caused by stress, but there was no severe stress in my life after 1969.

Furthermore, it was determined in the late 1980s that stress and spicy foods do not cause peptic ulcers. Instead, they are caused by bacterial infections (termed medically as *H. pylori Bacteria*). Since the military assumed the ulcers were caused by stress, it, along with hypertension, had a devastating effect on an officer's chances of obtaining command. I did not realize this until later, but before the real cause was known. I was treated at the Durham Medical Clinic in Carlisle in the late 1980s. They gave me antibiotics for about a month and my ulcer problem ended.

Florence also had to make four visits to Landstuhl because of blockages to her carotid arteries. On her first hospitalization in 1978, they opened and cleaned out the left carotid artery. She was in the hospital for about two weeks, and then she had to return after a month to ensure all was well. Truong stayed with her, living in a hospital guest room. Florence had to return to Landstuhl in February 1979 to have the right carotid cleaned out. Again, she was there for more than two weeks and she had to return in April to ensure there were no problems. Truong went along as before.

The Policy Section consisted of two offices with an administrative office between them. Colonel Peter H. Brumham from the British Army was the section chief when I arrived. He left in 1978, and another British colonel named Dennis W. Shuttleworth took over. The last British section chief was Colonel Brian H. Marciandi, who arrived in 1978/79.

In my office, there was, besides me, a Norwegian naval captain, Finn M. Moseng. He was married to a British woman named Marie. Then there was U.S. Army Lieutenant Colonel Richard L. Hopkins. Finally, a U.S. Marine colonel named Earl F. Pierson was the third officer in the office until Hopkins was assigned. Then, unfortunately, Earl came down with terminal cancer and departed early for the U.S.

A U.S. Navy commander, a UK wing commander, a German Army lieutenant colonel, and a Turkish Army lieutenant colonel named Hilmi Ozkok occupied the second office. Hilmi was married to a French woman whose name was Emel. Hilmi eventually became Commander-in-Chief of the Turkish Armed Forces.

My family and I made good friends with the Moseng family, who had arrived at SHAPE about the same time that we did. We also developed a close friendship with Hilmi and his wife.[1]

The Policy Section was part of the Plans and Policy Branch, consisting of the Force Programs Section and the Nuclear Policy Section. Brigadier General Robert L. Schweitzer (1928–2000) headed the Plans and Policy Branch. Schweitzer was at SHAPE with his five children and his wife, Nancy. He was an armor officer, and General Haig brought him to SHAPE from Germany, where he commanded an armored cavalry regiment. Schweitzer had served several times in Vietnam as a major and lieutenant colonel. His obituary mentions six tours, but some were cut short because of his many wounds. He served with Haig on the staff of the 1st Infantry Division, where he earned a DSC. He was also deputy commander of a cavalry regiment. Schweitzer's other combat decorations included three Silver Stars, a Distinguished Flying Cross, four Bronze Stars for valor, and seven Purple Hearts, one of which he later gave to President Regan after the assassination attempt.

In Chapter 18, I mentioned a quote from Colonel David Johnson's book. He says that my measured approach to every situation helped to dampen Colonel Emerson's temper and impulsiveness on many occasions. I was often used for the same purpose in the Policy Branch of SHAPE—called several times by Colonel R. J. Toner or Major F. X. Brennan to come and talk to the general. These episodes happened most often when the general had neglected to take some of his strong medications for the wounds he suffered in Vietnam and possibly his exposure to Agent Orange. Some of the severe effects of this agent were then beginning to be known.

Above the Policy Branch in the SHAPE hierarchy was the Plans and Policy Division, headed by Air Vice-Marshal P. R. Harding, RAF. This corresponded to DCSOPS in the Pentagon. I had few dealings with him, but he was the one who pinned on my eagles when promoted in an official ceremony with Florence and Truong present.

I did not have frequent dealings with Schweitzer in 1976, but all that changed during the last 32 months of my tour. Colonel R. J. Toner was Schweitzer's deputy. He had taken over from another Air Force Colonel named Glenn A. Carus. I am not sure when this change occurred. Major F. X. Brennan was Colonel Toner's assistant. Brennan's wife's name was Maureen, House Speaker Tip O'Neill's (1912–1994) niece.

My job description was as liaison officer to the French High Command. France had withdrawn from the military side of NATO, which caused SHAPE to move from the outskirts of Paris to Mons, Belgium. Except for a courtesy visit, I had no dealings with the French headquarters. The French had a liaison mission on a different floor in our building if I needed to see them, which was infrequent. However, I authored and coordinated a significant update to the French government and Allied Command Europe agreement.

I had been at SHAPE a few months when I received a call from the Policy Branch that SACEUR wanted to see me. I grabbed my notebook and headed for General Haig's office. To my surprise, I met Charles W. Dyke, who had been S-3 of 2/327 in Vietnam in 1965. He was now a brigadier general and working in Haig's office. After a few pleasantries, he told me Haig wanted a message drafted to another general or high official. I asked him why he and his legion of assistants could not do that. Bill Dyke (Bill was his nickname based on his middle name) asked me to step out into the corridor, where he mentioned Haig was looking for a new speechwriter and that I was a candidate. Bill told me that knowing I could treat it accordingly.

I did not want such a job and took the hint from Dyke. Therefore, I failed to use my best writing abilities and was not selected.

Lieutenant General Emerson came to SHAPE in 1976 to brief his classmate Haig on the fall maneuvers in Germany. Emerson's concept was to use his 18th Airborne Corps on the northern German plains. This placement was questionable for a corps with extraordinarily little armor. Nevertheless, General Haig voiced no criticism and I do not know what happened. Emerson and his aide visited our quarters that evening but could not stay for dinner because he had a busy schedule. That was the last time I saw him before his retirement, about six months later.

In the second and third years at SHAPE, I became the SHAPE coordinator for the Short-Term and Long-Term Defense Measures. These were initiatives launched by President Carter and were, of course, related to burden-sharing. The fact that I, as a lieutenant colonel, received the assignment demonstrates the feeling at SHAPE about its importance. I made several trips to NATO Headquarters in Brussels for meetings on the above subject, a couple of times in the company of Schweitzer, but more often alone.

Representatives from other countries at SHAPE provided inputs to the reports I prepared. It required an awful lot of coordination, but I was not assigned others to work with me.

It appeared to my co-workers and me that General Haig was preparing to become the Republican candidate for the presidential campaign in 1980. He made frequent visits to the U.S. in late 1978 or early 1979. As a result, my physical location changed temporarily to the Force Programs Section of the Policy Branch (across the hallway from Brigadier General Schweitzer's office). Here I had the help of two officers to prepare draft speeches for Haig that he planned to deliver to various organizations in the U.S. At times, what we wrote came back for changes and often caused us to work all night. I never thought it was right to use Army personnel in this manner.

In this period, I also became involved in trying to keep Portugal within the alliance. I made two or three trips to Lisbon, one with Brigadier General Schweitzer, for discussions with the U.S. Embassy and Portuguese officials. We had to change planes in Madrid. I went through the control points, but Schweitzer had troubles, forcing me to go back to help him. He was in uniform with his correct rank, but his ID card indicated he was a lieutenant colonel.

I vouched for his identity. He told me later he had never taken the time to obtain a new ID card. Schweitzer was a difficult officer to work for, and we had many arguments, but we respected each other. When I was on leave in Norway, he called me twice to get my opinion on minor issues. It usually dealt with the defense measures or Portugal. Once, he could not reach me because I was in one of the cabins, so he had Finn Moseng call the Norwegian police to find me. They showed up at my mother's home and caused a considerable commotion among her neighbors. This call dealt with Portugal, but it was not essential and could have waited until I returned.

In many ways, Schweitzer was a kind individual. He and his wife held a party for the Policy Branch officers at his house on 26 July 1978. When he learned that my mother was visiting us, he insisted she attend. Schweitzer walked out on the sidewalk to meet us as we drove up. He opened the door for my mother and helped her exit the car. Then Schweitzer escorted her into the house, introducing her in a short gracious speech. When we left, he walked my mother to the car and opened the door for her.

In early April 1978, Florence, Truong, and I took a short visit to the U.S. Truong had to renew her immigration papers. We tried to do this in Germany, but we needed to do it in Washington or Philadelphia. Florence also wanted to visit her mother. I came along to check on the rental homes in North Carolina. We picked up a rental car in New York and drove to Philadelphia, where the renewal of the immigration papers only took about an hour. Then we drove to Fayetteville, where we stopped for a day. After that, we drove back to New York, where I took a flight to Brussels, where we had left our car. I was only away six days, but Florence and Truong stayed another week in New York before returning.

I received notification on 28 December 1978 that I was on the list for promotion to colonel. This list was slow in appearing because the active Army's size had continued its decline from 1972. I was the only officer at SHAPE on the list. I received many congratulatory letters from officers I had worked for, including Major General Alexander Weyand (1928–2011), the S-3 of the 2/6th Battle Group in Berlin 18 years earlier. I also received a long letter from Major General DeWitt Smith.

Smith's letter began with the sentence, "You may or may not know that I was resurrected from the retired ranks 'busted' one grade and returned here to Carlisle for one more stint as Commandant." He was aware that both Florence and I had struggled with health issues at SHAPE. This letter was to a few selected officers he had come to know. Smith wanted to know what changes we would like to see in the curriculum. He mentioned that changes should only be thoughtful and purposeful. He noted that pendulum swings to meet perceived, short-term needs are generally disruptive and unlike to achieve fundamental needs.

"And education, more than training, is our responsibility." He wrote that he needed our help but wanted to keep the subject close since he did not consult the entire alumni.

I wrote Smith an answer and had it typed by my British secretary but delayed sending it until 19 February when I was sure Florence's operation was successful. I gave him my candid views on the issues. At the end of the letter, I noted I had received notification from the colonel's branch at OPO that I was considered for a Strategic Studies Institute (SSI) assignment at Carlisle. There was also talk of sending me to the U.S. Army Combat Development Command.

It resulted in a quick call from Smith, apologizing for not having mentioned this fact. He said that a project had come up, "right up my alley," and complemented the curriculum work. I stressed I did not want an assignment to teaching departments because it was not my strong side. Since I had told him earlier, Smith said I would go to SSI and only teach when I felt like it.

Brigadier General Schweitzer asked me about my next assignment on a drive to NATO headquarters in early May 1979. I told him about Smith's letter. Schweitzer did not think a tour at the USAWC would benefit my career and said he would see if he could get me assigned to the Armored Corps at Fort Hood in an operations slot. When the orders came, they were for assignment to the War College and they did not mention SSI. While I noted this, I felt Smith would have called me if there had been a change. Schweitzer said he would keep trying to bring me to Fort Hood, even if it meant I had to spend some time at Carlisle before arrangements could occur.

Before my promotion, my name appeared on the Combat Arms Command Selection Board list on 24 April 1979. I was designated an alternate for command in the Psychological Operations category, despite never serving in any psychological assignments. This shows that the specialty forced on me in 1973 had, in fact, caused severe damage to my career. There were four active Psychological Operations Groups in the U.S. Army in 1979, but only one airborne, my old nemesis the 4th. That position became open for a new commander about every two years, and that was a severe limitation on an alternate being chosen.

If they had designated me for command in my primary MOS, infantry, my chances for selection would have been much higher. If we eliminate the armored and cavalry divisions, there were eight infantry divisions with three brigades each. That makes 24 brigade command slots available every two years. To those, one can add the four active Special Forces Groups and the Ranger Regiment. That means that 14 or 15 colonel command slots in my primary MOS were coming open each year.[2]

While I felt this selection was terrible news, our time at SHAPE was quickly ending, and the activities forced me to delay doing anything about it until the following year. A German officer would take over the home where we lived, along with most of the things we had purchased. The Belgian packers were at the house for three days, doing the best job we had ever experienced. We spent a day cleaning, and on 14 June, we moved into the hotel we had lived in when we came to SHAPE. We drove to Norway on 26 June for a three-week leave. When we returned, I took the car to Rotterdam for shipment to Baltimore. We were booked on a flight to the U.S. on 16 July.

I received perfect OERs while at SHAPE, all recommending early brigade command and stating I was prime general officer material. My last visit with Schweitzer was at a ceremony when he awarded me my first Legion of Merit.

It may be appropriate to briefly mention the continuous career of two people I worked for at SHAPE, General Haig and Brigadier General Schweitzer. There was an assassination attempt in 1979 on General Haig in Mons as he was driving to NATO. The Red Army Faction had planted a mine under a bridge on the route he always used. Haig was not injured, but three of his bodyguards in a car that followed sustained wounds.

Both Haig and Schweitzer left SHAPE in 1979. Haig had already announced his retirement in January that year. Most had expected him to run for the presidency, but he entered private employment, and a few months later, he had a heart bypass operation. Nevertheless, President Reagan picked him as his Secretary of State in early 1981.

John Hinckley Jr. attempted to assassinate President Reagan outside the Hilton hotel in Washington, D.C., on 30 March 1981. The Secret Service rushed the injured president to the George Washington University Hospital. In the turmoil that followed, Alexander Haig used the poorly chosen words *I am in charge here*. He must have had a temporary lapse in his recall of the Constitution. He was the fourth in the succession line after Vice President George H. W. Bush, Speaker of the House Tip O'Neill, and President Pro Tempore of the Senate, Senator Strom Thurmond. The only one of the above not present in the White House was Vice President Bush, who was on his way.

There was much confusion about what Haig meant by his statement without waiting to determine that President Reagan could not carry out his duties. It may also have led the Soviets to alert their forces, knowing that Haig was a hardliner. It sounded to many like a putsch, which was probably also how it was viewed by the Soviets. The confusion eventually ended, but Haig's view of the Soviets continued to be a problem in an Administration where he did not have many friends.

It was, therefore, not a surprise that he submitted his resignation on 26 June 1982. Haig hinted on his departure that the reason was policy differences within the Administration. President Reagan announced his acceptance of Haig's resignation that same afternoon, also without mentioning any reasons. Reagan also stated he had nominated George Shultz to be Haig's replacement. Therefore, it remained unclear to many whether the resignation was at Haig's initiative or forced on him.

His resignation as Secretary of State was not the end of Haig's political ambitions. He entered the Republican primary for the 1988 election. He did very poorly in the early primary states, abandoned his campaign, and endorsed Senator Bob Dole. Haig and George H. W. Bush had apparently never had a good relationship. This came through in statements by Haig after the endorsement of Dole. In the end, Bush won the presidential election, which also brought Haig's political ambition to an end. He became head of a consulting firm, served as a director of businesses experiencing problems, and was frequently seen on TV.

Brigadier General Robert L. Schweitzer also arrived in Washington, D.C., in 1979. I believe I only talked to him once or twice on the telephone, and I met him in the Walter Reed Hospital parking lot in late 1980. Although I was depressed at the War College, I was always afraid Schweitzer would ask me to join him at the White House, but he never did. As a major general, he was the senior military adviser to the National Security Council about the same time as his mentor Alexander Haig became Secretary of State. Both had similar feelings about the danger posed by the Soviet Union. Schweitzer lost his job in 1981 because of a speech to the Association of the United States Army. It became known as the "drift toward war" presentation. He claimed the Soviets were on the move and were ready to strike. He described the danger as the greatest ever faced by the U.S.

The White House described the speech as "off the wall," and Major General Schweitzer was reassigned to the Pentagon the day following his remarks. He served in various positions in the Pentagon until he retired as a lieutenant general in 1987. His first marriage to Nancy, who we met at SHAPE, ended in a divorce, and Schweitzer married Marie. He had four sons and one daughter from the first marriage. Schweitzer died at Walter Reed Hospital from cancer in September 2000.

U.S. Army War College, 1979–1983

The flight to the U.S. was via London, where we had a plane change. We arrived in New York at 2000 hours the same day, rented a car, and spent the night with Florence's family before heading to Carlisle Barracks. Our arrival at Carlisle Barracks was on the afternoon of 17 July. My first stop was at the War College's main office to sign in. There I learned my presence was not required until 27 July when I would meet General Smith. After that news, we signed in at the USAWC Guest House, telling them we would head to North Carolina in a few days but return in about a week.

This 10-day delay was welcome news. It gave us time to take care of some essential things. We did not expect our car to arrive in Baltimore until the second half of August, so we purchased a used station wagon and a van. We drove the station wagon to North Carolina, where we stopped two days while placing one empty house for sale and instructing the realtor not to extend or relist the second house. We had an additional home that Passailaigue rented. We visited him and asked that he let us know a month before he left.

We returned to Carlisle on the evening of 25 July and checked into the post guest house pending my meeting with Major General Smith and assignment of quarters.

Friday 27 July 1979 was undoubtedly the worst day of my career. It concluded the bad career-oriented news, starting with the U.S. doctor at SHAPE telling me in early 1978 that the ulcer problem could adversely affect my career. Later in 1978, I was selected as alternate command of a Psyop group instead of a brigade in my primary specialty. These events had already caused me much disappointment before the meeting with Major General Smith.

It was less than a five-minute walk from the guest house to the first floor of the main War College building, and I reported to Major General Smith's secretary five minutes before my scheduled time. I was surprised to find Colonel Harry G. Summers also waiting to see the general.

The secretary brought us into DeWitt Smith's office at the appointed time. He rose from his chair and shook our hands, welcoming us to the USAWC, noting this was the second time he had done so for me. Then, after a few minutes of small talk, he got down to business. He mentioned first that Harry would be assigned to SSI to handle a project on the Vietnam War, not an easy task. Then he turned to me and said that I would go to the Department of National and International Security Studies (DNISS). In addition to teaching in that department, I would find myself heavily involved in curriculum changes.

I did not say anything. How do you tell a major general, an officer I respected and admired, that he was breaking promises made about a month earlier and do so in front of another officer? It would have been better if Smith had seen us separately. Instead, Summers asked me to join him in the coffee shop, where we talked primarily about the last months in the FPJMT. My mind was not on that subject at all but on the broken promise.

After the coffee call, I went back to General Smith's office, but he had left for the day, and I was told he was scheduled to be in Washington most of the following week. I was beginning to believe the joint appointment was no accident because he knew I would not challenge him in front of Summers.

I then saw the deputy commandant and caught him as he was about to leave the office for the day. I have forgotten his name and do not know whether he was military or civilian since he was in civilian clothes. I explained the situation to him and asked if he knew whether the project Smith had labeled as "right up my alley" was the same project now assigned to Colonel Summers. He answered that it was the same project as far as he knew. He told me that Major General Smith had been ordered by his superiors to assign the task to Colonel Summers.

I then told him that General Smith was fully aware that I did not want to end up in a teaching department, and he had assured me that would not happen, and I would be assigned to SSI and only teach when I felt like it. The deputy stated he knew nothing about that matter, but the change probably came about because of Summers's assignment.

I proceeded to the second floor to see Colonel Robert J. Gerard. I had forgotten it was lunchtime and a Friday. I had known Bob since I was a student when he was assigned to the Directorate of Academic Affairs. I wanted to tell him I had arrived and had been assigned to his department. Gerard's office was empty, and I saw no other officers in the department. I wrote Bob a message and stuck it in his downstairs mailbox.

I returned to the guest house to let Florence and Truong know what had happened. They suggested I call OPO to have my assignment changed. I talked to a colonel in the assignment branch, explained what had happened, and asked if the Institute of Land Warfare position at the Combat Development Command was still open. I was told they still had an opening for a colonel in that organization but noted that the Army would not allow two PCSs in one year unless it was an emergency.

I then walked to the Carlisle Barracks personnel office, close to the guest house. Unfortunately, they were busy processing new students. Still, I had a lengthy conversation with the senior NCO about my problem. He told me I had incurred a three-year military service obligation when I accepted the promotion to colonel and an additional one year in my latest PCS from overseas.

I told him the information he provided worsened my situation and asked him what he suggested I do. He then repeated what OPO had said to me about only one PCS allowed in one year. He told me that if I had decided to retire at the earliest opportunity, I should ask for a one-year extension to the tour at Carlisle and then retire in 1983. If that were denied and I accepted another assignment, I would not be able to retire until the summer of 1984.

Finally, he noted that I could request a release from my current posting in the summer of 1980. He doubted such a petition would be approved by the commandant and the Army unless they considered the new job critical. I thanked the NCO and headed back to the guest house.

That night Florence, Truong, and I walked the short distance to the officers' club to eat. After the meal, we headed back to the guest house. There were a couple of messages waiting for me. One was from housing requesting that we sign for our assigned quarters on Monday.

These quarters were on the ridge behind the War College, down the street from the commandants' quarters. Most of the houses in this area were small duplexes usually assigned to students. When I signed for our place, I was informed that more substantial quarters would not be available until the following year, and we could move at that time if we desired. The second message was from transportation informing me that our household goods would arrive on Thursday 2 August.

It was not much of a weekend as I was highly disappointed and depressed at the events that had unfolded. Florence and Truong tried to cheer me up by saying it was the Lord who had brought us back to Carlisle for some reason that we could only see in the future. To get out of the guest house, we went to an auction on Saturday. We took most of our meals at the officers' club while waiting for our quarters and household goods.

My first day of work at the college was Monday 6 August. I had met with Colonel Bob Gerard the previous week, and he told me what I would be doing during the academic year. My assignment and title were as Director of International Security Studies for Western Europe.

My duties in the department were, first, to teach and supervise one seminar group. Second, I would be the department's representative on the Curriculum Development Group. This group was chaired by Doctor Charles M. Hersh, Director of Academic Affairs. It functioned from Major General Smith's departure in the summer of 1980 and lasted for my whole tour of duty. Third, I would oversee the Washington Field Trip and its complicated coordination, with frequent changes. Fourth, I was the National Security Seminar (NSS) coordinator, a three-day annual event for students and invited guests. Its principal function was to examine current national security issues. Finally, I was the sponsor of the German International Fellow and his family, who attended the War College each year. This was also a time-consuming job for my whole family, but a pleasant one.

I was assigned a corner office on the second floor with an excellent view of the main entry gate and the street. My secretary for approximately the first 12–18 months was Kay Pressler. She was an exceedingly kind individual and an outstanding secretary. That is undoubtedly the reason she was stolen from me.

The social life described in the segment dealing with my year as a student was very active. I was expected to participate in all activities having to do with Europe and national security. Then there were travels to Europe to attend conferences or coordinate certain aspects of our mutual security concerns. I believe there were five such trips while I served there.

Florence and Truong also opened their business in 1979, and it appeared so promising that they rented a store in Carlisle in November 1979. Their activities involved me in the evenings and on weekends.

Discussion with Major General Smith

I had a couple of talks with Major General DeWitt Smith in early 1980 as he was getting ready to leave. In one such event, when we were alone, I brought up his promise in early 1979 that I would not be assigned to a teaching department. He was obviously uncomfortable with that issue. He briefly explained that the Army wanted Summers to write about Vietnam, but he still wanted me to come because a big struggle was brewing about the USAWC curriculum. He said this struggle could impact the role of the college in the Army school system. He noted I had shown a deeper understanding of his curriculum views than most in my answer to his earlier request to selected alumni.

I told the general I fully understood Summers's assignment, which his assistant explained was based on an order from Army superiors. I told Smith it was the failure to notify me that I would no longer be assigned to SSI but instead to a teaching department that concerned me. I pointed out I had informed him on numerous occasions that I did not want to teach. I stated to the general that I could have accepted the position at Combat Development Command, a better job for my career, and that I now considered retirement when this tour was over.

Smith answered that Combat Development Command's Institute of Land Warfare may have been better from the standpoint of my career. However, my work with the curriculum would hopefully lead to long-term benefits for our nation and a better understanding of the military's role in our society. He expressed his wish that I stay on active duty as long as possible. Furthermore, he did not accept my views that my future in the service was damaged by this posting.

I came away from this conversation understanding that Smith wanted the curriculum he had developed defended as vigorously as possible, particularly the points he had mentioned in his lengthy letter when I appeared on the promotion list at the end of 1978. He had now managed to elaborate on his most important wishes. Furthermore, in the process, he had informed me that a successful defense of these issues in the curriculum was vastly more important than my career. Unfortunately, the talk with Smith did nothing to ease my depression as I concluded I had again been used by someone I believed to be a friend.

Curriculum Development Group

The drive to make a significant overhaul of the War College curriculum predates my arrival at that organization. It was obviously in the works when Smith sent me his letter in late 1978. I do not know the driving force behind this change, but I believe it originated in the Pentagon, as did Colonel Summers's project. There was no direct linkage, but one complemented the other. Since this involved major revisions to Smith's curriculum over his two tours as commandant, I do not think much work had taken place at the college on this mammoth project before my arrival. Furthermore, it was evident that Smith's desire was for me to be one of those on the faculty to resist the most damaging changes.

Smith departed the War College in June 1980, and Major General Jack N. Merritt (1930–2018) became commandant. It was after that event that the Curriculum Development Group started its work. The real intent appeared to make the War College into a training rather than an educational institution. These were fundamental changes that would also affect the C&GSC. I saw it as my job to keep this development from doing too much damage to what many believed was the fundamental education of very senior officers.

One of my earliest inputs was a memo on 17 November 1980, making an institutional appraisal. This is one of several memos I kept from this assignment, and I have now used them in describing the curriculum issues. In the 17 November memo, I wrote that the general philosophy and mission of the USAWC was, in my view, essentially on the mark. The college should not be a trade school, a graduate course in social sciences, or a charm course for prospective general officers. Instead, the goal should be to prepare officers to perform duties they could be expected to undertake during the remaining 10 to 12 years of their careers. I then spent two pages outlining my initial suggestions.

I recommended that the present organizational structure needed modification so that lines of responsibility were clear. Furthermore, DNISS should be charged with responsibility for both national and military strategy. I pointed out it is not easy to separate these two elements in real life, and we should not try to do so in an academic environment. Furthermore, DNISS should emphasize the study of the Constitution and the role of the military in society. This should be followed by a segment on professionalism. Some aspects of this subject should be given to the Department of Command and Management. Department of Military Planning, Strategy and Operations (DMPSO) should focus on plans and operations at corps level and above.

I focused my efforts on departmental responsibilities to made them more logical. However, I suggested that the time devoted to self-assessment and domestic studies be shortened considerably. I proposed that self-assessment should be made before the students arrive at the college. I was also in favor of mailing students the readings in domestic studies, military history, and professionalism so they would not be faced with thousands of pages to read upon arrival. This would allow a cutback in the formal academic time devoted to these subjects. The freed-up time should be added to that devoted to the military's role in society, international, and strategy portion of the curriculum.

Among other things included in this memo and during the almost three years on the Curriculum Development Group were:

1. The elimination of the one-week New York trip. I felt it was debatable whether it had enough curriculum value to warrant the expenditure of time and money.
2. I recommended the lengthening of the Washington trip from one to three days to increase the time for visiting our legislators and government agencies and thus introduce more flexibility into the program.
3. Increase the number of faculty instructors in DNISS to cope with the increased workload.
4. Establish an administrative support section in DNISS under an officer with the rank of captain or major. This section would handle the coordination of the Washington, D.C., and New York (if retained) trips, the planning and coordination of guest speakers, and the planning and coordination for the National Security Seminar. I pointed out these duties were currently

performed by faculty members and detracted seriously from the time they had available for their primary functions as instructors.

The Curriculum Development Group was nearing its end in late 1982, with only some of my recommendations being implemented. The meetings were often acrimonious verbal exchanges between participants. Many of the participants who had been avid supporters of DeWitt Smith's curriculum had made a 180-degree turn in their thinking. They were going with the prevailing wind.

I informed Colonel Gerard in early 1982 that I needed reinforcement for the Curriculum Development Group, otherwise, I could not perform my job as an instructor, handle the Washington trip, and prepare for the NSS. This led to a second officer from DNISS joining me since so much was at stake for the department. The name of the additional officer was Colonel Littlefield.[3] I believe he soon grew as disturbed and flustered as I was. I had concluded that no matter how logical the proposals we made were, we dealt with an institution that had already decided to destroy DeWitt Smith's curriculum, developed over his two tours as commandant.

The main subject throughout the many meetings focused on organizing the curriculum. For ease in handling, it was eventually broken into segments. Still, much debating concentrated on placing these segments in the appropriate department and in a logical order. I wrote three memos in the period 2 February to 10 March 1982 on the above subjects, two for my signature and one for Colonel Gerard's signature since it was a departmental reply to the placements of the various segments. After that, I felt Colonel Littlefield and I had come very close to validating DeWitt Smith's wishes. However, this success carried a steep price. I made some bitter enemies on the faculty and staff in the process.

The only real issue remaining was student evaluations. This system was changed for Academic Year 1981 despite some strong objections. The personnel people in Washington were not happy with the reports received that year since they provided no discriminators.

I laid out my views, and Littlefield's, in a memorandum dated 1 October 1982. I stated that I was not surprised at the reaction from Washington. What we sent them in the new report was "garbage." It was not an evaluation, only a repetitive listing of the curriculum in which the student participated. However, I was not sure the earlier evaluations were any better. They consisted of a series of flowery phrases that may have made the recipients happy but were useless as a management tool.

We pointed out that one of the great values of the War College as an institution was its environment. Our students had spent their careers in a competitive and highly structured milieu. I stated that a formal evaluation system posed grave dangers to the educational philosophy of the War College institution. Colonel Littlefield and I recommended a revised evaluation system that gave the students credit for successfully attending the War College. These reports would identify the genuinely outstanding or less than mediocre individuals on an exceptional basis. This would retain the institutional environment while providing the personnel people in the Army with a managerial tool. The evaluation system recommended was close to that during Smith's years except for identifying the less than mediocre students.

Other Career and Business Events

In the summer of 1980, we were assigned to one of the large homes at Carlisle Barracks. We had to move at our own expense, but it was not expensive because the distance was only a half kilometer, and we moved all the small items ourselves. In 1980, I was again notified that I was an alternate for command in the Psyop category. Florence and Truong gave up their shop, which was too small, and leased another one on an annual basis on North Hannover Street in Carlisle.

In 1980 and early 1981, Colonel Summers repeatedly came to see me about his project. Unfortunately, his office was on the same floor as mine. I told him from the outset that using Karl von Clausewitz's writings as a model for examining war without front lines was meaningless. I challenged his statement that we had won every battle but lost the war. I reminded him that the bloody mountain battles in 1966–1967 were intended to draw as many maneuver battalions away from the populated areas as possible in preparation for the 1968 Tet Offensive. They achieved their goal, so our capturing mountaintops could not be labeled victories—it was the NVA that accomplished its mission. When it became apparent he could not convince me, our meetings ceased.

I had no further dealings with Summers's book except receiving a signed copy published in 1981. DeWitt Smith wrote a foreword for it. It was generous, recognizing the hard work involved and that it would be controversial. I would not be happy if I received such a foreword. He labeled the book as one man's opinion, in that it did not address the many faults of the U.S. military, and he found the use of the Clausewitz model noteworthy.[4]

Summers's book achieved the goals of those in the Pentagon who directed the project. It placed heavy blame for the debacle in Vietnam at the feet of Washington civilians and the U.S. media. I would never have reached such conclusions based on my decade-long dealings with that war. If I had been given that project, it would have led to my quick relief from that duty.

Unfortunately, Summers's book obfuscated some of the fundamental lessons from our conflict in Vietnam. It was seized upon by the right political spectrum, quoted in numerous articles and books, and even used in Congress. This may not have been Summers's intent, but in choosing to go along with those in the Pentagon who had insisted he be the writer, he certainly must bear some of the blame.

After retirement, I received a letter from Julie Sherman, Hackworth's co-author for *About Face*. They were still in Australia. They knew I had served as a member of the FPJMT in 1973–1974. She asked if I knew Colonel Tu, the chief of the DRV Delegation, and whether the statement attributed to him by Summers sounded right. She also asked if I had Tu's address.

The introduction to Summers's book had the following statements about a conversation with Colonel Tu on the last liaison flight to Hanoi on 25 April 1975. "You know you never defeated us on the battlefield," said the American colonel [Summers]. The North Vietnamese colonel pondered the remark a moment. "That may be so," he replied, "but it is also irrelevant."[5]

I talked to Summers about this statement in 1981 and asked him if something might have been lost in translation. He said no because he was accompanied by Captain Herrington, well known to me. I knew he spoke Vietnamese, but I did not know if he spoke it well enough to handle diplomatic nuances. Why would the DRV now admit they had troops in South Vietnam before the last offensive when they had denied it to the world for a decade?

I answered Julie Sherman honestly that I did not believe Tu had made the statement, and it was more likely a translation fiasco. I had sat across the table from Colonel Tu in some of our twice-weekly negotiations, in all private meetings, and accompanied him to Hanoi on at least one trip. I also told her that I did not have Tu's address, but Australia had diplomatic relations with Vietnam and their embassy would probably have it.

She sent me Colonel Tu's answer. He was then the military attaché to the Soviet Union. He had not read the book but denied making the statements in Summers's book. Colonel Tu failed to remember if the lieutenant colonel on the flight was Summers. There were no negotiations after June 1974, and it appears from the 1975 history that the USDFPJMT had only sporadic contacts with the DRV and PRG Delegations. Tu stated in his letter that the purpose of Summers and Herrington's travel was to get Giap to call off the attack on Saigon. Tu wrote that he called General Giap from the Gia Lam Airport, conveying their request.

As my three-year tour was coming to an end in 1982, I contacted the colonel's branch at OPO to see what they had in mind for me. In my earlier preference statement, I had asked for one of the Army Boards—such as the Infantry Board or the Airborne Board. I was told I would go overseas to utilize my secondary specialty. They mentioned I could go to Warsaw, Poland, as an army attaché, or to Stockholm, Sweden, as the military attaché. They asked for my reaction. I told them I did not like what was offered and that I would try to extend my War College tour by one year and then see what they had to offer.

It was another signal I could not get back to Infantry. However, the business in Carlisle and the market in Silver Springs continued to do well, with profit about three times that of my salary. We were well on the way to join the self-made millionaire class. Florence, Truong, and I decided to prepare for my retirement and begin house shopping, preferably one that could double as a residence and business. We settled on one in Shippensburg, about 20 kilometers west of Carlisle Barracks, and we were moved in by the end of June 1982. This was the same time Truong received her citizenship, delayed two years because of our tour at SHAPE. We also sold the two remaining homes in North Carolina.

Colonel Gerard retired during my last full year at the college. He came to see me in late 1981 to tell me that Al Paddock would be his replacement when he retired despite being "slightly" junior to me. He asked if I had any problems with this news. I answered promptly that his statement was analogous to describing a woman as slightly pregnant. After that, I told him I had no objections.

My recollection is that the above event took place after I lost Kay as my secretary. Fortunately, I obtained a replacement who was equally loyal and competent, Janet Moore. She remained my secretary until I retired. I could not have wished for a better secretary during those stressful years.

Colonel Alfred H. Paddock, Jr., was an OCS graduate at Fort Benning. I believe his alternate specialty was Psyop. In the Political/Military Division in the Pentagon, where we both served, he was Chief, Policy Planning. After that, he obtained a doctorate in history from Duke University and commanded the 4th Psyop Group before returning to Carlisle and the War College. Al had already spent a tour in DNISS. Unfortunately, Al Paddock and I had not worked well together.

In 1982 Paddock also assigned the New York trip as my responsibility which caused a virtual "revolt" of the secretaries, led by Kay and Janet. They went to see Colonel Paddock and pointed out I had the Washington trip, responsibility for coordinating the National Security Seminar, working on the Curriculum Development Group, and teaching. They pointed out to the department chair that this was happening while other officers had no extra duties. The New York trip was quickly given to someone else.

In early 1982, I applied for an extension to my tour at the War College as Carlisle Barrack Personnel Office had recommended in 1979. After asking me why I needed an extension, Paddock stated he could not recommend approval. I told him I only showed him the request as a gesture of courtesy. Furthermore, I told Al I would bring the request directly to the commandant. My statement caused Paddock to quickly change his mind.

I received calls from OPO in late 1982 offering me new assignments when my extended tour at Carlisle was over. Several proposed postings were as an adviser to reserve units or in charge of the ROTC at some universities. OPO called the next day again and asked if I would consider an operations slot in some command with an unfamiliar acronym, forgotten long ago. Within a couple of hours, I received a call from a friend at the Pentagon on a secure line warning me that the unit the assignment officer had offered me would go to Central Command, now being formed. Therefore, an assignment in an operation slot could not be guaranteed by anyone at this time. That was the end of this disingenuous offer.

I concluded I was receiving rotten treatment by the Army and decided, with the full support of Florence and Truong, not to allow OPO to jerk me around anymore. So I called OPO, rejected the offer, and asked my hard-working and loyal secretary, Janet Moore, to prepare my retirement papers. They were ready by the last week in February and sent to Washington.

Although my regular duties on the Curriculum Planning Group were over, I received a Departmental Missions memo dated 8 March 1983. I was asked to comment on it and its enclosure. I did so in a memorandum dated 11 March 1983. I said it was a step in the right direction but would not solve the "turf" battles unless specific responsibilities were further refined. I mentioned that we had, in the 1983 curriculum year, made curriculum changes without making the necessary organizational changes. The curriculum, students, and faculty suffered as a result. Now, for 1984, we were about to repeat that mistake by considering curriculum planning and organizational responsibilities separately as if no relations existed. I mentioned several problem areas:

1. What is the difference between the Spectrum of Application of Military Power, a DNISS responsibility, and the Spectrum of Warfare, a DMSPO responsibility?
2. How does National Strategic Planning differ from Joint Strategic Planning? We must spell out the difference if any.
3. Why is General War set aside as a DMSPO responsibility while all others are DNISS responsibility? After assigning the spectrum of warfare to one department, all elements of that spectrum should be the department's responsibility.
4. Nuclear issues are primarily strategic with a heavy emphasis on deterrence with less focus on warfighting. If we wish to reflect reality in our curriculum, DNISS should have prime responsibility in this area.
5. What is the difference between grand strategy, a DNISS responsibility, and global military strategy, a DMSPO responsibility? The lowest level at which global military strategy is articulated is the JCS, which should make it a DNISS responsibility.

The primary problem was precisely defining responsibilities, thereby eliminating "gray" areas that would cause future problems.

As I neared my retirement, the personnel section noted I had about 65 days of accrued leave. Therefore, I would lose at least five days. I told Paddock I would begin a 60-day leave on 2 May since my separation date was 1 July as specified in the DA retirement orders. He had no problems with my plans.

However, correspondence students were arriving for their mandatory summer presence. Paddock told me he had changed his mind as he needed me to participate in the instructions. I told Paddock I would take 30 days' leave in May and another 30 days in June, as we had agreed. Since the correspondence students would not arrive until June, I told him I was willing to come in during my leave when DNISS was responsible for instruction. Still, I requested that the department handle any seminar group preparations, such as providing handouts and reading requirements.

There was no ceremony by the War College for my retirement from the Army after 25 years. Neither the commandant, Major General Richard Lawrence (1930–2016), nor the deputy commandant, Brigadier General Dallas Brown (1932–2017), were available, so Colonel Thomas Leggett (1929–2008), Acting Secretary, gave me my second Legion of Merit. Earlier, there had been an informal farewell event in DNISS for Colonel Zane Finkelstein, and I was added to that gathering when my retirement papers were approved by DA.

I asked Janet Moore to join me in the coffee shop on my retirement day. I thanked her for her outstanding work and loyalty. If my memory is correct, I gave her a copy of the written evaluation I had submitted. In return, she gave me a card containing some very precious and meaningful words.

I stood my last Retreat with another retiree in the evening, and then Florence, Truong, and I adjourned to the officers' club for a few drinks. I had told various individuals we would buy drinks at the club. I know Janet showed up, as did a few other civilians from DNISS. Professor Hal Deutsch may have attended, but I am unsure. I am also uncertain if Kay attended, but I believe she did. The German International Fellow Colonel Manfred Gerber and his wife, Gudrun, also participated.

It was usual for alumni to be invited back to the War College for specific events, but I received no such invite during my retirement years. This was a sad way to leave the Army I had loved until my posting to the USAWC, but I felt then and now it was the right thing to do.

Retirement Years

I started working full-time in our business as soon as I retired, although I was not a partner. The owners remained Florence and Truong until 1992, when Florence withdrew for health reasons, and I became Truong's partner. We continued our brisk purchasing primarily in our store and our frequent trips to New York City's diamond district. Florida had become another important merchandise source. We also began using a personal computer after we purchased one in December 1982. It was a primitive machine compared to those we now use, but it allowed us to buy and sell via jewelry and coin sites. In addition, we increased our attendance at jewelry and coins shows. It was still a seven-day-a-week job. Each day consumed 18 hours of work because of the bookkeeping, commodity trade reports, and tax requirements that I handled, and Truong and Florence's repair and purchasing activities.

I continued making annual trips to Norway to see my mother. However, the frequency of these trips stopped after she died in the summer of 1989. We all attended my mother's funeral, and I ended up as the executor of the estate. Her death was followed by the death of my brother Ole in 1991 and my brother-in-law Birger in 2003. My brother Arthur died in 2007, and his wife Emma died the following year.

In 1990, we purchased a new beach-front property in Florida. It was our intention to use it as a vacation place after we retired. Unfortunately, I added to this senseless decision by purchasing a 42-foot two-masted Morgan sailboat. I spent the following year upgrading safety and communications, spending a large sum of money in upgrades as I was toying with the idea of sailing it across the Atlantic. Unfortunately, these plans crashed in 1993 when we were hit by a very rare winter hurricane in March. There was heavy damage to our under-insured home, leading the authorities to consider condemnation. Instead, we fixed and sold the house and returned to Pennsylvania. The Morgan family sold the sailboat for us in 1994.

We continued with our business, but the doctors suggested Florence needed to move to a warmer and preferably drier climate. We closed our business temporarily and spent a month looking at properties in the southwest part of the country and along the Gulf of Mexico. We also visited Lieutenant General Emerson, now living in Montana. Unfortunately, we found no property we liked on our trip.

Upon returning to Pennsylvania in 1995, we decided to close the business, which was still thriving. Unfortunately, we were all experiencing medical problems, and we were fully aware that it would take years to terminate a business and dispose of an extensive inventory with profit. Hence, we picked 2003 as the closing date.

By 2002, we had disposed of most of the inventory in installment sales to other businesses or through out-of-state wholesale. We listed our home for sale and found a buyer in June 2003, and our furniture was moved to temporary storage, pending a planned move to Florida.

Judy Hale, our realtor, had meanwhile come up with a new home in Chambersburg that she wanted us to look at. The asking price was $799,000. It was a beautiful place sitting on the top of a hill on 1.5 acres. The house was immense, the total square footage under the roof was about 7,000 with three finished floors. I don't know what I was thinking about, another unwise decision. It was built by a developer as his own place, but we learned later he had temporary cash flow problems.

As a goodwill gesture to Judy, who had worked hard to keep us in Pennsylvania, we made a low offer of $525,000 that we felt sure would be rejected and asked for a reply within 48 hours. To our surprise and regret, we received an acceptance of our offer the same day, forcing us to remain in Pennsylvania. We lived there for seven years. The purchase was a month after I had bought a Mercedes for myself and a BMW for Truong. Florence had given up driving after a bad accident.

More than a year after moving into our new home in 2004 and purchasing much new furniture, we decided to take a trip to California to visit relatives. We had gone as far as Memphis, Tennessee, when I became very sick, unable to breathe. I was rushed to a Baptist hospital. The doctors discovered a large mass on my left lung, and they recommended we abort the trip and return home. It was the beginning of medical problems that destroyed our retirement.

After the medical news, the first action was to call the VA in Lebanon, Pennsylvania, to tell them what had happened. They said the earliest appointment with an oncologist was May, more than four months in the future. I then called to meet with my civilian lung doctor, Doctor Khurshid from Saudi Arabia. He turned out to be the best pulmonologist I had over many years. He gave me a needle biopsy, and it came back as lymphoma. He said I needed to get to a good hospital as quickly as possible. The local oncologists seemed in no hurry, so Khurshid took over, ordering a PET scan and contacting Johns Hopkins in Baltimore, which he said would be his choice if he were in my position. So, I received a quick appointment at Johns Hopkins and spent the next few months in that excellent facility.

Truong also had back problems, and I wanted those tended to before my move to Baltimore. Both Doctor Swinnen in Baltimore and Truong's neurologist cooperated. Truong was operated on and spent only two days in the hospital.

Two needle biopsies at Johns Hopkins confirmed Khurshid's findings with a 99 percent assurance. However, that was not enough since Thoracic Surgery feared lung cancer cells could be in that large mass given my smoking history. I underwent a lung operation in early May, and they removed half my left lung (66 percent by volume), and after two weeks, I was sent back to Pennsylvania for rehab and chemotherapy. Doctor Lode Swinnen, my oncologist at Johns Hopkins, also told me this would be my last bite of the apple since a person of 70 or over was prevented by law from getting a stem cell transplant (also called bone marrow transplant).

I completed my rehab in late June 2006 and began 16 weeks of chemotherapy. Unfortunately, cataracts must favor chemo since I went legally blind, which worried my optometrist. He fixed one eye first and a week later the second. After that, I had another PET scan that did not show a trace of cancer.

We decided to restart the aborted trip to visit Florence's sister in San Diego. On our return trip, we spent a couple of days at the casinos in Henderson, Nevada. Unfortunately, I was not feeling well on the trip back home, so I saw Doctor Khurshid. He told me it looked like the cancer was back, this time in both the remnants of the left lung and in the right lung. This was confirmed by a PET scan. Khurshid contacted Johns Hopkins, and he was told to send me there, and they would handle all future care.

In late 2006, President George W. Bush issued an executive order removing the earlier prohibition of patients 70 years of age and over receiving stem cell transplants.

Consequently, I spent the next seven months at Johns Hopkins undergoing powerful chemo and having catheters placed in my arm and chest before drawing my blood and separating the white cells.

In early August, I was randomized to receive a drug never used for cancer before, Bexxar. But it was nuclear medicine and had to be brought from Texas by courier. It was fortunate because it gave me a chance to go home for a week.

I was given a small dose of Bexxar in mid-August to see if it was tolerated. It was, and they gave me the total prescribed amount and moved me into isolation for over 10 days while they drew my white cells to zero and left me like that for a couple days when they reinserted new stem cells. I made three trips to Johns Hopkins in 2009 to be revaccinated.

I was told when released to immediately go to a hospital if my temperature reached 101. It did in late November, but I was slow to react and collapsed on the floor. Florence called for an ambulance, and when I reached the hospital, I was in a coma. My local oncologist called Johns Hopkins and was told to give me liquid Avelox. That brought me out of the coma, and after my second painful bone marrow biopsy, I was released in about a week.

Florence and Truong still wanted to move to Florida. Consequently, we bought a home in Naples in 2010 and spent a winter there to see how we liked it. We did enjoy it and decided to sell our Chambersburg home, and the one we had purchased in Naples in 2010, and buy a larger home in Naples in 2011 because the one we had was too small for our furniture. So, the house in Chambersburg sold on 31 January 2011, the same day as the smaller Naples home.

Unfortunately, my immune system started to collapse again in late 2011, but my oncologist gave me Avelox tablets, restoring the system. However, I still need antibiotics when I have dental or dermatology appointments for frequent skin cancer.

I had written instructions to see Doctor Swinnen every six months. That was changed to once a year after moving to Florida and stopped in 2015 after I developed heart problems discovered by Doctor Swinnen.

Florence was not doing well health wise and was told she needed to have her carotid arteries cleaned out. We were told the operation was safe and straightforward, with less than 1 percent danger of anything going wrong. She was told they planned to release her the same day or the following. The doctor performing the surgery was informed that two cardiologists in Pennsylvania had warned us that her heart arteries were too small to be stented. The surgeon went in through the thigh, and I do not know how he reached the neck.

Florence began bleeding during the operation. She was moved to the ICU, but the bleeding could not be stopped. She died at the hospital hospice in Naples on 3 June 2012. It was a sad day. One evening, shortly before she died, she asked to see her three children, Truong and me. She said for Truong and me to marry as we needed to take care of each other. She added that we should not delay the marriage because she was not returning. I had difficulty keeping from crying since my welfare was still foremost in her mind after more than 47 years.

Truong and I married on 12 September 2012. We had no desire to stay in the Naples home because of the many memories and began looking for another place. We bought a lovely home in Cape Coral in February 2013, built in 2001. It is on a large canal leading to the ocean, so we constructed a dock and lift. I purchased a 28-foot cabin cruiser in 2013 but had to give it up in 2014 after I had the first of many falls. We spent a lot of money in the following years on upgrades.

I had open-heart surgery for a coronary bypass to eliminate five blockages in the heart in 2015. Doctor Comas performed the operation and he did an excellent job.

Unfortunately, my falls continued, and in late August 2020, I had one that crushed both hips. I spent a long time in the hospital receiving two new titanium hips and in recovery/rehab, not released until 29 October 2020. Neurologists told me later I would never again walk independently since several nerves in my legs were not responsive. I hope, somehow, to prove them wrong.

I had to do something to stay active during my lengthy illnesses, so I started writing. First, I concentrated on genealogy, a branch of history that has always fascinated me, and I wrote three books and five monographs in that field, published by Enoch Haga Publishers in California. Then I switched to writing military history and had four books published by Casemate. The first book was in progress when I was at Johns Hopkins in 2008. The copy-editor insisted I answer the many questions even though I was in the hospital and due to begin isolation. I turned the process over to my friend Colonel (Ret) Henry Gole. My books are still in print and selling. Two were published by foreign publishers, and I was told that one ended up on the bestseller list in the nonfiction category in Sweden. I am thankful that the Lord has given me the time to do all my writings, including this manuscript.

Epilogue

I considered America an exceptional nation, as could be expected from a teenager who came from Europe shortly after World War II, with parents who lived through two world wars, the worst pandemic in modern history, a great depression, the rise of tyranny, and the worst bloodletting since the Religious Wars.

By exceptional, I refer to the liberties and freedoms guaranteed by our amazingly wise—but flawed—Founders, the essential goodness and decency of Americans I came to know, and the virtually unbridled opportunities provided by our political and economic system. I do not support the very prevalent feeling our nation is omnipotent and omniscient. President John Kennedy, Doctor Arthur M. Schlesinger Jr., and President Richard M. Nixon denounced these delusions. Nevertheless, some commentators speak, even today, in this way, and our nation acts at times as if these delusions were facts. When used to denote superiority over others, it can be dangerous for our national security. At a minimum, we would lose friends' and allies' respect and confidence when it became evident that we are neither omnipotent nor omniscient.

My view of American exceptionalism began to erode at the end of my service and continued during my retirement years. Severe social cracks accompanied the political split in American society. These conditions are endangering American democracy. The political divisions should be evident because we came perilously close to becoming an autocracy at the end of 2020 and the beginning of 2021. The freedoms granted by Americans under the Constitution and Bill of Rights would be forever lost.

I will give a couple of examples of how our society has changed during my lifetime. For example, the attitude of caring for others has changed dramatically. If I had a flat tire or mechanical problem driving on a highway in the 1950s, other drivers invariably stopped and offered help. That seldom happens today, as I found out during the evacuation to escape Hurricane Irma. The current pandemic showed glaringly how the attitude toward caring for others has changed. Over 25 percent of the American population eligible for vaccination refused, although this posed a deadly threat against neighbors and friends. The younger generation refused to cancel trips home during the Thanksgiving and end-of-year holidays despite warnings from the scientific community; in this way, they showed total disregard for the safety of parents and grandparents to have their wishes fulfilled. This is a sharp departure from the caring society when I grew up. The unbelievable rise in deaths from shootings and drug overdoses, coming on top of 1 million dead from the pandemic, are not signs of an exceptional society. It appears we have become insensitive to avoidable deaths. Scientists and medical doctors are being demonized. Furthermore, we appear incapable of defending our borders as millions of illegals stream across our southern border each year or come in by aircraft and disappear among the multitude.

Let us take a close look at the economic inequities. There was already a sharp difference between the rich and the poor in the 1950s, but high taxes on the more fortunate kept the divergence within tolerable limits. Recent Federal data illustrates the current situation. They report the collective bottom 50 percent of Americans controlled $2.62 trillion of America's wealth. These are the poor and the lower one-third of the middle class as well as retirees on a fixed income. The wealthiest one percent held $41.52 trillion of the wealth. This means that the upper one percent of the population owned more than sixteen times what the lower half own. Poverty causes tens of millions of our fellow citizens to live on the edge.

It is necessary for the entrepreneurs in a capitalist democracy to receive special government incentives for taking risks that bring benefits and prosperity to all. Some of our richest individuals are becoming as strong politically as the plutocrats or moguls we denounce in Russia and China.

It is difficult to determine whether we have a clearer military advantage now than the one that existed when I served. The public knew our military structure was based on a two- and one-half war scenario. That was changed to a two-war scenario. In a paper titled "The National Military Strategy of the United States of America 2015" issued by the JCS, it spears we had gone to a one war scenario—war in one theater of operations while relying on deterrence against other threats.

However, our nuclear arsenal has been neglected since the fall of the Soviet Union. This became clear from the House briefing by our intelligence services. The only public statement by a member of the House Intelligence Committee was that Russia now has more nuclear weapons than the rest of the world combined, and Wikipedia states we will not catch up in the hypersonic missile field until late 2023 or 2024. After several failures, we had a successful launch of a hypersonic missile in mid-April 2022.

I feel compelled to comment on our propensity to get into "small wars" in regions labeled essential to American security. Sun-Tzu reminded us that a great power becoming involved increasingly in small wars is a sign of decline. The Duke of Wellington echoed this thought when he said great powers do not fight small wars.

It is also not correct to label these as critical for our security. Afghanistan, for example, started as a punitive action against the Taliban for providing refuge for Osama bin Laden. Still, eventually, we became nation builders in a tribal society that had existed for millennia. Wars are easy to get into but very difficult to end. I agree with President Biden that it was time to terminate our Afghan venture. However, I'm afraid I must disagree with the unprofessional way it was conducted. The cause may have been a lack of expertise at the highest levels in the new Administration.

The government admitted that intelligence estimated the takeover by the Taliban could take place in weeks, months, or even years. Military planners, faced with such diverse intelligence estimates, should focus on the estimate posing the greatest danger. Had they done so, the outcome could have been much different.

The evacuation from Afghanistan was a blow to Biden's popularity. Most Americans favored a withdrawal, but they felt that the way it was carried out was amateurish. This was the view of most Americans as well as our closest allies. The Administration resorted to hyperbole to put the evacuation in the best light by claiming it was the largest and most successful airlift in history. They are all too young to remember the Berlin airlift of 1948, or they were victims of our lack of historical remembrance. The Berlin airlift dwarfs our Afghanistan evacuation.

Many immigrants who came to this country in the late 1940s and 1950s feel that they can no longer recognize our society. What has brought us to this point? It would take a book to address this issue, but I believe the Immigration and Nationality Act of 1965 is a significant cause. It was enacted at the same time as President Johnson introduced U.S. combat forces in Vietnam.

This Congressional act did away with national quotas and opened the doors wide for people with no background in democracy. Furthermore, the technological revolution and steps taken by liberals led to the death of the long-standing melting-pot concept. Significant changes in the school curriculum away from the teaching of history, economics, civics, the study of the Constitution, and how the governments at various levels should operate have been very damaging.

Our move to an all-volunteer force in 1972 may also have caused damage. It intended to produce a smaller and better-trained force at a lower cost. I am no longer sure that the cost has been reduced much, as volunteers receive comparative pay with their civilian counterparts. The outsourcing of many military functions to civilian contractors has also increased the costs. About $161 billion, or 23 percent, of the defense budget is personnel costs—41 percent if you add retired pay. Wikipedia estimates that these costs will consume the entire defense budget by 2039.

Another reason was the opposition of most Americans to the Vietnam War. The all-volunteer force went far to break the traditional bond between the American public and their military, since only the families of the volunteers pay much attention to their military. It also broke the traditional service ideal of the American people. This situation makes it easier to get into questionable overseas ventures as most of the public does not have to worry that their own will be affected. It also translates to Congressional members not needing to worry about their seats by voting for military actions.

The election of President Biden ushered in new hopes for the future. Biden is the opposite of his predecessor in every way. He has great empathy, an excellent leadership quality, completely lacking in the former president. Biden is soft-spoken, and some listeners interpret this as a lack of certainty. President Biden may have to do what an earlier president said, 'walk softly but carry a big stick.'

Biden inherited a full plate of problems from the former Administration, including a pandemic and an opponent who refused to admit to losing the election. Climate change, with disastrous fires in the western states, drought in the west and middle states, and hurricanes and floods in the southern and eastern states, is no longer a theory but a fact. He also must deal with the unruly followers of the former president. They are engaging the Administration in both the political and social fields.

In appointing individuals to fill slots in his Administration, Biden used a yardstick not used before in my memory. He wanted his Administration to reflect American society and it included some who had worked for him or Obama before. Unfortunately, this approach does not necessarily lead to the best individuals filling critical positions and giving him sound advice.

One major problem for the new Administration is that while controlling both houses of Congress, it is with a razor-thin margin. The Senate ended up in a 50/50 split and is considered a Democratic Senate only because Vice President Harris can break a tie. The margin in the House of Representatives is likewise fragile. The House, voting on a simple majority, is still passing legislation, but sixty votes are needed for many legislative proposals when the legislation moves to the Senate.

There is also a problem in the Democratic camp. The Democratic voters cover the far left of the political spectrum. So, it is challenging for President Biden, a moderate, to hold the coalition together, both in the House of Representatives and the Senate.

Mid-term elections, like the one we face in November 2022, usually cause losses for the ruling party. I hope that this year is an exception to that rule. Otherwise, the Republican Party could have a majority in both the Senate and House. One way to retain the majority is for minorities, women, and the LGBT community to come out in droves as these groups are threatened.

Then in February 2022, the brutal former KGB officer in Moscow invaded Ukraine, virtually bringing Biden's agenda to a halt. It is the most severe threat to our country since 1962. Biden has managed it wisely despite his frequent speaking mistakes. He and his national security team know humanity's existence is at stake.

The war began strangely. Public sources estimated that the Russian forces that initially entered Ukraine consisted of 175,000 troops, going against a well-trained army estimated at 365,000 when ready reserves are included. It usually takes a ratio of *three* attackers against one defender for an attacker to be successful. Then, contrary to Soviet doctrine in World War II, they entered congested urban areas with armor without any visible infantry protection. During Operation *Bagration* (the most significant land battle in history) in 1944, the Soviets refused to be slowed down by urban warfare and bypassed the cities on their route. What was in Putin's mind? Even if one has intelligence that the enemy will not fight, you use overwhelming force from the beginning in case the intelligence is false.

The Russians are very sensitive to threats from the West and with good reasons since four major invasions have taken place from the West during the past four hundred years: Sweden in the early 1700s, Napoleon almost precisely one hundred years later, the German and Austro-Hungarian invasion in 1914, and Hitler's invasion in 1941. These invasions resulted in tens of millions of deaths.

In a heavily redacted State Department document, Secretary of State James Baker made the following statement to his Soviet counterpart Eduard Shevardnadze on 9 February 1990: "...There would, of course, have to be iron-clad guarantees that NATO's jurisdiction or forces would not move eastward. ..."[1]

President Clinton ignored these assurances in the 1990s, and President George Bush did likewise in 2004, as they brought virtually all former Warsaw Pact nations and three neutral countries into NATO. The Russians were unable to do anything about it. They did not possess the necessary military strength, but NATO moving east planted the seeds of future problems.

When there were rumors of Ukraine joining NATO, Putin decided to act because his nuclear arsenal was now up to par, and he had hypersonic missiles, as does China. This window of opportunity would not last longer than a couple of years.

The U.S. also looked weak, with a president who had shown a distaste for military ventures and political turmoil in this country. Usually, our nation unites behind its president in a foreign policy crisis, but not this time. NATO also appeared weak because it relies on Russia for much of its energy. The alliance countries have not seriously tried ending this dependence despite claims to the contrary.

Then there seems to be a misunderstanding in the public of the meaning of Article 5 of the NATO treaty. It does call an attack on one an attack against all. However, an escape clause insisted on by the U.S. leaves it up to the individual countries what action they take. The U.S. Congress was not about to surrender its war powers to an international organization.

Having noted all these faults and dangers, I hope my adopted country can overcome all and thereby return to the status of an exceptional nation. It will not be easy, and dangerous internal problems may be exacerbated.

I am satisfied with my life but regret my retirement was ruined for both my wife and me. The last vacation we had was 19 years ago.

I have always been determined to be the best at whatever I do. This became an obsession. As I reflect on my life, I feel blessed by all the experiences and successes I have enjoyed. I succeeded in anything I did, for which I feel humbled and appreciative.

I excelled in high school academically, although I was a newcomer to my adopted country. This performance continued as a university undergraduate in the 1950s and a graduate in the early 1970s. I was among the top in all military schools, including the prestigious USAWC.

Because of my demonstrated abilities, I received the most challenging positions in all my assignments. I was a planner in one of the most prestigious units in the U.S. Army, 1st Brigade, 101st Airborne Division. I accompanied that unit to Vietnam, where I became a company commander. Superiors, all the way up to General Westmoreland, singled out my unit for praise. On my second tour in the problem-ridden 9th Infantry Division, the battalion commander and I made our unit the best in the division. While realizing that promotions could be politically driven, I always strove to retain my integrity and was unafraid to call it as it was.

Business ventures were also in my blood. I dove into it with the same enthusiasm that characterized my military service. It resulted in huge earnings over the years.

This book may be my last unless the doctors find miraculous solutions to my ailments. I received encouragement to continue when I found out that Henry Kissinger, whom I admire, was publishing one at age 97.

Glossary

AA report	after-action report
ADC	Assistant Division Commander
AO	area of operations
APC	armored personnel carrier
ARVN	Army of the Republic of Vietnam
AWOL	Absent Without Leave
BAR	Browning Automatic Rifle
BIOC	Basic Infantry Officer Course
BOQ	bachelor officer quarters
B-Rations	mixture of hot and canned food
Bronze Star	for valor or meritorious service
C&C	Command and Control
C&GSC	Command and General Staff College
CIA	Central Intelligence Agency
CIDG	Civilian Irregular Defense Group
CINCPAC	Commander-in-Chief, Pacific
CMMI	Command Material Maintenance Inspection
CO	Commanding Officer
CONARC	Continental Army Command
CP	command post
C-Rations	cold canned meal
DA	Department of the Army
DAO	Defense Assistance Office
DCSOPS	Deputy Chief of Staff for Operations and Plans
DIC	Died in Captivity
DMG	Distinguished Military Graduate
DMSPO	Department of Military Strategy Plans and Operations
DNISS	Department of National and International Security Studies
DOD	Department of Defense
DRV	Democratic Republic of Vietnam
DSC	Distinguished Service Cross—decoration for valor
DZ	drop zone

EZ	extraction zone
FAC	Forward Air Controller
FBI	Federal Bureau of Investigation
FO	Artillery Forward Observer
FORSCOM	U.S. Army Forces Command
FPJMC	Four Party Joint Military Commission
FPJMT	Four Party Joint Military Team
Free-Fire Zone	an area pre-cleared for direct or indirect fire
FSO	Foreign Service Officer
FTX	Field Training Exercise
G-3, G-4	Staff Sections at division and corps
HD	Headquarters Detachment
HHC	Headquarters and Headquarter Company
ICC	International Control Commission
ICCS	International Commission for Control and Supervision
IFF	identify friend or foe
IG	Inspector General
INTERPOL	International Police
IOCC	Infantry Officer Career Course
J-3	Personnel, Intelligence and Operations Offices at a Joint Command
JCRC	Joint Casualty Resolution Center
JCS	Joint Chiefs of Staff
JROTC	Junior Reserve Officer Training Corps
KIA	killed in action
Lane Grader	officer instructor/umpire
LAPES	Low Altitude Parachute Extraction System
LOH	Light Observation Helicopter
LOLEX	Low-level Extraction System
Legion of Merit	medal for exceptional meritorious service
LST	Landing Ship Tank
LZ	landing zone
MA	Master of Arts
MACV	Military Assistance Command Vietnam
MATA	Military Assistance Training Adviser
Medevac	Medical Evacuation
MIA	missing in action
Medal of Honor	highest award for conspicuous gallantry
MOS	Military Occupational Specialty
MP	Military Police
MR	morning report

NATO	North Atlantic Treaty Organization
NCO	Non-Commissioned Officer
NKP	Nakhon Phanom Air Base in Thailand
NVA	North Vietnamese Army
OCS	Officer Candidate School
OD	Operational Detachment
OER	Officer Efficiency Report
OPO	Office of Personnel Operations at DA
ORT	Operational Readiness Test
PCS	permanent change of station
PhD	Doctorate degree
PLF	Parachute Landing Fall
PRG	Provisional Revolutionary Government of South Vietnam
R&R	rest and recuperation
RA	Regular Army
RIF	Reduction in Force
ROK	South Korean Army
ROTC	Reserve Officer Training Corps
RPG	rocket-propelled grenade
RTO	radio operator
RVN	Republic of Vietnam
S-1	personnel section at battalion and brigade
S-2	intelligence section at battalion and brigade
S-3	operations section at battalion and brigade
S-4	logistics section at battalion and brigade
SACEUR	Supreme Allied Commander Europe
SF	special forces
SHAPE	Supreme Headquarters Allied Powers Europe
SIGINT	Signal Intelligence
Silver Star	medal for Gallantry in Action
SJ	staff journal
SOP	standard operating procedure
SROTC	Senior Reserve Officer Training Corps
SSA	Social Security Administration
SSI	Strategic Studies Institute
SU	Syracuse University
TAC	Tactical Officer
TAOR	Tactical Area of Responsibility
TDY	temporary duty
TECOM	Test and Evaluation Command
TF	task force

TO&E	table of organization and equipment
TOC	Tactical Operations Center
TR	transportation request
UC	University of California
USAAESWB	U.S. Army Airborne, Electronic, and Special Warfare Board
USAIMA	U.S. Army Institute for Military Assistance
USAREUR	U.S. Army Europe
USARV	U.S. Army Vietnam
USATECOM	U.S. Army Test and Evaluation Command
USAWC	U.S. Army War College
USDFPJMT	U.S. Delegation, Four Party Joint Military Team
USNS	U.S. Navy Ship
UW	unconventional warfare
VA	Veterans Administration
VC	Viet Cong
VCSA	Vice Chief of Staff of the Army
WIA	wounded in action
WP	white phosphorus
YMCA	Young Men's Christian Association
XO	Executive Officer

Endnotes

Introduction

1 Google *Where did the saying toot your own horn come from* or Gore Vidal, *Inventing a Nation: Washington, Adams, Jefferson* (New Haven: Yale University Press, 2003), 61.
2 Charles B. McDonald, *Company Commander* (New York: History Book Club, 2006).
3 Colonel David H. Hackworth and Julie Sherman, *About Face: The Odyssey of an American Warrior* (New York: Simon and Schuster, 1989).
4 Anthony B. Herbert and James Wooten, *Soldier* (New York: Holt, Rinehart and Winston, 1973).
5 Those 24 notebooks—18 dealing with my first tour and six with my second tour—were severely damaged in March 1993 when our Florida home was flooded. Two notebooks dealing with my service in the 9th Infantry Division floated away. Some of the letters to and from the next of kin to those killed were likewise damaged to the point where some are unreadable. The extracts of more than 1,000 letters to my wife dealing with how I felt about various aspects of the war and description of military operations came to 114 single-space typewritten pages. These were located on the second floor and not damaged.
6 David Johnson, *Vietnam X3* (unpublished). He provided me a copy, and I urged him to have the book published. Dave's narrative is interspersed with comments by his wife Judith, and it is therefore a much better treatment of the problems faced by the families of those sent to Vietnam.
7 Barbara W. Tuchman, *The March of Folly from Troy to Vietnam* (New York: Knopf, 1984), 233–378.

Chapter 2: First Years in a New Country

1 My score was 192 out of a possible 200. Only the top eight are mentioned in the 15 May 1957 orders. Serge Demyanenko had a score of 184, placing him number eight.
2 The 17 December 1957 appointment list shows six selectees. Listed alphabetically, they were Cadet Rockwell C. Cramer, Cadet Serge P. C. Demyanenko, Cadet Janes B. Harbuck, Jr., Cadet Henrik O. Lunde, Cadet Robert H. Schumacher, and Cadet Howard Solvin. I do not know if all accepted the selection, as I never again met any of them except, of course, Serge.

Chapter 3: A Time of Preparation: Fort Benning 1958–1959

1 This is the position I was offered in early 1970.
2 The commandant of the Ranger School sent a very complimentary letter to my parents that they displayed with pride. Herbert's praise was referred to in the letter.
3 Herbert died in Colorado from cancer in June 2014.
4 After completing the course, wives were given the opportunity to be dropped from the towers. For safety reasons, the parachute did not separate from the cradle, and both parachute and cradle were dropped together. To her credit, Marion volunteered for this event.

Chapter 5: Secret Assignment, Personal Problems, and Refocusing, 1961–1964

1 Captain Adam Klys, on one of these jumps, landed on the roof of a barn in Bavaria. He penetrated into the interior of the barn. The U.S. Army ended up paying the owner for the damage. On return to Berlin, Adam was taken to the dispensary. I brought his boots to his wife Chris, who believed something profoundly serious had happened to her husband. She never forgot this prank by Adam and me.

Chapter 6: 1st Brigade, 101st Airborne Division

1 Hackworth, *About Face*, 452–453.
2 Major Herbert Dexter, who served on the brigade staff, had already spent a lot of time with the SF in Vietnam and his help was invaluable.
3 Hackworth, *About Face*, 463.

Chapter 7: A Command in Disarray

1 Arthur M. Schlesinger, Jr., *The Bitter Heritage: Vietnam and American Democracy 1941–1966* (Greenwich, Connecticut: Fawcett Publications, Inc., 1967), 71.
2 Hackworth, *About Face*, 464.
3 According to my military records, I made nine parachute jumps while in Vietnam, two at Bien Hoa, one at Don Ba Thien, two at An Khe, two at Cam Ranh Bay, and two at Phan Rang. I do not remember that many jumps in Vietnam.

Chapter 8: Provisional Cavalry Troop: Battle of An Ninh

1 A/2/17 Cavalry was under my operational control in May 1966 on the Cambodian border area, and its commander then was Captain George Hamilton.
2 The VC forces had suffered 80 casualties in the 3 September engagement according to the brigade prisoner interrogation reports.
3 Hackworth, *About Face*, 464–479.
4 Lieutenant Colonel Albert N. Garland (editor), *Infantry in Vietnam* (Fort Benning, Georgia: Infantry Magazine, 1967).
5 Mallon Faircloth, *Behind the Names: The Story of An Ninh the First Major Battle of Our War in Vietnam* (Columbus, Georgia: Brentwood Academic Press, 2003).
6 Ibid., 5–6. Judge Faircloth contacted me when he was writing his book. He said Hackworth had referred him to me. I cannot understand that referral since I had no part in the planning for, or execution of, *Gibraltar*. In retrospect, Dave Hackworth was already battling cancer, and it may be that he wanted to get this chore off his mind. In the interest of full disclosure, I told the judge the relations between Hackworth and me on one side and Smith on the other had not been the best and that this situation dated back to late 1964. I suggested he factor this into his evaluation, although my views would not have been different if the battalion commander had been someone else. I also told him my only first-hand knowledge of the battle came from radio traffic, a poor source, and from talking to my troops after assuming command of A/2/502. Finally, I gave him the names of officers on the brigade staff that could provide him with more accurate information.
7 Ibid., 28. Extract from 1st Brigade report and conversations after 1987 with Timothy and Hackworth. The sequence of events was also confirmed by personnel in the brigade S-3 section after Timothy gave me command of A/2/502.
8 Hackworth, *About Face*, 469.
9 *The First Screaming Eagles in Vietnam*, April 2012, 3–4. The article is based on after-action reports adapted by Captain James L. Sheppard. He wrote that he tried to contact Wilford (sic) Smith but never

received an answer. Faircloth also fails to mention receiving any information from Smith. It would have been natural for him to contact the former 2/502 commander. I did not know there was a Marine armored unit involved in the operation.

10 Faircloth, *Behind the Names*, 30–31.

11 The new casualty list for the 2/502, provided by Lieutenant Colonel (R) David Perrine, shows only 12 U.S. KIAs.

12 The 1st Air Cavalry Division at Bong Son captured this report the following year. It was translated by MACV, and I have a copy.

13 When the company was on the Cam Lao Peninsula, I received an award from the brigade headquarters. It was sent by Captain Terry McClain who wrote a letter dated 26 September 1965. He wrote, "I have heard Colonel Timothy go off at some length about 'Herr Lunde' and your exploits."

14 A/2/502 had no fatalities during Operation *Gibraltar* but had two deaths in August 1965. One was Private First Class G. Kilbuck, a Native American from Alaska, killed on 27 August. The other was Specialist 5 W. J. Suarez, listed as having died from an "accidental homicide" on 28 August.

15 His signature appears on my IOCC and Pathfinder School diplomas.

Chapter 9: Phan Rang, Ben Cat, the Iron Triangle, and Tuy Hoa

1 I later discovered that increased mobility and lightening the load of infantrymen became a main concern of the U.S. Army Combat Development Command at Fort Belvoir, Virginia. This led to new TO&Es discussed in chapter 19.

2 https://en.wikipedia.org/wiki/Iron_Triangle_(Vietnam). Much of the general information about the Iron Triangle is taken from Wikipedia as it provides a concise historical summary. During the French war from 1946 to 1954, the Viet Minh continued to expand on these underground facilities. After the French withdrawal, the problems in this area were inherited by the South Vietnamese and the Americans. Three large joint operations and numerous B-52 strikes in the 1966–1967 periods failed to destroy the VC underground system. In 1975, this strategically located area near both Saigon and Cambodia became the launching pad for the final attack on Saigon.

3 Recently, I learned that Private First Class Larry Greenhill had joined the company in the field on 8 or 9 December. He was immediately assigned to Sergeant Hawthorne's squad, and this would make the strength of that unit nine. Larry received a minor wound during the fighting but elected not to be evacuated.

4 Bob Bohler's family wrote in December. The family had sent a Christmas package, and they wanted to ensure we did not send it back but distributed the contents to the troops. He mentioned that the only thing to make them ever have any peace of mind is what Bob had written them: "Mom I know and believe in what we are fighting for." (From Thomas C. Leftwich in Lomita, California.) The company received hundreds of Christmas greetings and packages in December. It was mostly First Lieutenant Phil Mock's job to answer them. I remember one from the married sister of Sergeant Frank R. Mandl. She and her husband sent 106 dozen home-baked cookies that came in four packages. Mandl was one of the original troops who came over by ship in July 1965, and he was still in Vietnam when I departed; his name is on the tapestry titled *The Last Sixteen*. We were eventually so overwhelmed by cookies that the troops gave some to an orphanage. We also received some transistor radios and personal care items.

5 Thomas Taylor, *Where the Orange Blooms: One Man's War and Escape in Vietnam* (New York: McGraw-Hill Publishing Company, 1989), 73ff and several other places in the book. Emerson, now retired as a lieutenant general, found out there would be considerable coverage of the "hatchet incident" in the book and contacted Hackworth and me to try to convince Taylor to delete that part to save him embarrassment. Tom Taylor and I knew each other well, but we were never close friends like Robert Murphy and I were. When I called and recommended he delete or tone down his coverage of the hatchet incident, Taylor gave me a curt no. Taylor does not mention my call in his book, but Hackworth's intervention is discussed.

6 Hawthorne was awarded a DSC for the action near Ben Cat.

7 I explained my action at a meeting of my platoon leaders and asked them to pass it on to the troops. I also told them that if anyone wanted one of those gadgets, they should see the supply sergeant and give him $3.00. I never saw any of my troops carrying a hatchet.

8 Taylor, *Where the Orange Blooms*, 76.

9 Ibid. Malcolm Browne described what he witnessed: *We're turned into Animals!*

10 The brigade was also involved in Operation *Fillmore*, which began on 24 March and ended on 21 July 1966, but with the move of 2/502 and 1/327 to Phan Thiet and subsequently to the Cambodian border area, it was primarily 2/327 that participated in Operation *Fillmore.*

11 Hackworth, *About Face*, 532.

Chapter 10: Searching for and Finding the 95th NVA Regiment

1 Wikipedia, in its discussion of Operation *van Buren*, based on what was written by Major Elliot in his book *RAND in Southeast Asia: A History of the Vietnam Era* (Rand Corporation), 189–190. He wrote that "repeated massacres were reported to have been conducted in this operation by South Korean troops, with no distinction often being made between civilian and PAVN KIA. These areas became a hotbed for Viet Cong activity following this operation."

2 Wallace joined the company at the end of 1965. However, he had come to Vietnam on the *Eltinge* as a member of 2/502. His name is on the 31 July 1965 deployment roster and on at least one A/2/502 MR, the one for 30 September 1965. Otherwise, I did not see him until the end of 1965. Perrine believes Wallace was on special duty, either at Qui Nhon or at Nha Trang. This would also explain why some in his family thought he was killed in an accident in Nha Trang.

3 Schoonover had joined the company in December 1965. He previously served in A/2/502 as a platoon leader in the 3rd Platoon before deployment to Vietnam. After arriving in Vietnam, he served as Assistant S-1 on the brigade staff until he again joined his old company, receiving the same platoon with Sergeant First Class Ledford as his platoon sergeant.

4 The early generation of Starlight Night Vision devices was issued to the battalion around this time. It was primitive compared to what I have seen since. You needed a relatively clear sky and that limited its usefulness, but the factor that caused most companies not to use them was based on the security requirements imposed to keep this technology from falling into enemy hands.

5 The company MR for 3 February 1966 gives the names of those wounded and evacuated. They were Private First Class James K. Lingerfelt (foot wound), Private First Class Bobby L. Davis (foot wound), Specialist 4 Raleigh J. Pitre (foot wound) and Private First Class Ralph D. Tipton (knee wound). Three of the above were from the outpost commanded by Sergeant Richard C. Youngbear who was killed and evacuated.

6 On the company roster for 31 January 1966, Burges's name is given as "Burges-Sotomayor C," and it is also listed that way on the deployment roster dated 27 May 1965. In all correspondence with me, he uses the name Carlos Burgos, with an "o" instead of "e" in his last name. He never used a hyphenated last name. I have used the spelling of his name found in the rosters.

7 These two individuals are not listed in the MR as wounded on 4 February. A possible reason for this is that the two soldiers had life-threatening wounds and were flown directly to a hospital capable of treating them. Staff Sergeant Burges is mentioned in the 6 February MR. Lieutenant Colonel Perrine was able to locate a USARV General Order which awarded Burges a Purple Heart for wounds sustained on 4 February 1966. I have found no mention of Sergeant Nathaniel Franklin on any MR from February and March, but a Private First Class Nathaniel Franklin is mentioned in the company roster, but he is not the one who was wounded on 4 February. There are seven others mentioned along with Staff Sergeant Burges on the 6 February MR, but the columns showing why they are listed is so blurred that they are unreadable. Their names and ranks are readable, except for one. They are Specialist 4 Paul L. Jones, Private First Class Richard Laurel Jr., Sergeant Thomas S. Evans, Sergeant Harold W. Price (mentioned just before Burges and could be the one wounded on 4 February, not Nathaniel Franklin), Private First Class John N. Bergner and Specialist 4 Douglas Moss.

8 I did not recall using any air support, but one of my NCOs, Sergeant Earl Singeltary, told Lieutenant Colonel Perrine that we had air support. This explains a note I made in the field notebook after the operation cautioning the troops to stay away from the unexploded cluster shells. These antipersonnel bombs consisted of many bomblets housed in a larger canister. The canister exploded after dropped from an aircraft, and the bomblets fell to the ground and exploded individually, scattering pellets over a wide area. Hundreds of millions of these were dropped over Vietnam and Laos during the war. They had a 20–30 percent failure rate, and these were the ones I instructed the troops to avoid. Thousands of farmers and their families were wounded or killed by these unexploded bomblets. About 7,000 were reported maimed or killed in Quang Tri Province alone. Such weapons are no longer permitted under international conventions. A similar, but more confusing, change has taken place concerning the use of white phosphorus. The 1999 ST-100-3 Battle Book published by the U.S. Command and General Staff College states: "It is against the law of land warfare to employ white phosphorus against personnel targets." This is at the same time as other field manuals discuss the use of white phosphorus against personnel.

9 USARV lowered the award to a Silver Star.

10 Dave Johnson was one of the most excellent staff officers that I had the good fortune to serve alongside. He was also the S-1 in Lieutenant Colonel Donald Schroeder's battalion in the Delta in 1968 and I know that Schroeder felt the same way. He took over a company in the 9th Infantry Division and was wounded at the end of December 1968. Both Schroeder and I felt Dave would advance quickly to flag officer rank.

11 Dave Johnson, *Vietnam X3*, 36.

12 Those listed as wounded on the 4 February MR were Sergeant Norman L. McCarry, Private First Class Famous L. Lane, Private First Class Michael R. Lehmer, Sergeant Edward J. Laria, Sergeant Earl Singeltary, and Private First Class Dennis Morningstar.

13 The battalion AA report states that 30 enemy soldiers were killed by body count and 16 weapons captured. The report also relates that 15 enemy soldiers were estimated to have been killed and another 15 estimated wounded. These estimates did not come from Company A.

14 John Bartlett, *Bartlett's Familiar Quotations*. Sixteenth edition with Justin Kaplan as the general editor (Boston: Little, Brown and Company, 1992), 552.

15 We had typewriters in the company, but they were often left with the rear party. The letters were usually handwritten and taken to the battalion S-1 for typing. In the 9th Infantry Division, the battalion S-1 section was responsible for writing these letters, as I remember. It is a mistake to absolve the company commander of this task. The fallen soldier's immediate commander should be among the first to communicate with his family, if that is possible, and the task should not become a routine administrative function at some higher headquarters.

16 The MR for 8 February gives an assigned strength of 223 plus the usual 18–24 attachments.

17 In the article "Bayonets Unsheathed," in the October 1990 issue of *Vietnam Magazine*, Robert A. Lynn wrote on page 36 that Captain Murphy left the 1st and Weapons Platoons as security for the battalion CP. Captain Murphy confirms this in his input to Garland's book, *Infantry in Vietnam*, cited in note 19. The reason for leaving half of Company C as CP security makes no sense! My over-strength company was on Hill 51, and it became brigade reserve as Murphy departed.

18 The battalion AA report dated 12 February 1966 states that eight of the dead and 43 of the injured were from 2/502.

19 Hackworth, *About Face*, 501–509 wrote about My Canh (2); Lieutenant Colonel Albert N. Garland does the same in *Infantry in Vietnam*, 99–102; and in an article in the October 1990 issue of *Vietnam Magazine*, titled "Bayonets Unsheathed," written by Robert A. Lynn. He mentions that the battlefield report listed 66 NVA killed, which had increased to 108 by the time it reached the *Philadelphia Inquirer*. None of these writings explains the reasons for feeding the battlefield in driblets, shifting of AOs, and the reasons for command changes.

20 It appears these casualties are listed on the same MR as those from the 3rd Platoon. The date on the MR is 7 February, but that must be a mistake—it should be 8 February. The 1st Platoon's casualties were sustained during the night of 7/8 February, and 3rd Platoon did not have any casualties until

8 February. The two KIAs from the 3rd Platoon—Staff Sergeant Carlos K. Betancourt and Specialist 4 Sylvester Jackson Jr.—are also listed on this report although their status (KIA or MIA) were not known until we recovered the bodies around 1300 hours on 9 February. Instructions from Brigadier General Pearson were not to list these until we knew for sure whether they were MIA or KIA. Apparently, the staff did not get these instructions. Those listed as wounded are Private First Class Andrew J. Duvall, Private First Class David A. Lucero, Private First Class John F. Erlich, Specialist 4 Jose F. Deno, Private First Class Ronald Penn, Private First Class James A. Davenport, Sergeant Teyrone J. Adderley, and Private First Class David McDuffie. The high ratio of Privates First Class and Specialist 4s (7) versus one NCO was unusual for the company.

21 A/2/502 MR has them assigned on 6 February, but my notes make the first mention of these two officers on 5 February, and they must, therefore, have arrived that day or late on 4 February.

Chapter 11: Days of Flawed Decisions

1 When I attended the 50th Wedding Anniversary of Ray and Ruby Macias, I was reminded of this incident by my former first sergeant and some other NCOs. I guess it was the first time they had seen me lose my temper.

2 Lieutenant Colonel David Perrine had an interview with Colonel I Jim Schoonover regarding this action, and he gave me a copy. Jim's account is detailed, and I have no doubt it is more factual about the engagement than my notes and recollection. It appears from his interview that he had at least three wounded, but only one evacuated that evening. Schoonover, it seems, withdrew across the river because of an imminent B-52 strike to the southwest and he believed his platoon was in the danger zone. I do not recall any nearby B-52 strikes except for one made after it became evident that those encountered at My Canh (2) had withdrawn into the hills. That strike was a considerable distance from the 3rd Platoon. Those of us on Hill 51 were closer to the bombing than the 3rd Platoon, and the movement across the river was in the direction of the strike, although the move was no more than a kilometer. I still believe today that some of Schoonover's NCOs prevailed on him to put the river between them and the enemy. Schoonover makes no mention of the four sharp radio conversations he and I had during the night. Most surprising of all is the fact that he had at least two radio conversations with First Lieutenant Phil Mock about operational matters where I was mentioned. Phil did not tell me about these conversations. Phil told Jim I cleared the instructions he gave. They included detailed directions on how to retrieve the fallen soldiers. Being 6 kilometers away, I would not have involved myself in such details. I would also not have refused to let him take the whole platoon out to recover the fallen, as he reports Phil had stated. That was, in fact, the right thing to do. This was not the last time that Phil Mock made operational decisions without telling me.

3 This was the last time I saw Captain Murphy in Vietnam. That surprised me since we had both told Emerson we wanted to keep our commands until it was time for us to rotate back to the U.S.

4 Tom Clements was with my company for most of my tour in Vietnam and still there when I departed. He was the most excellent FO I ever encountered. He was singled out for written praise by his battalion, 2/320th Artillery, for the outstanding fire support plan he developed for Bu Gia Map.

5 Captain Phil Mock's draft article, "Chaos to Order", 2. I do not recall who sent me the article or when. It was probably after the 1993 flood since it is not water damaged.

6 The fact that Lieutenant Mock made this mistake so soon after his service in A/2/502 is difficult to understand. It is also curious that he wrote that the unit had been in Vietnam 10 months when the actual timespan was about six months. The distance from Tuy Hoa to the battlefield is also too short.

7 Garland, *Infantry in Vietnam*, Chapter XI, 314–319. I have the Garland book as well as the draft article, "Chaos to Order", submitted by Captain Mock to Captain James Sheppard. There are minor differences since the article is more detailed than Garland's book.

8 Specialist 5 Francis D. Faulkner, "Battle Diary: Long Night near Tuy Hoa", *Army Digest*, August 1966, 24–26. Faulkner was assigned to the information office of the 101st Airborne Division when he authored the article, but he was with the brigade in Vietnam.

9 *Battalion Staff Journal* extract for 9 February 1966, 1720 hours.
10 *Gunfighter* was Emerson's radio call sign during both tours in Vietnam.
11 Mock, "Chaos to Order", 5.

Chapter 12: Ambush: A Night of Terror

1 Faulkner, "Battle Diary", 24. At 1630, the decision to disengage had not been made, and the two deployed platoons were heavily engaged. Faulkner describes my initial maneuver after encountering the enemy as moving the 3rd Platoon to the left flank. This is incorrect—the 3rd Platoon was still at the entrance to the valley where we had left it.
2 091910 February entry in the *Battalion Staff Journal.*
3 Faulkner, "Battle Diary", 24. The focus of the article is on two soldiers from the 4th Platoon, who were separated from their unit and spent a frightful night surrounded by NVA troops. One died. The *Army Times* article also contains Fowler's statement.
4 Mock, "Chaos to Order", 4.
5 If this is the case, I find it strange that Settlemire did not tell me when I assigned him and the other two platoon leaders' sections of the perimeter where we had earlier left the 4th Platoon. It is possible that he believed Phil had told me his platoon had been moved and that I now wanted to return it to where it had been. Nevertheless, it is unfortunate that he or Phil did not warn the command group and the other two platoons heading for the wood line along the creek since they knew there were no friendly troops in that wood line. My best guess is that Bill believed Phil had told me. Nevertheless, I find the whole sequence of events very problematic.
6 The fact that this conversation is not mentioned in the SJ may seem unusual, but I know that Emerson received the message. I am sure Tom called Emerson directly because of its importance. Emerson may not have shared this with his staff immediately as was often the case (see chapter 15).
7 Phil Mock wrote in his article (p. 9) that when Sergeant Donald Bear eventually found us, we were only 50 yards from the rest of the company. Phil is sorely mistaken. The creek bed where we were located was about 200 meters from the knoll that Karl Beach used as the company assembly point. If it had been only 50 yards we could almost have talked to Beach without the use of radios. Mock wrote that it took his men four hours to reach the knoll, which he states were 200 meters from his location—I believe it was more than triple that distance and I do not believe it took him four hours to reach the knoll based on SJ entries. I also refer to my earlier discussion of distances in this chapter. Sergeant Bear found us the first time he searched for the command group. See later in this chapter. The distances and directions are wrong on all of Phil's sketches. Phil was in the creek until shortly after 2100 hours.
8 This is another indication that Mock had the location of his group wrong; otherwise, he would have been right next to us, not outside calling distance.
9 We had been issued very luminous wristwatches. I had cut off the top of an old pair of socks to cover the watch since the light could give away our position. All I had to do was peel the sock armband back to check the time. This watch helped me keep a somewhat accurate record of when an event took place, but these were not written in my notes until late 10 or early 11 February.
10 A *Battalion Staff Journal* entry at 092235 February notes that First Lieutenant Mock wanted B/2/502 to link up with us. Mock talked to Company B again according to another SJ entry at 100012 February. This means Mock must have been on the way to the assembly point at the time noted in the journal according to his own timetable. This timetable is obviously incorrect—it took him much less than four hours to reach the knoll. He must have reached the knoll before he sent the message at 2235 hours. This is further substantiated by the fact that Sergeant Bear had conducted two searches before 2400 hours of the area Phil had abandoned. The message he sent at 2235 hours was a violation of the order I had issued when we were both in the creek. The fact that neither Tom Taylor not Emerson reacted to the request is undoubtedly because of the cautionary message I gave Tom earlier. Knowing what I now know, Phil had obviously become unsettled by the intense pressure he had experienced. In his article, Phil Mock wrote that B/2/502 linked up with Company A, but that order was not issued until 100750 February. By that

time, Lieutenant Colonel Emerson had visited us, and two resupply/evacuation helicopters had landed and taken off. No mention was made about a link-up with B/2/502, as Emerson obviously cancelled it after we talked. I did not meet Captain Taylor until we reached the battalion forward CP the evening of the 10th.

11 A 092301 February entry in the battalion SJ has the following notation: "Flare ship in area—start it now. Wants gunships on call." No indication where this came from, but it was probably not from Mock because 26 minutes earlier he had sent a message—SJ entry 092235 February—that he "did not want light over area." After the operation, I was told that Tom Taylor had ordered the flares, which began around 100100 February, and that Karl Beach managed to get them stopped. There were no flares earlier. We had one operable radio until shortly after 0100 hours, but it was turned to the company command net and did not work well.

12 Mock, "Chaos to Order", 9.

13 Faulkner, "Battle Diary", 25–26, and 9 March *Army Times* article.

14 My award citation states that I turned command of the company over to Phil Mock during the night. This is a blatantly false statement and probably based on a supporting statement by Mock. I never turned command of the company over to anyone during the operation, but it was SOP for the XO to assume command after our last radio failed around 0100 hours on 10 February. This statement about relinquishing command doomed my chances of receiving a DSC, but my actions these two days did not deserve one.

15 This was the 2nd most significant encounter with the 95th NVA Regiment, the largest being the action at My Canh (2) on 6–8 February. The My Canh action is covered in a separate battalion AA report dated 12 February, and that is entirely understandable since it was a more substantial action and involved units from two battalions. The main after-action report was issued on 25 February and covered the long period from 15 January to 20 February. Company A's actions reported in the period after the fighting at My Canh appears to be a consolidation of what happened on 8 February and what transpired on 9–10 February and covered in seven lines in the report. The unusually extended period covered by the report results in it being hard to read, and the statistics given are difficult to match up with what happened on the ground.

16 The MR is difficult to read, and it appears to list one soldier twice, once as wounded, and once as having died.

17 In the brigade AA report for *Austin 2* and *6*, there is a statement in the Personnel and Administration enclosure to this report there is a paragraph labeled Programs (Paragraph 3, d). It reads "In order to expedite award of the Purple Heart to members of the brigade who were wounded in action but not evacuated, the brigade requested authority to award the Purple Heart." Lieutenant Colonel Perrine told me this request was approved by USARV. I had never heard about it. Since I rotated back to the U.S. before this AA report was published (5 June 1966), I can only hope it was somehow retroactive and that those who elected to remain with the company were recognized for their wounds and received the Purple Heart.

18 Barragy was killed when the helicopter he was on crashed on the way to Nhon Co on 4 May 1966, discussed in chapter 14.

19 Phil Mock claims that the camp "had been occupied by the Headquarters of the 95th North Vietnamese Regiment," "Chaos to Order," 9. We found nothing in the camp that indicated this was a valid statement, nor have I seen that claim anywhere else. We reported to battalion (SJ entry 101245 February) that it was a company-size camp.

Chapter 13: Operations, 17 February–4 April 1965

1 Lieutenant General (Ret) Henry Emerson's letter dated 1 December 2005.

2 S. L. A. Marshall, *Vietnam: Three Battles* (New York: Da Capo Press, Inc., 1982).

3 Master Sergeant Macias had made some changes in assignment for the senior NCOs in the company while I was away. I did not see Sergeant First Class Ledford when I returned. Sergeant First Class Jack was moved to the 1st Platoon, with Sergeant First Class Taylor taking over the 2nd Platoon. Staff

Sergeant James Castle took over as platoon sergeant of the 3rd Platoon. I am not sure who became platoon sergeant of the 4th Platoon, but it may have been Staff Sergeant Johnny Castro. The platoon sergeants also made some changes in squad leaders.

4 One box of cookies also arrived from a member of the Amidan family. Marilyn Amidan had written to the company in November/December 1965, as she was concerned since she had not heard from her brother, Private First Class Michael D. Amidan. If my recollection is correct, her brother had overstayed his R&R. I was proud of the fact that I never had to resort to non-judicial punishment (Article 15) for any of my troops. I found other ways to correct the situation. As punishment, I made Michael my driver. In the field, my driver served at my CP as runner. This was a dangerous assignment. The stateside package was only labeled as coming from Amidan. I assume it came from a member of his family.

5 Report from Lieutenant Colonel Perrine.

6 Operation *Harrison* ended on 25 March while we were in the mountains. Reported results were 288 VC/NVA killed while U.S. casualties were reported as 42 KIAs, 249 WIA, and two MIAs.

Chapter 14: Phan Thiet and Bu Prang

1 Punji stakes were mostly made of bamboo with very sharp tips, hidden by leaves and fallen branches. The tip of the bamboo was occasionally dipped in poison.

2 Battalion AA report records it as a 1962 truck. This must be a typing error.

3 The brigade AA report states that friendly casualties in this three-week operation were two killed and 15 wounded. The two killed were from Company A, as were six of the injured. The brigade had six rifle companies and two reconnaissance platoons in the Phan Thiet area, and the casualty statistics make me wonder what the other five companies and the two reconnaissance platoons were doing. The unequal distribution of casualties had started with the Ben Cat operation and continued through the Bu Gia Map operation.

4 S. L. A. Marshall, *Battles in the Monsoon: Campaigning in the Central Highlands, South Vietnam, Summer 1966* (New York: William Morrow & Company, Inc., 1966), 227.

5 The 5 June 1966 brigade AA report states the brigade began deployment from Phan Thiet by C-130 aircraft on 28 April 1966 using 172 sorties. All units had closed Nhon Co by 2 May.

6 The 2/502nd AA report, 24 May 1966, 3.

7 In 1995, I drove by Lupton, Arizona, the Navajo Reservation that Hawthorne came from. It is the first exit after crossing into Arizona from New Mexico on Interstate 40. The road leading north was named Hawthorne Road, and there was no doubt in my mind it was named for the legendary staff sergeant from my company. It was getting dark, and the road looked rough, so I decided to stop the next time I came through the area. I have since learned Hawthorne is buried in the Santa Fe National Cemetery in Santa Fe, New Mexico.

8 Marshall, *Battles in the Monsoon*, 227.

9 2/502 AA report, 24 May 1966, 2. For example, the day we made our attempt to reach the border, the AA report has my company providing CP security.

10 Ibid., at the bottom of the page.

Chapter 15: The Bu Gia Map Campaign, 6–10 May

1 Battalion AA report of 24 May, paragraph b (2) Concept of Operation.

2 Ibid., paragraph b (3) Execution.

3 A statement by Captain Ronald Brown for "The Bu Gia Map Campaign" in *The Battle of Bu Gia Map Special Study* by the 22nd Military History Detachment (after this referred to as the *Special Study).* Brown states the battalion made a helicopter assault by CH-47s on or about 7 May 1966. Another statement in the *Special Study* by 1st Lieutenant John B. Mooneyham also has 7 May as the starting date of the operation. These discrepancies call the accuracy of some of the dates and times before 9 May

into question. I believe both Ron and Mooneyham must have arrived in the afternoon of 6 May for Mooneyham to join the company before its departure shortly after 1400 hours on 6 May.

4 Hackworth, *About Face*, 533, and Taylor, *Where the Orange Blooms*, 109–113.

5 My notes for the early part of this operation are not as detailed as was usually the case. It was my last operation, and I had not anticipated its length. I believed there would be enough time to fill in the blanks before I turned over the command of the company. This was a mistake as the operation lasted until 17 May and involved several course changes and some heavy fighting. I resumed making detailed notes on 9 May.

6 I know my XO, Lieutenant Beach, was interviewed but he did not join us in the field until after the battle was over. I do not recall if he stayed for the pursuit, but most likely he returned to Nhon Co.

7 His doubts became known during the 1st Brigade reunion in Atlanta in 2006. Kim Coleman was there, and some of those in attendance had made some critical comments about her work. I did not meet Kim at the reunion, but Bob Murphy did. She was seeking information about the Bu Gia Map Operation, and Bob pointed me out as the ground commander, but she never approached me. After the reunion, Emerson sent me a copy of that part of the manuscript dealing with Bu Gia Map and asked me for my comments. Kim Coleman had asked him to write an introduction. After reading the manuscript, I concluded it was mostly a regurgitation of what Marshall had written, and I told Emerson it was, from a factual standpoint, no better. The end of the story was that Emerson did not write an introduction.

8 There is another problem, which further complicated my scarcity of notes. I made a sketch map at the end of the operation and gave it to the battalion S-3 section. I also made a copy for myself, but I must have been in a hurry since I left out the two grid intersection hash marks that are necessary to line up the sketch map properly. I also neglected to show a compass rose. These were maybe on the sketch map I turned in, and I just did not enter them on my copy. As a result, my first draft had our route about 2,000 meters further north than it was.

9 Mooneyham's report for the *Special Study*.

10 Marshall, *Battles in the Monsoon*, 233.

11 The battalion SJ confirms the time we intersected the trail as 1505 hours on 9 May and it gives the coordinates of the intersection as YU298340. Mooneyham's report has us finding the east–west trail on 8 May and receiving a resupply. He mentions nothing about the change in direction early on 8 May. I believe his use of the wrong starting date (7 May) caused this. We had our first resupply on 10 May.

12 Marshall, *Battles in the Monsoon*, 234.

13 The battalion AA report states this action took place at 1020 hours and gives a coordinate that is several kilometers too far west. The discrepancy in times is correct. I delayed reporting the engagement, pending more complete information.

14 I went to the Associated Press office in Saigon as I was leaving Vietnam as Henri Huét had asked me to. He gave me many pictures he had taken on the operation along with permission to use them. All used in this chapter are from Huét. Henri was the son of a French father and a Vietnamese mother, but he went to France when he was about six years old. He was killed on 10 February 1967 when two helicopters carrying journalists and photographers were shot down by anti-aircraft fire near the Laotian border.

15 Howell was killed later that summer, according to Lieutenant Colonel Perrine.

16 The brigade AA report (paragraph 27 of the intelligence portion of the report) identifies the prisoner as a master sergeant in the 2nd Squad, 1st Platoon, 2nd Company, 3rd Battalion, 141st Regiment and that he was occupying a guard post in front of his company when captured. This is not the information he gave us—I doubt a master sergeant in the NVA pulled guard duty. This was not a grab and snatch operation! He was captured 800 meters from his battalion and told us that he was leading a reconnaissance unit.

17 General Marshall and some of the other sources dealing with the upcoming battle do not mention the fact that I received operational control of all ground forces. It is mentioned by Hackworth and in the battalion AA report, which states the operational control remained in effect until we reached the Cambodian border. This is not mentioned in the brigade AA report, and I received the distinct

impression after the operation that the brigade commander was not aware of the fact I had operational control of all ground forces.

18 See, for example, Hackworth, *About Face*, 532, where he states Emerson landed at my location to question and pick up the prisoner.

19 Marshall, *Battles in the Monsoon*, 236.

20 Mrs. Settlemire sent us a copy of the front page of the weekend edition (14–15 May) of the *St. Louis Globe-Democrat* featuring the story of how we were saved from a deadly trap. Although her only child, Lieutenant William Settlemire, was killed in February, his mother still worried about Company A and showed pride in its activities.

21 Marshall, *Battles in the Monsoon*, 237–243.

22 A/2/17 Cavalry was attached to the battalion a few days earlier and was located on the Bu Gia Map airstrip when it was sent to reinforce us.

23 Marshall, *Battles in the Monsoon*, 237.

24 Ibid., 237–238.

25 The reason Company C was split up in this way was that it had only one officer. The Apache platoon was a form of reconnaissance platoon made up from the better-trained troops in the CIDG outfit. They were out to practice and improve their reconnaissance abilities when they were attached to TF Brown.

26 Marshall, *Battles in the Monsoon*, 242.

27 Ibid.

28 In his statement to the 22nd Military History Detachment, George Hamilton states the size of his task force alone was 250–300 men.

29 As reported by Captain Brown in his input to the *Special Study*.

30 The battalion AA report states A/2/502 linked up with TF Brown at 101700 May, 10 minutes after TF Hamilton arrived on the scene. It appears the battalion AA report is about one hour behind what Captain Hamilton and I reported.

31 Hamilton's report for the *Special Study*.

32 Marshall, *Battles in the Monsoon*, 242–244. This is wrong since reports found by Lieutenant Colonel Perrine state that A/2/17 Cavalry had only two wounded during the entire operation.

33 The 1st Brigade AA report on 5 June 1966 identifies the enemy regimental commander as Lieutenant Colonel Trac and Captain Than as the commander of 3rd Battalion.

34 Captain Brown wrote in his input to the *Special Study* that a perimeter was established by 1920 hours.

Chapter 16: Battle of Bu Gia Map and Pursuit

1 Marshall, *Battles in the Monsoon*, 245.

2 Hackworth, *About Face*, 533. He wrote that Emerson told me to plan the ground operation, and it worked like a charm.

3 Captain Taylor in his own book (*Where the Orange Blooms*, 111) has TF Brown as the enveloping force, and I have found no mention of the cavalry that struggled much in the impenetrable jungle to make the envelopment. Both Taylor's account and Marshall's version of what happened show the shortcomings of relating events in a battle where they were not present, basing their stories on second-hand information. Emerson could not remember receiving the post-battle sketches I left with the battalion S-3 section, which leads me to believe the S-3 may have thrown them away.

4 The report by 1st Lieutenant John B. Mooneyham states I left the Weapons Platoon (4th) as a reserve when I approached the enemy position. That was our original plan. We had expected the enemy front to be shorter than it was because we had assumed they were in a U-shaped position. When it turned out they were in a linear position, we needed all platoons to cover our extended front, and then some.

5 I am not sure how many aircraft were involved and how many sorties were flown, but I recall being told after the battle that 11 multi-aircraft attacks by fighter-bombers were conducted in our support. To us, on the ground, it sounded like a continuous stream of aircraft.

6 Headquarters 1st Brigade 101st Airborne Division, *Informal After Action Critique, Operation Austin 6*, dated 27 May 1966, 3, paragraph (4).

7 In his input to the *Special Study*, Major Allen V. Stott, S-3 of 2/320 Artillery, gives considerable praise to the FO (Lieutenant Clements) and concludes the infantry commander (me) used the fire support very effectively and achieved the best results up to then in the country.

8 There was nothing to do until the fighting was over. The finger was hanging by only flesh and skin. I wrapped that finger and the middle finger together in a piece of cloth. After the battle was over, a medic (a Specialist 4 whose name I have forgotten) made a finger splint and tried to reset the joint. He gave me a couple of aspirins and said if that did not work, they might have to cut the finger. I noticed that he winked at my RTO, and I told him, if that were the case, I would cut a couple of stripes from his sleeves. The finger functions fine but is partially crooked and I have difficulties getting my wedding band on.

9 Marshall, *Battles in the Monsoon*, 248.

10 Ibid., 249.

11 Kim Coleman's manuscript, 110–112. Ms. Coleman is an excellent and eloquent writer, but the accuracy of her research is lacking—this incident is only one example.

12 Enclosure 1, Development of Intelligence in the Bu Gia Map Area to Enclosure 2—Intelligence, to Combat Operations After Action Report, Operation *Austin*, 5 June 1966, paragraph 38.

13 I believe the number of weapons mentioned in the report is only a fraction of the many weapons or weapons' parts we found by 12 May.

14 *Combat Operations After Action Report AUSTIN*, 5 June 1966, 29, paragraph 11 b (3). We received no sniper fire on 11 May. This part of the report also mentions two NVA companies, and that we decimated the whole battalion. The NVA battalion consisted of a headquarters, three rifle companies and a heavy weapons company.

15 According to the battalion AA report and Major Stout's—S-3, 2nd Battalion, 320th Artillery (Abn)—report for the *Special Study*.

16 First Sergeant Lyn of A/2/17 Cavalry makes an almost identical observation, to what I wrote in my field notebook on the evening, 11 May, in his input to the *Special Study* as he walked through the battlefield.

17 Hackworth, *About Face*, 533.

18 It is strange that the sources are completely silent on this CBS visit to the field. I can only speculate that the various headquarters from brigade to MACV were eager to depict a large and successful operation to the public. However, when it quickly became apparent the visit itself might have caused the campaign to be less successful than it could have been, it became necessary to not mention it.

19 This contact is mentioned in the brigade AA, and the NVA is alleged to have worn U.S. uniforms. I do not recall Brown telling me about this incident.

20 I do not know if this is the same bombing as the brigade AA reports taking place along the Cambodian border on 14 May. We noticed no B-52 strikes on the 14th when we were at the Cambodian border, and I, therefore, believe brigade had the wrong date.

21 Marshall, *Battles in the Monsoon*, 257.

22 Taylor, *Where the Orange Blooms*, 112. Tom's call came after my talk with Emerson. Earlier in his book (109), Tom wrote he was still with the British (in Hong Kong in May and June). It was highly unusual for a brigade staff officer to communicate directly with a company commander—in fact, I cannot think of another example of this happening in the 1st Brigade.

23 This makes the total enemy killed by body count by my company and the two task forces 422 when the 23 reported by Brown on 10 May are added. That is the total reported by the three units in my task force and forms the basis for the reports by Hackworth and Marshall. Marshall must not have included the 24 my company killed on the way to the battlefield or the 32 who were killed during the pursuit. Hackworth must have reported these and that is why his number is 450, and the most accurate in my view. We did not report any estimated killed at Bu Gia Map, and I never used estimated counts in the 10 months I commanded a company size unit in Vietnam. The estimates were added at battalion and brigade levels.

24 I left Macias behind in the rear area during the Bu Gia Map campaign. He was nearing the end of his tour, had a large family (wife and five or six children) in Clarksville, Tennessee, and was in the habit of taking unnecessary risks. He was not happy about this, but I made it an order.

25 Awarded the Silver Star, recommended for the DSC (twice with the addition of the one for Bu Gia Map), recommended for two Oak Leaf Clusters for the Silver Star, and the Bronze Star with "V."

26 After I returned to the U.S. and had an opportunity to read some documents sent to me, Florence and I concluded that it was all done to further Emerson's reputation, unfortunately at my expense. Emerson did not need anyone to protect his reputation. He had leadership qualities, which I had recognized the first day we met, which alone secured his career in the Army.

Chapter 17: Airborne Test Division: The War in 1967

1 This proved to be a wise precaution. There were two letters from 2/502, dated 4 and 12 January 1967, referencing a package of award orders sent to our home address at 22 Brandywine Road in Clarksville from A/2/502. I never received that package and would not have known about them except for the fact they were mentioned in the 12 January letter. Based on this letter, the Airborne Test Division obtained copies, probably from DA, and I can only assume and hope they are the ones mentioned in the 12 January letter.

2 I was not aware of any published guidelines and relied on common sense. It was not until I joined the USAAESWB that I was required to sign a Public Affairs Guidance Document for personnel returning from Vietnam. The document gave advice for discussions with family, friends, and the press and other media outlets. The operative paragraph of the one-page document which I signed on 3 August 1966 read: "For broad guidance, military personnel should limit their remarks to unclassified information, within the scope of their own personal experience and responsibility. Otherwise, when your reply is not based on the facts of the matter, you may be doing harm to your country, your unit and yourself." It was a very mild and commonsense directive.

3 Alf Kvarme was able to obtain a video copy of the TV and radio interviews from the NRK files in August 2018, and I have those in my possession.

4 The NRK person who conducted the TV interview was named Brauteset. He also held the more extended radio interview for a weekly program called *Folk iforbifarten* (*People in Passing*).

5 USATECOM lists Lieutenant Colonel Rogers as Airborne Test Division Director from October 1966 to August 1967. Lieutenant Colonel C. W. Eckelsis listed as director from August 1967 to June 1968 at which time Lieutenant Colonel Robert E. Luttrell took over and served until June 1970.

6 Much of the information on the history of TECOM and the USAAESWB before my arrival is based on a paper issued by the Historical Office of the Test and Experimental Command at Fort Hood, Texas in October 1990. It is titled *The Airborne and Special Operations Test Board 1940–1990: A Commemorative History* (AD-A236 660).

7 *The Airborne and Special Operations Test Board 1940–1990*, 42.

8 Those six awards were two oak leaf clusters to the Silver Star I received at Phan Thiet, indicating three awards, a Bronze Star, the Air Medal with three numerals, and a Purple Heart. The DSC I was recommended for at Tuy Hoa on 9–10 February 1965 had been lowered to a Silver Star. The same happened to the DSC recommendation for the Battle of Bu Gia Map; it was also reduced to a Silver Star a few weeks after the ceremony and was presented to me by the board president, Colonel Strickland in an office ceremony before he departed. This award made the total of three oak leaves, indicating four awards. I had not expected a DSC for Tuy Hoa, as I really did not deserve one. The one for Bu Gia Map was different. I am sure I would have received one if the citation had stated that I commanded all ground forces both during the battle and pursuit. Furthermore, the OER for that period is equally unhelpful in not mentioning it. This is what caused Florence and I to conclude that the reason was to enhance Emerson's reputation. Both Emerson and Major Donald Schroeder had a hand in these actions. Emerson's conscience must have given him troubles because he sent me his DSC with the following words written on inside the box: "To Hank Lunde, the best combat leader of them all. Morally, this is yours. With great respect and gratitude. *Gunfighter* 25 Dec 94." I was furious and intended to return the award with an angry note. When Florence and June could not convince me not to return it, Florence called Hackworth and he told me not to do what I planned because it would break Emerson's heart. Consequently, I did not return the award and I am now glad.

9 Colonel Harry G. Summers, Jr., *Vietnam Almanac* (New York: Facts on File Publications, 1985), 215–217.
10 France's last major defeat 1953–1954 before their withdrawal.
11 Summers, *Vietnam Almanac*, 217.
12 Colonel Summers wrote that 205 Marines were killed at Khe Sanh while the NVA left 1,602 dead on the battlefield. Westmoreland, on the other hand, puts the NVA losses at 10,000–15,000!
13 A large framed humorous *facts and fiction* satire type poem about Florence and me was composed by the senior secretary of the Airborne Test Division, Shirley Hodnett, with the "enthusiastic" support of some of my "friends," like Arne Andersen, Richard Ezzard, Jack Miller, and Sergeant Eckstein. It was presented to Florence and me in a departure ceremony and is now in the possession of my grandnephew Asbjørn Ure. It alludes to me having a possible ulterior motive for assigning the project to James Dowdy. He was dating the daughter of one of the generals at Pope Air Force Base involved in the LAPES project and took much ribbing about the assignment, which was allegedly made by me to ease coordination with the Air Force.
14 The board president came to see me to ensure a junior officer such as Captain Dowdy could deal with more senior individuals in the Philippines and Vietnam. I assured him Dowdy would do an excellent job, but if he felt that I should also go, I would be willing to do so. I jokingly reminded him that my Irish wife may go on the warpath given her comments to him at a recent social event. In the end, he accepted my view of Captain Dowdy's abilities, and this was confirmed by many commendation letters received from the Air Force, Marines and USARV.
15 Summers, *Vietnam Almanac*, 40, 44.
16 For my brief summary of the Battle of Dak To, I have relied on a much longer and more detailed treatment of the subject by Wikipedia (https://en.wikipedia.org/wiki/Battle_of_Dak_To). Wikipedia relied on public domain material or documents at the United States Army Center of Military History.
17 Brigadier General Leo H. Schweiter had recently taken over command from my old battle group commander, Brigadier General John Deane.
18 Neil Sheehan, "David and Goliath in Vietnam," *New York Times* opinion article, 26 May 2017.
19 William G. Effros (compiler), *Quotations Vietnam 1945–1970* (New York: Random House, 1970), 85.
20 Ibid., 86.
21 Ibid.
22 Robert S. McNamara with Brian VanDeMark, *In Retrospect: The Tragedy and Lessons of Vietnam* (New York: Times Books a division of Random House, 1995), 5. He gives much praise to his time at UC, stating it opened a new world for him.
23 Ibid., 110 and 112–113.
24 Robert S. McNamara, James G. Blight, and Robert K. Brigham with Thomas J. Biersteker and Colonel Herbert Y. Schandler, *Argument Without End: In Search of Answer to the Vietnam Tragedy* (New York: Public Affairs, 1999).
25 When I met the North Vietnamese negotiators on my last tour in Vietnam, it became patently evident to me that we knew virtually nothing about North Vietnam as opposed to their extensive knowledge of our history, institutions, and political system.
26 Tuchman, *The March of Folly from Troy to Vietnam*, 317.
27 Ibid., 324.
28 Walter Millis, *Arms and Men: A Study in American Military History* (New York: G. P. Putman's Sons, 1956), and Walter Millis (editor), *American Military Thought* (Indianapolis: The Bobbs-Merrill Company, Inc., 1966). Samuel P. Huntington, *The Common Defense: Strategic Programs in National Politics* (New York: Columbia University Press, Fourth Printing 1969).
29 I do not have Earle's edition from the 1940s, but I do have a later version. Edward Mead Earle (editor), *The Makers of Modern Strategy: Military Thought from Machiavelli to Hitler* (Princeton: Princeton University Press, 1973).
30 Winston S. Churchill, *The Second World War: Volume 1, The Gathering Storm* (Boston: Houghton Mifflin Company, 1948), 319–320.

31 Clinton Rossiter (editor), *The Federalist Papers: Alexander Hamilton, James Madison, John Hay* (New York: Penguin Group, 1961), paper 63, probably authored by Madison, 382.
32 Sun-Tzu, *The Art of War*, new translation and commentary by Ralph D. Sawyer and Mei-chün Lee Sawyer (New York: Barnes & Noble, 1994), 173.
33 Ibid., 179.

Chapter 18: Arrival in Vietnam and Assignment as Brigade S-3

1 This is in addition to about 820,000 South Vietnamese troops, 8,000 Australian soldiers, about 50,000 South Korean troops, 6,000 Thai soldiers, 550 from New Zealand, and over 1,500 from the Philippines.
2 Effros, *Quotations Vietnam 1945–1970*, 87.
3 Ibid.
4 For the Battle for Saigon, I have relied heavily on "Battle for Saigon" by David T. Zabecki, which appeared in the summer 1989 issue of the *Vietnam Magazine*. For those who are interested in a more detailed treatment, I recommend the book by Keith William Noland, *The Battle for Saigon Tet 1968* (New York: Pocket Books, 1996) and, for the Tet Offensive as a whole, the incredibly detailed book, *The Viet-Cong Tet Offensive 1968*, edited and published by the Historical Division of the South Vietnamese General Staff in 1969.
5 Effros, *Quotations Vietnam 1945–1970*, 89.
6 Ibid.
7 Ibid., 90.
8 Carl O. Schuster (retired Navy captain), "Hanoi's Tet Deception," *Vietnam Magazine*, February 2020, 35. This is an excellent article by a former intelligence officer.
9 Maurice Matloff (editor), *American Military History* (2 volumes) (Conshohocken, Pennsylvania: Combined Books, 1996). Chapter 28 deals with Vietnam and is apparently based on what was written by Vincent H. Demma, who was a Center for Military History historian specializing in the Army role in the Vietnam conflict. It is stated in volume 2, chapter 28, 328 that "the Tet offensive began quietly in mid-January 1968" at Khe Sanh. I have already stated that I doubt this was the case. Instead, it may have been a continuation of the effort to draw U.S. and ARVN forces away from populated areas, and this is also what Demma concludes at the end of the paragraph on 328.
10 Schuster, "Hanoi's Tet Deception," 29–31.
11 The *USA Today* review of Mark Bowden's book *Huê 1968: A Turning Point of the American War in Vietnam* (New York: Atlantic Monthly Press, 2017).
12 John Hughes Wilson, *Military Intelligence Blunders* (New York: Carroll & Graf Publishers, Inc., 1999), 175.
13 Effros, *Quotations Vietnam 1945–1970*, 93.
14 Matloff, *American Military History*, vol. 2, 330
15 The president announced on 3 May 1968 that the U.S. and North Vietnam had agreed to begin formal peace talks in Paris beginning on 12 May. While Johnson also announced a temporary bombing halt of North Vietnam, that bombing halt became permanent at the end of October.
16 Operational Report 9th Infantry Division for the Period Ending 31 July 1968, dated 20 August 1968 (hereafter referred to as the 9th Division Report 20 August), 2.
17 Parrot's Beak was the name given to a protrusion of Cambodia in the direction of Saigon. Other elements of U.S. II Field Force were stationed on the north side of this protrusion.
18 9th Division Report, 20 August, 79.
19 Ibid., 11 and 90.
20 According to the 9th Infantry Division Report, 20 August 1968, Van Deusen was shot down and died on 3 July, and my notes give the time as about 1700 hours. There were 10 men on the helicopter, which was shot down and plunged into the Vam Co Tay River, near to Tan An. Three were rescued on 3 July, and the helicopter and the seven bodies were recovered on 4 July.

21 Colonel David Johnson in *Vietnam X3*, 51–52, wrote that "my quiet and measured approach to every situation helped to dampen Colonel Emerson's temper and impulsiveness on many occasions."
22 Henrik Lunde, *A Warrior Dynasty: The Rise and Fall of Sweden as a Military Superpower, 1611–1721* (Casemate Publishers: Havertown, Pennsylvania, and Oxford, 2014).
23 This was my first visit to the new "Pentagon East", almost completed. I became thoroughly familiar with this massive building during my third tour in Vietnam.

Chapter 19: Battalion Executive Officer

1 9th Division Operational Report, 20 August 1968, 94.
2 Specialist 5 Wayne Campbell, "Former home of VC now houses 2d-39th," 6 November 1968.
3 Virgil Ney, *Evolution of US Army Infantry Battalion: 1939–1968* (Fort Belvoir, Virginia: Combat Operations Research Group, United States Army Combat Development Command, October 1968). This is a detailed 207-page document.
4 Johnson, *Vietnam X3*, 54–55.
5 Ibid., 55.
6 Ibid., 54.
7 Lindsay had a distinguished career, retiring as general.
8 I was dubious about the enemy losses in this, as in other encirclements. We allegedly destroyed much of the encircled unit, reportedly found 66 enemies killed, but only 29 weapons. In encirclement, the number of weapons captured should be much closer to the number of enemies killed. I had been skeptical of the reliability of the body count in the 1st Brigade, 101st Airborne Division but, in the 9th Division, my skepticism turned to complete rejection of its truthfulness.
9 Operational Report of 9th Infantry Division for the Period Ending 31 January 1969, dated 15 February 1969. The reports show, on 75–76, that 11,399 awards of all types were issued from 1 November 1968 to 31 January 1969.
10 Refusal to deploy for combat usually, but not always, took place when they were loading on helicopters.
11 The prisoners were turned over to ARVN. Most of them were innocent civilians caught up in the engagement and were released. The six weapons captured when 64 enemies were reported killed had to be caused by a much-embellished body count.
12 I had violated my integrity before in the 2/502, but in those cases, it dealt with saving lives or sparing the feelings of the next of kin.
13 Our friendship did not end because of this episode. I believe he realized, after thinking about it, that I had shown full loyalty to him over the years, and that I had produced superior results and that some of the disagreements we had were meant to protect his interests. While this was our last combat tour together, I later served for him indirectly at Fort Bragg. We remained in continual contact after our retirements. I believe, based on what his nurse said, that Truong and I were the only two he summoned to Marathon, Florida, when he knew he was going to die. When he died, I felt I lost my best friend in the Army.
14 Colonel Geraci had an airborne and SF background, and I believe he came from Okinawa. Geraci was my OER endorser, covering the whole period I served in 2/39. He was a maverick, and we got along well. We remained in touch for a few years.
15 Geoffrey C. Ward and Ken Burns, *The Vietnam War: An Intimate History* (New York: Knopf Doubleday Publishers, 2017), 356–357.
16 These figures, given by Wikipedia and several other sources, do not agree with what is reported in the Operational Report of the 9th Division for Period Ending 31 January 1969, dated 15 February 1969, 17, but Operation *Speedy Express* continued for more than four months after the period covered by that report.
17 When Colonel Emerson was shot down, those of us from the 101st Airborne Division who had come over at his request lost our protector. Hunt treated all 101st field grade officers in a harsh and unjustified manner, particularly Lieutenant Colonels Schroeder and Hackworth. Emerson felt beholden to Hunt

for pulling him out of the helicopter, and that is understandable. After Emerson retired, both he and I received invitations to a 9th Division reunion in Maryland. He called me to see if I was going. I told him no, it would do injustice to the memory of Lieutenant Colonel Schroeder. I believe he received the same answer from Hackworth. It took some time, but eventually Emerson came to share our view about Hunt.

Chapter 20: Deputy G-3 Adviser, II ARVN Corps

1 Most information about my travel difficulties is taken from a three-page memorandum for record I prepared on 16 February 1969, enclosed to a complaint letter General Timothy wrote to USARV. The "letter-to" issued in Singapore, which also noted that travel cost was chargeable to Fund Cite: NVAL. CIC 19A-03, was attached.

2 Since charges showed up on my card from the Frankfurt area, it is likely the card was lost or stolen in Germany. I only had to pay $50.00 after I arrived at C&GSC.

3 I subsequently learned the complaint had results. The rules changed within a relatively brief time, giving priority to soldiers on emergency leave and reclassifying all empty seats as space available for any soldier heading for Vietnam.

4 The date given on the internet for his death is 13 February. This may be due to the date difference between the U.S. and Vietnam. It is equally possible that I made a mistake in my notes.

5 Johnson, *Vietnam X3*, 64.

6 Summers, *Vietnam Almanac*, 52.

7 This was the term given to incidents where soldiers attacked their superiors using fragmentation grenades.

8 The name of the corps commander while I was there was Lieutenant General Lu Mong Lan, born 1927, who had taken over the command on 1 March 1968. His name appears on both award citations, although one is so faded it is virtually impossible to read. He was a staunch supporter of President Thieu, and my guess is that he left the country in early 1973 with his wife and five children, although I do not know this for sure.

Chapter 21: Schooling and Battalion Command

1 A Federal Prison, which the students at C&GSC referred to as the "Long Course," is also located at Fort Leavenworth. The name of C&GSC has now changed to Command and General Staff School. The expanded functions are too involved and numerous to discuss in this work.

2 Since I had missed the graduation ceremonies at C&GSC, they sent me a brochure listing the graduates. I was on the Commandant's List, which meant I was in the top 10 percent of the class.

3 Ever since SU, I had sadly concluded the Army was determined to change my specialty. My MA in International Relations, rather than an interdisciplinary MA, pointed in that direction. My assignment to Detachment A with the assurance that it would not affect my specialty proved false. A future assignment in the field of psychological operations convinced me that my career was damaged beyond repair. Therefore, a tour with the SF was more acceptable as I would be among elite infantry troops.

4 Captain Dolighan was the temporary battalion XO when I arrived. His wife had accompanied Brigitte on her visit to Columbus, Georgia, in 1964. Soon after my assignment, I was assigned another major, Major Edward Perry Passailaigue (1932–2014), and Dolighan was given command of Company C.

5 The 5th Special Forces Group moved to Fort Campbell, Kentucky, in June 1988.

6 If my memory is correct, the 7th Special Forces Group had only two battalions at Fort Bragg. The other battalion must have been in Panama. The 7th Special Forces Group moved to Eglin Air Force Base, Florida in 2011.

7 Corson L. Hilton, Lieutenant Colonel, *United States Special Forces: From a Decade of Development to a Sustained Future*, (Carlisle Barracks: U.S. Army War College, 1991).

8 The lengthy time spent training led some wives of the officers in my battalion to bring the subject to Florence's attention at one of their social functions.

9 I had driven my 1965 VW for the first six months as battalion commander. The officers in the battalion did not feel it was a suitable car for their commander and I was finally shamed into trading it in on a new Triumph TR6.

10 Three of the officers were from the battalion HD. One was Major Lawrence C. Bruscas, the commander of A/3/5, the unit that would go to Iran in the autumn of 1973.

Chapter 22: Chief of Negotiation, U.S. Delegation FPJMT

1 Dana Crum, "Unforeseen Journey takes Miles from Military to Princeton," *Princeton Weekly Bulletin*, 13 June 2005.

2 https://en.Wikipedia.org/wiki/Graham Martin. This, plus articles in the *New York Times* and *Washington Post*, were used to describe the events in Ambassador Martin's earlier life, and his apparent tardiness in evacuating personnel and records before Saigon fell.

3 The Automatic Voice Network (AUTOVON) was a military telephone system developed by the US in 1963, designed to survive nuclear attacks. It allowed non-secure voice calls with priority override.

4 Pamphlet of 154 double-spaced pages by the FPJMT. It is titled *US Delegation Four Party Joint Military Team—A History 31 March—31 December 1973*. This pamphlet was written by the negotiations division and issued under a memorandum signed by Colonel Tombaugh. The reference refers to pp. II–III of this pamphlet.

5 Major Rich, in talking to Florence at her welcoming party, warned her to be careful because Vietnamese on mopeds were known to grab rings, necklaces, and watches from anyone when the windows were open. Two days later a passing moped ripped off Rich's Rolex watch in that manner and the poor guy underwent considerable ribbing.

6 I sent the coins that appeared uncirculated plus two key dates in the Barber series to have them certified and graded after we opened our business in 1979. The certification and grading came to over $300.00, so by the time they were all sold, we had a hefty profit. It was the most profitable C-130 ride I ever made.

7 Florence and I had become friends with Wallace and his wife, who had arrived before Florence and corresponded with her before she left the U.S. The Wallace family opened an import business in Bern, North Carolina. We learned this from Bekins.

8 I believe she became Tombaugh's wife after his divorce.

9 These type of incidents had happened earlier. The Polish delegation to the ICCS threatened to ram the gate to Camp Davis with their vehicle. The RVN replied that if they did that, RVN would open fire on the unarmed Poles. I do not know how it was finally resolved, but the other delegations to the ICCS probably lodged protests and it became apparent to the RVN that they risked the ire of the world community.

10 By the time I reached DA, Colonel Rosenblum had been promoted to brigadier general and was in the process of leaving the Army staff.

11 Letter from Lieutenant Colonel Miller dated 12 March 1974.

Chapter 23: Pentagon and U.S. Army War College

1 General Bernard W. Rogers was Army Chief of Staff from 1976 to 1979. Thereafter he was appointed Supreme Allied Commander Europe 1979 to 1987. He is alleged to have stated that for him happiness was the Pentagon in the rearview mirror, a feeling I share wholeheartedly.

2 While many sources list it as the second oldest, a Special Report by Samuel Stebbins, titled *America's Oldest Military Bases*, dated 9 March 2020, lists it as the oldest.

3 Most of the information on Alexander Haig's life before I met him is based on what is written on Wikipedia, https://en.wikipedia.org/wiki/Alexander_Haig#Early_life_and_education, as well as other public sources, such as Obituaries.

Chapter 24: SHAPE, USAWC, and Retirement

1 I corresponded with Finn Moseng (promoted to rear admiral) and his wife for many years. They also visited us in Shippensburg when he was stationed in Norfolk, Virginia, for a brief time. He died from Parkinson's disease. I likewise corresponded with Hilmi until well after my retirement, primarily through New Year cards.

2 The calculations of command slots becoming open each year for infantry officers are my own and may therefore not be accurate. Still, it demonstrates the damage caused by the switch in command categories.

3 While I have not met Colonel Littlefield since my retirement, I believe he is the same Colonel Richard Littlefield who died on 2 July 2021 in Newville, Pennsylvania. He had earlier lived in Mount Holly Springs, Pennsylvania, and I have a fleeting recollection that he lived there while working with me.

4 Harry G. Summers, Jr., Colonel of Infantry, *On Strategy: The Vietnam War in Context* (Carlisle Barracks, Pennsylvania: U.S. Army War College Strategic Studies Institute, 1981), 1.

5 Ibid.

Epilogue

1 Google for Memorandum of Conversation between James Baker and Eduard Shevardnadze in Moscow. This resulted from a Freedom of Information request.

Bibliography

Select List of Books and Manuscripts

Bartlett, John. *Bartlett's Familiar Quotations*. Sixteenth edition with Justin Kaplan general editor. Boston: Little, Brown and Company, 1992.

Bowden, Mark. *Hue 1968: A Turning Point of the American War in Vietnam*. New York: Atlantic Monthly Press, 2017.

Churchill, Winston S. *The Second World War: Volume 1, The Gathering Storm*. Boston: Houghton Mifflin Company, 1948.

Clausewitz, Karl von. *War, Politics & Power*. Selections from *On War*, and *I Believe and Profess*. Translated and edited Colonel Edward M. Collins, A Gateway Edition. Chicago: Henry Regnery Company, 1970.

Clausewitz, Karl von. *On War*. Washington, D.C.: Combat Forces Press, 1953.

Coleman, Kim. Unpublished Manuscript about the activities of 2/502, to include the Bu Gia Map campaign.

Earle, Edward Mead (editor). *The Makers of Modern Strategy: Military Thought from Machiavelli to Hitler*. Princeton: Princeton University Press, 1973.

Effros, William G. (compiler). *Quotations Vietnam 1945–1970*. New York: Random House,1970.

Elliot, Major. *RAND in Southeast Asia: A History of the Vietnam Era*. Rand Corporation, 2010.

Faircloth, Mallon. *Behind the Names: The Story of An Ninh the First Major Battle of Our War in Vietnam*. Columbus, Georgia: Brentwood Academic Press, 2003.

Garland, Lieutenant Colonel Albert N. (editor). *Infantry in Vietnam*. Fort Benning, Georgia: Infantry Magazine, 1967.

Griffin, Peter S. *When You Hear The Bugle Call: Battling PTSD and the Unraveling of the American Conscience*. New York: Trafford Publishing, Bloomington, Indiana, 2006.

Hackworth, Colonel David H and Julie Sherman. *About Face: The Odyssey of an American Warrior*. New York: Simon and Schuster, 1989.

Herbert, Anthony B. and James Wooten. *Soldier*. New York: Holt, Rinehart, and Winston, 1973.

Hilton, Lieutenant Colonel Corson L. *United States Special Forces: From a Decade of Development to a Sustained Future*. Carlisle Barracks: U.S. Army War College, 1991.

Huntington, Samuel P. *The Common Defense: Strategic Programs in National Politics*. New York: Columbia University Press, Fourth Printing, 1969.

Johnson, David. *Vietnam X3*. Unpublished Manuscript in the form of a paperback book.

Kronenberg, Philip G. (editor). *Planning U.S. Security*. Washington, D.C.: National Defense University Press, 1981.

Liddell-Hart, B. H. *Strategy*. New York: Praeger Publishers, Second Revised Edition, 1972.

Lunde, Henrik. *A Warrior Dynasty: The Rise and Fall of Sweden as a Military Superpower, 1611–1721*. Havertown, Pennsylvania and Oxford: Casemate Publishers, 2014.

Marshall, Brigadier General (Ret) S. L. A. *Battles in the Monsoon: Campaigning in the Central Highlands, South Vietnam Summer 1966*. New York: William Morrow & Company, Inc., 1966.

Marshall, Brigadier General (Ret) S. L. A. *Vietnam: Three Battles*. New York: Da Capo Press, 1982.
Matloff, Maurice (editor). *American Military History*. Conshohocken, Pennsylvania: Combined Books, 1996.
McDonald, Charles B. *Company Commander*. Washington, D.C.: Infantry Journal Press, 1947.
McNamara, Robert S. with James Blight, Robert Brigham, Thomas Biersteker and Colonel Herbert Schandler. *Argument Without End: In Search of Answers to the Vietnam Tragedy*. New York: Public Affairs, 1999.
McNamara, Robert S. with Brian VanDeMark. *In Retrospect: The Tragedy and Lessons of Vietnam*. New York: Times Books a division of Random House, 1995.
Millis, Walter. *Arms and Men: A Study in American Military History*. New York: G. P. Putman Sons, 1956.
Millis, Walter (editor). *American Military Thought*. Indianapolis: The Bobbs-Merrill Company, Inc., 1966.
Noland, Keith William. *The Battle for Saigon Tet 1968*. New York: Pocket Books, 1996.
Phillipa, Brigadier General Thomas R. *Roots of Strategy*. Harrisburg, Pennsylvania: The Military Service Publishing Company.
Rossiter, Clinton (editor). *The Federalist Papers: Alexander Hamilton, James Madison, John Hay*. New York: Penguin Group, 1961.
Schlesinger, Arthur M. Jr. *The Bitter Heritage: Vietnam and American Democracy 1941–1966*. Greenwich, Connecticut: Fawcett Publications, Inc., 1967.
South Vietnamese General Staff, Historical Division 1969. *The Viet-Cong Tet Offensive 1968*.
Summers, Colonel Harry G. Jr. *Vietnam Almanac*. New York: Facts on File Publications, 1985.
Summers, Colonel of Infantry Harry G. Jr. *On Strategy: The Vietnam War in Context*. Carlisle Barracks, Pennsylvania: Strategic Studies Institute U.S. Army War College, 1981.
Sun-Tzu, *The Art of War*. Translation and commentary by Ralph D. Sawyer and Mei-chün Lee Sawyer. New York: Barnes & Nobles, 1994.
Taylor, Thomas. *Where the Orange Blooms: One Man's Escape in Vietnam*. New York: McGraw-Hill Publishing Company, 1989.
Tuchman, Barbara W. *The March of Folly From Troy to Vietnam*. New York: Knopf, 1984.
Vidal, Gore. *Inventing a Nation: Washington, Adams, Jefferson*. New Haven: Yale University Press, 2003.
Ward, Geoffrey C., and Ken Burns. *The Vietnam War: An Intimate History*. New York: Knopf Doubleday Publishers, 2017.
Wilson, John Hughes. *Military Intelligence Blunders*. New York: Carroll & Graf Publishers, Inc., 1999.

Field Manuals, Pamphlets, and Studies

Department of the Army Field Manual 27-10, July 1956. *The Law of Land Warfare*.
Department of the Army, Pamphlet 27-44. *Protocols to the Geneva Convention of 12 August 1949*. September 1979.
Historical Office, Test and Experimental Command, *The Airborne and Special Operations Test Board 1940–1990: A Commemorative History (AS-A236-660)*. October 1990.
Ney, Virgil. *Evolution of the U.S. Army Infantry Battalion: 1939–1968*. Technical Operations, Combat Operations Research Group, Combat Developments Command, 1968.
Stebbins, Samuel. A Report, *America's Oldest Military Base*, 9 March 2020.
U.S. Army 22nd Military History Detachment. I have used inputs from six participants in the Bu Gia Map Battle Study.
U.S. Command and General Staff College. 1999 *ST-100-3 Battle Book*.
U.S. Delegation FPJMT, *History of the United States Delegation, Four Party Joint Military Team 31 March 1973 to 30 April 1975*.

Articles

"Assessing a Murderous Cease Fire." *Time Magazine*, 31 December 1973.

Campbell, SP5 Wayne, "Former home of VC now houses 2d-39th." It may have been an article written for *Octofoil*, the 9th Division magazine.

"CPT Lunde Leaves the Brigade." *First Screaming Eagles in Vietnam*, July–August 1966.

Faley, Colonel (Ret) Thomas E. Jr. "101st Airborne vs Viet Cong at An Ninh." *Vietnam Magazine*, August 1997.

Faulkner, Specialist 5 Francis D. "Battle Diary: Long Night near Tuy Hoa." *Army Digest*, August 1966.

First Screaming Eagles in Vietnam, January 2015: 30–31. This is an extract from the History of the 2/17 Cavalry and these two pages deal with the role of A/2/17 Cavalry in the Battle of Bu Gia Map.

Lunde, Lieutenant Colonel Henrik O. *North Sea Oil: Implications for NATO Nations. Parameters*, Volume VI, 1976, Number 1.

Lynn Robert A. "Bayonets Unsheathed." *Vietnam Magazine*, October 1990.

Mock, Captain Phil. "Chaos to Order." Draft article for *Infantry in Vietnam*

New York Times, 14 March 1974 article dealing with death in captivity repatriation

"PFC Sweats Long Night After Hell Opens Up: Fear Turns To Numbness In Total Darkness." *Army Times*, 9 March 1966.

Schuster, Carl O. "Hanoi's Tet Deception." *Vietnam Magazine*, February 2020.

Sheehan, Neil. "David and Goliath in Vietnam." *New York Times*, 26 May 2017.

Shepard, Captain James L. "Into the frying pan." AA Report Adaptation. *The First Screaming Eagles in Vietnam*, April 2012.

Zabecki, David T. "Battle for Saigon." *Vietnam Magazine*, Summer 1989.

Unit Reports and Miscellaneous Sources

Battalion After Action Reports.

Battalion Staff Journals.

Contemporaneous *Field Notebooks.*

US Delegation to FPJMT Pamphlet, *U.S. Delegation Four Party Joint Military Team—A History 31 March–31 December 1973.*

US Delegation to FPJMT A short pamphlet titled *History of the United States Delegation, Four Party Joint Military Team 31 March 1973–30 April 1975.*

Hundreds of conversations I had with my former troops over the years, in-person or by telephone. Most of these took place in the 1980s, after my retirement.

Nearly 200 *Morning Reports* from 2/502, mostly for A/2/502.

Personnel Rosters of the units or organizations to which I was assigned.

USARV General Orders dealing with awards for some soldiers in A/2/502.

Virtual contemporaneous extracts from more than 1,000 letters to my wife and family. The total came to 114 single-spaced typewritten pages.

1st Brigade, 101st Airborne Division *After Action Reports.*

1st Brigade, 101st Airborne Division *Casualty Lists.*

9th Infantry Division Operational Report for the Period Ending 31 July 1968, dated 20 August 1968.

9th Infantry Division Operational Report for the Period Ending 31 January 1969, dated 15 February 1969.

Written statement by Sergeant Earl Singeltary to Lieutenant Colonel Perrine.

Written statement by Private First Class Clifford Rosseau to Lieutenant Colonel Perrine.

Verbal statement by Colonel (Ret) Jim Schoonover to Lieutenant Colonel Perrine.

Written statement by Colonel (Ret) Karl Beach to Lieutenant Colonel Perrine.

Index